Evolutionary Multi-objective Optimization: An Honorary Issue Dedicated to Professor Kalyanmoy Deb

Evolutionary Multi-objective Optimization: An Honorary Issue Dedicated to Professor Kalyanmoy Deb

Editors

Carlos Coello
Erik Goodman
Kaisa Miettinen
Dhish Saxena
Oliver Schütze
Lothar Thiele

MDPI • Basel • Beijing • Wuhan • Barcelona • Belgrade • Manchester • Tokyo • Cluj • Tianjin

Editors

Carlos Coello	Erik Goodman	Kaisa Miettinen
CINVESTAV-IPN	Michigan State University	University of Jyvaskyla
Mexico	USA	Finland
Dhish Saxena	Oliver Schütze	Lothar Thiele
Indian Institute of Technology	CINVESTAV-IPN	ETH Zürich
India	Mexico	Switzerland

Editorial Office
MDPI
St. Alban-Anlage 66
4052 Basel, Switzerland

This is a reprint of articles from the Special Issue published online in the open access journal *Mathematical and Computational Applications* (ISSN 2297-8747) (available at: https://www.mdpi.com/journal/mca/special_issues/K_Deb).

For citation purposes, cite each article independently as indicated on the article page online and as indicated below:

LastName, A.A.; LastName, B.B.; LastName, C.C. Article Title. *Journal Name* **Year**, *Volume Number*, Page Range.

ISBN 978-3-0365-6980-2 (Hbk)
ISBN 978-3-0365-6981-9 (PDF)

© 2023 by the authors. Articles in this book are Open Access and distributed under the Creative Commons Attribution (CC BY) license, which allows users to download, copy and build upon published articles, as long as the author and publisher are properly credited, which ensures maximum dissemination and a wider impact of our publications.

The book as a whole is distributed by MDPI under the terms and conditions of the Creative Commons license CC BY-NC-ND.

Contents

About the Editors vii

Preface to "Evolutionary Multi-objective Optimization: An Honorary Issue Dedicated to Professor Kalyanmoy Deb" ix

Carlos Coello, Erik Goodman, Kaisa Miettinen, Dhish Saxena, Oliver Schütze and Lothar Thiele
Interview: Kalyanmoy Deb Talks about Formation, Development and Challenges of the EMO Community, Important Positions in His Career, and Issues Faced Getting His Works Published
Reprinted from: *Math. Comput. Appl.* **2023**, *28*, 34, doi:10.3390/mca28020034 1

Ankur Sinha and Jyrki Wallenius
MCDM, EMO and Hybrid Approaches: Tutorial and Review
Reprinted from: *Math. Comput. Appl.* **2022**, *27*, 112, doi:10.3390/mca27060112 11

Carlos Ignacio Hernández Castellanos and Oliver Schütze
A Bounded Archiver for Hausdorff Approximations of the Pareto Front for Multi-Objective Evolutionary Algorithms
Reprinted from: *Math. Comput. Appl.* **2022**, *27*, 48, doi:10.3390/mca27030048 39

Siyuan Xing and Jian-Qiao Sun
Multi-Objective Optimization of an Elastic Rod with Viscous Termination
Reprinted from: *Math. Comput. Appl.* **2022**, *27*, 94, doi:10.3390/mca27060094 77

Kiran Pannerselvam, Deepanshu Yadav and Palaniappan Ramu
Scarce Sample-Based Reliability Estimation and Optimization Using Importance Sampling
Reprinted from: *Math. Comput. Appl.* **2022**, *27*, 99, doi:10.3390/mca27060099 91

Antonio J. Nebro, Jesús Galeano-Brajones, Francisco Luna and Carlos A. Coello Coello
Is NSGA-II Ready for Large-Scale Multi-Objective Optimization?
Reprinted from: *Math. Comput. Appl.* **2022**, *27*, 103, doi:10.3390/mca27060103 121

Henrik Smedberg, Carlos Alberto Barrera-Diaz, Amir Nourmohammadi, Sunith Bandaru and Amos Ng
Knowledge-Driven Multi-Objective Optimization for Reconfigurable Manufacturing Systems
Reprinted from: *Math. Comput. Appl.* **2022**, *27*, 106, doi:10.3390/ mca27060106 139

Octavio Ramos-Figueroa, Marcela Quiroz-Castellanos, Efrén Mezura-Montes and Nicandro Cruz-Ramírez
An Experimental Study of Grouping Mutation Operators for the Unrelated Parallel-Machine Scheduling Problem
Reprinted from: *Math. Comput. Appl.* **2023**, *28*, 6, doi:10.3390/mca28010006 157

Hao Wang, Michael Emmerich, André Deutz, Víctor Adrián Sosa Hernandez and Oliver Schütze
The Hypervolume Newton Method for Constrained Multi-Objective Optimization Problems
Reprinted from: *Math. Comput. Appl.* **2023**, *28*, 10, doi:10.3390/mca28010010 187

Santiago Sinisterra-Sierra, Salvador Godoy-Calderón and Miriam Pescador-Rojas
COVID-19 Data Analysis with a Multi-Objective Evolutionary Algorithm for Causal Association Rule Mining
Reprinted from: *Math. Comput. Appl.* **2023**, *28*, 12, doi:10.3390/mca28010012 209

Xilu Wang and Yaochu Jin
Knowledge Transfer Based on Particle Filters for Multi-Objective Optimization
Reprinted from: *Math. Comput. Appl.* **2023**, *28*, 14, doi:10.3390/mca28010014 . . . . **225**

António Gaspar-Cunha, Paulo Costa, Francisco Monaco and Alexandre Delbem
Many-Objectives Optimization: A Machine Learning Approach for Reducing the Number of Objectives
Reprinted from: *Math. Comput. Appl.* **2023**, *28*, 17, doi:10.3390/mca28010017 . . . . **239**

Raktim Biswas and Deepak Sharma
Single-Loop Multi-Objective Reliability-Based Design Optimization Using Chaos Control Theory and Shifting Vector with Differential Evolution
Reprinted from: *Math. Comput. Appl.* **2023**, *28*, 26, doi:10.3390/mca28010026 . . . . **259**

About the Editors

Carlos Coello

Carlos Coello received a PhD in Computer Science from Tulane University (USA) in 1996. His research has mainly focused on the design of new multi-objective optimization algorithms based on bio-inspired metaheuristics (e.g., evolutionary algorithms), which is an area he has made pioneering contributions to. He has received several awards, including the National Research Award (in 2007) from the Mexican Academy of Science and the 2012 National Medal of Science in Physics, Mathematics and Natural Sciences from Mexico's presidency, the 2013 IEEE Kiyo Tomiyasu Award, the 2016 The World Academy of Sciences (TWAS) Award in "Engineering Sciences", and the 2021 IEEE Computational Intelligence Society Evolutionary Computation Pioneer Award. Since January 2011, he has been an IEEE Fellow. He is currently the Editor-in-Chief of the IEEE Transactions on Evolutionary Computation. He is Full Professor with distinction (Investigador Cinvestav 3F) at the Computer Science Department of CINVESTAV-IPN in Mexico City, Mexico.

Erik Goodman

Erik Goodman was PI and Director of BEACON Center for the Study of Evolution in Action, an NSF Center headquartered at Michigan State University, from 2010-2018. He was Professor of Electrical and Computer Engineering and Mechanical Engineering and Computer Science and Engineering until he retired in 2022. He co-founded Red Cedar Technology (1999, now part of Siemens), and developed the HEEDS SHERPA commercial design optimization software now widely used in industry. Honors include Michigan Distinguished Professor of the Year, 2009; MSU Distinguished Faculty Award, 2011; Senior Fellow, International Society for Genetic and Evolutionary Computation, 2004; Founding Chair, ACM SIG on Genetic and Evolutionary Computation (SIGEVO), 2005-2007, and continuing service on its Executive Committee and Advisory Committee.

Kaisa Miettinenn

Kaisa Miettinen is Professor of Industrial Optimization at the University of Jyvaskyla. Her research interests include theory, methods, applications and software of nonlinear multiobjective optimization including interactive and evolutionary approaches, in particular, different types of hybrid methods. She heads the Research Group on Multiobjective Optimization and is the director of the thematic research area called Decision Analytics, utilizing Causal Models and Multiobjective Optimization (DEMO, www.jyu.fi/demo). She has authored over 200 refereed journal, proceedings, and collection papers, edited 19 proceedings, collections and special issues and written a monograph on 'Nonlinear Multiobjective Optimization'. She is a member of the Finnish Academy of Science and Letters, Section of Science, and has served as the President of the International Society on Multiple Criteria Decision Making (MCDM). She belongs to the editorial boards of seven international journals and the Steering Committee of Evolutionary Multiobjective Optimization. She has previously worked at IIASA, International Institute for Applied Systems Analysis in Austria, KTH Royal Institute of Technology in Stockholm, Sweden and Helsinki School of Economics, Finland. She has received the Georg Cantor Award of the International Society on MCDM for independent inquiries to develop innovative ideas in the theory and methodology of MCDM.

Dhish Saxena

Dhish Saxena is an Associate Professor at the Department of Mechanical and Industrial Engineering and Mehta Family School of Data Science and Artificial Intelligence at the Indian Institute of Technology Roorkee. Prior to joining IIT Roorkee, Dhish worked with Cranfield University and Bath University, UK (2008-12). His research has focused on development of evolutionary multi- and many-objective optimization algorithms; their performance enhancement through machine learning; their termination criterion; decision support based on redundancy determination and preference ranking of objectives and constraints. He is also an Associate Editor for Elsevier's *Swarm and Evolutionary Computation* journal.

Oliver Schütze

Oliver Schütze is a Full Professor at the Cinvestav-IPN in Mexico City, Mexico. His main research interests are numerical and evolutionary optimization. He is the co-author of more than 150 publications, including two monographs, five school textbooks, and ten edited books. He is recipient of the C. S. Hsu Award 2022. Two of his papers have received the IEEE Transactions on Evolutionary Computation Outstanding Paper Award (in 2010 and 2012). He is the founder of the Numerical and Evolutionary Optimization (NEO) workshop series. He is Editor-in-Chief of the journal *Mathematical and Computational Applications* and is a member of the Editorial Board of the journals *Engineering Optimization, Computational Optimization and Applications, IEEE Transactions on Evolutionary Computation, Research in Control and Optimization*, and *Applied Soft Computing*. He is a member of the Mexican Academy of Sciences and the National System of Researchers (SNI III).

Lothar Thiele

Lothar Thiele joined ETH Zurich, Switzerland, as a full Professor of Computer Engineering in 1994. His research interests include bioinspired optimization techniques; models, methods, and software tools for the design of real-time embedded systems; cyberphysical systems; embedded software. In 1986, he received the "Dissertation Award" of the Technical University of Munich, in 1987, the "Outstanding Young Author Award" of the IEEE Circuits and Systems Society, in 1988, the Browder J. Thompson Memorial Award of the IEEE, and in 2000-2001, the "IBM Faculty Partnership Award". In 2004, he joined the German Academy of Sciences Leopoldina. In 2005, he was the recipient of the Honorary Blaise Pascal Chair of University Leiden, the Netherlands. Since 2010, he is a member of the Academia Europea. In 2013, he joined the National Research Council of the Swiss National Science Foundation SNF. Lothar Thiele received the "EDAA Lifetime Achievement Award" in 2015. Since 2017, Lothar Thiele has been Associate Vice President of ETH for Digital Transformation. Lothar Thiele has been elected IFIP Fellow by the International Federation for Information Processing (IFIP) as part of its first cohort of fellows in 2020. In 2021, he received the IEEE TCRTS Achievement and Leadership Award.

Preface to "Evolutionary Multi-objective Optimization: An Honorary Issue Dedicated to Professor Kalyanmoy Deb"

This volume is a reprint of the Honorary Special Issue dedicated to the 60th birthday of Professor Dr. Kalyanmoy Deb, published in the journal Mathematical and Computational Applications (MCA). Kalyanmoy Deb is a pioneer and highly impactful and influential proponent of Evolutionary Multi-objective Optimization (EMO) since 1994. He is currently a Koenig Endowed Chair Professor and University Distinguished Professor in the Department of Electrical and Computer Engineering at Michigan State University, USA, and holds additional appointments in Mechanical Engineering and in Computer Science and Engineering. Professor Deb's research interests are in evolutionary optimization and its application in multi-objective optimization, modeling, machine learning, and in multi-objective decision making. He has been a visiting professor at various universities across the world, including IITs in India, Aalto University in Finland, the University of Skovde in Sweden, and Nanyang Technological University in Singapore. He was awarded the IEEE Evolutionary Computation Pioneer Award, the Infosys Prize, the TWAS Prize in Engineering Sciences, the CajAstur Mamdani Prize, the Distinguished Alumni Award from IIT Kharagpur, the Edgeworth Pareto Award, the Bhatnagar Prize in Engineering Sciences, and the Bessel Research Award from Germany. He is a fellow of IEEE, ASME, and three Indian science and engineering academies.

He has published over 600 research papers, with Google Scholar citations of over 180,000 and with an h-index of 131. More information about his research contributions can be found from https://www.coin-lab.org. This volume contains one interview, one review paper, and 11 regular papers. We briefly present all of these contributions in the following. The regular papers are organized chronologically by their publication times in MCA.

In Chapter 1, Kalyanmoy Deb gives an interview to the guest editors of the Honorary Special Issue. In this interview, Dr. Deb talks about formation, development and challenges of the Evolutionary Multi-objective Optimization (EMO) community, important points in his career, and issues he has faced in getting his work published.

In Chapter 2, Sinha and Wallenius first review the classic interactive approaches from the field of Multiple Criteria Decision Making (MCDM), followed by the underlying idea and methods in the field of EMO. Next, they consider and discuss several promising MCDM and EMO hybrid approaches that aim to capitalize on the strengths of these two domains. Finally, they conclude with discussions on important behavioral considerations related to the use of such approaches and possible paths of future work.

In Chapter 3, Hernández Castellanos and Schütze propose a new bounded archiver, ArchiveUpdateHD, aiming for Hausdorff approximations of the Pareto front of a multi-objective optimization problem. It is shown that an application of this archiver yields, under certain (mild) assumptions with a probability one after finitely many steps, a Δ^+ approximation of the Pareto front, where Δ^+ is computed by the archiver within the run of the algorithm without any prior knowledge of the Pareto front. Numerical results using ArchiveUpdateHD as an external archiver within state of the art multi-objective evolutionary algorithms (MOEAs) indicate the benefit of the novel strategy.

In Chapter 4, Xing and Sun study a multi-objective optimization problem related to the viscous boundary condition of an elastic rod. For the numerical treatment of this problem they use the algorithm GA-SCN, a hybrid of the multi-objective evolutionary algorithm NSGA-II and cell mapping techniques. Finally, several optimal designs are illustrated and discussed.

In Chapter 5, Pannerselvam et al. use importance sampling to deal with scarce sample based reliability estimation and optimization. More precisely, they propose to approximate the probability density function and the cumulative distribution function using kernel functions and employ these approximations to find the parameters of the importance sampling density to eventually estimate the reliability. The proposed approach is finally tested on several benchmark reliability examples.

In Chapter 6, Nebro et al. investigate the applicability of the evolutionary algorithm NSGA-II to large scale multi-objective optimization problems. To this end, the authors use the automated algorithmic tuning method irace together with a highly configurable version of NSGA-II available in the jMetal framework. The resulting tuned algorithm is then tested on the continuous ZDT test functions with up to $2^{17} = 131,072$ decision variables and on a particular binary problem with thousands of bits. Results show that significant improvements can be obtained compared to the original NSGA-II.

In Chapter 7, Smedberg et al. investigate a novel knowledge driven optimization (KDO) approach to speed up the convergence in reconfigurable manufacturing systems (RMS) applications. This approach generates generalized knowledge from previous scenarios, which is then applied to improve the efficiency of the optimization of new scenarios. The proposed approach is then applied to a multi-part flow line RMS. The results demonstrate how a KDO approach leads to convergence rate improvements in a real world RMS case.

In Chapter 8, Ramos Figueroa et al. present a comparative experimental study of different mutation operators for a Grouping Genetic Algorithm 2 (GGA) designed to solve the parallel machine scheduling problem with unrelated machines and makespan minimization. The focus is on identifying the strategies involved in the mutation operations and their adaptation to the characteristics of the studied problem. Experimental results indicate that the state of the art GGA performance considerably improves by replacing the original mutation operator with the new one.

In Chapter 9, Wang et al. extend the recently proposed Hypervolume Newton Method (HVN) to the treatment of constrained multi-objective optimization problems with in principle any number of objectives. This Newton method is defined on the space of (vectorized) fixed cardinality sets of decision space vectors for a given multi-objective problem (MOP) with the aim to maximize the hypervolume indicator. Numerical results are presented of the method both as standalone algorithm as well as local search engine within a multi-objective evolutionary algorithm.

In Chapter 10, Sinisterra Sierra et al. propose an evolutionary multi-objective algorithm based on NSGA-II to guide the mining process in datasets. In particular they consider the dataset composed of 15.5 million records with official data describing the COVID-19 pandemic in Mexico. The proposed algorithm generates, recombines, and evaluates patterns, focusing on recovering promising high quality rules with actionable cause effect relationships among the attributes to identify which groups are more susceptible to disease or what combinations of conditions are necessary to receive certain types of medical care.

In Chapter 11, Wang and Jin propose a novel particle filter based multi-objective optimization algorithm (PF-MOA) by transferring knowledge acquired from the search experience. The key insight adopted here is that, if one can construct a sequence of target distributions that can balance the multiple objectives and make the degree of the balance controllable, one can approximate the Pareto optimal solutions by simulating each target distribution via particle filters. Experimental results on several test functions show that PF-MOA achieves competitive performance compared to state of the art MOEAs on most test instances.

In Chapter 12, Gaspar-Cunha et al. propose a novel machine learning methodology, called

FS-OPA, to reduce the number of objectives within a many-objective optimization problem. The new method is first assessed using the DTLZ benchmark problems, where the method shows good performance compared to similar algorithms. Finally, the strength of the method is demonstrated on a difficult real world application coming from polymer processing.

Finally, in Chapter 13, Biswas and Sharma propose a single loop multi-objective reliability based design optimization formulation that approximates 3 reliability analysis using Karush Kuhn Tucker (KKT) optimality conditions. Further, chaos control theory is used to avoid convergence issues. Numerical results demonstrate that the proposed method, MORBDO, is highly competitive to double loop variants of multi-objective differential evolution algorithms.

We warmly thank the authors who contributed to this special issue as well as the reviewers for their constructive comments. We hope the readers enjoy to study these works as much as we enjoyed editing them. Among others, these works demonstrate that Evolutionary Multi objective Optimization is still an active and fruitful research field after three decades of its existence.

Carlos Coello, Erik Goodman, Kaisa Miettinen, Dhish Saxena, Oliver Schütze and Lothar Thiele
Editors

Editorial

Interview: Kalyanmoy Deb Talks about Formation, Development and Challenges of the EMO Community, Important Positions in His Career, and Issues Faced Getting His Works Published

Carlos Coello [1], Erik Goodman [2], Kaisa Miettinen [3], Dhish Saxena [4], Oliver Schütze [1,*] and Lothar Thiele [5]

1. Depto de Computacion, CINVESTAV-IPN, Mexico City 07360, Mexico; coello@cs.cinvestav.mx
2. BEACON Center for the Study of Evolution in Action, Michigan State University, East Lansing, MI 48824, USA; goodman@egr.msu.edu
3. University of Jyvaskyla, Faculty of Information Technology, P.O. Box 35 (Agora), FI-40014 University of Jyvaskyla, Finland; kaisa.miettinen@jyu.fi
4. Department of Mechanical and Industrial Engineering, Indian Institute of Technology, Roorkee 247667, India; dhish.saxena@me.iitr.ac.in
5. Computer Engineering and Networks Laboratory, ETH Zürich, CH-8092 Zurich, Switzerland; thiele@tik.ee.ethz.ch
* Correspondence: schuetze@cs.cinvestav.mx

1. Introducing Kalyanmoy Deb

Kalyanmoy Deb was born in Udaipur, Tripura, the smallest state of India at the time, in 1963. He is the eldest of four siblings. Like him, his other brothers are also engineers, one in academics, one in an industry, and the other is a freelancer. Educated in the IIT system in India, he worked for two years in a reputed engineering design company, before heading for his graduate studies in the USA. After his return to India, he taught at IIT Kanpur for 20 years. He is currently a University Distinguished Professor and Koenig Endowed Chair Professor in the Department of Electrical and Computer Engineering at Michigan State University, USA. Prof. Deb's research interests are in evolutionary optimization and its application in multi-criterion optimization, modeling, and machine learning. He has been a visiting professor at various universities across the world including the University of Skövde in Sweden, ETH Zurich in Switzerland, Aalto University in Finland, Nanyang Technological University in Singapore, and a few IITs in India. He was awarded the IEEE Evolutionary Computation Pioneer Award for his pioneering work in EMO, Infosys Prize, TWAS Prize in Engineering Sciences, CajAstur Mamdani Prize, Distinguished Alumni Award from IIT Kharagpur, Edgeworth-Pareto Award, Bhatnagar Prize in Engineering Sciences, and Bessel Research Award from Germany. He has received an honorary doctorate degree from the University of Jyvaskyla, Finland. He is a fellow of ACM, ASME, IEEE, and three Indian science and engineering academies. He has published over 600 research papers. He is married to Debjani Sarkar, who is an academic specialist at Michigan State University. Their son runs a start-up on AI and their daughter works in a reputed company as a marketing manager.

2. Introducing Evolutionary Multi-Objective Optimization (EMO)

Multi-objective optimization (MO) problems give rise to not one, but a set of Paretooptimal solutions, each of which makes a trade-off among the associated objectives with another solution. Between a pair of solutions, if one is better on one objective, it must be worse in at least one other objective. Although a single solution is desired as an outcome of a multi-objective optimization task, finding a representative set of Pareto-optimal solutions can be helpful in the process of making a decision. There exist different scalarizationbased multi-objective optimization methods that scalarize multiple objectives into a single

parameterized one and apply a single-objective optimization method to find the respective optimal solution. Most scalarization techniques ensure that the resulting optimal solution is a Pareto-optimal one but the scalarization technique must be selected carefully to be able to reach any Pareto-optimal solution.

Evolutionary multi-objective optimization (EMO) methods work with a population of solutions in every iteration and can find multiple well-diversified solutions simultaneously. Because of their heuristic nature, they cannot usually guarantee Pareto-optimality, but they approximate Pareto optimal solutions. Early EMO methods could handle two and three objectives well, but the new methods, known as evolutionary many-objective optimization (EMaO) methods, are demonstrated to handle as many as 15 to 20 objectives. EMO and EMaO methods use an implicitly parallel search process introduced by the evolutionary operators, and a partial ordering and diversity-preserving-based selection mechanism. Aided by modular and flexible structures, EMO and EMaO methods are regularly used to solve challenging academic and industrial problems. They have also been commercialized into software packages and public-domain codes for their use at large. The discovery of a representative set of Pareto-optimal solutions has a number of advantages for users. First, the set of solutions can be analyzed to understand the comprehensive nature of possible variations of objectives and their trade-offs, which can provide useful information to the users to follow an informed decision-making task for picking a single preferred solution for deployment. Second, the knowledge of alternate Pareto-optimal solutions can utilize them to use in a platform-based solution philosophy, in which every Pareto-optimal solution can become a potential solution for a different hardware or system platform. Third, an application of machine learning techniques to multiple Pareto-optimal solutions can bring out essential common principles hidden in them. These common principles can reveal valuable insights for constructing optimal solutions for a problem. Fourth, the EMO and EMaO philosophies are increasingly being used to introduce helper objectives in the search process to find optimal solutions for original objectives faster and with more accuracy.

EMO and EMaO methods have uniquely utilized evolutionary algorithm's (EO) population approach to finding and storing multiple optimal solutions. The matching of MO and EO philosophies could not be any better. MO gives rise to multiple alternate solutions and EO's population approach provides a platform to find and capture them. For the past three decades, EMO researchers have not only exploited this match to develop efficient MO algorithms, but they also have launched various related studies to make EMO a field of study with hundreds of PhD theses, commercial and public-domain software, dedicated conference/seminar series, and a record number of publications. Many new ideas for improving existing algorithms, new areas of applications, and new ways to utilize them for various problem-solving areas are continuously emerging. EMO has undoubtedly become a unique and ubiquitous medium for solving multi-objective problems.

It is perhaps an excellent time to celebrate the moment and recognize every EMO researcher's hard work, passion, and collaborative efforts over the past three decades.

3. Interview

The following is an interview with Prof. Kalyanmoy Deb. The editor's question is stated first, followed by Deb's response.

1. Kalyan, thank you very much for taking some of your valuable time for this interview that we are doing as part of the Special Issue dedicated to your 60th birthday. The title of this SI is "Evolutionary Multi-objective Optimization" (EMO) which leads us directly to the first questions, since you are a pioneer and highly impactful and influential proponent of EMO since 1994. Can you recall for us your first steps that, looking back, helped in the formation of what we today call the EMO community?

First of all, I am touched and humbled by your initiative in compiling this Special Issue for the occasion of my 60th birthday. It is a great honor for me. I also take this opportunity to thank all authors and reviewers of the papers published in this Special

Issue. My appreciation also goes to the MDPI journal on Mathematical and Computational Applications for publishing this Special Issue.

It has been a long journey, hasn't it! The birth of EMO studies and the start of my academic career as an assistant professor at Indian Institute of Technology Kanpur (IITK) in India, happened almost concurrently. After completing my graduate studies and a short post-doctoral stay in the USA, I returned to India in early 1993 and took the Assistant Professor position at IITK. During my graduate studies (1987–1991), I was fortunate enough to have been exposed to genetic algorithms (GAs)—a fascinating concept for solving search and optimization problems using principles of natural selection and genetics–from the Evolutionary Computation pioneer David Goldberg. A 10-line outline of a plausible GA-based multi-objective optimization algorithm in Goldberg's 1989 pioneering book (Addison-Wesley) caught my attention, while I took the GA course from Goldberg. In an earlier attempt by David Schaffer in 1985, Goldberg observed that a proactive diversity-preserving operator was missing in Schaffer's vector-evaluated GA (VEGA). Having worked on niche-based GAs in my master's thesis, I immediately realized that Goldberg's suggestion for building a working EMO algorithm was just on the horizon. However, by that time, I was already quite advanced with my PhD topic on the development of messy GAs—a variable-length GA that could solve complex problems including deceptive problems, which were found difficult to solve by standard GAs. I temporarily put off my interest on multi-objective optimization research and waited until I had my first graduate student, Nidamurthy Srinivas, at IITK, to begin working on Goldberg's suggestion. The use of non-domination sorting (NS) and niche- preservation based on a sharing function approach in the GA's selection operator confirmed Goldberg's intuition. There came one of the first EMO algorithms—NSGA. We submitted our paper to Evolutionary Computation Journal of MIT Press in 1993 and the paper appeared in print in 1995. Those days, the internet was not that accessible and soon thereafter I came across two other papers which used Goldberg's idea in slightly different ways and produced two other successful EMO algorithms: multi-objective GA (MOGA) and niched Pareto GA (NPGA). Each of these methods showed that a stable population of Pareto- optimal solutions could be found and maintained for successive generations on two-objective problems. In my opinion, these three studies during 1993–1995 have initiated the birth of the EMO field, although there were a few other EMO studies that came soon thereafter which did not use Goldberg's idea literally.

Of course, a few papers or even one great idea does not often fan out to be a successful field of research and application which has lasted for about three decades now. I narrate some of the systematic and chronological developments in which I took a major part. First, more efficient EMO algorithms with fewer tunable parameters and elite preservation appeared. My 2002 NSGA-II paper (IEEE Transactions on Evolutionary Computation (TEVC)) is one such EMO algorithm, in addition to Zitzler and Thiele's Strength Pareto Evolutionary Algorithm (SPEA) and Knowles and Corne's Pareto-Archived Evolution Strategy (PAES). The simplicity and modularity in these algorithms and the availability of their public-domain codes make EMO accessible to researchers and applicationists within and outside the computer science and engineering communities. These algorithms have helped mature the EMO field and attracted many newcomers. Second, with every new algorithm being proposed, I started to realize the need for a test suite through which algorithms can be tested and compared with each other. I found a mechanism in my 1999 test problem construction paper (MIT Press's ECJ) by which existing single-objective challenging test problems can be channeled to construct similarly difficult test problems for multi-objective optimization. That study led to a collaboration with Eckart Zitzler and Lothar Thiele to formulate a two- objective Zitzler-Deb-Thiele (ZDT) test suite with discernable Pareto-optimal fronts. Although largely concurred, ZDT problems are still used as the first problems to test a new algorithm on. Third, with the existence of efficient algorithms to apply to challenging test problems, researchers proposed various performance metrics to measure convergence and diversity of obtained solutions. In my opinion, this three-pronged development of

"Algorithm-Test-suite–Performance-metric" allowed more researchers to introduce new ideas and industries to venture into solving their problems for multiple objectives. All these activities started the EMO revolution, and there was no stopping it.

2. The growing interest in EMO even led to, among other things, a new conference series dedicated to this topic, called Evolutionary Multi-Criterion Optimization. Its first edition was held in Zurich (Switzerland) in 2001, and is since been held biannually and very successfully until now. Can you tell us a bit about the evolutionary history of this event series?

The opportunity offered by EMO algorithms to solve problems for multiple objectives attracted many bright PhD students. Journals started to accept EMO papers and major evolutionary computation (EC) conferences accepted EMO-related papers in their regular tracks. It became clear to everyone that EC's population approach provided a unique niche for solving multi-objective problems and EMO was being flagged as a success story of EC. To push the EMO activities further and to let everyone know about others' work closely, I realized that a dedicated conference on EMO was the need of the time. It was December of 1999 and I was on a flight from Delhi to travel to Zurich to examine the PhD thesis of Eckart Zitzler. I pondered on how nice it would be to hold the first EMO conference in Zurich. I expressed my thoughts to Eckart and Lothar, and before I realized it, Lothar was on the phone to find an available date of ETH's auditorium to host the proposed conference. The first international conference on EMO was held in March of 2001 at ETH Zurich with about 50 papers presented. Springer agreed to publish the proceedings under its Lecture Notes in Computer Science (LNCS) series. We prepared the conference for about 60 participants, but 90+ participants attended the conference. If I recall correctly, we had to order extra proceedings from Springer and post them later to many participants. The conference was a huge success, and three proposals for hosting the second one were received. To involve more key EMO researchers in the decision-making of future EMO conference events, Eckart, Lothar and I decided to form an EMO Steering Committee with a total of seven members, which has been recently extended to have 11 members. The steering committee decided to host the conference every two years and adopted a couple of practices from the very first EMO conference: (i) there will be no parallel sessions, so everyone is in the same room for all presentations, thereby giving every paper a wide attention, and (ii) there will be Multi-Criterion Decision-Making (MCDM) events within EMO conferences. Since 2001, the EMO conference series has been held every odd year.

3. For the treatment of multi-objective optimization problems you mainly use evolutionary techniques. However, you have always promoted the use of mathematical programming and multi-criterion decision-making (MCDM) techniques within EMO, which has had a significant impact on the formation of the community. Could you comment on that?

I consider myself a problem solver rather than particularly an EC or an optimization researcher. I strongly believe that a successful researcher should always acquire a good knowledge of the fundamentals associated with the topic before starting to work on it. This not only provides a deeper understanding of the topic for making any fundamental changes, but it also paves the way to know other contemporary approaches as possible alternatives. As you have correctly pointed out, mathematical programming and MCDM fields are two related and contemporary fields which deal with multi-objective problem-solving. While I understand that it is not easy and always uncomfortable to go out of one's own comfort zone and mingle with people in a different field to understand their trades, the trouble is worth taking for two reasons. First, it allows one to evaluate one's methods with other competing methods, and the process can eventually motivate developing hybrid methods. Second, it helps to propagate one's methods to the other contemporary fields.

It was evident from the beginning that multi-objective problem-solving tasks should end up or involve somehow a decision-making activity in arriving at a single preferred solution. I was fortunate to be invited to attend a few MCDM events in 1999 and the years following thereafter, and I came to know the existence of an MCDM field which had been addressing multi-objective problem solving since the early seventies. While they were mainly interested in scalarizing multiple objectives into a single one and in involving a decision-maker directly to provide preference information to move to new scalarized problems iteratively, I realized that EMO studies could definitely benefit by working with MCDM researchers. EMO's ability to find multiple representative near-Pareto solutions can be combined with MCDM-based preference incorporation ideas to make the whole EMO-MCDM approach holistic. To create this merger, I planned a few events.

First, at the EMO-2001 conference, we invited two prominent MCDM researchers: Kaisa Miettinen and Ralph Steuer, both being authors of popular MCDM books, to give a tutorial and a keynote speech on MCDM topics for EMO researchers to be aware of. This tradition has been followed in a number of future EMO conferences.

Second, in 2004, during my Bessel Research Prize visit to the University of Karlsruhe, Germany, I joined hands with my hosts Juergen Branke and Hartmut Schmeck, along with the above-mentioned MCDM researchers, to propose a Dagstuhl Seminar at Schloss Dagstuhl, Saarbrucken, Germany by inviting 30 EMO and 30 MCDM researchers. It was the first time these two groups met and openly exchanged ideas with each other. Of course, EMO being about 20 years younger than MCDM in terms of its inception, EMO researchers strikingly found that many of their ideas were already proposed by their elder counterparts. However, the seminar provided a breeding ground for the two groups to plan future collaborative studies. I must say that MCDM researchers were also exposed to the EMO philosophy and the later publication records of some of the leading MCDM researchers clearly support my assertion. The success of the first Dagstuhl seminar motivated us to repeat it at regular intervals. The epitome of the merger was the publication of an edited book (under Springer's LNCS series, edited by four founding organizers) in which most chapters were jointly written by EMO and MCDM authors.

Third, I was invited to visit Helsinki School of Economics (now Aalto University School of Business) as a Finland Distinguished Professor for two years and to collaborate with Kaisa Miettinen, Jyrki Wallenius and Pekka Korhonen – three stalwarts in the MCDM community. With this collaboration, I had a better appreciation of the MCDM philosophy and met other prominent MCDM researchers who regularly visited the university. I began to combine EMO and MCDM methods, a process which resulted in reference-point-based NSGA-II, reference-direction-based NSGA-II, light-beam-search-based EMO, progressively interactive EMO, and others which also combined EMO with MCDM methods to find a single preferred Pareto-optimal solution at the end.

Fourth, during my Helsinki visit, I also worked with Jyrki and others to make EMO an area topic for the Journal of Multi-Criterion Decision Analysis (Wiley) and served as an area editor from 2009 until 2018.

Fifth, in 2008, I worked with the International Society on MCDM to establish an EMO track within their bi-annual MCDM conferences and reciprocated the same, with the advice of the EMO steering committee, by instituting an MCDM track within EMO conferences soon thereafter. I am happy that these practices are still being continued.

My quest for fundamental understanding has helped me tremendously in evaluating EC's scope as an optimization algorithm compared to mathematical optimization literature, although I must admit that I do not have the adequate mathematical background to understand all of their detailed theoretical intricacies. However, I have been fortunate to have a few colleagues in mathematical optimization and operations research areas with whom I have not only pursued some fundamental convergence studies, but also co-taught multi-objective optimization courses, exposing students to both mathematical and computational worlds of optimization. Using variational principles, we were able to estimate a Karush-Kuhn-Tucker Proximity Measure (KKTPM) for any feasible or infeasible solution from the KKT-based Pareto-optimal set without actually knowing the location of the Pareto-optimal set. Although the KKTPM measure requires computation of derivatives of objective and constraint functions, the idea brought in useful EMO operators aiding guaranteed convergence to EMO studies.

To reiterate the importance of associated knowledge around a field, the next example is illustrative. I was exposed to a resource allocation problem from an industry which involved about 50,000 integer decision variables. While it was a linear programming problem, the integer restriction of variables made all the differences between a fast and guaranteed solution methodology for the real-parameter version of the problem and an exponentially worse algorithm for its integer version. Well-known operations research software packages could not find the optimal solution for 2000 or more variables. We developed a customized EC-based procedure that recombined two or more solutions meaningfully in the context of the problem and used local adjustments to try to make infeasible solutions feasible. The procedure not only found near-optimal solutions (within a maximum of 0.03% deviation from the true optimum) in 2000 or even 50,000 variables, but to a staggering one billion variable version of the problem in polynomial computational time. I believe more such defining contributions are possible and are worth pursuing, but this will require a good understanding of the associated literature and strengths and weaknesses of various alternative methodologies.

4. How do you see the current development of the EMO community?

I am absolutely certain that the EMO field is in good hands. I am happy that a simple idea on the use of a population-based optimization method to find multiple Pareto-optimal solutions simultaneously survived almost three decades and provided EMO researchers with plenty of opportunities to formulate new research ideas, extended to solve various types of problems, and helped merge multiple fields together.

Looking at the recent publications, a major thrust in EMO research today is clearly in the area of evolutionary many-objective optimization (EMaO), which focuses on addressing four or more objectives. While several efficient EMaO algorithms are in place based on reference vectors, the idea is interesting enough to be pursued further.

Another current development in EMO is in the use of machine learning (ML) methods for enhancing performance of EMO and EMaO algorithms. In the past two decades, ML has experienced a surge of activities, mainly due to the availability of data and the need for finding intelligence from data. Evolving a population of solutions and their objective/constraint values within an EMO algorithm can also be seen as a series of evolving data. ML methods can mine the data to reveal interesting search patterns and directions, which in turn can help make EMO methods faster and more reliable. Various such efforts in utilizing ML to improve EMO are underway. On a different note, EMO researchers should also find ways to utilize EC and EMO algorithms for enhancing ML's performance to make EMO an integral part of the current ML revolution.

Surrogate-assisted EMO is another area which is getting significant attention for its own right. Optimizing for a budget of solution evaluations will keep EMO applications practically viable.

Challenging test-problem development for benchmarking EMO algorithms should always be a constant thrust of EMO researchers. I am happy to see the original ZDT and DTLZ-based philosophies are being constantly extended to create more challenging test problems and EMO algorithms are improving consistently as a result.

5. What do you think are the most important challenges EMO has to face in the future?

EMO and EMaO algorithms are now quite capable of addressing different kinds of multi- and many-objective problems, although further improvements are always necessary. They have performed well on challenging test problems and some small-sized engineering problems, but their real test will come when they are extensively applied to large-scale real-world problems. Industries are slowly but surely embracing EMO algorithms for solving two- and three- objective problems mostly (thanks to the use of dedicated commercial software and public-domain codes on EMO!) and it may be a while before they move to addressing more objectives. In the meantime, EMO researchers should advance the current practices as well.

First, more representative problems from real-world problems need to be identified and used to test our best EMaO algorithms for their working. In this direction, a direct collaboration with commercial software companies and researchers in application industries would be helpful.

Second, many-objective problems demand an easy and insightful visualization technique to understand trade-offs among Pareto-optimal solutions. There is a lack of a suitable visualization technique for understanding trade-offs, feasible search spaces, Pareto boundaries, etc., conveniently. Let us accept that the standard parallel coordinate plot (PCP) or radial visualization (RadViz) or scatter plots do not cut it. We may get influenced by high-dimensional data analysis literature for a clue here, but let us understand that our data have a special property – they possess a trade-off among the dimensions, in which generic data analysis folks may not be particularly interested. Hence, EMO researchers may have to find a solution for many-objective Pareto-optimal data visualization themselves.

Third, I strongly believe optimization algorithms must be customized for specific problem classes to make them more efficient both in terms of computational time and solution accuracy. While ML methods can be of help here (as alluded to before), practical use of EMO algorithms must be accompanied by an interactive platform which enables monitoring and aiding in the solution process by real users during the optimization process. Users' many years of experience on the problem can be utilized to customize an algorithm on the fly. Optimization algorithms discover useful variable interactions and patterns through their iterations, and a user's interaction can be made more fruitful if such discoveries can be shared with the user for their feedback on the relevance of the discoveries. Preference-related feedback can also be integrated here for multi-objective problems. We should soon see more such interactive EMO platforms being developed.

In most EMO and EMaO studies, we have focused on developing selection mechanisms for handling multiple objectives and have not spent much time on creation mechanisms for finding new and effective solutions. Unless new and diverse solutions are created by EMO's generation process, the multi-objective selection operator cannot do much. We should start focusing on hybrid genetic and local search methods and focus on creating more solutions directly in places where there is a lack of non-dominated solutions in the current population.

EMO has matured enough now to be applied to address large-scale societal and industrial problems. Problems affecting societies, such as climate change, obesity, forest management, agricultural management problems involving water, energy and food, and others, involve many conflicting objectives in terms of operating and installation costs, environmental effects, sustainability issues, etc., having numerous variables that can be adjusted with time and having constraints which must be satisfied to make a solution implementable. Finding a few alternative Pareto-optimal solutions by EMO algorithms customized to such problems can provide policy-makers with a new and transparent solution approach. Industrial problems such as supply-chain management, large manufacturing system operation, and integrated multi-level design tasks are other areas.

EMO algorithms, like single-objective EC methods, are stochastic and cannot ever have a theoretical convergence proof for any arbitrary problem, as supported by the no-free-lunch theorem. However, an EMO algorithm's population approach and its recombination operator help establish an implicit parallel search, which makes the EMO algorithm unique and different from other optimization methods. Collectively, we should find and focus on addressing problems that are difficult to solve by existing point-based methods, but a clever design of an EMO method can help find acceptable solutions.

6. During your career, you have held numerous important positions. You have already mentioned your times in Dortmund and the ETH Zurich as visiting professor. Your

main affiliation has been at the IIT Kanpur in India. After 15 years of service you decided to take a position in Helsinki (Finland). What was your main motivation for that?

I started my professional academic career at IIT Kanpur in India in 1993, when GAs were then mostly unheard of and their practice was questioned in engineering departments. I kept working on some key issues needed to popularize EC and make EC an effective tool for search and optimization in practice. I am happy that a few of these contributions have become popular over the years, including my parameter-less constraint handling approach, real-parameter recombination (SBX) and polynomial mutation operators, multi-objective optimization algorithm (NSGA series), multi-objective test problem construction, two textbooks on optimization, and others. I had the good fortune to have extremely dedicated students with excellent programming skills to help me execute these studies.

From time to time I realized that I needed to get feedback and have real discussions with experts in the field. I took a few opportunities that came my way to visit and interact with key EC experts: University of Dortmund with the Humboldt Fellowship from Alexander von Humboldt Foundation, Germany during 1998–1999, ETH Zurich with visiting professorship in 2001, University of Karlsruhe with Bessel Research Prize Award from Alexander von Humboldt Foundation, Germany in 2003, Nanyang Technological University, Singapore with A* project visit in 2006, Helsinki School of Economics with Finland Distinguished Professorship from the Academy of Finland during 2007–2009, and a number of bilateral project visits between India and European countries. These extended visits not only put me on the right track, but also exposed my work to experts in the field. Although such frequent visits came at the expense of relocating my family, I would recommend to young and isolated researchers to embrace such research visits as opportunities, rather than a disadvantage. I thank my family for their sacrifice and adjustments which I sincerely hope have given them better exposure and made them better individuals.

7. The next—and until now last—major change came in 2011 where you moved to East Lansing (USA) to become Professor and Koenig Endowed Chair at Michigan State University, which definitely came with new challenges for you and your family.

The genetic algorithms research was started in Michigan in early sixties. Michigan State University (MSU) is one of the few universities in USA which traditionally had a strong focus in evolutionary computation field. The BEACON center for the study of evolution in action funded by National Science Foundation (NSF) at MSU enabled a major research collaboration opportunity in various aspects of evolution led by Prof. Erik Goodman. When an endowed chair faculty position was offered to me at MSU, I did not have any second thought. Thus, far, I had the opportunity to work with several MSU colleagues from various disciplines, visiting researchers from various countries, and automobile and chemical industries in Michigan to have a better fulfillment of my research career. The move also provided great educational opportunities to my children at a critical time of their careers.

8. Finally, we come to another topic that might be very interesting, in particular, for younger scholars. We recall a Keynote Talk of yours where you presented a new evolutionary algorithm for a particular resource allocation problem. While the results were amazing, you mentioned that you have faced major issues to get the related paper published. Many readers might assume that publication of a paper that contains such great results and that comes from a renowned researcher like you should just be a formality. Apparently, this is not always the case. Could you comment on that?

Most researchers may have faced such incidents in their careers. Since you mentioned it, let me address it to hopefully make a remark on the current paper review system in our field. What I thought was a great EC-application study which showcased an EC-based solution methodology to solve a billion-variable resource allocation problem (never done before), editors and reviewers of a leading EC journal suggested that I 'compare' my approach with a few recommended existing EC methods. Upon a survey, I found that the suggested EC methods addressed completely different kinds of problems having only 500 to 1000 variables. It was obvious that these methods were generic and would not have worked on a specific problem class involving million to billion-variable integer variables. We developed a customized EC algorithm for solving such large-scale problems and our purpose was to demonstrate that the population-based approach with customized recombination and mutation operators was a better answer to this type of exa-scale optimization problems rather than the standard point-based structured algorithms. I really wanted the paper to appear in an EC-based journal so we, as a community, could celebrate and propagate EC techniques with such defining studies. Anyway, the paper was eventually published in a non-EC journal, after I withdrew the paper from the EC journal.

With this experience and from a few other recent reviews on my papers, I am increasingly convinced that most of our current reviewers expect that every article, to be published, must fall into certain patterns. A paper should have a new idea, but no matter how small or incremental the idea is, it must be compared with many existing algorithms, it must produce page-long tables presenting comparative results, and it must end by citing papers from most renowned authors in the field. Such a mindset of reviewers is harmful for the field in the long run. While there is a need for comparative studies, there is also a need for new and direction-providing papers, addressing bigger issues of the field, providing first-time ideas which cannot be compared with anything from the past, and defining applications that will keep EC alive and meaningful to practitioners. Let us be more inclusive and open-minded.

9. NSGA-III is one of the most cited and most widely used multi-objective evolutionary algorithms. Rumors say that it was also not easy for you to get the two initial works on this algorithm published. Is this true?

It is true that the NSGA-III paper was rejected at first. Apparently, the paper exceeded the strict maximum two-time review policy restriction. Apparently, we failed to follow the suggestion of a reviewer to remove one of the three application problems, as the reviewer thought the paper was too long. I blame it to the lack of patience everyone has these days to pick signals from noise, but it is disturbing to think how many such trivial but harsh decisions are ruining the fate of important studies. I am glad that the decision was overturned eventually and the paper made its way to see the light of day, enriching the journal and EMO community and receiving significant attention to date.

Another not-so-fortunate outcome occurred with the Deb-Thiele-Laumanns- Zitzler (DTLZ) scalable test suite development paper, which never appeared in a journal due to its rejection, but its book-chapter version is probably one of the most highly-cited EMO articles today. I am sure everyone has such examples to cite, but we should all collectively plan for ways and means to reduce such unfortunate events, as these important studies, if can be envisioned by editors and reviewers about their possible future impact, could not only help the field, they will enhance the citation profile of our journals and conferences.

10. Finally, do you have a message for the authors out there that are struggling to get their research published?

I actually have messages for both authors, reviewers and editors. I believe as an author of any work, we should first be "satisfied" and "happy" with our work. If the author is not happy about its content, how can the author convince reviewers or readers to pay attention to it? Thus, my message for authors is to keep improving your work until you think you have tried enough to bring the work to a logical conclusion and in your opinion the work contributes to advance the field. Then, look for a journal/conference which is most suitable for the work. If you are a budding researcher, I understand that you need a good "quantity" of papers, so work on as many ideas as you can, collaborate with as many researchers as you can, and publish. However, once in a while, take a break, and think big and look at your field from 10,000 feet above and identify areas that need deeper attention. Work on these challenging ideas and see if you can make a crack. These works will give you fame, inspire you, and keep you alive.

As to the reviewers, my message is to have a bit of patience. Every article to be conceived worked on and written needs a lot of effort, taking many months to years, which every one of us has experience with. Treat others' papers the same way you would expect your articles to be treated. Here is an idea! Instead of assuming that the article you are reviewing is a reject to start with and looking for positive aspects to decide if you would accept the paper, think the other way. Assume every article is an accept to start with and then evaluate to see if it has enough new messages/results for it to be an accept or reject. Know that every author expects some constructive comments, particularly when the paper is rejected. If you are rejecting the article, please provide enough feedback so that authors find directions to modify it. As a reviewer, always know that you are in some sense in charge of what should be published and what should not be. You need to elevate yourself to decide the article's contribution to the overall growth and advancement of the field. You are a key component in this endeavor and everyone in the EMO community thanks you profusely for your time and efforts.

In my opinion, editors of journals and proceedings are the most influential persons in a field, indirectly controlling the focus of the field. They should not be intermediaries who simply count the number of accepts and rejects to decide the fate of a submission. They are the leaders of the field. They can judge a paper on their own very well and should be courageous enough to change a reviewer's comments and decisions if they think otherwise. Let every stakeholder in the review system (authors, editors and reviewers) care only about our field, its overall advancement and acceptance to contemporary other fields, rather than any other matter.

We have come a long way with all-round and well-grounded activities. Let us all together make the EMO research and application unbiased, top-notch, rewarding, and enjoyable. Let us all feel proud to be a part of the EMO revolution.

Acknowledgments: The opinions of Kalyanmoy Deb presented in this article are solely his own and does not reflect the views of anyone else, including his current and past employers and collaborators. His frank opinion and criticism, if any, is meant for no specific individual or entity, and the sole purpose of their mention here was to improve general quality of the state-of-the art of the EMO field.

Conflicts of Interest: The authors declare no conflict of interest.

Disclaimer/Publisher's Note: The statements, opinions and data contained in all publications are solely those of the individual author(s) and contributor(s) and not of MDPI and/or the editor(s). MDPI and/or the editor(s) disclaim responsibility for any injury to people or property resulting from any ideas, methods, instructions or products referred to in the content.

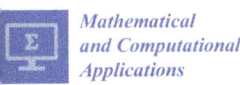

Review

MCDM, EMO and Hybrid Approaches: Tutorial and Review

Ankur Sinha [1,*] and Jyrki Wallenius [2]

1 Centre for Innovation Incubation and Entrepreneurship (CIIE), Indian Institute of Management Ahmedabad, Ahmedabad 380015, India
2 School of Business, Aalto University, P.O. Box 11000, 00076 Aalto, Finland
* Correspondence: asinha@iima.ac.in

Abstract: Most of the practical applications that require optimization often involve multiple objectives. These objectives, when conflicting in nature, pose both optimization as well as decision-making challenges. An optimization procedure for such a multi-objective problem requires computing (computer-based search) and decision making to identify the most preferred solution. Researchers and practitioners working in various domains have integrated computing and decision-making tasks in several ways, giving rise to a variety of algorithms to handle multi-objective optimization problems. For instance, an *a priori* approach requires formulating (or eliciting) a decision maker's value function and then performing a one-shot optimization of the value function, whereas an *a posteriori* decision-making approach requires a large number of diverse Pareto-optimal solutions to be available before a final decision is made. Alternatively, an *interactive* approach involves interactions with the decision maker to guide the search towards better solutions (or the most preferred solution). In our tutorial and survey paper, we first review the fundamental concepts of multi-objective optimization. Second, we discuss the classic interactive approaches from the field of Multi-Criteria Decision Making (MCDM), followed by the underlying idea and methods in the field of Evolutionary Multi-Objective Optimization (EMO). Third, we consider several promising MCDM and EMO hybrid approaches that aim to capitalize on the strengths of the two domains. We conclude with discussions on important behavioral considerations related to the use of such approaches and future work.

Keywords: evolutionary multi-objective optimization; multi-criteria decision making; interactive optimization

1. Introduction

Multi-Criteria Decision Making (MCDM) as a scientific field is some 60 years old. Its roots are in Goal Programming [1] and Multi-Attribute Utility Theory (MAUT) [2]. A subsequently popular subfield, interactive man–machine multi-objective optimization, developed greatly during the 1970s. The common frameworks used a discrete set of choices and a mathematical programming problem formulation (optimization) to solve multi-objective problems. With the interactive approaches, phases of decision making and computing would alternate. The aim was to converge towards the most preferred solution on the Pareto-optimal frontier.

Independently from MCDM, the Evolutionary Multi-Objective Optimization (EMO) approaches started developing during the 1980s [3]. Many of the EMO scholars had an engineering or a computer science background. EMO algorithms [4,5] have been applied to problems with multiple objectives for the task of finding a well-representative set of Pareto-optimal solutions. These methods [6,7] have been successful in solving a wide variety of problems with two or three objectives. However, these methodologies are criticized for their excessive computational expense, and they often tend to suffer while solving problems with objectives higher than three [8,9]. The major hindrances in handling a higher number of objectives relate to stagnation in search, increased dimensionality of Pareto-optimal front, large computational cost, and difficulty in visualization of the objective space. These difficulties are inherent to optimization problems having a large number of objectives and are not easy to eliminate; rather, procedures to handle such difficulties need to be explored. EMO methods that are better equipped at handling a larger number of objectives are being continuously explored [10–12]. Some of these approaches aim for solutions that are near Pareto-optimal and provide a discretized and diverse representation of the high-dimensional frontier for many-objective (i.e., more than two or three objectives) problems. However, the level of discretization for an accurate and well-represented many-objective frontier would require a very large number of points. Even if a fine-grained discretization is achieved with a large number of points, the decision-making challenges still remain.

The areas of MCDM and EMO were solving similar problems; therefore, the researchers working in these domains decided to pursue active collaboration through formal channels such as common conferences and seminars. As a result, Branke, Deb, Miettinen, and Słowiński organized the first Dagstuhl seminar [13] in 2004 to allow collaboration between the two communities. This led to researchers combining ideas from MCDM to EMO and vice-versa. Since then, the Dagstuhl seminar has been organized every few years to enhance the collaboration and flow of ideas from one research community to the other. In this article, we evaluate the classic studies in MCDM and EMO and also the hybrid approaches that have been proposed for handling many-objective problems. Some of the review papers that talk about interactive multi-objective optimization are [14,15]. This article takes a tutorial-cum-review approach to discuss the classic ideas published in the areas of MCDM, EMO, and their intersection and is structured as follows. In Section 2, we cover the theoretical concepts on optimization and decision making that arise in the multi-objective literature. This is followed by Section 3, where we discuss how search and decision making can be integrated together in various ways to find the most preferred point for the decision maker (DM). Thereafter, we discuss the classic MCDM (Section 4), EMO (Section 5), and hybrid (Section 6) approaches that have been discussed in the literature over the past few decades. We conclude the article in Section 7 with discussions on behavioral considerations and future work.

2. Multi-Objective Optimization

Multi-objective optimization [4,16–18] involves two or more conflicting objectives that are supposed to be simultaneously optimized subject to a given set of constraints. These problems arise in various fields of science, engineering, economics, and mathematics and have been widely studied in the literature. However, modern applications keep posing challenges with an increasing level of complexity. The complexity depends on a number of factors, such as number of objectives, number of decision variables, type of decision variables (continuous, discrete), number of constraints, and functional form of the functions in the optimization problems (linear, convex, non-convex, non-differentiable, etc.) that may lead to non-separability and multi-modality. While many of the above difficulties are common to single-objective optimization as well, multi-objective optimization poses additional challenges as such problems do not have a single solution which would simultaneously maximize/minimize each of the objectives; instead, there is a set of solutions from which a rational DM should choose. These solutions are called Pareto-optimal solutions. Choosing the most preferred solution from the set of Pareto-optimal solutions requires an additional step of decision making, which is often subjective and not straightforward to model. The challenges posed by multi-objective optimization often include inability to generate a complete ordering of points and requirement of maintaining a pool of non-dominated points. A feasible point in multi-objective optimization is considered to be non-dominated within a set when there does not exist any other feasible point that is better than the former in terms of some objective and is not worse than the former in terms of other objectives. The concept is discussed in detail in Section 2.1. Difficulty in representation and visualization of the solutions in objective space, especially while working with many objectives, makes decision making difficult, and therefore requires preference learning while searching for the point most preferred by the DM. Below, we describe a general multi-objective problem ($p \geq 2$):

$$\begin{aligned}
\text{Maximize} \quad & \mathbf{f}(\mathbf{x}) = (f_1(\mathbf{x}), \ldots, f_p(\mathbf{x})) \\
\text{subject to} \quad & \mathbf{g}(\mathbf{x}) \geq \mathbf{0}, \mathbf{h}(\mathbf{x}) = \mathbf{0} \\
& \mathbf{x}^{(L)} \leq \mathbf{x} \leq \mathbf{x}^{(U)}
\end{aligned} \quad (1)$$

In the above formulation, $\mathbf{x} = (x_1, x_2, \ldots, x_n)$ is the n-dimensional decision variable vector which represents the decision space. A search is expected to be performed within the constrained region of the decision space that is determined by the inequality constraints ($\mathbf{g}(\mathbf{x}) \geq \mathbf{0}$), equality constraints ($\mathbf{h}(\mathbf{x}) = \mathbf{0}$) and box constraints ($\mathbf{x}^{(L)} \leq \mathbf{x} \leq \mathbf{x}^{(U)}$). We refer to the set of solutions which are feasible with respect to the constraints and are *non-dominated* with respect to all feasible solutions, as *Pareto-optimal* solutions. Among the Pareto-optimal solutions, the solution that is the most preferred by the DM will be referred to as the *most preferred solution*. We provide formal definitions for these terms in the next sections.

Note that the objective vector $\mathbf{f}(\mathbf{x})$ is the image of the decision vector $\mathbf{x}$ under the objective function $\mathbf{f}$. In a single-objective optimization ($p = 1$) problem, the feasible set is completely ordered according to the objective function $\mathbf{f}(\mathbf{x}) = f_1(\mathbf{x})$, such that for solutions, $\mathbf{x}^{(1)}$ and $\mathbf{x}^{(2)}$ in the decision space, either $f_1(\mathbf{x}^{(1)}) \geq f_1(\mathbf{x}^{(2)})$ or $f_1(\mathbf{x}^{(2)}) \geq f_1(\mathbf{x}^{(1)})$. Therefore, for two solutions in the objective space, there are two possibilities with respect to the $\geq$ relation. However, when several objectives ($p \geq 2$) are involved, the feasible set is not necessarily completely ordered but partially ordered. In multi-objective problems, for any two objective vectors, $\mathbf{f}(\mathbf{x}^{(1)})$ and $\mathbf{f}(\mathbf{x}^{(2)})$, the relations $=$, $>$ and $\geq$ can be extended as follows:

- $\mathbf{f}(\mathbf{x}^{(1)}) = \mathbf{f}(\mathbf{x}^{(2)}) \Leftrightarrow f_i(\mathbf{x}^{(1)}) = f_i(\mathbf{x}^{(2)}) : i \in \{1, 2, \ldots, p\}$
- $\mathbf{f}(\mathbf{x}^{(1)}) \geq \mathbf{f}(\mathbf{x}^{(2)}) \Leftrightarrow f_i(\mathbf{x}^{(1)}) \geq f_i(\mathbf{x}^{(2)}) : i \in \{1, 2, \ldots, p\}$
- $\mathbf{f}(\mathbf{x}^{(1)}) > \mathbf{f}(\mathbf{x}^{(2)}) \Leftrightarrow f_i(\mathbf{x}^{(1)}) > f_i(\mathbf{x}^{(2)}) : i \in \{1, 2, \ldots, p\}$

While comparing the multi-objective scenario with the single-objective case, we find that for two solutions in the objective space there are three possibilities with respect to the $\geq$ relation. These possibilities are: $\mathbf{f}(\mathbf{x}^{(1)}) \geq \mathbf{f}(\mathbf{x}^{(2)})$, $\mathbf{f}(\mathbf{x}^{(2)}) \geq \mathbf{f}(\mathbf{x}^{(1)})$ or $\mathbf{f}(\mathbf{x}^{(1)}) \not\geq \mathbf{f}(\mathbf{x}^{(2)}) \wedge \mathbf{f}(\mathbf{x}^{(2)}) \not\geq \mathbf{f}(\mathbf{x}^{(1)})$. If any of the first two possibilities are met, it allows to rank or order the solutions independent of any preference information (or a DM). On the other hand, if the first two possibilities are not met, the solutions cannot be ranked or ordered without incorporating preference information (or involving a DM). Drawing analogy from the above discussion, the relations $<$ and $\leq$ can be extended in a similar way.

2.1. Dominance Concept

Based on the established binary relations for two vectors in the previous section, the following dominance concept [16] can be constituted:

- $\mathbf{x}^{(1)}$ strongly dominates $\mathbf{x}^{(2)} \Leftrightarrow \mathbf{f}(\mathbf{x}^{(1)}) > \mathbf{f}(\mathbf{x}^{(2)})$;
- $\mathbf{x}^{(1)}$ (weakly) dominates $\mathbf{x}^{(2)} \Leftrightarrow \mathbf{f}(\mathbf{x}^{(1)}) \geq \mathbf{f}(\mathbf{x}^{(2)}) \wedge \mathbf{f}(\mathbf{x}^{(1)}) \neq \mathbf{f}(\mathbf{x}^{(2)})$;
- $\mathbf{x}^{(1)}$ and $\mathbf{x}^{(2)}$ are non-dominated with respect to each other $\Leftrightarrow \mathbf{f}(\mathbf{x}^{(1)}) \not\geq \mathbf{f}(\mathbf{x}^{(2)}) \wedge \mathbf{f}(\mathbf{x}^{(2)}) \not\geq \mathbf{f}(\mathbf{x}^{(1)})$.

In the case of weak dominance, it is common to drop the word *weak* and refer to it only with *dominance*, which is why we use the word *weak* in brackets. Dominance of $\mathbf{x}^{(1)}$ over $\mathbf{x}^{(2)}$ essentially means that no component of $\mathbf{f}(\mathbf{x}^{(1)})$ is less than the corresponding component of $\mathbf{f}(\mathbf{x}^{(2)})$, and at least one component of $\mathbf{f}(\mathbf{x}^{(1)})$ is greater than the corresponding component of $\mathbf{f}(\mathbf{x}^{(2)})$. The above dominance concept is also explained in Figure 1 for a two-objective maximization case. In Figure 1, two shaded regions are shown in reference to point A. The shaded region in the north-east corner (excluding the lines) is the region which strongly dominates point A, the shaded region in the south-west corner (excluding the lines) is strongly dominated by point A, and the non-shaded region is the non-dominated region.

Therefore, point A strongly dominates point B, and points A, E, and D are non-dominated with respect to each other. Note that point A weakly dominates point C. From hereon, we only talk about dominance by avoiding the word *weak*.

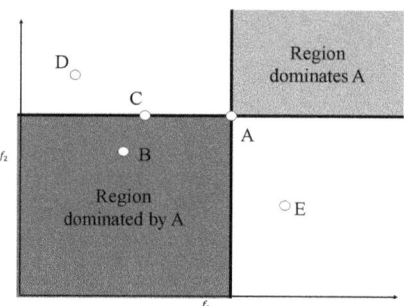

Figure 1. Dominance concept for a maximization problem where A dominates B and C; A, D, and E are non-dominated.

Many of the existing evolutionary multi-objective optimization algorithms use the dominance principle to converge towards the Pareto-optimal set of solutions. The concept allows us to partially order two decision vectors based on the corresponding objective vectors in the absence of any preference information. The algorithms which operate with a sparse set of solutions in the decision space and the corresponding images in the objective space usually give priority to a solution which dominates another solution. The solution which is not dominated with respect to any other solution in the sparse set is referred to as a *non-dominated solution* within that set.

In case of a discrete set of solutions: the subset whose solutions are not dominated by any solution in the discrete set is referred to as the *non-dominated set* within the discrete set. When the set in consideration is the entire search space, the resulting non-dominated set is referred to as a *Pareto-optimal set*, or the frontier formed with these points is referred to as the *Pareto-optimal front*. To formally define a Pareto-optimal front, consider a set $\mathbf{X}$ which constitutes the entire decision space with solutions $\mathbf{x} \in \mathbf{X}$. The subset $\mathbf{X}^* : \mathbf{X}^* \subset \mathbf{X}$, containing solutions $\mathbf{x}^*$ which are not dominated by any $\mathbf{x}$ in the entire decision space, forms the Pareto-optimal front.

The concept of a Pareto-optimal front and a non-dominated set are illustrated in Figure 2. The shaded region in the figure represents $\mathbf{f}(\mathbf{x}) : \mathbf{x} \in \mathbf{X}$. It is the image in the objective space of the entire feasible region in the decision space. The bold curve represents the Pareto-optimal front for a maximization problem. Mathematically, this curve is $\mathbf{f}(\mathbf{x}^*) : \mathbf{x}^* \in \mathbf{X}^*$, which are all the optimal points for the two objective optimization problem. A number of points are also plotted in the figure, which constitute a discrete set. Among this set of points, the points connected by broken lines are the points which are not dominated by any point in the discrete set. Therefore, these points constitute a non-dominated set within the discrete set. The other points which do not belong to the non-dominated set are dominated by at least one of the points in the non-dominated set.

In the field of MCDM, a Pareto-optimal point $\mathbf{f}(\mathbf{x}^*)$ in the objective space is often referred to as a non-dominated point, as it is not dominated by any feasible point in the objective space. The corresponding decision vector $\mathbf{x}^*$ is referred to as an *efficient point*. Similarly, if $\mathbf{f}(\mathbf{z})$ is a dominated point in the objective space, then $\mathbf{z}$ would be referred to as an *inefficient point* in the decision space. In other words, a point is efficient if and only if it is the inverse image of a non-dominated objective vector, and it is inefficient if and only if it is an inverse image of a dominated objective vector.

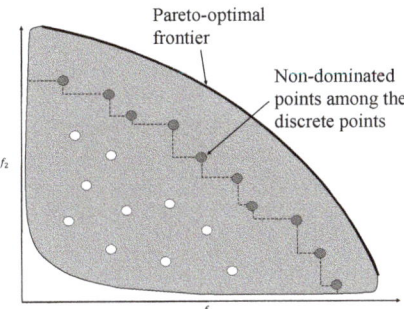

Figure 2. Non-dominated set from a discrete set of points and a Pareto-optimal front that dominates the entire search space.

2.2. Decision Making

Even though there are multiple potentially optimal solutions to a multi-objective problem, there is often just a single solution which is of interest to the DM; which is termed as the *most preferred solution*. Search and decision making are two intricacies [19] involved in handling any multi-objective problem. Search requires an intensive exploration in the decision space to get close to the Pareto-optimal solutions; on the other hand, decision making is required to provide preference information over the available non-dominated solutions in pursuance of the most preferred solution.

In a decision-making context, the solutions can be compared and ordered based on the preference information, though there can be situations where strict preference of one solution over the other is not obtained, and the ordering is partial. For instance, consider two vectors, $x^{(1)}$ and $x^{(2)}$, in the decision space, having their images, $f(x^{(1)})$ and $f(x^{(2)})$, in the objective space. A preference structure can be defined using three binary relations $\succ$, $\sim$, and $\|$. The meaning of the binary relations are provided below:

- $x^{(1)} \succ x^{(2)} \Leftrightarrow x^{(1)}$ is preferred over $x^{(2)}$;
- $x^{(1)} \sim x^{(2)} \Leftrightarrow x^{(1)}$ and $x^{(2)}$ are equally preferable;
- $x^{(1)} \| x^{(2)} \Leftrightarrow x^{(1)}$ and $x^{(2)}$ are incomparable;

where the preference relation, $\succ$, is asymmetric, the indifference relation, $\sim$, is reflexive and symmetric, and the incomparability relation, $\|$, is irreflexive and symmetric. A weak preference $\succeq$ relation can be established as $\succeq = \succ \cup \sim$ such that

- $x^{(1)} \succeq x^{(2)} \Leftrightarrow x^{(1)}$ is either preferred over $x^{(2)}$ or they are equally preferred.

As already mentioned, preference can easily be established for pairs where one solution dominates the other. However, for pairs which are non-dominated with respect to each other, a DM's input is required to establish a preference. The following is the inference for preference choice which can be drawn from dominance:

- If $x^{(1)}$ dominates $x^{(2)} \Rightarrow x^{(1)} \succ x^{(2)}$.

It is common to emulate a DM with a value function, $V(f_1(x), \ldots, f_p(x))$, which is scalar in nature and assigns a value or a measure of satisfaction to each of the solutions. For two solutions, $x^{(1)}$ and $x^{(2)}$:

- If $x^{(1)} \succ x^{(2)} \Leftrightarrow V(f(x^{(1)})) > V(f(x^{(2)}))$;
- If $x^{(1)} \sim x^{(2)} \Leftrightarrow V(f(x^{(1)})) = V(f(x^{(2)}))$;
- If $x^{(1)} \succeq x^{(2)} \Leftrightarrow V(f(x^{(1)})) \geq V(f(x^{(2)}))$.

2.3. Preference Eliciting and Modeling

There are several ways of eliciting preference information from the DM that can be used to create a preference model to be incorporated in the search process. Some of the approaches are listed below:

1. Asking about goals or aspiration levels for the objectives;
2. Pairwise comparisons of solutions in objective space;
3. Asking the DM which objectives and by how much they would be willing to worsen to allow improvements in other objectives;
4. Asking the DM to specify exact marginal rates of substitution between objectives and a reference objective (trade-offs);
5. Directly asking for the search direction;
6. Directly asking the importance of each objective to get an idea of weights or to rank the objectives;
7. Yes–no questions, for instance: Do you like this search direction?

After the preferences are obtained from the DM, there are various ways in which the information is incorporated in the search process. For instance, value functions could be generated based on the preferences expressed by the DM. Methods differ based on the kind of value function, i.e., linear or non-linear, that is chosen to model preference information. While some methods generate a single maximum discriminating value function fitting preference information, others generate multiple value functions fitting the same preference information. Scalarizing functions (for example, see [20]), weighted sum of objectives (similar to a linear value function), and the ϵ-constraint method [21] are other approaches to convert the multi-objective problem into a single-objective problem that aligns with the DM's preferences. Sometimes, the dominance principle is modified to search in a region that better fits the preferences of the DM.

There are other very interesting approaches to modeling preferences in MCDM. Such approaches are outranking relations and rule-based models. Outranking methods were developed by B. Roy in the late 1960s, originating from criticism of utility theory in solving practical problems (see [22,23]). An outranking relation is a binary relation. It is based on the ideas of concordance and discordance. "Loosely speaking", alternative **x** outranks **y**, if there are enough arguments (attributes favoring **x** over **y**) to declare that **x** is at least as good as **y** while there is no essential reason to refute this statement. Decision rules are expressions of the form "if, then" [24]. Procedures for generating decision rules use an inductive learning principle. The authors distinguish three types of rules: certain, possible, and approximate. Certain rules are generated from lower approximations of unions of classes; possible rules are generated from upper approximations of unions of classes and approximate rules are generated from boundary regions. To structure the data prior to the induction of rules, the authors suggest using the Dominance-based Rough Set Approach (DRSA) [25]. As an illustrative example, the authors consider the problem of evaluating high school students based on performance in some of the subjects using "if, then" rules. Multi-criteria classification and sorting are frequently considered problems in rule-based preference modeling, although the ideas can be extended for the problem of identifying the most preferred alternative. Both outranking relations and rule-base preference modeling were originally developed for the problem of choosing among discrete (known) alternatives, and not the mathematical programming or EMO context. Hence, we do not extensively cover them in our survey and tutorial. There are some exceptions, though. For example, the Light Beam search approach (which is based on utilizing outranking relations) was developed for solving multi-objective mathematical programming problems [26]. In a later section, we illustrate how the Light Beam approach is used in an EMO context.

In the later part of the paper, we discuss approaches that elicit and model the preferences of the DM in different ways while searching for the most preferred point.

3. Incorporating Decision Maker's Preferences

Searching and decision making can be combined in various ways to generate procedures which can be classified into three broad categories.

3.1. A Priori Approach

In this approach, DM's preferences are elicited before the start of the algorithm, then the optimization algorithm is executed by incorporating the preference information, and the most preferred solution is identified. Figure 3 shows the process followed to arrive at the most preferred solution. This approach has been common among MCDM practitioners, who realized the complexities involved in decision making for such problems. Their approach to the problem is to ask simple questions from the DM before starting the search process.

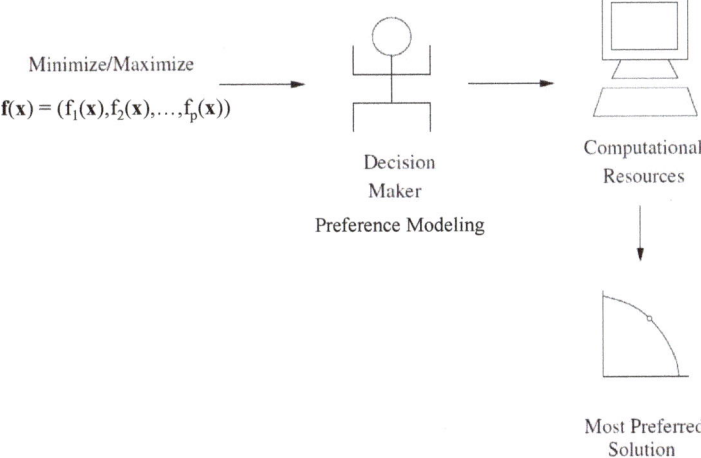

Minimize/Maximize

$\mathbf{f}(\mathbf{x}) = (f_1(\mathbf{x}), f_2(\mathbf{x}), \ldots, f_p(\mathbf{x}))$

Decision Maker
Preference Modeling

Computational Resources

Most Preferred Solution

Figure 3. *A priori* approach.

After eliciting information from the DM, the multi-objective problem is usually converted into a single-objective problem. One of the early approaches, that is, MAUT [2], used the initial information from the DM to construct a utility function which reduced the problem to a single-objective optimization problem. Scalarizing functions (for example, [20]) are also commonly used by the researchers in this field to convert a multi-objective problem into a single-objective problem.

Since information is elicited towards the beginning, the solution obtained after executing the algorithm may not be close to the most preferred solution. Moreover, the DM's preferences might be different for solutions close to the Pareto-optimal front, and the initial inputs taken from them may not conform to it. Therefore, relying on this approach, it may be difficult to get close to the actual solution which meets the requirements of the DM. The approach is also highly error-prone, as even slight deviations in providing preference information at the beginning may lead to entirely different solutions. Such errors are common because of the inability of the DM to reliably express preferences in case of not knowing the solution space or having no precise understanding of own preferences at the beginning of the preference elicitation process. To avoid the errors due to deviations, researchers in the EMO field used the approach in a slightly modified way. They produced multiple solutions in the region of interest to the DM (often close to the Pareto-optimal front) [27–30], and then elicited the DM's preferences. We discuss this approach next.

3.2. A Posteriori Approach

In this approach, after a set of (approximate) Pareto-optimal solutions are obtained using an optimization algorithm, decision making is performed to find the most preferred solution. Figure 4 shows the process followed to arrive at the final solution which is most preferred to a DM. This approach is based on the assumption that a complete knowledge of all the alternatives helps in taking better decisions. The research in the field of evolutionary multi-objective optimization has been directed along this approach, where the aim is to produce all the possible alternatives for the DM to make a choice. Until relatively recently, the community has largely ignored decision-making aspects and has been striving towards producing all the possible optimal solutions.

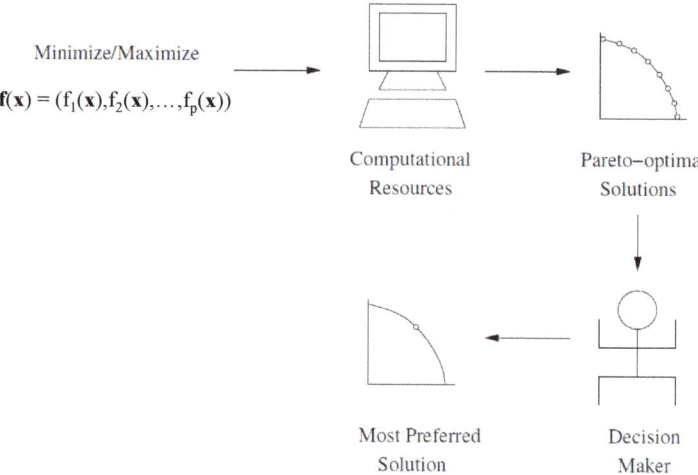

Figure 4. *A posteriori* approach.

There are enormous difficulties in finding the entire Pareto-optimal front for a many-objective problem. Even if it is assumed that an algorithm can approximate the Pareto-optimal front for a high-objective problem with a huge set of points, the herculean task of choosing the best point from the set still remains. For two and three objectives where the solutions in the objective space could be represented geometrically, making decisions might be easy (though even such an instance could be, in reality, a difficult task for a DM). Imagine a multi-objective problem with more than three objectives for which an evolutionary multi-objective algorithm is able to produce the entire front. The front is approximated with a large number of points and high accuracy. Since a graphical representation is not possible for the Pareto-points, how is a DM going to choose the most preferred point? There are of course decision aids available, but the limited accuracy with which the final choice could be made using these aids questions the purpose of producing the entire front with high accuracy. Binary comparisons can be a solution to choose the best point out of a set, but this can only be utilized if the points are very few in number. Therefore, offering the entire set of Pareto-points should not be considered as a complete solution to the problem. However, the difficulties related to decision making have been realized by EMO researchers only after copious research has already gone towards producing the entire Pareto-front for many-objective problems. Most of the EMO algorithms [6,7,10–12,31–33] that aim to produce the entire Pareto-optimal front would lie in this category.

3.3. Interactive Approach

In this approach, the DM interacts with the optimization algorithm and has multiple opportunities to provide preference information to the algorithm. The interaction between the DM and the optimization algorithm continues until a solution acceptable to the DM is obtained. The process is represented in Figure 5. Based on the type of interaction of the DM with the optimization algorithm, this approach is often implemented in two ways.

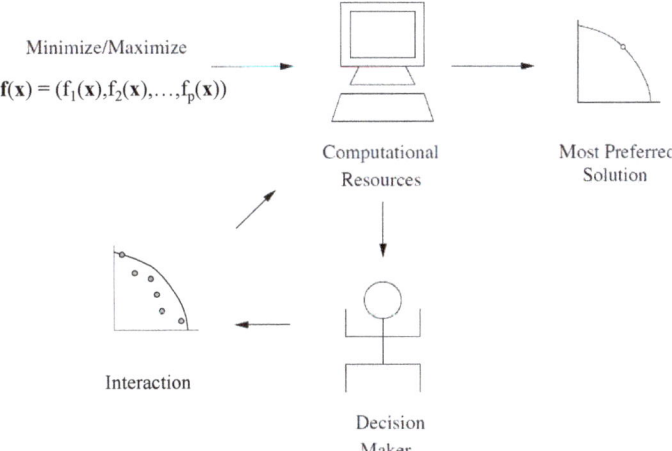

Figure 5. Interactive approach.

The first approach involves elicitation of preference information and execution of the optimization algorithm to obtain one or many Pareto-optimal solutions. If a solution acceptable to the DM is obtained, the process is terminated; otherwise, the process is restarted and continued until a satisfactory solution is found. In this approach, the progression towards the most preferred solution may take place on the Pareto-optimal frontier. MCDM researchers following an interactive approach usually elicit preference information and find a solution conforming to the inputs given by the DM. They iterate this process until a satisfactory solution is obtained. For example, when using a scalarization function, multiple reference points (or starting points) could be provided by the DM. Once a reference point is available, the computer provides a projection of that point on the Pareto-optimal frontier. This process converts the problem into a single-objective optimization problem and produces one of the Pareto-optimal points as the solution. If the point finally produced is not to the liking of the DM, the search is continued with new reference points and projections. This process is continued until a solution acceptable to the DM is obtained. The iterations of a simple algorithm using this approach are shown in Figure 6. The figure shows that a DM is able to find a satisfactory solution in three iterations.

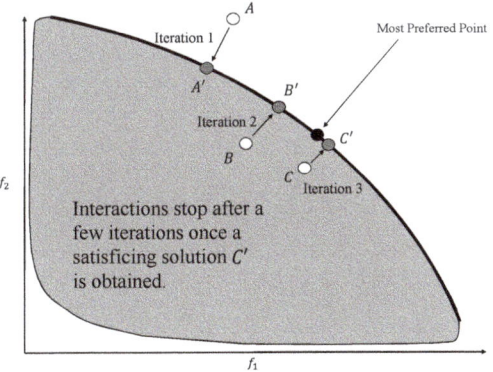

Figure 6. Interaction after a run.

EMO researchers have taken cues from their MCDM counterparts, wherein they used the powerful evolutionary search tool to produce multiple solutions in the region of interest to the DM or generate a small part of the Pareto-front which the DM finds interesting. This is a similar approach where interactions happen before and after a complete run of the EMO. The algorithm produces multiple solutions in a particular region or multiple regions of the Pareto-optimal front in a single run. Once the solutions are produced, another decision-making task is performed, and the solution to the liking of the DM is chosen. If none of the solutions are acceptable to the DM, the process of elicitation and search is repeated until a satisfactory solution is found. Some examples of evolutionary procedures which have used this approach are [34,35].

The second approach involves elicitation of preference information periodically from a DM while the optimization algorithm is progressing towards the Pareto-optimal frontier. In this approach, preference information is taken at the intermediate steps of the search algorithm, and the algorithm proceeds towards the most preferred point. This is an effective integration of the search and decision-making process, as both work simultaneously towards the exploration of the solution. Such an integration avoids multiple optimization runs and is therefore preferable for problems that are computationally expensive. It also allows the DM to better understand the consequences of their actions, as they can immediately see how the convergence direction changes. Some previous works which have been conducted in a similar vein in the MCDM field are [36,37], and in the EMO field, are [38–44]. The iterations of an algorithm that uses this approach, commonly referred to as a progressively interactive approach, is shown in Figure 7. The DM is presented with a set of points and is expected to choose one of the points to start the search. The choice of the DM gives clues to the search algorithm about the search direction, and the algorithm progresses towards the most preferred solution. The DM may change their preference structure as the search progresses, and the algorithm is able to adapt to such changes.

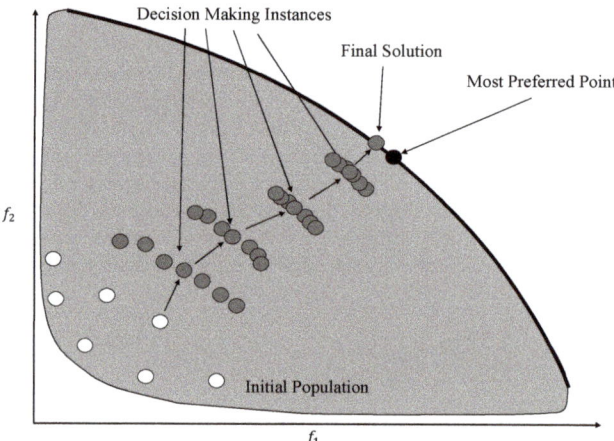

Figure 7. Progressive interaction during the run.

4. MCDM Interactive Techniques

Linear Programming (LP) was rather popular in large Western companies in the 1960s and 1970s, as well as in Gosplan (central government agency) for government level planning in the Soviet Union. To address the need to solve multi-objective LPs, Charnes and Cooper developed Goal Programming [1] in late 1950s and coined the name in the early 1960s. In Goal Programming, the DM is asked to specify aspiration levels in terms of objectives. The algorithm then finds a feasible solution that would minimize the weighted deviations from the aspiration levels. The original version of Goal Programming was for solving multiple-objective LPs. Goal Programming was not an interactive approach, and there was not an option to update the aspiration levels. In multi-objective linear programs, the concept of an optimum was being replaced by a "compromise" or a "non-dominated solution".

With simultaneous advances in computer technology (teletypes accessing main frame computers), the idea of interactively or progressively solving multi-objective optimization problems was proposed in early 1970s. In the interactive approach:

1. Phases of computing and decision making would alternate: the human would guide the computer (algorithm) towards the most preferred solution;
2. The human and the computer were performing tasks that they were good at;
3. Learning (of one's preferences) was possible;
4. The ideas were based on using linear programming or non-linear programming;
5. Systematic progress towards the most preferred solution would take place;
6. The methods would generally operate with non-dominated solutions, in other words, allow exploration of the Pareto-optimal (non-dominated) frontier.

We review the following classic interactive multi-objective optimization methods, which all represented the state of the art at the time:

1. STEP method due to Benayoun et al. (1971) [45];
2. GDF method due to Geoffrion, Dyer, and Feinberg (1972) [36];
3. ZW method due to Zionts and Wallenius (1976) [37];
4. Reference point method due to Wierzbicki (1980) [20];
5. Reference direction method due to Korhonen and Laakso (1986) [46];
6. Pareto Race due to Korhonen and Wallenius (1988) [47];

4.1. STEP Method (Benayoun et al., 1971) [45]

The ancestor of the STEP method [45] was the Progressive Orientation Procedure (POP) by Benayoun and Tergny [48]. In the POP method, a subset of efficient extreme points is computed and presented to the DM for her evaluation. The DM can either choose the most preferred solution, or choose an attractive subset, and so forth. The STEP method was one of the first truly interactive approaches for solving multi-objective LPs. In this man–model symbiosis, phases of computation alternate with phases of decision. The process allows the DM to learn to recognize good solutions and the relative importance of the objectives.

In the STEP method, each objective is optimized one at a time to obtain the ideal point of the problem. For a maximization problem, the components of the ideal point describe the upper bounds of the individual objectives for the points corresponding to the Pareto-optimal front. Similarly, the nadir point (not used in STEP method) is defined as the lower bounds of the individual objectives for the points corresponding to the Pareto-optimal front. Denote the ideal point as $\mathbf{M} = (M_1, M_2, \ldots, M_p)$. At each iteration, the following LP problem is solved to obtain the feasible compromise solution $\mathbf{x}^{(k)}$ (k is the iteration counter), which is nearest in the *minimax* sense to $\mathbf{M}$:

$$\begin{array}{ll} \text{Minimize} & q \\ \text{subject to} & q \geq (M_i - f_i(\mathbf{x}))\lambda_i \ \forall \ i \in 1, \ldots, p \\ & \mathbf{x} \in B^k \\ & q \geq 0 \end{array} \quad (2)$$

where B^k is the feasible region at iteration k, $f_i(\mathbf{x})$ is the function for the ith objective at decision $\mathbf{x}$, and λ_i is the set of normalized weights (not specified by the DM). At the decision phase, the objective function vector associated with the compromise solution $\mathbf{x}^{(k)}$ is presented to the DM. Next, the DM must choose the objectives f_{i^*} (if any), where $i^* \subset \{1, \ldots, p\}$, which they would be willing to worsen to allow an improvement in the unsatisfactory ones. Then, the DM must specify the maximal amount of relaxation in the above objectives. At the next iteration, the feasible region is modified as $B^{k+1} = \{\mathbf{x} : f_j(\mathbf{x}) \geq f_i(\mathbf{x}^k) - \Delta f_j, f_i(\mathbf{x}) \geq f_i(\mathbf{x}^k) \ \forall \ i \notin i^*, j \in i^*\}$. The weights of the objectives to be relaxed are set to 0, and the next calculation phase is performed. The process is terminated as soon as the DM has found a satisfactory solution. The solutions at termination are not necessarily always non-dominated, but with modifications, they can all be made non-dominated. Note that the *minimax* operation corresponds to minimizing the Chebycheff norm.

4.2. GDF Algorithm (Geoffrion, Dyer, and Feinberg, 1972) [36]

In Geoffrion, Dyer, and Feinberg's algorithm [36], the problem is formulated as follows:

$$\begin{aligned} \text{Maximize} \quad & U(f_1(\mathbf{x}), \ldots, f_p(\mathbf{x})) \\ \text{subject to} \quad & \mathbf{x} \in \mathbf{X} \end{aligned} \quad (3)$$

where $\mathbf{X}$ is the feasible set (convex and compact), f_i are objective functions of the decision vector $\mathbf{x}$, and U is the overall utility (or value) function defined over the values of the objectives, assumed to be concave (under maximization) and differentiable. Everything else, except for U, is assumed to be explicitly known. U, however, is only assumed to be implicitly known. (If U were explicitly known, the problem would be an ordinary non-linear program.)

The GDF algorithm uses a modification of the Frank–Wolfe [49] algorithm from 1956. Note that the Frank-Wolfe algorithm is a steepest ascent algorithm. Two problems alternate: the direction-finding problem and the step-size problem. Let us ignore for the moment that U is not explicitly known, then the algorithm progresses as follows:

1. Choose an initial solution $\mathbf{x}^{(1)} \in \mathbf{X}$. Set $k = 1$ (iteration counter).
2. Determine an optimal solution $\mathbf{y}^{(k)}$ of the direction-finding problem

$$\begin{aligned} \text{Maximize} \quad & \nabla_\mathbf{x} U(f_1(\mathbf{x}), \ldots, f_p(\mathbf{x}))\mathbf{y} \\ \text{subject to} \quad & \mathbf{y} \in \mathbf{X}. \end{aligned} \quad (4)$$

3. Set $\mathbf{d}^{(k)} = \mathbf{y}^{(k)} - \mathbf{x}^{(k)}$. This step determines the "best" search direction based on a linear (first-order Taylor expansion) approximation of U.
4. Next, solve the step-size problem for an optimal t:

$$\begin{aligned} \text{Maximize} \quad & U(f_1(\mathbf{x}^{(k)} + t\mathbf{d}^{(k)}), \ldots, f_p(\mathbf{x}^{(k)} + t\mathbf{d}^{(k)})) \\ \text{subject to} \quad & 0 \leq t \leq 1. \end{aligned} \quad (5)$$

5. Set $\mathbf{x}^{(k+1)} = \mathbf{x}^{(k)} + t^k \mathbf{d}^{(k)}, k = k+1$, and return to the direction-finding problem. Theoretical termination criterion is satisfied if $\mathbf{x}^{(k)}$ and $\mathbf{x}^{(k+1)}$ are equal.

Now, assume that we do not know U. The gradient of U can be replaced with the sum of the product of weights w_i^k times the gradient of f in terms of $\mathbf{x}$.

$$\begin{aligned} \text{Maximize} \quad & \Sigma_{i=1}^p w_i^k \nabla_\mathbf{x} f_i(\mathbf{x}^{(k)}) y_i \\ \text{subject to} \quad & \mathbf{y} \in \mathbf{X} \end{aligned} \quad (6)$$

where we define $w_i^k = \frac{\partial U / \partial f_i^{(k)}}{\partial U / \partial f_j^{(k)}}, i = 1, \ldots, p$ with f_j being arbitrarily chosen as the reference criterion. The weights reflect the DM's tradeoff between f_j and f_i (at the current point), and must be elicited from the DM. We determine what change Δf_j in the reference criterion exactly compensates for a change Δf_i: $w_i^k = -\frac{\Delta f_j}{\Delta f_i}$. This is the Marginal Rate of Substitution (MRS) between the objectives.

The step-size problem must be solved directly by the DM. In early work, the computer would tabulate the values of the objectives at selected intervals and let the DM choose from this numerical display their most preferred solution.

4.3. ZW Method (Zionts and Wallenius, 1976) [37]

The Zionts–Wallenius method [37] is a simple-to-use multi-objective "simplex method", which companies could easily adopt for relatively large-scale problems. The authors initially made the assumption that the DM's underlying (implicit) value function would be linear (in terms of the objectives). LP theory suggests that the optimal solution would be a non-dominated extreme point solution. Hence, it would be sufficient to operate with efficient extreme point solutions. The authors first developed a *naïve* approach, which starts with an efficient extreme point and asks the DM about neighboring extreme points: Do you prefer any of the neighboring points to the current point? If yes, the DM is moved to one of the preferred neighbors and the method continues. If not, the optimal solution (or most preferred solution) is assumed to be found. The problem with the *naïve* approach is that the convergence was awfully slow for even moderately large problems. Therefore, a more elaborate approach had to be thought through to make the algorithm more efficient.

In the elaborate approach, the process starts by assuming some arbitrary (positive) weights for the objectives. If no other information exists, one may start with equal weights. The method uses the current set of weights to generate a non-dominated solution, and then asks the DM to tell whether any of the "efficient" neighboring solutions are preferred to the current solution (or a unit movement in that direction = trade-offs). If not, the most preferred solution is found, otherwise, the process continues. Note that the trade-offs can be obtained from the simplex table corresponding to the objective function rows and the non-basic variable columns.

The following so-called "λ-problem" tells how the weights are updated based on the DM's yes/no answers:

$$\begin{array}{ll} \text{Maximize} & \epsilon \\ \text{subject to} & \sum_{i=1}^{p} \lambda_i x_i^{(r)} - \epsilon \geq \sum_{i=1}^{p} \lambda_i x_i^{(s)} \ \forall \ \mathbf{x}^{(r)} \in \mathbf{X}_r, \mathbf{x}^{(s)} \in \mathbf{X}_s \\ & \sum_{i=1}^{p} \lambda_i = 1 \\ & \lambda_i > 0, i \in 1, \ldots, p \end{array} \quad (7)$$

The sets $\mathbf{X}_r$ and $\mathbf{X}_s$ contain points where every element in $\mathbf{X}_r$ is preferred to every element in $\mathbf{X}_s$, i.e., $\mathbf{x}^{(r)} \succ \mathbf{x}^{(s)} \ \forall \ r, s$. The updated weights are used to generate an improved non-dominated extreme point solution and the process is repeated. The process terminates when none of the neighboring extreme point solutions are preferred to the current solution, which is assumed to be the optimal solution. Note that, in this approach, it is not necessary to ask the DM about all neighboring extreme point solutions, but only the *efficient* ones. The algorithm was tested for moderately sized LP problems with 3–4 objectives.

4.4. Reference Point Method (Wierzbicki, 1980) [20]

The Reference Point method [20] asks the DM to provide aspiration levels for the objectives. The aspiration point is then projected to the non-dominated frontier. Note that it does not matter whether the aspiration point provided by the DM is feasible or not. In the projection, Wierzbicki used the so-called Achievement Scalarizing Function (ASF), which was minimized as:

$$\begin{array}{ll} \text{Min} & \text{Max}_{i=1}^{p} \left(\frac{g_i - f_i(\mathbf{x})}{w_i} \right) + \rho \sum_{i=1}^{p} \frac{g_i - f_i(\mathbf{x})}{w_i} \\ \text{subject to} & \mathbf{x} \in \mathbf{X} \end{array} \quad (8)$$

where $w_i > 0$ is a set of weights, ρ is a small number, and g_i is the vector of aspiration levels. Note that when $\rho = 0$, the indifference contours being optimized are orthogonal (90 degree angle); when $\rho > 0$, the indifference contours being optimized form an angle between 90 and 180 degrees. Once the non-dominated projection of the aspiration levels is found, the method asks the DM to update the aspiration levels. The method stops when the DM is satisfied with the solution. In contrast with the GDF and ZW methods, no assumptions of U are made.

4.5. Reference Direction Approach (Korhonen and Laakso, 1986) [46]

Instead of projecting a single reference point using Wierzbicki's ASF, Korhonen and Laakso [46] suggested projecting multiple directions to the efficient frontier. The projection was determined by solving the following parametric program:

$$\begin{aligned}&\text{Min} && \epsilon \\ &\text{subject to} && f_i(\mathbf{x}) + \epsilon w_i \geq q_i + td_i,\ i \in 1,\ldots,p \\ & && \mathbf{x} \in \mathbf{X}\end{aligned} \qquad (9)$$

where $w_i > 0$ is a set of weights, q_i is any vector in the criterion space, and $d_i = g_i - q_i$ is a reference direction, with g_i being an aspiration level or a reference goal in the spirit of Wierzbicki's reference point approach. When the parameter t in the above problem is varied from zero to infinity, an efficient curve emanating from point $\mathbf{q}$ is obtained.

The interface of the reference direction method is similar to the GDF method. When the DM has identified the most preferred solution along the projection, then they are asked to revise their aspiration point, and the process is repeated. An extension and application of the reference direction approach on multi-objective quadratic linear programming can be found in [50].

4.6. Pareto Race (Korhonen and Wallenius, 1988) [47]

Pareto Race [47] is a visual, dynamic search procedure for exploring the non-dominated frontier of a multi-objective LP problem. It is based on the idea of projecting reference directions on the efficient frontier. However, no aspiration levels are elicited from the DM. Instead, if the DM wants to improve the value of a certain objective, they press the number key (one or more times, depending on the relative desired improvement in that objective) of the corresponding objective.

There is an analogy to driving an automobile (on the efficient frontier). The user sees the objective function values on a display in numeric form and as bar graphs as they travel along the non-dominated frontier. Keyboard controls include accelerator, gears, breaks, and a steering mechanism. Technically, two parameters are used to control the motion: the reference direction (direction) and step size (speed). Figure 8 shows the interactive dashboard used in the Pareto Race approach.

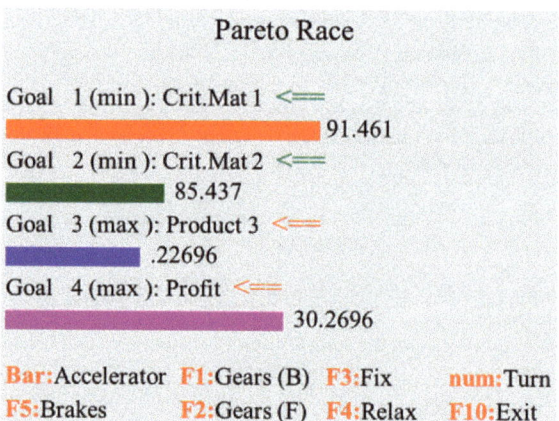

Figure 8. Pareto Race interface.

5. EMO Introduction and History

An evolutionary algorithm is a general population-based optimization algorithm which uses a mechanism inspired by biological evolution, i.e., selection, crossover, mutation, and replacement. The common underlying idea behind an evolutionary technique is that, for a given population of individuals, the environmental pressure causes natural selection, which leads to a rise in fitness of the population. A comprehensive discussion of the principles of an evolutionary algorithm can be found in [51–55]. In contrast to classical algorithms, which iterate from one solution point to the other until termination, an evolutionary algorithm works with a population of solution points. Each iteration of an evolutionary algorithm results in an update of the previous population by eliminating inferior solution points and including the superior ones. In the terminology of evolutionary algorithms, an iteration is commonly referred to as a generation and a solution point as an individual. A pseudo-code for a general genetic algorithm, which is a type of evolutionary algorithm, is provided below:

Step 1: Create a random initial population (i.e., a set of solution points in the decision space).

Step 2: Evaluate the individuals (i.e., the solution points) in the population with respect to objective(s) and constraints, if present, and assign fitness (i.e., quality measure).

Step 3: Repeat the generations (i.e., iterations of the evolutionary algorithm) until termination.

   Substep 1: Select the fitter individuals (referred to as parents) from the population for reproduction (i.e., producing new solution points through genetic operators of crossover and mutation).

   Substep 2: Produce new individuals (referred to as offspring) through crossover and mutation operators.

   Substep 3: Evaluate the new individuals and assign fitness.

   Substep 4: Replace the low-fitness individuals in the population with high-fitness individuals that may have been generated through crossover and mutation.

Step 4: Report the highest fitness individual as the output.

Along with the pseudo-code presented above, a flowchart for a general evolutionary algorithm is presented in Figure 9. In evolutionary algorithms, to begin with, a pool of individuals is generated by randomly creating points in the search space, which is called the population. Each individual in the population is evaluated on objective(s) and constraints (if any) and is assigned a fitness. For instance, while solving a single-objective maximization problem, a solution point with a higher function value is better than a solution point with lower function value when both solutions are feasible. Therefore, in such cases, the individual with higher function value is assigned a higher fitness. While comparing two infeasible solutions, the solution with a smaller constraint violation is often assigned a higher fitness as compared with the solution with larger constraint violation. In the presence of multiple constraints, the constraint violation for a particular point is defined as the sum of violation of those constraints that are infeasible with respect to that point. While comparing a feasible solution against an infeasible solution, a feasible solution is often assigned a higher fitness as compared with the infeasible solution. There can, of course, be other ways to assign fitness. For an unconstrained maximization problem, the function value itself can be treated as the fitness value and, for an unconstrained minimization problem negative of the function value, may serve the purpose of fitness. In all such cases, the algorithm searches for a higher fitness solution.

In a multi-objective context, the requirement is to produce a set of solutions that approximate the Pareto-optimal front. Fitness assignment based on constraint violation can be performed in the multi-objective case in a similar manner as the single-objective case. Moreover, a feasible solution point which dominates another feasible solution point can be assigned a higher fitness. However, fitness assignment for two solutions that are non-dominated with respect to each other is tricky. In such cases, algorithms often consider a measure of diversity or crowdedness [4] in the objective space to assign fitness and prefer one solution over the other. The measure for crowdedness prefers solutions that are isolated over solutions that are in crowded regions to enhance diversity in the population and to obtain a "well-spread" set of solutions approximating the Pareto-optimal front. A multi-objective evolutionary procedure, therefore, assigns fitness to each of the solution points based on their superiority over other solution points in terms of constraints, dominance, and diversity in the objective space. Different algorithms use different quality functions to assign fitness to an individual in a population. Once an initial population is generated and the fitness is assigned, a few of the better candidates from the population are chosen as parents. Crossover and mutation are performed to generate new solutions. Crossover is an operator applied to two or more selected individuals and results in one or more new individuals. Mutation is applied to a single individual and results in one new individual. Executing crossover and mutation lead to offspring that compete, based on their fitness, with the individuals in the population, for a place in the next generation. An iteration of this process often leads to a rise in the average fitness of the population and, over iterations, helps the algorithm converge towards the optimum in a single-objective case and towards the Pareto-optimal front in a multi-objective case.

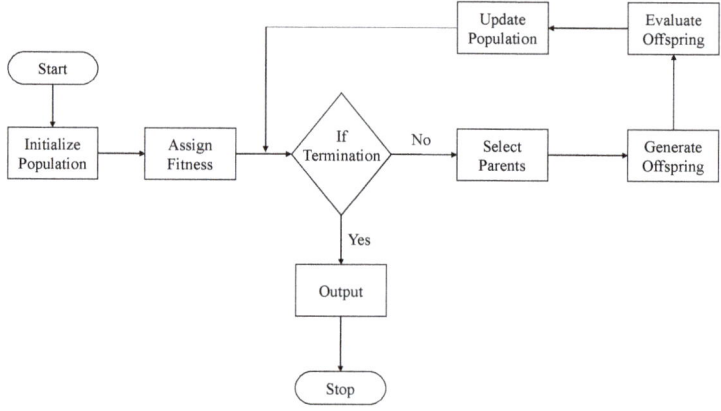

Figure 9. A flowchart for a general evolutionary algorithm.

Using the described evolutionary framework, a number of algorithms have been developed which successfully solve a variety of optimization problems. Their strength is particularly observable in handling two- to three-objective optimization problems and generating the entire Pareto-front. The aim of an EMO algorithm is to produce solutions which are (ideally) Pareto-optimal and uniformly distributed over the entire Pareto-front, so that a complete representation is provided. In the domain of EMO algorithms, these aims are commonly referred to as convergence and diversity. Figure 10 shows the working of a typical EMO algorithm that starts with a random initial population and aims to converge to the efficient frontier with a diverse set of solutions. The researchers in the EMO community have so far regarded an *a posteriori* approach to be an ideal approach where a representative set of Pareto-optimal solutions are found and then a DM is invited to select the most preferred point. The assertion is that only a DM who is well-informed is in a position to take a right decision. A common belief is that decision making should be based on complete knowledge of the available alternatives; current research in the field of EMO algorithms has taken inspiration from this belief. Though the belief is true to a certain extent, there are inherent difficulties associated with producing the entire set of alternatives and performing decision making thereafter, which many a time renders the approach ineffective.

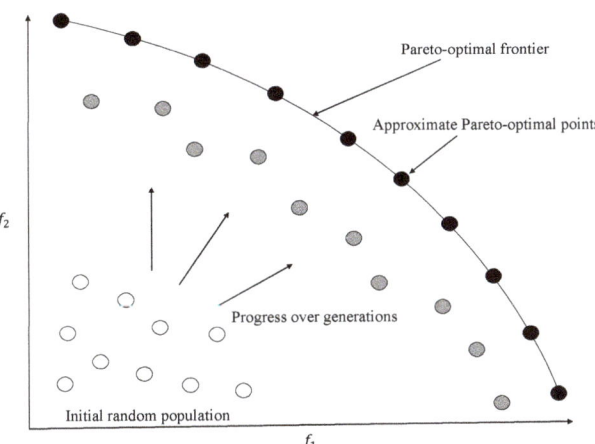

Figure 10. The working of a general evolutionary multi-objective optimization (EMO) algorithm.

The EMO approaches can be divided into three broad categories based on the idea that they use to achieve convergence and diversity. The categories are:

1. Pareto-based Methods [6,7,31,32,56]
2. Indicator-based Methods [11,57–59]
3. Decomposition-based Methods [10,12,33,60,61]

While Pareto-based approaches have been popular for solving two- or three-objective test problems, their efficiency deteriorates on problems with a higher number of objectives. Many of these methods are based on the approach of non-dominated sorting of the population as the primary driver. In problems with a large number of objectives, most of the solutions generated by these approaches are non-dominated in the comparison set leading to deterioration in progress towards the Pareto-frontier. Indicator-based approaches attempt to optimize a particular indicator that accounts for both convergence and diversity but did not become popular because of high computational costs involved in computing the indicator metric (for example, Hypervolume or Inverted Generational Distance) in many-objective problems. Despite these issues, both Pareto-based and indicator-based methods still hold promise, as non-dominated sorting in Pareto-based approaches is one of the fundamental ideas for partial ordering that cannot be ignored; similarly, faster computation of indicator metrics would make the indicator-based approaches competitive.

An alternative to Pareto-based approaches and indicator-based approaches are decomposition-based approaches, which have been effective in handling a larger number of objectives by decomposing the original problem into a set of subproblems, either multiple single-objective problems or multiple simplified multi-objective problems. These multiple problems are solved simultaneously in a collaborative manner and lead to better convergence and diversity, as the convergence is guaranteed by ensuring that each subproblem is properly optimized, and diversity is guaranteed by implicitly distributing the subproblems in an even manner. Interestingly, the decomposition-based methods utilize MCDM approaches while decomposing the multi-objective problems into subproblems. For instance, a distributed set of reference directions from the ideal point (or sometimes from the nadir point) towards the Pareto-front would lead to a well-distributed set of Pareto-optimal solutions if the front is uniform in shape. The methods that rely on decomposition solve these subproblems in a parallel manner and differ mostly on the basis of how the subproblems are created, how information between subproblems is shared during the generations, and how the subproblems may adapt during intermediate generations. However, note that if one considers a 10-objective problem, with a discretization of 10 along each objective, one would need 10^{10} points to approximate the frontier. Moreover, even if the points are produced by a computationally efficient algorithm, the decision-making challenge still remains. If the Pareto-front is not found with sufficient discretization, the DM may expect the method to explore additional solutions. For the purpose of evaluating the EMO approaches, a large body of literature exists on test problem toolkits [62–65] and performance assessment metrics [66–70] that allow the developers to compare the performance of various algorithms.

6. Hybrid Methods

In this section, we focus on hybrid approaches that incorporate decision making within EMO. As already highlighted, the aim of the EMO algorithms is to find a diverse set of solutions close to the Pareto-optimal front, and the DM is then expected to choose the most preferred point from the objective space. However, approximating the entire Pareto-optimal front with a set of points is not always easy and may not serve the purpose, especially in the context of problems with a large number of objectives. To alleviate these problems associated with *a posteriori* EMO approaches, some EMO researchers taking cues from their MCDM counterparts have attempted an *a priori* approach, where a small set of Pareto-optimal points in the region of interest to the DM is targeted. As soon as the region of interest becomes smaller, certain problems associated with the high dimensionality of the problem in the objective space gets alleviated. Greenwood et al. [30] used an evolutionary approach to optimize a linear value function obtained from the DM through ranking of a few alternatives. In this method, the preference information is employed before optimization, and therefore this qualifies as an *a priori* method. Other studies in this direction are the cone-dominance-based EMO [71], biased-niching-based EMO [27], the light beam approach based EMO [35], and reference-point-based EMO approaches [28,29].

In [71], the authors modify the dominance principle based on interactions with the DM. For every pair of objectives, the DM specifies maximally acceptable trade-offs, i.e., what is the improvement of one unit in one objective (say f_1) worth in terms of degradation of another objective (say f_2). If the degradation is worth at most a_{12} in f_2 when f_1 improves by unity, and at most a_{21} in f_1 when f_2 improves by unity, then the dominance scheme $x \succ y$ is modified as follows with a strict inequality in at least one case:

$$(f_1(x) + a_{12}f_2(x) \leq f_1(y) + a_{12}f_2(y)) \wedge (a_{21}f_1(x) + f_2(x) \leq a_{21}f_1(y) + f_2(y))$$

Incorporating the above principle in an EMO is straightforward, as one can simply replace objectives f_1 and f_2 with Ω_1 and Ω_2, respectively, where Ω_1 and Ω_2 are defined below, and solve the problem with the standard dominance principle.

$$\Omega_1(\mathbf{x}) = f_1(\mathbf{x}) + a_{12}f_2(\mathbf{x})$$
$$\Omega_2(\mathbf{x}) = a_{21}f_1(\mathbf{x}) + f_2(\mathbf{x})$$

The approach can be incorporated in any EMO and does not lead to any increase in complexity.

Figures 11 and 12 indicate the working of the light beam approach based EMO [35] and the reference-direction-based EMO [28,29] approaches, respectively. In their study, Jaskiewicz and Branke [40] showed that it is difficult for an EMO algorithm alone to find a good spread of solutions in five- to ten-objective problems, and when solutions around the most preferred point are targeted, the hybrid approaches are able to find satisfactory solutions.

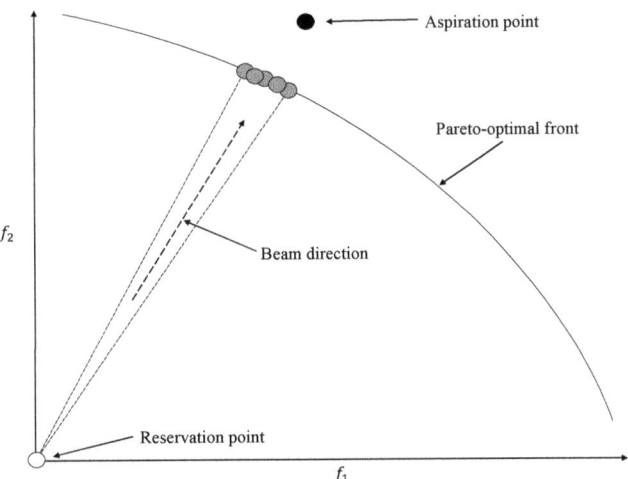

Figure 11. A light beam approach integrated within an EMO that finds a crowded set of points close to the Pareto-frontier based on the aspirations of the DM.

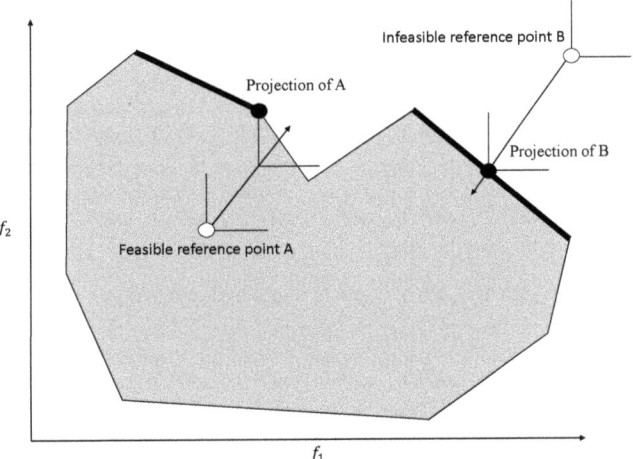

Figure 12. Projection of a feasible and infeasible reference point on the Pareto-optimal frontier within an EMO.

Preference-based EMO algorithms can differ from each other based on the following aspects:
1. Stage at which preference is incorporated;
2. Manner in which preference information is elicited;
3. Type of preference modeling performed;
4. Integration of preference model with EMO search;
5. Choice of the EMO, i.e., Pareto-based, indicator-based or decomposition-based.

Apart from a priori and a posteriori approaches, a more seamless and effective way to incorporate DMs' preferences in the EMO would be to collect and incorporate preferences at the intermediate generations of the EMO algorithm to guide the search towards the most preferred point. Such an approach is commonly referred to as a progressively interactive EMO approach. We discuss, in detail, some of the progressively interactive techniques studied in the literature.

6.1. Phelps and Köksalan (2003) [38]

Phelps and Köksalan [38] presented one of the first hybrid approaches, where they optimized a linearly weighted utility function during the iterations of an evolutionary algorithm. The decision maker makes a number of binary comparisons that leads to the weights of the utility function. For a given parameter t and ideal point $f_k^* = \text{Max}_{x \in X}\{f_k(x)\}$, the authors solve the following optimization problem to obtain the weights w_k, $k = 1, \ldots, p$.

$$\begin{aligned}
\text{Max} \quad & \varepsilon \\
\text{s.t.} \quad & \sum_{k=1}^{p} w_k = 1 \\
& \sum_{k=1}^{p} w_k \left(f_k^* - f_k\left(\mathbf{x}^{(i)}\right)\right)^t \leq \sum_{k=1}^{p} w_k \left(f_k^* - f_k\left(\mathbf{x}^{(j)}\right)\right)^t - \varepsilon \; \forall \; \mathbf{x}^{(i)} \succ \mathbf{x}^{(j)} \\
& w_k \geq \varepsilon \; \forall \; k = 1, \ldots, p
\end{aligned}$$

The above problem is an LP that leads to $\mathbf{w}^*$ used in calculating the fitness of each point using the following utility function:

$$U(\mathbf{x}) = -\sum_{k=1}^{p} w_k^* (f_k^* - f_k(\mathbf{x}))^t$$

The preference from the DM is taken initially or during the execution of the algorithm to modify the fitness function. The authors considered linear utility functions in their study.

To incorporate the properties of an implicit quasi-concave utility function into an EMO, Fowler et al. [39] developed an interactive EMO approach using convex preference cones. They used feasibility, dominance, and preference cones to order the population members and used that information for fitness calculation. They tested their algorithm on multi-dimensional (up to four dimensions) knapsack problems using a similar interactive genetic algorithm framework to that of Phelps and Köksalan [38]. Jaszkiewicz [40] constructed an achievement scalarizing function using random weights. The random weights are preferred if the scalarizing function generated conforms to the preference information provided by the DM. The EMO search is then guided by the scalarizing function generated with random weights.

6.2. Branke, Greco, Słowiński, and Zielniewicz (2009) [41]

Branke et al. [41] implemented the GRIP [72] methodology, in which the DM-provided pairwise information is used to find all possible compatible additive value functions (not necessarily linear). A preference-based dominance relationship and a preference-based diversity preserving operator is used in an EMO to find new solutions for the next few generations. In their approach, they make pairwise comparisons after every few generations in order to develop the preference structure. It is also possible for the DM to specify the intensities of preference. The authors use robust ordinal regression on information obtained through interaction with the DM to determine the set of all compatible value functions. Thereafter, the EMO procedure performs a parallel search for all non-dominated solutions that are preferred with respect to the compatible value functions. The authors demonstrated their procedure on a two-objective test problem. The study was later extended to solve up to five-objective test problems in [73]. The study takes a robustness approach to avoid arbitrary selection of a value function, which makes it different from most of the other studies that determine the single most discriminating value function. The use of preference information in a robust manner in EMO is a significant contribution of this study. Other recent studies that use a set of instances of the preference model compatible with the DM's preference information are [74,75]. These studies generate multiple instances of the preference model using Monte Carlo simulation and utilize the instances as search directions in a decomposition-based EMO approach.

6.3. Deb, Sinha, Korhonen, and Wallenius (2010) [42]

Based on earlier interactive MCDM approaches [76,77], this paper proposes a preference-based EMO to guide a DM to the most preferred solution by creating non-linear value functions in the intermediate generations of the algorithm. The approach accepts preference information in the form of complete or partial ranking, i.e., the DM may prefer one solution over the other or the DM may be indifferent between two solutions. The authors do not consider the situation where the DM is unable to compare two solutions. Through an extensive computational study on two- to five-objective problems, the authors evaluated the performance of their approach when the DM interacts less/more frequently with the EMO approach, as well as the impact on the quality of the solution produced when the DM provides erroneous preference information. The approach utilized the approximated value function in an innovative manner by partitioning the objective space into two areas using the value function. They also utilized the value function for performing local search and termination of the method.

In this paper, the authors fit a polynomial value function with the following structure for two objectives.

$$V(f_1, f_2) = (f_1 + k_1 f_2 + l_1)(f_2 + k_2 f_1 + l_2)$$

where f_1, f_2 are the objective functions
and k_1, k_2, l_1, l_2 are the value function parameters

For a higher number of objectives, they use a higher-order polynomial function of the following kind:

$$V(\mathbf{f}) = \prod_{i=1}^{p} \left(\sum_{j=1}^{p} \left[k_{ij} f_j + k_{i(p+1)} \right] \right)$$

where $\sum_{j=1}^{p} k_{ij} = 1$ for all i, and $k_{ij} \geq 0$ for $j \leq p$ and for all i. The value function is fitted by solving the following optimization problem with respect to the value function parameters when preference information is available:

Maximize ϵ
subject to V is non-negative at every point $\mathbf{x}^{(i)}$
V is strictly increasing at every point $\mathbf{x}^{(i)}$
$V(\mathbf{x}^{(i)}) - V(\mathbf{x}^{(j)}) \geq \epsilon$, for all (i,j) pairs satisfying $\mathbf{x}^{(i)} \succ \mathbf{x}^{(j)}$
$\left| V(\mathbf{x}^{(i)}) - V(\mathbf{x}^{(j)}) \right| \leq \delta_V$, for all (i,j) pairs satisfying $\mathbf{x}^{(i)} \sim \mathbf{x}^{(j)}$

A look into the above optimization problem reveals that it attempts to find a value function for which the minimum difference in the value function values between the ordered pairs of points is maximum. At the same time, it also ensures that the difference in the value function values for a pair of indifferent points is smaller than a threshold that is proposed to be $\delta_V = 0.1\epsilon$. Figures 13 and 14 show how the preference structure is captured using the value function when points have a complete or a partial order, respectively. An extension of this study suggested a generalized polynomial value function [78]; however, any attempt to fit a very complex value function to user preference is not always advisable. Unless there are errors or conflicts in preference information, the preference structure in a region can often be captured using relatively simple value functions.

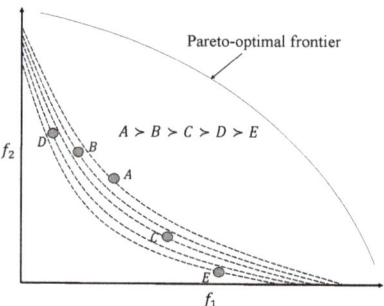

Figure 13. Value function fitting when the points are ordered.

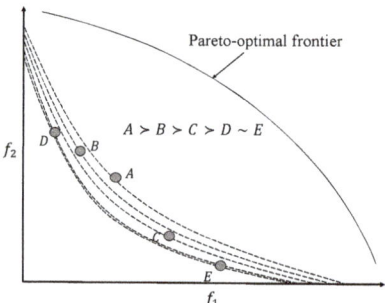

Figure 14. Value function fitting when the points are partially ordered.

6.4. Sinha, Deb, Korhonen, and Wallenius (2014) [43]

In this study, Sinha et al. [43] generate the most preferred solution on the Pareto-optimal frontier in a fixed budget of decision-making calls. Most of the earlier hybrid approaches did not assume that the DM will be available for providing preferences only for a fixed number of times. In fact, in most of the procedures, there is no control on the number of DM calls, or the DM calls are not utilized effectively. The assumption in most of the interactive approaches is that the DM would be available for as many interactions as desired by the method until a satisfactory solution is found; however, this is not a wise assumption to make. The approach discussed in this section attempts to address this concern by solving the problem in a fixed number of interactions with the DM. The study also deviated from constructing value functions and, instead, suggested constructing polyhedral cones heuristically to guide the EMO. The authors tested their approach on two- to five-objective test problems and studied the impact of increasing or decreasing the budget of DM calls on the performance of the algorithm in getting close to the most preferred point.

The algorithm requires the ideal point at start. Once the ideal point is known, the initial random population is created, and the point in the initial population closest to the ideal point is chosen. Let the distance be denoted as D_I. This distance D_I is divided into certain equal parts (say d_I) based on the budget of DM calls available. Thereafter, the EMO run starts, and preference from the DM is elicited only after a progress of d_I has been made. During the progress, the algorithm stores all non-dominated solutions produced in an archive set, and preference from the DM is taken in terms of the most preferred point from the archive set.

The method heuristically constructs a polyhedral cone using the most preferred solution suggested by the DM from the archive set and the end points along each of the objectives. For a p-objective problem, a polyhedral cone is formed using $p + 1$ points. Figures 15 and 16 show the construction of cones in two and three dimensions. Once the polyhedral cone is determined, it provides an idea for a search direction. The normal unit vectors (V_i) of all the p hyperplanes can be summed up to obtain a heuristic search direction ($\vec{W} = \sum_{i=1}^{p} V_i$), which is used in the algorithm for the purpose of local search.

As an extension, a mathematically driven preference-cone-based approach was later proposed in [79], where the user's preferences were assumed to follow an unknown quasi-concave and increasing value function. In addition to considering the preference cones as a tool for eliminating non-preferred solutions, the authors also presented how the cones could be leveraged in approximating the steepest ascent direction to guide an evolutionary algorithm. A merit function is proposed that the authors use for fitness calculations in the algorithm. In addition to test problems, a mixed-integer facility location problem was solved in the later study.

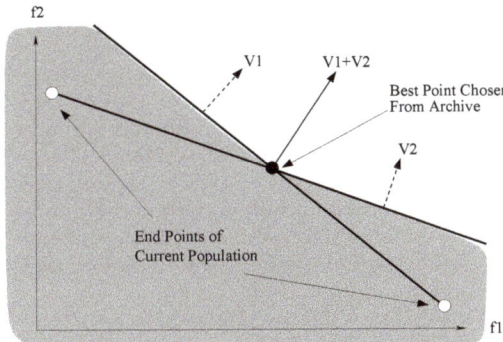

Figure 15. Polyhedral cone in 2 dimensions.

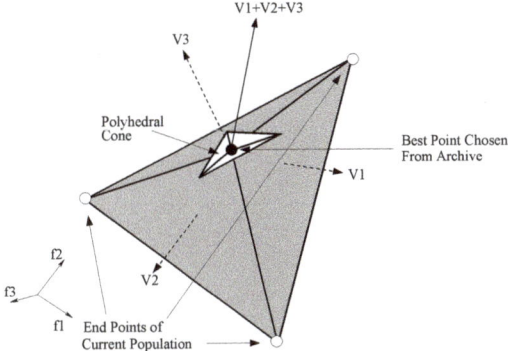

Figure 16. Polyhedral cone in 3 dimensions.

7. Interaction Styles, Behavioral Considerations, and Future Work

Given that preferences can be elicited in a number of ways, developers of a specific method normally think that the interaction style embedded in their approach is the best. However, we need more research to answer what kind of cognitive load is caused by the interaction style (preference elicitation) and which interaction style leads closer to the true most preferred solution. An interesting approach is to use neuro-physiological measurement instruments to measure the DM's cognitive and emotional load. Scholars in the 1970s pioneered the idea of interactively solving multi-objective problems, which was remarkable considering the state of the art of computer technology in the early to mid 1970s. No personal computers, nor computer graphics capabilities, were available before the early 1980s. Scholars had to access the main frame computer via teletypes (time sharing). Their contribution was not the development of the concept of efficient or Pareto-optimal solution, rather, it was Pareto who introduced the ideas of non-dominance. However, the scholars during the period made it possible to explore or move around the non-dominated frontier in an effective way. Problems studied were largely limited to LP framework (convex and compact feasible sets).

With computation becoming faster, newer applications arising in practice, and numerical or computational techniques for more general classes of problems being developed, researchers started looking beyond LPs. However, the decision-making difficulties did not receive the attention they deserved. For instance, there has been only limited effort in trying to solve multi-objective problems in a fixed number of interactions with the DM [43,80]. The decision-making calls are often assumed to be an unlimited resource, with the expectation that the DM is available for a large number of interactions.

Termination criterion for methods involving human–machine interaction is a challenge. Optimization methods may terminate based on gradient-based criterion, Karush–Kuhn–Tucker-based criterion, or improvement-based criterion. However, with the DM interacting with the method, it is difficult to terminate the process, as one does not know in advance the proximity of the current best solution for the DM to the true most preferred solution. Effort is also required on visualization techniques to reduce the burden on the DM during the decision-making process. Many of the visualization techniques focus on commonly used descriptive approaches, such as scatter plots, bar charts, value plots, etc. However, very few of the techniques offer an immersive experience to the DM, where the DM can easily navigate in the search space, understand trade-offs, possible improvements, and then make a decision. A comprehensive review of visualization-based approaches can be found in [81,82].

Other challenges in the decision-making context which have led to difficulties in preference modeling are as follows:

1. DM providing erroneous preferences;
2. DM providing conflicting or inconsistent preferences;
3. DM preference structure changing in different regions of the objective space;
4. DM preference structure changing as a function of learning;
5. DM becoming biased (anchored) based on the initial set of options presented;
6. DM unable to compare two options in terms of either dominance or indifference.

Significant effort is still required towards developing decision-making and search techniques that are robust to the above mentioned issues.

Author Contributions: Authors A.S. and J.W. have contributed equally in conceptualization, investigation and writing of the manuscript. All authors have read and agreed to the published version of the manuscript.

Funding: This research received no external funding.

Conflicts of Interest: The authors declare no conflict of interest.

References

1. Charnes, A.; Cooper, W. Management models and industrial applications of linear programming. *Manag. Sci.* **1957**, *4*, 38–91. [CrossRef]
2. Keeney, R.L.; Raiffa, H. *Decisions with Multiple Objectives: Preferences and Value Tradeoffs*; Wiley: New York, NY, USA, 1976.
3. Schaffer, J.D. Multiple objective optimization with vector evaluated genetic algorithms. In *Proceedings of the First International Conference of Genetic Algorithms and Their Application*; Psychology Press: New York, NY, USA, 1985, pp. 93–100.
4. Deb, K. *Multi-Objective Optimization Using Evolutionary Algorithms*; Wiley: Chichester, UK, 2001.
5. Coello, C.A.C.; VanVeldhuizen, D.A.; Lamont, G. *Evolutionary Algorithms for Solving Multi-Objective Problems*; Kluwer: Boston, MA, USA, 2002.
6. Zitzler, E.; Laumanns, M.; Thiele, L. SPEA2: Improving the Strength Pareto Evolutionary Algorithm for Multiobjective Optimization. In Proceedings of the Evolutionary Methods for Design, Optimization and Control with Applications to Industrial Problems, Athens, Greece, 19–21 September 2001; pp. 95–100.
7. Deb, K.; Agrawal, S.; Pratap, A.; Meyarivan, T. A fast and Elitist multi-objective Genetic Algorithm: NSGA-II. *IEEE Trans. Evol. Comput.* **2002**, *6*, 182–197. [CrossRef]

8. Deb, K.; Saxena, D. Searching for Pareto-Optimal Solutions through Dimensionality Reduction for Certain Large-Dimensional Multi-Objective Optimization Problems. In Proceedings of the World Congress on Computational Intelligence (WCCI-2006), Vancouver, BC, Canada, 16–21 July 2006; pp. 3352–3360.
9. Knowles, J.; Corne, D. Quantifying the Effects of Objective Space Dimension in Evolutionary Multiobjective Optimization. In Proceedings of the Fourth International Conference on Evolutionary Multi-Criterion Optimization (EMO-2007), Matsushima, Japan, 5–8 March 2007; pp. 757–771.
10. Zhang, Q.; Li, H. MOEA/D: A multiobjective evolutionary algorithm based on decomposition. *IEEE Trans. Evol. Comput.* **2007**, *11*, 712–731. [CrossRef]
11. Bader, J.; Zitzler, E. HypE: An algorithm for fast hypervolume-based many-objective optimization. *Evol. Comput.* **2011**, *19*, 45–76. [CrossRef] [PubMed]
12. Deb, K.; Jain, H. An evolutionary many-objective optimization algorithm using reference-point-based nondominated sorting approach, Part I: Solving problems with box constraints. *IEEE Trans. Evol. Comput.* **2013**, *18*, 577–601. [CrossRef]
13. Branke, J.; Deb, K.; Miettinen, K.; Słowiński, R. *Multiobjective Optimization: Interactive and Evolutionary Approaches*; Springer: Heidelberg, Germany, 2008; Volume 5252.
14. Wang, H.; Olhofer, M.; Jin, Y. A mini-review on preference modeling and articulation in multi-objective optimization: Current status and challenges. *Complex Intell. Syst.* **2017**, *3*, 233–245. [CrossRef]
15. Xin, B.; Chen, L.; Chen, J.; Ishibuchi, H.; Hirota, K.; Liu, B. Interactive multiobjective optimization: A review of the state-of-the-art. *IEEE Access* **2018**, *6*, 41256–41279. [CrossRef]
16. Steuer, R.E. *Multiple Criteria Optimization: Theory, Computation and Application*; Wiley: New York, NY, USA, 1986.
17. Miettinen, K. *Nonlinear Multiobjective Optimization*; Springer Science & Business Media: Berlin, Germany, 2012; Volume 12.
18. Cohon, J.L. Multicriteria programming: Brief review and application. In *Design Optimization*; Gero, J.S., Ed.; Academic Press: New York, NY, USA, 1985; pp. 163–191.
19. Horn, J. Multicriterion decision making. In *Handbook of Evolutionary Computation*; Institute of Physics Publishing: Bristol, UK; Oxford University Press: New York, NY, USA, 1997; pp. F1.9:1–15.
20. Wierzbicki, A.P. The use of reference objectives in multiobjective optimization. In *Multiple Criteria Decision Making Theory and Applications*; Fandel, G.; Gal, T., Eds.; Springer: Berlin, Germany, 1980; pp. 468–486.
21. Haimes, Y.Y.; Lasdon, L.S.; Wismer, D.A. On a bicriterion formulation of the problems of integrated system identification and system optimization. *IEEE Trans. Syst. Man Cybern.* **1971**, *1*, 296–297.
22. Roy, B. The outranking approach and the foundations of ELECTRE methods. In *Readings in Multiple Criteria Decision Aid*; Springer: Heidelberg, Germany, 1990; pp. 155–183.
23. Roy, B.; Vanderpooten, D. The European school of MCDA: Emergence, basic features and current works. *J. Multi-Criteria Decis. Anal.* **1996**, *5*, 22–38. [CrossRef]
24. Greco, S.; Matarazzo, B.; Słowiński, R. Decision rule preference model. In *Wiley Encyclopedia of Operations Research and Management Science*; John Wiley & Sons, Inc.: New York, NY, USA, 2011; pp. 1–16.
25. Greco, S.; Matarazzo, B.; Słowiński, R. Rough sets theory for multicriteria decision analysis. *Eur. J. Oper. Res.* **2001**, *129*, 1–47. [CrossRef]
26. Jaszkiewicz, A.; Słowiński, R. The light beam search—Outranking based interactive procedure for multiple-objective mathematical programming. In *Advances in Multicriteria Analysis*; Springer: Heidelberg, Germany, 1995; pp. 129–146.
27. Branke, J.; Deb, K. Integrating user preferences into evolutionary multi-objective optimization. In *Knowledge Incorporation in Evolutionary Computation*; Jin, Y., Ed.; Springer: Hiedelberg, Germany, 2004; pp. 461–477.
28. Deb, K.; Sundar, J.; Uday, N.; Chaudhuri, S. Reference Point Based Multi-Objective Optimization Using Evolutionary Algorithms. *Int. J. Comput. Intell. Res.* **2006**, *2*, 273–286.
29. Thiele, L.; Miettinen, K.; Korhonen, P.; Molina, J. A preference-based interactive evolutionary algorithm for multi-objective optimization. *Evol. Comput. J.* **2009**, *17*, 411–436. [CrossRef] [PubMed]
30. Greenwood, G.W.; Hu, X.; D'Ambrosio, J.G. Fitness functions for multiple objective optimization problems: Combining preferences with pareto rankings. *Found. Genet. Algorithms* **1996**, 437–455.
31. Murata, T.; Ishibuchi, H. MOGA: Multi-objective genetic algorithms. In Proceedings of the Second IEEE International Conference on Evolutionary Computation, Perth, Western Australia, 29 November–1 December 1995; pp. 289–294.
32. Kukkonen, S.; Lampinen, J. GDE3: The third Evolution Step of Generalized Differential Evolution. In Proceedings of the 2005 Congress on Evolutionary Computation (CEC 2005), Scotland, UK, 2–5 September 2005; pp. 443–450.
33. Wang, R.; Purshouse, R.C.; Fleming, P.J. Preference-inspired co-evolutionary algorithms using weight vectors. *Eur. J. Oper. Res.* **2015**, *243*, 423–441. [CrossRef]
34. Deb, K.; Kumar, A. Interactive evolutionary multi-objective optimization and decision-making using reference direction method. In Proceedings of the Genetic and Evolutionary Computation Conference (GECCO-2007), London, UK, 7–11 July 2007; The Association of Computing Machinery (ACM): New York, NY, USA, 2007; pp. 781–788.
35. Deb, K.; Kumar, A. Light Beam Search Based Multi-objective Optimization using Evolutionary Algorithms. In Proceedings of the Congress on Evolutionary Computation (CEC-07), Singapore, Singapore, 25–28 September 2007; pp. 2125–2132.
36. Geoffrion, A.M.; Dyer, J.S.; Feinberg, A. An interactive approach for multi-criterion optimization with an application to the operation of an academic department. *Manag. Sci.* **1972**, *19*, 357–368. [CrossRef]

37. Zionts, S.; Wallenius, J. An interactive programming method for solving the multiple criteria problem. *Manag. Sci.* **1976**, *22*, 656–663. [CrossRef]
38. Phelps, S.; Koksalan, M. An interactive evolutionary metaheuristic for multiobjective combinatorial optimization. *Manag. Sci.* **2003**, *49*, 1726–1738. [CrossRef]
39. Fowler, J.W.; Gel, E.S.; Köksalan, M.; Korhonen, P.; Marquis, J.L.; Wallenius, J. Interactive evolutionary multi-objective optimization for quasi-concave preference functions. *Eur. J. Oper. Res.* **2010**, *206*, 417–425. [CrossRef]
40. Jaszkiewicz, A. Interactive multiobjective optimization with the pareto memetic algorithm. *Found. Comput. Decis. Sci.* **2007**, *32*, 15–32.
41. Branke, J.; Greco, S.; Słowiński, R.; Zielniewicz, P. Interactive evolutionary multiobjective optimization using robust ordinal regression. In Proceedings of the Fifth International Conference on Evolutionary Multi-Criterion Optimization (EMO-09), Nantes, France, 7–10 April 2009; Springer: Berlin, Germany, 2009; pp. 554–568.
42. Deb, K.; Sinha, A.; Korhonen, P.; Wallenius, J. An Interactive Evolutionary Multi-Objective Optimization Method Based on Progressively Approximated Value Functions. *IEEE Trans. Evol. Comput.* **2010**, *14*, 723–739. [CrossRef]
43. Sinha, A.; Korhonen, P.; Wallenius, J.; Deb, K. An interactive evolutionary multi-objective optimization algorithm with a limited number of decision maker calls. *Eur. J. Oper. Res.* **2014**, *233*, 674–688. [CrossRef]
44. Sinha, A.; Saxena, D.K.; Deb, K.; Tiwari, A. Using objective reduction and interactive procedure to handle many-objective optimization problems. *Appl. Soft Comput.* **2013**, *13*, 415–427. [CrossRef]
45. Benayoun, R.; de Montgolfier, J.; Tergny, J.; Laritchev, P. Linear programming with multiple objective functions: Step method (STEM). *Math. Program.* **1971**, *1*, 366–375. [CrossRef]
46. Korhonen, P.; Laakso, J. A visual interactive method for solving the multiple criteria problem. *Eur. J. Oper. Res.* **1986**, *24*, 277–287. [CrossRef]
47. Korhonen, P.; Wallenius, J. A Pareto race. *Nav. Res. Logist.* **1988**, *35*, 615–623. [CrossRef]
48. Benayoun, R.; Tergny, J. Mathematical Programming with multi-objective functions: A solution by P.O.P. (Progressive Orientation Procedure). *Revue METRA* **1970**, *9*, 279–299.
49. Frank, M.; Wolfe, P. An algorithm for quadratic programming. *Nav. Res. Logist. Q.* **1956**, *3*, 95–110. [CrossRef]
50. Korhonen, P.; Yu, G.Y. A reference direction approach to multiple objective quadratic-linear programming. *Eur. J. Oper. Reseaech* **1997**, *102*, 601–610. [CrossRef]
51. Goldberg, D.E. *Genetic Algorithms for Search, Optimization, and Machine Learning*; Addison-Wesley: Reading, MA, USA, 1989.
52. Koza, J.R. *Genetic Programming: On the Programming of Computers by Means of Natural Selection*; MIT Press: Cambridge, MA, USA, 1992.
53. Fogel, D.B. *Evolutionary Computation*; IEEE Press: Piscataway, NY, USA, 1995.
54. Bäck, T. *Evolutionary Algorithms in Theory and Practice*; Oxford University Press: New York, NY, USA, 1996.
55. Mitchell, M. *Introduction to Genetic Algorithms*; MIT Press: Ann Arbor, MI, USA, 1996.
56. Srinivas, N.; Deb, K. Multi-Objective function optimization using non-dominated sorting genetic algorithms. *Evol. Comput. J.* **1994**, *2*, 221–248. [CrossRef]
57. Zitzler, E.; Künzli, S. Indicator-Based Selection in Multiobjective Search. In *International Conference on Parallel Problem Solving from Nature (PPSN VIII)*; Springer: Berlin/Heidelberg, Germany, 2004; Volume 3242, pp. 832–842.
58. Beume, N.; Naujoks, B.; Emmerich, M. SMS-EMOA: Multiobjective selection based on dominated hypervolume. *Eur. J. Oper. Res.* **2007**, *181*, 1653–1669. [CrossRef]
59. Sun, Y.; Yen, G.G.; Yi, Z. IGD indicator-based evolutionary algorithm for many-objective optimization problems. *IEEE Trans. Evol. Comput.* **2018**, *23*, 173–187. [CrossRef]
60. Murata, T.; Ishibuchi, H.; Gen, M. Cellular genetic local search for multi-objective optimization. In Proceedings of the 2nd Annual Conference on Genetic and Evolutionary Computation, Las Vegas, NV, USA, 10–12 July 2000; pp. 307–314.
61. Wu, M.; Li, K.; Kwong, S.; Zhou, Y.; Zhang, Q. Matching-based selection with incomplete lists for decomposition multiobjective optimization. *IEEE Trans. Evol. Comput.* **2017**, *21*, 554–568. [CrossRef]
62. Zitzler, E.; Deb, K.; Thiele, L. Comparison of multiobjective evolutionary algorithms: Empirical Results. *Evol. Comput. J.* **2000**, *8*, 125–148. [CrossRef] [PubMed]
63. Deb, K.; Thiele, L.; Laumanns, M.; Zitzler, E. Scalable multi-objective optimization test problems. In Proceedings of the Congress on Evolutionary Computation (CEC-2002), Honolulu, HI, USA, 12–17 May 2002; pp. 825–830.
64. Huband, S.; Hingston, P.; Barone, L.; While, L. A review of multiobjective test problems and a scalable test problem toolkit. *IEEE Trans. Evol. Comput.* **2006**, *10*, 477–506. [CrossRef]
65. Deb, K.; Sinha, A.; Kukkonen, S. Multi-objective Test Problems, Linkages, and Evolutionary Methodologies. In Proceedings of the 8th Annual Genetic and Evolutionary Computation Conference (GECCO 2006), Seattle, WA, USA, 8–12 July 2006; ACM Press: New York, NY, USA, 2006; pp. 1141–1148.
66. Zitzler, E.; Thiele, L. Multiobjective optimization using evolutionary algorithms – A comparative case study. In Proceedings of the Parallel Problem Solving from Nature V (PPSN-V), Amsterdam, The Netherlands, 27–30 September 1998; pp. 292–301.
67. Fonseca, V.G.D.; Fonseca, C.M.; Hall, A.O. Inferential performance assessment of stochastic optimisers and the attainment function. In *International Conference on Evolutionary Multi-Criterion Optimization*; Springer: Berlin/Heidelberg, Germany, 2001; pp. 213–225.

68. Zitzler, E.; Thiele, L.; Laumanns, M.; Fonseca, C.M.; Fonseca, V.G.d. Performance assessment of multiobjective optimizers: An analysis and review. *IEEE Trans. Evol. Comput.* **2003**, *7*, 117–132. [CrossRef]
69. Jiang, S.; Ong, Y.; Zhang, J.; Feng, L. Consistencies and contradictions of performance metrics in multiobjective optimization. *IEEE Trans. Cybern.* **2014**, *44*, 2391–2404. [CrossRef]
70. Audet, C.; Bigeon, J.; Cartier, D.; Le Digabel, S.; Salomon, L. Performance indicators in multiobjective optimization. *Eur. J. Oper. Res.* **2021**, *292*, 397–422. [CrossRef]
71. Branke, J.; Kaußler, T.; Schmeck, H. Guidance in evolutionary multi-objective optimization. *Adv. Eng. Softw.* **2001**, *32*, 499–507. [CrossRef]
72. Figueira, J.; Greco, S.; Słowiński, R. Building a set of additive value functions representing a reference preorder and intensities of preference: GRIP method. *Eur. J. Oper. Res.* **2009**, *195*, 460–486. [CrossRef]
73. Branke, J.; Greco, S.; Słowiński, R.; Zielniewicz, P. Learning value functions in interactive evolutionary multiobjective optimization. *IEEE Trans. Evol. Comput.* **2015**, *19*, 88–102. [CrossRef]
74. Tomczyk, M.K.; Kadziński, M. Decomposition-based interactive evolutionary algorithm for multiple objective optimization. *IEEE Trans. Evol. Comput.* **2019**, *24*, 320–334. [CrossRef]
75. Tomczyk, M.K.; Kadziński, M. Decomposition-based co-evolutionary algorithm for interactive multiple objective optimization. *Inf. Sci.* **2021**, *549*, 178–199. [CrossRef]
76. Korhonen, P.; Moskowitz, H.; Wallenius, J. A progressive algorithm for modeling and solving multiple-criteria decision problems. *Oper. Res.* **1986**, *34*, 726–731. [CrossRef]
77. Korhonen, P.; Moskowitz, H.; Salminen, P.; Wallenius, J. Further developments and tests of a progressive algorithm for multiple criteria decision making. *Oper. Res.* **1993**, *41*, 1033–1045. [CrossRef]
78. Sinha, A.; Deb, K.; Korhonen, P.; Wallenius, J. Progressively Interactive Evolutionary Multi-Objective Optimization Method Using Generalized Polynomial Value Functions. In Proceedings of the 2010 IEEE Congress on Evolutionary Computation (CEC-2010), Barcelona, Spain, 18–23 July 2010; IEEE Press: Piscataway, NJ, USA, 2010; pp. 1–8.
79. Sinha, A.; Malo, P.; Kallio, M. Convex preference cone-based approach for many objective optimization problems. *Comput. Oper. Res.* **2018**, *95*, 1–11. [CrossRef]
80. Miettinen, K.; Eskelinen, P.; Ruiz, F.; Luque, M. NAUTILUS method: An interactive technique in multiobjective optimization based on the nadir point. *Eur. J. Oper. Res.* **2010**, *206*, 426–434. [CrossRef]
81. Miettinen, K. Survey of methods to visualize alternatives in multiple criteria decision making problems. *OR Spectr.* **2014**, *36*, 3–37. [CrossRef]
82. Korhonen, P.; Wallenius, J. Visualization in the multiple objective decision-making framework. In *Multiobjective Optimization*; Springer: Heidelberg, Germany, 2008; pp. 195–212.

Mathematical and Computational Applications

Article

A Bounded Archiver for Hausdorff Approximations of the Pareto Front for Multi-Objective Evolutionary Algorithms

Carlos Ignacio Hernández Castellanos [1,*,†] and Oliver Schütze [2,*,†]

1. Instituto de Investigaciones en Matemáticas Aplicadas y Sistemas (IIMAS), Universidad Nacional Autónoma de México (UNAM), Mexico City 04510, Mexico
2. Computer Science Department, CINVESTAV-IPN, Mexico City 07360, Mexico
* Correspondence: carlos.hernandez@iimas.unam.mx (C.I.H.C.); schuetze@cs.cinvestav.mx (O.S.)
† These authors contributed equally to this work.

Abstract: Multi-objective evolutionary algorithms (MOEAs) have been successfully applied for the numerical treatment of multi-objective optimization problems (MOP) during the last three decades. One important task within MOEAs is the archiving (or selection) of the computed candidate solutions, since one can expect that an MOP has infinitely many solutions. We present and analyze in this work ArchiveUpdateHD, which is a bounded archiver that aims for Hausdorff approximations of the Pareto front. We show that the sequence of archives generated by ArchiveUpdateHD yields under certain (mild) assumptions with a probability of one after finitely many steps a Δ^+-approximation of the Pareto front, where the value Δ^+ is computed by the archiver within the run of the algorithm without any prior knowledge of the Pareto front. The knowledge of this value is of great importance for the decision maker, since it is a measure for the "completeness" of the Pareto front approximation. Numerical results on several well-known academic test problems as well as the usage of ArchiveUpdateHD as an external archiver within three state-of-the-art MOEAs indicate the benefit of the novel strategy.

Keywords: evolutionary multi-objective optimization; archiving; convergence

1. Introduction

This work is dedicated to the 60th birthday of Professor Kalyanmoy Deb, a pioneer and highly impactful and influential proponent of Evolutionary Multi-Objective Optimization (EMO) for the last three decades. In particular, the seminal work *Combining Convergence and Diversity in Evolutionary Multiobjective Optimization* by Marco Laummans, Lothar Thiele, Kalyanmoy Deb, and Eckart Zitzler [1] has been a motivation of the second author to consider the challenging and fruitful field of archiving in EMO.

Multi-objective optimization problems (MOPs), i.e., problems where several conflicting objectives have to be optimized concurrently, naturally arise in many real-world applications (e.g., [2–8]). While one can expect *one* optimal solution if "only" one objective is being considered, the solution set of an MOP (the so-called Pareto set, respectively, its image, the Pareto front) typically forms at least locally a manifold of a certain dimension [9]. One important task in multi-objective optimization (MOO) is hence to identify a "suitable" finite size approximation of these solution sets. Multi-objective evolutionary algorithms (MOEAs) represent an important class of algorithms for the numerical treatment of such problems. MOEAs have caught the interest of researchers and practitioners due to their global nature and robustness and since they require only minimal assumptions on the model (e.g., [2,10]). The process to elect a subset of the candidate solutions generated by the MOEA is called *selection* or *archiving*. Existing archiving/selection strategies can be roughly divided into two classes (see subsequent section for more details): (i) mechanisms that maintain sets those cardinalities are equal or do not exceed a certain pre-defined cardinality—which we will call bounded archivers in the following—and (ii) archivers that are based on the concept of ϵ-dominance. Such archivers generate sequences of archives A_i with monotonic behavior, i.e., no deterioration of cyclic behavior can be observed during the run of an algorithm. Furthermore, for $i \to \infty$, these archives yield certain limit approximation qualities that can be adjusted a priori, mainly by choosing the values of $\epsilon \in \mathbb{R}^k$ which comes rather naturally at least if the MOP arises from a real-world application. On the other hand, the magnitudes of the final archives are entirely determined by ϵ and some other design parameters, which are set a priori and are supposed to remain fixed during the computation, and the size of the Pareto front, which is a priori of course unknown. It has turned out that most EMO researchers prefer to have a fixed number of elements in the archives, e.g., for the sake of a better comparison to other methods but also to avoid the necessity of storing an unexpected large amount of candidate solutions. The latter problem is apparently by construction not given by bounded archives. For most strategies from class (i), however, no theoretical analyses such as convergence properties are known. For many distance-based methods, it is further known that cyclic behavior and deterioration can occur during the run of the algorithm. It is hence fair to say that these methods do not tap the full potential, since any MOEA using such a strategy will not converge regardless of the regions they explore during the run of the algorithm. An exception is the bounded archive proposed in [11], which yields under certain (mild) assumptions and with the probability of one ϵ-Pareto set in the limit, where $\epsilon \in \mathbb{R}$ is the smallest possible value with respect to to the bound of the archives.

In this paper, we propose a bounded archiver that is based on distance, dominance and ϵ-dominance that offers quasi-monotonic behavior and yields approximation qualities in the limit. More precisely, ArchiveUpdateHD aims for Hausdorff approximations of the Pareto front (i.e., evenly spread solutions along the Pareto front). Under certain (mild) assumptions on the generation process, it will be shown that the Hausdorff distances of the images of the archives $F(A_i)$ and the Pareto front $F(P_Q)$ are bounded by a value Δ^+, which is computed by the archiver during the run of the algorithm. Numerical experiments show that this value indeed represents a good approximation of the actual Hausdorff distance (while a better strategy is proposed for bi-objective problems). During the run of the algorithm, two design parameters are adjusted adaptively during the run of the algorithm (one being the value of ϵ for the ϵ-dominance). Since these values will become stationary during the search process, one can expect monotonic behavior from a certain stage of the search process. The knowledge of the Hausdorff distance of $F(A_i)$ and $F(P_Q)$ is important information for the decision maker (DM), since it represents the maximal error in the approximation. If not needed (i.e., depending on the chosen initial design parameters), the magnitudes of the archivers will not reach the pre-defined size N. Else, the value Δ^+ computed by the archiver is an important piece of information, since it tells the DM if the approximation is "complete enough" or not. In the latter case, the computation may have to be repeated using an increased value of N. A preliminary version of this work can be found in [12], which is restricted to bi-objective problems and contains fewer empirical results.

The rest of this document is structured as follows: Section 2 briefly summarizes the background that is required for the understanding of the sequel and presents the related work. In Section 3, the new archiver ArchiveUpdateHD is discussed and analyzed, first for bi-objective problems and after that for the general number of objectives. In Section 4, some numerical results and comparisons are presented and discussed. Finally, in Section 5, conclusions are drawn, and possible paths for future research are mentioned.

2. Background and Related Work

Here, we consider continuous multi-objective optimization problems (MOPs) that can be expressed as follows:

$$\min_{x \in Q} F(x). \tag{MOP}$$

The map F is defined by the individual objective functions f_i, i.e.,

$$F : Q \to \mathbb{R}^k, \quad F(x) = (f_1(x), \ldots, f_k(x))^T, \tag{1}$$

where each $f_i : Q \to \mathbb{R}, i = 1, \ldots, k$, is assumed to be continuous. We stress, however, that the archiver presented below can also be applied to discrete problems. Q is the domain or feasible set of the problem, which is typically expressed by equality and inequality constraints. We assume Q to be compact (i.e., closed and bounded). If $k = 2$ objectives are considered, the problem is also termed a bi-objective problem (BOP).

In order to define optimality in multi-objective opimization, the concept of dominance can be used: for two vectors $x, y \in \mathbb{R}^k$ we say that x is less than y ($x <_p y$) if $x_i < y_i$, $i \in \{1, \ldots, k\}$, analogously for the relation $\leq_p$. We say that $y \in Q$ is *dominated* by $x \in Q$ ($x \prec y$) with respect to (MOP) if $F(x) \leq_p F(y)$ and $F(x) \neq F(y)$, else we say that y is non-dominated by x. Finally, $x^* \in Q$ is called Pareto optimal or simply optimal with respect to (MOP) if there exists no $y \in Q$ that dominates x. The Pareto set P_Q is the set of all optimal solutions with respect to (MOP), and its image $F(P_Q)$ is called the Pareto front. One can expect that both the Pareto set and Pareto front are from at least locally objects of dimension $k - 1$, where k is the number of objectives considered in the MOP [9].

For the convergence analysis, we will consider a very general class of algorithms, called Generic Stochastic Search Algorithm (GSSA), first considered by Laumanns et al. [1]. An algorithm of this class consists of a process to generate new candiate solutions together with an update strategy. Algorithm 1 shows the pseudocode of GSSA.

Algorithm 1 Generic Stochastic Search Algorithm

1: $P_0 \subset Q$ drawn at random
2: $A_0 = ArchiveUpdate(P_0, \emptyset)$
3: **for** $j = 0, 1, 2, \ldots$ **do**
4: $\quad P_{j+1} = Generate(P_j)$
5: $\quad A_{j+1} = ArchiveUpdate(P_{j+1}, A_j)$
6: **end for**

In the following, we define the Hausdorff distance d_H and the averaged Hausdorff distance Δ_p, which we will use to assess the approximation qualities of the obtained Pareto front approximations (toward the actual Pareto fronts).

Definition 1. *Let $u \in \mathbb{R}^n$ and $A, B \subset \mathbb{R}^n$. The semi-distance $dist(\cdot, \cdot)$ and the Hausdorff distance $d_H(\cdot, \cdot)$ are defined as follows:*

(a) $dist(u, A) := \inf_{v \in A} \|u - v\|_\infty$

(b) $dist(B, A) := \sup_{u \in B} dist(u, A)$

(c) $d_H(A, B) := \max\{dist(A, B), dist(B, A)\}$

Definition 2 ([13])**.** *Let $A, B \subset \mathbb{R}^n$ be finite sets. The value*

$$\Delta_p(A, B) = \max(GD_p(A, B), IGD_p(A, B)), \tag{2}$$

where

$$GD_p(A, B) = \left(\frac{1}{|A|} \sum_{a \in A} dist(a, B)^p \right)^{1/p}$$

$$IGD_p(A, B) = \left(\frac{1}{|B|} \sum_{b \in B} dist(b, A)^p \right)^{1/p}, \tag{3}$$

and $p \in \mathbb{N}$, is called the averaged Hausdorff distance between A and B.

We further define some objects that specify certain approximation qualities of Pareto front approximations. All of these objects are based on the concept of ϵ-dominance, which we will define first.

Definition 3 (ϵ-dominance). Let $\epsilon = (\epsilon_1, \ldots, \epsilon_k)^T \in \mathbb{R}_+^k$ and $x, y \in \mathbb{R}^n$. x is said to ϵ-dominate y (in short: $x \prec_\epsilon y$) with respect to (MOP) if

$$F(x) - \epsilon \leq_p F(y) \quad \text{and} \quad F(x) - \epsilon \neq F(y). \tag{4}$$

Definition 4 (ϵ-(approximate) Pareto front, [1]). Let $\epsilon \in \mathbb{R}_+^k$ and $A \subset \mathbb{R}^n$.
(a) $F(A)$ is called an ϵ-approximate Pareto front of (MOP) if every point $x \in Q$ is ϵ-dominated by at least one $a \in A$, i.e.,

$$\forall x \in Q : \exists a \in A : \quad a \prec_\epsilon x. \tag{5}$$

(b) $F(A)$ is called an ϵ-Pareto front if $F(A)$ is an ϵ-approximate Pareto front and if every point $a \in A$ is a Pareto point of (MOP).

Definition 5 (Δ-tight ϵ-(approximate) Pareto front, [14]). Let $\epsilon \in \mathbb{R}_+^k$ and $A \subset \mathbb{R}^n$.
(a) $F(A)$ is called a Δ-tight ϵ-approximate Pareto front of (MOP) if A is an ϵ-approximate Pareto front of (MOP) and if in addition

$$\text{dist}(F(P_Q), F(A)) \leq \Delta. \tag{6}$$

(b) $F(A)$ is called a Δ-tight ϵ-Pareto front if A is an ϵ-Pareto front of (MOP) and if in addition

$$d_H(F(P_Q), F(A)) \leq \Delta. \tag{7}$$

The archiver we propose in this work, ArchiveUpdateHD, aims for Δ-tight ϵ-Pareto fronts for particular values of Δ and ϵ. The sole usage of ϵ-dominance for the Pareto front approximations may lead to gaps in particular when parts of the front are flat. The Δ-tight ϵ-(approximate) Pareto fronts also take into account the distance of the Pareto front toward the candidate set, leading to better approximations in the Hausdorff sense (see Figure 1).

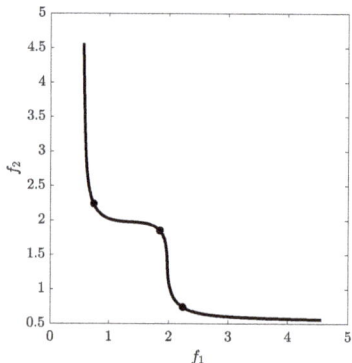 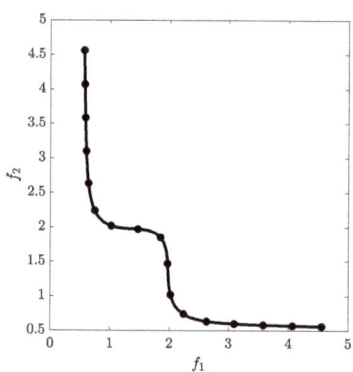

Figure 1. Gaps in the approximation can occur when ϵ-dominance is used exclusively in the selection/archiving of the candidate solutions (**left**). Δ-tight ϵ-(approximate) Pareto fronts also consider the distance of the Pareto front toward the archive (**right**).

Since one can expect infinitely many solutions for a continuous MOP, it is inevitable in (continuous) evolutionary multi-objective optimization (EMO) that not all promising solutions can be kept during the run of an algorithm. Instead, one has to elect a subset of candiate solutions in each iteration so that this sequence eventually leads to a "suitable" representation of the Pareto set/front of the given problem. This process is typically called "selection" within MOEAs and "archiving" if an external set of candidate solutions (archive) is maintained during the run of a MOEA (though of course both terms can be used interchangeably).

Three main classes of MOEAs exist: (a) dominance-based [15–18], (b) decomposition-based [19–25], and (c) indicator-based [26–30] algorithms. The selection strategies for MOEAs of class (b) or (c) are rather straightforward: the selection in a decomposition-based MOEA is done implicitly by the chosen scalarizing functions, and the selection in an indicator-based MOEA is typically handled via considering the indicator contributions. These two approaches come on the one hand with a monotonic behavior of the sequence of approximations (i.e., no deterioration can occur). On the other hand, these selection strategies do not guarantee convergence toward the best approximation (e.g., [29,31]). The selection of the first dominance-based MOEAs is based on non-dominated sorting in combination with niching techniques (e.g., [32–34]). Due to missing elite preservation, none of these methods converge in the mathematical sense. Later MOEAs such as SPEA [35], PAES [18], SPEA-II [16], and NSGA-II [15] include such elite preservation leading to much better overall performance. However, also for these algorithms, no convergence properties (again, in the mathematical sense) are known. Rudolph [36–39] and Hanne [40–43] have studied convergence properties of MOEA frameworks. These studies are mainly concerned with the convergence of individuals of the populations toward the Pareto set/front, while the magnitudes and the distributions of the resulting populations are not considered.

Archiving strategies with bounded archive size based on adaptive grid selection have been considered in [44–46]. Bounded archivers in particular for hypervolume approximations have been proposed in [47,48]. Both archivers yield monotonic behavior in the approximation qualities of the obtained sequence of archives.

Laumanns et al. considered the class of algorithms GSSA as described above [1,49] which allows to focus on the archiver under certain (mild) assumptions on the generator. In both studies, archivers were considered, aiming for several ϵ approximations of the Pareto front, where finitely many iterations were considered. Later, further archivers have been proposed based on ϵ-dominance using the framework of GSSA to perform convergence analysis [14,50–54].

In [11], Laumanns and Zenklusen propose two bounded archivers that use adaptive schemes to obtain ϵ approximations of the Pareto front. Another adaptive archiving strategy is proposed in [55] that utilizes a particular discretization of the objective space of the given problem. A strategy that is based on the convex hull of individual minima in order to increase diversity of the solutions is proposed in [56].

Recently, the use of external archives has become more popular [57–62] in particular for the treatment of real-world applications where function evaluations are expensive, and where it is hence advisable to maintain all promising candidate solutions. Consequently, most of these archivers are unbounded [63–67]. For the treatment of in particular MOPs with many objectives—also called many objective problems—MOEAs have been proposed that utilize *two* archives, one aiming for convergence and one aiming for diversity [68,69].

3. ArchiveUpdateHD

We will in this section propose and discuss the novel archiver ArchiveUpdateHD. Since the considerations of the distances as well as the Hausdorff approximations can be done more accurately for $k = 2$—where we can assume the Pareto front to locally form a curve, and hence, the elements of the approximations can be arranged via a sorting in objective space—we first address the bi-objective case and will afterwards consider the archiver for problems with $k > 2$.

3.1. The Bi-Objective Case

The pseudocode of ArchiveUpdateHD for bi-objective problems is shown in Algorithm 2. This archiver aims for approximations of the Pareto front of a given BOP in the Hausdorff sense (i.e., for solutions that are evenly spread along the Pareto front). The archiver is based (i) on the distances among the candidate solutions (lines 18–36 of Algorithm 2), (ii) "classical" dominance or elite preservation (lines 5 and 9) as well as (iii) the concept of ϵ-dominance (line 5). The archiver can roughly be divided into two parts: an acceptance strategy to decide if an incoming candidate solution p should be considered (line 5), and a pruning technique (mainly lines 18–36, but also lines 11–14) which is applied if the size of the archive has exceeded a predefined budget N of archive entries.

In the following, we will describe ArchiveUpdateHD as in Algorithm 2 in more detail. This algorithm contains several elements that have to be incorporated in order to guarantee convergence. After the convergence analysis (Theorem 1), we will discuss more practical realizations of the algorithm.

In line 5, it is decided if a candidate solution p should be (at least temporarily) added to the existing archive A. This is the case if (a) none of the entries $a \in A$ $\Theta\epsilon$-dominates p ($\Theta \in (0,1)$ being a safety factor needed to guarantee convergence, see below for practical realizations), or if (b) none of the entries $a \in A$ dominates p and for none of the entries $a \in A$ the distance $\|F(a) - F(p)\|$ is less or equal than $\Theta\Delta$. Throughout this work, $\|\cdot\|$ denotes the Euclidean norm. We stress that this acceptance strategy is identical to the one of the archiver ArchiveUpdateTight2 [14], which we will need for the upcoming convergence analysis.

If the candidate solution p is accepted, it will be added to A. Next, all other entries $a \in A$ dominated by p will be discarded (lines 8–10). Hence, all archives generated by ArchiveUpdateHD only contain mutually non-dominated elements (elite preservation). If the distance $\|F(p) - F(a)\|$ is larger than ϵ for any of these dominated archive entries a, a "reset" is executed for Δ and ϵ: Δ_{min} is set to $\kappa\Delta_{min}$ (where $\kappa > 1$ another safety factor). Next, Δ and ϵ are updated using this new minimal value. The idea behind this reset is as follows: if $p \prec a$ and the distance of $F(a)$ and $F(p)$ is larger than Δ, then p and a could be located in different connected components of the set of (local) solutions of the bi-objective problem. Since the values both of Δ and ϵ are determined by the length of the (known) Pareto front, their values have to be set back, since a "jump" to a new connected component may lead to a new length. See Figure 2 for a hypothetical scenario. The value of Δ_{min} has to be (slightly) increased in each reset in order to avoid the possible of a cyclic behavior in the sequence of archives (which, in fact, has not been observed in our computations).

If $|A|$ exceeds the predefined magnitude N, it is decided in lines 18–36 which of the elements of A has to be discarded (pruning). For $k = 2$ objectives, we can order all the entries of the archives (e.g., as done here: in ascending order wrt objective f_1). Then, the vector $d \in \mathbb{R}^N$ of distances can be simply computed via:

$$d_i := \|F(a_{i+1}) - F(a_i)\|, \quad i = 1, \ldots, N. \tag{8}$$

For an index m chosen from arg min d, either a_m or a_{m+1} is then removed from A, which is done in lines 23–33. The aim of ArchiveUpdateHD is to maintain good approximations of the end points of the Pareto front. Accordingly, a_2, respectively, a_N, are always discarded instead of a_1 and a_{N+1}, respectively (lines 23–26). The rationale behind the selection in lines 28–33 is to keep the archive of size N with the most evenly distributed elements.

Algorithm 2 ArchiveUpdateHD

Require: Problem (MOP), where $k = 2$, P: current population, A_0: current archive, $\Delta_0 > 0$: current value of Δ, Δ_{min}: minimal value of Δ, $\Theta \in (0,1)$, $\kappa > 1$: safety factors, N: upper bound for archive size

Ensure: updated archive A, updated values for Δ, Δ_{min}, and ϵ

1: $A := A_0$
2: $\Delta := \Delta_0$
3: $\epsilon := (\Delta, \ldots, \Delta)^T$
4: **for all** $p \in P$ **do**
5:    **if** $\nexists a \in A : a \prec_{\Theta \epsilon} p$, or $\nexists a \in A : a \prec p$ and $\forall a \in A : \|F(a) - F(p)\| > \Theta \Delta$ **then**
6:       $A := A \cup \{p\}$
7:    **end if**
8:    **for all** $a \in A$ **do**
9:       **if** $p \prec a$ **then**
10:          $A := A \cup \{p\} \backslash \{a\}$
11:          **if** $\|F(p) - F(a)\|_\infty > \Delta$ **then**   ▷ reset Δ and ϵ
12:             $\Delta_{min} := \kappa \Delta_{min}$
13:             $\Delta := \Delta_{min}$
14:             $\epsilon := (\Delta, \ldots, \Delta)^T$
15:          **end if**
16:       **end if**
17:    **end for**
18:    **if** $|A| = N + 1$ **then**   ▷ apply pruning
19:       $\Delta := \frac{N+1}{N} \Delta$
20:       $\epsilon := \frac{N+1}{N} \epsilon$
21:       sort A (e.g., according to f_1)
22:       compute $d \in \mathbb{R}^N$ as in (8)
23:       choose $m \in \arg\min d$
24:       **if** $m = 1$ **then**
25:          $A := A \backslash \{a_2\}$ ▷ remove 2nd entry
26:       **else if** $m = N$ **then**
27:          $A := A \backslash \{a_N\}$ ▷ remove 2nd but last entry
28:       **else**
29:          $dl := \|F(a_{m+1}) - F(a_{m-1})\|$
30:          $dr := \|F(a_{m+2}) - F(a_m)\|$
31:          **if** $dl < dr$ **then**
32:             $A := A \backslash \{a_m\}$
33:          **else**
34:             $A := A \backslash \{a_{m+1}\}$
35:          **end if**
36:       **end if**
37:    **end if**
38: **end for**
39: **return** $\{A, \epsilon, \epsilon_{min}, \Delta\}$

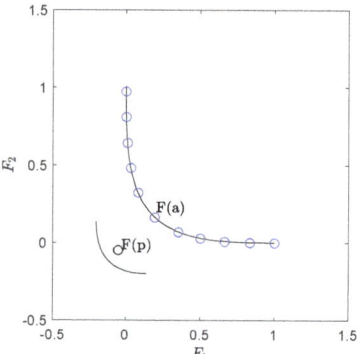

Figure 2. A hypothetical scenario that can happen for multi-modal problems: first, a front that is only locally optimal is detected by the search process and approximated by the archiver. If later, a candidate p is computed such that $F(p)$ lies on a "better" front, the current values of Δ and ϵ may not be adequate any more to suitably approximate this front.

In the following, we investigate the limit behavior of ArchiveUpdateHD.

Theorem 1. *Let (MOP) be given and $Q \subset \mathbb{R}^n$ be compact, and let there be no weak Pareto points in $Q \backslash P_Q$. Furthermore, let F be continuous and injective, and*

$$\forall x \in Q \text{ and } \forall \delta > 0: \quad P(\exists l \in \mathbb{N} \,:\, P_l \cap B_\delta(x) \cap Q \neq \emptyset) = 1. \tag{9}$$

Then, an application of Algorithm 1, where ArchiveUpdateHD (Algorithm 2) is used to update the archive, leads to a sequence of archives $A_l, l \in \mathbb{N}$, where the following holds:

(a) *There exists a $l_1 \in \mathbb{N}$ and $\Delta^+ > 0$ such that*

$$\Delta_l = \Delta^+, \quad \forall l \geq l_1, \quad \text{with probability one.}$$

(b) *There exists with probability one a $l_2 \in \mathbb{N}$ such that A_l is a Δ^+-tight ϵ-approximate Pareto front with respect to (MOP) for all $l \geq l_2$, where $\epsilon = (\Delta^+, \ldots, \Delta^+)^T$.*

(c)
$$\lim_{l \to \infty} dist(A_l, P_Q) = 0, \quad \text{with probability one.}$$

(d) *There exists a $l_3 \in \mathbb{N}$ such that*

$$d_H(F(A_l), F(P_Q)) \leq \Delta^+, \quad \forall l \geq l_3, \quad \text{with probability one.}$$

Proof. We first show that during the run of the algorithm, only finitely many changes of the value of Δ (and hence also of ϵ) can occur. Since F is continuous and the domain $Q \subset \mathbb{R}^n$ is compact, also the image $F(Q)$ is compact, and hence, in particular bounded. ArchiveUpdateHD changes the value of Δ in two cases: if (i) a reset of Δ and ϵ is executed (line 12) or if (ii) the pruning technique is applied (line 19). In case of (i), the value of Δ_{min} is increased by a constant factor $\kappa > 1$. The value of Δ after the i-th reset is hence equal to or larger than $\kappa^i \Delta_{min}^0$, where $\Delta_{min}^0 > 0$ denotes the value of Δ_{min} at the start of the algorithm. A reset is applied if the distance of the image of the candidate solution p to the image of an archive element a is larger than the current value of Δ (line 11). Since $F(P_Q)$ is bounded, only a finite number of such resets can be applied during the run of the algorithm.

Case (ii) happens if the magnitude of the current archive is $N + 1$. New candidate solutions p are added to the archive in lines 5 and 6 and lines 9 and 10. Lines 9 and 10 describe a dominance replacement which does not increase the magnitude of the archive.

Hence, such replacements do not lead to an application of the pruning. A candidate p can be further added to the current archive A if one of the following statements is true (line 5):

$$\begin{aligned} &\mathcal{E}_1 \quad \nexists a \in A : a \prec_{\Theta\epsilon} p, \text{ or} \\ &\mathcal{E}_2 \quad \nexists a \in A : a \prec p \text{ and } \forall a \in A : \|F(a) - F(p)\| > \Theta\Delta \end{aligned} \quad (10)$$

Since $F(Q)$ is bounded, there exists for every $a \in Q$ a (large enough) $\Delta_a > 0$ so that $a \prec_{\Theta\epsilon} p$, where $\epsilon = (\Delta_a, \ldots, \Delta_a)^T$. Similarly, $\|F(a) - F(p)\| < \Theta\Delta_a$ if Δ_a is large enough. Since in each pruning step, the value of Δ is increased by the factor of $(N+1)/N$ and since only finitely many resets are executed, also only finitely many prunings can be applied during the run of the algorithm.

Note that ArchiveUpdateHD differs from ArchiveUpdateTight2 in two parts: the reset strategy (lines 11–15) and the pruning technique (lines 18–37), and that both these parts come with a change of the values of Δ and ϵ. In other words, ArchiveUpdateHD is identical to ArchiveUpdateTight2 as long as no change in Δ and ϵ occurs. For this case, we can hence apply the theoretical results on ArchiveUpdateTight2 for ArchiveUpdateHD. Now, consider a fixed value of Δ (and hence also ϵ). During the run, it can either be the case that (i) all magnitudes of A_l are less than or equal to N (i.e., no pruning is applied), or that (ii) this magnitude is $N+1$ at one point, leading to an application of the pruning technique. In case (i), we can use Theorem 7.4 of [54] on ArchiveUpdateTight2: there exists with probability of one a $\bar{l} \in \mathbb{N}$ such that the sets $F(A_l)$ form a Δ-tight ϵ-approximate Pareto front for all $l \geq \bar{l}$. Note that once $F(A_l)$ forms an object, no more resets can occur: assume there exists a candidate solution p that dominates an element $a \in A_l$, and where $\|F(p) - F(a)\|_\infty > \Delta$. The latter means that

$$\max_{i=1,\ldots,k} f_i(a) - f_i(p) > \Delta \quad (11)$$

which in turn means that a does not ϵ-approximate p, which is a contradiction to the assumption on A_l. In case (ii), the value of Δ is simply not large enough for the N-element archive to form a Δ-tight ϵ- approximate Pareto front. Again, by Theorem 7.4 of [54], there exists in this case with a probability of one a finite iteration number where the magnitude will exceed N. As discussed above, the pruning can only be applied finitely many times during the run of the algorithm. Hence, the value of Δ will, with a probability of one, stay fixed from one iteration onwards, which proves part (a).

Parts (b) and (c) follow from Theorem 7.4 of [54] and part (a), and finally, part (d) follows from parts (b) and (c) and the definition of the Hausdorff distance. □

Remark 1. (a) Equation (9) is an assumption that has to be made on the generation process. It means that every neighborhood of every feasible point $x \in Q$ will be "visited" with probability one by Generate() after finitely many steps. For MOEAs, this, e.g., ensured if Polynomial Mutation [70,71] is used or another mutation operator for which the support of the probability density functions equal to Q (at least for box-constrained problems). We hence think that this assumption is rather mild.
(b) The complexity of the consideration of one candidate solution p is $O(N \log(N))$, which is determined by the sorting of the current archive A in line 20.
(c) $\Theta \in (0, 1)$ and $\kappa > 1$ are safety factors needed to guarantee the convergence properties. In our computations, however, we have not observed any impact of these values if both are chosen near to one. We hence suggest to use $\Theta = \kappa = 1$ (i.e., practically not to use these safety factors).
(d) The above consideration is done for $\epsilon = (\Delta, \ldots, \Delta)^T \in \mathbb{R}^k$, i.e., using the same value for all entries of ϵ. If the values for the objectives along the Pareto front differ significantly, one

can of course instead use $\Delta = \epsilon = (\Delta_1, \ldots, \Delta_k)^T$ using different values Δ_i. In that case, the following modifications have to be done: (i) the last condition in line 5 has to be replaced by

$$\nexists a \in A \, : \, |f_i(a) - f_i(p)| \leq \Delta_i, \quad i = 1, \ldots, k.$$

Furthermore, (ii) the condition for the reset in line 11 has to be replaced by

$$\exists i \in \{1, \ldots, k\} \, : \, |f_i(p) - f_i(a)| > \Delta_i.$$

(e) The value of Δ computed throughout the algorithm yields an approximation quality of the archivers in the Hausdorff sense. The theoretical upper bound of the final value Δ^+ is twice the value of the actual Hausdorff approximation as the following discussion shows (refer to Figure 3): assume we are given a linear front with slope -1, and we are given a budget of $N = 2$ elements (the discussion is analog for general N). The ideal archive as computed by ArchiveUpdateHD is in this case $A = \{a_1, a_2\}$, where the a_i's are the end points of the Pareto set. Assume we have $F(a_1) = (0, 1)^T$ and $F(a_2) = (1, 0)^T$; then, the Hausdorff distance of the Pareto front and A is $1/2$ determined by the point $y_m = (1/2, 1/2)^T$. Given this archive, for any value $\Delta < 1$ and assuming that $F(Q)$ is large enough, there exists a candidate p such that p is not dominated by a_1 or a_2 and that $\|F(a_i) - F(p)\| > \Delta, i = 1, 2$. Hence, p will be added to the archiver—and later on discarded (lines 23–26). The latter leads to an increase of Δ.

On the one hand, one suggesting strategy would be to take $\frac{1}{2}\Delta^+$ as a Hausdorff approximation of the Pareto front in particular, since most Pareto fronts have at least one element where the slope of the tangent space is -1. On the other hand, the use of ϵ-dominance prevents that the images $F(a), a \in A$, are perfectly evenly distributed along the Pareto front so that $\frac{1}{2}\Delta^+$ is not that accurate for some problems. In fact, this factor of two can only be observed for linear fronts, while Δ^+ already yields a good approximation in general (see, e.g., the subsequent results for MOPs with more than two objectives). However, we have observed that the following estimation gives even better approximations of the Hausdorff distances: given $A = \{a_1, \ldots, a_N\}$, which is sorted (e.g., according to objective f_1), the current Hausdorff approximation h is computed as follows:

$$\tilde{d}_i := \begin{cases} \|F(a_{i+1}) - F(a_i)\|, & \text{if } \|F(a_{i+1}) - F(a_i)\| \leq 2\Delta \\ 0, & \text{else} \end{cases}, \quad i = 1, \ldots, N-1 \quad (12)$$

$$h := \frac{1}{2} \max_{i=1, \ldots, N-1} \tilde{d}_i.$$

Note that the distance is set to 0 if the distance between two neighboring candidate solutions is larger or equal to 2Δ, which has been done to take into account approximations of Pareto fronts that fall into several connected components.

(f) Several norms are used within the algorithm. While one is—except in line 11, see the above proof—in principle free for the choice of the norms, we suggest taking the infinity norm in line 5 in order to reduce the issue mentioned in the previous part, and the 2 norm in lines 28 and 29 in order to obtain a (slightly) better distribution of the entries along the Pareto front.

Algorithm 3 shows the modifications of ArchiveUpdateHD discussed above, which have been used for the calculations presented in this work. Hereby, $\Delta_{min} \in \mathbb{R}^k_+$ denotes the vector of minimal elements for each entry Δ_i.

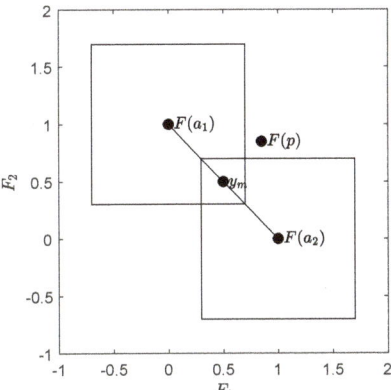

Figure 3. Linear Pareto front with slope -1. If for $N = 2$, the archive is given by $A = \{a_1, a_2\}$ such that $F(a_1)$ and $F(a_2)$ are the end points of the Pareto front, then the Hausdorff distance of A and the Pareto front is given by $h = \|F(a_1) - y_m\|_\infty$, where y_m is the arithmetic mean of $F(a_1)$ and $F(a_2)$. For $\Delta < 2h$, there may exist candidate solutions p that will be considered by the archive (line 5 of Algorithm 1) but discarded in the same step (lines 23 to 26 of Algorithm 1), leading to an increase of Δ.

Remark 2. *For the performance assessment of MOEAs, it is typically advisable to take instead of the Hausdorff distance d_H the averaged Hausdorff distance Δ_p. The main reason for this is that MOEAs may compute a few outliers in particular if the MOP contains weakly dominated solutions that are not optimal (also called dominance resistance solutions [72]). On the other hand, we stress that Δ_p, opposed to d_H, is not a metric in the mathematical sense, since the triangle inequality does not hold. We refer, e.g., to [13,38,73,74] for more discussion on this matter.*

In the following, we discuss one possibility to obtain an approximation of the value of Δ_p from a given archive A. To this end, we first investigate the value of Δ_p if the elements of A are perfectly located around a linear connected Pareto front (if N is large enough, we can expect that this approximation works fine for any connected Pareto front). That is, all a_i values are optimal. Furthermore, if A is sorted, $F(a_1)$ and $F(a_N)$ are the end points of the Pareto front, and the distance of two consecutive elements $F(a_i)$ and $F(a_{i+1})$ is given by $2h$ (leading to $d_H = h$). Since all the a_i values are optimal, the Δ_p value is hence given by the value of IGD_p, which can be computed as follows:

$$\Delta_p(F(A), F(P_Q)) = IGD_p(F(A), F(P_Q)) = \left(\frac{1}{F(a_N) - F(a_1)} \int_{F(a_1)}^{F(a_N)} dist(t, F(A))^p dt \right)^{\frac{1}{p}}$$

$$= \left(\frac{1}{(N-1)2h} 2(N-1) \int_0^h t^p dt \right)^{\frac{1}{p}}$$

$$= \left(\frac{1}{h} \left[\frac{1}{p+1} t^{p+1} \right]_0^h \right)^{\frac{1}{p}} = \left(\frac{1}{h} \frac{1}{p+1} h^{p+1} \right)^{\frac{1}{p}} \qquad (13)$$

$$= \sqrt[p]{\frac{1}{p+1}} \cdot h$$

Hereby, we have used the formulation of IGD_p for continuous Pareto fronts as discussed in [73]. It remains to compute h. Since the assumption that all the images of the a_i values are evenly spread is ideal, we cannot simply take $\frac{1}{2}\|F(a_{i+1}) - F(a_i)\|$ for an arbitrarily index $i \in \{1, \ldots, N-1\}$. Instead, it makes sense to use the average of these distances:

$$h \approx \frac{\sum_{i=1}^{N-1} \tilde{d}_i}{2m}, \tag{14}$$

where $\tilde{d}_i$ is as in (12) and m denotes the number of elements of $\tilde{d}_i$ that are not equal to zero. This leads to the approximation d_p of the averaged Hausdorff distance Δ_p of the Pareto front by a given archive A:

$$d_p := \sqrt[p]{\frac{1}{p+1} \cdot \frac{\sum_{i=1}^{N-1} \tilde{d}_i}{2m}}. \tag{15}$$

In order to obtain a first impression on the effect of the archiver, we apply it to several test problems. More precisely, we use ArchiveUpdateHD together with the generator, which is simply choosing candidate solutions uniformly at random from the domain of the problem. As test problems, we use CONV (convex front), DENT ([75], convex-concave front), RUD1 and RUD2 (disconnected fronts), LINEAR (linear front) and RUD3 (convex front). The first five test problems are uni-modal, while RUD3 has next to the Pareto front eight local fronts. RUD3 is taken from [76], and RUD1 and RUD2 are straightforward modifications of RUD3 to obtain the given Pareto front shapes.

Figure 4 shows the final approximations of the fronts using $N = 30$ for the archive size and initial values of Δ small enough so that this threshold is reached for all problems. As it can be seen, in all cases, evenly distributed solutions along the Pareto fronts have been obtained. Figure 5 shows the actual Hausdorff and averaged Hausdorff values of the computed archives in each step for one run of the algorithm (d_H and Δ_2, i.e., $p = 2$ has been used for the averaged Hausdorff distance), together with their approximations h and d_2. For all problems, the archiver is capable of quickly determining a good approximation of both d_H and Δ_2 during the run of the algorithm. Tables A1 and A2 show the approximation qualities averaged over 30 independent runs, which support the observations from Figure 5. Figure 6 shows the evolution of the value of Δ during one run of the algorithm for DENT and RUD3. For the uni-modal problem DENT, the value of Δ is essentially increasing monotonically (i.e., not counting the first few iteration steps), while for the multi-modal problem RUD3, more than 10 restarts occur. Nevertheless, in both cases, a final value Δ^+ is reached, which is in accord with Theorem 1.

Figure A1 shows the box collections

$$C(A_f) := \bigcup_{a \in A_f} B_{\Delta_f}(F(a)) \tag{16}$$

of the final archives A_f and the final value Δ_f for the test problems, where $B_\Delta(x)$ denotes the Δ-ball around x using the maximum norm. The figure indicates that the Hausdorff distance of $F(A_f)$ and the respective Pareto fronts is indeed less or equal to Δ_f for all problems.

Algorithm 3 $\{A, \Delta, h\} := ArchiveUpdateHD(P, A_0, \Delta_0, N)$

Require: Problem (MOP), where $k = 2$, P: current population, A_0: current archive, $\Delta_0 \in \mathbb{R}_+^k$: current values of Δ, N: upper bound for archive size
Ensure: updated archive A, updated values for Δ, Hausdorff approximation h

1: $A := A_0$
2: $\Delta := \Delta_0$
3: $\epsilon := \Delta$
4: **for all** $p \in P$ **do**
5:   **if** $\nexists a \in A : a \prec_\epsilon p$, or $\nexists a \in A : a \prec p$ and $\nexists a \in A : |f_i(a) - f_i(p)| \leq \Delta_i$, $i = 1, \ldots, k$ **then**
6:     $A := A \cup \{p\}$
7:   **end if**
8:   **for all** $a \in A$ **do**
9:     **if** $p \prec a$ **then**
10:       $A := A \cup \{p\} \setminus \{a\}$
11:       **if** $\exists i \in \{1, \ldots, k\} : f_i(a) - f_i(p) > \Delta_i$ **then**   ▷ reset Δ and ϵ
12:         $\Delta := \Delta_{min}$
13:         $\epsilon := \Delta$
14:       **end if**
15:     **end if**
16:   **end for**
17:   **if** $|A| = N + 1$ **then**   ▷ apply pruning
18:     $\Delta := \frac{N+1}{N} \Delta$
19:     $\epsilon := \frac{N+1}{N} \epsilon$
20:     sort A (e.g., according to f_1)
21:     compute $d \in \mathbb{R}^N$ as in (8)
22:     choose $m \in \arg\min d$
23:     **if** $m = 1$ **then**
24:       $A := A \setminus \{a_2\}$ ▷ remove 2nd entry
25:     **else if** $m = N$ **then**
26:       $A := A \setminus \{a_N\}$ ▷ remove 2nd but last entry
27:     **else**
28:       $dl := \|F(a_{m+1}) - F(a_{m-1})\|_2$
29:       $dr := \|F(a_{m+2}) - F(a_m)\|_2$
30:       **if** $dl < dr$ **then**
31:         $A := A \setminus \{a_m\}$
32:       **else**
33:         $A := A \setminus \{a_{m+1}\}$
34:       **end if**
35:     **end if**
36:   **end if**
37: **end for**
38: sort A (e.g., according to f_1)   ▷ compute Hausdorff approximation
39: compute $\tilde{d}_i, i = 1, \ldots, |A| - 1$ as in (12)
40: $h := \frac{1}{2} \max_{i=1,\ldots,|A|-1} \tilde{d}_i$
41: **return** $\{A, \Delta, h\}$

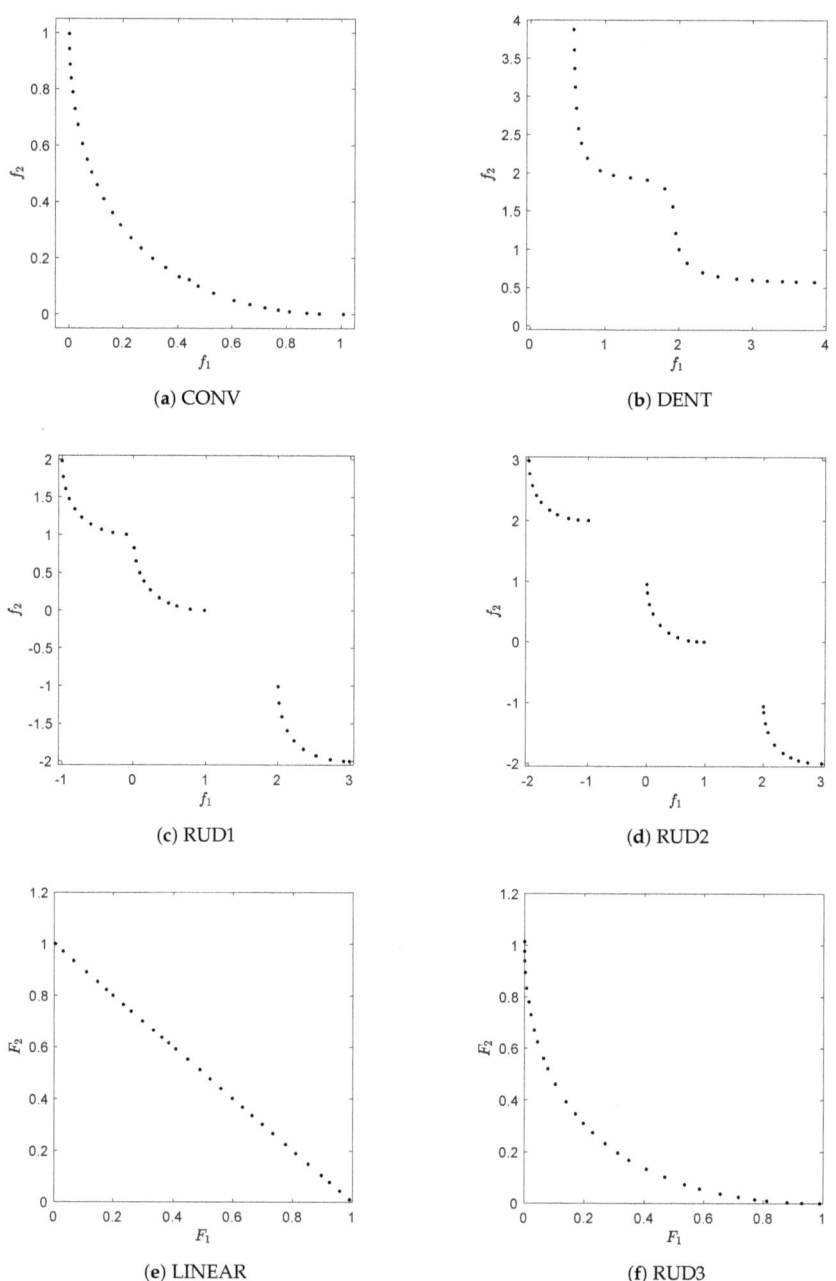

Figure 4. Numerical results of ArchiveUpdateHD on six BOPs with different shapes of the Pareto fronts. For the sake of clarity, we omitted the fronts that already become apparent by the approximations.

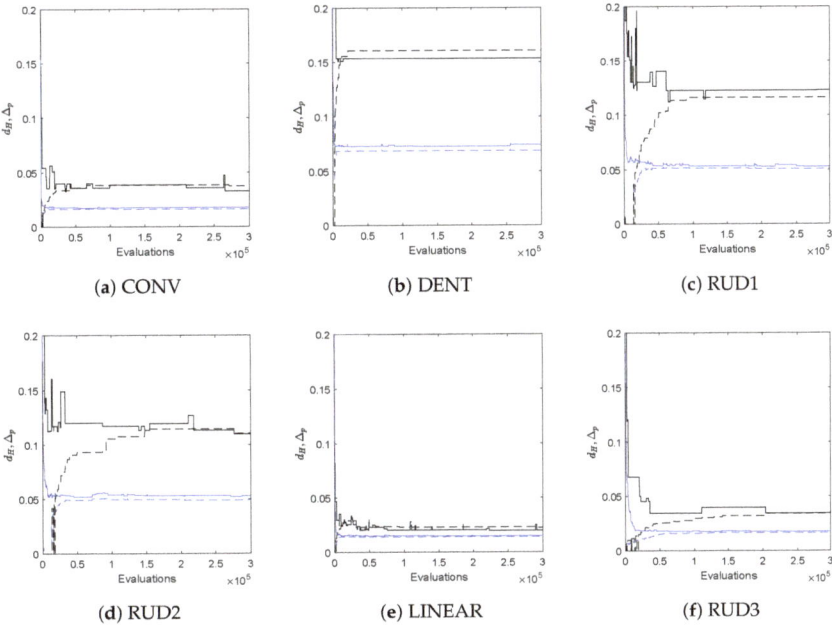

Figure 5. Hausdorff and averaged Hausdorff approximations (d_h and Δ_2, respectively) obtained by ArchiveUpdateHD for one single run for six bi-objective problems (see Figure 4) together with their approximations h and d_2. d_H is plotted black solid, h is black dashed, Δ_2 is blue solid, and d_2 is blue dashed.

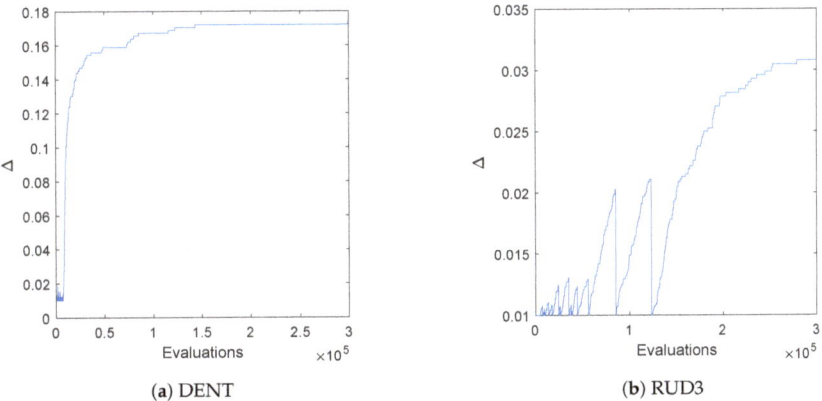

Figure 6. Evolution of the value of Δ for one run of the algorithm on DENT and RUD3.

3.2. The General Case

Next, we consider the archiver for MOPs with more than two objectives. Algorithm 4 shows the pseudocode of ArchiveUpdateHD for such problems. The archiver is essentially identical to the one for BOPs; however, it comes with two modificatons, since one cannot expect the Pareto front to form a one-dimensional object any more and another one prevents too many unnecessary resets during the run of the algorithm.

1. The distances cannot be be sorted any more as in (8). Instead, one has to consider the distances
$$d_{i,j} = \|F(a_i) - F(a_j)\|, \quad i,j = 1,\ldots,|A|, \quad j > i, \tag{17}$$
for a given archive A. Furthermore, more sophisticated considerations of the distances as, e.g., in lines 27 and 28 of Algorithm 3 cannot be considered any more. Instead, we have chosen to first compute
$$d_{i_m,j_m} \in \arg \min_{\substack{i,j=1,\ldots,N+1 \\ j>i}} d_{i,j}, \tag{18}$$
and then to remove a_l from the archiver, where l is chosen randomly from $\{i_m, j_m\}$. Similar as for the bi-objective case, an exception can of course be made for the best found solutions for each objective value.
2. The approximation of the Hausdorff distance cannot be done as in (12) any more. Instead, we choose the value of Δ as an approximation for $d_h(F(A), F(P_Q))$, which is motivated by Theorem 1.
3. The reset is completed if there exists an entry a of the current archive A and a candidate solution p that dominates a and
$$f_i(a) - f_i(p) > \Delta_i \quad i = 1,\ldots,k.$$

That is, the improvement is larger than Δ_i for *all* objectives. It has been observed that if one only asks for an improvement in one objective (as done for the bi-objective case), too many resets are performed in particular for MOPs that contain a "flat" region of the Pareto front.

Note that none of these changes affects the statements made in Theorem 1. Hence, the statements of Theorem 1 also hold if Algorithm 4 is used for MOPs with $k > 2$ objectives. We stress that this algorithm can of course also be used for the treatment of BOPs; however, in that case, Algorithm 3 seems to be better suited, since both distance considerations and Hausdorff approximation are more sophisticated.

Figure 7 shows an application of Algorithm 4 on the test function DTLZ2 with three objectives (concave and connected Pareto front) for $N = 300$ and $N = 500$. The evolution of the approximated value Δ of the Hausdorff distance $d_h(F(A), F(P_Q))$ together with the real value can be found in Figure 8. Hereby, we have used ArchiveUpdateHD as the external archiver of NSGA-II. The same result could have been obtained using randomly chosen test points within the domain Q, however, for a much higher amount of test points. Figures 9 and 10 show the respective results for DTLZ7, whose Pareto front is disconnected and convex-concave. In all cases, the archiver is capable of finding evenly spread solutions along the Pareto front, and the value of Δ is already after some iterations quite close to the actual Hausdorff distance. In order to suitably handle weakly optimal solutions, we have used the approach we describe in the following remark.

Remark 3. *It is known that distance-based archiving/selection for MOPs that contains weakly optimal solutions that are not optimal (dominance-resistant solutions) may lead to unsatisfactory results, since candidates may be included in the archive that are far away from the Pareto front. In [77], it has been suggested to consider the modified objectives*
$$\tilde{f}_i(x) = (1-\alpha)f_i(x) + \frac{\alpha}{m}\sum_{i=1}^{k} f_i(x), \quad i = 1,\ldots,k, \tag{19}$$
where $\alpha > 0$ is "small", instead of the orginal objectives f_i, $i = 1,\ldots,k$. We have adopted this approach for the treatment of the ZDT and DTLZ functions in this work, using $\alpha = 0.02$.

Algorithm 4 $\{A, \Delta\} := ArchiveUpdateHD(P, A_0, \Delta_0, N)$

Require: Problem (MOP), P: current population, A_0: current archive, $\Delta_0 \in \mathbb{R}_+^k$: current value of Δ, N: upper bound for archive size
Ensure: updated archive A, updated value of Δ

1: $A := A_0$
2: $\Delta := \Delta_0$
3: $\epsilon := \Delta$
4: **for all** $p \in P$ **do**
5:    **if** $\nexists a \in A : a \prec_\epsilon p$, or $\nexists a \in A : a \prec p$ and $\nexists a \in A : |f_i(a) - f_i(p)| \leq \Delta_i, \ i = 1, \ldots, k$ **then**
6:       $A := A \cup \{p\}$
7:    **end if**
8:    **for all** $a \in A$ **do**
9:       **if** $p \prec a$ **then**
10:          $A := A \cup \{p\} \setminus \{a\}$
11:          **if** $f_i(a) - f_i(p) > \Delta_i, \ i = 1, \ldots, k,$ **then**   ▷ reset Δ and ϵ
12:             $\Delta := \Delta_{min}$
13:             $\epsilon := \Delta$
14:          **end if**
15:       **end if**
16:    **end for**
17:    **if** $|A| = N + 1$ **then**   ▷ apply pruning
18:       $\Delta := \frac{N+1}{N} \Delta$
19:       $\epsilon := \frac{N+1}{N} \epsilon$
20:       compute $d_{i,j}$ as in (17)
21:       choose $d_{i_m, j_m} \in \arg\min_{\substack{i,j=1,\ldots,N+1 \\ j>i}} d_{i,j}$
22:       choose l randomly from $\{i_m, j_m\}$
23:       $A := A \setminus \{a_l\}$
24:    **end if**
25: **end for**
26: **return** $\{A, \Delta\}$

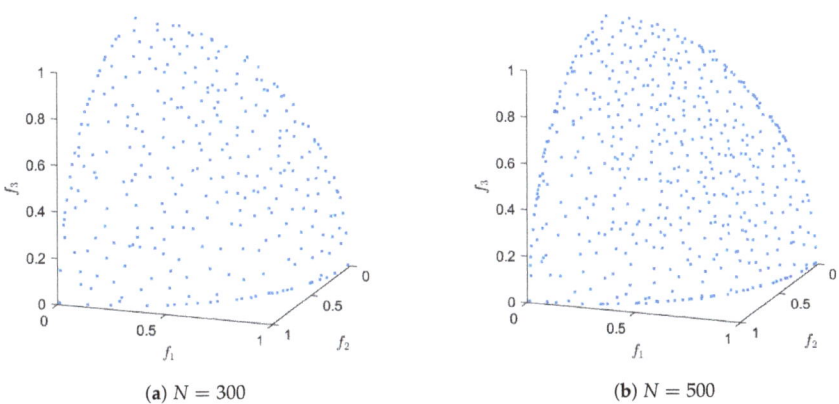

(a) $N = 300$ (b) $N = 500$

Figure 7. Results of ArchiveUpdateHD on DTLZ2 for different values of N.

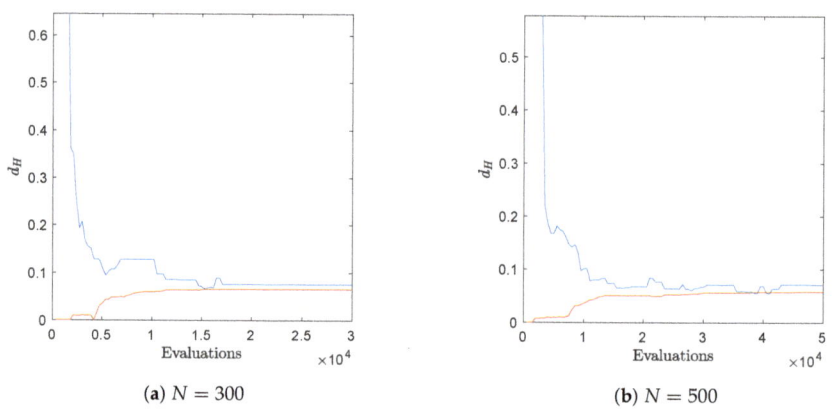

(a) $N = 300$ (b) $N = 500$

Figure 8. Real (blue) and approximated (red) Hausdorff distances during the run of one algorithm for DTLZ2.

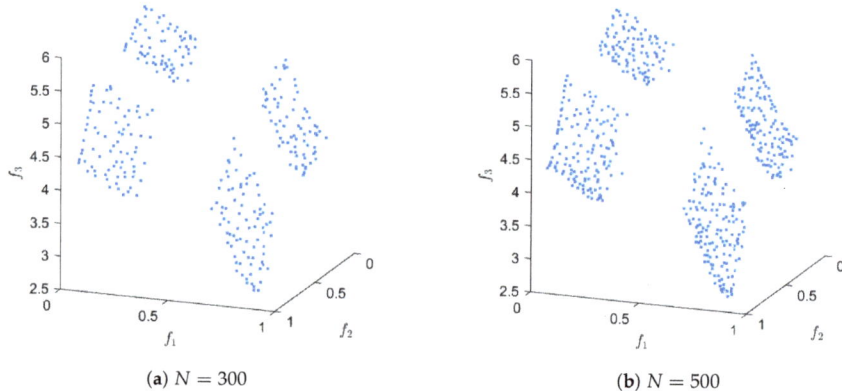

(a) $N = 300$ (b) $N = 500$

Figure 9. Results of ArchiveUpdateHD on DTLZ7 for different values of N.

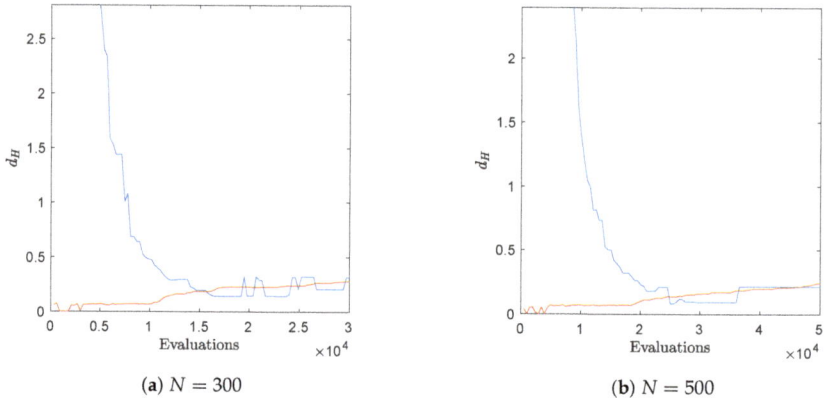

(a) $N = 300$ (b) $N = 500$

Figure 10. Real (blue) and approximated (red) Hausdorff distances during the run of one algorithm for DTLZ7.

Remark 4. We finally stress that the archiver A only reaches the magnitude N if Δ (and hence ϵ) is chosen "small enough", which does not represent a drawback in our opinion. In real-world applications, the values of Δ have a physical meaning. As a hypothetical example, consider that one objective in the design of the car is its maximal speed (e.g., $f_1 = s_{max}$), and the decision maker considers two cars to have different maximal speeds if s_{max} differs by at least 10 km/h. In this case $\Delta_1 = 10$ is a suitable choice for ArchiveUpdateHD. Hence, depending on these values and the size of the Pareto front, it may happen that less than N elements are needed to suitably represent the solution set. In turn, if Δ^+ is (significantly) larger than the target values, this gives a hint to the decision maker that N has to be increased and that the computation has to be repeated in order to obtain a "complete" approximation. Figure 11 shows two results of ArchiveUpdateHD on CONV for two different starting values of Δ.

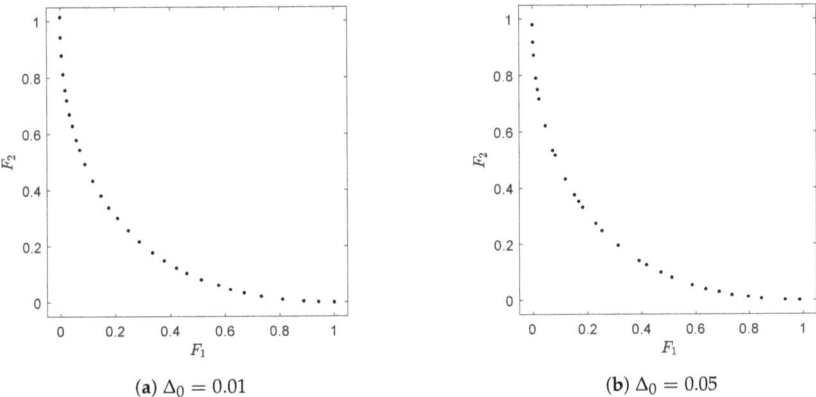

(a) $\Delta_0 = 0.01$ (b) $\Delta_0 = 0.05$

Figure 11. Results of ArchiveUpdateHD on CONV for two different initial values of Δ using $N = 30$. For $\Delta_0 = 0.01$, the final archive contains 30 elements, while there are only 28 elements for $\Delta_0 = 0.05$. The solutions on the left are more evenly spread along the Pareto front due to distance considerations in the pruning technique. For the solution on the right, no pruning technique has been applied during the run of the algorithm.

4. Numerical Results

In this section, we show some more numerical results to further demonstrate the advantage of the proposed archiver. As base MOEAs, we have chosen to take the state-of-the-art algorithms NSGA-II (dominance based), MOEA/D (decomposition based), and SMS-EMOEA (indicator based). We have used the implementations of the algorithms as well as the reference fronts provided by PlatEMO [78]. For sake of a fair comparison, we will in the following equip these MOEAs with ArchiveUpdateHD as an external archiver, where the upper bound N is chosen equal to the population sizes. For each run of an algorithm, we have fed the archiver with exactly the same candidate solution as for the respective base MOEA.

Motivated by Theorem 1 and by the discussion made in Remark 2, we will primarily use Δ_p ($p = 2$) for the performance assessment of the MOEA results. However, we will also use the Hpyervolume indicator [79], leading to some surprising results.

We first make a comparison with NSGA-II to investigate possible cyclic behavior during the run of an algorithm. It is known that distance-based selection/archiving strategies may lead to such cyclic behavior, which means that from a certain stage of the search, no more improvements can be expected (and in particular no convergence). The selection strategy of NSGA-II is mainly distance based (since from a certain point on, all individuals of the population are mutually non-dominated). For this, we have set both population size and N to 50 and have run NSGA-II for 1000 generations, using $P_c = 1$ and $\eta_c = 20$ for SBX, and $P_m = 1/N$ and $\eta_m = 20$ for polynomial mutation.

For ArchiveUpdateHD, we have chosen the first ϵ_0 small enough so that archive size $|A| = N$ was reached for all problems. In Figure 12, typical evolutions of the values of the approximation qualities Δ_p are shown over time for six selected BOPs (similar plots are obtained for all problems considered in this study). Hereby, "NSGA-II" stands for the population of the MOEA, and "NSGA-II-A" stands for the respective archive that was fed with the same candidate solutions as NSGA-II. While NSGA-II reveals clear cyclic behavior in all cases, this is not the case for NSGA-II-A. The latter is due to the acceptance strategy of ArchiveUpdateHD that is based on ϵ-dominance. As discussed above, the value of Δ (and hence also of ϵ) will become large enough during the run of the algorithm so that only dominance replacements will occur, which, however, cannot lead to cyclic behavior.

Apart from the "quasi-monotonic" behavior, one can also observe that the Δ_2 values of NSGA-II-A are for all test problems significantly lower than the ones of NSGA-II.

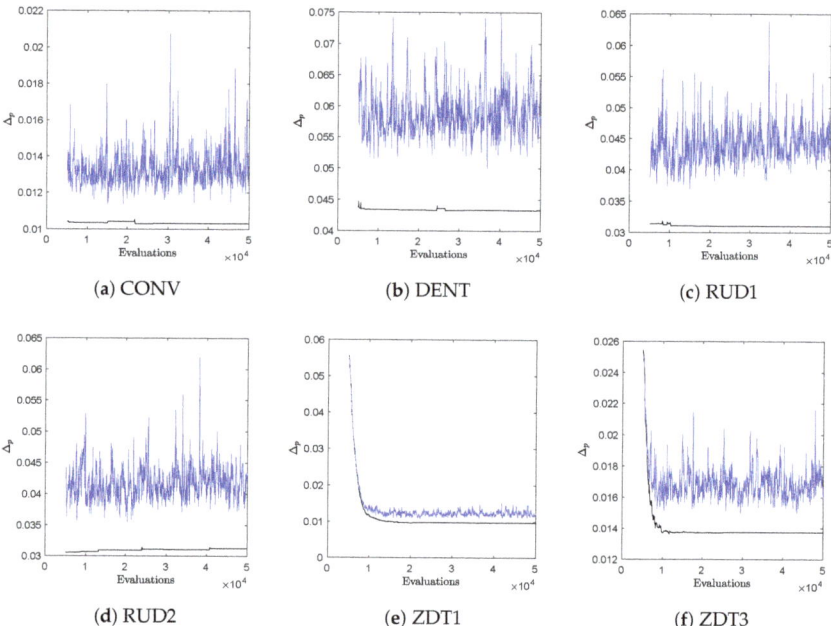

Figure 12. Approximation qualities of the Pareto fronts (measured by Δ_2) during one run of the algorithm for NSGA-II (blue) and the archives NSGA-II-A (black) for six selected BOPs.

Next, we investigate the performance of ArchiveUpdateHD as an external archive for the three MOEAs using an extended set of test functions. We first consider bi-objective problems. For this, we have chosen the ZDT problems [80], where we have used the modified objectives as expressed in (19) using $\alpha = 0.02$ to handle weak Pareto optimal solutions that are not optimal. Next to these six test problems, we have taken another four BOPs, which were selected due to the shapes of their fronts: LIN ([81], linear front), CONV (convex front), as well as DENT and SSW [82], which have both convex–concave Pareto fronts. The boxplots of the results are shown in Figures 13 and 14, based on 30 independent runs, for each using 1000 generations and a population size of 50. The Wilcoxon rank-sum is shown in Table 1. In the following, we will compare the results of the base algorithms against the respective solutions that use ArchiveUpdateHD.

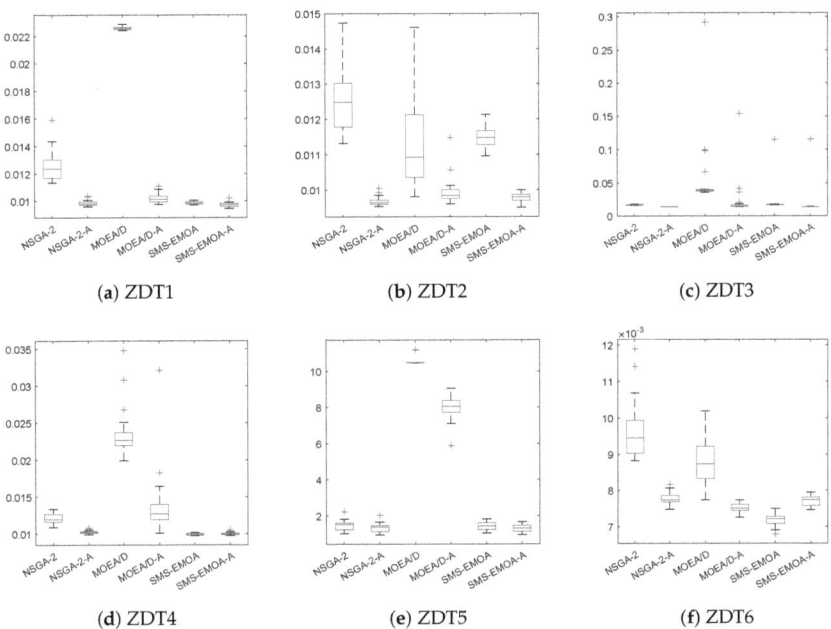

Figure 13. Boxplots for the obtained results for the ZDT test functions.

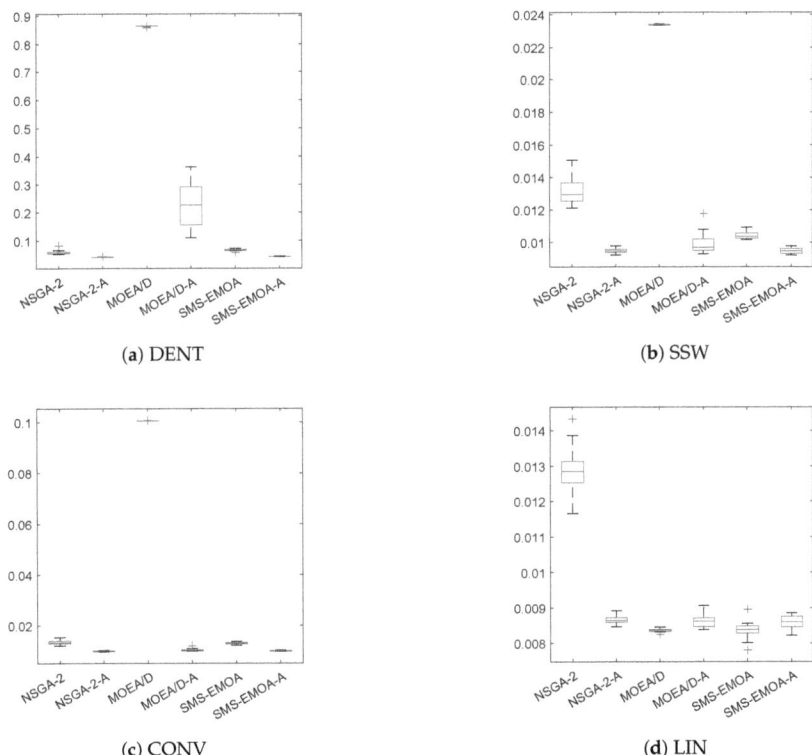

Figure 14. Boxplots for the obtained results for DENT, SSW, CONV and LIN.

The performance of the external archives is better in 10 out of 10 cases for NSGA-II, in 9 out of 10 cases for MOEA/D, and in 8 out of 10 cases for SMS-EMOA. ArchiveUpdateHD loses against the MOEA/D and SMS-EMOA on test problem LIN, which has a linear and thus most possible regular Pareto front. Both MOEA/D and SMS-EMOA are able to compute perfect solutions for this problem. Such perfect approximations cannot be expected from ArchiveUpdateHD due to its acceptance strategy. While this strategy is responsible for suppressing any cyclic behavior, it also prevents that all the solutions even of the limit archive are perfectly evenly spread along the Pareto front. For more complex Pareto fronts, the situation, however, changes. Figures A2 and A3 show the average results obtained by the different methods on problems DENT and ZDT, respectively. For DENT, the use of ArchiveUpdateHD leads in all three cases to significantly better Pareto front approximations. This is similar to ZDT3, while the improvements are less, since all three base MOEAs can already detect very good approximations.

Table 1. Comparison (wins/ties/losses) of the results of the base MOEAs against their archive equipped variants on the bi-objective test problems. The Wilcoxon rank-sum test has been used for statistical significance, where p-value < 0.05.

Method 1	Method 2	Wins	Ties	Losses
NSGA-2	NSGA-2-A	0	0	10
MOEA/D	MOEA/D-A	1	0	9
SMS-EMOA	SMS-EMOA-A	2	0	8

In a next step, we investigate the effect of ArchiveUpdateHD on several test problems with $k = 3$ objectives. For this, we have chosen the seven DLTZ test problems, the test functions IDTLZ1 and ITDLZ2 [21] with "inverted" fronts, and MaF1 to 5 [83]. Table 2 shows the Wilcoxon rank-sum for these 14 test problems using the indicators Δ_p, HV, as well as the classical Hausdorff distance d_H. Figure A4 shows the boxplots for all algorithms and test problems for Δ_p, Figures A5 and A6 show the results of the algorithms on IDTLZ1 and MaF2, respectively, and Figure A7 shows the selected behaviors of the Hausdorff approximations. For the latter, we have taken the median runs with respect to Δ_p. As it can be seen from Table 2, the use of ArchiveUpdateHD as the external archiver is highly beneficial in almost all cases. More precisely, starting with Δ_p, NSGA-II-A is better than NSGA-II in 12 out of 14 cases, and it only becomes (slightly) beaten on DTLZ5 and 6, which is likely owed to the degeneration the Pareto fronts of these two test problems (which has to be investigated in more detail in the future). MOEAD-A is superior to MOEAD in 10 out of 14 cases with one tie (DTLZ4) and 3 losses (DLTZ1-3), which is due to the regular structure of these Pareto fronts where MOEA/D can hardly be beaten. Finally, SMS-EMOA-A yields better results in all of the 14 cases. The situation is quite similar when considering the other two performance indicators. While this was expected for d_H, the results are surprising for HV: note that SMS-EMOA-A also outperforms SMS-EMOA on all of the 14 test functions when considering the hypervolume indicator.

Finally, Figures A8 and A9 show evolutions of the obtained Hausdorff distances of NSGA-II-A for the same test problems but now using $k = 4$ and $k = 5$ objectives. The results already give evidence that the values of Δ obtained by ArchiveUpdateHD yield satisfying approximations of the actual values of d_H also for problems with more objectives. The only exceptions are DTLZ5 and DTLZ6 (both for four and five objectives) as well as MaF4 for $k = 5$. By Theorem 1, we know that the runs of the algorithms have simply not been long enough, while it is in turn unclear how long these runs should have been. While these results are satisfying, more investigation has to be done in particular for the treatment of many objective problems, which we leave for future study.

Table 2. Comparison (wins (1) / ties (0) / losses (−1)) of the results of the base MOEAs against their archive equipped variants on the 14 three-objective test problems. The Wilcoxon rank-sum test has been used for statistical significance, where p-value < 0.05.

Indicator	Method 1	Method 2	Result	GroupCount
Δ_2	NSGA-2	NSGA-2-A	−1	12
Δ_2	NSGA-2	NSGA-2-A	0	0
Δ_2	NSGA-2	NSGA-2-A	1	2
Δ_2	MOEAD	MOEAD-A	−1	10
Δ_2	MOEAD	MOEAD-A	0	1
Δ_2	MOEAD	MOEAD-A	1	3
Δ_2	SMS-EMOA	SMS-EMOA-A	−1	14
Δ_2	SMS-EMOA	SMS-EMOA-A	0	0
Δ_2	SMS-EMOA	SMS-EMOA-A	1	0
HV	NSGA-2	NSGA-2-A	−1	11
HV	NSGA-2	NSGA-2-A	0	1
HV	NSGA-2	NSGA-2-A	1	2
HV	MOEAD	MOEAD-A	−1	9
HV	MOEAD	MOEAD-A	0	1
HV	MOEAD	MOEAD-A	1	4
HV	SMS-EMOA	SMS-EMOA-A	−1	14
HV	SMS-EMOA	SMS-EMOA-A	0	0
HV	SMS-EMOA	SMS-EMOA-A	1	0
d_H	NSGA-2	NSGA-2-A	−1	13
d_H	NSGA-2	NSGA-2-A	0	1
d_H	NSGA-2	NSGA-2-A	1	0
d_H	MOEAD	MOEAD-A	−1	10
d_H	MOEAD	MOEAD-A	0	1
d_H	MOEAD	MOEAD-A	1	3
d_H	SMS-EMOA	SMS-EMOA-A	−1	14
d_H	SMS-EMOA	SMS-EMOA-A	0	0
d_H	SMS-EMOA	SMS-EMOA-A	1	0

5. Conclusions and Future Work

In this paper, we have presented and analyzed the archiving strategy ArchiveUpdateHD for use within set-based stochastic search algorithms such as multi-objective evolutionary algorithms (MOEAs) for the treatment of multi-objective optimization problems (MOPs). ArchiveUpdateHD is a bounded archiver that is based on distance dominance, ϵ-dominance and the distances among the candidate solutions and that aims for evenly spread solutions along the Pareto front of a given MOP. We have shown that the images $F(A_i)$ of the sequence of archives A_i generated by this archiver form under certain (mild) conditions of the process to generate candidate solutions with a probability of one of a Δ^+-approximation of the Pareto front in the Hausdorff sense, and all entries of A_i converge to Pareto optimal solutions with a probability of one and for $i \to \infty$. Furthermore, the value Δ^+ is computed by ArchiveUpdateHD during the run of the algorithm (without any prior knowledge of the Pareto front). Since this value represents the maximal error in the representation, it is of important value for the decision maker (DM). In particular, if the magnitude of the archives reaches the pre-defined value N, the value of Δ^+ gives a feedback if the approximation is "complete enough" or not. Empirical studies on several benchmark test problems have shown the benefit of the novel strategy, among others, that the obtained value Δ^+ gives a good approximation of the actual Hausdorff approximation. For bi-objective problems, we have presented an alternative way to compute this value, which can even be considered to be tight from the practical point of view. Finally, we have used ArchiveUpdateHD as the external archiver for three state-of-the-art MOEAs (NSGA-II, MOEA/D, and SMS-EMOA), indicating that it is capable of significantly improving the overall performance of these algorithms.

One important next step which we will leave for future work is to use the mechanisms behind ArchiveUpdateHD as the selection strategy within an MOEA. If an external archiver is used, two archives (instead of only one) have to be maintained, leading to an additional overhead, which could be avoided. It is hence intended to utilize ArchiveUpdateHD to design a new class of MOEAs that aims for (averaged) Hausdorff approximations of the Pareto fronts (as, e.g., done in [84–86]).

Author Contributions: C.I.H.C. and O.S. have contributed equally to this work. All authors have read and agreed to the published version of the manuscript.

Funding: This research received no external funding.

Data Availability Statement: The codes will be made publicly available after acceptance.

Conflicts of Interest: The authors declare no conflict of interest.

Appendix A

Table A1. Hausdorff distances d_H and approximations h computed by ArchiveUpdateHD for the six bi-objective problems.

Problem	Mean d_H	std d_H	Mean h	std h
CONV	0.0345	0.0014861	0.036105	0.0016771
DENT	0.15428	0.012059	0.15872	0.0091187
RUD1	0.11337	0.0075653	0.10027	0.024311
RUD2	0.11295	0.0083812	0.085445	0.038149
LINEAR	0.02094	0.0019671	0.01977	0.0068899
RUD3	0.035354	0.0023404	0.025694	0.011484

Table A2. Averaged Hausdorff distances Δ_2 and approximations d_2 computed by ArchiveUpdateHD for the six bi-objective problems.

Problem	Mean Δ_2	std Δ_2	Mean d_2	std d_2
CONV	0.016626	0.00021014	0.01602	4.9072×10^{-5}
DENT	0.070802	0.00075385	0.069309	0.00036096
RUD1	0.052171	0.00072633	0.050631	0.0022879
RUD2	0.050967	0.00068389	0.049108	0.00034928
LINEAR	0.014494	0.00033184	0.013892	0.00018454
RUD2	0.016653	0.00028272	0.01595	0.00034355

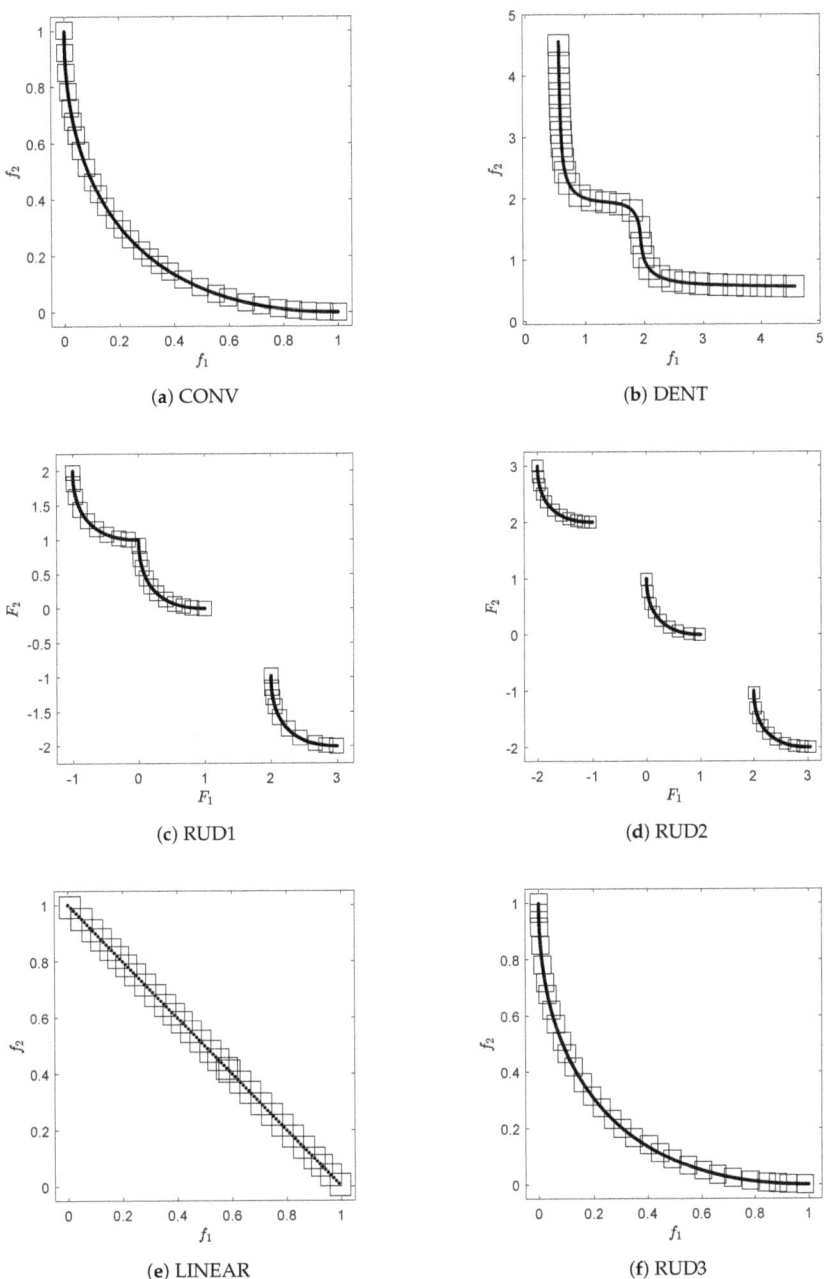

Figure A1. The box coverings $C(A_f)$ for the final archives incidate that the Hausdorff distance between $F(A_f)$ and the Pareto fronts is less than the final value Δ_f computed by ArchiveUpdateHD for all test problems.

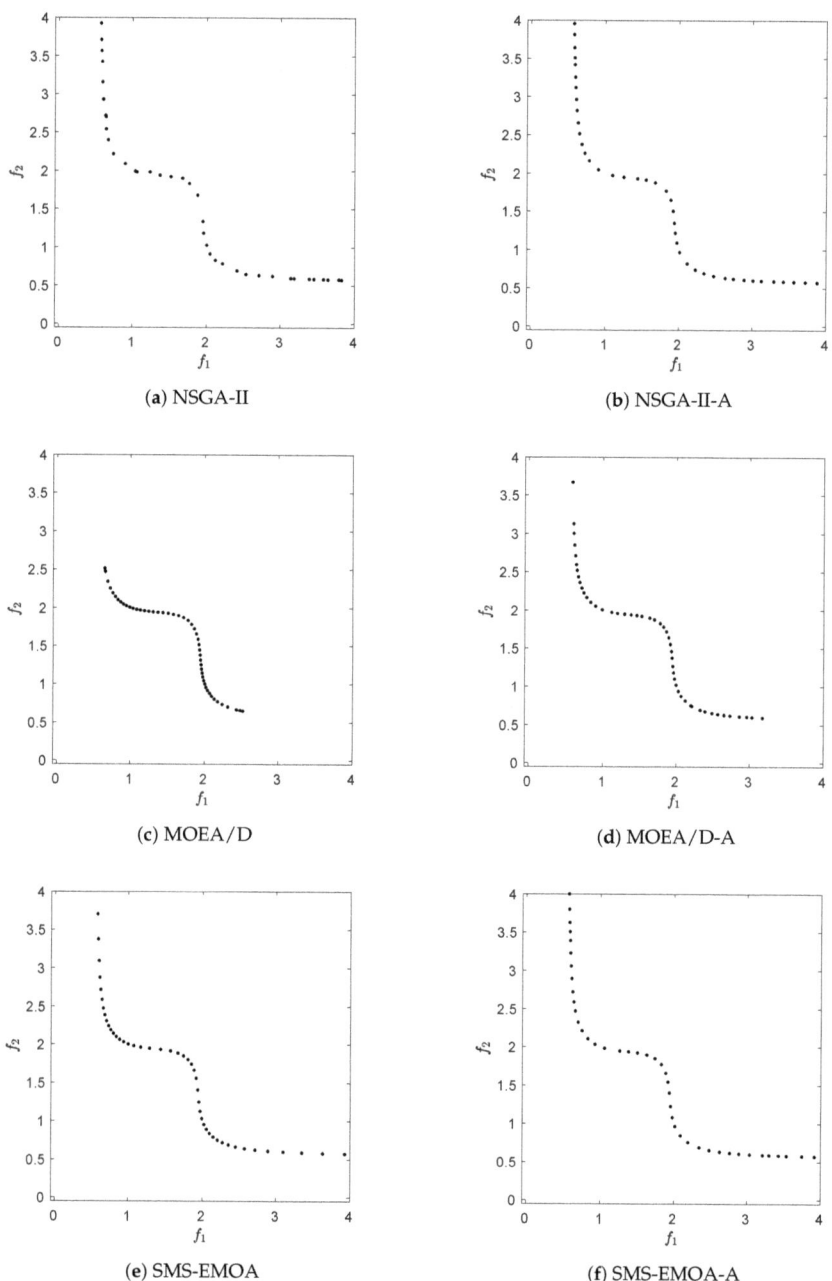

Figure A2. Numerical results of the different algorithms and archiving/selection strategies on DENT.

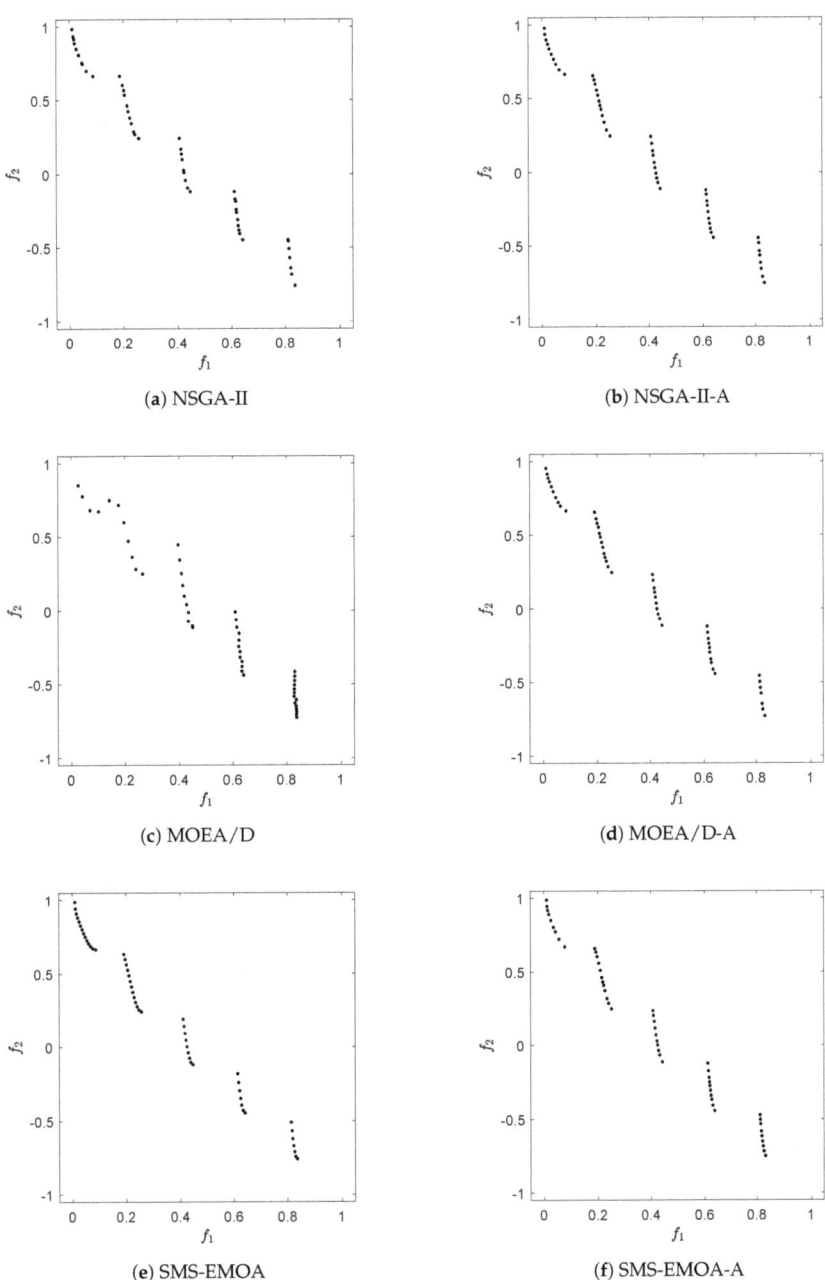

Figure A3. Numerical results of the different algorithms and archiving/selection strategies on ZDT3.

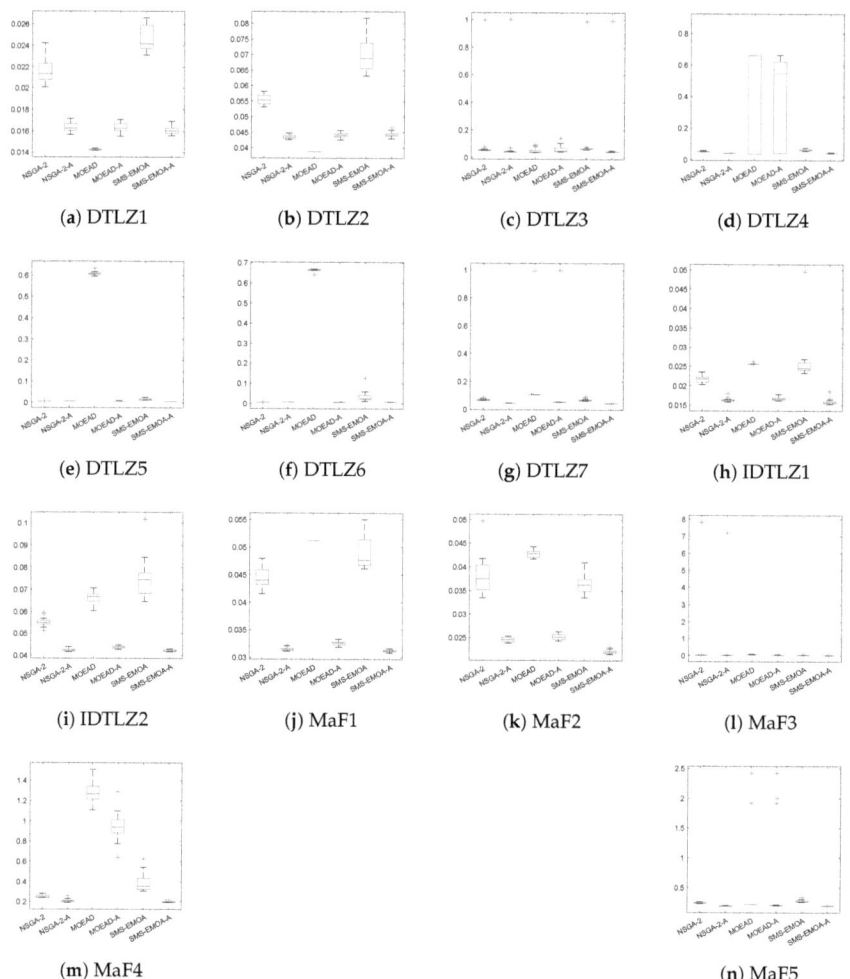

Figure A4. Boxplots for the considered three-objective test functions.

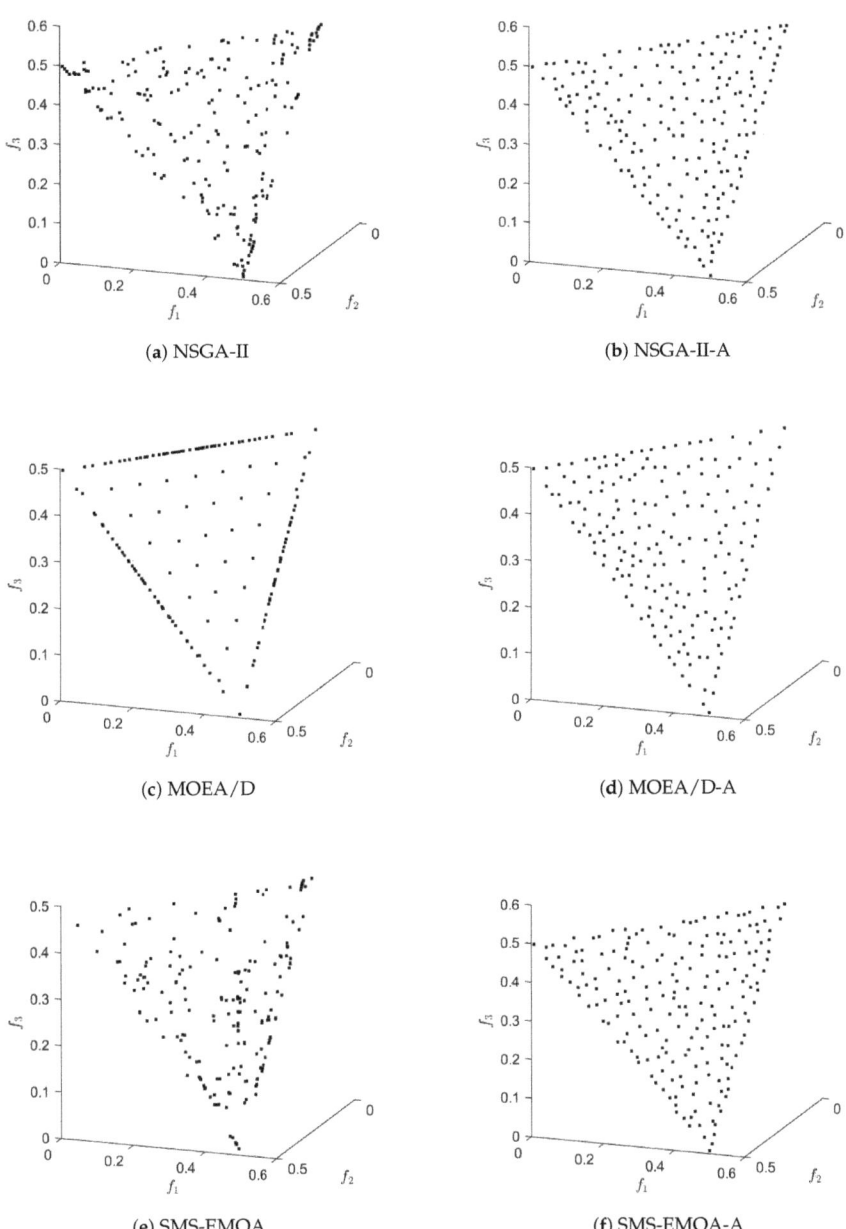

Figure A5. Numerical results of the different algorithms and archiving/selection strategies on IDTLZ1 for $k = 3$.

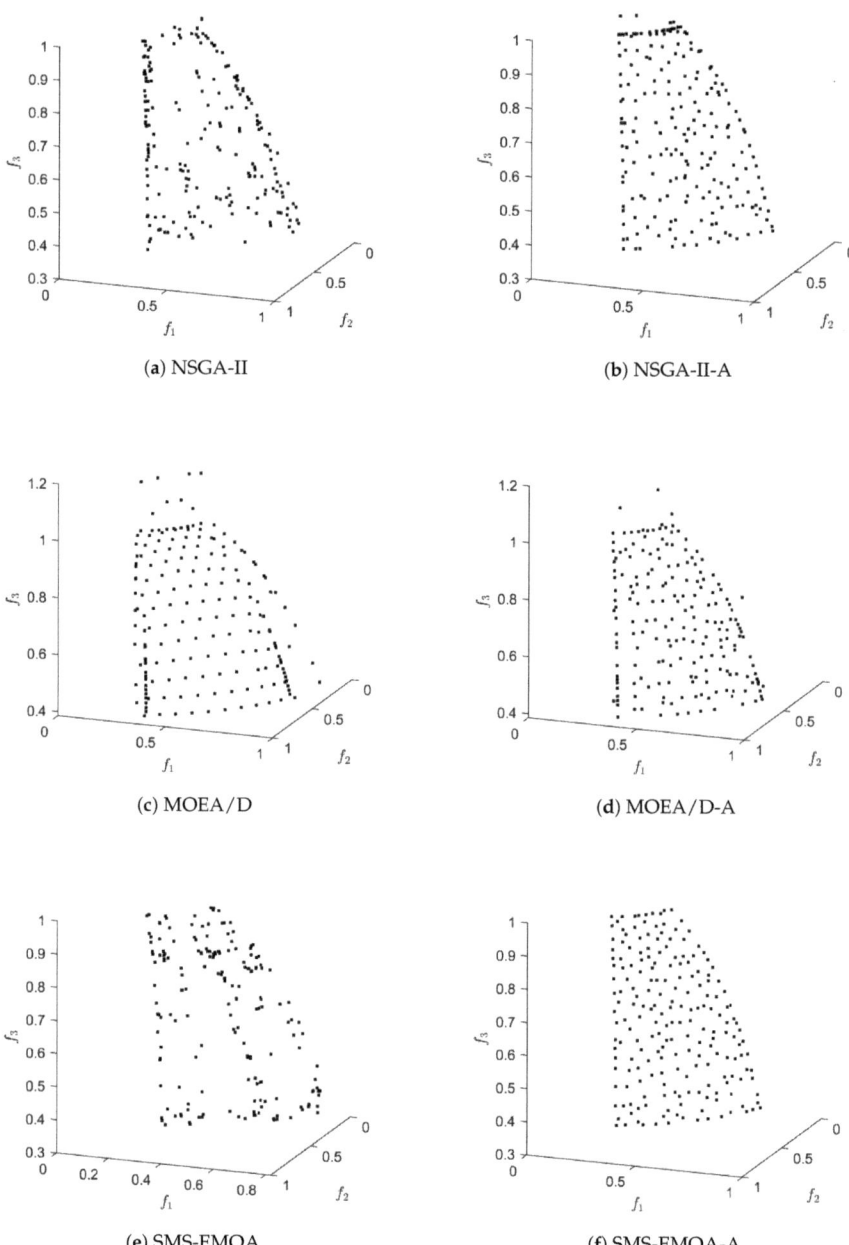

Figure A6. Numerical results of the different algorithms and archiving/selection strategies on MaF2 for $k=3$.

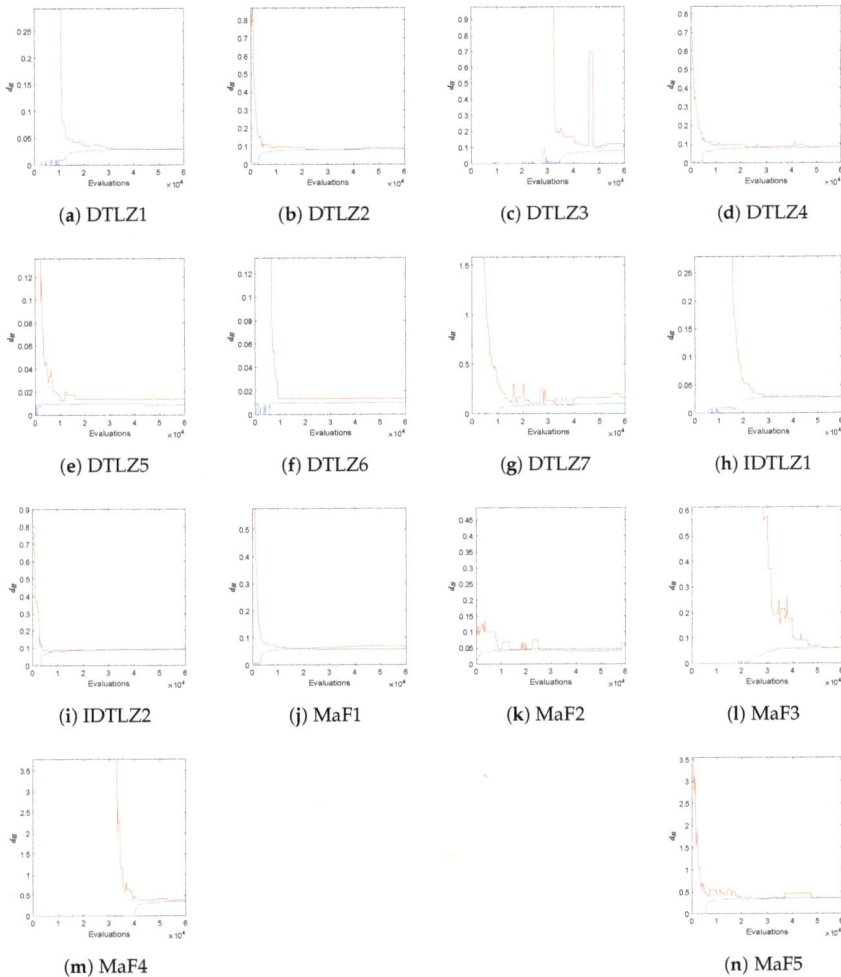

Figure A7. Evolution of the Hausdorff distances $d_H(F(A), F(P_Q))$ of NSGA-II-A and the computed approximations Δ for several test functions, using $k = 3$ objectives.

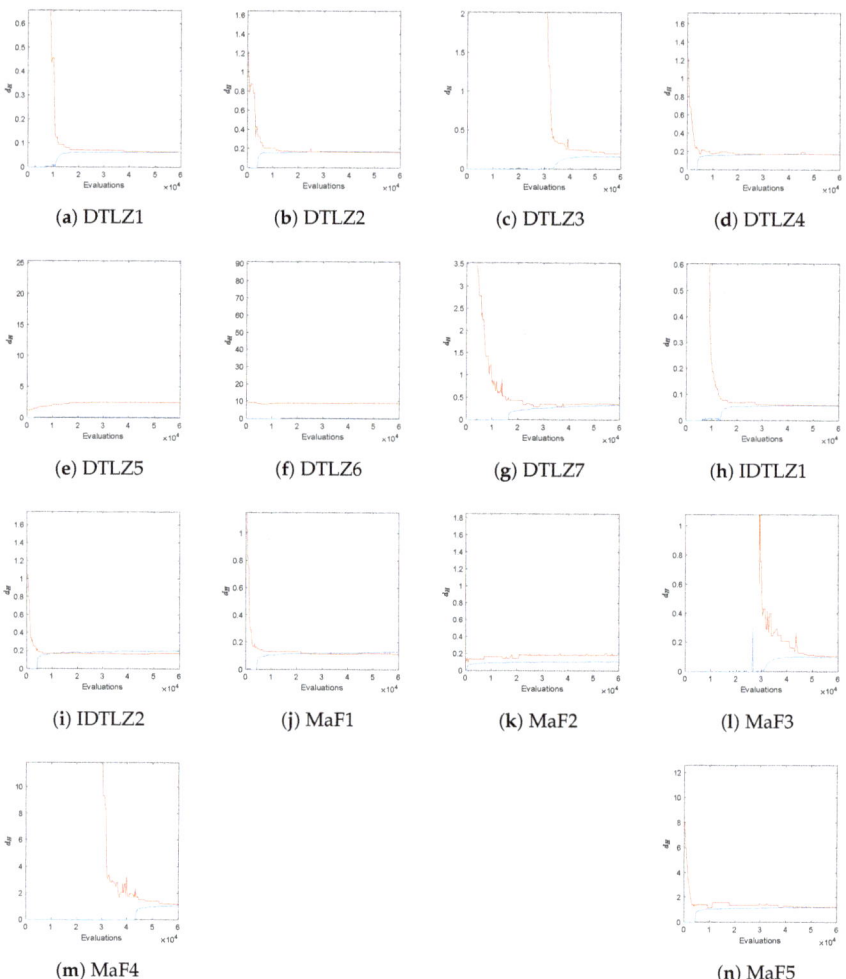

Figure A8. Evolution of the Hausdorff distances $d_H(F(A), F(P_Q))$ of NSGA-II-A and the computed approximations Δ for several test functions, using $k = 4$ objectives.

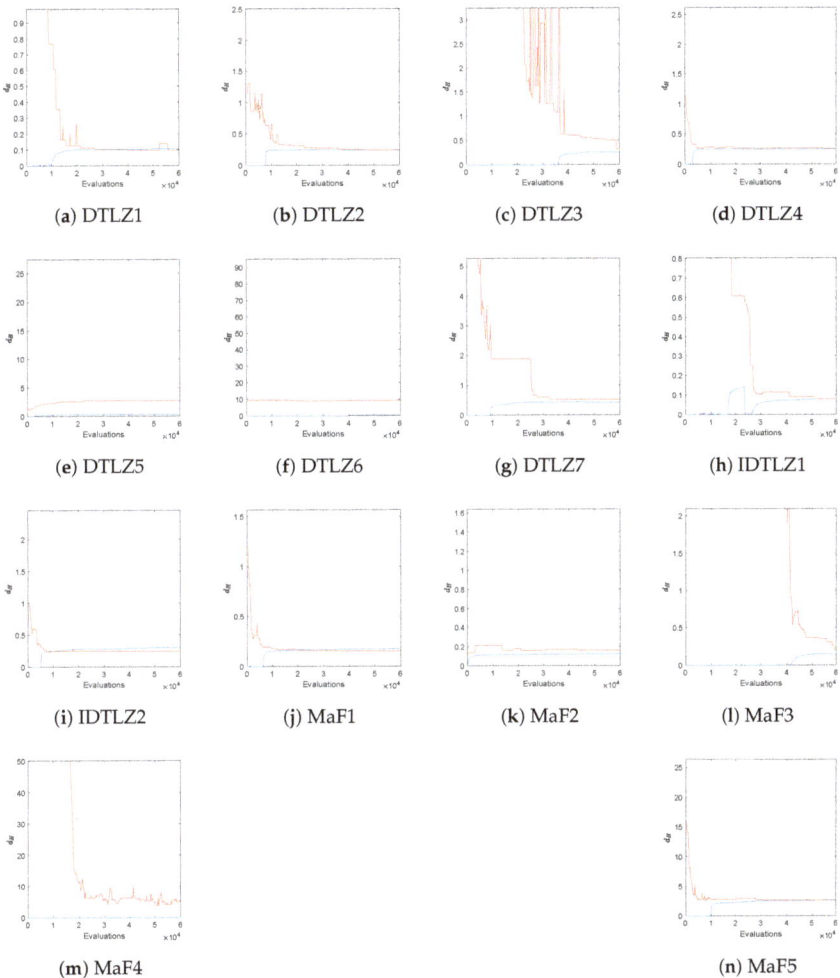

Figure A9. Evolution of the Hausdorff distances $d_H(F(A), F(P_Q))$ of NSGA-II-A and the computed approximations Δ for several test functions, using $k = 5$ objectives.

References

1. Laumanns, M.; Thiele, L.; Deb, K.; Zitzler, E. Combining convergence and diversity in evolutionary multiobjective optimization. *Evol. Comput.* **2002**, *10*, 263–282. [CrossRef] [PubMed]
2. Deb, K. *Multi-Objective Optimization Using Evolutionary Algorithms*; John Wiley & Sons: Chichester, UK, 2001; ISBN 0-471-87339-X.
3. Stewart, T.; Bandte, O.; Braun, H.; Chakraborti, N.; Ehrgott, M.; Göbelt, M.; Jin, Y.; Nakayama, H. Real-World Applications of Multiobjective Optimization. In *Proceedings of the Multiobjective Optimization*; Lecture Notes in Computer Science; Slowinski, R., Ed.; Springer: Berlin/Heidelberg, Germany, 2008; Volume 5252, pp. 285–327.
4. Sun, J.Q.; Xiong, F.R.; Schütze, O.; Hernández, C. *Cell Mapping Methods—Algorithmic Approaches and Applications*; Springer: Berlin/Heidelberg, Germany, 2019.
5. Aguilera-Rueda, V.J.; Cruz-Ramírez, N.; Mezura-Montes, E. Data-Driven Bayesian Network Learning: A Bi-Objective Approach to Address the Bias-Variance Decomposition. *Math. Comput. Appl.* **2020**, *25*, 37. [CrossRef]
6. Estrada-Padilla, A.; Lopez-Garcia, D.; Gómez-Santillán, C.; Fraire-Huacuja, H.J.; Cruz-Reyes, L.; Rangel-Valdez, N.; Morales-Rodríguez, M.L. Modeling and Optimizing the Multi-Objective Portfolio Optimization Problem with Trapezoidal Fuzzy Parameters. *Math. Comput. Appl.* **2021**, *26*, 36. [CrossRef]

7. Frausto-Solis, J.; Hernández-Ramírez, L.; Castilla-Valdez, G.; González-Barbosa, J.J.; Sánchez-Hernández, J.P. Chaotic Multi-Objective Simulated Annealing and Threshold Accepting for Job Shop Scheduling Problem. *Math. Comput. Appl.* **2021**, *26*, 8. [CrossRef]
8. Castellanos-Alvarez, A.; Cruz-Reyes, L.; Fernandez, E.; Rangel-Valdez, N.; Gómez-Santillán, C.; Fraire, H.; Brambila-Hernández, J.A. A Method for Integration of Preferences to a Multi-Objective Evolutionary Algorithm Using Ordinal Multi-Criteria Classification. *Math. Comput. Appl.* **2021**, *26*, 27. [CrossRef]
9. Hillermeier, C. *Nonlinear Multiobjective Optimization: A Generalized Homotopy Approach*; Springer Science & Business Media: Berlin/Heidelberg, Germany, 2001; Volume 135.
10. Coello Coello, C.A.; Lamont, G.B.; Van Veldhuizen, D.A. *Evolutionary Algorithms for Solving Multi-Objective Problems*, 2nd ed.; Springer: New York, NY, USA, 2007.
11. Laumanns, M.; Zenklusen, R. Stochastic convergence of random search methods to fixed size Pareto front approximations. *Eur. J. Oper. Res.* **2011**, *213*, 414–421. [CrossRef]
12. Hernández, C.; Schütze, O. A Bounded Archive Based for Bi-objective Problems based on Distance and epsilon-dominance to avoid Cyclic Behavior. In Proceedings of the Genetic and Evolutionary Computation Conference (GECCO-2022), Boston, MA, USA, 9–13 July 2022.
13. Schütze, O.; Esquivel, X.; Lara, A.; Coello, C.A.C. Using the averaged Hausdorff distance as a performance measure in evolutionary multi-objective optimization. *IEEE Trans. Evol. Comput.* **2012**, *16*, 504–522. [CrossRef]
14. Schütze, O.; Laumanns, M.; Tantar, E.; Coello, C.A.C.; Talbi, E.G. Computing gap free Pareto front approximations with stochastic search algorithms. *Evol. Comput.* **2010**, *18*, 65–96. [CrossRef]
15. Deb, K.; Pratap, A.; Agarwal, S.; Meyarivan, T. A fast and elitist multiobjective genetic algorithm: NSGA-II. *Evol. Comput. IEEE Trans.* **2002**, *6*, 182–197. [CrossRef]
16. Zitzler, E.; Laumanns, M.; Thiele, L. SPEA2: Improving the Strength Pareto Evolutionary Algorithm for Multiobjective Optimization. In Proceedings of the Evolutionary Methods for Design, Optimisation and Control with Application to Industrial Problems (EUROGEN 2001), Athens, Greece, 19–21 September 2001; Giannakoglou, K., Tsahalis, D., Périaux, J., Papailiou, K., Fogarty, T., Eds.; International Center for Numerical Methods in Engineering (CIMNE): Barcelona, Spain, 2002; pp. 95–100.
17. Fonseca, C.M.; Fleming, P.J. An overview of evolutionary algorithms in multiobjective optimization. *Evol. Comput.* **1995**, *3*, 1–16. [CrossRef]
18. Knowles, J.D.; Corne, D.W. Approximating the nondominated front using the Pareto Archived Evolution Strategy. *Evol. Comput.* **2000**, *8*, 149–172. [CrossRef] [PubMed]
19. Zhang, Q.; Li, H. MOEA/D: A Multi-objective Evolutionary Algorithm Based on Decomposition. *IEEE Trans. Evol. Comput.* **2007**, *11*, 712–731. [CrossRef]
20. Deb, K.; Jain, H. An evolutionary many-objective optimization algorithm using reference-point-based nondominated sorting approach, part I: Solving problems with box constraints. *Trans. Evol. Comput.* **2014**, *18*, 577–601. [CrossRef]
21. Jain, H.; Deb, K. An Evolutionary Many-Objective Optimization Algorithm Using Reference-Point Based Nondominated Sorting Approach, Part II: Handling Constraints and Extending to an Adaptive Approach. *IEEE Trans. Evol. Comput.* **2014**, *18*, 602–622. [CrossRef]
22. Martínez, S.Z.; Coello, C.A.C. A multi-objective particle swarm optimizer based on decomposition. In Proceedings of the Genetic and Evolutionary Computation Conference (GECCO-2011), Dublin, Ireland, 12–16 July 2011; pp. 69–76.
23. Zuiani, F.; Vasile, M. Multi Agent Collaborative Search based on Tchebycheff decomposition. *Comput. Optim. Appl.* **2013**, *56*, 189–208. [CrossRef]
24. Moubayed, N.A.; Petrovski, A.; McCall, J. (DMOPSO)-M-2: MOPSO Based on Decomposition and Dominance with Archiving Using Crowding Distance in Objective and Solution Spaces. *Evol. Comput.* **2014**, *22*, 47–77. [CrossRef] [PubMed]
25. Zapotecas-Martínez, S.; López-Jaimes, A.; García-Nájera, A. Libea: A Lebesgue indicator-based evolutionary algorithm for multi-objective optimization. *Swarm Evol. Comput.* **2019**, *44*, 404–419. [CrossRef]
26. Beume, N.; Naujoks, B.; Emmerich, M. SMS-EMOA: Multiobjective selection based on dominated hypervolume. *Eur. J. Oper. Res.* **2007**, *181*, 1653–1669. [CrossRef]
27. Zitzler, E.; Thiele, L.; Bader, J. SPAM: Set Preference Algorithm for multiobjective optimization. In Proceedings of the Parallel Problem Solving From Nature PPSN X, Dortmund, Germany, 13–17 September 2008; pp. 847–858.
28. Wagner, T.; Trautmann, H. Integration of Preferences in Hypervolume-based multiobjective evolutionary algorithms by means of desirability functions. *IEEE Trans. Evol. Comput.* **2010**, *14*, 688–701. [CrossRef]
29. Schütze, O.; Domínguez-Medina, C.; Cruz-Cortés, N.; de la Fraga, L.G.; Sun, J.Q.; Toscano, G.; Landa, R. A scalar optimization approach for averaged Hausdorff approximations of the Pareto front. *Eng. Optim.* **2016**, *48*, 1593–1617. [CrossRef]
30. Sosa-Hernández, V.A.; Schütze, O.; Wang, H.; Deutz, A.; Emmerich, M. The Set-Based Hypervolume Newton Method for Bi-Objective Optimization. *IEEE Trans. Cybern.* **2020**, *50*, 2186–2196. [CrossRef] [PubMed]
31. Bringmann, K.; Friedrich, T. Convergence of Hypervolume-Based Archiving Algorithms. *IEEE Trans. Evol. Comput.* **2014**, *18*, 643–657. [CrossRef]
32. Fonseca, C.M.; Fleming, P.J. Genetic algorithms for multiobjective optimization: Formulation, discussion, and generalization. In Proceedings of the 5th International Conference on Genetic Algorithms, Urbana-Champaign, IL, USA, 17–21 June 1993; pp. 416–423.

33. Srinivas, N.; Deb, K. Multiobjective optimization using nondominated sorting in genetic algorithms. *Evol. Comput.* **1994**, *2*, 221–248. [CrossRef]
34. Horn, J.; Nafpliotis, N.; Goldberg, D.E. A niched Pareto genetic algorithm for multiobjective optimization. In Proceedings of the First IEEE Conference on Evolutionary Computation, IEEE World Congress on Computational Computation, Orlando, FL, USA, 27–29 June 1994; IEEE Press: Piscataway, NJ, USA, 1994; pp. 82–87.
35. Zitzler, E.; Thiele, L. Multiobjective evolutionary algorithms: A comparative case study and the strength Pareto approach. *IEEE Trans. Evol. Comput.* **1999**, *3*, 257–271. [CrossRef]
36. Rudolph, G. Finite Markov Chain results in evolutionary computation: A Tour d'Horizon. *Fundam. Inform.* **1998**, *35*, 67–89. [CrossRef]
37. Rudolph, G. On a multi-objective evolutionary algorithm and its convergence to the Pareto set. In Proceedings of the IEEE International Conference on Evolutionary Computation (ICEC 1998), Anchorage, AK, USA, 4–9 May 1998; IEEE Press: Piscataway, NJ, USA, 1998; pp. 511–516.
38. Rudolph, G.; Agapie, A. Convergence Properties of Some Multi-Objective Evolutionary Algorithms. In Proceedings of the 2000 IEEE Congress on, Evolutionary Computation (CEC), La Jolla, CA, USA, 16–19 July 2000; IEEE Press: Piscataway, NJ, USA, 2000.
39. Rudolph, G. Evolutionary Search under Partially Ordered Fitness Sets. In Proceedings of the International NAISO Congress on Information Science Innovations (ISI 2001), Dubai, United Arab Emirates, 17–21 March 2001; ICSC Academic Press: Sliedrecht, The Netherlands, 2001; pp. 818–822.
40. Hanne, T. On the convergence of multiobjective evolutionary algorithms. *Eur. J. Oper. Res.* **1999**, *117*, 553–564. [CrossRef]
41. Hanne, T. Global multiobjective optimization with evolutionary algorithms: Selection mechanisms and mutation control. In Proceedings of the Evolutionary Multi-Criterion Optimization, First International Conference, EMO 2001, Zurich, Switzerland, 7–9 March 2001; Springer: Berlin/Heidelberg, Germany, 2001; pp. 197–212.
42. Hanne, T. A multiobjective evolutionary algorithm for approximating the efficient set. *Eur. J. Oper. Res.* **2007**, *176*, 1723–1734. [CrossRef]
43. Hanne, T. A Primal-Dual Multiobjective Evolutionary Algorithm for Approximating the Efficient Set. In Proceedings of the 2007 IEEE Congress on Evolutionary Computation (CEC), Singapore, 25–28 September 2007; IEEE Press: Piscataway, NJ, USA, 2007; pp. 3127–3134.
44. Knowles, J.D.; Corne, D.W. Properties of an adaptive archiving algorithm for storing nondominated vectors. *IEEE Trans. Evol. Comput.* **2003**, *7*, 100–116. [CrossRef]
45. Corne, D.W.; Knowles, J.D. Some multiobjective optimizers are better than others. In Proceedings of the IEEE Congress on Evolutionary Computation, Canberra, Australia, 8–12 December 2003; IEEE Press: Piscataway, NJ, USA, 2003; pp. 2506–2512.
46. Knowles, J.D.; Corne, D.W. Bounded Pareto archiving: Theory and practice. In *Proceedings of the Metaheuristics for Multiobjective Optimisation*; Springer: Berlin/Heidelberg, Germany, 2004; pp. 39–64.
47. Knowles, J.D.; Corne, D.W.; Fleischer, M. Bounded archiving using the Lebesgue measure. In Proceedings of the IEEE Congress on Evolutionary Computation, Canberra, Australia, 8–12 December 2003; IEEE Press: Piscataway, NJ, USA, 2003; pp. 2490–2497.
48. López-Ibáñez, M.; Knowles, J.D.; Laumanns, M. On Sequential Online Archiving of Objective Vectors. In Proceedings of the Evolutionary Multi-Criterion Optimization (EMO 2011), Ouro Preto, Brazil, 5–8 April 2011; Springer: Berlin/Heidelberg, Germany, 2011; pp. 46–60.
49. Laumanns, M.; Zitzler, E.; Thiele, L. On the effects of archiving, elitism, and density based selection in evolutionary multi-objective optimization. In Proceedings of the International Conference on Evolutionary Multi-Criterion Optimization, Zurich, Switzerland, 7–9 March 2001; Springer: Berlin/Heidelberg, Germany, 2001; pp. 181–196.
50. Schütze, O.; Laumanns, M.; Coello, C.A.C.; Dellnitz, M.; Talbi, E.G. Convergence of Stochastic Search Algorithms to Finite Size Pareto Set Approximations. *J. Glob. Optim.* **2008**, *41*, 559–577. [CrossRef]
51. Schütze, O.; Lara, A.; Coello, C.A.C.; Vasile, M. On the Detection of Nearly Optimal Solutions in the Context of Single-Objective Space Mission Design Problems. *J. Aerosp. Eng.* **2011**, *225*, 1229–1242. [CrossRef]
52. Schütze, O.; Vasile, M.; Coello, C.A.C. Computing the Set of Epsilon-Efficient Solutions in Multiobjective Space Mission Design. *J. Aerosp. Comput. Inf. Commun.* **2011**, *8*, 53–70. [CrossRef]
53. Schütze, O.; Hernandez, C.; Talbi, E.G.; Sun, J.Q.; Naranjani, Y.; Xiong, F.R. Archivers for the Representation of the Set of Approximate Solutions for MOPs. *J. Heuristics* **2019**, *5*, 71–105. [CrossRef]
54. Schütze, O.; Hernández, C. *Archiving Strategies for Evolutionary Multi-Objective Optimization Algorithms*; Springer: Berlin/Heidelberg, Germany, 2021.
55. Luong, H.N.; Bosman, P.A.N. Elitist Archiving for Multi-Objective Evolutionary Algorithms: To Adapt or Not to Adapt. In *Proceedings of the Parallel Problem Solving from Nature—PPSN XII*; Springer: Berlin/Heidelberg, Germany, 2012; pp. 72–81.
56. Zapotecas Martínez, S.; Coello Coello, C.A. An archiving strategy based on the Convex Hull of Individual Minima for MOEAs. In Proceedings of the 2010 IEEE Congress on Evolutionary Computation (CEC), Barcelona, Spain, 18–23 July 2010; IEEE Press: Piscataway, NJ, USA, 2010; pp. 1–8.
57. Cai, X.; Li, Y.; Fan, Z.; Zhang, Q. An External Archive Guided Multiobjective Evolutionary Algorithm Based on Decomposition. *IEEE Trans. Evol. Comput.* **2015**, *19*, 508–523.
58. Wang, F.; Zhang, H.; Li, Y.; Zhao, Y.; Rao, Q. External archive matching strategy for MOEA/D. *Soft Comput.* **2018**, *22*, 7833–7846. [CrossRef]

59. Tanabe, R.; Ishibuchi, H. An analysis of control parameters of MOEA/D under two different optimization scenarios. *Appl. Soft Comput.* **2018**, *70*, 22–40. [CrossRef]
60. Bezerra, L.C.T.; López-Ibáñez, M.; Stützle, T. Archiver effects on the performance of state-of-the-art multi- and many-objective evolutionary algorithms. In Proceedings of the Genetic and Evolutionary Computation Conference (GECCO '19), Prague, Czech Republic, 13–17 July 2019; pp. 620–628.
61. Hernández, C.I.; Schütze, O.; Sun, J.Q.; Ober-Blöbaum, S. Non-Epsilon Dominated Evolutionary Algorithm for the Set of Approximate Solutions. *Math. Comput. Appl.* **2020**, *25*, 3. [CrossRef]
62. Patil, M.B. Improved performance in multi-objective optimization using external archive. *Sādhanā* **2020**, *45*, 1–10. [CrossRef]
63. Brockhoff, D.; Tran, T.D.; Hansen, N. Benchmarking numerical multiobjective optimizers revisited. In Proceedings of the 2015 Annual Conference on Genetic and Evolutionary Computation, Madrid, Spain, 11–15 July 2015; pp. 639–646.
64. Wang, R.; Zhou, Z.; Ishibuchi, H.; Liao, T.; Zhang, T. Localized weighted sum method for many-objective optimization. *IEEE Trans. Evol. Comput.* **2016**, *22*, 3–18. [CrossRef]
65. Pang, L.M.; Ishibuchi, H.; Shang, K. Algorithm Configurations of MOEA/D with an Unbounded External Archive. *arXiv* **2020**, arXiv:2007.13352.
66. Ishibuchi, H.; Pang, L.M.; Shang, K. Solution Subset Selection for Final Decision Making in Evolutionary Multi-Objective Optimization. *arXiv* **2020**, arXiv:2006.08156.
67. Ishibuchi, H.; Pang, L.M.; Shang, K. A New Framework of Evolutionary Multi-Objective Algorithms with an Unbounded External Archive. In *ECAI 2020*; IOS Press: Amsterdam, The Netherlands, 2020; pp. 283–290.
68. Praditwong, K.; Yao, X. A New Multi-objective Evolutionary Optimisation Algorithm: The Two-Archive Algorithm. In Proceedings of the Computational Intelligence and Security, Harbin, China, 15–19 December 2007; Wang, Y., Cheung, Y.M., Liu, H., Eds.; Springer: Berlin/Heidelberg, Germany, 2007; pp. 95–104.
69. Wang, H.; Jiao, L.; Yao, X. Two_Arch2: An Improved Two-Archive Algorithm for Many-Objective Optimization. *IEEE Trans. Evol. Comput.* **2015**, *19*, 524–541. [CrossRef]
70. Deb, K.; Agrawal, S. A niched-penalty approach for constraint handling in genetic algorithms. In Proceedings of the International Conference on Artificial Neural Networks and Genetic Algorithms (ICANNGA-99), Portoroz, Slovenia, 6–9 April 1999; Springer: Berlin/Heidelberg, Germany, 1999; pp. 235–243.
71. Deb, K.; Deb, D. Analysing mutation schemes for real-parameter genetic algorithms. *Int. J. Artif. Intell. Soft Comput.* **2014**, *4*, 1–28. [CrossRef]
72. Ikeda, K.; Kita, H.; Kobayashi, S. Failure of Pareto-based MOEAs: Does non-dominated really mean near to optimal? In Proceedings of the 2001 IEEE Congress on Evolutionary Computation (CEC), Seoul, Korea, 27–30 May 2001; pp. 957–962.
73. Bogoya, J.M.; Vargas, A.; Cuate, O.; Schütze, O. A (p, q)-Averaged Hausdorff Distance for Arbitrary Measurable Sets. *Math. Comput. Appl.* **2018**, *23*, 51. [CrossRef]
74. Vargas, A.; Bogoya, J. A Generalization of the Averaged Hausdorff Distance. *Computación y Sistemas* **2018**, *22*, 331–345. [CrossRef]
75. Witting, K. Numerical Algorithms for the Treatment of Parametric Multiobjective Optimization Problems and Applications. Ph.D. Thesis, Deptartment of Mathematics, University of Paderborn, Paderborn, Germany, 2012.
76. Rudolph, G.; Naujoks, B.; Preuss, M. Capabilities of EMOA to Detect and Preserve Equivalent Pareto Subsets. In *Proceedings of the Evolutionary Multi-Criterion Optimization: 4th International Conference, EMO 2007, Matsushima, Japan, 5–8 March 2007*; Obayashi, S., Deb, K., Poloni, C., Hiroyasu, T., Murata, T., Eds.; Springer: Berlin/Heidelberg, Germany, 2007; pp. 36–50.
77. Ishibuchi, H.; Matsumoto, T.; Masuyama, N.; Nojima, Y. Effects of dominance resistant solutions on the performance of evolutionary multi-objective and many-objective algorithms. In Proceedings of the Genetic and Evolutionary Computation Conference (GECCO '20), Cancún, Mexico, 8–12 July 2020; Coello, C.A.C., Ed.; ACM: New York, NY, USA, 2020; pp. 507–515. [CrossRef]
78. Tian, Y.; Cheng, R.; Zhang, X.; Jin, Y. PlatEMO: A MATLAB Platform for Evolutionary Multi-Objective Optimization. *IEEE Comput. Intell. Mag.* **2017**, *3*, 73–87. [CrossRef]
79. Zitzler, E.; Thiele, L. Multiobjective optimization using evolutionary algorithms—A comparative case study. In *Proceedings of the Parallel Problem Solving from Nature—PPSN V*; Eiben, A.E., Bäck, T., Schoenauer, M., Schwefel, H.P., Eds.; Springer: Berlin/Heidelberg, Germany, 1998; pp. 292–301.
80. Zitzler, E.; Deb, K.; Thiele, L. Comparison of multiobjective evolutionary algorithms: Empirical results. *Evol. Comput.* **2000**, *8*, 173–195. [CrossRef]
81. Emmerich, M.; Deutz, A. Test problems based on Lamé superspheres. In *Proceedings of the Evolutionary Multi-Criterion Optimization: 4th International Conference, EMO 2007, Matsushima, Japan, 5–8 March 2007*; Obayashi, S., Deb, K., Poloni, C., Hiroyasu, T., Murata, T., Eds.; Springer: Berlin/Heidelberg, Germany, 2007; pp. 922–936.
82. Schaeffler, S.; Schultz, R.; Weinzierl, K. Stochastic Method for the Solution of Unconstrained Vector Optimization Problems. *J. Optim. Theory Appl.* **2002**, *114*, 209–222. [CrossRef]
83. Cheng, M.; Tian, Y.; Zhang, X.; Yang, S.; Jin, Y.; Yao, X. A benchmark test suite for evolutionary many-objective optimization. *Complex Intell. Syst.* **2017**, *3*, 67–81. [CrossRef]
84. Rudolph, G.; Trautmann, H.; Sengupta, S.; Schütze, O. Evenly Spaced Pareto Front Approximations for Tricriteria Problems Based on Triangulation. In Proceedings of the Evolutionary Muti-Criterion Optimization Conference (EMO 2013), Sheffield, UK, 19–22 March 2013; pp. 443–458.

35. Rudolph, G.; Grimme, C.; Schütze, O.; Trautmann, H. An Aspiration Set EMOA based on Averaged Hausdorff Distances. In Proceedings of the Learning and Intelligent Optimization Conference (LION 2014), Gainesville, FL, USA, 16–21 February 2014; pp. 153–156.
36. Rudolph, G.; Schütze, O.; Grimme, C.; Domínguez-Medina, C.; Trautmann, H. Optimal averaged Hausdorff archives for bi-objective problems: Theoretical and numerical results. *Comput. Optim. Appl.* **2016**, *64*, 589–618. [CrossRef]

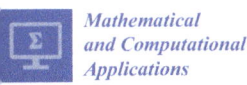

Article

Multi-Objective Optimization of an Elastic Rod with Viscous Termination

Siyuan Xing [1] and Jian-Qiao Sun [2,*]

[1] Department of Mechanical Engineering, California Polytechnic State University, San Luis Obispo, CA 93047, USA; sixing@calpoly.edu
[2] Department of Mechanical Engineering, School of Engineering, University of California Merced, Merced, CA 95343, USA
* Correspondence: jsun3@ucmerced.edu

Abstract: In this paper, we study the multi-objective optimization of the viscous boundary condition of an elastic rod using a hybrid method combining a genetic algorithm and simple cell mapping (GA-SCM). The method proceeds with the NSGAII algorithm to seek a rough Pareto set, followed by a local recovery process based on one-step simple cell mapping to complete the branch of the Pareto set. To accelerate computation, the rod response under impulsive loading is calculated with a particular solution method that provides accurate structural responses with less computational effort. The Pareto set and Pareto front of a case study are obtained with the GA-SCM hybrid method. Optimal designs of each objective function are illustrated through numerical simulations.

Keywords: multi-objective optimization; genetic algorithm; simple cell mapping; rod vibration; mass–damper–spring termination; impulse response

1. Introduction

Structures with viscous boundaries have been applied to diverse areas for vibration reduction [1], sound absorption [2], and boundary control [3]. One recent example is the railway bridge design for high-speed trains where the soil interacting with the bridge has been modeled as mass–damper–spring terminations of the structure [4]. The best design of structures has always been the pursuit of engineers. The optimal structural design must usually accommodate multiple objectives such as the settling time of vibrations, the response amplitude, and the shaping of the frequency response, leading to multi-objective optimization problems (MOPs). This paper presents a study of the multi-objective optimal design of a one-dimensional elastic rod with a mass–damper–spring termination.

The multi-objective nature of the optimization problem leads to a set of optimal solutions called the Pareto set, making set-oriented methods such as simple cell mapping (SCM) [5] suitable for solving such problems. The cell mapping method was initially developed by Hsu [6] for investigating the global behavior of nonlinear dynamical systems, then extended by Sun and his coworkers [7–9] for MOPs. The method seeks optimal solutions by constructing cell mappings based on the local dominance relation of cells in the discretized design space until the optimal solutions are achieved. Although the method is effective for low-dimensional problems, it suffers from the curse of dimensionality for high-dimensional problems because the searching space grows exponentially with the increase of the dimensions.

In terms of solving MOPs with relatively high dimensions, the evolutionary algorithms such as the genetic algorithm (GA) [10], immune algorithm [11], particle swarm optimization (PSO) [12], and ant colony optimization [13] are the mainstream methods for MOPs. The evolutionary algorithms are stochastic methods that mimic the biological evolutionary process using the evolution laws defined based on the Pareto dominance of fitness functions. Such methods can escape the local optima and rapidly discover the domains containing the solutions. However, the results of evolutionary algorithms can be sensitive to the selection of the hyperparameters.

Recently, Sun and colleagues [5,14] proposed a hybrid method that incorporates NSGAII and simple cell mapping (SCM). The method begins with NSGAII to generate a rough set from several generations such that the domains containing optimal solutions can be outlined. Using the rough set, SCM performs a local recovery method to complete the branches of the Pareto set through iterative refinement of the design space. With the power of NSGAII, the searching domain of the simple cell mapping method has been substantially reduced, making it possible to apply SCM for high-dimensional problems. On the other hand, the SCM method can complement the GA since obtaining outlined optimal domains using the GA is not very sensitive to the selection of the hyperparameters and is much easier than obtaining detailed Pareto optimal solutions using the GA. This can reduce the burden of parameter tuning with the GA. This paper will present a new case study of MOPs by the hybrid GA-SCM method. For more discussions on the advantage of the GA-SCM method and a comparison with different methods, the reader is referred to [5] and the references therein.

To accelerate the MOP algorithms for structural design, a fast and accurate solver that can predict structural response under external loading is needed. Traditional methods such as the finite-element method for calculating structural response can result in considerable computational load. However, obtaining such a solver for structures with viscous terminations is not an easy task. This is because viscous boundary conditions lead to non-self-adjoint boundary value problems that cannot be solved by the traditional method of eigenvalue expansion. To address this issue, several analytical methods have been developed. Hull et al. [15] presented a method that applies modal expansion in the augmented spatial interval where orthogonal eigenmodes exist. Jayachandran and Sun [16] transformed the problem into a self-adjoint boundary value problem in Hilbert space. Oliveto et al. [17] proposed a complex modal expansion method, which requires formulating new orthogonality conditions. Jovannovic [18] formulated the steady-state solution in the form of Fourier series in the state space by reconstructing the differential operator of the equations of motion. Recently, Xing and Sun [19] applied a particular solution method to study the impulsive response of a 1D elastic rod subject to a mass–damper–spring termination.

In this study, we will continue the effort in [19] to optimize the viscous termination of a 1D elastic rod under impulsive loading using the GA-SCM method. The solution of this problem has many potential applications in structural and acoustic design. The dynamic response of the rod will be predicted by the particular solution method. Firstly, we will define the multi-objective optimization problem, followed by the introduction of the GA-SCM hybrid method. Then, we will formulate the impulse response of the structural problem using the particular solution method and introduce the multi-objective functions for the structural optimization problem. We will demonstrate the effectiveness of the GA-SCM method through a case study.

2. Multi-Objective Optimization

A continuous multi-objective optimization problem (MOP) can be defined as

$$\min_{\mathbf{x} \in \mathcal{R}^n} \mathbf{F}(\mathbf{x}),$$
$$\text{with } g_i(\mathbf{x}) \leq 0, \ i = 1, \ldots, l, \tag{1}$$
$$h_j(\mathbf{x}) = 0, \ j = 1, \ldots, m,$$

where $\mathbf{x}$ is a variable of the design space and g_i and h_j are the design constraints. $\mathbf{F}$ is a map comprised of objective functions f_i ($i = 1, 2, \ldots, k$), i.e.,

$$\mathbf{F}(\mathbf{x}) = \{f_1(\mathbf{x}), \ldots, f_k(\mathbf{x})\}, \tag{2}$$

where $f_i : Q \to \mathcal{R}$. Herein, Q is the feasible set represented by

$$Q = \{\mathbf{x} \in \mathcal{R}^n \mid g_i(\mathbf{x}) \leq 0, \ i = 1, \ldots, l,$$
$$\text{and } h_j(\mathbf{x}) = 0, \ j = 1, \ldots, m\}. \tag{3}$$

The optimal solution of the multi-objective problem is defined in the sense of Pareto optimality, which requires the introduction of the following definitions.

Definition 1 (Dominance relation [5]).
(a) A vector $\mathbf{y} \in Q$ is called strictly dominated (or simply dominated by a vector $\mathbf{x} \in Q$ ($\mathbf{x} \prec \mathbf{y}$) if

$$\mathbf{F}(\mathbf{x}) <_p \mathbf{F}(\mathbf{y}) \text{ and } \mathbf{F}(\mathbf{x}) \neq \mathbf{F}(\mathbf{y}),$$

where $<_p$ is an elementwise less-than-or-equal-to relation.
(b) A vector $\mathbf{y} \in Q$ is called weakly dominated by a vector $\mathbf{x} \in Q$ ($\mathbf{x} \preceq \mathbf{y}$) if $\mathbf{F}(\mathbf{x}) \leq_p \mathbf{F}(\mathbf{y})$.

The dominance relation defines the "good" solution in the sense of Pareto optimality. This is a strong relation, which can lead to many optimal solutions, because objective functions are considered as equally "good" solutions when they partially satisfy the inequality relations. To define the sets of optimal solutions and their objective functions, we introduce the Pareto set and Pareto front.

Definition 2 (Pareto point, Pareto set, Pareto front [5]).
(a) A point $\mathbf{x} \in Q$ is called Pareto optimal or a Pareto point of (1) if there is no $\mathbf{y} \in Q$ that dominates $\mathbf{x}$.
(b) A point $\mathbf{x} \in Q$ is called locally (Pareto) optimal or a local Pareto point of (1) if there exists a neighborhood $N_\mathbf{x}$ of $\mathbf{x}$ such that there is no $\mathbf{y} \in Q \cap N_\mathbf{x}$ that dominates $\mathbf{x}$.
(c) A point $\mathbf{x} \in Q$ is called a weak Pareto point or weakly optimal if there exists no $\mathbf{y} \in Q$ such that $\mathbf{F}(\mathbf{y}) <_p \mathbf{F}(\mathbf{x})$.
(d) The set of all Pareto optimal solutions is called the Pareto set, i.e.,

$$\mathcal{P} = \mathcal{P}_Q := \{\mathbf{x} \in Q \ : \ \mathbf{x} \text{ is a Pareto point of } (1)\}. \tag{4}$$

(e) The image $\mathbf{F}(\mathcal{P})$ of $\mathcal{P}$ is called the Pareto front.

3. GA-SCM Hybrid Method

We apply a hybrid method combining genetic algorithms (GAs) and cell mapping methods [14] to solve an MOP with multi-objective performance indices to be defined in Section 4. The hybrid method is initiated with a genetic algorithm (NSGAII) to generate a rough Pareto set in the design space, which is then used by a cell-mapping-based recovery method to seek a complete branch of the Pareto set through iterative refinement of the cellular space of the design parameters, which will be defined in Section 5. The pseudo code of the GA-SCM method is listed in Algorithm 1. The pseudo code for recovering the Pareto optimal solution is listed in Algorithm 2.

As shown in Algorithm 2, the recovery process firstly discretizes the design space and then iterates through elements of the rough Pareto set from the GA or the previous cell partition, performing a one-step simple cell mapping to search local Pareto points. If a cell is mapped to itself (i.e., a local sink is found), then the cell is pushed into the candidate set, followed by an operator to gather nearby solutions into the set to be visited (S_tovisit) as long as they dominate some elements in the Pareto set $\mathcal{P}_s$. Otherwise, the destination cell of the cell mapping is pushed to S_tovisit. Then, the same iterative procedure will be performed on the set S_tovisit until no new cells can be brought into S_tovisit. At last, a dominance check is carried out to remove non-dominant points from the Pareto set. More detail on the method can be seen in [5].

Algorithm 1 GA-SCM algorithm.

Input: Design space Q, cell space partition N, refinement partition sub, GA population size n, objective functions $\mathbf{F}$, refinement number k
Output: Pareto set $\mathcal{P}_s$, Pareto front $\mathcal{P}_f$
1: **Initialization** $S_r \leftarrow GA(n, Q)$ {finding a rough candidate set using the GA}
2: $S_c \leftarrow$ cell creation$(S_r, \mathbf{F})$
3: **while** $i \leq k$ **do** {seeking Pareto set and front using SCM-based local recovery processes}
4: $\quad \mathcal{P}_s, \mathcal{P}_f \leftarrow$ recover$(S_c, \mathbf{F}, N, Q)$
5: $\quad S_c \leftarrow$ refine$(\mathcal{P}_s, N, sub)$
6: $\quad N \leftarrow N \times sub$ {refining cell space}
7: $\quad i \leftarrow i + 1$
8: **end while**

Algorithm 2 SCM-based recovering algorithm.

Input: Rough Pareto set $\mathcal{P}_s$, rough Pareto front $\mathcal{P}_f$, objective functions $\mathbf{F}$, cell space partition N, design space Q, max iteration n
Output: Pareto set $\mathcal{P}_s$, Pareto front $\mathcal{P}_f$ (under the cell space partition N)
1: **Initialization** Discretize design space Q based on the cell space partition N
2: $S_{\text{visiting}}, S_{\text{visited}} \leftarrow \mathcal{P}_s, S_c \leftarrow \emptyset$ {S_c stores candidate solutions.}
3: **while** $S_{\text{visiting}} \neq \emptyset$ **do**
4: $\quad S_{\text{tovisit}} \leftarrow \emptyset$
5: $\quad$ **for** $q \in S_{\text{visiting}}$ **do**
6: $\quad\quad C_d \leftarrow$ simple cell mapping(q, S_{visited})
7: $\quad\quad$ **if** $C_d \neq q$ and $C_d \notin \mathcal{P}_s$ **then**
8: $\quad\quad\quad S_{\text{tovisit}} \leftarrow S_{\text{tovisit}} \cup \{C_d\}$
9: $\quad\quad$ **else**
10: $\quad\quad\quad S_c \leftarrow S_c \cup \{C_d\}$
11: $\quad\quad\quad S_{\text{tovisit}} \leftarrow S_{\text{tovisit}} \cup \{\mathbf{x}|\mathbf{x} \in neighbor(q) \text{ and } \mathbf{x} \prec \mathbf{y} \text{ where } \mathbf{y} \in \mathcal{P}_s\}$ {collecting neighbors that dominate some element(s) in $\mathcal{P}_s$}
12: $\quad\quad$ **end if**
13: $\quad$ **end for**
14: $\quad S_{\text{visiting}} \leftarrow S_{\text{tovisit}}$
15: $\quad \mathcal{P}_s \leftarrow \mathcal{P}_s \cup S_c, \mathcal{P}_f \leftarrow \mathcal{P}_f \cup \mathbf{F}(S_c)$
16: **end while**
17: $\mathcal{P}_s, \mathcal{P}_f \leftarrow$ dominance check$(\mathcal{P}_s, \mathcal{P}_f)$

The detail of the one-step simple cell mapping algorithm is listed in Algorithm 3. The method finds the local optimal solution by checking the dominance relation between a cell and its neighbor. The optimal solution is defined as the most distant cell that dominates the source cell.

Algorithm 3 Simple cell mapping algorithm.

Input: Objective functions $\mathbf{F}$, cell C_s, visited cell set S_{visited}
Output: Destination cell C_d, visited cell set S_{visited}
1: $S_{\text{nbr}} \leftarrow neighbor(C_s)$
2: **for** N in S_{nbr} **do**
3: $\quad$ **if** $N \prec C_s$ **and** constraints satisfied **then** {$\mathbf{F}(N)$ can be fetched from visited set directly if N is visited.}
4: $\quad\quad$ Store N
5: $\quad\quad S_{\text{visited}} \leftarrow S_{\text{visited}} \cup \{N\}$
6: $\quad$ **end if**
7: **end for**
8: $C_d \leftarrow \arg\{\max\|q_s - q_{nbr}\|_2\}$ {q_s and q_{nbr} are the cell centers of C_s and S_{nbr}}

Given the numerical computation of the impulse response of the rod is the most time-consuming subroutine in this problem, we record all visited cells using a dictionary structure, whose key is the cell index and whose values consist of the multi-objective functions. This way, the algorithm can search for the values in the dictionary with a time complexity $O(1)$, eliminating the repeated computation for cells that have been visited. In addition, the key of a dictionary is unique. Pushing a visited cell to the dictionary will automatically replace the repeated one. Therefore, our implementation, different from that in [14], does not require combining the repeated cells in the visited set.

4. Multi-Objective Optimization of Mass–Damper–Spring Termination

4.1. Impulse Response

The one-dimensional elastic rod with a mass–damper–spring termination is shown in Figure 1. An impact loading $f(t) = f_0 \delta(t)$ is applied to its free end. Young's modulus, the cross-section area, and the length of the rod are denoted by E, A, and L, respectively. We split total response $u(x,t)$ into the sum of rigid-body and elastic responses such that

$$u(x,t) = u_r(x,t) + u_e(x,t), \text{ with } 0 \leq x \leq L, t \geq 0. \tag{5}$$

where u_r is the rigid-body response and u_e is the elastic response. From [19], the equations of motion of the system in Figure 1 are in the form

$$\rho A L \ddot{u}_r + M \ddot{u}_r + c \dot{u}_r + k u_r + \tag{6}$$

$$\rho A \int_0^L \frac{\partial^2 u_e(x,t)}{\partial t^2} dx + M \ddot{u}_e(L,t) + c \dot{u}_e(L,t) + k u_e(L,t) = 0,$$

$$c_p^2 \frac{\partial^2 u_e}{\partial x^2} = \ddot{u}_r + \frac{\partial^2 u_e}{\partial t^2}, \tag{7}$$

where ρ is the density and $c_p = \sqrt{E/\rho}$ is the speed of the longitudinal stress wave. The corresponding boundary conditions are

$$EA \frac{\partial u_e(0,t)}{\partial x} = 0, \tag{8}$$

$$EA \frac{\partial u_e}{\partial x}(L,t) = -M[\ddot{u}_r + \frac{\partial^2 u_e}{\partial t^2}(L,t)]$$
$$- c[\dot{u}_r + \frac{\partial u_e}{\partial t}(L,t)] - k[u_r + u_e(L,t)]. \tag{9}$$

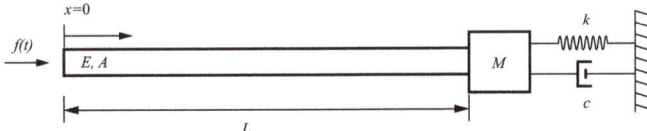

Figure 1. A uniform elastic rod with a mass–damper–spring termination. An impact loading $f(t)$ is applied to the free end. The material coordinate system is fixed to the free end of the rod.

The non-homogeneous boundary condition of Equation (9) leads to a non-orthogonal eigenvalue problem. We attack this problem using a method of a particular solution, which expresses the elastic motion $u_e(x,t)$ in the form

$$u_e(x,t) = u_h(x,t) + u_p(x,t), \tag{10}$$

where $u_h(x,t)$ is the homogeneous solution with free–free boundary conditions such that

$$u_h(x,t) = \sum_{i=1}^{n} \phi_i(x) y_i(t), \tag{11}$$

where

$$\int_0^L \phi_i(x)\phi_j(x)\,dx = \delta_{ij}, \tag{12}$$

and $u_p(x,t)$ is the particular solution such that

$$u_p(x,t) = \left(\frac{x}{L}\right)^2 \alpha(t). \tag{13}$$

Substitution of Equations (10)–(13) into Equations (5)–(9) yields a state space form [19]

$$\dot{\mathbf{Z}} = \mathbf{AZ}, \tag{14}$$

where

$$\mathbf{Z} = [z(t); \dot{z}(t)], \tag{15}$$

$$\mathbf{A} = \begin{bmatrix} \mathbf{0} & \mathbf{I} \\ -\mathbf{M}^{-1}\mathbf{K} & -\mathbf{M}^{-1}\mathbf{C} \end{bmatrix}, \tag{16}$$

$$z(t) = [u_r(t), \alpha(t), y_1(t), y_2(t), \ldots, y_n(t)]. \tag{17}$$

The formal solution of Equation (14) reads

$$\mathbf{Z}(t) = e^{\mathbf{A}t}\mathbf{Z}_0, \tag{18}$$

where $\mathbf{Z}_0$ is the initial condition generated from the impulsive input (see Appendix A). The numerical error analysis of the method was performed in [19]. We incorporate this method into the GA-SCM method to optimize the termination of the structure.

4.2. Objective Functions

We define the multi-objective performance indices of terminal response as

$$\mathbf{F} = (t_s^{e_3}, |u(L)|_{max}, 1/\delta), \tag{19}$$

where $t_s^{e_3}$ is the settling time of the third elastic mode, $|x(L)|_{max}$ is the maximal absolute displacement at termination, and δ is the log decrement of the strain response at termination.

$t_s^{e_3}$ is an indirect indicator for the settling time of the rod response. The reason for using $t_s^{e_3}$ is twofold. Firstly, the settling time of higher modes produced by the model cannot properly capture the physical phenomena that the response of high-frequency modes usually decays more rapidly than that of low-frequency modes. Secondly, identifying the settling time of the total response from the numerical simulation could lead to extensive computational load. Therefore, the settling time of the third elastic mode is used and defined in the form

$$t_s^{e_3} = \frac{4}{|Real(\lambda_{e_3})|}, \tag{20}$$

where e_3 stands for the third elastic mode. The selection of the third mode is based on trial and error.

δ is also an indirect indicator to estimate the decay of the impact wave. After the impact load is applied, an impulsive wave will be produced at the left terminal and a response wave due to the rigid-body motion will be generated at the right terminal. The two waves will propagate along the rod and be reflected at both ends. Although the strain response is the superposition of two waves, the impact wave dominates the response when it is propagated to the right terminal for the first few times. We define δ in the form

$$\delta = \frac{1}{n-1} \log \frac{|u_x(t_1, L)|}{|u_x(t_n, L)|}, \tag{21}$$

where t_1 and t_n represent the first and n-th time when the impulse wave is propagated to the right end, respectively. The larger δ is, the more the impact wave is suppressed. We let $n = 3$ in this study.

5. A Case Study

We considered an elastic rod with Young's modulus $E = 10$, density $\rho = 10$, length $L = 2$, cross-section area $A = 0.1$, and excitation force magnitude $f_0 = 1.0$. The design space was chosen as

$$Q = \{\mathbf{x}|\mathbf{x} \in [0.1, 2.0] \times [1.0, 6.0] \times [10, 20]\}, \tag{22}$$

subject to a constraint

$$\delta > 0, \tag{23}$$

where $\mathbf{x}$ is the tuple (m, c, k). We calculated the first 15 s rod response under the impact loading through the numerical integration of Equation (14), because the max displacement appears quickly after impact, and the impact wave dominates the terminal response when it is propagated at the right end during this time period. Thirty elastic modes were adopted, which, based on our observation, are sufficient to approximate the values of performance indices within the design space.

We first discover a rough Pareto set using the NSGAII algorithm with a population size 1000, number of generations 10, and mutation rate 0.05. Other configurations of NSGAII can be seen in Table 1. With the numerical predictor, the NSGAII algorithm was completed in 66 s on a desktop with an Intel core i-7 CPU, producing a rough Pareto set as the input to the SCM method. In the SCM method, the $m - c - k$ design space is discretized into a $10 \times 20 \times 20$ cellular grid as shown in Table 2. The elements of the Pareto set are the cells in the design space. The local search and recovery algorithm are performed twice, the first time with the initial grid and the second time with the refined grid, which divides the initial grid by three. We stop the program after the refinement because the desired resolution 0.06 $\times$ 0.08 $\times$ 0.166 in the parameter space is achieved. The computational time was 36 s with the initial grid and 2000 s with the refined grid.

Table 1. Configuration of NSGAII.

Encoding	Population	Mutation Rate	Crossover	Generation Number
Binary	1000	0.05	two-point	10

Table 2. Configuration of SCM.

Initial Cell Partition	Sub Partition
$10 \times 20 \times 20$	3

There are 5392 cells in the Pareto set. The Pareto set and front of the mass–damper–spring termination are presented in Figure 2. Generally, either larger stiffness or damping will lead to better design. The majority of optimal design is achieved with either moderate or small mass. The Pareto front can be divided into three regions, labeled in Figure 2b. Region 1 minimizes displacement at the cost of long settling time and moderate damping performance. Region 2 balances the performance of three objective functions. Region 3 achieves premium damping performance at the expense of large displacement and moderate settling time.

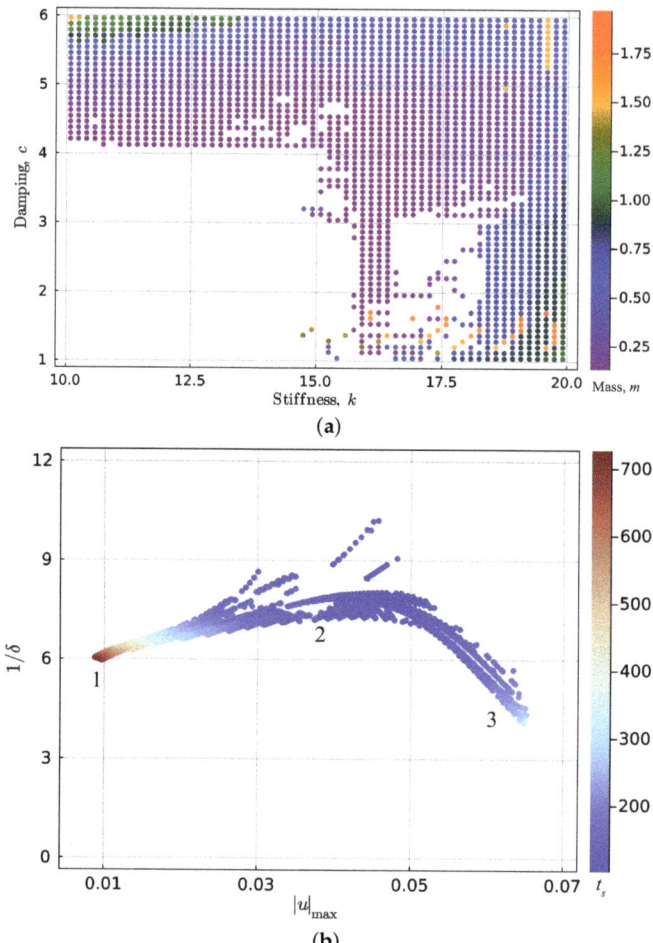

Figure 2. The Pareto set and front of the $m - c - k$ termination design of the elastic rod. (**a**) Pareto set. (**b**) Pareto front. Design parameters $m \in [0.1, 2.0]$, $c \in [1.0, 6.0]$, $k \in [10.0, 20.0]$. The labels "1", "2", and "3" indicate the regions where optimal terminal displacement, balanced performance of objective functions, and optimal damping performance are achieved.

The optimal designs of each performance index are presented in Figures 3–5. The corresponding design parameters, as well as performance indices are listed in Table 3.

Table 3. Design parameters and performance indices of optimal designs in Figures 3–5.

Figure	Design Parameters			Performance Indices		
	M	c	k	δ	$t_s^{e_3}$	$|u(L)|_{max}$
3	1.4617	4.9583	18.7500	0.1103	103.4239	0.0482
4	1.0183	1.0416	19.9167	0.2428	324.5931	0.0648
5	0.1316	5.9583	19.9167	0.0414	724.9264	0.0088

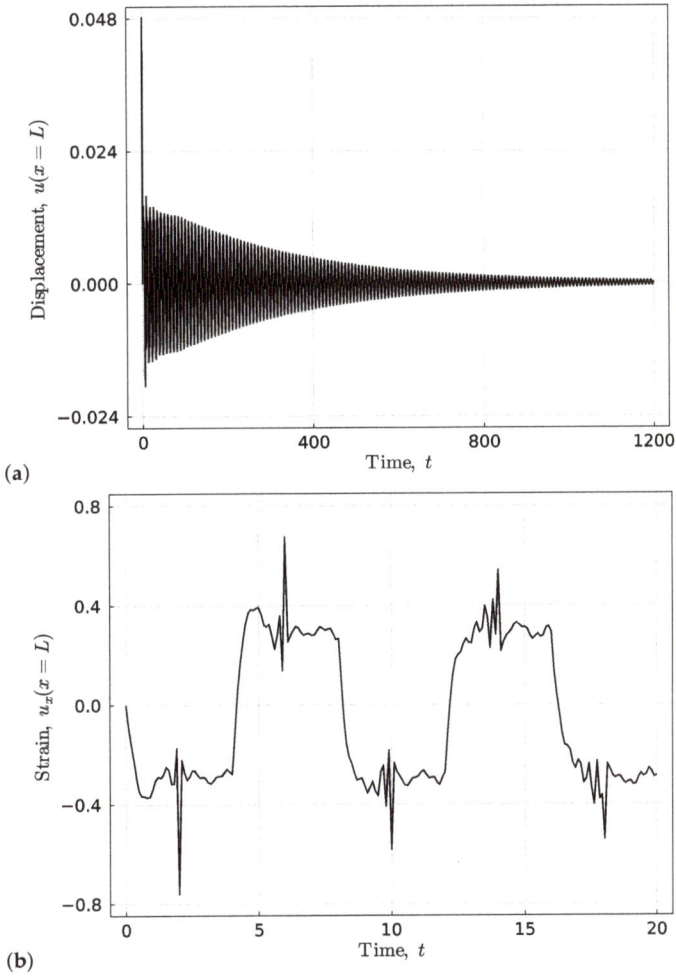

Figure 3. The optimal design of settling time. The corresponding (**a**) terminal displacement and (**b**) strain responses of the rod. The response is computed with $N = 30$.

5.1. Optimal Design: Minimal Settling Time

Figure 3 shows the optimal design of the settling time. The settling time of the total response approximates 1200 s. While the performance index of the settling time is significantly smaller than this number, it still correctly reflects the trend of the settling time change in comparison to other designs such as those in Figures 4 and 5. The large mass in this design can increase the portion of energy transmitted to the mass after impact, which can be more effectively dissipated through the heavily damped boundary condition.

5.2. Optimal Design: Maximal Decay of Impact Wave

The time response of the optimal design maximizing the decay of the impact wave is presented in Figure 4. The impact wave propagates to the right end when $t = 2, 6, 10 \ldots$. The suppression of the impact wave is evident. However, this is at the cost of at least a five-times longer settling time and a slight increase of the maximal displacement. When compared to the other two designs, this design considerably reduces the damping coefficient. This could be attributed to the velocity change of the mounted mass in response to the impact wave hitting the terminal. Such a change will immediately alter the viscous force produced by the damper, which in turn can lead to higher strain at the terminal. A small damping coefficient can reduce the magnitude of the reflected impact wave.

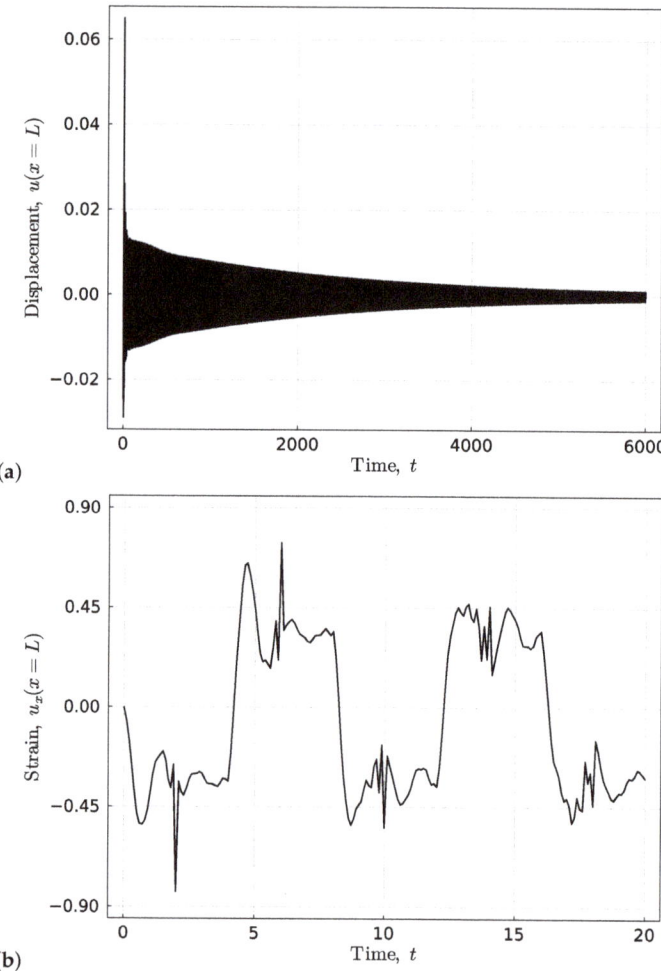

Figure 4. The optimal design of the decay of the impact wave. The corresponding (**a**) terminal displacement and (**b**) strain response of the rod. The response is calculated with $N = 30$.

5.3. Optimal Design: Minimal Peak Displacement at Termination

The optimal design of terminal peak displacement in Figure 5 has the same stiffness, but much smaller mass and larger damping as the design in Figure 4. This makes sense because the terminal displacement is identical to the displacement of the mounted mass. Using small inertia and large stiffness and damping, one can effectively reduce the maximal terminal displacement. However, smaller inertia also leads to less energy distributed to the mass. Because the energy can only be dissipated through the damper attached to the mass, this choice can also significantly amplify the settling time.

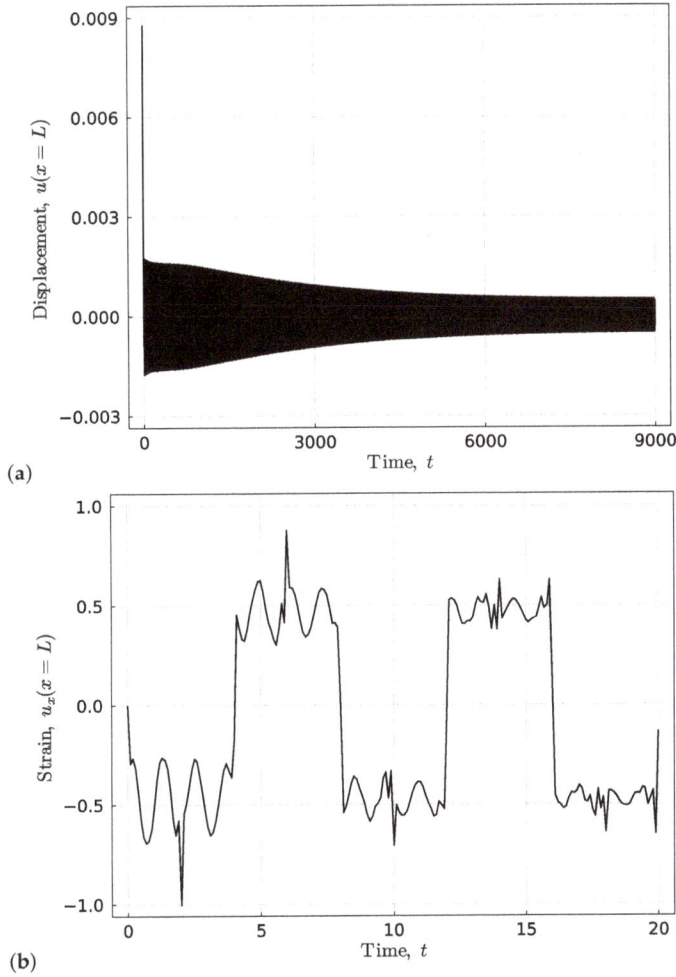

Figure 5. The optimal design of the maximal terminal displacement. The corresponding (**a**) terminal displacement and (**b**) strain responses of the rod. The response is calculated with $N = 30$.

6. Conclusions

In this paper, a multi-objective optimization problem of the terminal response of an elastic rod with a viscous boundary condition was formulated. The terminal response of the rod was predicted through a computationally effective and accurate particular solution method. The Pareto set and front of the MOP were obtained with the GA-SCM hybrid method. The proposed objective functions can effectively capture the dynamic response of the structure. The optimal design strategies were presented and analyzed. The amount of energy distributed to the terminal mass after impact was significant for the optimization of the terminal design.

The computational load of this work was due to the repeated computations of the impulse response with different parameter sets. Although the solver adopted in this paper can be computationally more effective and accurate than finite-element methods, it still requires a sufficient number of modes to capture the non-smooth impulsive response when highly accurate results are desired. The computational load can be further reduced using a surrogate (metamodel) model [20]. One future direction is to use neural operators such as

DeepONet [21] to approximate the impulsive response, with the neural operator trained using data from the adopted solver.

Author Contributions: Conceptualization, methodology, and supervision, J.-Q.S.; software, formal analysis, investigation, and writing—original draft preparation, S.X.; writing—review and editing, J.-Q.S. All authors have read and agreed to the published version of the manuscript.

Funding: The first author would like to thank for the release time support from the Donald E. Bently Center for Engineering Innovation at California Polytechnic State University.

Conflicts of Interest: The authors declare no conflict of interest.

Appendix A

From [19], the initial conditions of Equation (18) are

$$\rho A L \dot{u}_{r0} + M \dot{u}_{r0} = f_0, \tag{A1}$$

$$\dot{u}_{r0} + \sum_{i=1}^{n} \phi_i(0) \dot{y}_{i0} = \frac{f_0}{\rho A}, \tag{A2}$$

$$u_{r0} + \sum_{i=1}^{n} y_{i0} + \left(\frac{x}{L}\right)^m \alpha_0 = 0, 0 \leq x \leq L, \tag{A3}$$

$$\sum_{i=1}^{n} \phi_i(x) \dot{y}_{i0} + \left(\frac{x}{L}\right)^m \dot{\alpha}_0 = 0, 0 < x \leq L, \tag{A4}$$

where $u_{r0} = u_r(0)$, $\alpha_0 = \alpha(0)$, and $y_{i0} = y_i(0)$. Equation (A1) leads to

$$\dot{u}_{r0} = f_0 / (\rho A L + M). \tag{A5}$$

By uniformly sampling spatial points on the rod and applying the least-mean-squares method, the initial conditions of the particular solution and response of elastic modes can be obtained in the form

$$\dot{\mathbf{y}}_0 = (\mathbf{\Phi}^T \mathbf{\Phi})^{-1} \mathbf{\Phi}^T \mathbf{F}, \tag{A6}$$

where $\dot{\mathbf{y}}_0 = [\dot{\alpha}_0, \dot{y}_{10}, \cdots, \dot{y}_{n0}]$, $\mathbf{F} = [f_0/(\rho A) - \dot{u}_{r0}, 0, 0, ...0]^T$ and

$$\mathbf{\Phi} = \begin{bmatrix} 0 & \phi_1(0) & \phi_2(0) & \cdots & \phi_n(0) \\ (x_1/L)^m & \phi_1(x_1) & \phi_2(x_1) & \cdots & \phi_n(x_1) \\ \vdots & \vdots & \vdots & \ddots & \vdots \\ (L/L)^m & \phi_1(L) & \phi_2(L) & \cdots & \phi_n(L) \end{bmatrix}. \tag{A7}$$

References

1. Feng, Q.; Shinozuka, M. Control of Seismic Response of Structures Using Variable Dampers. *J. Intell. Mater. Syst. Struct.* **1993**, *4*, 117–122. [CrossRef]
2. Jayachandran, V.; Sun, J.Q. Impedance Characteristics of Active Interior Noise Control Systems. *J. Sound Vib.* **1998**, *211*, 716–727. [CrossRef]
3. Udwadia, F.E. Boundary Control, Quiet Boundaries, Super-stability and Super-instability. *Appl. Math. Comput.* **2005**, *164*, 327–349. [CrossRef]
4. Hirzinger, B.; Adam, C.; Salcher, P. Dynamic Response of a Non-classically Damped Beam with General Boundary Conditions Subjected to a Moving Mass-spring-damper System. *Int. J. Mech. Sci.* **2020**, *185*, 105877. [CrossRef]
5. Sun, J.Q.; Xiong, F.R.; Schütze, O.; Hernández, C. *Cell Mapping Methods—Algorithmic Approaches and Applications*; Springer: New York, NY, USA, 2018.
6. Hsu, C.S. *Cell-to-Cell Mapping—A Method of Global Analysis for Nonlinear Systems*; Springer: New York, NY, USA, 1987.
7. Sardahi, Y.; Naranjani, Y.; Liang, W.; Sun, J.Q.; Hernandez, C.; Schuetze, O. Multi-objective Optimal Control Design with the Simple Cell Mapping Method. In Proceedings of the ASME International Mechanical Engineering Congress & Exposition, San Diego, CA, USA, 15–21 November 2013. [CrossRef]
8. Xiong, F.R.; Qin, Z.C.; Xue, Y.; Schütze, O.; Ding, Q.; Sun, J.Q. Multi-objective Optimal Design of Feedback Controls for Dynamical Systems with Hybrid Simple Cell Mapping Algorithm. *Commun. Nonlinear Sci. Numer. Simul.* **2014**, *19*, 1465–1473. [CrossRef]

9. Hernández, C.; Naranjani, Y.; Sardahi, Y.; Liang, W.; Schütze, O.; Sun, J.Q. Simple Cell Mapping Method for Multi-objective Optimal Feedback Control Design. *Int. J. Dyn. Control* **2013**, *1*, 231–238. [CrossRef]
10. Deb, K.; Pratap, A.; Agarwal, S.; Meyarivan, T. A Fast and Elitist Multi-objective Genetic Algorithm: NSGA-II. *IEEE Trans. Evol. Comput.* **2002**, *6*, 182–197. [CrossRef]
11. Khoie, M.; Salahshoor, K.; Nouri, E.; Sedigh, A.K. PID Controller Tuning Using Multi-objective Optimization Based on Fused Genetic-Immune Algorithm and Immune Feedback Mechanism. In *Lecture Notes in Computer Science—Advanced Intelligent Computing Theories and Applications*; Springer: Berlin, Germany, 2012; Volume 6839.
12. Poli, R.; Kennedy, J.; Blackwell, T. Particle Swarm Optimization. *Swarm Intell.* **2007**, *1*, 33–57. [CrossRef]
13. Chiha, I.; Liouane, N.; Borne, P. Tuning PID Controller Using Multiobjective Ant Colony Optimization. *Appl. Comput. Intell. Soft Comput.* **2012**, *2012*, 11. [CrossRef]
14. Naranjani, Y.; Hernández, C.; Xiong, F.R.; Schütze, O.; Sun, J.Q. A Hybrid Method of Evolutionary Algorithm and Simple Cell Mapping for Multi-objective Optimization Problems. *Int. J. Dyn. Control* **2017**, *5*, 570–582. [CrossRef]
15. Hull, A.J.; Radcliffe, C.J.; Miklavcic, M.; Maccluer, C.R. State Space Representation of the Nonself-adjoint Acoustic Duct System. *J. Vib. Acoust.* **1990**, *112*, 483–488. [CrossRef]
16. Jayachandran, V.; Sun, J.Q. The Modal Formulation and Adaptive-passive Control of the Nonself-adjoint One-dimensional Acoustic System with a Mass-spring Termination. *J. Appl. Mech.* **1999**, *66*, 242–249. [CrossRef]
17. Oliveto, G.; Santini, A.; Tripodi, E. Complex Modal Analysis of a Flexural Vibrating Beam with Viscous End Conditions. *J. Sound Vib.* **1997**, *200*, 327–345. [CrossRef]
18. Jovanovic, V. A Fourier Series Solution for the Longitudinal Vibrations of a Bar with Viscous Boundary Conditions at Each End. *J. Eng. Math.* **2013**, *79*, 125–142. [CrossRef]
19. Xing, S.Y.; Sun, J.Q. Impulse Response of an Elastic Rod with a Mass-damper-spring Termination. *J. Vib. Test. Syst. Dyn.* **2023**, accepted.
20. Chugh, T.; Sindhya, K.; Hakanen, J.; Miettinen, K. A Survey on Handling Computationally Expensive Multiobject Optimization Problems with Evolutionry Algorithms. *Soft Comput.* **2019**, *23*, 3137–3166. [CrossRef]
21. Lu, L.; Jin, P.; Pang, G.; Karniadakis, G.E. Learning Nonlinear Operators via DeepONet Based on the Universal Approximation Theorem of Operators. *Nat. Mach. Intell.* **2021**, *3*, 218–229. [CrossRef]

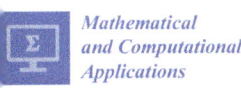

Article

Scarce Sample-Based Reliability Estimation and Optimization Using Importance Sampling

Kiran Pannerselvam, Deepanshu Yadav and Palaniappan Ramu *

Advanced Design, Optimization and Probabilistic Techniques (ADOPT) Laboratory, Department of Engineering Design, Indian Institute of Technology Madras, Chennai 600036, India
* Correspondence: palramu@iitm.ac.in; Tel.: +91-4422574738; Fax: +91-4422574732

Abstract: Importance sampling is a variance reduction technique that is used to improve the efficiency of Monte Carlo estimation. Importance sampling uses the trick of sampling from a distribution, which is located around the zone of interest of the primary distribution thereby reducing the number of realizations required for an estimate. In the context of reliability-based structural design, the limit state is usually separable and is of the form Capacity (C)–Response (R). The zone of interest for importance sampling is observed to be the region where these distributions overlap each other. However, often the distribution information of C and R themselves are not known, and one has only scarce realizations of them. In this work, we propose approximating the probability density function and the cumulative distribution function using kernel functions and employ these approximations to find the parameters of the importance sampling density (ISD) to eventually estimate the reliability. In the proposed approach, in addition to ISD parameters, the approximations also played a critical role in affecting the accuracy of the probability estimates. We assume an ISD which follows a normal distribution whose mean is defined by the most probable point (MPP) of failure, and the standard deviation is empirically chosen such that most of the importance sample realizations lie within the means of R and C. Since the probability estimate depends on the approximation, which in turn depends on the underlying samples, we use bootstrap to quantify the variation associated with the low failure probability estimate. The method is investigated with different tailed distributions of R and C. Based on the observations, a modified Hill estimator is utilized to address scenarios with heavy-tailed distributions where the distribution approximations perform poorly. The proposed approach is tested on benchmark reliability examples and along with surrogate modeling techniques is implemented on four reliability-based design optimization examples of which one is a multi-objective optimization problem.

Keywords: reliability; importance sampling; scarce data; surrogate; RBDO; MOO

1. Introduction

Reliability-based design optimization (RBDO) is a design approach that is used to generate reliable designs by accounting for uncertainties in the system variables such as material properties, loading conditions and geometry. Probabilistic approaches use probability distributions to model the uncertainties. In such approaches, the reliability of the system is measured as the probability of failure to satisfy a performance criterion. Mathematically, this involves calculating the hyper-volume of a multi-dimensional probability density function (PDF) under the failure region. This calculation becomes infeasible when the number of dimensions are large. Even in low dimensions, this calculation could become intractable due to complicated geometry of the failure region [1]. Attractive alternatives are analytical methods or sampling-based approaches.

Analytical methods, such as first-order and second-order reliability methods (FORM and SORM), transform the probability distributions to standard normal space and use linear or quadratic approximations of the performance function to estimate the failure

probability at the most probable point (MPP) of failure [2–4]. In essence, analytical methods can estimate failure probability within a reasonable number of evaluations for linear or slightly non-linear performance functions. However, if the failure boundary is highly non-linear, analytical approaches are likely to lead to erroneous estimation. Additionally, other factors, such as island failure regions and multiple failure modes, limit their performance [5,6].

Sampling-based approaches such as Monte Carlo methods are highly effective for complex failure boundary problems and multi-modal failure problems [7]. In high-reliability applications where the failure probability is very low, MCS requires a very large number of model evaluations to obtain an accurate estimate. Most RBDO applications involve evaluating high-fidelity models which are computationally expensive, thus rendering MCS prohibitive for reliability estimation.

The computational burden of RBDO can be reduced by using surrogate-based methods wherein surrogate models which are cheaper to evaluate are constructed using limited high-fidelity model evaluations. Uncertainty from the random variables is then propagated through these surrogate models to obtain reliability estimates. Various surrogate modeling approaches, such as polynomial response surface (PRS), radial basis function (RBF), support vector machine (SVM) and Kriging among others have been adopted for reliability estimation [8]. Li and Xiu [9] proposed using cheaper to evaluate surrogates away from the limit state and high-fidelity model evaluations close to the limit state to improve accuracy and reduce cost. Dai et al. [10] proposed an SVM-based radial basis function to approximate the limit state function which is then used to estimate failure probability. Dubourg et al. [11] used error measure derived from Kriging to refine the surrogate during subset-simulation-based reliability estimation. Reliability estimation using surrogates may carry forward the bias from the surrogate approximation [12]. Surrogate modeling can also be used to build approximation models for reliability metrics instead of limit state function. Foschi et al. [13] used the combination of response surface, FORM and importance sampling to perform reliability estimation. Qu and Haftka [14] compared the accuracy of surrogates of different reliability metrics, such as failure probability, reliability index and probabilistic sufficiency factor (PSF) during RBDO. They conclude that inverse measure, such as PSF operating in performance space, performs better compared to a classical reliability metric. A survey of various surrogate-based RBDO frameworks is provided in [15]. The choice between surrogate for reliability estimation versus surrogate for limit state is a trade-off based on the number of design variables and the number of random variables as well as the cost of building the surrogate and cost of reliability estimate [16].

Employing variance reduction techniques to improve the efficiency and accuracy of Monte Carlo estimations is another way to alleviate the computational burden of RBDO. Several variance reduction techniques, such as importance sampling (IS) [17–19], subset simulation (SS) [1,20] and separable Monte Carlo (SMC) [21,22], are used to improve the accuracy of failure probability estimates while reducing the required number of high-fidelity model evaluations.

Importance sampling improves the accuracy of the estimate by drawing the sample realizations of the input random variables that have greater impact on the estimate, more often. In order to do that, an alternate sampling density known as importance sampling density (ISD) is chosen which enables sampling the important values more frequently. This introduces a bias in the estimator which is corrected by weighing the sample realizations. A good choice of ISD is proven to improve accuracy and in contrast, incorrect choice of ISD could lead to spurious estimates. Hence, the choice of ISD is critical, and several approaches have been explored to find the optimal ISD. Melchers [17] applied importance sampling for assessing reliability of parallel and series structural systems, where a multi-normal PDF centered at MPP was chosen as the ISD. Using the original distribution shifted to MPP, multivariate normal distribution located at MPP with various choices for the co-variance matrix ranging from the same as the original distribution to using only diagonal elements of the original co-variance matrix have been studied [23].

In cross-entropy-based methods [24], ISD is found by minimizing the Kullback–Leibler (KL) divergence between theoretical optimal ISD and a chosen family of distributions. Kurtz and Song [25] used a Gaussian mixture to obtain a non-parametric multi-modal PDF for ISD. It was observed that the coefficient of variation of the failure probability estimate converged as the number of Gaussian densities in the mixture increased. Cao and Choe [26] used an expectation-maximization (EM) algorithm to obtain a Gaussian mixture as the near optimal ISD. Cross-entropy information criterion (CIC) was used to select the number of Gaussian densities in the mixture. Geyer et al. [27] proposed a modified version of EM algorithm for updating the Gaussian-mixture-based ISD. For selecting the number of distributions in the mixture, density-based spatial clustering of applications with noise (DBSCAN) algorithm was used. In cross-entropy-based IS, one still requires the joint PDF of the original random variables to compute the near optimal ISD.

Kernel-based IS is another way to obtain the alternate sampling density wherein a kernel sampling density is constructed instead of choosing from a family of distributions [28,29]. Au and Beck [30] proposed Markov Chain Monte Carlo (MCMC) to distribute samples asymptotically according to the optimal ISD, and subsequently a kernel sampling density is constructed from these samples. Dai et al. [31] proposed a wavelet density estimation technique to construct the ISD from the MCMC samples. Botev et al. [32] proposed combining MCMC and IS to address the issues of biased sampling estimators that result from MCMC. Various adaptive importance sampling procedures have gained popularity recently. Dalbey and Swiler [33] proposed a Gaussian-process-based adaptive importance sampling where a Gaussian process surrogate is used to identify the likely regions of failure to adaptively improve the sampling density estimate. Zhao et al. [34] constructed a Kriging surrogate from the initial MCMC samples which is improved using an active learning process, and subsequently the surrogate is used for limit state evaluations for adaptive improvement of ISD. Wang and Song [35] used cross-entropy-based adaptive importance sampling for high-dimensional reliability analysis. Here, ISD is obtained by minimizing the KL divergence between a von Mises–Fisher mixture model and near optimal ISD.

In all the literature discussed above, while employing IS, determination of the appropriate ISD is considered to be the challenge. The probabilistic distributions and the corresponding parameters of the original random variables, however, are assumed to be known [22,36]. However, this is not necessarily always true. Here, we propose a framework to employ the importance sampling method for separable failure boundary of the form Capacity (C)–Response (R) using only scarce realizations of the R and C where no information about their distributions is known. We make use of tail-modeling techniques to approximate the cumulative distribution function (CDF) of the capacity and response. These approximations are used to locate a Gaussian ISD whose standard deviation is empirically chosen. Sample realizations drawn from the ISD are used to compute the failure probability. During this computation, kernel density estimates of PDF of response are utilized along with CDF approximation of capacity. Furthermore, bootstrap samples are generated from the original scarce samples of R and C. The proposed framework is applied on the bootstrap samples to obtain the confidence bounds for the reliability estimate. Reliability estimates obtained from scarce samples using the proposed approach are used to construct a surrogate of reliability index which is used for constraint evaluation during RBDO.

The rest of the paper is organized as follows. Section 2 presents the theoretical background of importance sampling in the context of reliability estimation. In Section 3, the methodology is discussed, and in later sections we present the results from the proposed method when applied to test cases and RBDO applications including a multi-objective optimization (MOO) application. Appendices A and B are used to provide short descriptions of kernel density estimation (KDE) and the third-order polynomial normal transformation (TPNT) technique.

2. Reliability Estimation Using Importance Sampling for Separable Limit States

In structural engineering, limit states are useful in prescribing performance requirements of a design. Thus, a limit state decomposes the design space of a system into safe and failure regions. Violation of a limit state is considered to be failure. and reliability is a measure of probability of such violations. For most structural problems, limit state can be expressed as the difference of Capacity (C) and Response (R), as presented in Equation (1), where R and C are functions of independent sets of random variables. This is referred to as a separable limit state [21,22,37], and we consider such limit states in this work.

$$G(C, R) = C - R \tag{1}$$

The system is said to fail when $C \leq R$ and safe when $C > R$. When either capacity or response or both are functions of variables that are random, a probabilistic measure such as the probability of failure is as presented in Equation (2)

$$p_f = \iint_{G \leq 0} f_{CR}(c, r) \, dc \, dr \tag{2}$$

where f_{CR} is the joint probability distribution function (PDF), and $G \leq 0$ is the failure region. In the case of separable limit state, the joint PDF of capacity and response can be decomposed into the product of the marginal PDFs of capacity and response as presented in Equation (3)

$$p_f = \int_{-\infty}^{\infty} \int_{-\infty}^{c \leq r} f_C(c) f_R(r) \, dc \, dr \tag{3}$$

$$p_f = \int_{-\infty}^{\infty} F_C(x) f_R(x) \, dx \tag{4}$$

where $f_C(c)$ and $f_R(r)$ are the marginal density functions of C and R, respectively. Equation (3) can also be written in a single integral form as presented in Equation (4). Here, $F_C(c)$ is the cumulative distribution function (CDF) of capacity. For low failure probabilities of order 10^{-4}, to obtain a Monte Carlo estimate with 10% coefficient of variation, the sample size required is $100 \times \frac{1}{p_f} = 10^6$. Generating 10^6 instances of expensive computer models is not feasible. To reduce such computational burden, importance sampling is used as in Equation (5).

$$p_{f_{IS}} = \int_{-\infty}^{\infty} \frac{F_C(x) f_R(x)}{h_x(x)} h_x(x) \, dx \tag{5}$$

where $h_x(x)$ is the alternate sampling density, and $p_{f_{IS}}$ is the failure probability computed using the importance sampling approach. It is the expectation of the integrand $\frac{F_C(x) f_R(x)}{h_x(x)}$ computed with respect to the ISD, h_x. Consequently, if $x_1, x_2, \ldots, x_N$ is an independent identically distributed (i.i.d.) random sample from h_x, then the expectation has an unbiased estimator:

$$\widehat{p_{f_{IS}}} = \sum_{i=1}^{N} \frac{F_C(x_i) f_R(x_i)}{h_x(x_i)}, \quad x_i \sim h_x \tag{6}$$

Alternatively, if the marginal distribution of the response ($f_R(r)$) is integrated in Equation (3), then the importance sampling estimator of p_f would be expressed as:

$$\widehat{p_{f_{IS}}} = \sum_{i=1}^{N} \frac{(1 - F_R(x_i)) f_C(x_i)}{h_x(x_i)}, \quad x_i \sim h_x \tag{7}$$

As mentioned in Section 1, in most of the literature, importance sampling is used when the distributions of R and C are known, and it becomes computationally expensive to draw samples in the region where tails of R and C overlap. Figure 1 presents a schematic of such a scenario where the limit state is of the separable form. Here, the region of interest lies in the tails of the distributions of R and C, and it contains the most probable point (MPP) of failure. Hence, it is only logical to locate the ISD at the MPP [3,17,22].

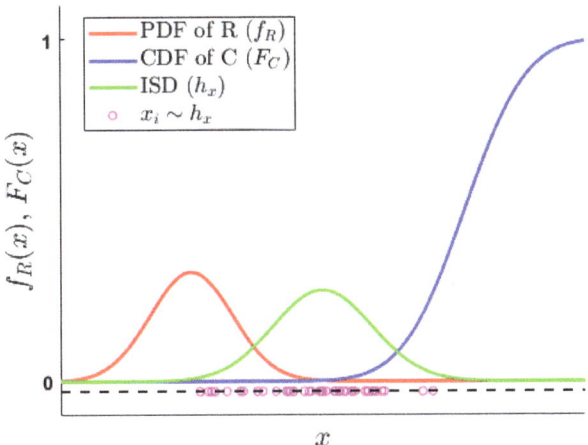

Figure 1. Basic C–R problem: a schematic of importance sampling.

Figure 1 depicts a Gaussian ISD for which MPP serves as the mean of the distribution and is usually found by solving a constrained optimization problem. Once the mean of the ISD is determined, the spread of the distribution needs to be chosen. In order to have a finite variance for the importance sampling estimator, the ISD should not have a lighter tail than the original distribution [38]. In the literature [22,23], using the same co-variance matrix and sometimes using strictly the diagonal elements of the co-variance matrix of the original distribution is suggested. This has been shown to work for a range of possible limit states. However, sometimes a designer does not necessarily know the original distributions of input variables but has only a few realizations of R and C either through expensive computer simulations or physical experiments. Generally, response is considered to be the source of randomness since it is a measured quantity. However, capacity can also be a random variable. For instance, an example of capacity is yield strength which is a measured quantity. We know that it is random and hence modeled using probability distributions [39,40]. Other examples of capacity that are considered to be random include: member capacity under seismic loading [41], maximum flow capacity in measuring hydraulic reliability of water distribution system [42], and material fatigue properties [43,44].

In this work, we first characterize the distributions of R and C from limited samples and use the concept of importance sampling to estimate low failure probabilities. A Gaussian distribution is chosen as the ISD which is fully described by its two parameters, the mean and variance. Section 3 describes the procedure employed to identify the parameters of ISD. In the proposed framework, to demonstrate the methodology, distribution information of original input random variables is used only to generate the initial limited samples. However, the distribution information is not utilized anywhere afterwards.

3. Identifying Parameters of Gaussian ISD

Figure 2 presents an example scenario [23] of a separable limit state where the response and capacity follow normal distributions. It can be observed that the functional $F_C f_R$ integrated in Equation (4) is maximum at the point ($x \sim 11.55$), near the point of intersection between the PDF of response and the CDF of capacity, i.e., $f_R(x) = F_C(x)$. In importance sampling, MPP is used to locate the ISD to maximize sampling of the failure probability content. Hence, it is only logical to define this point of intersection as the MPP and use it as the mean of Gaussian ISD.

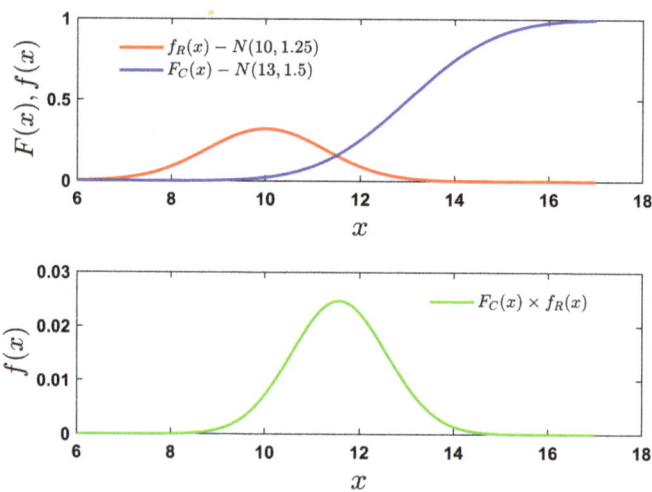

Figure 2. Probabilistic view of MPP for a separable limit state scenario.

This point can be anywhere within the bounds of capacity and response. In high-reliability scenarios, it is located at the tails of one of the distributions or both, so we need to extrapolate into the tails of R and C. The available PDF approximation methods capture the central part of the distribution better than the tails, whereas the main focus of the tail modeling techniques applied for CDF estimation is at the tails of the distribution. Hence, we can reduce the errors in finding the MPP by using the intersection of $1 - F_R$ and F_C instead of the intersection point of the curves f_R and F_C. Here, $1 - F_R$ is the complementary CDF of R. It is to be noted that the suitability of such a modification has been tested for only uni-modal type response. For multi-modal response, using a single MPP will only capture partial failure region. However, the approach can be extended by using a mixture of Gaussian distributions by using a summed failure probability integral as described in [45]. Algorithm 1 presents the bracketing procedure followed in the current work to find the MPP, while the same process is visually presented in Figure 3.

In Steps 3 and 6 of Algorithm 1, it is stated that the CDF approximations of capacity ($\widehat{F_C}$) and response ($\widehat{F_R}$) are obtained through a TPNT technique (details provided in Appendix B); however, it is an independent block in the proposed approach and hence can be replaced by any other suitable technique based on user discretion. In effect, the MPP finding problem reduces to finding the zeroes of the function $\widehat{F_C}(x) - (1 - \widehat{F_R}(x))$. Hence, root finding algorithms can also be applied to find the MPP. However, it is advised to use derivative-free approaches to avoid numerical issues.

Algorithm 1 Finding μ_h.

1: Obtain samples of response $\mathbf{r} = \{r_1, r_2, \ldots, r_M\}$ and capacity $\mathbf{c} = \{c_1, c_2, \ldots, c_N\}$ as in Figure 3a.
2: **for** $i = 1, 2, \ldots, M$ **do**
3:    $\widehat{F_C}(r_i), \widehat{F_R}(r_i) \leftarrow$ TPNT approximations of CDF of response and capacity at response sample $\mathbf{r}$.
4:    Obtain point A in Figure 3b $\leftarrow$ maximum of $\mathbf{r_x} = \{r_i | \widehat{F_C}(r_i) - (1 - \widehat{F_R}(r_i)) < 0\}$.
5: **for** $i = 1, 2, \ldots, N$ **do**
6:    $\widehat{F_C}(c_i), \widehat{F_R}(c_i) \leftarrow$ TPNT approximations of CDF of response and capacity at capacity sample $\mathbf{c}$.
7:    Obtain point B in Figure 3c $\leftarrow$ minimum of $\mathbf{c_x} = \{c_i | \widehat{F_C}(c_i) - (1 - \widehat{F_R}(c_i)) > 0\}$.
8: Generate a set of evenly spaced points $\mathbf{x} = \{x_i : i = 1, 2, \ldots, 100\}$ between points A and B.
9: Obtain mean of ISD, $\mu_h \leftarrow$ maximum of $\mathbf{x} = \{x_i | \widehat{F_C}(x_i) - (1 - \widehat{F_R}(x_i)) < 0\}$. (Alternatively, minimum of $\mathbf{x} = \{x_i | \widehat{F_C}(x_i) - (1 - \widehat{F_R}(x_i)) > 0\}$ can also be used.)

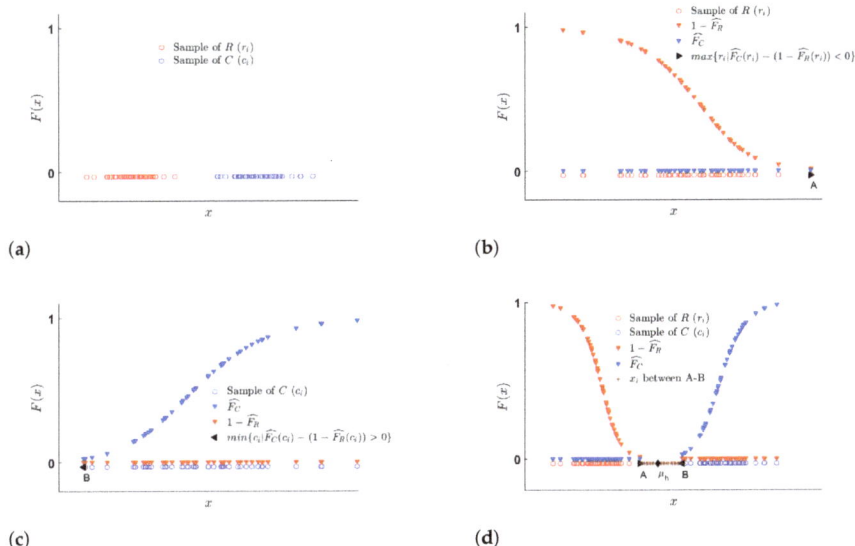

Figure 3. Procedure for identifying mean of Gaussian ISD (μ_h). (**a**) Scarce samples of R and C. (**b**) Finding point A using response sample r_i as per Step 4 in Algorithm 1. (**c**) Finding point B using capacity sample c_i as per Step 7 in Algorithm 1. (**d**) μ_h identified between points A and B as per Step 9 in Algorithm 1.

In very low failure probability estimation, the region corresponding to the estimation is quite small, and it has been observed that aspects such as non-uniqueness of MPP and non-linearity of the limit states have little effect on the estimation [5]. Similarly, we find that errors in the MPP estimation have lesser effect on the reliability estimation compared to a poor choice of standard deviation.

The standard deviation of the ISD determines the importance ascribed to region around the MPP during sampling. The region of sampling itself could be bounded by the supports of capacity and response distributions. Different measures of spread could be applied based on the available knowledge. In this work, a 10% coefficient of variation (CoV) was used to calculate the standard deviation of the ISD to investigate the effect. Such a measure was found to be suitable for scarce samples of normally distributed capacity and response. Different measures of spread were investigated while testing the formulation on samples simulated to be belonging to a different distribution. The spread parameter obtained through Equation (8) was found to be appropriate as such a measure allows one to restrict 68% percent of importance sample realizations within the means of capacity and response.

$$\sigma_h = \frac{\bar{x}_C - \bar{x}_R}{2} \quad (8)$$

where $\bar{x}_C$ is the sample mean of capacity, and $\bar{x}_R$ is the sample mean of the response.

4. Estimation of Reliability and Its Confidence Bounds

$$\widehat{p_f} = \sum_{i=1}^{N} \frac{\widehat{F_C}(x_i)\widehat{f_R}(x_i)}{h_x(x_i)}, \quad x_i \sim h_x : \mathcal{N}(\mu_h, \sigma_h^2) \quad (9)$$

Using the now defined ISD, sample points are drawn at which the PDF of response and CDF of capacity are obtained to be used in the computation of failure probability as per Equation (6). However, instead of the actual values, approximations $\widehat{F_C}(x_i)$, $\widehat{f_R}(x_i)$ are used during the computation as presented in Equation (9). As mentioned earlier, TPNT is used to approximate CDF ($\widehat{F_C}$), whereas for PDF approximation ($\widehat{f_R}$) an adaptive kernel density estimation method is employed. Both of these methods are distribution-free methods; however, other suitable methods of approximation [46,47] can also be used. Despite the accuracy of the method chosen, errors from the approximations are bound to result in loss of accuracy in the failure probability estimate. Hence, it becomes necessary to quantify the confidence on the estimate. Here, confidence bounds on the estimate are computed using a non-parametric bootstrap method.

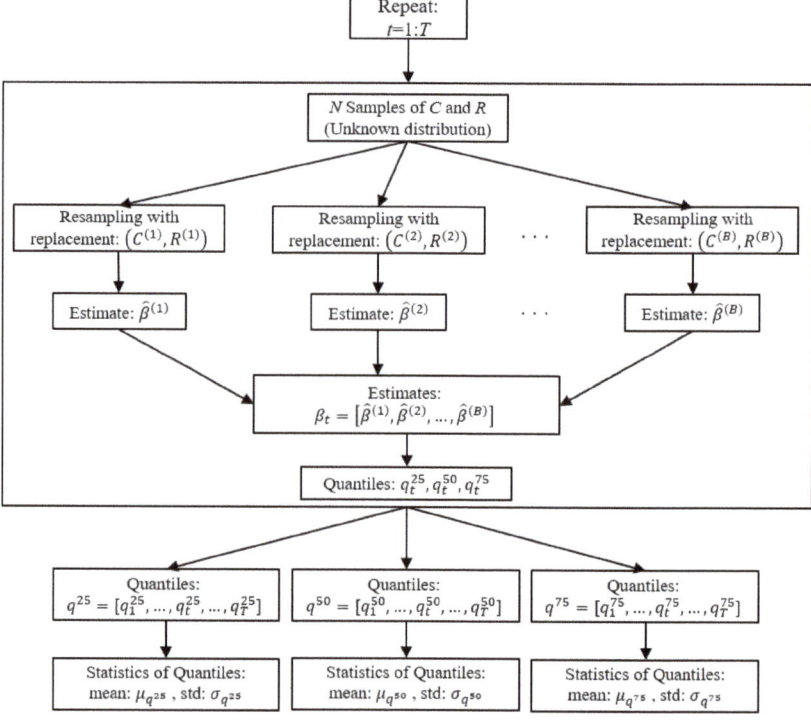

Figure 4. Schematic representation of bootstrapping.

The underlying idea of a non-parametric bootstrap method is to recreate samples from the original sample by sampling with the replacement. The sample size of bootstrap samples must be the same as the original sample. From each of the bootstrap samples, a statistical quantity of interest (such as failure probability) can be estimated. By repeating the process many times (say B times), one can obtain a distribution around the estimate from the original sample. In the current work, the proposed approach is applied to the bootstrap samples of C and R to obtain confidence bounds on the reliability estimate. Since the original samples of C and R are themselves scarce, this process of bootstrapping is repeated for T ($=100$) original samples of C and R. Thus, the quantiles of $\hat{\beta}$ obtained from T ($=100$) iterations are compared with mean and standard deviation of quantiles of $\hat{\beta}_{boot}$ from the bootstrap samples. Figure 4 presents a schematic representation of the bootstrapping procedure followed in the current work.

In order to test the efficacy of the formulation, different tails for capacity and response were considered. To simulate samples of response and capacity belonging to different tail types, generalized extreme value (GEV) distribution is used which takes the shape parameter (ξ) as an input along with location (θ) and scale (σ) parameters. Shape parameter or tail index is a measure of heaviness of tails of a distribution. In GEV distributions, the shape parameter affects the lower-tail and upper-tail differently. In this study, the parameters are chosen such that response distributions are positively skewed, while capacity distributions are negatively skewed to better simulate the difficulties of sampling in tails. Individually, the shape parameters (ξ_r, ξ_c) correspond to three types of tail heaviness: heavy, medium and light. Here, tail heaviness is considered for the upper-tail of R and the lower-tail of C. The location parameter of the capacity distribution (θ_c) is changed while keeping the response location (θ_r) stationary so that each combination corresponds to a failure probability of 10^{-4}. Nine study cases result because of the different combination of tails possible for both R and C. The parameters for the nine study cases are presented in Table 1. The distribution parameters are only utilized to generate scarce samples of R and C. It is to be noted that the GEV distributions used here are continuous over the real line ($\mathbb{R}$) and can have negative values. Though this does not reflect the real-world scenario, it does not deter in evaluating the performance of the proposed formulation.

Table 1. GEV distributions parameters of R and C for nine study cases.

Response Tail	$\xi_r, \theta_r, \sigma_r$	Capacity Tail	$\xi_c, \theta_c, \sigma_c$
Heavy	$(0.2, 1, 0)$	Heavy	$(-1.8, 1, 33.5)$
		Medium	$(-1, 1, 26.5)$
		Light	$(-0.52, 1, 26.2)$
Medium	$(0, 1, 0)$	Heavy	$(-1.8, 1, 30)$
		Medium	$(-1, 1, 10.7)$
		Light	$(-0.52, 1, 9.5)$
Light	$(-0.12, 1, 0)$	Heavy	$(-1.8, 1, 30)$
		Medium	$(-1, 1, 9.4)$
		Light	$(-0.52, 1, 6.4)$

To capture sampling variability, multiple iterations are carried out, and the procedure employed for identifying the variability in the estimates and bootstrap bounds is presented in Algorithm 2.

Algorithm 2 Confidence bounds using bootstrap.

1: **for** $j = 1, 2, \ldots, T$ **do**
2:    $\mathbf{r}_{j \times M} \sim GEV(\xi_r, \theta_r, \sigma_r)$, $\mathbf{c}_{j \times N} \sim GEV(\xi_c, \theta_c, \sigma_c)$ ← Generate samples of response and capacity.
3:    $\widehat{p_{f_j}}$ ← Estimate failure probability by applying proposed approach to samples $\mathbf{r}_{j \times M}$ and $\mathbf{c}_{j \times N}$.
4:    **for** $i = 1, 2, \ldots, B$ **do**
5:        $\mathbf{rb}_{i \times M}, \mathbf{cb}_{i \times N}$ ← Generate bootstrap samples from original samples $\mathbf{r}_{j \times M}$ and $\mathbf{c}_{j \times N}$.
6:        $\widehat{p_{fb_j}}$ ← Estimate failure probability by applying proposed approach to bootstrap samples $\mathbf{rb}_{i \times M}$ and $\mathbf{cb}_{i \times N}$.
7: 25th, 50th, 75th percentiles ← $\{\widehat{p_f}\}_{T \times 1}$.
8: 25th$_{1 \times T}$, 50th$_{1 \times T}$, 75th$_{1 \times T}$ percentiles ← $\{\widehat{p_{fb}}\}_{B \times T}$.

$$\beta_{IS} = \Phi^{-1}(1 - \widehat{p_f}) \quad (10)$$

The failure probability estimates calculated through Algorithm 2 for each study case are converted into reliability indices using Equation (10). To facilitate comparison, the estimates are divided by the actual reliability index ($\beta_a = 3.71$). For all nine study cases, the sample size of response (M) and capacity (N) are considered to be 50. The results of applying the formulation to each study case are presented in Table 2. Values under the 'Original sample' column represent the percentiles of ratio of the estimates from the original samples (from Step 7 of Algorithm 2) repeated for T (=100) iterations. Mean and standard deviation of the percentiles (from Step 8 of Algorithm 2) from the bootstrap repetitions ($B = 100$) are presented under the 'Bootstrap' column. An accurate estimate of the reliability index would be indicated with a value of one, and high precision is indicated by low variability between the percentiles and low standard deviation in the bootstrap percentiles. It is observed that the estimation is poorer in the case of heavy-tailed response and medium-tailed capacity and heavy-tailed response and light-tailed capacity. In both these cases, the failure region is situated further into the tail of the heavy-tailed response where the scarce sample-based PDF estimation is prone to high errors. In many instances, the probability density drops to zero prematurely which results in overestimation of reliability.

Table 2. Both R and C unknown case: percentiles of β_{IS}/β_a.

		Heavy C		Medium C		Light C	
	Percentile	Original Sample	Bootstrap Mean (Std)	Original Sample	Bootstrap Mean (Std)	Original Sample	Bootstrap Mean (Std)
Heavy R	25th	0.96	1.10 (0.26)	1.21	1.42 (0.29)	1.79	2.08 (0.61)
	50th	1.06	1.17 (0.29)	1.50	1.54 (0.32)	2.13	2.46 (0.89)
	75th	1.22	1.36 (0.31)	1.76	1.77 (0.33)	2.59	3.08 (1.31)
Medium R	25th	0.93	1.03 (0.20)	0.85	0.95 (0.18)	1.01	1.09 (0.21)
	50th	1.02	1.09 (0.21)	0.97	1.01 (0.19)	1.13	1.20 (0.25)
	75th	1.18	1.25 (0.23)	1.08	1.14 (0.22)	1.30	1.40 (0.32)
Light R	25th	0.91	1.04 (0.23)	0.78	0.85 (0.14)	0.85	0.91 (0.12)
	50th	1.01	1.10 (0.25)	0.88	0.91 (0.14)	0.94	0.98 (0.13)
	75th	1.18	1.28 (0.26)	0.99	1.04 (0.17)	1.03	1.09 (0.18)

In certain reliability applications, either f_R or f_C is known, or it is easier to obtain samples from one of the distributions of R and C. The proposed method is tested for such scenarios where only one of the distributions is unknown, and during this exercise, the same combinations of tails for R and C are assumed. Tables 3 and 4 present the results for R unknown and C unknown cases, respectively, using the proposed approach. From Table 3, it is observed that both the accuracy and precision of the estimation improved for most of the tail combinations compared to both R and C unknown cases. In the case of heavy-tailed response and medium-tailed and light-tailed capacity, and in addition, medium-tailed response and light-tailed capacity, the bias in the estimate has increased. This is again due to the erroneous PDF estimation of heavier-tailed response distribution using a scarce sample. Lesser bias in both R and C unknown cases is due to the interaction between the PDF and CDF approximation.

In Table 4, larger errors are observed for heavy-tailed capacity and medium-tailed response and heavy-tailed capacity and light-tailed response. This suggests that estimating heavy-tailed distribution further into the tails results in larger errors; this is akin to the observations made for the R unknown case. Furthermore, the largest errors observed in the C unknown case are smaller compared to the largest errors from the R unknown case which suggests that TPNT is a better approximation for CDF of heavy tailed distributions compared to adaptive KDE used for PDF approximation. To demonstrate that this is indeed the case, the alternate form of the importance sampling estimator presented in Equation (7) is used for the R unknown scenario, wherein CDF of the response distribution is approximated instead of the PDF. Table 5 presents the results, from which it is observed that the bias has reduced compared to the PDF approximation-based estimation. However, this also results in underestimation of reliability in the case of light-tailed response and light-tailed capacity. This is a trade-off between the choice of adaptive-kernel-based PDF approximation and TPNT-based CDF approximation. From these observations, it can be surmised that it would be beneficial to know the heaviness of R and C so that appropriate estimator can be chosen based on the efficacy of the approximation methods available.

Table 3. R unknown case: failure probability estimated as per Equation (6); (PDF approximation of R): percentiles of β_{IS}/β_a.

		Heavy C		Medium C		Light C	
	Percentile	Original Sample	Bootstrap Mean (Std)	Original Sample	Bootstrap Mean (Std)	Original Sample	Bootstrap Mean (Std)
Heavy R	25th	1.02	1.02 (9×10^{-3})	1.67	1.71 (0.15)	3.16	3.63 (0.66)
	50th	1.03	1.03 (7×10^{-3})	1.78	1.72 (0.15)	3.64	3.67 (0.67)
	75th	1.04	1.04 (5×10^{-3})	1.81	1.79 (0.06)	4.00	4.09 (0.30)
Medium R	25th	0.99	0.99 (2×10^{-3})	1.02	1.03 (0.06)	1.25	1.32 (0.20)
	50th	1.00	1.00 (2×10^{-3})	1.05	1.04 (0.05)	1.37	1.34 (0.20)
	75th	1.00	1.00 (2×10^{-3})	1.08	1.07 (0.03)	1.45	1.51 (0.14)
Light R	25th	0.99	0.99 (2×10^{-3})	0.99	0.99 (0.02)	0.98	1.03 (0.10)
	50th	1.00	1.00 (2×10^{-3})	1.00	1.00 (0.02)	1.07	1.06 (0.10)
	75th	1.00	1.00 (2×10^{-3})	1.02	1.01 (0.02)	1.12	1.13 (0.07)

An additional observation is that for one (either R or C) unknown case, the bootstrap standard deviation is larger when the bias in the estimates from the original samples are larger and smaller for more accurate cases. Thus, in practice where there is no actual value to compare with, bootstrap standard deviation can be used to discern the accuracy of the estimate. However, this does not track well in the case of both R and C unknown.

Table 4. C unknown case: failure probability estimated as per Equation (6); (CDF approximation of C): percentiles of β_{ls}/β_a.

		Heavy C		Medium C		Light C	
	Percentile	Original Sample	Bootstrap Mean (Std)	Original Sample	Bootstrap Mean (Std)	Original Sample	Bootstrap Mean (Std)
Heavy R	25th	0.96	0.98 (0.10)	0.99	0.99 (6×10^{-3})	1.00	1.00 (2×10^{-3})
	50th	1.03	1.00 (0.08)	1.00	1.00 (3×10^{-3})	1.00	1.00 (2×10^{-3})
	75th	1.06	1.04 (0.05)	1.00	1.00 (2×10^{-3})	1.00	1.00 (2×10^{-3})
Medium R	25th	0.93	1.13 (0.31)	0.87	0.92 (0.12)	0.96	0.96 (0.05)
	50th	1.12	1.24 (0.35)	0.96	0.96 (0.11)	0.99	0.98 (0.04)
	75th	1.42	1.52 (0.33)	1.03	1.02 (0.07)	1.00	1.00 (0.02)
Light R	25th	0.91	1.05 (0.23)	0.82	0.90 (0.13)	0.87	0.89 (0.09)
	50th	1.03	1.12 (0.25)	0.93	0.95 (0.14)	0.94	0.94 (0.09)
	75th	1.20	1.29 (0.29)	1.03	1.06 (0.14)	1.00	0.99 (0.08)

Table 5. R unknown case: failure probability estimated as per Equation (7); (CDF approximation of R): percentiles of β_{ls}/β_a.

		Heavy C		Medium C		Light C	
	Percentile	Original Sample	Bootstrap Mean (Std)	Original Sample	Bootstrap Mean (Std)	Original Sample	Bootstrap Mean (Std)
Heavy R	25th	0.95	0.96 (0.09)	0.95	1.14 (0.29)	0.92	1.13 (0.31)
	50th	1.02	0.99 (0.07)	1.13	1.22 (0.31)	1.11	1.23 (0.35)
	75th	1.03	1.03 (0.02)	1.43	1.42 (0.30)	1.38	1.51 (0.41)
Medium R	25th	0.99	0.99 (0.02)	0.84	0.89 (0.12)	0.77	0.89 (0.18)
	50th	0.99	0.99 (0.01)	0.94	0.94 (0.11)	0.93	0.96 (0.20)
	75th	1.00	1.00 (2×10^{-3})	1.02	1.01 (0.09)	1.08	1.11 (0.21)
Light R	25th	0.99	0.99 (2×10^{-3})	0.91	0.93 (0.07)	0.79	0.84 (0.12)
	50th	1.00	1.00 (1×10^{-3})	0.97	0.96 (0.06)	0.87	0.90 (0.12)
	75th	1.00	1.00 (1×10^{-3})	1.00	0.99 (0.04)	0.99	0.98 (0.12)

Tail-Index Estimation

Estimation of tail index is sometimes part of the distribution identification process and in turn CDF estimation where methods such as Hill estimator [48], Pickands estimator, Generalized Pareto fits and others are applied. Hill estimator considers k upper order statistics from a sample to evaluate the tail heaviness. Equation (11) presents the estimator for a positive sample of size n with the order statistics, $X_{1,n} \leq X_{2,n} \leq \ldots X_{n,n}$.

$$H_{k,n} = \frac{1}{k} \sum_{i=0}^{k-1} \log \frac{X_{n-i,n}}{X_{n-k,n}} \qquad (11)$$

The estimate of tail heaviness is sensitive to the number of order statistics (k) used and shifting of sample. Different modifications that address such sensitivity issues exist in the literature [49,50]. As we only require comparing between tails of R and C, especially when they are very different, obtaining exact estimates is of low priority. Hence, a modified Hill estimator is used where the sample is mean-shifted, and k is considered to be 10%

of the sample size. For upper-tail estimation, the largest k values are used and for lower-tail estimation, the absolute values of the smallest k values are used. The Modified Hill estimator is applied to assess the tail-heaviness of upper-tail of response and lower-tail of capacity, and the sample with the heavier tail is chosen for CDF approximation, and thereby the appropriate form of the estimator is chosen for failure probability estimation.

In both unknown scenarios, the heavy-tailed R and the light-tailed C which showed the largest deviation from the actual value was chosen to test the tail index estimate-based improvement on the proposed formulation. Results presented in Table 6 show the use of tail index estimation improved the estimates. It is to be noted that the modified Hill estimator was successful in contrasting between heaviness of tails of R and C 81 out of 100 iterations.

Table 6. Heavy R and light C: Percentiles of β_{IS}/β_t from tail estimation-based improved formulation.

Percentile	Original Sample	Bootstrap Mean (Std)
25th	0.93	1.19 (0.39)
50th	1.12	1.32 (0.53)
75th	1.39	1.70 (1.02)

5. Reliability Estimation Examples

Based on the flowchart of the proposed approach in Figure 5, benchmark reliability estimation examples are tested in this section. In all examples, to account for sample variability 100 iterations are used with samples of size 50 for R and C in each iteration. For each iteration, bootstrap samples for R and C are generated 100 times.

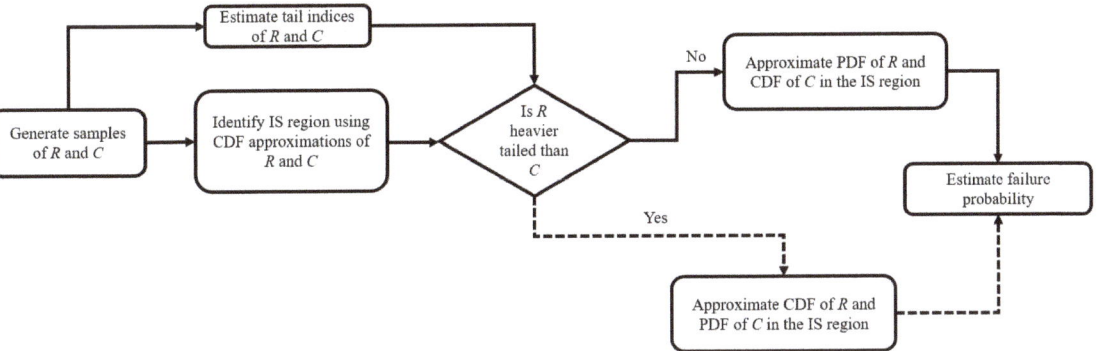

Figure 5. Flowchart representing failure probability estimation using proposed IS approach.

5.1. Example 1: Concave Limit State 1

This is a concave limit state example taken from [51].

$$G = 2.62 - u_2 - 0.15u_1^2 \qquad (12)$$

Both u_1 and u_2 are standard normal variables, and the concave limit state is of the separable form. Here, R is taken as $0.15u_1^2$, and C is taken as $2.62 - u_2$.

Table 7. Concave limit state-1: percentiles of β_{IS}/β_t for $\beta_t = 2.39$.

Percentile	Original Sample	Bootstrap Mean (Std)
25th	0.84	0.96 (0.20)
50th	0.96	1.03 (0.20)
75th	1.12	1.20 (0.22)

Note: β_t is computed through MCS with 10^8 samples.

From tail-index estimates in 88 out of 100 iterations, response R is determined to be heavier-tailed than C which is consistent with the analytical form of R and C. The response distribution resulting from squaring a standard normal variable is an χ^2-distribution with one degree of freedom. In this case, the χ^2-distribution has a heavier tail than the standard normal distribution.

Table 7 provides the results obtained for a target reliability $\beta_t = 2.39$. It is observed that the true value is contained within the percentile bounds (0.84–1.12) from the original sample estimates, and the bootstrap bounds obtained for each percentile also contain the true value. The variability of the estimates from the original sample is high, and the standard deviation computed from the bootstrap estimates is reflective of the variability presented in the original sample estimates.

5.2. Example 2: Concave Limit State 2

Example 2 is a concave limit state taken from [51].

$$G = u_1^2 - 5u_2^2 + 45 \tag{13}$$

Both u_1 and u_2 are standard normal variables, and the concave limit state is of the separable form where R is taken as $5u_2^2$ and C is taken as $u_1^2 + 45$.

Table 8 presents the numerical results obtained for this example by applying the proposed IS approach. From tail-index estimates, in 100 out of 100 iterations, response R is determined to be heavier-tailed than C. Here, both the response and capacity distributions resulting from squaring standard normal variables u_1 and u_2 are χ^2-distributions. However, the upper tail of response is heavier because scaling a χ^2-distribution results in an increase of tail heaviness.

Table 8. Concave limit state-2: percentiles of β_{IS}/β_t for $\beta_t = 2.82$.

Percentile	Original Sample	Bootstrap Mean (Std)
25th	0.82	0.89 (0.16)
50th	0.90	0.95 (0.16)
75th	1.02	1.08 (0.19)

Note: β_t is computed through MCS with 10^8 samples.

The percentiles of β_{IS}/β_t from the original samples show that the target value is contained within the first and third quartile bounds. For all the percentiles, it is observed that the bootstrap bounds also contain the target reliability.

5.3. Example 3: Roof Truss Example

This example is discussed as a case study for reliability estimation in [45]. The schematic in Figure 6 presents a roof truss subjected to a uniformly distributed load q which is transformed into the nodal load $P = \frac{ql}{4}$. Equation (14) presents the limit state constructed for perpendicular deflection Δ_C at node C as:

$$G(x) = 0.03 - \Delta_C \tag{14}$$

where

$$\Delta_C = \frac{ql^2}{2}\left(\frac{3.81}{A_c E_c} + \frac{1.13}{A_s E_s}\right) \qquad (15)$$

Here, A_c and A_s are areas of cross sections of the concrete reinforced bars and steel bars, respectively. Similarly, the variables E_c and E_s represent the moduli of elasticity, while l denotes the length. The input variables are considered to be mutually independent random variables, distributed normally. The parameters of their distributions are as presented in Table 9.

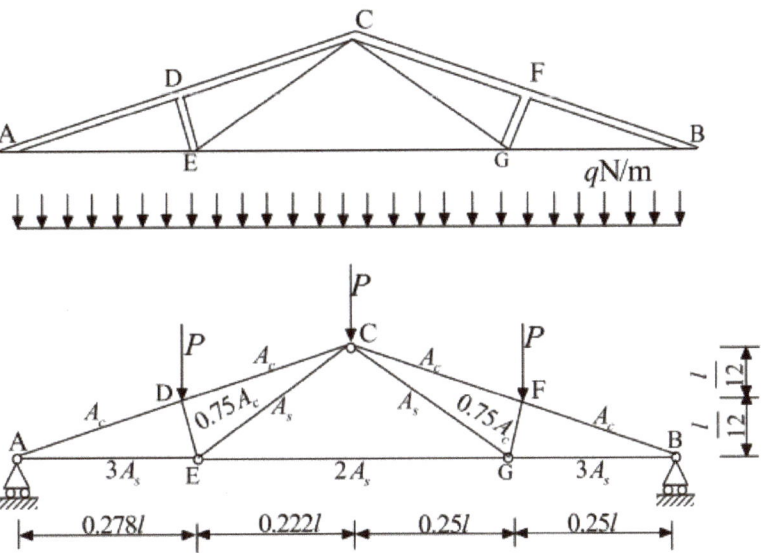

Figure 6. Schematic of roof truss.

Table 9. Mean and SD of random variables for roof truss example.

Random Variable	Mean (SD)
q (N/m)	20,000 (1600)
l (m)	12 (0.24)
A_s (m^2)	9.82×10^{-4} (5.89×10^{-5})
A_c (m^2)	0.04 (0.008)
E_s (N/m^2)	1.2×10^{11} (8.4×10^9)
E_c (N/m^2)	3×10^{10} (2.4×10^9)

The limit state is transformed into $G(C, R) = C - R$ form where $C = \frac{0.03}{q}$ and $R = \frac{\Delta_C}{q}$ becomes a function of five random variables that correspond to the geometry and material properties of the truss members.

Table 10 provides the estimates of reliability and the corresponding bootstrap bounds for a target reliability of $\beta_t = 3.4$. It is observed that at each of the percentiles, the bootstrap bound captures the target reliability. From tail-index estimates, in 77 out of 100 iterations, response R is determined to be heavier-tailed than C.

Table 10. Roof truss example: percentiles of β_{IS}/β_t for $\beta_t = 3.4$.

Percentile	Original Sample	Bootstrap Mean (Std)
25th	0.84	0.94 (0.17)
50th	0.94	1.02 (0.20)
75th	1.07	1.18 (0.29)

Note: β_t is computed through MCS with 10^8 samples.

5.4. Example 4: Propped Cantilever Beam Example

Figure 7 presents the schematic of the example which is taken from [52]. Equation (16) presents the original limit state for the maximum deflection of the beam v_{max} against the maximum allowable deflection v_{crit}:

$$G = v_{max} - v_{crit} \tag{16}$$

where deflection of the beam $v(x)$ is measured as per Equation (17), and for the considered loading condition, the maximum deflection (v_{max}) is obtained at $x = 0.5528L$.

$$v(x) = \frac{q_0 x^2}{120 L E I}(4L^3 - 8L^2 x - 5Lx^2 - x^3) \tag{17}$$

where

$$I = \frac{b_f d^3 - (b_f - t_w)(d - 2t_f)^3}{12} \tag{18}$$

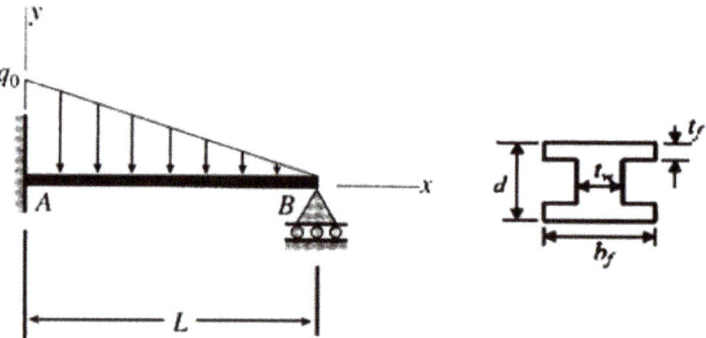

Figure 7. Propped cantilever beam with triangular distributed loading.

The limit state is modified to convert into $G(C,R) = C - R$ form, where $C(v_{crit}, E) = v_{crit}E$, and R is a function of remaining seven random variables. Mean and standard deviation (SD) of the normally distributed random variables is presented in Table 11. The critical displacement v_{crit} is changed between 4–5 mm to generate three target reliability situations.

Table 11. Mean and SD of random variables for propped cantilever beam example.

Random Variable	Mean (SD)
q_0 (kN/m)	20 (2)
L (m)	6 (0.3)
E (GPa)	210 (10)
d (cm)	25 (0.5)
b_f (cm)	25 (0.5)
t_w (cm)	2 (0.2)
t_f (cm)	2 (0.2)

Note: All random variables follow normal distribution.

Table 12 presents the results obtained from the proposed IS formulation for different target reliability indices (β_t). As the target reliability increases, the variability from both the original sample estimates and bootstrap sample estimates remain similar.

Table 12. Propped cantilever beam: percentiles of β_{IS}/β_t for different v_{crit} and β_t.

Percentiles	$v_{crit} = 4.0$ mm, $\beta_t = 2.98$		$v_{crit} = 4.5$ mm, $\beta_t = 3.50$		$v_{crit} = 5.0$ mm, $\beta_t = 3.97$	
	Original	Bootstrap Mean (Std)	Original	Bootstrap Mean (Std)	Original	Bootstrap Mean (Std)
25th	0.84	1.03 (0.30)	0.82	0.99 (0.27)	0.81	0.99 (0.30)
50th	0.99	1.13 (0.36)	0.99	1.09 (0.32)	0.96	1.12 (0.39)
75th	1.29	1.31 (0.42)	1.24	1.29 (0.44)	1.26	1.35 (0.52)

Note: β_t values are computed through MCS with 10^8 samples.

6. Application to RBDO Examples

The proposed importance sampling approach is demonstrated on two benchmark and two real-world RBDO examples. Algorithm 3 delineates the steps followed to perform RBDO using the proposed approach of reliability estimation. For the benchmark examples, efficiency between the proposed approach and a crude Monte Carlo approach is compared using the total number of limit state evaluations which is computed as $N_{doe} \times N_{is}$ for the proposed approach and $N_{doe} \times N_{mcs}$ for the MCS-based approach. For the real-world examples, MCS is used only to validate the optima obtained through the proposed approach.

Algorithm 3 RBDO using proposed importance sampling approach.

1: $\mathbf{d} = \{d_1, d_2, \ldots, d_{N_{doe}}\} \leftarrow$ Generate a design of experiment (DoE) in design variable space.
2: **for** $i = 1, 2, \ldots, N_{doe}$ **do**
3:     Propagate uncertainty at DoE points.
4:     $\mathbf{r}, \mathbf{c} \leftarrow$ Obtain response and capacity samples through simulations or physical experiments. In the examples, analytical functions are utilized.
5:     $\widehat{p_{f_i}} \leftarrow$ Apply proposed importance sampling formulation to samples $\mathbf{r}, \mathbf{c}$.
6:     $\beta_{IS_i} \leftarrow$ Transform failure probability to reliability index using (10).
7: $\widehat{fi_{IS}} \leftarrow$ Construct surrogate model for reliability index using $\{\beta_{IS_i}\}$ and $\mathbf{d}$.
8: $d^* \leftarrow$ Optimization using $\widehat{fi_{IS}}$ for evaluation of reliability constraint.

6.1. Cantilever Beam Example

This is a standard RBDO example taken from [53]. In this example, the weight of a cantilever beam (shown in Figure 8) is minimized while considering two failure modes:

bending stress does not exceed yield strength (19) and the tip displacement does not exceed the allowable displacement limit of 2.5 in (20).

$$G_s = \sigma_y - \frac{6L}{wt}\left(\frac{X}{w} + \frac{Y}{t}\right) \tag{19}$$

$$G_d = D_0 - \frac{4L^3}{Ewt}\sqrt{\left(\frac{Y}{t^2}\right)^2 + \left(\frac{X}{w^2}\right)^2} \tag{20}$$

The length of the beam (L) and the density are held constant, while the width (w) and thickness (t) of the beam are allowed to change which transforms the objective function from weight to area of cross section, $A = wt$. The horizontal (X) and vertical (Y) loads along with modulus of elasticity (E) are random variables whose uncertainty characteristics are presented in Table 13.

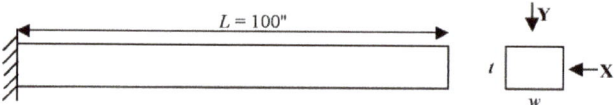

Figure 8. Cantilever beam under horizontal and vertical loads.

Table 13. Random variables for cantilever beam example.

Random Variable	Mean (SD)
X (lb)	500 (100)
Y (lb)	10^3 (100)
σ_y (psi)	4×10^4 (2×10^3)
E (psi)	2.9×10^7 (1.45×10^6)

Note: All random variables follow normal distribution.

RBDO of the cantilever beam requires that the failure probability of both the limits states does not exceed 1.35×10^{-3} which translates to a target reliability index $\beta_t \geq 3$. Thus, the optimization is formulated as:

$$\begin{aligned} \min_{w,t} \quad & A = wt \\ \text{s.t.} \quad & g1 = \Phi^{-1}(1 - Pr(G_s \leq 0)) \geq 3 \\ & g2 = \Phi^{-1}(1 - Pr(G_d \leq 0)) \geq 3 \end{aligned} \tag{21}$$

As stated in Algorithm 3, a DoE of size ($N_{doe} = 40$) is created in $d = (w, t)$ space using latin hypercube sampling (LHS). Additionally, four corner points are added to the DoE. At each design point (d_i), samples of response and capacity for both limit states are obtained by simulating uncertainty as per Table 13, considering a sample size of $N_{is} = 50$. For limit state G_s, σ_y is considered as capacity, while the rest of the equation is considered as a response. Similarly, for limit state G_d, $D_0 \times E$ is taken as capacity by regrouping the random variables in the limit state function to convert it into a separable form [54]. Using these samples, failure probability estimates for both limit states are obtained through the proposed approach. A surrogate model for reliability index β is constructed, and this surrogate is used for constraint evaluation during optimization.

In a similar fashion, MCS-based failure probability estimates are also obtained at the design points using samples of size $N_{mcs} = 10^6$. A surrogate model using the MCS estimates is constructed for a reliability index, and optimization is carried out. At design points that are closer to the lower and upper bounds, failure probability estimates could be either zeros or ones. These estimates when converted into reliability indices become $-\infty$

and ∞; hence, these are modified during surrogate construction. These singularities are more common in the case of MCS estimation compared to IS estimation.

The optima obtained from both MCS and IS are compared in Table 14. As the cost of the knowledge of random variables is not quantified, computational cost is only compared with MCS. Additionally, different surrogate choices, such as PRS, RBF, Kriging and weighted average surrogate (WAS), were considered for $\hat{f}_i$ construction, and the optima obtained by using WAS model are presented. The accuracy of the surrogate for both constraints is evaluated using a generalized mean square error (GMSE) metric. GMSE for constraint g_1 using IS-based estimates is reported as 0.91 (mean of reliability estimates = 2.21), whereas the error from the MCS-based surrogate is 0.09 (mean of reliability estimates = 1.97). For constraint g_2, GMSE (vs. mean) is reported as 0.70 (vs. 1.98) for the IS surrogate and 0.12 (vs. 1.41) for the MCS surrogate.

To validate the results, at the optima, a reliability index is calculated using MCS with sample size of 10^7 which is also presented in the Table 14. It is observed that the surrogate from IS estimates has less global accuracy. However, reliability indices obtained at the optima using MCS (β_{MCS} at d^*) suggest that the surrogate is reasonably approximated at the constraint boundaries. The optima obtained from IS and MCS are very close, but the computational savings are hugely in favour of IS (50 vs. 10^6).

Table 14. RBDO results of cantilever beam example.

Surrogate Model for β Constraints	Reliability Estimation	Optima (d^*)		Objective Function Value	$\hat{\beta}$ at d^*		β_{MCS} at d^*	
		w (in)	t (in)	A (in^2)	g_1	g_2	g_1	g_2
WAS	IS	2.59	3.74	9.69	3.00	3.64	3.25	3.69
	MCS	2.59	3.66	9.50	3.00	3.44	2.95	3.39

6.2. Bracket Structure Example

This is originally from [55] where a bracket structure is subjected to a tip load (P) in addition to its own weight due to gravity (g) as presented in Figure 9. The weight of the bracket structure is optimized while considering two failure modes:

(i) Maximum bending stress of beam CD at point B (σ_B) does not exceed its yield strength (f_y),
(ii) Maximum axial load on beam AB (F_{AB}) does not exceed the Euler critical buckling load ($F_{buckling}$).

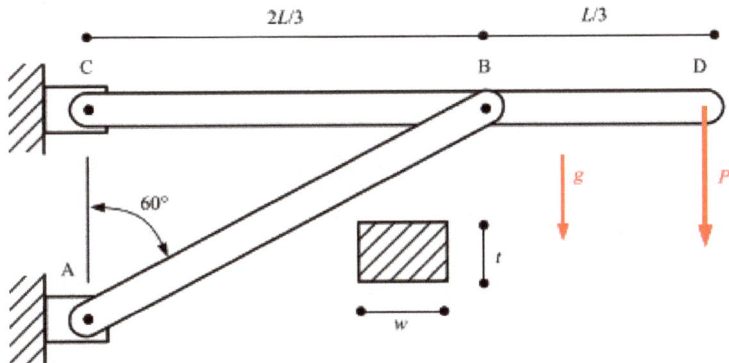

Figure 9. Bracket structure subjected to a tip load.

Equations (22) and (23) present the limit states as:

$$G_{CD} = f_y - \sigma_B, \quad \text{where} \tag{22a}$$

$$\sigma_B = \frac{6M_B}{w_{CD} t^2} \tag{22b}$$

$$M_B = \frac{PL}{3} + \frac{\rho g w_{CD} t L^2}{18} \tag{22c}$$

$$G_{AB} = F_{buckling} - F_{AB}, \quad \text{where} \tag{23a}$$

$$F_{buckling} = \frac{\pi^2 E t w_{AB}^3 9 \sin \theta^2}{48 L^2} \tag{23b}$$

$$F_{AB} = \frac{1}{\cos \theta} \left(\frac{3P}{2} + \frac{3\rho g w_{CD} t L}{4} \right) \tag{23c}$$

During RBDO of the bracket structure, the target reliability index for both limit states is $\beta \geq 2$, and the design parameters are means of the geometrical parameters of the structure: width of CD ($\mu_{w_{CD}}$), width of AB ($\mu_{w_{AB}}$) and thickness of AB and CD (μ_t) which are bounded between 50 mm and 300 mm. The uncertainty characteristics of the random variables is presented in Table 15. Thus, the RBDO is formulated as:

$$\min_{w_{CD}, w_{AB}, t} C = \mu_\rho \mu_t \mu_L \left(\frac{4\sqrt{3}}{9} \mu_{w_{AB}} + \mu_{w_{CD}} \right)$$

$$\text{s.t.} \quad g1 = \Phi^{-1}(1 - Pr(G_{CD} \leq 0)) \geq 2 \tag{24}$$

$$g2 = \Phi^{-1}(1 - Pr(G_{AB} \leq 0)) \geq 2$$

$$50 \leq \mu_{w_{CD}}, \mu_{w_{AB}}, \mu_t \leq 300 \text{ (in mm)}$$

Table 15. Random variables for bracket structure example.

Type	Variable	Distribution	Mean	C.o.V
Random	P (kN)	Gumbel	100	15%
	E (GPa)	Gumbel	200	8%
	f_y (MPa)	Lognormal	225	8%
	ρ (kg·m^{-3})	Weibull	7860	10%
	L (m)	Gaussian	5	5%
Design	w_{AB} (mm)	Gaussian	$\mu_{w_{AB}}$	5%
	w_{CD} (mm)	Gaussian	$\mu_{w_{CD}}$	5%
	t (mm)	Gaussian	μ_t	5%

The steps enumerated in Algorithm 3 are followed using a DoE of size ($N_{doe} = 60$), and scarce sample sizes of R and C during the IS approach are considered as $N_{is} = 75$, while $N_{mcs} = 10^6$ realizations are used in MCS. The RBDO results are presented in Table 16 which has the same format as the first example. GMSE (vs. mean) for constraint g_1 using IS-based estimates is reported as 0.58 (1.37), whereas the error from the MCS-based surrogate is 0.24 (1.02). For constraint g_2, GMSE (vs. mean) is reported as 0.97 (vs. 3.72) for the IS surrogate and 0.30 (vs. 3.08) for the MCS surrogate. It is observed that the IS estimate-based surrogate has less global accuracy; however, the MCS-based reliability indices computed at the optima show that it approximates reasonably well near the constraint boundaries. It is to be noted that in both engineering examples, we assume that both R and C are unknown. Any knowledge of the uncertainty characteristics of either R or C will only improve the accuracy of the reliability estimates.

Table 16. RBDO results of bracket structure example.

Surrogate Model for β Constraints	Reliability Estimation	Optima (d^*)			Objective Function Value	$\hat{\beta}$ at d^*		β_{MCS} at d^*	
		w_{AB} (mm)	w_{CD} (mm)	t (mm)	Weight (kg)	g_1	g_2	g_1	g_2
WAS	IS	58	89	300	1576	2.00	2.00	2.59	2.87
	MCS	62	77	300	1474	2.00	2.00	2.02	3.55

6.3. Torque Arm Example

This example presents RBDO of torque arm where the mass of the component is to be minimized adhering to a probabilistic constraint on the allowable stress. Unlike previous examples, there is no analytical expression available for limit state evaluation in this case. It is a shape optimization problem originally from Bennett and Botkin [56]. Researchers have used it as a benchmark example for reliability estimation [52,57]. Rahman and Wei [58] perform RBDO where a constant allowable stress limit is considered.

In the current study, seven design variables (see Figure 10) as per [59] are considered for altering the shape of the torque arm. Figure 11 presents the base design of the torque arm around which the optimization is to be performed. Here, a horizontal load ($F_x = -2789$ N) and a vertical load ($F_y = 5066$ N) are applied at the right hole while the left hole is fixed. The torque arm has modulus of elasticity $E = 207 \times 10^5$ N·cm^{-2}, density $\rho = 7.850 \times 10^{-3}$ kg·cm^{-3} and Poisson's ratio $\nu = 0.3$.

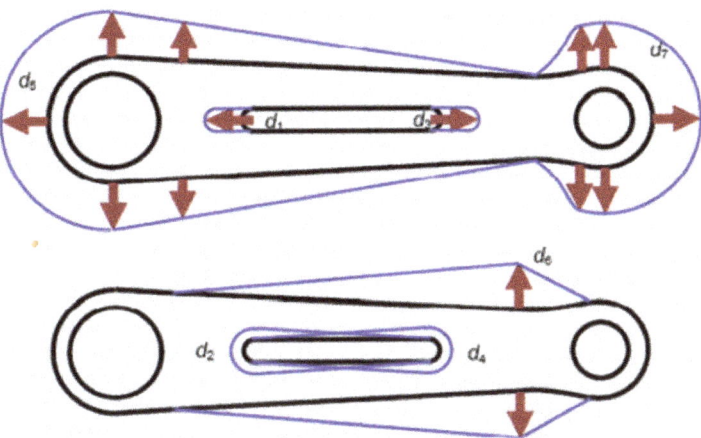

Figure 10. Design variables used to modify the shape of the torque arm [59].

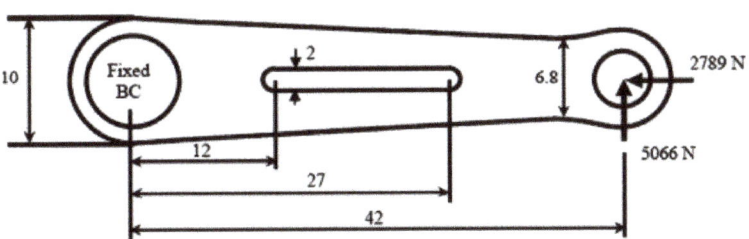

Figure 11. Loading and boundary conditions with base design parameter values (in cm) [59].

Equation (25) presents the limit state equation for the torque arm.

$$G = \sigma_{max}(d_i, F_x, F_y) - \sigma_{all} \tag{25}$$

where σ_{max} is the maximum von Mises stress developed in the torque arm, and σ_{all} is the allowable stress limit. Since there is no analytical expression that relates the design variables with the response σ_{max}, finite-element analysis is used to compute the stresses developed in the torque arm for a given loading condition. A MATLAB finite-element toolbox developed by CALFEM [60] is used for this purpose. The thickness of the finite-elements in the mesh is considered to be 0.3 cm. At the end of each finite-element analysis, the maximum of the stresses is used as σ_{max} in Equation (25).

For RBDO, the design variables (d_1 to d_7), loads (F_x and F_y) and the allowable stress (σ_{all}) are considered to be uncertain. Each design point (d_i) is considered to be normally distributed about itself with a coefficient of variation of 10%. The uncertainty characteristics of the remaining random variables is presented in Table 17.

Table 17. Mean and SD of random variables in torque arm example.

Random Variable	Distribution Type	Mean; SD
F_x (N)	Normal	−2789; 278.9
F_y (N)	Normal	5066; 506.6
σ_{all} (MPa)	Lognormal	800; 80

Equation (26) presents the RBDO formulation of the torque arm where a target reliability index of three is considered.

$$\begin{aligned} \min_{\{d_1,\ldots,d_7\}} \quad & Mass \\ \text{s.t.} \quad & g = \Phi^{-1}(1 - Pr(G \leq 0)) \geq 3 \end{aligned} \tag{26}$$

As per Algorithm 3, a DoE of size ($N_{doe} = 200$) is generated where reliability is estimated using an IS approach. Sample sizes of $R = \sigma_{max}$ and $C = \sigma_{all}$ during IS approach are considered as $N_{is} = 100$. An RBF-based surrogate is constructed using IS-based reliability estimates. The error (GMSE vs. range) for the RBF surrogate of β is found to be 6% which indicates a good fit. This surrogate is used for constraint (g) evaluation during optimization.

The stress contour of the torque arm design obtained as a result of the optimization is presented in Figure 12. Here, mean values for design parameters and mean loading condition are considered. The maximum von Mises stress is observed to be 523.92 MPa for the optimum design. The optimal mass of the torque arm is 0.801 kg. It can be observed that the mass is distributed to meet the target reliability. An MCS (with 10^5 sample size) is used to validate the reliability of RBDO optima obtained from the IS approach, and it is observed that $\beta_{MCS} = 3.00$. For the Monte Carlo simulation of 10^5 simulations, it took 8.7 h using parallel computing toolbox of MATLAB on a system with the following specifications: Intel Xeon 10 Core 2.20 GHz 64 bit processor, with 32GB RAM. Table 18 presents the design variable bounds and the optimum design obtained from RBDO.

Though the errors in the individual reliability estimations are quantified via bootstrap, they were not propagated into the surrogate model during RBDO. Using the surrogate model for reliability index evaluation instead of direct evaluation enabled the smoothing of noise from the IS-based estimation which leads to better convergence during optimization. From MCS validation at the optima, it is observed that the proposed approach results in heavier but safer designs. Further analysis is required to understand the error propagation from different stages of the proposed approach.

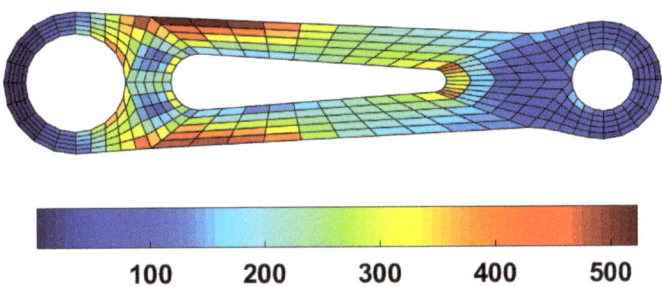

Figure 12. Stress (von Mises stress in MPa) contour of optimum design with mean design parameters (d^*) and loading condition of $F_x = -2789$ N and $F_y = 5066$ N.

Table 18. Design variable bounds and optimum design of torque arm (in cm).

DV	d_L	d_U	d^* (Optimum)
d_1	1.80	3.20	2.15
d_2	1.25	1.60	1.28
d_3	1.20	4.60	1.59
d_4	−0.10	0.40	−0.09
d_5	−0.30	0.30	0.30
d_6	−0.90	0.80	0.30
d_7	0.40	1.80	0.54

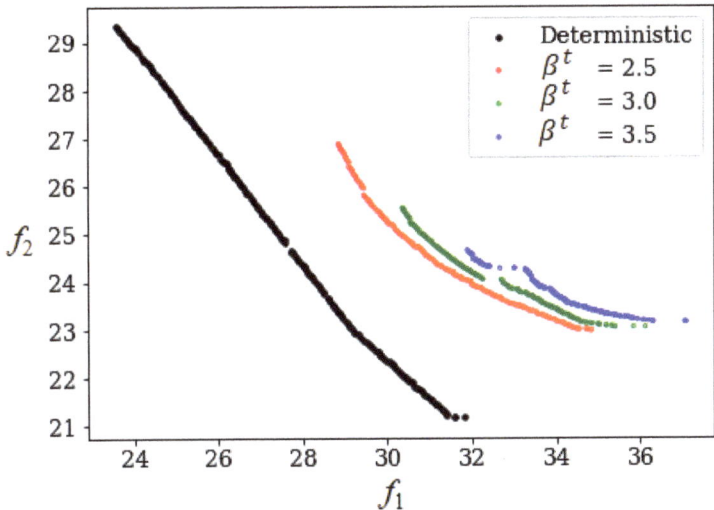

Figure 13. Pareto optimal front corresponding to different values of reliability index estimated through polynomial response surface (PRS).

6.4. Car Side-Impact Problem—A Multi-Objective Reliability-Based Design Optimization (MORBDO) Example

We demonstrate the proposed methodology on an MORBDO example taken from [61]. In this example, the objective is to minimize the weight (f_1) of a car as well as the average rib deflection (f_2) during a crash. A car is subjected to a side-impact based on European Enhanced Vehicle-Safety Committee (EEVC) procedures. The effect of the side-impact on a dummy in terms of head injury criteria, load in the abdomen, pubic symphysis force, viscous criterion, and rib deflections at the upper, middle and lower rib locations are considered as constraints. The MORBDO formulation is made up of seven uncertain design variables $(x_1, \ldots, x_7)$ and four random variables $(p_1, \ldots, p_4)$. Equation (27) presents the optimization formulation of the car side-impact problem:

$$\min_{\mu_x} \quad f_1 = f(\mu_x, \mu_p)$$
$$\min_{\mu_x} \quad f_2 = \frac{g_2(\mu_x, \mu_p) + g_3(\mu_x, \mu_p) + g_4(\mu_x, \mu_p)}{3} \quad (27)$$
$$\text{s.t.} \quad \Phi^{-1}\left(1 - \Pr(g_i(\mathbf{x},\mathbf{p})) \leq b_i\right) \geq \beta_t,$$
$$i = 1, \ldots, 10.$$

where

$g_1(\mathbf{x},\mathbf{p}) \equiv$ Abdomen load ≤ 1 kN
$g_2(\mathbf{x},\mathbf{p}) \equiv$ Upper rib deflection ≤ 32 mm
$g_3(\mathbf{x},\mathbf{p}) \equiv$ Middle rib deflection ≤ 32 mm
$g_4(\mathbf{x},\mathbf{p}) \equiv$ Lower rib deflection ≤ 32 mm
$g_5(\mathbf{x},\mathbf{p}) \equiv$ Upper viscous criteria ≤ 0.32 m/s
$g_6(\mathbf{x},\mathbf{p}) \equiv$ Middle viscous criteria ≤ 0.32 m/s
$g_7(\mathbf{x},\mathbf{p}) \equiv$ Lower viscous criteria ≤ 0.32 m/s
$g_8(\mathbf{x},\mathbf{p}) \equiv$ Pubic symphysis force ≤ 4.0 kN
$g_9(\mathbf{x},\mathbf{p}) \equiv$ Velocity of B-pillar at middle point
≤ 10 mm/ms
$g_{10}(\mathbf{x},\mathbf{p}) \equiv$ Velocity of front door at B-pillar
≤ 15.7 mm/ms;

$1.0 \leq x_1 \leq 1.5, 0.45 \leq x_2 \leq 1.0, 0.5 \leq x_3 \leq 1.5,$
$0.5 \leq x_4 \leq 1.5, 0.875 \leq x_5 \leq 2.625, 0.4 \leq x_6 \leq 1.2,$
$0.4 \leq x_7 \leq 1.2, \mu_{p_1} = 0.345, \mu_{p_2} = 0.192, \mu_{p_3} = \mu_{p_4} = 0.$

Analytical expressions of the objective functions and constraints as well as the physical descriptions of the design variables $(x_1 - x_7)$, and random variables $(p_1 - p_4)$ are presented in Appendix C.

In order to solve the MORBDO problem as per Algorithm 3, a DoE of size $(N_{doe} = 200)$ is generated within the design bounds where reliability of the ten constraints $(g_1, \ldots, g_{10})$ is estimated using the IS approach. In this example, the number of design variables is seven; hence, $2^7 = 128$ corner points have been sampled. Next, we performed a space-filling sampling using LHS. In each dimension, we sampled 10 points (in total $7 \times 10 = 70$) using LHS design as per a thumb rule in DoE sampling [62]. Without loss of generalization, we added two to make a round sampling number. Sample sizes of response and capacity during IS are considered as $N_{is} = 50$. PRS surrogate for reliability indices of the ten constraints is constructed using the IS-based estimates. In order to improve the surrogate accuracy, an additional DoE of size 200 is generated within adjusted design bounds. The final surrogate errors (GMSE vs. range) for all constraints is found to range between 3.76% and 8.38%. Using these surrogates for constraint evaluation, the MOO problem presented in Equation (27) is solved using NSGA-II [63].

The Pareto optimal front corresponding to the different target reliability indices $(\beta^t = [2.5, 3.0, 3.5])$ along with the deterministic Pareto optimal front is presented in

Figure 13. The NSGA-II algorithm is applied for the four instances using the population size of 200 for 100 generations. The GA uses the following parameters: number of offspring is 50, probability (p_c) of simulated binary crossover (SBX) is 0.9, crossover parameter (η_c) is 20, probability of mutation (p_m) is 0.9, and the mutation parameter (η_m) is 50.

It is evident from Figure 13 that as the targeted reliability increases, the respective reliable Pareto optimal front shifts inside the feasible criterion space and away from the deterministic Pareto optimal front to ensure more reliable solutions. The Pareto solutions were further validated using MCS ($N_{mcs} = 10^6$), and all the solutions were found to meet the target reliability.

7. Conclusions

A scarce sample-based importance sampling approach to estimate reliability is proposed when there is little or no information about the uncertainty characteristics of the random variables involved. The proposed formulation was tested on different tail heaviness for R and C distributions. In the case of one of the distributions being heavy-tailed, a tail-index estimate-based improvement to choose between PDF and CDF approximation was employed and shown to improve the accuracy (50th percentile by 1.9 times). Confidence bounds on the reliability estimate obtained through the bootstrap procedure have been shown to be indicative of the accuracy of the estimate. The proposed IS approach has been applied for reliability estimation and RBDO examples and found to be effective in terms of computational savings ($50 \times 44 = 2200$ for cantilever beam and $75 \times 60 = 4500$ for bracket structure example) as compared to MCS where the sample size for each reliability estimate was 10^6. The approach is demonstrated on a non-analytical RBDO example which yielded a design that met the target reliability index (validated by MCS). The proposed approach has also been demonstrated on the car side-impact problem which is a multi-objective reliability-based design optimization example.

While the tail-index estimate-based alternative reduces the errors from the approximation, establishing the superiority of CDF approximation versus PDF approximation was only achieved through post-analysis of results for the specific methods used in this work. Future work could include incorporating region-wise best methods for both PDF and CDF approximation, using a suite of methods assessed through cross-validation errors. Active learning approaches could be employed during optimization to further reduce the number of design points, thereby reducing the number of reliability estimations required to obtain the optima.

Author Contributions: Conceptualization, K.P. and P.R.; investigation, K.P. and D.Y.; methodology, K.P. and P.R.; supervision, P.R.; validation, K.P. and D.Y.; writing—original draft, K.P.; writing—review and editing, K.P., D.Y. and P.R. All authors have read and agreed to the published version of the manuscript.

Funding: This research received no external funding.

Data Availability Statement: MATLAB® codes used to generate the results shall be provided upon request.

Conflicts of Interest: The authors declare that they have no conflict of interest.

Appendix A. Kernel Density Estimation (KDE)

Let $(x_1, x_2, ..., x_n)$ be an i.i.d. sample from a distribution with a PDF (f), then the kernel density estimate of f is given as

$$\hat{f}_h(x) = \frac{1}{nh} \sum_{i=1}^{n} K\left(\frac{x - x_i}{h}\right) \tag{A1}$$

where h is a smoothing parameter called bandwidth, n is the sample size, and $K(.)$ is a kernel, which is non-negative, integrates to one and is centered at zero. Different kernel functions can be used, such as normal, uniform, Epanechnikov, triangle and others, and the bandwidth is selected based on the sample data chosen. The choice of the bandwidth influences the variance and the bias of the estimator. The performance of the kernel density estimator is more dependent on the choice of the bandwidth rather than kernel choice. Despite being the most popular non-parametric approach to density estimation, there are some implementation issues, such as bandwidth selection, local adaptivity and boundary bias. While KDE works well for data following a normal distribution, it performs poorly while estimating heavy-tailed distributions, especially in the tail region which is our region of interest, hence adaptive KDE proposed by [64] is chosen. The Matlab® implementation of adaptive KDE for 1D [65] was employed in the current work for PDF approximation.

Appendix B. Third-Order Polynomial Normal Transformation Technique (TPNT)

Hong and Lind [66] proposed this method of approximating a CDF where given the order statistics $\zeta_1 \leq \zeta_2 \leq \ldots \leq \zeta_N$ obtained from a sample realization of a random variable Z, through "sample rule" the fractiles are constrained in the following manner:

$$\{\zeta_i, F_Z(\zeta_i)\} = \{\zeta_i, \frac{i}{N+1}\}, \quad i = 1, 2, \ldots, N \tag{A2}$$

where $F_Z(.)$ is the cumulative distribution function of Z. In this method, a third-order polynomial relationship between ζ and a normal transformation of $F_Z(\zeta)$ is assumed as presented in Equation (A3)

$$\zeta = \sum_{k=0}^{3} a_k \eta^k \tag{A3}$$

where

$$\eta = \Phi^{-1}(F_Z(\zeta)) \tag{A4}$$

Here, $\Phi^{-1}(.)$ is the inverse of the standard normal distribution function. The coefficients of the polynomial in Equation (A3) are found through least squares minimization of the error, ε:

$$\varepsilon = \sum_{j \in J_s} \left(\zeta_j - \sum_{k=0}^{3} a_k (\eta_j)^k\right) \tag{A5}$$

where J_s is a set of data points chosen for the parameter estimation which is usually the same as sample size N. Two constraints $a_2^2 - 3a_1 a_3 > 0$, $a_3 > 0$ are imposed to ensure monotonicity in the third-order polynomial curve.

At a new fractile ζ_0, the probability $F_Z(\zeta_0)$ is determined through $\Phi(\eta_0)$, where η_0 is obtained by solving Equation (A3), with substitution of ζ by ζ_0.

Appendix C. Car Side-Impact Problem

The analytical expression of the objective function and constraint functions are given below:

$$f_1(\mathbf{x}) = 1.98 + 4.9x_1 + 6.67x_2 + 6.98x_3 + 4.01x_4 + \\ 1.78x_5 + 0.00001x_6 + 2.73x_7,$$

$$g_1(\mathbf{x},\mathbf{p}) = 1.16 - 0.3717x_2x_4 - 0.00931x_2p_3 - \\ 0.484x_3p_2 + 0.01343x_6p_3,$$

$$g_2(\mathbf{x},\mathbf{p}) = 28.98 + 3.818x_3 - 4.2x_1x_2 + 0.0207x_5p_3 \\ + 6.63x_6x_9 - 7.7x_7x_8 + 0.32p_2p_3,$$

$$g_3(\mathbf{x},\mathbf{p}) = 33.86 + 2.95x_3 + 0.1792p_3 - 5.057x_1x_2 - \\ 11x_2p_1 - 0.0215x_5p_3 - 9.98x_7p_1 + 22p_1p_2,$$

$$g_4(\mathbf{x},\mathbf{p}) = 46.36 - 9.9x_2 - 12.9x_1p_1 + 0.1107x_3p_3,$$

$$g_5(\mathbf{x},\mathbf{p}) = 0.261 - 0.0159x_1x_2 - 0.188x_1p_1 - 0.019x_2x_7 + \\ 0.0144x_3x_5 + 0.0008757x_5p_3 + 0.08045x_6x_9 + \\ 0.00139p_1p_4 + 0.00001575p_3p_4,$$

$$g_6(\mathbf{x},\mathbf{p}) = 0.214 + 0.00817x_5 - 0.131x_1p_1 - 0.0704x_1p_2 + \\ 0.03099x_2x_6 - 0.018x_2x_7 + 0.0208x_3p_1 \\ + 0.121x_3p_2 - 0.00364x_5x_6 + 0.0007715x_5p_3 - \\ 0.0005354x_6p_3 + 0.00121p_1p_4 + \\ 0.00184x_9p_3 - 0.018x_2x_2,$$

$$g_7(\mathbf{x},\mathbf{p}) = 0.74 - 0.61x_2 - 0.163x_3p_1 + 0.001232x_3p_3 - \\ 0.166x_7p_2 + 0.227x_2x_2,$$

$$g_8(\mathbf{x},\mathbf{p}) = 4.72 - 0.5x_4 - 0.19x_2x_3 - 0.0122x_4p_3 + \\ 0.009325x_6p_3 + 0.000191p_4p_4,$$

$$g_9(\mathbf{x},\mathbf{p}) = 10.58 - 0.674x_1x_2 - 1.95x_2p_1 + 0.02054x_3p_3 - \\ 0.0198x_4p_3 + 0.028x_6p_3,$$

$$g_{10}(\mathbf{x},\mathbf{p}) = 16.45 - 0.489x_3x_7 - 0.843x_5x_6 + 0.0432p_2p_3 - \\ 0.0556p_2p_4 - 0.000786p_4p_4.$$

Description of the design variables ($x_1 - x_7$) and random variables ($p_1 - p_4$) (standard deviation in bracket)

$x_1 = $ Thickness of B-Pillar inner (0.03),
$x_2 = $ Thickness of B-Pillar reinforcement (0.03),
$x_3 = $ Thickness of floor side inner (0.03),
$x_4 = $ Thickness of cross members (0.03),
$x_5 = $ Thickness of door beam (0.05),
$x_6 = $ Thickness of door belt line reinforcement (0.03),
$x_7 = $ Thickness of roof rail (0.03),
$p_1 = $ Material of B-Pillar inner (0.006),
$p_2 = $ Material of floor side inner (0.006),
$p_3 = $ Barrier height (10),
$p_4 = $ Barrier hitting position (10).

References

1. Au, S.K.; Beck, J.L. Estimation of small failure probabilities in high dimensions by subset simulation. *Probabilistic Eng. Mech.* **2001**, *16*, 263–277. [CrossRef]
2. Hohenbichler, M.; Gollwitzer, S.; Kruse, W.; Rackwitz, R. New light on first- and second-order reliability methods. *Struct. Saf.* **1987**, *4*, 267–284. [CrossRef]
3. Schuëller, G.I.; Stix, R. A critical appraisal of methods to determine failure probabilities. *Struct. Saf.* **1987**, *4*, 293–309. [CrossRef]
4. Rackwitz, R. Reliability analysis-a review and some perspective. *Struct. Saf.* **2001**, *23*, 365–395. [CrossRef]
5. Engelund, S.; Rackwitz, R. A benchmark study on importance sampling techniques in structural reliability. *Struct. Saf.* **1993**, *12*, 255–276. [CrossRef]
6. Zhi, P.; Yun, G.; Wang, Z.; Shi, P.; Guo, X.; Wu, J.; Ma, Z. A Novel Reliability Analysis Approach under Multiple Failure Modes Using an Adaptive MGRP Model. *Appl. Sci.* **2022**, *12*, 8961. [CrossRef]
7. Tsompanakis, Y.; Papadrakakis, M. Large-scale reliability-based structural optimization. *Struct. Multidiscip. Optim.* **2004**, *26*, 429–440. [CrossRef]
8. Chatterjee, T.; Chakraborty, S.; Chowdhury, R. A critical review of surrogate assisted robust design optimization. *Arch. Comput. Methods Eng.* **2019**, *26*, 245–274. [CrossRef]
9. Li, J.; Xiu, D. Evaluation of failure probability via surrogate models. *J. Comput. Phys.* **2010**, *229*, 8966–8980. [CrossRef]
10. Dai, H.; Zhao, W.; Wang, W.; Cao, Z. An improved radial basis function network for structural reliability analysis. *J. Mech. Sci. Technol.* **2011**, *25*, 2151–2159. [CrossRef]
11. Dubourg, V.; Sudret, B.; Deheeger, F. Metamodel-based importance sampling for structural reliability analysis. *Probabilistic Eng. Mech.* **2013**, *33*, 47–57. [CrossRef]
12. Chaudhuri, A.; Kramer, B.; Willcox, K.E. Information Reuse for Importance Sampling in Reliability-Based Design Optimization. *Reliab. Eng. Syst. Saf.* **2020**, *201*, 106853. [CrossRef]
13. Foschi, R.; Li, H.; Zhang, J. Reliability and performance-based design: A computational approach and applications. *Struct. Saf.* **2002**, *24*, 205–218. [CrossRef]
14. Qu, X.; Haftka, R.T. Reliability-based design optimization using probabilistic sufficiency factor. *Struct. Multidiscip. Optim.* **2004**, *27*, 314–325. [CrossRef]
15. Moustapha, M.; Sudret, B. Surrogate-assisted reliability-based design optimization: A survey and a unified modular framework. *Struct. Multidiscip. Optim.* **2019**, *60*, 2157–2176. [CrossRef]
16. Bichon, B.J. Efficient Surrogate Modeling for Reliability Analysis and Design. Ph.D. Thesis, Graduate School of Vanderbilt University, Nashville, TN, USA, 2010.
17. Melchers, R.E. Importance sampling in structural systems. *Struct. Saf.* **1989**, *6*, 3–10. [CrossRef]
18. Melchers, R.E. Search-based importance sampling. *Struct. Saf.* **1990**, *9*, 117–128. [CrossRef]
19. West, N.; Swiler, L. Importance sampling: Promises and limitations. In Proceedings of the 51st AIAA/SAE/ASEE Joint Propulsion Conference, Orlando, FL, USA, 12–15 April 2010; pp. 1–14. [CrossRef]
20. Yin, C.; Kareem, A. Computation of failure probability via hierarchical clustering. *Struct. Saf.* **2016**, *61*, 67–77. [CrossRef]
21. Smarslok, B.P.; Haftka, R.T.; Carraro, L.; Ginsbourger, D. Improving accuracy of failure probability estimates with separable Monte Carlo. *Int. J. Reliab. Saf.* **2010**, *4*, 393. [CrossRef]
22. Chaudhuri, A.; Haftka, R.T. Separable Monte Carlo combined with importance sampling for variance reduction. *Int. J. Reliab. Saf.* **2013**, *7*, 201. [CrossRef]
23. Melchers, R.E. *Structural Reliability Analysis and Prediction*; John Wiley & Sons: Hoboken, NJ, USA, 2002.
24. De Boer, P.T.; Kroese, D.P.; Rubinstein, R.Y. A Tutorial on the Cross-Entropy Method. *Ann. Oper. Res.* **2005**, *134*, 19–67. [CrossRef]
25. Kurtz, N.; Song, J. Cross-entropy-based adaptive importance sampling using Gaussian mixture. *Struct. Saf.* **2013**, *42*, 35–44. [CrossRef]
26. Cao, Q.D.; Choe, Y. Cross-entropy based importance sampling for stochastic simulation models. *Reliab. Eng. Syst. Saf.* **2019**, *191*, 106526. [CrossRef]
27. Geyer, S.; Papaioannou, I.; Straub, D. Cross entropy-based importance sampling using Gaussian densities revisited. *Struct. Saf.* **2019**, *76*, 15–27. [CrossRef]
28. Ang, G.L.; Ang, A.H.; Tang, W.H. Optimal importance-sampling density estimator. *J. Eng. Mech.* **1992**, *118*, 1146–1163. [CrossRef]
29. Zhang, P. Nonparametric Importance Sampling. *J. Am. Stat. Assoc.* **1996**, *91*, 1245–1253. [CrossRef]
30. Au, S.; Beck, J. A new adaptive importance sampling scheme for reliability calculations. *Struct. Saf.* **1999**, *21*, 135–158. [CrossRef]
31. Dai, H.; Zhang, H.; Rasmussen, K.J.R.; Wang, W. Wavelet density-based adaptive importance sampling method. *Struct. Saf.* **2015**, *52*, 161–169. [CrossRef]
32. Botev, Z.I.; L'Ecuyer, P.; Tuffin, B. Markov chain importance sampling with applications to rare event probability estimation. *Stat. Comput.* **2013**, *23*, 271–285. [CrossRef]
33. Dalbey, K.; Swiler, L. Gaussian process adaptive importance sampling. *Int. J. Uncertain. Quantif.* **2014**, *4*, 133–149. [CrossRef]
34. Zhao, H.; Yue, Z.; Liu, Y.; Gao, Z.; Zhang, Y. An efficient reliability method combining adaptive importance sampling and Kriging metamodel. *Appl. Math. Model.* **2015**, *39*, 1853–1866. [CrossRef]
35. Wang, Z.; Song, J. Cross-entropy-based adaptive importance sampling using von Mises-Fisher mixture for high dimensional reliability analysis. *Struct. Saf.* **2016**, *59*, 42–52. [CrossRef]

36. Lee, G.; Kim, W.; Oh, H.; Youn, B.D.; Kim, N.H. Review of statistical model calibration and validation—from the perspective of uncertainty structures. *Struct. Multidisc. Optim.* **2019**, *60*, 1619–1644. [CrossRef]
37. Acar, E. A reliability index extrapolation method for separable limit states. *Struct. Multidiscip. Optim.* **2016**, *53*, 1099–1111. [CrossRef]
38. Rubinstein, R.Y.; Kroese, D.P. *Simulation and the Monte Carlo Method*; John Wiley & Sons: Hoboken, NJ, USA, 2009; p. 345.
39. Ramakrishnan, B.; Rao, S. A general loss function based optimization procedure for robust design. *Eng. Optim.* **1996**, *25*, 255–276. [CrossRef]
40. Lee, D.; Rahman, S. Robust design optimization under dependent random variables by a generalized polynomial chaos expansion. *Struct. Multidiscip. Optim.* **2021**, *63*, 2425–2457. [CrossRef]
41. Dymiotis, C.; Kappos, A.J.; Chryssanthopoulos, M.K. Seismic reliability of RC frames with uncertain drift and member capacity. *J. Struct. Eng.* **1999**, *125*, 1038–1047. [CrossRef]
42. Li, D.; Dolezal, T.; Haimes, Y.Y. Capacity reliability of water distribution networks. *Reliab. Eng. Syst. Saf.* **1993**, *42*, 29–38. [CrossRef]
43. Zhao, J.; Tang, J.; Wu, H.C. A generalized random variable approach for strain-based fatigue reliability analysis. *J. Press. Vessel Technol.* **2000**, *122*, 156–161. [CrossRef]
44. Ramu, P.; Arul, S. Estimating probabilistic fatigue of Nitinol with scarce samples. *Int. J. Fatigue* **2016**, *85*, 31–39. [CrossRef]
45. Yun, W.; Lu, Z.; Jiang, X. A modified importance sampling method for structural reliability and its global reliability sensitivity analysis. *Struct. Multidiscip. Optim.* **2018**, *57*, 1625–1641. [CrossRef]
46. Cortés López, J.C.; Jornet Sanz, M. Improving kernel methods for density estimation in random differential equations problems. *Math. Comput. Appl.* **2020**, *25*, 33. [CrossRef]
47. Coles, S. Classical extreme value theory and models. In *An Introduction to Statistical Modeling of Extreme Values*; Springer: Berlin/Heidelberg, Germany, 2001; pp. 45–73.
48. Hill, B.M. A Simple General Approach to Inference About the Tail of a Distribution. *Ann. Stat.* **1975**, *3*, 1163–1174. [CrossRef]
49. Aban, I.B.; Meerschaert, M.M. Shifted hill's estimator for heavy tails. *Commun. Stat. Part B Simul. Comput.* **2001**, *30*, 949–962. [CrossRef]
50. Nguyen, T.; Samorodnitsky, G. Tail inference: Where does the tail begin? *Extremes* **2012**, *15*, 437–461. [CrossRef]
51. Yao, W.; Tang, G.; Wang, N.; Chen, X. An improved reliability analysis approach based on combined FORM and Beta-spherical importance sampling in critical region. *Struct. Multidiscip. Optim.* **2019**, *60*, 35–58. [CrossRef]
52. Acar, E. Reliability prediction through guided tail modeling using support vector machines. *Proc. Inst. Mech. Eng. Part C J. Mech. Eng. Sci.* **2013**, *227*, 2780–2794. [CrossRef]
53. Wu, Y.T.; Shin, Y.; Sues, R.H.; Cesare, M.A. Safety-factor based approach for probability-based design optimization. In Proceedings of the 19th AIAA Applied Aerodynamics Conference, Baltimore, MD, USA, 23–25 September 1991. [CrossRef]
54. Ravishankar, B.; Smarslok, B.; Haftka, R.; Sankar, B. Separable sampling of the limit state for accurate Monte Carlo Simulation. In Proceedings of the 50th AIAA/ASME/ASCE/AHS/ASC Structures, Structural Dynamics, and Materials Conference 17th AIAA/ASME/AHS Adaptive Structures Conference, Palm Springs, CA, USA, 4–7 May 2009; p. 2266.
55. Chateauneuf, A.; Aoues, Y. Advances in solution methods for reliability-based design optimization. In *Structural Design Optimization Considering Uncertainties*; CRC Press: Boca Raton, FL, USA, 2008; pp. 217–246. [CrossRef]
56. Bennett, J.; Botkin, M. *The Optimum Shape*; Springer: New York, NY, USA, 1986. [CrossRef]
57. Acar, E. Guided tail modelling for efficient and accurate reliability estimation of highly safe mechanical systems. *Proc. Inst. Mech. Eng. Part C: J. Mech. Eng. Sci.* **2011**, *225*, 1237–1251. [CrossRef]
58. Rahman, S.; Wei, D. Reliability-based design optimization by a univariate decomposition method. In Proceedings of the 13th AIAA/ISSMO Multidisciplinary Analysis and Optimization Conference 2010, Fort Worth, TX, USA, 13–15 September 2010; pp. 1–14. [CrossRef]
59. Picheny, V.; Kim, N.H.; Haftka, R.; Queipo, N. Conservative predictions using surrogate modeling. In Proceedings of the 49th AIAA/ASME/ASCE/AHS/ASC Structures, Structural Dynamics, and Materials Conference, Schaumburg, IL, USA, 7–10 April 2008; p. 1716.
60. Lindemann, J.; Persson, K. CALFEM, A finite element toolbox to MATLAB. 1999. Available online: http://www-amna.math.uni-wuppertal.de/~ehrhardt/TUB/NumPar/calfem/calfem.pdf (accessed on 14 September 2022).
61. Deb, K.; Gupta, S.; Daum, D.; Branke, J.; Mall, A.K.; Padmanabhan, D. Reliability-based optimization using evolutionary algorithms. *IEEE Trans. Evol. Comput.* **2009**, *13*, 1054–1074. [CrossRef]
62. Stein, M. Large sample properties of simulations using Latin hypercube sampling. *Technometrics* **1987**, *29*, 143–151. [CrossRef]
63. Deb, K.; Pratap, A.; Agarwal, S.; Meyarivan, T. A fast and elitist multiobjective genetic algorithm: NSGA-II. *IEEE Trans. Evol. Comput.* **2002**, *6*, 182–197. [CrossRef]
64. Botev, Z.I.; Grotowski, J.F.; Kroese, D.P. Kernel density estimation via diffusion. *Ann. Stat.* **2010**, *38*, 2916–2957. [CrossRef]
65. Botev, Z.I. Adaptive Kernel Density Estimation in One-Dimension—MATLAB Central File Exchange. 2016. Available online: https://www.mathworks.com/matlabcentral/fileexchange/58309-adaptive-kernel-density-estimation-in-one-dimension (accessed on 14 September 2022).
66. Hong, H.P.; Lind, N.C. Approximate reliability analysis using normal polynomial and simulation results. *Struct. Saf.* **1996**, *18*, 329–339. [CrossRef]

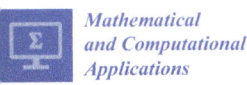

Article

Is NSGA-II Ready for Large-Scale Multi-Objective Optimization?

Antonio J. Nebro [1,2], Jesús Galeano-Brajones [3], Francisco Luna [1,2,*] and Carlos A. Coello Coello [4]

1. ITIS Software, University of Málaga, Ada Byron Research Building, 29071 Málaga, Spain
2. Departamento de Lenguajes y Ciencias de la Computación, University of Málaga, E.T.S. de Ingeniería Informática, 29071 Málaga, Spain
3. Departamento de Ingeniería de Sistemas Informáticos y Telemáticos, Universidad de Extremadura, Centro Universitario de Mérida, 06800 Badajoz, Spain
4. Evolutionary Computation Group, CINVESTAV-IPN, Ciudad de México 07360, Mexico
* Correspondence: flv@lcc.uma.es

Abstract: NSGA-II is, by far, the most popular metaheuristic that has been adopted for solving multi-objective optimization problems. However, its most common usage, particularly when dealing with continuous problems, is circumscribed to a standard algorithmic configuration similar to the one described in its seminal paper. In this work, our aim is to show that the performance of NSGA-II, when properly configured, can be significantly improved in the context of large-scale optimization. It leverages a combination of tools for automated algorithmic tuning called irace, and a highly configurable version of NSGA-II available in the jMetal framework. Two scenarios are devised: first, by solving the Zitzler–Deb–Thiele (ZDT) test problems, and second, when dealing with a binary real-world problem of the telecommunications domain. Our experiments reveal that an auto-configured version of NSGA-II can properly address test problems ZDT1 and ZDT2 with up to $2^{17} = 131,072$ decision variables. The same methodology, when applied to the telecommunications problem, shows that significant improvements can be obtained with respect to the original NSGA-II algorithm when solving problems with thousands of bits.

Keywords: NSGA-II; auto-configuration and auto-design of metaheuristics; large-scale multi-objective optimization; real-world problems optimization

1. Introduction

Since the publication of the seminal paper of Deb et al. [1] presenting the Non-dominated Sorting Genetic Algorithm-II (NSGA-II) over twenty years ago, this algorithm has become the standard metaheuristic for solving multi-objective optimization problems. Since then, NSGA-II has been included in a large number of works as a reference against which newly proposed approaches are compared (e.g., [2–4]). Additionally, it is normally the first-choice solver for dealing with real-world problems [5–8]. Its popularity can be easily assessed by looking at the number of citations to [1] (e.g., in Google Scholar or Clarivate Analytics).

NSGA-II is a generational genetic algorithm characterized by applying a dominance ranking scheme to foster convergence and the crowding distance density estimator to promote diversity. These components are used in the replacement step prior to building up the population for the next generation of the algorithm. In most of the studies involving NSGA-II, particularly when continuous problems are tackled, it is configured according to a parameterization mimicking the one used when it was originally introduced in [1], namely: population and offspring population size of 100, Simulated Binary Crossover (probability: 0.9, distribution index: 20.0), and Polynomial-based Mutation (probability: $1/L$, where L is the number of decision variables of the problem, distribution index: 20.0).

It is well known that the performance of metaheuristics in solving a given problem depends, to a large extent, on its correct parameter settings [9], so the motivation behind this work is to carry out an experimental study to determine to what extent the search capacity of NSGA-II can be improved if it is properly configured. We focus this study on the context of large-scale optimization problems, i.e., those problems having more than 100 decision variables.

The methodology that we have applied consists, first, of using a highly configurable version of NSGA-II, which is available in jMetal, a Java-based optimization framework [10,11]. We assume that any multi-objective genetic algorithm using dominance ranking and the crowding distance in the replacement step is an NSGA-II variant. That version, referred to as AutoNSGA-II, has been made more extensible and flexible so that: (i) it can adopt an external archive to store the non-dominated solutions, (ii) the offspring population size can be different from the population size, and (iii) the variation operators can be taken from an extended set of different crossover and mutation operators besides Simulated Binary Crossover and Polynomial-based Mutation. Second, we use the `irace` tool [12] to automatically find the best AutoNSGA-II configurations from a set of training instance problems.

We are going to consider two scenarios, one consisting of solving the Zitzler–Deb–Thiele (ZDT) [13] test suite, starting with 2048 decision variables and another one dealing with a real-work binary telecommunication problem where the solutions can have thousands of bits, which aims to minimize the energy consumption and increase the provided bandwidth in an ultra-dense 5G (fifth generation) network. It is important to emphasize that the purpose of this work is not to compare NSGA-II against state-of-the-art algorithms designed to solve large-scale multi-objective problems but to empirically assess up to what extent the performance of NSGA-II can be enhanced when properly configured in the two scenarios previously considered.

The rest of this paper is organized as follows. The next section reviews the related literature and identifies the research gap covered in this work. Section 3 elaborates on the components required to auto-configure NSGA-II with `irace`, as well as the two target scenarios used to assess the performance of AutoNSGA-II. The results obtained in the experiments conducted are analyzed in Section 4. Finally, Section 5 discusses the main conclusions drawn and proposes some lines for future research.

2. Related Work

The auto-configuration (or auto-tuning) of metaheuristics is an open research field that studies the design of tools that follow the machine learning approach of, given a set of problems used as a training set, automatically finding an accurate parameterization of the algorithm that it is expected to work well on a validation test and, consequently, on similar problems. A further step is the auto-design of metaheuristics, which, given a set of components, is able to create a full algorithm specifically tailored to the training and validation sets. In the field of multi-objective metaheuristics, these issues have been studied in several papers, such as in [14–16].

Focusing on NSGA-II, the idea of auto-tuning a configurable version of it by combining jMetal and `irace` was presented in [17], where the Walking Fish Group (WFG) [18] test suite was used as the training set, and the resulting NSGA-II variant was validated with the same problems plus the Deb–Thiele–Laumanns–Zitzler (DTLZ) [19] test suite. The reported results showed that that version globally outperformed the original NSGA-II in most of the problems when applying four quality indicators. A similar approach has been used in this paper to address large-scale multi-objective optimization problems.

Indeed, the context of large-scale multi-objective optimization is a hot research topic that is mainly motivated because many real-world problems contain hundreds or even thousands of decision variables (e.g., the training of deep neural networks). Consequently, the search space becomes huge and traditional metaheuristics have difficulties finding accurate solutions. One of the first works in this line is [20], where eight multi-objective metaheuristics, including NSGA-II, were tested on the ZDT problems scaling the variables up to 2048. Paper [21] presents a survey of recent proposals, but none of them is based on applying auto-configuration to an existing algorithm.

3. Materials and Methods

In this section, we describe the configurable version of NSGA-II available in jMetal and the experimental methodology adopted, which includes the two scenarios considered, the auto-configuration process with `irace`, and the computing environments.

3.1. Component-Based NSGA-II

The implementations of NSGA-II in jMetal have evolved over time. Keeping as a reference the behavior of a generic evolutionary algorithm, following the pseudo-code included in Algorithm 1, the first implementation provided by the release presented in [10] was based on a single and large method (130 lines of Java code) that contained all the steps of the algorithm. In the jMetal 5 release [11], this approach was replaced by an abstract class that closely mimicked the pseudo-code, which improved the modularity and reusability of the code. The last implementation, presented in [17], is based on a component-based architecture, where all the steps of an evolutionary algorithm are objects; this scheme offers an enhanced degree of flexibility that allows the generation of evolutionary algorithms in a dynamic way from a repository of components. This architecture is the basis of the AutoNSGA-II algorithm that we will use in this work.

Algorithm 1 Pseudo-code of an evolutionary algorithm.

1: $P(0) \leftarrow$ GenerateInitialSolutions()
2: $t \leftarrow 0$
3: Evaluation($P(0)$)
4: **while not** TerminationCriterionIsMet() **do**
5:     $P'(t) \leftarrow$ Selection($P(t)$)
6:     $Q(t) \leftarrow$ Variation($P'(t)$)
7:     Evaluate($Q(t)$)
8:     $P(t+1) \leftarrow$ Replacement($P(t), Q(t)$)
9:     $t \leftarrow t+1$
10: **end while**

The component types and some of the available instances are shown in Table 1. Therefore, we see that there are three strategies to create a population of solutions: random, Latin hypercube sampling, and the strategy used in some scatter search algorithms (e.g., AbySS [22]). The evaluation of a population can be performed sequentially or in parallel using the processor cores (multithreaded evaluation). We can observe that there are four components to indicate the stopping condition, ranging from the typical computation of a maximum number of evaluations to reach a certain level in a quality indicator; in the latter case, a maximum number of evaluations must also be set to cope with situations where the stopping condition is never fulfilled. The most commonly used selection scheme in NSGA-II is a binary tournament, but we have generalized it to an n-ary tournament and added a random selection. As NSGA-II is a genetic algorithm, the variation component applies both crossover and mutation, and the replacement component characterizing NSGA-II is the one based on ranking and a density estimator.

Table 1. Component catalog in jMetal for evolutionary algorithms.

Solutions Creation	Evaluation	Termination
- Random - Latin hypercube sampling - Scatter search	- Sequential - Multithreaded	- By evaluations - By time - By keyboard - By quality indicator
Selection	**Variation**	**Replacement**
- N-ary tournament - Random - Neighbour - Differential evolution	- Crossover and mutation - Differential evolution	- Ranking and density estimator - $(\mu + \lambda)$ - (μ, λ)

3.2. Parameter Space for Auto-Configuring NSGA-II

The automatic configuration of our AutoNSGA-II is based on a parameter space that is composed of several elements coming both from the particular selected components and from specific algorithmic parameters. We have to take into account that a number of components are fixed: the evaluation is sequential, the termination is by evaluations, and the replacement is performed based on a ranking procedure (non-dominated sorting) and the use of a density estimator (crowding distance).

Currently, the implementation of AutoNSGA-II can deal with both continuous and binary problems. The full parameter space for solving both types of problems is detailed in Table 2. There is a first group of common parameters that is not dependent on the encoding, and then we include those that are specific for either continuous or binary decision variables.

Given a population size, which we have fixed to 100 solutions, the algorithm can optionally use an external archive to store the non-dominated solutions of capacity 100; in that case, the result of the algorithm will be either the external archive or, otherwise, the population. Furthermore, when using an archive, the population size can vary from 10 to 200, and the crowding distance estimator is used to promote diversity when the archive is full (i.e., the solution having the lowest crowding distance value is removed). While the standard NSGA-II is a generational evolutionary algorithm, we can configure the offspring population size from 1 (i.e., steady-state) to a maximum of 400 solutions.

Next, we describe the parameters for real-coded multi-objective optimization problems. As commented in the previous section, there are three possible strategies for creating the initial population (random, Latin hypercube sampling, and scatter search). The variation component can choose between two crossover operators (SBX and BLX_ALPHA) and four mutation operators (uniform, polynomial, linked polynomial, and non-uniform). The operators can have common parameters (e.g., the crossover probability) and specific parameters (e.g., the distribution index for the SBX crossover is a value in the range [5.0, 400.0]). The mutation probability is problem-dependent, usually set to $1/n$ (where n is the number of decision variables), so we consider a mutation probability factor, which is a value between 0.0 and 2.0, in such a way that the effective mutation probability will be the multiplication of that factor and $1/n$. The repair strategies (random, round, bounds) are applied when a variation operator produces values out of bounds:

- random: the variable takes a random value within the bounds.
- bounds: if the value is lower/higher than the lower/upper bound, the variable is assigned the lower/upper bound.
- round: if the value is lower/higher than the lower/upper bound, the variable is assigned the upper/lower bound.

Table 2. Parameter space of AutoNSGA-II for real- and binary-coded problems.

Parameter	Domain	
algorithmResult	{externalArchive, population}	
populationSizeWithArchive	[10, 200]	s.t. algorithmResult == externalArchive
externalArchive	crowdingDistanceArchive	s.t. algorithmResult == externalArchive
offspringPopulationSize	[1, 400]	
selection	{tournament, random}	
selectionTournamentSize	(2, 10)	s.t. selection == tournament
Real-coded variables		
createInitialSolutions	{random, latinHypercubeSampling, scatterSearch}	
variation	crossoverAndMutationVariation	
crossover	{SBX, BLX_ALPHA}	
crossoverProbability	[0.0, 1.0]	
crossoverRepairStrategy	{random, round, bounds}	
sbxDistributionIndex	[5.0, 400.0]	s.t. crossover == SBX
blxAlphaCrossoverAlphaValue	[0.0, 1.0]	s.t. crossover == BLX_ALPHA
mutation	{uniform, polynomial, linkedPolynomial, nonUniform}	
mutationProbabilityFactor	[0.0, 2.0]	
mutationRepairStrategy	{random, round, bounds}	
polynomialMutationDistributionIndex	[5.0, 400.0]	s.t. mutation ∈ {polynomial, linkedPolinomial}
uniformMutationPerturbation	[0.0, 1.0]	s.t. mutation == uniform
nonUniformMutationPerturbation	[0.0, 1.0]	s.t. mutation == nonUniform
Binary-coded variables		
createInitialSolutions	random	
variation	crossoverAndMutationVariation	
crossover	{singlePoint, HUX, uniform}	
crossoverProbability	[0.0, 1.0]	
mutation	{bitflip}	
mutationProbabilityFactor	[0.0, 2.0]	

The operators and parameters used to solve binary problems include single-point, HUX, and uniform crossover, while the mutation operator is bit-flip. We have also used here a mutation factor between 0.0 and 2.0 to modulate the effect of the mutation operator.

3.3. Experimental Methodology

Our aim in this paper is to carry out an empirical study to determine if NSGA-II can address large-scale multi-objective optimization problems if it is properly configured. To this end, we designed two trial scenarios (a real-coded benchmark problem and a binary-coded real-world problem) and conducted a set of experiments divided into two phases, namely, auto-configuring NSGA-II with irace with a simple set of instances and performance assessment over a wider testbed.

3.3.1. Scenarios

The first scenario faces continuous benchmark problems; concretely, we have chosen the ZDT instances. These problems were used in the scalability study presented in [20], where a number of algorithms, including NSGA-II, were applied to optimize the problem family configured with up to 2048 variables. In that work, the solvers stopped the search when they found an approximated front whose Hypervolume (HV) was higher than 95% of the HV of the front used as reference. Those algorithms requiring the fewest number of evaluations to fulfill that condition were considered the fastest. A limit of ten million evaluations was also set so that an algorithmic execution reaching such a limit before obtaining an acceptable front was considered unsuccessful. In our scenario, we keep the same stopping condition, but the limit for failed executions is raised to

25 million evaluations and we configure ZDT instances starting from 2048 variables until 131,072 variables.

The second scenario considers a binary real-world problem from the domain of telecommunications, specifically in the context of 5G networks. A key enabling technology for these networks to meet their expected performance in terms of data rates, latency, etc. [23], lies in deploying many small base stations (SBS) close to end-users, which allows better re-use of the electromagnetic spectrum, as well as improving the signal quality and reducing the communication latency [24]. They are known as Ultra-Dense Networks (UDNs). Dimensioned to satisfy a given demand, UDNs incur considerable power consumption because of the number of SBSs that are operating. If no action is taken, this energy consumption also appears even in periods of low demand (e.g., commercial centers, office buildings, out of business hours, etc.). A well-known and standardized approach to reducing the electricity bill is to switch off a subset of the SBSs when they are underutilized. This poses a multi-objective optimization problem, named CSO (cell switch-off), which, given a set of SBSs, has to determine which subset must be turned on/off (binary decision) in order to minimize the power consumption and maximize the capacity provided to the users [25–27]. A detailed definition of the problem can be found in Appendix A. Recall that this is a large-scale multi-objective optimization problem, as seminal studies have anticipated that deployments with SBS every few meters might be required [24]. We have scaled up to about 12,000 cells per km^2 in this work. Figure 1 shows an example of a UDN deployment with macro and micro base stations and small cells, where the on-off state of each one corresponds to one bit of the solutions.

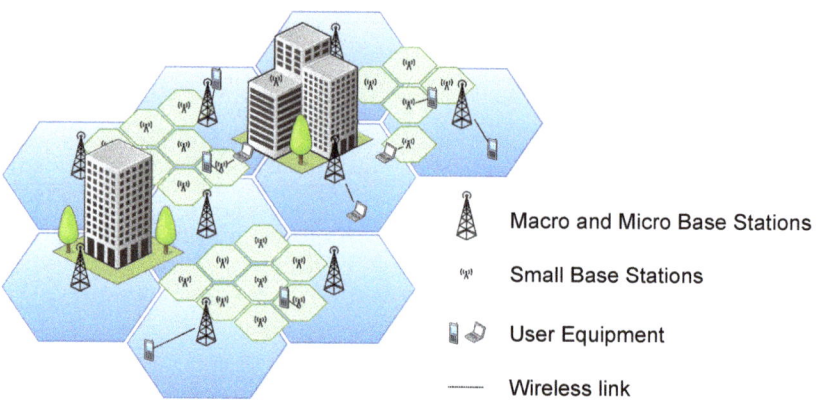

Figure 1. An example of a UDN.

3.3.2. Auto-Configuration and Performance Assessment

We now describe the phases of the experiments, namely, the use of irace to approximate the best configurations of AutoNSGA-II and the comparison of the obtained NSGA-II versions with the original one. We would like to point out that irace uses an iterative approach that samples the space of all possible configurations defined in Table 2 according to a particular distribution, selects the best configurations from the newly sampled ones by means of racing, and updates the sampling distribution to bias the sampling towards the best configurations. Therefore, it is a heuristic algorithm that does not guarantee the global optimal algorithmic configuration is found, as the sampling is limited to a maximum number of evaluations for which the algorithm is run with the sampled configuration on a given instance.

In order to use irace, a number of inputs are required:

- A file describing the parameter space included in Table 2.
- A set of problems used for training.

- An executable program that, for each combination of problem and configuration selected by `irace`, returns an indicator value so that `irace` can compare different configurations.
- The total number of different configurations to generate. The default value is 100,000.

In the continuous benchmark problem scenario, common parameters for real-coded variables are used. The training set consists of five ZDT problems with their default number of decision variables: 30 for ZDT1, ZDT2, and ZDT3, and 10 for ZDT4 and ZDT6. The executable is a jar file including jMetal code that, after solving a problem with a particular AutoNSGA-II configuration, applies the hypervolume quality indicator by using a reference front for the problem (as the ZDT are synthetic problems, reference fronts representing a subset of the Pareto fronts are available). Once `irace` has found a compromised configuration for AutoNSGA-II for the training set, this version of NSGA-II is compared with the original NSGA-II.

In the case of the CSO problem, `irace` receives the common and binary-coded parameters of Table 2. Evaluating a typical instance of this problem requires a significant amount of time, so generating and evaluating 100,000 configurations is infeasible. Our approach has been to define a small instance (with 1170 bits) that is used for training. As the Pareto front for this problem is unknown, we have defined a reference point (which is the requirement to apply the hypervolume) after inspecting several approximated fronts reached in a number of pilot tests. We have taken the extreme points of these fronts and added an offset in a conservative way to ensure that any approximated front computed by AutoNSGA-II would dominate those points. The reference point is then the result of taking the highest values per dimension of the extreme points. As with benchmark problems, the configuration found for AutoNSGA-II will be compared with the standard NSGA-II on a set of realistic problem instances.

3.3.3. Computing Environments

Running `irace` for algorithm auto-configuration can require a significant amount of computer power. The experiments on the ZDT problems have been executed in a virtualization environment located at the Ada Byron Research Center at the University of Málaga (Spain). We have used a virtual machine with Intel(R) Xeon(R) Platinum 8358 CPU @ 2.60 GHz processor (64 cores) and 64 GB of RAM. The operating system is Ubuntu 21.04, and the versions of Java and `irace` are, respectively, JDK 14 and 3.4.1. The version of jMetal is 6.0-SNAPSHOT.

The experimentation conducted on the CSO problem, which is very computationally demanding, has been deployed on the facilities of the Supercomputing and Bioinformatics Center of the Universidad de Málaga, named Picasso. It is a heterogeneous computing platform composed of several clusters with up to 30.616 computing cores. The full hardware description can be found at http://www.scbi.uma.es/site/scbi/hardware, accessed on 25 October 2022. As the stopping condition here is to reach a predefined number of function evaluations because the true Pareto front is not known for this real-world problem, executions can be performed in this heterogeneous environment because runtimes are not relevant for this study. As such, each of these executions is submitted to Picasso using `slurm`, a cluster job manager, which allocates them to the first available computing core.

4. Results

In this section, we present and analyze the results obtained after applying the experiments in the two scenarios described above.

4.1. ZDT Benchmark

In Table 3, we include the default settings of NSGA-II and the configuration of AutoNSGA-II found by `irace`. If we compare the two algorithms, we observe that none of the default parameters of NSGA-II is kept by AutoNSGA-II. The auto-configured algorithm uses an external archive with population and offspring populations sizes of 56 and 14, respectively (the default values are 100 in both populations). It is worth noting that the traditionally used Simulated Binary Crossover (SBX) and Polynomial-based Mutation are replaced by BLX_alpha crossover and non-uniform mutation. The configuration obtained by irace sets a value of $\alpha = 0.94$ for BLX_alpha, which introduces an additional diversity in the population that aims to properly integrate the controlled effect of the non-uniform mutation with the $1/n$ scheme used for the mutation rate in the search, and both the perturbation = 0.3 and the mutation factor of 0.45.

Table 3. Settings of NSGA-II and AutoNSGA-II for the ZDT problems.

Default Settings for NSGA-II	Settings of AutoNSGA-II
algorithmResult: population	algorithmResult: externalArchive
populationSize: 100	populationSizeWithArchive: 56
offspringPopulationSize: 100	offspringPopulationSize: 14
variation: crossoverAndMutationVariation	variation: crossoverAndMutationVariation
crossover: SBX	crossover: BLX_ALPHA
crossoverProbability: 0.9	crossoverProbability: 0.88
crossoverRepairStrategy: random	crossoverRepairStrategy: bounds
sbxDistributionIndexValue: 20.0	blxAlphaCrossoverAlphaValue: 0.94
mutation: polynomial	mutation: nonUniform
mutationProbabilityFactor: 1	mutationProbabilityFactor: 0.45
mutationRepairStrategy: random	mutationRepairStrategy: round
polynomialMutationDistributionIndex: 20.0	nonUniformMutationPerturbation: 0.3
selection: tournament	selection: tournament
selectionTournamentSize: 2	selectionTournamentSize: 9

We have executed both NSGA-II variants in the first scenario. The results obtained are presented in Table 4, which includes the computing times and evaluations required to reach the stopping condition. It is worth mentioning that we conducted a set of preliminary experiments, which revealed that the computing times and a number of evaluations per algorithm–problem combination were roughly similar, so performing a number of independent runs and reporting mean values would not add relevant information. This has to be taken into account, as it should be noted that some runs take hours or even days to complete. Consequently, the figures in Table 4 are the result of single executions.

If we focus on ZDT1 and 2048 variables, we observe that AutoNSGA-II needs 182,356 evaluations against the 1,250,500 required by NSGA-II. As a consequence, the computing times are reduced from 0.13 to 0.02 h (453 and 87 s, respectively), so the AutoNSGA-II is about 4.6 times faster than NSGA-II. This behavior continues until the number of variables increases up to 16,384, as NSGA-II is unable to solve ZDT1 with 32,768 variables; however, AutoNSGA-II is able to reach an approximated front that satisfies the stopping condition for the 131,072 decision variables of ZDT1 (95% of the HV of the reference front). The figures of ZDT2 are similar to those of ZTD1.

In the case of ZDT3, the number of evaluations decreases for NSGA-II compared to the ones of ZDT1 and ZDT2, while they increase for AutoNSGA-II, which is around 4.2 times faster. For this problem, NSGA-II fails to solve ZDT3 with 32,768 variables, while AutoNSGA-II is not capable of doing so with the largest number of variables. The results for ZDT6 reveal that AutoNSGA-II is about 18 times faster than NSGA-II in solving the problem with up to 65,356 variables, while NSGA-II can only solve it with 8192. The ZDT4 problem deserves special attention. Neither algorithm was able to solve it for 2048 variables, so we decided to re-run the auto-configuration process by using only ZDT4 as the training set. The settings obtained by irace are similar to those shown in Table 3 except for the mutation operator, which is linked polynomial mutation [28] (distributed index = 18.49, mutation probability factor = 0.28, and mutation repair strategy = random). With these parameter values, AutoNSGA-II has been able to solve ZDT4 with 2048 variables in less than 25 million evaluations.

Table 4. Results for NSGA-II and AutoNSGA-II on the ZDT benchmark. The last row shows the time and evaluations of AutoNSGA-II using a specific configuration for the ZDT4 problem.

		Time (h)		Evaluations	
Problem	Variables	NSGA-II	AutoNSGA-II	NSGA-II	AutoNSGA-II
ZDT1	2048	0.13	0.02	1,250,500	182,356
	4096	0.51	0.12	2,906,100	484,356
	8192	2.40	0.50	6,622,600	1,039,156
	16,384	11.19	2.15	14,741,200	2,180,656
	32,768	-	9.04	-	4,605,556
	65,356	-	31.66	-	9,494,556
	131,072	-	120.02	-	19,359,356
ZDT2	2048	0.14	0.02	1,472,800	164,756
	4096	0.62	0.10	3,433,100	429,156
	8192	2.77	0.49	7,676,600	986,556
	16,384	12.30	2.28	17,059,600	2,358,056
	32,768	-	9.28	-	4,736,056
	65,356	-	39.19	-	10,081,856
	131,072	-	138.85	-	21,703,556
ZDT3	2048	0.10	0.03	1,089,800	253,356
	4096	0.47	0.16	2,514,200	610,956
	8192	2.08	0.62	5,463,000	1,267,656
	16,384	9.18	2.68	11,877,500	2,820,556
	32,768	-	11.39	-	6,158,256
	65,356	-	40.69	-	11,912,856
	131,072	-	-	-	-
ZDT4 *	2048	-	2.62	-	21,746,882
ZDT6	2048	0.45	0.04	5,401,100	291,856
	4096	1.82	0.16	11,482,400	659,956
	8192	7.16	0.66	24,897,300	1,374,056
	16,384	-	3.08	-	3,221,156
	32,768	-	15.51	-	7,941,156
	65,356	-	63.79	-	17,685,556
	131,072	-	-	-	-

* This instance has used a specifically tuned configuration by `irace`.

From these results, we can state that the use of auto-configuration for NSGA-II produces a variant that is not only faster than NSGA-II on all problems except for ZDT4 but is also capable of scaling up to more than 100,000 variables in the case of problems ZDT1 and ZDT2, which is a remarkable outcome of our study. Using the five instances as a training set for the auto-configuration process has had the consequence of finding a suitable parameterization for four problems at the expense of a detriment in ZDT4.

The ZDT benchmark was proposed more than 20 years ago, and its problems are considered easy to solve, so we could consider our findings as a kind of lower bound of the capabilities of NSGA-II to solve scalable problems. We could also argue that the time required to solve ZDT1 and ZDT2 with 131,072 variables is more than four days, but we have to consider that we have used virtual machines and we have not applied any optimization technique (e.g., parallelism), so those times could be significantly reduced.

4.2. The CSO Problem

The resulting configuration of AutoNSGA-II and how it contrasts with the typical NSGA-II settings for binary encodings is shown in Table 5. In this case, the main differences are again the presence of an external archive, the size reduction in the two populations (from 100 to 93 and 32 individuals, respectively), almost doubling the mutation impact (to 1.7) and higher selection pressure since a tournament size of 9 is adopted instead of 2.

Table 5. Settings for NSGA-II and AutoNSGA-II for the CSO problem.

Default Settings for NSGA-II	Settings of AutoNSGA-II
algorithmResult: population	algorithmResult: externalArchive
populationSize: 100	populationSizeWithArchive: 93
offspringPopulationSize: 100	offspringPopulationSize: 32
variation: crossoverAndMutationVariatio	variation: crossoverAndMutationVariation
crossover: singlePoint	crossover: singlePloint
crossoverProbability: 0.90	crossoverProbability: 0.89
mutation: bitFlip	mutation: bitFlip
mutationProbabilityFactor: 1	mutationProbabilityFactor: 1.7
selection: tournament	selection: tournament
selectionTournamentSize: 2	selectionTournamentSize: 9

In this experimental scenario, the goal is not to reach an approximated Pareto front with a given quality level but to approximate the best possible set of non-dominated solutions. To do so, we have used nine different families of CSO instances with an increasing density, not only in the SBSs deployed in the network (i.e., the problem size) but also in the number of existing users that represents the actual demand for data traffic. Three density levels for each parameter have been considered, namely Low, Medium, and High (L, M, and H, respectively), whose full specification is included in Table A1 in the Appendix. The combination of these density levels results in nine families of instances that have already been addressed in previous works [26,27]. We would like to emphasize that we have used the term "family" because the generation of these instances involves random processes for the deployment of both users and SBSs. To address this issue, we have considered here the same 50 random seeds for the two algorithms so that both NSGA-II and AutoNSGA-II face exactly the same generated instances. Two statistical measures of the HV indicator of the approximated Pareto fronts are computed: the mean and the standard deviation (see Table 6). Finally, as we do not have the true Pareto front for this real-world problem, the stopping condition is slightly different from that of the benchmarking problems addressed in the previous section. In fact, a maximum number of function evaluations has been used, which increases with the size of the instances: 100,000, 150,000, and 250,000 for L{X}, M{X}, and H{X}, respectively, with X = {L,M,H}. To obtain a reliable value of the HV indicator, we have first composed a reference Pareto front composed of all the non-dominated solutions found by all the algorithms for each instance, and then we have normalized each approximated front prior to computing the HV value, thus avoiding the effect of the different scaling in the problem objectives.

Table 6. HV indicator for the nine CSO problem families (Mean$_{\pm\text{Standard deviation}}$).

	NSGA-II	AutoNSGA-II
LL	$0.733_{\pm 0.074}$	$0.857_{\pm 0.041}$
LM	$0.726_{\pm 0.077}$	$0.834_{\pm 0.044}$
LH	$0.707_{\pm 0.116}$	$0.814_{\pm 0.071}$
ML	$0.619_{\pm 0.084}$	$0.871_{\pm 0.030}$
MM	$0.659_{\pm 0.098}$	$0.843_{\pm 0.048}$
MH	$0.685_{\pm 0.099}$	$0.823_{\pm 0.067}$
HL	$0.699_{\pm 0.080}$	$0.868_{\pm 0.034}$
HM	$0.644_{\pm 0.128}$	$0.792_{\pm 0.119}$
HH	$0.725_{\pm 0.103}$	$0.812_{\pm 0.086}$

The HV values reached by NSGA-II and AutoNSGA-II are shown in Table 6, where we have used a gray background to highlight the best (highest) value of the indicator. The conclusion is clear: AutoNSGA-II consistently outperforms NSGA-II in all combinations of densities in the UDN. These differences are remarkable, considering the normalization of the approximated fronts. If we analyze the effect of the density in more detail, we can also observe that when the density of users is Low, i.e., families {X}L (rows 1, 4 and 7), the average HV improvement of AutoNSGA-II is 0.18 over NSGA-II, whereas it is slightly lower for families {X}M and {X}H, which is 0.15 and 0.11, respectively. This showcases a very interesting point for the radio network designer (the decision-maker in the CSO problem) because substantially improved solutions can be reached in periods of very low demand, thus saving more energy consumption. All these results are shown to have statistical significance at a 95% level using either an ANOVA I or a Kruskal–Wallis depending on the normality of the samples, which is checked beforehand by a Kolmogorov–Smirnov test.

In order to better support these claims, in Figure 2, we also show the *50%-attainment surfaces* [29] of the nine families of CSO instances. It can be seen that, averaged over all the approximated fronts, the attainment surfaces of AutoNSGA-II cover regions of the solution space with very large energy savings (left-hand side of the plots), where NSGA-II is unable to reach. This particularly holds in the plots of the first column (i.e., families {X}L), corroborating the previous analysis of the HV values. Note that this is a key issue in the deployment of 5G networks, as this problem objective actually computes the instantaneous power consumption, so even small reductions have a deep impact on the electricity bill over a month/year timeframe for a network operator.

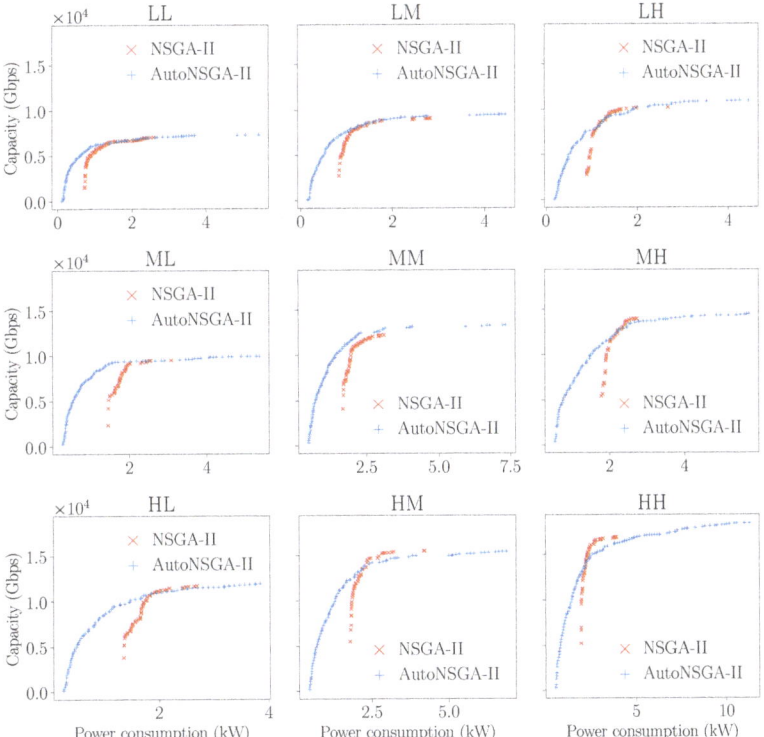

Figure 2. Attainment surfaces for the nine CSO instance families.

5. Conclusions

This work has shown how a well-designed optimization software in combination with an automatic configuration tool such as `irace` allows tuning the NSGA-II algorithm to deal with large-scale multi-objective optimization problems. By properly adjusting the algorithm components in a methodology that involves not only updating the application rates but also the type of operators used, the auto-configured version of NSGA-II, named AutoNSGA-II, has been successfully evaluated over fairly different scenarios. On the one hand, AutoNSGA-II has been able to address instances of the continuous ZDT problem family (ZDT1 and ZDT2) with up to $2^{17} = 131,072$ decision variables, being considerably faster (in terms of the number of function evaluations and thus the execution time) than the canonical NSGA-II in reaching approximated Pareto fronts with 95% of the HV indicator of the true Pareto front. On the other hand, in a more application-oriented context, AutoNSGA-II has been able to improve upon NSGA-II when addressing a combinatorial optimization problem in ultra-dense 5G networks, where a subset of cells have to be selected to be switched off in order to reach a trade-off between energy consumption and quality of service. The newly algorithmic configuration has been able to reach approximated Pareto fronts with, specifically, higher energy-efficient solutions than those computed by the standard NSGA-II.

A line of work that is worth addressing in the future is to repeat our experiments with the ZDT problems but using each problem separately as a training set aimed at determining, first, whether the performance of AutoNSGA-II can be improved (in terms of reducing the number of evaluations and then reducing the computing time) and, second, to analyze the obtained NSGA-II configurations for each problem to detect common parameter values or components.

The usefulness of using a methodology for automated algorithm tuning, such as NSGA-II, makes sense in the context of dealing with real-world problems, as our study with the CSO has shown. The application of this approach with our combination of jMetal and irace to other problems is also further research work.

Author Contributions: Conceptualization, A.J.N., J.G.-B., F.L. and C.A.C.C.; methodology, A.J.N., F.L. and C.A.C.C.; software, A.J.N. and J.G.-B.; validation, A.J.N., J.G.-B and F.L.; analysis, A.J.N., J.G.-B., F.L. and C.A.C.C.; writing—original draft preparation, A.J.N. and J.G.-B.; writing—review and editing, A.J.N., J.G.-B., F.L. and C.A.C.C.; All authors have read and agreed to the published version of the manuscript.

Funding: This work has been partially funded by the Spanish Ministry of Science and Innovation via grants PID2020-112540RB-C41 and PID2020-112545RB-C54, by the European Union NextGenerationEU/PRTR under grant and TED2021-131699B-I00 (AEI/FEDER, UE), and the Andalusian PAIDI program with grants P18-RT-2799, A-TIC-608-UGR20, P18.RT.4830, and PYC20-RE-012-UGR. Carlos A. Coello Coello acknowledges support from CONACyT grant no. 2016-01-1920 (Investigación en Fronteras de la Ciencia 2016).

Data Availability Statement: A repository containing the source codes will be publicly available if the paper is accepted.

Acknowledgments: The authors would like to thank Picasso, the supercomputer at the Supercomputing and Bioinformatics centre of the Universidad de Málaga, for providing its services to perform the experiments (http://www.scbi.uma.es/, accessed on 25 October 2022).

Conflicts of Interest: The authors declare no conflict of interest.

Appendix A. UDN Modeling and Instances

This work considers a service area of 500×500 meters, which has been discretized using a grid of 100×100 points (also called "pixels" or area elements), each covering a $25\ \text{m}^2$ area, where the signal power is assumed to be constant. In addition to that, vertical densification has been taken into account by considering three vertical area elements, i.e., 25 m of height.

Ten different regions have been defined with different propagation conditions. To compute the received power at each point, $P_{rx}[dBm]$, the following model has been used:

$$P_{rx}[dBm] = P_{tx}[dBm] + PLoss[dB] \tag{A1}$$

where P_{rx} is the received power in dBm, P_{tx} is the transmitted power in dBm, and $PLoss$ is the global signal losses, which depend on the given propagation region, and are computed as:

$$PLoss[dB] = GA + PA \tag{A2}$$

where GA is the total gain of both antennas, and PA is the transmission losses in space, computed as:

$$PA[dB] = \left(\frac{\lambda}{2 \cdot \pi \cdot d}\right)^K \tag{A3}$$

where d is the Euclidean distance to the corresponding sector at the SBS, and K is the exponent loss, which randomly ranges in [2.0, 4.0] for each of the 10 different regions. The Signal-to-Interference plus Noise Ratio (SINR) for UE k, is computed as:

$$SINR_k = \frac{P_{rx,j,k}[mW]}{\sum_{i=1}^{M} P_{rx,i,k}[mW] - P_{rx,j,k}[mW] + P_n[mW]} \tag{A4}$$

where $P_{rx,j,k}$ is the received power by UE k from the cell j, the summation is the total received power by UE k from all the cells operating at the same frequency that j, and P_n is the noise power, computed as:

$$P_n[dBm] = -174 + 10 \cdot \log_{10} BW_j \tag{A5}$$

where BW_j is the bandwidth of cell j, defined as 10% of the SBS operating frequency, which is the same for all the cells it deploys (see Table A1).

Finally, the UE's capacity has been calculated according to the MIMO depicted in [30]. Thus, we assume that the transmission power from each antenna is P_{tx}/n_{tx}, where n_{tx} indicates the number of transmitting antennas. Then, if we consider the subchannels to be uncoupled, their capacities can add up, and the overall channel capacity of the UE k can be estimated using the Shannon capacity formula:

$$C_k^j[bps] = BW_k^j[Hz] \cdot \sum_{i=1}^{r} \log_2\left(1 + \frac{SINR_k \cdot \lambda_i}{n_{tx}}\right) \tag{A6}$$

where $\sqrt{\lambda_i}$ is the singular value of the channel matrix **H**, of dimensions $n_{rx} \times n_{tx}$ (i.e., # receiving antennas × # transmitting antennas). Note that both n_{rx} and n_{tx} depend on the cell type (see Table A1). BW_k^j is the bandwidth assigned to UE k when connected to cell j, assuming a round-robin schedule, that is:

$$BW_k^j = \frac{BW_j}{N_j} \tag{A7}$$

where N_j is the number of UEs connected to cell j, and the UEs are connected to the cell that provides the highest SINR, regardless of its type.

In order to build a heterogeneous network, three different types of cells of increasing size and decreasing frequency are considered: femtocells, picocells, and microcells. Recall that these cells are generated by the antennas installed in a given sector of an SBS. Figure A1 illustrates the three configurations used in our modeling. In the first row, the three SBSs have the three sectors, and all their cells switched on (in operation). Thus the mapping to the binary string that represents a tentative solution, included below each subfigure, does have all the genes set to 1. In the second row, we have included several solutions with a subset of cells switched off, with the corresponding genes set to 0. It should also be noted that the number of transmitting antennas of each cell type increases with frequency, being 8, 64, and 256 transmitting antennas, respectively, for micro, pico, and femtocells. In the same way, we assume that high-capacity UEs, which will preferably connect to small cells (pico and femtocells), will implement a higher number of receiving antennas (4 and 8 for pico and femtocells, respectively).

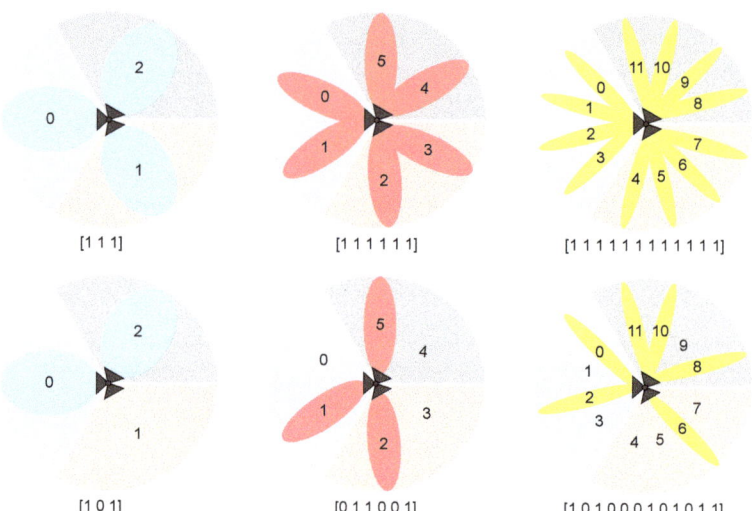

Figure A1. Configuration of the SBSs, sectors, and cells used in this work, as well as its mapping into a binary encoded representation.

With the system configuration described above, the actual deployment of the cells is carried out via the placement of SBSs in the working area, using a random rotation angle for the sectors, which determines the orientation of the different cell beams. Then, both SBSs and UEs are deployed using independent Poisson Point Processes (PPP) with different densities, defined by λ_P^{Cells} and λ_P^{UE}), respectively.

The power consumption of a transmitter is computed based on the model presented in [31], which considers that the device is transmitting over the fiber backhauling. Therefore, the regular power consumption of cell j, P_j, is expressed as:

$$P_j = \alpha \cdot P + \beta + \delta \cdot S + \rho \tag{A8}$$

where P denotes the transmitted or radiated power of the transmitter, coefficient α represents the efficiency of the transmission power produced by a radio frequency amplifier and feeder losses, the power dissipated due to signal processing and site cooling is denoted by β, and the dynamic power consumption per unit of data is given by δ, where S is the actual traffic demand provided by the serving cell. Finally, the power consumption of the transmitting device is represented by the coefficient ρ. However, in order to consider an accurate power consumption model, the power consumed by the air conditioning and power supply of the SBS should also be taken into account [32]. This has been called maintenance power and is set to 2W/SBS for any SBS containing at least one active cell.

The detailed parametrization of the scenarios addressed is included in Table A1, in which the column equation links the parameter to the corresponding equation in the formulation detailed above. The names in the last nine columns, XY, represent the deployment densities of SBSs and UEs, respectively, so that X = {L, M, H}, meaning either low, medium, or high-density deployments (λ_P^{Cell} parameter of the PPP), and Y = {L, M, H}, indicate a low, medium, or high density of deployed UEs (λ_P^{UE} parameter of the PPP), in the last row of the table. The parameters G_{tx} and f of each type of cell refer to the transmission gain and the operating frequency (and its available bandwidth) of the antenna, respectively, where n_{tx} and n_{rx} are the number of transmitting and receiving antennas. Finally, the parameters of the previously described power consumption model are also included. Nine instances have been, therefore, used in this work in order to assess the performance of the different metaheuristics and their hybridization with the problem-specific operators.

Table A1. Model parameters for users and base stations.

Cell	Parameter	Equation	LL	LM	LH	ML	MM	MH	HL	HM	HH
Micro	G_{tx}	(A2)					12				
	f	(A5)				5 GHz (BW = 500 MHz)					
	α	(A8)					15				
	β	(A8)					10000				
	δ	(A8)					1				
	$\rho[W]$	(A8)					1				
	n_{tx}						8				
	n_{rx}						2				
	λ_P^{micro} (Cells/km²)		300	300	300	600	600	600	900	900	900
Pico	G_{tx}	(A2)					20				
	f	(A5)				20 GHz (BW = 2000 MHz)					
	α	(A8)					9				
	β	(A8)					6800				
	δ	(A8)					0.5				
	$\rho[W]$	(A8)					1				
	n_{tx}						64				
	n_{rx}						4				
	λ_P^{pico} (Cells/km²)		1500	1500	1500	1800	1800	1800	2100	2100	2100
Femto	G_{tx}	(A2)					28				
	f	(A5)				68 GHz (BW = 6800 MHz)					
	α	(A8)					5.5				
	β	(A8)					4800				
	δ	(A8)					0.2				
	$\rho[W]$	(A8)					1				
	n_{tx}						256				
	n_{rx}						8				
	λ_P^{femto} (Cells/km²)		3000	3000	3000	6000	6000	6000	9000	9000	9000
UEs	λ_P^{UE} (UE/km²)		1000	2000	3000	1000	2000	3000	1000	2000	3000

Problem Formulation and Objectives

Let $\mathcal{B}$ be the set of randomly deployed SBSs. A solution to the CSO problem is a binary string $s \in \{0,1\}^{|\mathcal{B}|}$, where s_i indicates whether the cell i of a given SBS is activated or not. The first objective to be minimized is, therefore, computed as:

$$\min f_{Power}(s) = \sum_{i=1}^{|\mathcal{B}|} s_i \cdot P_i \qquad (A9)$$

where P_i is the power consumption of SBS i (Equation (A8)). Note that P_i includes both the transmission power of every cell i in the SBSs and its maintenance power.

Let $\mathcal{U}$ be the set of UEs also deployed, as described in the previous section, and $\mathcal{U}$ be the entire set of cells contained in $\mathcal{B}$. Subsequently, in order to compute the total capacity of the system, UEs are first assigned to the active cell that provides it with the highest SINR. Let $\mathcal{A}(s) \in \{0,1\}^{|\mathcal{U}| \times |\mathcal{C}|}$ be the matrix where $a_{ij} = 1$ if $s_j = 1$ and the Cell j serves UE i

with the highest SINR, and $a_{ij} = 0$ otherwise. Then, the second objective to be maximized, which is the total capacity provided to all UEs, is calculated as:

$$\max f_{Cap}(s) = \sum_{i=1}^{|\mathcal{U}|} \sum_{j=1}^{|\mathcal{C}|} s_j \cdot a_{ij} \cdot BW_i^j \quad (A10)$$

where BW_i^j is the shared bandwidth of cell j provided to UE i (Equation (A7)). We would like to remark that these two problem objectives are clearly conflicting with each other since switching off base stations leads to a reduction in the power consumption of the network, but it also damages the capacity received by the user, as the UE–cell distance increases (rising the propagation losses) at the same time as the available bandwidth to serve users is reduced.

References

1. Deb, K.; Pratap, A.; Agarwal, S.; Meyarivan, T. A Fast and Elitist Multiobjective Genetic Algorithm: NSGA-II. *IEEE Trans. Evol. Comput.* **2002**, *6*, 182–197. [CrossRef]
2. Li, H.; Zhang, Q. Multiobjective Optimization Problems With Complicated Pareto Sets, MOEA/D and NSGA-II. *IEEE Trans. Evol. Comput.* **2009**, *13*, 284–302. [CrossRef]
3. Reyes Sierra, M.; Coello Coello, C.A. Improving PSO-Based Multi-objective Optimization Using Crowding, Mutation and ϵ-Dominance. In *Evolutionary Multi-Criterion Optimization*; Coello Coello, C.A., Hernández Aguirre, A., Zitzler, E., Eds.; Springer: Berlin/Heidelberg, Germany, 2005; pp. 505–519.
4. Nebro, A.J.; Durillo, J.J.; García-Nieto, J.; Coello, C.A.C.; Luna, F.; Alba, E. SMPSO: A new PSO-based metaheuristic for multi-objective optimization. In Proceedings of the 2009 IEEE Symposium on Computational Intelligence in Multi-Criteria Decision-Making (MCDM 2009), Nashville, TN, USA, 30 March–2 April 2009; pp. 66–73. [CrossRef]
5. Zavala, G.R.; Nebro, A.J.; Luna, F.; Coello, C.A.C. A survey of multi-objective metaheuristics applied to structural optimization. *Struct. Multidiscip. Optim.* **2014**, *49*, 537–558. [CrossRef]
6. Becerra, D.; Sandoval, A.; Restrepo-Montoya, D.; Nino, L.F. A parallel multi-objective Ab initio approach for protein structure prediction. In Proceedings of the 2010 IEEE International Conference on Bioinformatics and Biomedicine, Houston, TX, USA, 9–12 December 2010; pp. 137–141.
7. Fang, W.; Guan, Z.; Su, P.; Luo, D.; Ding, L.; Yue, L. Multi-Objective Material Logistics Planning with Discrete Split Deliveries Using a Hybrid NSGA-II Algorithm. *Mathematics* **2022**, *10*, 2871. [CrossRef]
8. Turkson, R.F.; Yan, F.; Ahmed Ali, M.K.; Liu, B.; Hu, J. Modeling and multi-objective optimization of engine performance and hydrocarbon emissions via the use of a computer aided engineering code and the NSGA-II genetic algorithm. *Sustainability* **2016**, *8*, 72. [CrossRef]
9. Adenso-Díaz, B.; Laguna, M. Fine-tuning of algorithms using fractional experimental designs and local search. *Oper. Res.* **2006**, *54*, 99–114. [CrossRef]
10. Durillo, J.; Nebro, A. jMetal: A Java framework for multi-objective optimization. *Adv. Eng. Softw.* **2011**, *42*, 760–771. [CrossRef]
11. Nebro, A.; Durillo, J.J.; Vergne, M. Redesigning the jMetal Multi-Objective Optimization Framework. In Proceedings of the Companion Publication of the 2015 Annual Conference on Genetic and Evolutionary Computation (GECCO Companion '15), Madrid, Spain, 11–15 July 2015; ACM: New York, NY, USA, 2015; pp. 1093–1100. [CrossRef]
12. López-Ibáñez, M.; Dubois-Lacoste, J.; Pérez Cáceres, L.; Stützle, T.; Birattari, M. The irace package: Iterated Racing for Automatic Algorithm Configuration. *Oper. Res. Perspect.* **2016**, *3*, 43–58. [CrossRef]
13. Zitzler, E.; Deb, K.; Thiele, L. Comparison of Multiobjective Evolutionary Algorithms: Empirical Results. *Evol. Comput.* **2000**, *8*, 173–195. [CrossRef] [PubMed]
14. Blot, A.; Hoos, H.H.; Jourdan, L.; Kessaci-Marmion, M.É.; Trautmann, H. MO-ParamILS: A Multi-objective Automatic Algorithm Configuration Framework. In *Learning and Intelligent Optimization*; Festa, P., Sellmann, M., Vanschoren, J., Eds.; Springer International Publishing: Cham, Switzerland, 2016; pp. 32–47.
15. Bezerra, L.C.T.; López-Ibáñez, M.; Stützle, T. Automatic Component-Wise Design of Multiobjective Evolutionary Algorithms. *IEEE Trans. Evol. Comput.* **2016**, *20*, 403–417. [CrossRef]
16. Bezerra, L.C.T.; López-Ibáñez, M.; Stützle, T. Automatically Designing State-of-the-Art Multi- and Many-Objective Evolutionary Algorithms. *Evol. Comput.* **2020**, *28*, 195–226. [CrossRef] [PubMed]
17. Nebro, A.J.; López-Ibáñez, M.; Barba-González, C.; García-Nieto, J. *Automatic Configuration of NSGA-II with jMetal and Irace*; Association for Computing Machinery, Inc.: New York, NY, USA, 2019; pp. 1374–1381. [CrossRef]
18. Huband, S.; Barone, L.; While, R.; Hingston, P. A Scalable Multi-objective Test Problem Toolkit. In Proceedings of the Third International Conference on Evolutionary MultiCriterion Optimization, EMO 2005, Guanajuato, Mexico, 9–11 March 2005; Coello, C., Hernández, A., Zitler, E., Eds.; Springer: Berlin, Germany, 2005; Lecture Notes in Computer Science; Volume 3410, pp. 280–295.

19. Deb, K.; Thiele, L.; Laumanns, M.; Zitzler, E. Scalable Test Problems for Evolutionary Multiobjective Optimization. In *Evolutionary Multiobjective Optimization. Theoretical Advances and Applications*; Abraham, A., Jain, L., Goldberg, R., Eds.; Springer: Berlin/Heidelberg, Germany, 2001; pp. 105–145.
20. Durillo, J.J.; Nebro, A.J.; Coello, C.A.C.; Garcia-Nieto, J.; Luna, F.; Alba, E. A Study of Multiobjective Metaheuristics When Solving Parameter Scalable Problems. *IEEE Trans. Evol. Comput.* **2010**, *14*, 618–635. [CrossRef]
21. Tian, Y.; Si, L.; Zhang, X.; Cheng, R.; He, C.; Tan, K.C.; Jin, Y. Evolutionary Large-Scale Multi-Objective Optimization: A Survey. *ACM Comput. Surv.* **2021**, *54*, 174. [CrossRef]
22. Nebro, A.J.; Luna, F.; Alba, E.; Dorronsoro, B.; Durillo, J.J.; Beham, A. AbYSS: Adapting Scatter Search to Multiobjective Optimization. *IEEE Trans. Evol. Comput.* **2008**, *12*, 439–457. [CrossRef]
23. Bohli, A.; Bouallegue, R. How to Meet Increased Capacities by Future Green 5G Networks: A Survey. *IEEE Access* **2019**, *7*, 42220–42237. [CrossRef]
24. Lopez-Perez, D.; Ding, M.; Claussen, H.; Jafari, A.H. Towards 1 Gbps/UE in Cellular Systems: Understanding Ultra-Dense Small Cell Deployments. *IEEE Commun. Surv. Tutorials* **2015**, *17*, 2078–2101. [CrossRef]
25. González González, D.; Mutafungwa, E.; Haile, B.; Hämäläinen, J.; Poveda, H. A Planning and Optimization Framework for Ultra Dense Cellular Deployments. *Mob. Inf. Syst.* **2017**, *2017*, 9242058. [CrossRef]
26. Luna, F.; Luque-Baena, R.; Martínez, J.; Valenzuela-Valdés, J.; Padilla, P. Addressing the 5G Cell Switch-off Problem with a Multi-objective Cellular Genetic Algorithm. In Proceedings of the IEEE 5G World Forum, 5GWF 2018—Conference Proceedings, Silicon Valley, CA, USA, 9–11 July 2018; pp. 422–426. [CrossRef]
27. Luna, F.; Zapata-Cano, P.H.; González-Macías, J.C.; Valenzuela-Valdés, J.F. Approaching the cell switch-off problem in 5G ultra-dense networks with dynamic multi-objective optimization. *Future Gener. Comput. Syst.* **2020**, *110*, 876–891. [CrossRef]
28. Zille, H.; Ishibuchi, H.; Mostaghim, S.; Nojima, Y. Mutation operators based on variable grouping for multi-objective large-scale optimization. In Proceedings of the 2016 IEEE Symposium Series on Computational Intelligence (SSCI), Athens, Greece, 6–9 December 2016; pp. 1–8. [CrossRef]
29. Knowles, J. A summary-attainment-surface plotting method for visualizing the performance of stochastic multiobjective optimizers. In Proceedings of the 5th ISDA, Washington, DC, USA, 8–10 September 2005; pp. 552–557.
30. Vucetic, B.; Yuan, J. Performance Limits of Multiple-Input Multiple-Output Wireless Communication Systems. In *Space-Time Coding*; John Wiley & Sons, Ltd.: Hoboken, NJ, USA, 2005; chapter 1, pp. 1–47.
31. Piovesan, N.; Fernandez Gambin, A.; Miozzo, M.; Rossi, M.; Dini, P. Energy sustainable paradigms and methods for future mobile networks: A survey. *Comput. Commun.* **2018**, *119*, 101–117. [CrossRef]
32. Son, J.; Kim, S.; Shim, B. Energy Efficient Ultra-Dense Network Using Long Short-Term Memory. In Proceedings of the 2020 IEEE Wireless Communications and Networking Conference (WCNC), Seoul, Republic of Korea, 25–28 May 2020; pp. 1–6.

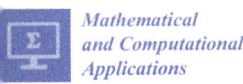

Article

Knowledge-Driven Multi-Objective Optimization for Reconfigurable Manufacturing Systems

Henrik Smedberg [1,*], Carlos Alberto Barrera-Diaz [1], Amir Nourmohammadi [1], Sunith Bandaru [1] and Amos H. C. Ng [1,2]

[1] Division of Intelligent Production Systems, School of Engineering Science, University of Skövde, P.O. Box 408, 54128 Skövde, Sweden
[2] Division of Industrial Engineering and Management, Department of Civil and Industrial Engineering, Uppsala University, P.O. Box 256, 75105 Uppsala, Sweden
* Correspondence: henrik.smedberg@his.se

Abstract: Current market requirements force manufacturing companies to face production changes more often than ever before. Reconfigurable manufacturing systems (RMS) are considered a key enabler in today's manufacturing industry to cope with such dynamic and volatile markets. The literature confirms that the use of simulation-based multi-objective optimization offers a promising approach that leads to improvements in RMS. However, due to the dynamic behavior of real-world RMS, applying conventional optimization approaches can be very time-consuming, specifically when there is no general knowledge about the quality of solutions. Meanwhile, Pareto-optimal solutions may share some common design principles that can be discovered with data mining and machine learning methods and exploited by the optimization. In this study, the authors investigate a novel knowledge-driven optimization (KDO) approach to speed up the convergence in RMS applications. This approach generates generalized knowledge from previous scenarios, which is then applied to improve the efficiency of the optimization of new scenarios. This study applied the proposed approach to a multi-part flow line RMS that considers scalable capacities while addressing the tasks assignment to workstations and the buffer allocation problems. The results demonstrate how a KDO approach leads to convergence rate improvements in a real-world RMS case.

Keywords: multi-objective optimization; knowledge discovery; reconfigurable manufacturing system; simulation

1. Introduction

Current trends in the manufacturing industry are challenging companies to cope with demand variations and fluctuating production volumes. Companies are required to rapidly adjust the functionalities of their manufacturing systems to critically manage the needs of this dynamic market to stay competitive [1]. By implementing Reconfigurable Manufacturing Systems (RMSs), companies can efficiently meet the requirements of the competitive market [2]. RMSs enable cost-effective means to meet dynamic market demands by reconfiguring, among other aspects, their resources (e.g., machines, operators, buffers, etc.) and the process plan of the manufacturing system [3].

Today's manufacturing industry is affected by disruptions and shortages of components caused by extraordinary situations such as a global pandemic or war. These disruptions, combined with an increasingly shortened product life-cycle trend, mean that manufacturing organizations are required to ramp up and down products more frequently by modifying their production volumes more often than ever before [4]. Therefore, findings regarding how dynamic market demands of today can be addressed more efficiently constitutes a crucial research area in the RMS community.

Although an RMS may be able to meet the dynamic requirements in the market, designing and configuring the RMS is no trivial task. Simulation techniques, particularly discrete event simulation, have proven to be a powerful tool for the manufacturing industry to assess the capabilities of their production systems [5,6]. Often, several conflicting objectives are used to simultaneously measure the quality of the system. Combining simulation techniques with Multi-Objective Optimization (MOO), i.e., Simulation-based Multi-objective Optimization (SMO), has been a successful approach for optimizing RMSs in the literature [4,7,8]. A general Multi-Objective Optimization Problem (MOOP) can be defined as:

$$\text{Minimize:} \quad F(\mathbf{x}) = [f_1(\mathbf{x}), \ldots, f_M(\mathbf{x})]^T$$
$$\text{Subject to:} \quad \mathbf{x} \in S$$

for M number of objective functions, in the constrained and feasible search space S, where $\mathbf{x} = [x_1, \ldots, x_N]^T$ is a vector of N decision variables. Due to the structure of MOOPs, a MOOP solution can be seen to inhabit two distinct spaces: the decision space and the objective space, and the objective functions can be seen as a mapping from the decision space to the objective space. The goal of MOO is to find a set of solutions that together represent the so-called Pareto-optimal front—the set of solutions that outperform or *dominate* all other solutions to the MOOP in S.

Due to complex aspects, such as the stochastic failures of resources and equipment that can be modeled using simulation techniques, exact methods are often omitted from consideration when optimizing SMO problems; instead, evolutionary algorithms are used. Multi-Objective Evolutionary Algorithms (MOEAs) are optimization techniques that are developed to mimic fundamental principles of evolution found in nature such as the well-known algorithm Non-dominated Sorting Genetic Algorithm II (NSGA-II) [9], which is inspired by Darwinian survival of the fittest and evolves a population of solutions over a number of generations to converge on the Pareto-optimal front.

Although MOEAs are a powerful tool to solve all kinds of MOOPs, they generate many non-optimal solutions during the optimization process. Since these are largely eliminated during optimization and rarely considered in the decision-making process, one can see the wasted computational effort in evaluating them, specifically given the very time-consuming simulations in SMO. After the observation that most of the analysis of MOOP solutions is focused solely on the objective space, and mostly disregarding the dominated solutions, the authors of [10] present Knowledge Driven Optimization (KDO), which is the idea to employ knowledge discovery methods to describe decision-makers (DMs) preferences in the objective space, in terms of knowledge about the solutions in the decision space, and then use this knowledge to drive the search towards faster convergence on more optimal solutions. This can be achieved in two ways, either *offline* where knowledge is generated related to a previous scenario or case, and used to improve the convergence in a future scenario, or *online* where knowledge discovery is integrated into the optimization process as part of the MOEA itself to drive the search towards better convergence in the current scenario. In this paper, we investigate an offline KDO approach.

In this work, we employ a knowledge-driven NSGA-II for a real-world Multi-Part Flow Line (MPFL) to optimize the RMS configuration by considering scalable capacities and fluctuating production volumes. The MOOP formulation addresses task allocation to workstations as well as buffer allocation while maximizing throughput (THP) and minimizing total buffer capacity (TBC). In Section 5, we show how the new approach is able to speed up the convergence towards non-dominated solutions for new scenarios by utilizing knowledge discovered from initial scenarios. The scope of the paper is limited to proposing and showcasing this knowledge-driven approach and comparing the effects of utilizing knowledge in the form of decision rules discovered from one variant of the considered RMS, to speed up the convergence rate of another variant of the same RMS.

2. Background

Simulation and optimization techniques have successfully been used in the context of manufacturing in the literature. However, the analysis of solutions is often limited to manual methods and mostly focus on the objective space. This section offers a background of simulation and optimization, knowledge discovery in MOO, and knowledge-driven optimization.

2.1. Simulation and Optimization in Manufacturing Systems

Regardless of the benefits of RMS compared to traditional manufacturing systems in achieving demand and capacity fluctuations, the design and management of these systems are considered a complex combinatorial NP-hard problem which therefore can be handled by the employment of simulation and optimization tools [7,11,12]. When it comes to RMS problems, meta-heuristic methods such as genetic algorithms have become very popular in the literature because they have shown better performance in generating near-optimal solutions [7]. In addition, simulation has been a satisfactory tool to support the modeling and analysis of manufacturing systems for many years [13]. Because of the complexity and dynamism inherent in manufacturing systems, engineers and DMs supported by simulation tools can perform better analysis and, therefore, obtain a better understanding of the real-world systems [14]. Concerning RMS, simulation has been identified in the literature as a supportive technique to handle the uncertainty found in these types of dynamic, evolving systems [15]. Still, considering that the complexity of today's manufacturing systems is growing and that they need to consider a range of possible scenarios with a large number of variables to model and analyze, the use of simulation tools becomes nonfunctional. Alternatively, optimization methods could be employed to solve larger-scale NP-hard problems [7]. However, the majority of prior studies that applied optimization methods to RMS reduced the problem by excluding variability and stochasticity (e.g., machine failures) and therefore providing imprecise solutions. Therefore, studies that employed simulation and optimization separately have shown some of the above-mentioned shortcomings. Against these drawbacks, simulation-based optimization combines the benefits of simulation and optimization. In the literature, simulation-based optimization has successfully led to improvements in manufacturing systems. Consequently, SMO could lead to improvements in current RMSs [11,13].

RMSs need to address three main challenges, namely: (i) the system configuration, (ii) the process planning, and (iii) the components of the system [3]. The system configuration targets the physical arrangement of the resources (e.g., operators, machines, etc.) in the system [2]. This challenge is usually addressed by optimizing the resource assignment to workstations (WSs). The process planning targets the task allocation and balancing throughout the WSs [16]. This challenge is usually addressed by optimizing the work tasks allocation. Lastly, the components of the system address the appropriate number and type of components (e.g., buffers, operators, machines, etc.) in the system to reach the established capacity goal [13]. This challenge is usually addressed by optimizing the number of resources to perform the tasks. Although simulation-based optimization has been employed to address RMS problems previously in the literature, the use of SMO to address several or all of these challenges simultaneously is sporadic.

2.2. Knowledge Discovery in MOO

Methods for knowledge discovery in the decision space of MOO solutions are not conventional in the multi-criteria decision-making literature, which mostly focus on manual methods for analyzing the solutions in the objective space. However, Ref. [10] offers a survey of data mining and machine learning methods that have been employed for knowledge discovery to support decision-making in MOO. The process of *innovization* [17] was developed as a way of finding innovative design principles to describe the Pareto-optimal front. Innovization was initially described as a manual process of formulating relationships between correlated regions of the objective space using appropriate regression models; however, it has since been automated using genetic programming [18]. Simulation Based Innovization (SBI) is another method for knowledge discovery in MOO [19,20]. SBI trains a decision tree with the distance to a user-defined reference point (a point describing a DMs aspiration) in the objective space as the regression target. The DM then chooses a threshold for the distance to the reference point to find rules that describe the decision space for the solutions within this threshold. A further application of knowledge discovery methods used in the analysis of solutions is offered by [21] where the authors used clustering in both the objective and decision spaces, as well as association rule analysis in cantilever design optimization problems.

Flexible Pattern Mining

Although previous approaches have successfully utilized common data mining and machine learning methods for knowledge discovery, these methods were not developed specifically for the indented use in MOO, and may not fully be able to manage the typical characteristics of MOOP solutions, such as different variable types (continuous, discrete and ordinal, and nominal) [10]. However, a method that has been specifically developed for knowledge discovery in MOO is Flexible Pattern Mining (FPM) [22]. FPM was developed to extend sequential pattern mining [23] using the a priori algorithm [24] for finding decision rules. While sequential pattern mining finds rules of the form $\{x_i = c\}$ for a variable x_i and constant value c, FPM is further able to find rules on the forms $\{x_i \neq c\}$, $\{x_i < c\}$, $\{x_i \leq c\}$, $\{x_i > c\}$ and $\{x_i \geq c\}$. To run FPM, the DM is required to supply a *selected* and an *unselected* set of solutions, and these selections are made in the objective space. With these selections as input, FPM then generates rules that separate the selected set from the unselected set in terms of the variables in the decision space. Typically, the DM may choose the non-dominated solutions as the selected set and the remaining solutions as the unselected set. Each rule generated by FPM has an associated *significance* or *sig* value, which is the fraction of solutions in the selected set that are covered by the rule, and a similar *unselected significance* or *unsig* for the fraction of solutions in the unselected set. An interesting and meaningful FPM-rule would have a high *sig* while having a low *unsig*, and thereby be describing only the solutions in the selected set. Rule interactions can also be considered by combining several FPM-rules and evaluating their combined *sig* and *unsig*. The three individual rules $\{x_1 < c_1\}$, $\{x_2 > c_2\}$ and $\{x_3 = c_3\}$ can be combined into the three-level rule interaction $\{x_1 < c_1 \land x_2 > c_2 \land x_3 = c_3\}$.

2.3. Knowledge-Driven Optimization

Knowledge discovery methods can be a powerful tool in decision-making; however, in this manner, the knowledge is only used by the DMs. The term *Knowledge-Driven Optimization* (KDO) is used when knowledge discovered from good or preferred MOOP solutions is fed back into the optimization algorithm to affect the convergence behaviour, or used to update the MOOP formulation itself to make the search more efficient. The former is called online KDO, while the latter refers to offline KDO [10].

A key difference between online and offline KDO is that, since the knowledge used for the former is discovered during the search process from the best-so-far solutions, it does not necessarily describe the optimal solutions to the MOOP. On the other hand, with the assumption that an optimizer converges close to the Pareto-optimal front, offline KDO has access to "pure" knowledge directly describing the optimal (or preferred) solutions.

2.3.1. Online KDO

Online KDO in a MOEA involves a specific knowledge discovery step to generate knowledge from previous or current solutions, and is able to use this knowledge to affect the convergence behaviour and more effectively generate better or preferred solutions. Online KDO algorithms have been implemented to involve an additional step after the ordinary evolutionary process that finds knowledge for feeding into the evolutionary operators for the next generation. An example of an approach like this is shown in [25,26], where FPM rules are generated to build a distribution over the preferred solutions close to the reference point in preference-based MOO. This distribution is then sampled in a new mutation operator for the next generation of solutions. Another approach using FPM rules is presented in [27], where the rules are used as constraints in the decision space.

Approaches that train a classifier between *good* and *bad* solutions have also been proposed. In [28], a classifier was trained online to differentiate between dominated and non-dominated solutions, and in [29], a classifier is trained online to find constraint violating solutions. In both papers, the classifier was used before the solutions were evaluated, in order to save time by not evaluating poor solutions. Recently, approaches that use innovization online have also been proposed [30,31].

2.3.2. Offline KDO

Offline KDO refers to when knowledge about MOOP solutions is generated offline, after an optimization run has finished and is used to benefit future optimizations of the same or similar cases, or to give insights that can lead to an updated MOOP formulation. Only when DMs fully understand the MOOP and its solutions are they able to make an informed decision.

In [32], SBI was used to find decision rules about solutions close to a user-defined reference point, and then used as constraints in a second optimization run, to generate more non-dominated solutions. This method served both as a way to discover more preferred solutions, but also to validate the method and show that it generates actionable knowledge. Previously, it has also been found that leveraging domain knowledge can also greatly benefit the optimization [33,34]. This type of knowledge is not generated from previous optimizations, but from the experience and intuitions of veteran DMs. In [35], domain knowledge was used to develop specialized design heuristics to speed up the convergence of a multi-objective satellite design system problem.

Offline KDO is similar to the concept of *transfer learning* in the machine learning literature [36], where a model able to perform a specific task is also able to perform or jump-start the learning process of another related task. In this paper, we focus on using offline KDO in order to generate knowledge from an initial scenario that can be applied to benefit the search in a new scenario. In the next section, we present an illustration of how offline KDO can be implemented.

3. Illustration of Offline KDO

Knowledge generated from MOOP solutions obtained in one scenario may be beneficial for future scenarios of similar MOOPs. Preferred solutions in the objective space may have a certain structure in the decision space that can be exploited to ensure a faster convergence towards the Pareto-optimal front or a greater density of preferred solutions. In this paper, we consider the knowledge generated through the FPM procedure [22] and the openly available implementation in the web-based decision support system Mimer (Mimer: https://assar.his.se/mimer/, accessed on 6 October 2022).

In this section, we want to showcase an example of how simple knowledge about non-dominated solutions can help to speed up the convergence and generate even more non-dominated solutions. We show how knowledge in the form of FPM-rules can be applied as constraints in the decision space to focus the search for non-dominated solutions in different parts of the Pareto-front.

Illustrative Example

We showcase an example of offline KDO on the RE3-5-4 problem from the RE suite of real-world (inspired) test-problems [37]. We show how it is possible to use FPM to generate rules that describe non-dominated solutions, and then use these rules as box-constraints for the decision variables of the MOOP for a different optimization run. Without first generating knowledge about an initial solution set, this approach would not be possible. We also compare this offline approach with simply constraining the decision space to focus the search without relying on any knowledge.

The RE3-5-4 is a three-objective engineering problem with a mathematical formulation, based on the vehicle crash-worthiness design problem described in [38]. The objectives to RE3-5-4 are: (f_0) minimize the weight of the vehicle, (f_1) minimize the acceleration characteristics in the crash, and (f_2) minimize the toe-board intrusion during the crash, while the variables (x_0–x_4) each relate to the thickness of a different support member in the frontal structure in the vehicle.

Figure 1 shows non-dominated solutions generated from a single run on the RE3-5-4 problem with a budget of 6000 function evaluations, which resulted in 2344 non-dominated solutions. The structure of the objective space clearly shows three distinct, disconnected clusters of solutions. A DM would not only be interested in what causes solutions to end up in these different clusters in terms of the decision space, but also how to focus the search to further saturate these regions with more trade-off solutions. We can use FPM for each of the clusters, to find knowledge for the respective solutions in terms of the decision space. The FPM procedure requires a selected and an unselected set of solutions. We run FPM three times using Mimer, each time with the non-dominated solutions from one of the clusters as the selected set and the remaining solutions from the entire solution set as the unselected set, thus finding rules that describe the non-dominated solutions in each cluster. The resulting FPM rules are shown in Table 1.

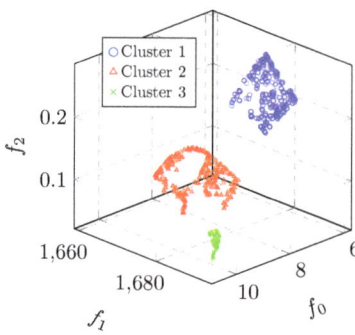

Figure 1. Non-dominated solutions from RE3-5-4.

Table 1. Rule interactions found by using FPM for each of the clusters shown in Figure 1.

Cluster	Rule Interaction	Sig	Unsig
1	$x_2 > 2.01 \wedge x_3 < 1.06 \wedge x_0 < 1.08 \wedge x_1 > 2.63$	100%	10.91%
2	$x_2 < 1.03 \wedge x_3 < 1.49 \wedge x_0 < 1.93$	100%	22.68%
3	$x_1 > 2.99 \wedge x_4 > 2.78 \wedge x_2 < 1.02 \wedge x_0 > 1.02 \wedge x_3 < 2.53$	100%	5.12%

FPM was run with a minimum significance of 100% in each case, meaning that all discovered rules completely covered the selected set, and the results still show that the rules discriminate between the selected and unselected set, given the low unselected significance. However, the rule interaction found for cluster 2 had an *unsig* of 22.68%. This means that the rule interaction also describes 22.68% of the solutions in the unselected set, which would lead to a lower search pressure towards the non-dominated solutions within this cluster when used for offline KDO.

With this knowledge about the different clusters in hand, we run additional optimizations, focusing on each of these clusters separately. We used the rule interactions found using FPM as bounds to constrain the decision space, and ran an optimization with a total of 2000 function evaluations for each respective rule interaction. These three solution sets where then combined, and the non-dominated solutions from these combined runs are shown in Figure 2. This offline approach resulted in 3070 non-dominated solutions, with the same total function evaluations (6000) as the original run.

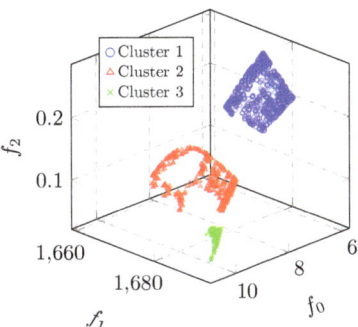

Figure 2. Non-dominated solutions from RE3-5-4 using offline KDO.

We also compare this offline KDO approach with the crude method of simply constraining the objective space to focus the search on the three clusters. The clusters can be classified by the objective space bounds shown in Table 2. To be fair against the offline KDO approach, we gave this crude method a budget of 4000 function evaluations for each cluster since the offline KDO approach was able to utilize knowledge from an initial 6000 solutions. We combined the final solutions sets from each cluster into one. This approach resulted in 2858 total non-dominated solutions, which are shown in Figure 3.

Table 2. Objective space bounds for each of the clusters as shown in Figure 1.

Cluster	Bounds
1	$f_2 > 0.13$
2	$f_2 < 0.13 \wedge f_0 < 1680$
3	$f_2 < 0.13 \wedge f_0 > 1680$

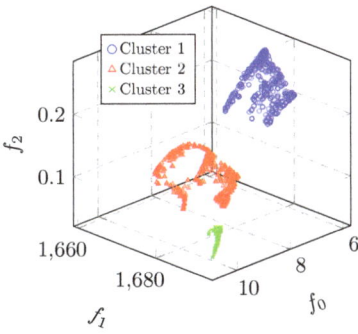

Figure 3. Non-dominated solutions from RE3-5-4 using bounded objective space.

We compare the baseline run with the offline KDO approach and the bounded objective space approach, by using the hypervolume metric (HV) [39] and by counting the contribution of each run to the composite front produced by combining the solutions from the three approaches. The composite front is shown in Figure 4 and the resulting HV and contribution to the composite front is shown in Table 3. The offline KDO approach resulted in a slightly greater HV and a greater contribution to the composite front, meaning that this approach gives superior performance over the other approaches.

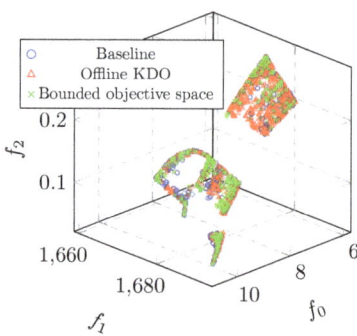

Figure 4. Composite front of the solutions from Figures 1–3.

Table 3. HV score and contribution to composite front of the three approaches.

Approach	HV	Contribution (n)	Contribution (%)
Baseline	1.034324	1134	20.38
Offline KDO	1.037663	2542	45.68
Bounded objective space	1.037533	1889	33.94

Since the offline KDO approach is utilizing knowledge discovered from a previous run, it is expected to have a higher performance. However, this example demonstrates that simply adding knowledge as box constraints in the decision space is enough to greatly improve the performance of an optimization run. This example also highlighted that applying a similar approach, by constraining the objective space, is not as effective as this offline KDO approach. This example shows the potential of incorporating offline knowledge into a MOO pipeline by spending a portion of the function evaluation budget on generating solutions, then finding knowledge about high performing solutions, and then utilizing this knowledge offline, for the remaining function evaluation budget, to reach a faster convergence on more preferred solutions.

4. Real-World RMS Problem

The considered RMS comes from a MPFL setup implemented in a truck manufacturer in Sweden. The case is based on a pedal car production, where two product families are manufactured. The MPFL is composed of three reconfigurable WSs able to add, relocate, or remove operators from them in order to cope with production changes (e.g., volumes or capacity changes). Both products need to be produced at specific volumes. As the total production capacity or the production volumes fluctuate, the system configuration, the process plan, and the components of the systems change to meet the new scenario. The changes include the number of operators employed, the assignments of operators to the WSs, the tasks' assignments to WSs, and the buffers' capacities. The company was interested in different scenarios. Initially, they wanted to investigate the system's capacity with seven operators for the specific production volumes, 70/30 and 30/70. These different proportions of production volumes determine the total proportion to be produced of the two product parts. For example, a proportion of 70/30 refers to the fact that 70% of the total parts produced should be of part A, and the remaining 30% should be of part B. Furthermore, the company also wanted to investigate how much capacity could be gained by adding one and two extra operators to the system, including the information regarding how to reconfigure the system, how to re-balance the tasks, and a re-assessment of the capacities of the buffers. Therefore, as the proportion and volume changes, the RMS evolve accordingly. The assumptions of the RMS are:

- A MPFL consisting of several WSs produce several products under different volumes;

- The resources of the RMS are subjected to disturbances, such as breakdowns, setup times, and variability of the tasks;
- Each WS has a number of parallel and identical resources that execute the same sequence of tasks;
- Each WS has reserved space for adding or reallocating resources;
- There are buffers with variable capacity in-between the WSs;
- The manufacturing tasks of the considered products are subjected to a precedence relationship and technological constraints that ensure a feasible sequence to be performed in each WS.

The mathematical problem formulation for the considered MPFL-RMS is detailed in [40].

In this paper, we consider an SMO problem using Throughput (THP) and Total Buffer Capacity (TBC) as objectives while striving for the optimal buffer and tasks allocation for the different scenarios. The total manufacturing time for the production is 336.38 s for part A and 293.38 s for part B divided into 29 and 24 tasks, respectively. The tasks precedence relations for both products are shown in Figure 5. Note that each task can be assigned to only one WS.

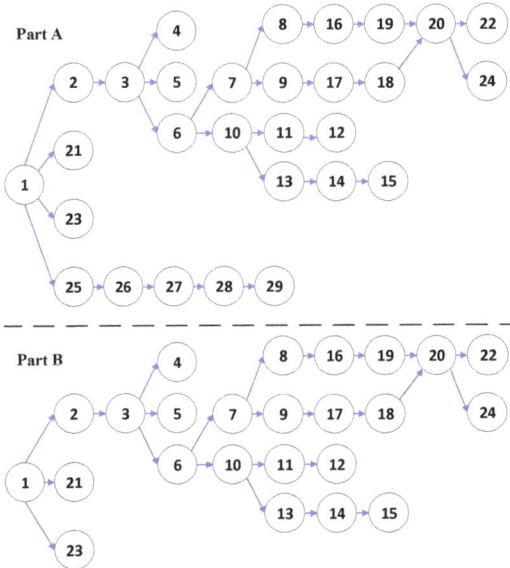

Figure 5. Precedence relation of the tasks for both products.

SMO Approach

The architecture of the SMO approach used can be divided into two major components: the simulation engine and the optimization engine, which are tightly integrated. For the simulation engine, the discrete event simulation software FACTS Analyzer [41] was employed for modeling the production system and simulating the studied scenarios. The optimization engine was implemented in the well-known platform MATLAB. The integration between the simulation and optimization engines allows an accurate representation of a realistic production line involving many types of model variables regardless of their nature (e.g., failure, availability, mean time to repair, process time) while avoiding the simplification found in other production line optimization studies. The process begins in the optimization engine where custom-made encoding and decoding mechanisms generate feasible RMS solutions to, later on, be automatically mapped to the simulation engine. The simulation engine then uses the received combination of input variables to run the simulation on the model. The results from the simulation experiments are fed back to the optimization engine in order to be evaluated by the optimization algorithm in terms of the designated conflicting objectives. This process in which the optimization engine evaluates the output of the optimization for instructing a new combination of input parameters to be simulated is repeated until the results converge to a set of optimal solutions or the stopping criterion is reached (i.e., a predefined number of generations).

Due to the outstanding performance in handling up to three conflicting objectives and being known as an effective MOEA when handling complex combinatorial problems, a customized NSGA-II with specific encoding and decoding mechanisms for RMS was implemented within the optimization engine to generate feasible solutions [4,12]. There are three main factors behind the success of NSGA-II, the fast non-dominated sorting which establishes a dominance relationship between each pair of solutions, the elitism mechanism to keep the best solutions, and the crowding distance calculation that ensures that ranks the solutions of each individual front maintaining diversity. The general steps of the customized NSGA-II for RMS are shown in Algorithm 1.

Algorithm 1 Enhanced SMO-NSGA-II

Require: Generation limit G_{max}; Population size; Precedence relation; RMS inputs regarding WSs, buffers, resources and constraints
1: Create a population of priority-based representation vectors
2: Initialize generation counter g
3: **while** $g \leq G_{max}$ **do**
4:    Using the custom-made encoding and decoding mechanisms, ensure a population of RMS feasible solutions
5:    Use the simulation engine to evaluate the fitness functions for all solutions
6:    Rank the solutions using fast non-dominated sorting
7:    Calculate the crowding distance of each solution in each individual front
8:    Select parents for crossover using tournament selection
9:    Using crossover and mutation operators, generate a new set of offspring
10:   Using elitist replacement mechanism, preserve best individuals
11:   Increment g
12: **end while**
13: **return** The Pareto-optimal solutions for RMS

Due to the differences in how the considered RMS is encoded from a standard MOOP solved by NSGA-II, the variables for the number of WSs, and task- and buffer assignment are encoded as random keys in the enhanced algorithm, and on Line 4, they are decoded as feasible input for the simulation model. On Line 5, these decoded solutions are sent to and evaluated by the simulation engine, and the objective values are sent back to the algorithm. A complete description of the enhanced algorithm is provided in [40].

5. Experimental Results

In this section, we present the results from the initial optimizations, the knowledge we were able to discover from the solutions to these optimizations, and new results from an offline KDO study using this discovered knowledge. We investigate the improvement in convergence towards the Pareto-optimal front by applying FPM rules as constraints in the decision space. All optimizations refer to the real-world RMS problem described in Section 4. All knowledge discovery was performed using the openly available web-based decision-support system Mimer, enabling the knowledge discovery framework described in [42].

5.1. Optimization Results

We ran six optimizations initially, one scenario for each pair of number of operators (7, 8, 9) and proportion (70/30, 30/70). Each optimization run had a budget of 500 generations and a population size of 50. The resulting non-dominated solutions from these runs are shown in terms of their task allocation in Figure 6, where each row represents one solution and each column represents one task for either product A or B, and the color of the cell shows the WS it was assigned to. In total, 72 non-dominated solutions were found in these scenarios altogether.

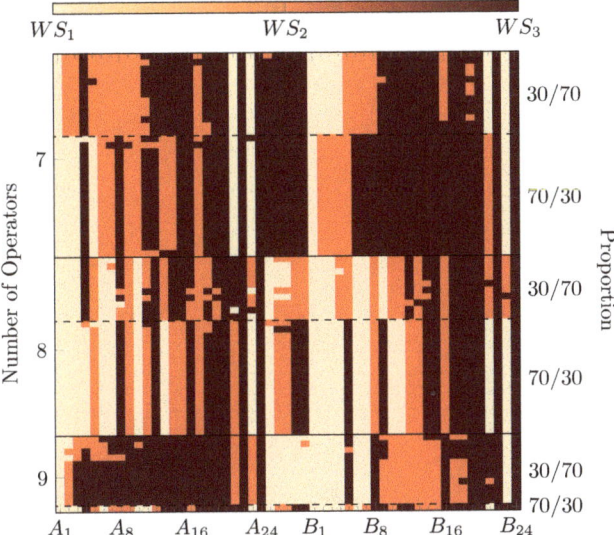

Figure 6. Task allocations from the non-dominated solutions from all scenarios in the initial optimizations.

From the figure, it is clear that most of the non-dominated solutions in each scenario share common task allocations. However, all solutions shown in Figure 6 are distinct and have varying buffer allocations which are not shown here.

The number of non-dominated solutions from each scenario is shown in Table 4, where we can see that the number of non-dominated solutions in each scenario varies from 10–19, except for the scenario of nine operators with a proportion of 70/30 where only one non-dominated solution was found. The objective space of the non-dominated solutions from all scenarios is also shown in Figure 7, where it is very clear how increasing the number of operators, as expected, has a definite impact on the throughput.

Table 4. Number of non-dominated solutions found for each scenario in the initial optimizations.

NO	Proportion	Solutions (n)
7	30/70	13
7	70/30	19
8	30/70	10
8	70/30	18
9	30/70	11
9	70/30	1

5.2. Knowledge Discovery

Due to the ability of the system to both increase and decrease the number of operators and to change the proportion between the two parts, in this paper, we are interested in finding generalized knowledge about each of the different number of operators and the different proportions. In other words, if we can generate knowledge from the previous scenarios with seven operators that can be generalized to improve the optimization process for future scenarios with seven operators but new proportions, and if we can generate knowledge from the scenarios with a proportion of 30/70 and use it in future scenarios with different numbers of operators, and so on for each group of scenarios.

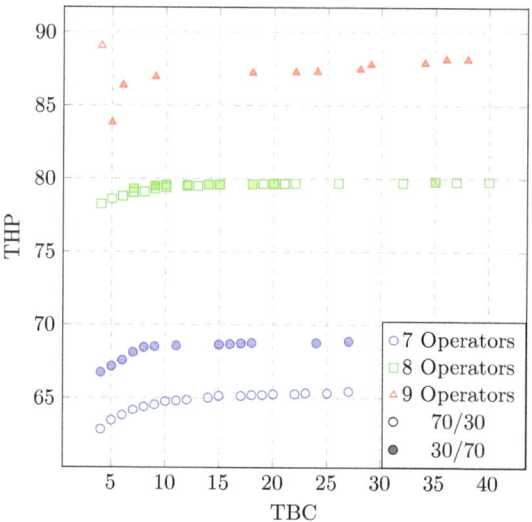

Figure 7. Objective space of the non-dominated solutions from all scenarios in the initial optimizations.

We generate knowledge in the form of decision rules using the FPM procedure. From the initial results, we are interested in five groups of scenarios to generate knowledge from. The scenarios wherein the numbers of operators equal 7, 8, and 9, and where the proportions equal 30/70 and 70/30. In order to run FPM, we merged the solutions from all optimization scenarios into one combined dataset so that the different scenarios can take all cases into account. For each group, we ran FPM with the non-dominated solutions from the scenarios in the group as the selected set, and all remaining solutions (dominated and non-dominated) from all scenarios as the unselected set. In this way, the generated knowledge is general between scenarios in the MOOP.

For this knowledge discovery, we only focus on the task allocation. Even so, the number of decision variables is high (53) which affects the run-time of the FPM procedure. For this reason, the maximum level of rule interactions was limited to 4, i.e., only interactions of four FPM-rules are considered. As we can see in Figure 6, many non-dominated solutions in one scenario share the same task allocations for many tasks. Therefore, FPM is expected to find many rules with high significance. However, it is the rules that have a high significance while simultaneously having a low unselected significance, which are descriptive, since these rules more accurately distinguish between the selected and unselected sets of solutions.

Table 5 shows the FPM rules discovered for each scenario, indicating the tasks that distinguish the non-dominated solutions in the groups of scenarios more from the other solutions. For all groups, the parameter for the minimum required significance was kept constant at 90% when running the FPM procedure. For the scenarios with seven operators, a rule interaction was found with a significance of 100% and an unselected significance of 10.13%, meaning that all non-dominated solutions in the scenarios support the rules, while only 10.13% of the solutions in the unselected set support the rules. The rule interaction with the highest ratio between significance and unselected significance was found in the scenarios with nine operators, perhaps indicating that the non-dominated solutions in these scenarios are easier to distinguish from the rest. The scenarios with the lowest ratio are where the proportion is 30/70, perhaps indicating that the non-dominated solutions in these scenarios are more difficult to distinguish.

Table 5. Rule interactions found by using FPM for each of the scenarios from the initial optimization.

NO	Group Proportion	Rule Interaction	Sig	Unsig
7		$A_{10} = 2 \wedge B_4 \neq 3 \wedge B_5 = 2 \wedge B_{23} = 1$	100%	10.13%
8		$A_{17} = 2 \wedge A_{27} \neq 3 \wedge B_7 = 1 \wedge B_{16} = 2$	96.43%	12.89%
9		$A_{28} = 1 \wedge B_7 = 1 \wedge B_8 = 3 \wedge B_9 \neq 1$	91.67%	4.89%
	30/70	$A_{14} = 3 \wedge B_3 = 1 \wedge B_{10} \neq 1 \wedge B_{23} \neq 3$	97.06%	29.23%
	70/30	$A_{14} = 2 \wedge A_{17} = 2 \wedge B_4 \neq 3 \wedge B_{11} \neq 2$	92.11%	10.89%

5.3. Offline Knowledge-Driven Optimization

The rules for the different groups were applied to ten new scenarios, using the proportions of 40/60 and 60/40 between parts A and B for 7, 8, and 9 operators, and using 6 and 10 operators with the proportions of 30/70 and 70/30. We compare standard optimization runs for the new scenarios versus runs using the offline KDO approach of applying the rules presented in Table 5 as constraints in the decision space. Due to the high computational cost involved in the evaluation of each solution, each scenario was given an evaluation budget of 2500 solutions (50 generations with a population size of 50).

We compare the rate of convergence of the standard MOO approach and the offline KDO approach in each separate scenario by plotting the Hypervolume (HV) [39] contribution at each generation. Figure 8 shows the convergence plots for all scenarios. We also consider the Area Under the Curve (AUC) of the convergence plots as a quantitative score for the convergence rate. The AUC scores for all scenarios are shown in Table 6.

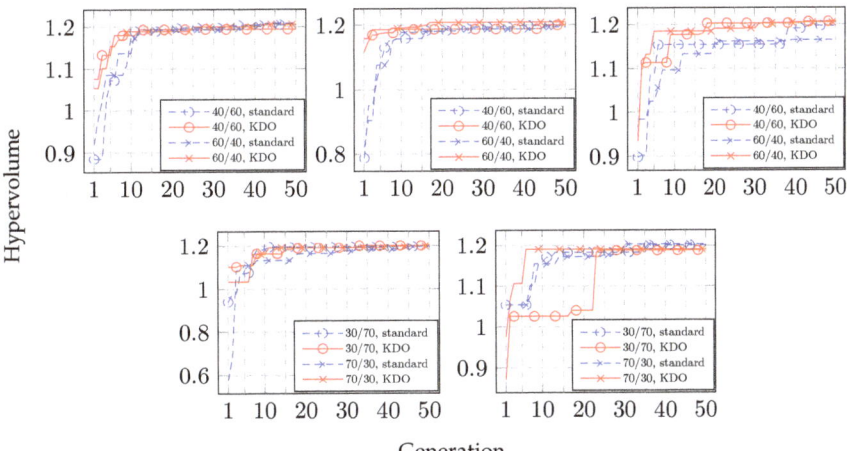

Figure 8. Convergence plots of the scenarios with 7 operators (**top left**), 8 operators (**top center**), 9 operators (**top right**), 6 operators (**lower left**), and 10 operators (**lower right**).

The results show that the offline KDO approach leads to faster convergence in all scenarios with operators equal to 7, 8, and 9 and the new proportions of 40/60 and 60/40 compared with the standard approach, and most of the scenarios using the proportions of 30/70 and 70/30 and the new numbers of operators of 6 and 10. In fact, only in the scenario with 10 operators and a proportion of 30/70 did the offline KDO approach not lead to faster convergence. However, the convergence plots for six operators are very similar for both approaches. This indicates that the offline KDO approach leads to an improved convergence rate for the current RMS MOOP when considering new proportions for the initial assignment of 7, 8, or 9 operators, but may be slightly less fruitful for scenarios with new numbers of operators and the original proportions.

Table 6. Area Under the Curve (AUC) of the convergence plots shown in Figure 8 for the different cases of Number of Operators (NO), proportion, and optimization approach.

NO	Proportion	Standard	Offline KDO
7	40/60	5.649×10^1	$\mathbf{5.804 \times 10^1}$
	60/40	5.688×10^1	$\mathbf{5.802 \times 10^1}$
8	40/60	5.650×10^1	$\mathbf{5.836 \times 10^1}$
	60/40	5.644×10^1	$\mathbf{5.883 \times 10^1}$
9	40/60	5.580×10^1	$\mathbf{5.776 \times 10^1}$
	60/40	5.507×10^1	$\mathbf{5.772 \times 10^1}$
6	30/70	5.759×10^1	$\mathbf{5.781 \times 10^1}$
	70/30	5.617×10^1	$\mathbf{5.750 \times 10^1}$
10	30/70	$\mathbf{5.729 \times 10^1}$	5.474×10^1
	70/30	5.727×10^1	$\mathbf{5.786 \times 10^1}$

Bold values indicate higher AUC scores.

6. Discussion

The initial results provided solutions found for six different scenarios from the same real-world RMS MOOP involving task allocation. The approach presented in this paper demonstrates the use of a knowledge discovery method to generate decision rules which are applied in future, different scenarios to help the optimization algorithm reach faster convergence on non-dominated solutions. We grouped scenarios where the numbers of operators were the same and proportions were different, in order to find if there is generalized knowledge that can be applied across scenarios with the same number of operators as well as the same for scenarios with the same proportions and different numbers of operators.

Although the initial optimization runs had a very high evaluation budget, they did not produce many non-dominated solutions in each scenario. In the scenario with nine operators and a proportion of 70/30, only a single non-dominated solution was found. This means that the optimization did not find a diverse set of solutions for this scenario, which might in turn means that the knowledge generated is not general enough. However, despite this, as shown in Figure 8 and Table 6, the offline KDO approach did result in faster convergence compared to the standard approach for both scenarios with nine operators.

To generate knowledge about the different scenarios, we used Flexible Pattern Mining (FPM) to find decision rules. However, the number of aspects in terms of decision variables considered by this study increases the complexity of the SMO and its knowledge discovery post-optimal analysis exponentially. For this reason, the number of rule interactions considered in each scenario was limited to four. Nonetheless, the rules extracted reveal knowledge regarding which tasks are more important and therefore need to be prioritized for finding competitive solutions with respect to different criteria. However, finding more complex rule interactions could potentially lead to more precise knowledge which might be of further benefit.

FPM is expected to identify the rules that are the most interesting to the decision-maker. Considering the rules discovered by FPM and shown in Table 5, we can see that, out of all groups of scenarios, some tasks are repeated in the rule interactions, namely A_{14}, A_{17}, B_4, B_7 and B_{23}. Indicating that these tasks have higher importance for more general scenarios, however, since no rules are common in all scenario groups, likely no rule describes a completely general scenario for the considered RMS MOOP. Only half of these tasks (A_{17}, B_4, B_7) have the same rule in the different scenario groups.

In the presented offline KDO approach, we applied the discovered rule as hard constraints in the decision space by limiting the values that the corresponding variables could take on. Although this approach did result in faster convergence in most cases, it does not guarantee that the solutions found are Pareto-optimal since it limits the search space. Secondly, the significance of the rule interactions used might also impact the quality of the final non-dominated solutions found. This point is driven further by the possibility that the solutions found in the initial optimization runs did not convergence close to the true Pareto-optimal front. However, in the case of SMO where each evaluation can take a very long time, decision-makers are more interested in finding *good enough* solutions fast rather than finding the true Pareto-optimal solutions.

We used knowledge found from six initial scenarios to drive the search for faster convergence in 10 new scenarios. The results show a bigger increase in the convergence rate in the scenarios with the initial numbers of operators and different proportions than the scenarios with the initial proportions and different numbers of operators, when using the offline KDO approach. This indicates that, for the considered MOOP, more general knowledge may be derived for the scenarios grouped by considering the different numbers of operators. The rule interactions also confirm this for the scenarios grouped by the proportion of 30/70, where the unselected significance is high compared to the rest of the scenario groups. This implies that it was more difficult to find rules that distinguish this group. One possible explanation for why the offline KDO approach did not lead to more of an improvement in a convergence rate for these scenarios is that no simple rule interaction is able to capture the distinguishing features regarding the proportions in the initial results. Tasks that are more important for changes in the proportion may be overshadowed by tasks more important for differences in the number of operators.

In this paper, we only considered the variables related for task allocation in the knowledge discovery and offline KDO approach. However, it would also be interesting to investigate the possible convergence rate improvement by generating knowledge also about the operators' assignments to WSs and the capacities of the inter-station buffers.

7. Conclusions

In this paper, we propose the use of an offline KDO approach for increased convergence rates in a real-world reconfigurable manufacturing system simulation-based multi-objective optimization problem. We first showcase an offline KDO approach for populating non-dominated solutions in the real-world inspired test problem RE3-5-4, by dividing found solutions into different clusters and finding specific knowledge for each cluster. This knowledge was then used to constrain the decision space to guide the optimization to converge on more non-dominated solutions. This approach was also shown to outperform a crude approach of constraining the objective space. We use a similar offline KDO approach on the real-world RMS problem.

RMSs are considered a key enabler for manufacturing systems to produce the required capacity and volume when needed. However, prior research in real-scale industrial applications is sporadic and seemingly ignores the importance of post-optimal analysis on the combined decision-objective space for supporting decision-making about the requirements of the future system. The use of offline KDO on SMO data sets of RMS is a novel area that can support the RMS research community, and accordingly, this paper illustrates an example of how it can be achieved.

In this paper, we considered knowledge discovery through the FPM procedure to generate if-then decision rules about the decision variables in relation to selections made in the objective space of the solutions. We considered variables related to task assignment in workstations. The results show how the offline KDO approach was able to lead the optimization to faster convergence in the majority of tested scenarios of new proportions and numbers of operators; however, for the considered MOOP, the offline KDO approach leads to a greater improvement in scenarios based on new proportions.

In additional to offline KDO, rules discovered through the FPM procedure can also be used to inform the decision-maker about various aspects about the MOOP and the solutions. Actionable insights from a post-optimal analysis using FPM for knowledge discovery may lead to improvements in the MOOP formulation and be a tool in decision-making.

For the future work, we would like to further investigate how the qualities of the generated rules correlate with the convergence when using offline KDO on more real-world applications. In this study, only knowledge in the form of FPM-rules was considered for offline KDO. Future work should also be focused on finding other appropriate knowledge representations for RMS applications.

Author Contributions: Conceptualization, H.S., C.A.B.-D., S.B. and A.H.C.N.; methodology, H.S. and C.A.B.-D.; software, H.S., C.A.B.-D. and A.N.; validation, H.S. and C.A.B.-D.; formal analysis, H.S.; investigation, H.S. and C.A.B.-D.; data curation, H.S. and C.A.B.-D.; writing—original draft preparation, H.S. and C.A.B.-D.; writing—review and editing, H.S., C.A.B.-D., S.B., A.H.C.N. and A.N.; visualization, H.S.; supervision, S.B. and A.H.C.N.; project administration, H.S. and C.A.B.-D.; funding acquisition, A.H.C.N. All authors have read and agreed to the published version of the manuscript.

Funding: This work was funded by the Knowledge Foundation (KKS), Sweden, through the KKS Profile Virtual Factories with Knowledge-Driven Optimization, VF-KDO, Grant No. 2018-0011.

Data Availability Statement: All reported data will be made available upon acceptance for publication.

Conflicts of Interest: The authors declare no conflict of interest. The funders had no role in the design of the study; in the collection, analyses, or interpretation of data; in the writing of the manuscript; or in the decision to publish the results.

References

1. Koren, Y. *The Global Manufacturing Revolution: Product-Process-Business Integration and Reconfigurable Systems*; John Wiley & Sons: Hoboken, NJ, USA, 2010.
2. Koren, Y.; Heisel, U.; Jovane, F.; Moriwaki, T.; Pritschow, G.; Ulsoy, G.; Van Brussel, H. Reconfigurable manufacturing systems. *CIRP Ann.* **1999**, *48*, 527–540. [CrossRef]
3. Koren, Y.; Gu, X.; Guo, W. Reconfigurable manufacturing systems: Principles, design, and future trends. *Front. Mech. Eng.* **2018**, *13*, 121–136. [CrossRef]
4. Diaz, C.A.B.; Aslam, T.; Ng, A.H. Optimizing Reconfigurable Manufacturing Systems for Fluctuating Production Volumes: A Simulation-Based Multi-Objective Approach. *IEEE Access* **2021**, *9*, 144195–144210. [CrossRef]
5. Mourtzis, D.; Doukas, M.; Bernidaki, D. Simulation in manufacturing: Review and challenges. *Procedia Cirp* **2014**, *25*, 213–229. [CrossRef]
6. Haddou Benderbal, H.; Dahane, M.; Benyoucef, L. Modularity assessment in reconfigurable manufacturing system (RMS) design: An Archived Multi-Objective Simulated Annealing-based approach. *Int. J. Adv. Manuf. Technol.* **2018**, *94*, 729–749. [CrossRef]
7. Renzi, C.; Leali, F.; Cavazzuti, M.; Andrisano, A.O. A review on artificial intelligence applications to the optimal design of dedicated and reconfigurable manufacturing systems. *Int. J. Adv. Manuf. Technol.* **2014**, *72*, 403–418. [CrossRef]
8. Delorme, X.; Malyutin, S.; Dolgui, A. A multi-objective approach for design of reconfigurable transfer lines. *IFAC-PapersOnLine* **2016**, *49*, 509–514. [CrossRef]
9. Deb, K.; Agrawal, S.; Pratap, A.; Meyarivan, T. A fast elitist non-dominated sorting genetic algorithm for multi-objective optimization: NSGA-II. In Proceedings of the International Conference on Parallel Problem Solving from Nature, Paris, France, 3 September 2000; Springer: Berlin, Germany, 2000; pp. 849–858.
10. Bandaru, S.; Ng, A.H.; Deb, K. Data mining methods for knowledge discovery in multi-objective optimization: Part A-Survey. *Expert Syst. Appl.* **2017**, *70*, 139–159. [CrossRef]
11. Bortolini, M.; Galizia, F.G.; Mora, C. Reconfigurable manufacturing systems: Literature review and research trend. *J. Manuf. Syst.* **2018**, *49*, 93–106. [CrossRef]
12. Michalos, G.; Makris, S.; Mourtzis, D. An intelligent search algorithm-based method to derive assembly line design alternatives. *Int. J. Comput. Integr. Manuf.* **2012**, *25*, 211–229. [CrossRef]
13. Diaz, C.A.B.; Fathi, M.; Aslam, T.; Ng, A.H. Optimizing reconfigurable manufacturing systems: A Simulation-based Multi-objective Optimization approach. *Procedia CIRP* **2021**, *104*, 1837–1842. [CrossRef]
14. Mourtzis, D. Simulation in the design and operation of manufacturing systems: State of the art and new trends. *Int. J. Prod. Res.* **2020**, *58*, 1927–1949. [CrossRef]
15. Petroodi, S.E.H.; Eynaud, A.B.D.; Klement, N.; Tavakkoli-Moghaddam, R. Simulation-based optimization approach with scenario-based product sequence in a reconfigurable manufacturing system (RMS): A case study. *IFAC-PapersOnLine* **2019**, *52*, 2638–2643. [CrossRef]
16. Koren, Y. The rapid responsiveness of RMS. *Int. J. Prod. Res.* **2013**, *51*, 6817–6827. [CrossRef]
17. Deb, K.; Srinivasan, A. Innovization: Innovating design principles through optimization. In Proceedings of the 8th Annual Conference on Genetic and Evolutionary Computation, Seattle, WA, USA, 8–12 July 2006; pp. 1629–1636.
18. Bandaru, S.; Deb, K. A dimensionally-aware genetic programming architecture for automated innovization. In Proceedings of the International Conference on Evolutionary Multi-Criterion Optimization, Sheffield, UK, 19–22 March 2013; Springer: Berlin, Germany, 2013; pp. 513–527.

19. Ng, A.; Deb, K.; Dudas, C. Simulation-based innovization for production systems improvement: An industrial case study. In Proceedings of the International 3rd Swedish Production Symposium, SPS'09, Göteborg, Sweden, 2–3 December 2009; pp. 278–286.
20. Dudas, C.; Ng, A.H.; Pehrsson, L.; Boström, H. Integration of data mining and multi-objective optimisation for decision support in production systems development. *Int. J. Comput. Integr. Manuf.* **2014**, *27*, 824–839. [CrossRef]
21. Sato, Y.; Izui, K.; Yamada, T.; Nishiwaki, S. Data mining based on clustering and association rule analysis for knowledge discovery in multiobjective topology optimization. *Expert Syst. Appl.* **2019**, *119*, 247–261. [CrossRef]
22. Bandaru, S.; Ng, A.H.; Deb, K. Data mining methods for knowledge discovery in multi-objective optimization: Part B-New developments and applications. *Expert Syst. Appl.* **2017**, *100*, 119–138. [CrossRef]
23. Agrawal, R.; Srikant, R. Mining sequential patterns. In Proceedings of the Eleventh International Conference on Data Engineering, Taipei, Taiwan, 6–10 March 1995; pp. 3–14.
24. Agrawal, R.; Srikant, R. Fast algorithms for mining association rules. In Proceedings of the 20th International Conference on Very Large Data Bases, VLDB, Santiago de Chile, Chile, 12–15 September 1994; Volume 1215, pp. 487–499.
25. Smedberg, H. Knowledge-driven reference-point based multi-objective optimization: First results. In Proceedings of the Genetic and Evolutionary Computation Conference Companion, Prague, Czech Republic, 13–17 July 2019; pp. 2060–2063.
26. Smedberg, H.; Bandaru, S. A Modular Knowledge-Driven Mutation Operator for Reference-Point Based Evolutionary Algorithms. In Proceedings of the 2022 IEEE Congress on Evolutionary Computation (CEC), Padua, Italy, 18–23 July 2022; pp. 1–8.
27. Karlsson, I.; Bandaru, S.; Ng, A.H. Online Knowledge Extraction and Preference Guided Multi-Objective Optimization in Manufacturing. *IEEE Access* **2021**, *9*, 145382–145396. [CrossRef]
28. Zhang, J.; Zhou, A.; Tang, K.; Zhang, G. Preselection via classification: A case study on evolutionary multiobjective optimization. *Inf. Sci.* **2018**, *465*, 388–403. [CrossRef]
29. Nojima, Y.; Tanigaki, Y.; Masuyama, N.; Ishibuchi, H. Multiobjective Evolutionary Data Mining for Performance Improvement of Evolutionary Multiobjective Optimization. In Proceedings of the 2018 IEEE International Conference on Systems, Man, and Cybernetics (SMC), Miyazaki, Japan, 7–10 October 2018; pp. 745–750.
30. Mittal, S.; Saxena, D.K.; Deb, K.; Goodman, E.D. A learning-based innovized progress operator for faster convergence in evolutionary multi-objective optimization. *ACM Trans. Evol. Learn. Optim. (TELO)* **2021**, *2*, 1–29. [CrossRef]
31. Mittal, S.; Saxena, D.K.; Deb, K.; Goodman, E.D. Enhanced Innovized Progress Operator for Evolutionary Multi-and Many-objective Optimization. *IEEE Trans. Evol. Comput.* **2021**, *26*, 961–975. [CrossRef]
32. Dudas, C.; Ng, A.H.; Bostroem, H. Post-analysis of multi-objective optimization solutions using decision trees. *Intell. Data Anal.* **2015**, *19*, 259–278. [CrossRef]
33. Bonissone, P.P.; Subbu, R.; Eklund, N.; Kiehl, T.R. Evolutionary algorithms+ domain knowledge= real-world evolutionary computation. *IEEE Trans. Evol. Comput.* **2006**, *10*, 256–280. [CrossRef]
34. Mahbub, M.S.; Wagner, M.; Crema, L. Incorporating domain knowledge into the optimization of energy systems. *Appl. Soft Comput.* **2016**, *47*, 483–493. [CrossRef]
35. Hitomi, N.; Selva, D. Incorporating expert knowledge into evolutionary algorithms with operators and constraints to design satellite systems. *Appl. Soft Comput.* **2018**, *66*, 330–345. [CrossRef]
36. Weiss, K.; Khoshgoftaar, T.M.; Wang, D. A survey of transfer learning. *J. Big Data* **2016**, *3*, 1–40. [CrossRef]
37. Tanabe, R.; Ishibuchi, H. An easy-to-use real-world multi-objective optimization problem suite. *Appl. Soft Comput.* **2020**, *89*, 106078. [CrossRef]
38. Liao, X.; Li, Q.; Yang, X.; Zhang, W.; Li, W. Multiobjective optimization for crash safety design of vehicles using stepwise regression model. *Struct. Multidiscip. Optim.* **2008**, *35*, 561–569. [CrossRef]
39. Zitzler, E.; Thiele, L. Multiobjective evolutionary algorithms: A comparative case study and the strength Pareto approach. *IEEE Trans. Evol. Comput.* **1999**, *3*, 257–271. [CrossRef]
40. Barrera-Diaz, C.A.; Nourmohammdi, A.; Smedberg, H.; Aslam, T.; Ng, A.H.C. An enhanced simulation-based multi-objective optimization approach with knowledge discovery for reconfigurable manufacturing systems. *arXiv* **2022**, arXiv:cs.SY/2212.00581.
41. Ng, A.H.; Bernedixen, J.; Moris, M.U.; Jägstam, M. Factory flow design and analysis using internet-enabled simulation-based optimization and automatic model generation. In Proceedings of the 2011 Winter Simulation Conference (WSC), Phoenix, AZ, USA, 11–14 December 2011; pp. 2176–2188.
42. Smedberg, H.; Bandaru, S. Interactive knowledge discovery and knowledge visualization for decision support in multi-objective optimization. *Eur. J. Oper. Res.* **2022**. [CrossRef]

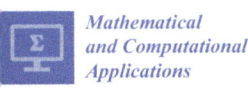

Article

An Experimental Study of Grouping Mutation Operators for the Unrelated Parallel-Machine Scheduling Problem

Octavio Ramos-Figueroa *, Marcela Quiroz-Castellanos, Efrén Mezura-Montes and Nicandro Cruz-Ramírez

Artificial Intelligence Research Institute, Universidad Veracruzana, Campus Sur, Calle Paseo Lote II, Sección Segunda 112, Nuevo Xalapa, Veracruz 91097, Mexico
* Correspondence: oivatco.rafo@gmail.com

Abstract: The Grouping Genetic Algorithm (GGA) is an extension to the standard Genetic Algorithm that uses a group-based representation scheme and variation operators that work at the group-level. This metaheuristic is one of the most used to solve combinatorial optimization grouping problems. Its optimization process consists of different components, although the crossover and mutation operators are the most recurrent. This article aims to highlight the impact that a well-designed operator can have on the final performance of a GGA. We present a comparative experimental study of different mutation operators for a GGA designed to solve the Parallel-Machine scheduling problem with unrelated machines and makespan minimization, which comprises scheduling a collection of jobs in a set of machines. The proposed approach is focused on identifying the strategies involved in the mutation operations and adapting them to the characteristics of the studied problem. As a result of this experimental study, knowledge of the problem-domain was gained and used to design a new mutation operator called 2-Items Reinsertion. Experimental results indicate that the state-of-the-art GGA performance considerably improves by replacing the original mutation operator with the new one, achieving better results, with an improvement rate of 52%.

Keywords: grouping genetic algorithm; grouping mutation operator; grouping problem; unrelated parallel-machine scheduling

1. Introduction

Over the last decades, the interest of the scientific community in solving Combinatorial Optimization Problems (COPs) has grown considerably since these types of problems emerge in many practical issues in industry, logistics, and engineering. In general, the optimization of a COP comprises the search of the suitable values for a set of discrete variables, so that the objective function is optimized, satisfying the given conditions and constraints. Thus, the solution of this type of problems can involve a feasible disposition, grouping, order, or selection of discrete objects that typically are finite in number [1]. It is well-known that many COPs have high complexity, and in the worst-case scenario, there is no efficient algorithm that solves all their possible cases optimally. Such problems belong to the NP-hard class [2]. In this order of ideas, this work focuses on grouping problems, a special type of COPs that in general consist of looking for an efficient arrangement of a set of elements among a collection of groups [1].

Parallel-Machine Scheduling (PMS) is a classical NP-hard grouping problem, consisting of looking for the most efficient sequential scheduling of a set of n jobs $N = \{j_1, \ldots, j_n\}$ among a collection of m parallel-machines $M = \{i_1, \ldots, i_m\}$, in such a way that each machine i can process only one job j at a time, and each job j must be processed by a single machine i [3].

The PMS variants can consider different parameters in the problem definition, such as resource and scheduling environments, job characteristics, and optimization criteria, among others. The most general classification of PMS problems is according to the machine environment. In this sense, this work focuses on a variant that belongs to the class with unrelated machines, i.e., each machine can require a different time to process each job, and there is not a behavior pattern with respect to the speed of the machines with a machine always being the fastest or the slowest one (Unrelated Parallel-Machine Scheduling, UPMS). This problem family has received much recognition due to its numerous real-world applications [4–6]. Although a large number of mathematical models have been proposed, the exact approaches can solve only small instances in a reasonable time [7]. Given the complexity of several UPMS variants, most approaches are metaheuristic algorithms, such as local searches, swarm intelligence, and evolutionary algorithms. The state of the art contains local searches such as the Hill Climbing [8], the Iterated Greedy Algorithm [9], the Variable Neighborhood Descent [10], and the GRASP Algorithm [11]. In the same spirit, the literature includes several swarm intelligence algorithms, such as the Worm Optimization Algorithm [12], the Firefly Algorithm [13], the Artificial Bee Colony [14], and the Fruit Fly Optimization Algorithm [15]. Additionally, we identified several evolutionary algorithms such as the Genetic Algorithm [16], the Genetic Programming [17], and the Imperialist Competitive Algorithm with memory [18]. Finally, the specialized literature includes some memetic algorithms [19,20]. The literature review reveals that there are a wide variety of UPMS problems, each with particular characteristics and challenges. Given the increasing appearance of these problems, there exists a trend to explore the algorithmic behavior of different metaheuristic approaches that can work well or badly according to the properties of the variant of the problem to solve. One of the main challenges in the development of high-performance algorithms for UPMS problems is the design of efficient strategies that work together with the features of the problem variant to find high-quality solutions.

This work addresses the UPMS variant known as the $R||C_{max}$ problem, where the machines $\{i_1, \ldots, i_m\}$ are unrelated, jobs $\{j_1, \ldots, j_n\}$ have no-preemptions, and the objective of interest is the reduction of the maximum completion time C_{max}, i.e., the processing time C_i required by the machine i that finishes at the end.

It is well-known that the problem $R||C_{max}$ belongs to the class NP-hard [2]. Hence, over the past forty years, different approaches have been studied to try to solve it efficiently. The specialized literature includes deterministic methods [21,22], two-phase algorithms (or rounding methods) [23,24], and branch and bound algorithms [3,25]. The literature also includes distinct metaheuristic algorithms for $R||C_{max}$, covering proposals based on local searches [3,26], the swarm intelligence algorithm Particle Swarm Optimization (PSO) [1], the Genetic Algorithm (GA) [27], and some hybrid approaches [3]. According to the scope of this review, the approaches based on local searches have shown the best performance on solving the problem $R||C_{max}$. The state of the art highlights the results reached by the Iterated Greedy Local Search (NVST-IG+) proposed by Fanjul-Peyro and Ruiz in 2009, considered one of the best solution methods designed for the problem of interest so far. The success key of the NVST-IG+ performance is the incorporation of some techniques to control the way in which the jobs and machines are selected and manipulated during the construction of the neighborhoods [26].

In [1], we presented one of the most recent related works; the experimental results suggested that a GA with a group-based representation GGA has a better performance than a GA with an extended permutation solution encoding and a PSO with a machine-based representation scheme for the 1400 test instances studied. Such GGA was an adaptation of the GGA-CGT designed by Quiroz-Castellanos et al. for the Bin Packing Problem [28]. According to Quiroz-Castellanos et al., the performance of the GGA-CGT is related mainly to the mutation operator, which alone is capable of finding quality solutions. The mutation is one of the most used genetic operators in GGAs. Commonly, mutation operators promote the exploration of the search space by slightly altering the solution genetic material. This behavior is useful for a GGA mainly when it is converging to a local optimum since it provides the capacity to redirect the search to other areas. Section 2.5 includes an experimental study with different parameter configurations that allows observing how the performance of the GGA proposed in [1] is mainly related to the crossover operator, while the mutation operator has a low impact. The above motivates this work that aims to study the performance of different grouping mutation operators to identify the strategies that they use and that positively impact their performance, to employ them in the design of a new operator, and to incorporate that operator into the GGA in order to improve its performance when solving $R||C_{max}$.

This paper continues as follows. Section 2 describes the components and the problem-domain heuristics of the GGA for $R||C_{max}$. Section 3 reviews the state-of-the-art grouping mutation operators. Section 4 contains the experimental design proposed to analyze the impact of different strategies in the performance of grouping mutation operators. Section 5 compares the GGA performance with the new and the old mutation operators to analyze the improvement rate. Finally, Section 6 summarizes the conclusions and future paths of research.

2. Grouping Genetic Algorithm for $R||C_{max}$

The state of the art suggests that the GGA is one of the most used metaheuristics to solve grouping problems. Such popularity is related to its promising results and its flexibility to adopt new ideas to handle the constraints and conditions of the problem to be solved [1,29,30].

The GGA is an extension to the standard GA; therefore, it has a similar procedure. The GGA starts with the generation of the initial population, generally in a random way. Next, selection strategies and variation operators, mainly crossover and mutation, are used iteratively so as to find better solutions. Each iteration represents a generation that starts utilizing a selection strategy to pick some individuals of the population based on their fitness values; then, the genetic material of the selected individuals is recombined with the crossover operator to generate offspring. Subsequently, the offspring are added to the population using a replacement strategy. Finally, some individuals, chosen with a selection strategy, are slightly modified with the mutation operator. In this way, the GGA iterates performing the before-mentioned procedure until some stopping criterion (e.g., the maximum number of generations, the maximum search time, convergence of solutions, or finding an optimal solution) is met.

One of the main features of the GGA is the group-based scheme that it uses to encode and manage solutions in the search space. According to Falkenauer, this is a more natural way of representing solutions to grouping problems. Moreover, it helps to reduce the search space since it produces fewer isomorphic solutions than a traditional representation scheme [31]. In this encoding, each gene represents a group that contains the collection of elements that correspond to it. Therefore, the length of a solution is equal to the number of groups that it includes.

Another important aspect to consider when developing a GGA is the design of variation operators such as crossover and mutation since they must work at the group level. With this feature, operators can perform procedures in a more controlled way, determining which groups and elements vary according to the constraints and objectives of the problem to solve. The crossover operator uses two or more solutions of the current population to recombine their genetic material, creating offspring with new characteristics. This operator is used to give GGA the ability to converge on the most promising areas identified during the search. One of the advantages of crossover operators for the group-based encoding is that they can use the quality of the groups to determine how parents transmit the genetic material to their offspring to perform a more controlled search. On the other hand, the mutation operator provides GGA the ability to explore new areas of the search space, producing small modifications to the genetic material of some solutions. This procedure is helpful for a GGA, mainly to address highly constrained grouping problems, where there are large possibilities of converging to local optimums. These slight alterations performed by the mutation operator can generate solutions in other regions of the search space, avoiding premature convergence [32].

The next sections describe the elements of the state-of-the-art GGA for $R||C_{max}$, the object of study in this work, including the population initialization strategy, the variation operators, selection and replacement strategies, and the problem-domain heuristics. This algorithm is an adaptation of the Grouping Genetic Algorithm with Controlled Gene Transmission (GGA-CGT) introduced by Quiroz-Castellanos et al. to solve the Bin Packing problem [28]. The details of the heuristic used to generate the initial population, as well as the mutation and crossover operators appear in the work of Ramos-Figueroa et al. [1], while the remaining mechanisms and operators, as well as the parameter settings can be consulted in the work of Quiroz-Castellanos et al. [28].

2.1. Genetic Encoding, Fitness Function, and Initial Population

The GGA uses the group-based representation scheme to encode and manipulate solutions, where each machine i is a gene (or group) G_i that will include a set of jobs. Therefore, all solutions have the same number of genes, equal to the number of machines m. The quality of each machine i is equal to the time it takes to process its assigned jobs, denoted as C_i. Thus, the quality of a solution C_{max} is equal to the C_i value of the machine with the longest processing time. The initial population is generated in a random manner by running the well-known Min() heuristic on random permutations of the n jobs [33]. For each job j, Min() calculates the equation $C_i = C_i + p_{ij}$ for all the machines, where p_{ij} indicates the time that the machine i needs to process the job j. In this way, Min() assigns the job j to the machine i that generates the lowest C_i value.

Figure 1 describes the procedure followed by the population initialization strategy. To give a comprehensive description, Figure 1a includes an example instance I represented as a matrix with $m = 4$ machines depicted by the columns and $n = 10$ jobs represented by the rows. Thus, the example starts from a permutation (Figure 1b) of the ten jobs, $\{j_9, j_5, j_2, j_6, j_3, j_8, j_4, j_7, j_1, j_{10}\}$, used to generate the partial solution, shown in Figure 1c. The construction of the partial solution can be calculated from the first nine jobs in the permutation, $\{j_9, j_5, j_2, j_6, j_3, j_8, j_4, j_7, j_1,\}$ and the instance I using the heuristic Min(). To exemplify how this heuristic Min() works, Figure 1d shows a complete solution, resulting from the assignment of the last job in the permuted list (i.e., j_{10}) to the solution. Therefore, following the Min() procedure mentioned above, the processing time C_i of each machine plus the time that they require to process the job j_{10} results in the following way: $C_1 = 26 + 8$, $C_2 = 25 + 20$, $C_3 = 20 + 18$, and $C_4 = 10 + 28$. Hence, Min() assigned the job j_{10} to the machine i_1 since it generated the lowest C_i value. It is important to note that if two or more machines produce the same C_i value, this allocation heuristic assigns the job in turn to the machine i that appears first from i_1 to i_m. Finally, Figure 1d also shows the fitness value of the generated solution that is equal to the longest processing time C_i, in this case, the $C_1 = 34$, outlined in bold.

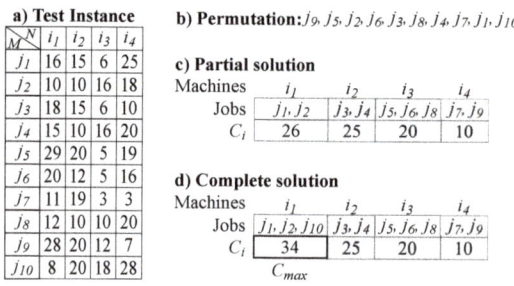

Figure 1. Population initialization strategy.

2.2. Adapted Gene-Level Crossover Operator

The GGA uses the Adapted Gene-Level Crossover (AGLX) operator, a variant of the GLX operator proposed by Quiroz-Castellanos et al. [28] that produces two children solutions by using two parent solutions. Algorithm 1 presents the procedure of AGLX. We denote $S' = \text{Sort}(S)$ the solution derived from S by sorting its machines in increasing order concerning its C_i values (lines 1 and 2). Thus, AGLX first transmits the machines that process their jobs fastest and then the slowest ones (lines 3–6). In this way, the first child C_1 starts inheriting the fastest machine from the first parent S_1, next the fastest machine from the second parent S_2, then the second-fastest machine from the first parent S_1, and so on (line 4). Similarly, the second child C_2 receives genes alternately from both parents but starting with the fastest machine from the second parent S_2 (line 5). We denote $C = \text{Inherit}(C, i_a, i_b)$ the child solution C upgraded with the machines i_a and i_b, one for each parent. It is important to remark that before inheriting each machine, the Inherit() function verifies that it has not already been transmitted by the other parent to the child C. Otherwise, the machine is discarded. Likewise, before inheriting each job, this function validates that it has not already been transmitted. Otherwise, it is discarded to avoid infeasible solutions. It is important to note that in most of cases this procedure generates infeasible solutions, since some jobs can be missed during the crossover process. Therefore, it is necessary to re-insert the jobs to transform the solutions into feasible ones (lines 7 and 8). We denote $MJ[] = \text{MissedJobs}(C)$ the set of jobs missed during the genetic material transmission of a child C. Finally, the missed jobs MJ are permuted and re-inserted with the Min() heuristic described above (lines 9–12). We denote $MJ[]' = \text{Permute}(MJ[])$ the set of jobs derived from $MJ[]$ by permuting it with a uniform distribution and $C' = \text{Min}(C, MJ[]')$ the child solution obtained from the re-insertion of the jobs in $MJ[]'$ to the solution C.

Algorithm 1 AGLX operator

    Input: Two parent solutions S_1 and S_2, and the number of machines m.
    Output: Two offspring solutions C_1' and C_2'.
1: $S_1' = \text{Sort}(S_1)$;
2: $S_2' = \text{Sort}(S_2)$;
3: **for each** machine i in S_1' and S_2' **do**
4:     $C_1 = \text{Inherit}(C_1, S_1'[i], S_2'[i])$;
5:     $C_2 = \text{Inherit}(C_2, S_2'[i], S_1'[i])$;
6: **end for**
7: $MJ_1[] = \text{MissedJobs}(C_1)$;
8: $MJ_2[] = \text{MissedJobs}(C_2)$;
9: $MJ_1[]' = \text{Permute}(MJ_1[])$;
10: $MJ_2[]' = \text{Permute}(MJ_2[])$;
11: $C_1' = \text{Min}(C_1, MJ_1[]')$;
12: $C_2' = \text{Min}(C_2, MJ_2[]')$;
13: **end process.**

Figure 2 describes the process of the AGLX operator with an example that contains two parent solutions for the test instance of Figure 1a with four machines (groups). The ten jobs, from j_1 to j_{10}, are distributed among the four machines, from i_1 to i_4, and the time that each machine i requires to process its assigned jobs from C_1 to C_4 is stored in the vector C_i. Figure 2a depicts the transmission process. Therefore, it shows the two parents with their groups in increasing order, which indicates the gene transmission sequence, i.e., from best (Lowest C_i) to worst (Highest C_i). Figure 2b indicates the way the repeated genetic material is handled. Thus, it contains the two solutions produced during the transmission process, which only keep the machine i of the parent in which it appears first according to the gene transmission sequence. Furthermore, this figure includes the repeated jobs, highlighted in bold, that must be removed from the machine with the highest processing time C_i. Lastly, this figure shows a list with the jobs missed MJ during the transmission process. Figure 2c contains the partial solution resulting from the transmission process without the repeating genetic material, as well as a permutation of the jobs in MJ. Finally, Figure 2d shows the complete solutions resulting from the assignment of the missed jobs with the heuristic Min(). The processing time C_i of each machine i, as well as the operations performed by the Min() heuristic to assign the missed jobs, can be calculated using the example instance presented in Figure 1a.

Given two parent solutions for the test instance of Figure 1a, the Adapted Gene-level crossover operator (AGLX) proposed by Ramos-Figueroa et al. [1] works as follows:

a) Transmission process	Machines Jobs C_i	i_4 j_7, j_9 10	i_3 j_5, j_6, j_8 20	i_2 j_3, j_4 25	i_1 j_1, j_2, j_{10} 34	First Parent	
	Machines Jobs C_i	i_2 j_2 10	i_3 j_1, j_3, j_6, j_7 20	i_1 j_5, j_9 57	i_4 j_4, j_8, j_{10} 68	Second Parent	
b) Repeated genetic material	Machines Jobs C_i	i_4 j_7, j_9 10	i_2 j_2 10	i_3 j_5, j_6, j_8 20	i_1 j_5, j_9 57	First Child	MJ j_1, j_3, j_4, j_{10}
	Machines Jobs C_i	i_2 j_2 10	i_4 j_7, j_9 10	i_3 j_1, j_3, j_6, j_7 20	i_1 j_5, j_9 57	Second Child	MJ j_4, j_8, j_{10}
c) Partial solution	Machines Jobs C_i	i_1 0	i_2 j_5, j_6, j_8 10	i_3 20	i_4 j_7, j_9 10	First Child	Permutation j_{10}, j_4, j_3, j_1
	Machines Jobs C_i	i_1 j_5 29	i_2 j_2 10	i_3 j_1, j_3, j_6 17	i_4 j_7, j_9 10	Second Child	Permutation j_8, j_{10}, j_4
d) Offspring	Machines Jobs C_i	i_1 j_1, j_{10} 24	i_2 j_2, j_4 20	i_3 j_5, j_6, j_8 20	i_4 j_3, j_7, j_9 20	First Child	
	Machines Jobs C_i	i_1 j_5 29	i_2 j_2, j_4, j_8 30	i_3 j_1, j_3, j_6, j_{10} 17	i_4 j_7, j_9 10	Second Child	

Figure 2. AGLX operator.

2.3. Download Mutation Operator

The GGA includes the Download mutation operator that uses two phases to modify two genes in a solution. Algorithm 2 contains the procedure of the Download mutation operator. In the first stage, called download, the operator clusters the genes (machines) among two sets, W and O (line 1). We denote $W, O = \text{Cluster}(S)$ the sets derived by grouping the machines in the solution S, in such a way that W includes the machines with a processing time C_i equal to the makespan C_{max}, while O holds the ones with an assigned processing time C_i less than the makespan C_{max}. Next, from each set (W and O), one machine (w and o) is randomly selected (lines 2 and 3). We denote $i=\text{Pick}(M)$ the machine i randomly selected from the set of machines M with a uniform distribution. Subsequently, the jobs in the selected machines are released (line 4). We denote $S', RJ[] = \text{Download}(S, w, o)$ the solution derived by releasing the jobs of the machines o and w, which are placed in the set $RJ[]$. Finally, the arrangement of the jobs in $RJ[]$ is modified with the permute() function mentioned above, giving rise to the set $RJ'[]$ (line 5). Later, in the second stage, the released jobs are redistributed among the selected machines w and o with the heuristic Best() (lines 6–8). We denote $S'' = \text{Best}(S', j, w, o)$ the solution obtained by applying the Best() heuristic. For each job j, this heuristic calculates the equations $C_w = C_w + p_{wj}$ and $C_o = C_o + p_{oj}$, where C_w and C_o represent the assigned processing time of machines w and o, respectively, and p_{wj} and p_{oj} the processing time required for machines w and o to process the job j. In this way, Best() assigns j to the machine that generates the lowest C_i value. It is important to highlight that the main difference between the reassignment heuristics Min() and Best() is that Min() re-inserts the jobs considering all the machines, while Best() re-inserts them by considering only the two selected machines o and w.

Algorithm 2 Download mutation operator

    Input: A solution S.
    Output: A mutated solution S''.
1: $W, O = \text{Cluster}(S)$;
2: $w = \text{Pick}(W)$;
3: $o = \text{Pick}(O)$;
4: $S', RJ[] = \text{Download}(S, w, o)$;
5: $RJ'[] = \text{Permute}(RJ[])$;
6: **for all** job $j \in RJ'[]$ **do**
7:     $S'' = \text{Best}(S', j, w, o)$;
8: **end for**
9: **end process.**

Figure 3 describes the mutation process of the Download operator with an example that contains an initial solution for the instance presented in Figure 1a with four genes (groups). The ten jobs, from j_1 to j_{10}, are distributed among four groups, from i_1 to i_4, and the time that each group i requires to process its assigned jobs from C_1 to C_4 is stored in the vector C_i. Figure 3a shows the result of clustering the machines with processing time C_i equal to the makespan C_{max} in the set $W = \{i_1\}$ and the remaining machines in set $O = \{i_2, i_3, i_4\}$. Figure 3b indicates the machines $w = i_1$ and $o = i_4$, outlined in bold, randomly selected from the sets W and O, respectively. Figure 3c contains the solution with the selected machines to be altered, outlined in bold, downloaded by releasing their jobs and placing them in the box of released jobs RJ. Finally, Figure 3d shows a permutation of the jobs in RJ and the result of reinserting them with the allocation heuristic Best(). The calculation of the processing time C_i of each machine i, as well as the operations performed by the allocation heuristic Best() to assign the released jobs, can be calculated using the example instance I presented in Figure 1a. As this example shows, the quality of the mutated solution is better than that of the initial solution, demonstrating the effectiveness of the Download mutation operator.

Given the following potential solution for the test instance of Figure 1a:

		Solution		
Machines	i_1	i_2	i_3	i_4
Jobs	j_1, j_2, j_{10}	j_3, j_4	j_5, j_6, j_8	j_7, j_9
C_i	34	25	20	10

The Download mutation operator proposed by Ramos-Figueroa et al. [1] works as follows:

a) Machines in the sets W and O	i_1 W		i_2, i_3, i_4 O			
b) Selecting machines w and o	Machines Jobs C_i	i_1 j_1, j_2, j_{10} 34 w	i_2 j_3, j_4 25	i_3 j_5, j_6, j_8 20	i_4 j_7, j_9 10 o	
c) Download	Machines Jobs C_i	i_1 0	i_2 j_3, j_4 25	i_3 j_5, j_6, j_8 20	i_4 0	RJ $j_1, j_2, j_7, j_9, j_{10}$
d) Reinsertion	Machines Jobs C_i	i_1 j_1, j_{10} 24	i_2 j_3, j_4 25	i_3 j_5, j_6, j_8 20	i_4 j_2, j_7, j_9 28	Permutation $j_1, j_{10}, j_2, j_9, j_7$

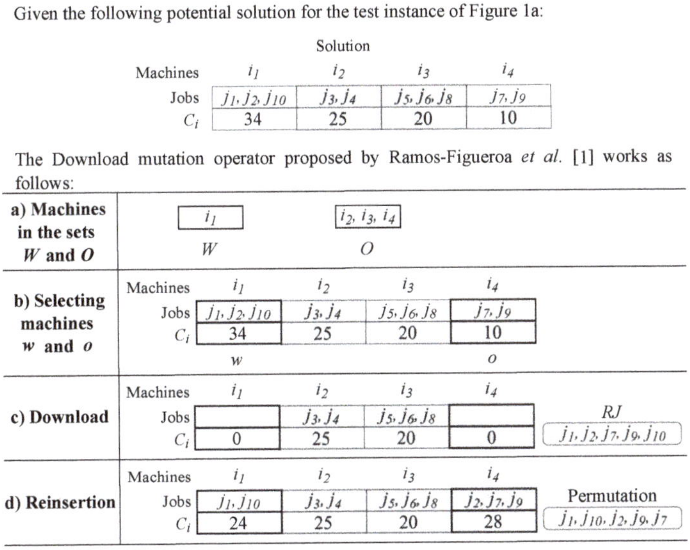

Figure 3. Download mutation operator.

2.4. Selection and Replacement Strategies

The GGA employs an adaptation of the controlled reproduction technique proposed by Quiroz-Castellanos et al. [28], which uses an elitist approach together with two inverted rankings to give all the solutions a chance to contribute to the next generation but forcing the survival of the best solutions. The replacement strategy preserves the population diversity and the best solutions by replacing duplicated fitness individuals and the worst fitness solutions with new offspring. Algorithm 3 contains the procedure of the ranking strategy. First, this algorithm ranks the population (line 1). We denote $P' = \text{Rank}(P)$ the individuals arranged by sorting them from best to worst according to their fitness. Next, if there are solutions with repeated fitness, only one solution is kept in the ranked, and the others are placed at the end of the ordered list (line 2). We denote $P'' = \text{Rearrange}(P)$ the population rank resulting from placing the similar solutions at the end of the ordered list. Subsequently, the solutions in P'' are distributed among the sets G, R, and B (line 3). We denote $G, R, B = \text{Distribution}(P'')$ the sets obtained by placing the ranked solutions in the sets G, R, B. In this way, G includes the best n_c solutions, where n_c is a parameter to be configured that determines the number of individuals selected for the crossover process of each generation. On the other hand, the set R contains the solutions in the population P'' without the best $n_c/2$ solutions. Finally, the set B holds the best $|B|$ individuals, called elite solutions, that receive special treatment since they have the best characteristics of the population. Therefore, $|B|$ is another parameter to be configured.

Algorithm 3 Ranking strategy

    Input: The population P.
    Output: The population rearranged en sets the G, R, and B.
1: $P' = \text{Rank}(P)$;
2: $P'' = \text{Rearrange}(P)$;
3: $G, R, B = \text{Distribution}(P'')$;
4: **end process.**

Given this solution hierarchical structure, $n_c/2$ parent solutions are randomly taken from the set G, and the remaining $n_c/2$ parents are randomly picked up from the solutions in the set R. In this way, each pair of parents is created with a parent selected from the set G and the other one from the set R. Hence, it is necessary to validate that parent pairs do not have the same solution since some solutions can be selected more than once. After applying the crossover operator to each pair of parents, the new individuals are incorporated into the ranked population P'' in the following way. Half of the generated children replace the parents selected from the set R, and the remaining offspring replace first the solutions with repeated fitness and then those with worse fitness, i.e., the solutions at the end of the ranked population P''.

Once the replacement strategy is applied, the population is rearranged again with the same ranking strategy, described in Algorithm 3, to later select the best n_m solutions for mutation, where n_m is a parameter to be configured that determines the number of mutated solutions each generation. When applying the mutation operator, if a solution belongs to the elite group B, the solution is first cloned and later mutated. The clones can be entered into the population, replacing first the solutions with repeated fitness and then those with worse fitness.

2.5. Impact Analysis of Crossover and Mutation Rate on GGA

In order to identify the impact of each variation operator (crossover and mutation) on the GGA performance, an experimental study was performed by using three different values for the number of individuals selected for the crossover process (n_c) and the number of solutions to be mutated (n_m): 20, 40, and 60. In this way, GGA was run with the 9 configurations ($Conf$) generated from all possible combinations of these three parameters: $Conf_1$:

$n_c = 20$, $n_m = 20$, $Conf_2$: $n_c = 20$, $n_m = 40$, ... $Conf_9$: $n_c = 60$, $n_m = 60$. Figure 4 shows a bar graph of the results obtained from this study, where each bar represents 1 of the 9 configurations grouped according to the number of mutated solutions (n_m), and each pattern indicates the number of selected individuals for the crossover process (n_c): squares $= 20$, waves $= 40$, and circles $= 60$. As Figure 4 indicates, the GGA performance tends to improve (lower error rate) as the number of individuals considered for the crossover and mutation processes increases, although the crossover operator shows a higher impact on its performance. This behavior is different from the one presented by the GGA-CGT, where the mutation operator has the greatest positive impact on the final performance of this algorithm. The results and conclusions obtained from this study motivated the review of the mutation operator, exploring different strategies to include those that contribute to the impact improvement of this operator on the GGA final performance on solving the $R||C_{max}$ problem.

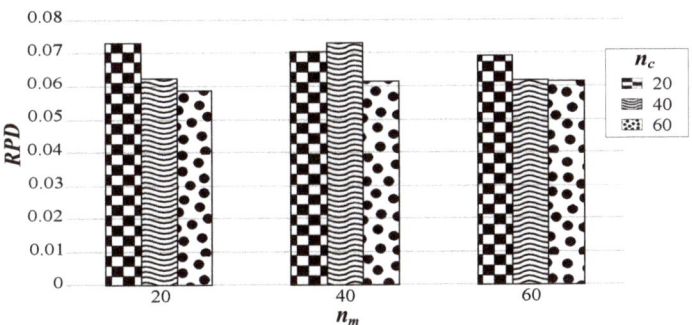

Figure 4. Impact analysis of the parameters: number of individuals selected for crossover n_c and number of mutated solutions n_m in the GGA final performance.

3. Grouping Mutation Operators

The mutation is a genetic operator generally used to control population diversity during the GGA search process. The mutation operators for the GGA are called grouping mutation operators since they work at the group level. That is, they select g groups using some criterion (such as selecting the best, the worst, or random groups) to slightly modify them employing different operations. According to Ramos-Figueroa et al. [32], the specialized literature holds seven mutation operators designed for GGAs in addition to the Download operator. Three of them, the Swap, the Insertion, and the Item Elimination, perform small alterations in the solutions with operations directly applied to some items of the selected groups. In contrast, the remaining operators, called Elimination, Creation, Merge and Split, and Reordering, promote more severe disturbances in solutions since they perform operations involving all the items of the selected groups.

The seven mutation operators have been used to solve a wide variety of grouping problems with different conditions and constraints. Due to these differences, mutation operators must be adapted to the characteristics of the problem to be solved. As a result, grouping mutation operators for the $R||C_{max}$ problem can differ in the tactics that they use to select the jobs and machines involved in the mutation operations, the strategies employed to handle the jobs and the selected machines, and the problem-domain heuristics included. The following sections show the general procedure of four state-of-the-art grouping mutation operators: Swap, Insertion, Elimination, and Merge and Split. This study contemplates the best state-of-the-art mutation operators that apply for the $R||C_{max}$ problem, discarding the infeasible ones and those which have not shown outstanding performance. However, in [32] a more detailed description of the seven group-oriented mutation operators procedure can be found, as well as a compilation of other mutation operators applied to different grouping problems and the parameter settings approach that they use. It is important to note that in addition to the Download operator, none of the four mutations described below have been used to solve the $R||C_{max}$ grouping problem. The above motivates this experimental study, whose main objective is to explore the performance of the most used mutation operators to solve $R||C_{max}$.

3.1. The Swap Operator

The Swap operator selects two groups to later pick k items from each selected group and exchange the items from one group to another. Due to its way of working, it can be adapted and used to solve grouping problems with different constraints and conditions. Thanks to this quality, the Swap operator has been used to solve classic problems such as Bin Packing [34] as well as new problems such as Maximally Diverse [35].

3.2. The Insertion Operator

Similar to the Swap operator, the Insertion operator selects two groups to later pick k items from one selected group and insert them to the other group. This operator has been used to solve from classic problems such as Graph Coloring [36] to newer problems such as Group Stock Portfolio [37], covering problems with different constraints and conditions [38].

3.3. The Elimination Operator

The Elimination operator chooses g groups to remove them, release their items, and re-insert them by applying problem-domain heuristics, for example, the heuristic Min() used by the state-of-the-art GGA for $R||C_{max}$. According to the scope of the literature review, this is the most used mutation operator to solve grouping problems because it has shown promising results, mainly in classic problems such as Bin Packing [28], Cell Formation [39], Multiple Knapsack [40], and Timetabling [41].

3.4. The Merge and Split Operator

The Merge and Split, also known as Division and Combination operator, works in two phases. In the first stage, it selects two groups and transforms them into a single one. Then, in the second stage, it picks a group to distribute its items between two distinct groups. Merge and Split has been used to solve grouping problems such as Cell Formation [42] and Multivariate Micro-aggregation [43].

4. Computational Experiments

This section presents the experimental design proposed to analyze the way different elements involved in the mutation process can impact the performance of grouping mutation operators. The objective of this work is to design an efficient grouping mutation operator that includes the best features identified during the experimentation, to later incorporate it to the state-of-the-art GGA for $R||C_{max}$ to improve its performance [1]. The experimental design consists of four phases. The first stage covers the analysis of the state-of-the-art grouping mutation operators to determine which one has the best performance for $R||C_{max}$. The second phase comprises an exploratory analysis to observe the influence of the numbers of machines and jobs involved in mutation operations. The third phase includes the assessment of different machine selection strategies, including biased, random, and mixed approaches. Finally, the fourth phase studies the contribution of distinct rearrangement heuristics based on insertion and swap operations. The main objective of these strategies is to reorganize some jobs of the solutions applying more complex and expensive processes. Although they involve a computational cost, they are of vital importance when the mutation operator alone is unable to leave a local optimum. The information collected is used to design an efficient grouping mutation operator for $R||C_{max}$.

The performance assessment of each operator involves solving 1400 test instances introduced by Fanjul-Peyro in 2010, distributed among 7 sets [26]. The first 5 sets differ in the range employed to generate the p_{ij} values with a uniform distribution: $U(1, 100)$,

$U(10, 100)$, $U(100, 120)$, $U(100, 200)$, and $U(1000, 1100)$. From the remaining sets, one includes instances with correlated machines (*MacCorr*) and the other instances with correlated jobs (*JobsCorr*). These instances can consider 100, 200, 500, or 1000 jobs and 10, 20, 30, 40, or 50 machines. Each set contains 200 instances, 10 for each combination of the number of machines m and jobs n.

To analyze the performance of each operator, we generate a population of 100 individuals with the heuristic Min() to later mutate them for 500 generations. For a fair comparison, we use the same seed for each operator. Finally, we use the average Relative Percentage Deviation (*RPD*) to compare the operators performance. Given an instance i, the *RPD* is defined as in (1), where $C_{max}(i)$ depicts the C_{max} value found by the operator, and $C^*_{max}(i)$ represents the best C_{max} found using two hours of the commercial solver CPLEX. Thus, *RPD* indicates the deviation from the evaluated grouping mutation operators to CPLEX.

$$RPD = \frac{C_{max}(i) - C^*_{max}(i)}{C^*_{max}(i)} \qquad (1)$$

4.1. State-of-the-Art Mutation Operators

This experiment aims to study the performance of the state-of-the-art grouping mutation operators in the problem $R||C_{max}$. Recalling from Section 3, this study comprises four operators: Swap, Insertion, Elimination, and Merge and Split, since this work focuses on the best state-of-the-art mutation operators that apply for the $R||C_{max}$ problem. However, the specialized literature contains other mutation operators applied to various grouping problems with different constraints and conditions [32]. Next, the procedures of the four mutation operators adapted to work with the constraints and conditions of the problem $R||C_{max}$ are presented. This information is reinforced by Algorithms 4–7 and Figure 5 that includes an example for each operator.

Algorithm 4 contains the procedure of the Swap mutation operator. First, it selects two machines i_A and i_B (lines 1 and 2). We denote $i=$ PickMachine(S) the machine i randomly selected from the solution S with a uniform distribution. Later, this operator selects one job for each chosen machine (lines 3 and 4). We denote $j=$ PickJob(i) the job j randomly selected from the machine i with a uniform distribution. Finally, the operator interchanges the two picked up jobs (line 5). We denote $S' =$ Interchange(S, i_A, i_B, j_A, j_B) the solution derived by interchanging the jobs j_A and j_B in machines i_A and i_B. Figure 5a explains the mutation process of the Swap operator adapted to solve the problem $R||C_{max}$ with an example in which the jobs $j_A = j_1$ and $j_B = j_7$, selected from machines $i_A = i_1$ and $i_B = i_4$, respectively, are exchanged. In this way, in the initial individual (*Solution*), the machines i_A and i_B outlined in bold and the jobs in bold j_A and j_B depict the machines and the jobs selected, respectively; and the final individual (*Mutation*) shows the jobs in their new position.

Algorithm 4 Swap operator

 Input: A solution S.
 Output: A mutated solution S'.
1: $i_A=$ PickMachine(S);
2: $i_B=$ PickMachine(S);
3: $j_A=$ PickJob(i_A);
4: $j_B=$ PickJob(i_B);
5: $S' =$ Interchange(S, i_A, i_B, j_A, j_B);
6: **end process**.

Given a test instance of $R||C_{max}$ with $n=9$ jobs from j_1 to j_9 and $m=4$ machines from i_1 to i_4 where each cell indicates the processing time p_{ij} that each machine i requires to process every job j, as well as a solution where each gene represents a machine i that contains its assigned jobs and the processing time C_i that it needs to process such jobs:

Test Instance

M\N	i_1	i_2	i_3	i_4
j_1	20	15	10	12
j_2	10	12	16	18
j_3	18	15	11	10
j_4	15	17	16	11
j_5	10	20	11	19
j_6	20	12	15	16
j_7	11	19	20	13
j_8	12	10	18	20
j_9	15	20	12	11

Solution

Machines	i_1	i_2	i_3	i_4
Jobs	j_1, j_9	j_2, j_4	j_5, j_8	j_3, j_6, j_7
C_i	35	29	29	39

The four group-oriented mutation operators work as follows:

a) Swap

Machines	i_1	i_2	i_3	i_4	
Jobs	j_1, j_9	j_2, j_4	j_5, j_8	j_3, j_6, j_7	Solution
C_i	35	29	29	39	
	i_A			i_B	

Machines	i_1	i_2	i_3	i_4	
Jobs	j_7, j_9	j_2, j_4	j_5, j_8	j_1, j_3, j_6	Mutation
C_i	26	29	29	38	

b) Insertion

Machines	i_1	i_2	i_3	i_4	
Jobs	j_1, j_9	j_2, j_4	j_5, j_8	j_3, j_6, j_7	Solution
C_i	35	29	29	39	
	i_B			i_A	

Machines	i_1	i_2	i_3	i_4	
Jobs	j_1, j_7, j_9	j_2, j_4	j_5, j_8	j_3, j_6	Mutation
C_i	46	29	29	26	

c) Elimination

Machines	i_1	i_2	i_3	i_4	
Jobs	j_1, j_9	j_2, j_4	j_5, j_8	j_3, j_6, j_7	Solution
C_i	35	29	29	39	
			i_A	i_B	

Machines	i_1	i_2	i_3	i_4		RJ
Jobs	j_1, j_9	j_2, j_4			Incomplete Solution	j_3, j_5, j_6, j_7, j_8
C_i	35	29				

Machines	i_1	i_2	i_3	i_4		Permutation
Jobs	j_1, j_9	j_2, j_4, j_8	j_5, j_6	j_3, j_7	Mutation	j_6, j_7, j_5, j_3, j_8
C_i	35	39	26	23		

d) Merge & Split

Machines	i_1	i_2	i_3	i_4	
Jobs	j_1, j_9	j_2, j_4	j_5, j_8	j_3, j_6, j_7	Solution
C_i	35	29	29	39	
			i_A	i_B	

Machines	i_1	i_2	i_3	i_4		$i_A \cup i_B$
Jobs	j_1, j_9	j_2, j_4			Incomplete Solution	j_3, j_5, j_6, j_7, j_8
C_i	35	29				

Machines	i_1	i_2	i_3	i_4		Permutation
Jobs	j_1, j_9	j_2, j_4	j_5, j_6, j_8	j_3, j_7	Mutation	j_6, j_7, j_5, j_3, j_8
C_i	35	29	44	23		

Figure 5. Group-oriented mutation operators adapted for $R||C_{max}$.

Similarly, Algorithm 5 includes the procedure of the Insertion mutation operator. First, it uses the before-mentioned PickMachine() function to select two machines i_A and i_B (lines 1 and 2). Next, it employs the PickJob() function described above to select a job j_A from the first selected machine i_A (line 3). Finally, this operator inserts the job j_A into the second selected machine i_B (line 4). We denote $S' =$ Insertion(S, i_A, i_B, j_A) the solution derived by inserting the job j_A from machine i_A into machine i_B. Figure 5b describes the mutation process of the Insertion operator implemented to solve the problem $R||C_{max}$ with an example, where the job $j_A = j_7$, selected from machine $i_A = i_4$, is inserted into machine $i_B = i_1$. For a clear explanation, the example outlines in bold the selected machines i_A and i_B and highlights the inserted item in bold j_A in the initial individual (*Solution*). Thus, the final individual (*Mutation*) shows the picked job j_A in its new position.

Algorithm 5 Insertion operator

Input: A solution S.
Output: A mutated solution S'.
1: $i_A =$ PickMachine(S);
2: $i_B =$ PickMachine(S);
3: $j_A =$ PickJob(i_A);
4: $S' =$ Insertion(S, i_A, i_B, j_A);
5: **end process.**

On the other hand, Algorithm 6 describes the procedure of the Elimination operator. Like the Swap and the Insertion operators, the Elimination process starts by picking up two machines i_A and i_B by using the PickMachine() function (lines 1 and 2). Next, it places all the jobs of both machines in the set of released jobs RJ, employing the before-mentioned Download() function (line 3). It is important to remark that this process is performed instead of the elimination, since the machines cannot be removed due to the characteristics of the problem. Subsequently, the location of the jobs in RJ is modified by using the Permute() function (line 4). Finally, the permuted jobs in $RJ'[]$ are re-inserted with the Min() heuristic (lines 5–7). Figure 5c explains the mutation process of the Elimination operator adapted to solve the problem $R||C_{max}$ with an example, where the machines outlined in bold $i_A = i_3$ and $i_B = i_4$ depict the machines selected to remove their jobs $j_3, j_5, j_6, j_7,$ and j_8 highlighted in bold from the initial individual (*Solution*). The *Incomplete Solution* shows the chromosome without the released items placed in the box RJ. Lastly, the box *Permutation* represents the jobs in RJ reordered randomly, and the final solution *Mutation* depicts the chromosome generated by assigning the jobs in the box *Permutation* by using the problem-domain heuristic Min().

Algorithm 6 Elimination operator

Input: A solution S.
Output: A mutated solution S''.
1: $i_A =$ PickMachine(S);
2: $i_B =$ PickMachine(S);
3: $S', RJ[] =$ Download(S, i_A, i_B);
4: $RJ'[] =$ Permute($RJ[]$);
5: **for all** job $j \in RJ'[]$ **do**
6: $\quad S'' =$ Min($S', RJ'[]$);
7: **end for**
8: **end process.**

Lastly, Algorithm 7 contains the procedure of the Merge and Split operator. Similar to the before-described mutation operators, Merge and Split begins by choosing two machines i_A and i_B in a random way with the PickMachine() function (lines 1 and 2). Later, it locates the jobs of the selected machines in the set of released jobs RJ with the Download() function (line 3). As can be seen, it is a similar case to the elimination since the machines cannot be joined or split. Hence, the operator uses the Permute() function to modify the location of the jobs in RJ (line 4), and later, it simulates the splitting part by re-inserting the permuted jobs in $RJ'[]$ among the two selected machines i_A and i_B using the above-described heuristic Best() (lines 5–7). Figure 5d includes the mutation process of the Merge and Split operator with an example that contains an initial individual (*Solution*) with the two selected machines i_A and i_B outlined in bold and the released jobs j_3, j_5, j_6, j_7, and j_8 highlighted in bold. Moreover, the example contains the *Incomplete Solution* without the jobs in $i_A \cup i_B$ placed in a box with the same name ($i_A \cup i_B$). Lastly, this figure includes the final solution *Mutation* that depicts the chromosome resulting from the allocation of the jobs in *Permutation* (a box with the jobs in $i_A \cup i_B$ reordered randomly) by applying the problem-domain heuristic Best().

Algorithm 7 Merge and Split operator

    Input: A solution S.
    Output: A mutated solution S''.
1: i_A = PickMachine(S);
2: i_B = PickMachine(S);
3: S', $RJ[]$ = Download(S, i_A, i_B);
4: $RJ'[]$ = Permute($RJ[]$);
5: **for all** job $j \in RJ'[]$ **do**
6:     S'' = Best(S', j, w, o);
7: **end for**
8: **end process.**

Table 1 shows the results obtained from the computational experiments. For a comprehensive study, the performance of the operators was analyzed considering the number of jobs n, the number of machines m, the distribution of the processing times p_{ij}, and the 1400 instances together. In this way, the first column indicates the criterion used to study the performance of the operators, the second one contains the classes covered for each grouping criterion, and the following columns represent the average *RPD* (Relative Percentage Deviation) achieved by each operator: Swap, Insertion, Merge and Split, and Elimination, respectively. Finally, this table highlights in bold the results obtained by the best operator for each group of instances. From Table 1, it can be observed that the Elimination operator excelled in all the criteria used to distribute the instances. It is important to note that the four operators had a similar performance since their average *RPD* differs only by hundredths.

Moreover, it is remarkable that the Download mutation operator procedure of the studied GGA is quite similar to the state-of-the-art mutation operator Merge and Split, since although the operations merge and split cannot be applied to groups explicitly due to the characteristics and conditions of the problem, they can be emulated by considering the jobs. In this way, the first stage of the Download mutation operator represents the combination of the groups, where the jobs of the two selected machines are released and placed in a single set. Similarly, the second stage depicts the split operation, where the jobs are redistributed among the selected machines. Finally, it is also important to mention that the only difference between the Merge and Split operator and the Elimination operator (the two operators with the best performance) is the job reassignment strategy they work with, since Merge and Split re-inserts the jobs only on the two selected machines, while the Elimination operator tries to re-insert the jobs on all the machines.

The following stages of this experimental study contain the analysis of different aspects involved in the mutation operator with the reassignment heuristic that considers all the machines, such as the number of machines to handle, the number of jobs to remove, the machine selection strategy, and the rearrangement heuristics.

Table 1. Comparison of Swap, Insertion, Merge and Split, and Elimination mutation operators using RPD.

	Instance Set	Swap	Insertion	Merge and Split	Elimination
n	100	0.1213	0.1219	0.1071	**0.0804**
	200	0.1408	0.1432	0.1353	**0.1154**
	500	0.1365	0.1371	0.1372	**0.1281**
	1000	0.1380	0.1381	0.1387	**0.1350**
m	10	0.1291	0.1290	0.1291	**0.1178**
	20	0.1391	0.1402	0.1344	**0.1229**
	30	0.1256	0.1252	0.1220	**0.1074**
	40	0.1310	0.1331	0.1270	**0.1084**
	50	0.1460	0.1478	0.1353	**0.1172**
P_{ij}	$U(1, 100)$	0.2802	0.2740	0.2632	**0.2107**
	$U(10, 100)$	0.2080	0.2060	0.2039	**0.1802**
	$U(100, 120)$	0.0417	0.0438	0.0408	**0.0384**
	$U(100, 200)$	0.1230	0.1248	0.1198	**0.1164**
	$U(1000, 1100)$	0.0218	0.0230	0.0214	**0.0201**
	JobsCorr	0.1259	0.1307	0.1194	**0.1049**
	MacsCorr	0.1385	0.1432	0.1384	**0.1326**
	1400 instances	0.1341	0.1351	0.1296	**0.1147**

4.2. Handled Machines and Removed Jobs

After observing that the four operators of the state of the art showed quite similar performance and that the Elimination operator slightly excelled, the second phase of the experimental study focused on analyzing how the number of handled machines and removed jobs impact the performance of the mutation operator. To analyze this phenomenon, we explore thirty-five variants of the operator. This study consists of evaluating the suitability of removing 1, 2, 3, 4, 6, 8, and 10 jobs from 2, 4, 6, 8, and 10 different machines, where each combination of removed jobs and managed machines results in an operator. For this study, we designed an enhanced version of the Elimination operator, called Elimination operator-v2. Algorithm 8 contains the procedure of this version that is able to adapt itself to the number of machines f and jobs h to handle. Therefore, this version receives the solution and the number of machines and jobs to consider. Thus, it starts by using a cycle to select the machines with the PickMachine() function (lines 1 and 2). Furthermore, for each machine, it employs another cycle to choose the h jobs with the PickJob() function and place them in the set of released jobs RJ (lines 3–5). It is important to highlight that if a machine does not have enough jobs h, all of them are released and placed in RJ. Finally, the functions Permute() and Min() are used to modify the location of the jobs and re-insert them, respectively (lines 7–10).

For a fair comparison, all the operators use randomness to select the machines and the jobs that intervene in their mutation process. Thus, each operator releases k jobs from g machines and then re-inserts them with the heuristic Min(). As in the first phase, for each operator, 100 individuals were generated and mutated during 500 generations using the same seed.

Table 2 shows the experimental results of the thirty-five variants of the mutation operator. The first column indicates the number of machines that each operator manages, the second one represents the number of jobs removed from each of the handled machines, and the last column contains the average RPD of each operator for the 1400 test instances, highlighting in bold the result obtained by the best variant of the thirty-five mutation operators.

Algorithm 8 Elimination operator-v2

Input: A solution S, number of machines f and jobs h handle.
Output: A mutated solution S''.

1: **for each** machine i from 1 to f **do**
2: $\quad i=$ PickMachine(S);
3: $\quad$ **for each** job j from 1 to h **do**
4: $\quad\quad RJ[] =$ PickJob(i);
5: $\quad$ **end for**
6: **end for**
7: $RJ'[] =$ Permute($RJ[]$);
8: **for all** job $j \in RJ'[]$ **do**
9: $\quad S'' =$ Min(S', $RJ'[]$);
10: **end for**
11: **end process.**

Table 2. Comparison of handled machines and removed jobs using RPD.

Handled Machines	Removed Jobs	RPD
2	1	0.091437
	2	0.094475
	3	0.097644
	4	0.100010
	6	0.102259
	8	0.103456
	10	0.103984
4	1	0.093067
	2	0.100647
	3	0.104505
	4	0.107246
	6	0.109475
	8	0.111302
	10	0.111263
6	1	0.095776
	2	0.105834
	3	0.109519
	4	0.111925
	6	0.114454
	8	0.115151
	10	0.115754
8	1	0.09889
	2	0.109016
	3	0.112681
	4	0.114861
	6	0.116797
	8	0.117525
	10	0.117800
10	1	0.102228
	2	0.110804
	3	0.114677
	4	0.116184
	6	0.117627
	8	0.118031
	10	0.117819

It appears from Table 2 that the operators that release only one job from each machine perform better than those that release more and that the best option is to consider only two machines. Moreover, to graphically observe the behavior of the 35 designed operators, the 1400 instances were grouped into 20 groups concerning each combination of jobs (100, 200, 500, and 1000) and machines (10, 20, 30, 40, and 50) to calculate the average RPD of each group and analyze the impact of each operator in more detail, e.g., the group where $m = 10$ and $n = 100$, the group where $m = 10$ and $n = 200$, and so on. Figures 6 and 7 contain two representative graphs of the behavior presented by the thirty-five mutation operator variants, which allow observing the impact of the two evaluated features, i.e., the number of machines to be handled and the number of jobs to be removed from each machine.

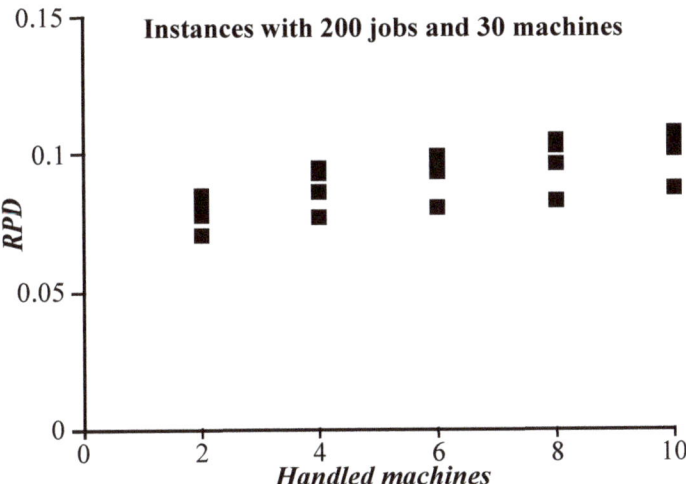

Figure 6. Behavior of the mutation operators grouped by the number of handled machines.

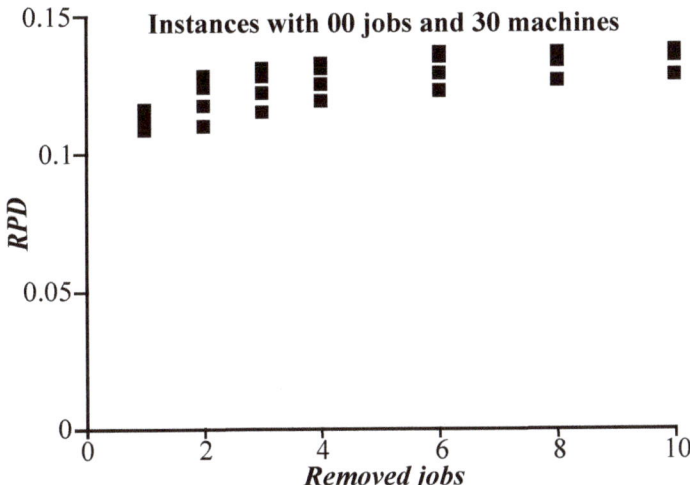

Figure 7. Behavior of the mutation operators grouped by the number of removed jobs from each handled machine.

Figure 6 allows observing the behavior of the operator's performance grouped according to the number of machines that they handle for all instances with 200 jobs and 30 machines. The x-axis of this figure indicates the number of machines handled, and the y-axis contains the average RPD reached for each operator. On the other hand, Figure 7 groups the operators according to the number of jobs removed from each machine in instances with 500 jobs and 20 machines. The x-axis contains the operators grouped according to the number of jobs that they remove, and the y-axis contains the average RPD reached for each operator. In this way, Figure 6 allows graphically observing that the performance of the operators improves as the number of handled machines decreases, while Figure 7 shows that the operators removing fewer jobs have better performance. In this fashion, the analysis suggests that the operators handling a fewer number of machines and releasing fewer jobs are more suitable.

4.3. Machines Selection Strategy

Once identifying that the variant that considers two machines and releasing one job from each machine has the best performance, in this stage, we evaluate the performance of four machine selection strategies, Random, Worst, Worst Best, and Worst Random, to analyze how they affect the performances of the mutation operators. Given a solution to be mutated, these strategies work as follows. Random chooses the two machines randomly. Worst selects the two machines with the worst C_i values (i.e., the machines with the highest loads). Worst Best picks the worst and the best machine (i.e., the machines with the highest and the lowest loads). If there are several machines with the lowest or highest load, first, they are identified to later use a uniform distribution to select one of them randomly. Finally, Worst Random divides the machines into two groups (W and O) in such a way that W contains the machines with $C_i = C_{max}$ and O the remaining machines. Next, it randomly selects the machines w and o from sets W and O, respectively. It is important to note that for each machine selection strategy, the two released jobs are selected randomly using a uniform distribution and later re-inserted employing the heuristic Min().

Table 3 shows the experimental results of the operators with the four machine selection strategies. As can be seen, this table has the same structure as Table 1. That is, it clusters the instances according to the number of jobs n, the number of machines m, the distribution of the processing times p_{ij} of the instances, and the 1400 test instances together. Therefore, the first column indicates the criterion used to study the performance of the operators, the second one contains the classes covered for each grouping criterion, and the following columns represent the average RPD (Relative Percentage Deviation) achieved by the operators with each machine selection strategy: Random, Worst, Worst Best, and Worst Random. Finally, this table highlights in bold the results obtained by the best mutation operator for each group of instances. The experimental results in Table 3 suggest that the most suitable machine selection strategy is Worst Random, with an average RPD of 0.0674 since the other approaches (Random, Worst, and Worst Best) reached higher RPD averages of 0.0913, 0.0875, and 0.0912, respectively.

Table 3. Comparison of mutation operators with selection strategies Random, Worst, Worst Best, and Worst Random using RPD.

	Instance Set	Random	Worst	Worst Best	Worst Random
n	100	0.0605	0.0577	0.0618	**0.0296**
	200	0.0848	0.0797	0.0832	**0.0533**
	500	0.1030	0.0987	0.1028	**0.0827**
	1000	0.1175	0.1147	0.1178	**0.1046**
m	10	0.0873	0.0857	0.0894	**0.0718**
	20	0.0978	0.0942	0.0977	**0.0752**
	30	0.0842	0.0824	0.0854	**0.0635**
	40	0.0908	0.0853	0.0885	**0.0631**
	50	0.0963	0.0900	0.0951	**0.0634**
p_{ij}	$U(1,100)$	0.1430	0.1470	0.1522	**0.1146**
	$U(10,100)$	0.1321	0.1319	0.1362	**0.1003**
	$U(100,120)$	0.0351	0.0309	0.0329	**0.0244**
	$U(100,200)$	0.1017	0.0939	0.0970	**0.0740**
	$U(1000,1100)$	0.0182	0.0155	0.0171	**0.0123**
	JobsCorr	0.0909	0.0820	0.0810	**0.0576**
	MacsCorr	0.1179	0.1112	0.1220	**0.0888**
	1400 instances	0.0913	0.0875	0.0912	**0.0674**

4.4. Rearrangement Heuristics

After identifying the machine selection strategy that provides the best performance to the mutation operator, we noted that there are high possibilities that the genetic material of many solutions does not undergo any alteration during the mutation process. Such a phenomenon can occur because it is likely that the two released jobs can be re-inserted in the same machine to which they belonged. In order to analyze the above, we evaluated the success rate (i.e., the number of the alterations in the genetic material divided by the mutation attempts) of the mutation operator with the best properties identified in the two previous stages. The experimental results revealed that only about the 42% of the mutation attempts are successful.

The above motivates this stage of the experimental study that consists of evaluating the utility of incorporating two rearrangement heuristics, called Insertion and Assemble, to increase the operator's success rate and improve its performance. These heuristics are only used if, after releasing and reinserting the jobs, the genetic material of the mutated solution has not been altered.

The rearrangement heuristic Insertion seeks to reduce the number of jobs in one of the two selected machines by trying to insert each of their jobs into the other ones. Algorithm 9 has the procedure of the rearrangement heuristic Insertion. We denote $S' = $ Insertion(S, j_{sm}, sm, i) the solution derived from S by inserting job j_{sm} (j_w or j_o) from the selected machine sm (w or o) into machine i. As can be seen, this heuristic goes through the jobs j_w and j_o of the machines w and o selected with the machine selection strategy Worst Random (line 1). Thus, for each pair of jobs (j_w and j_o), this algorithm traverses the m machines (line 2). In this way, for each machine i different from machine w and o (line 3 and line 9), it tries to insert the job j_w of the worst machine w (line 3) and then the job j_o from the other machine o (line 7) following two conditions, denoted as Cnd_1 and Cnd_2.

Algorithm 9 Rearrangement heuristic Insertion

Input: A solution S and two machines w and o.
Output: A mutated solution S'.

1: **for all** job $j_w \in w$ & $j_o \in o$ **do**
2:    **for** machine i in S **do**
3:       **if** $i \mathrel{!}= w$ **then**
4:          **if** Cnd_1(S, j_w, w, i) and Cnd_2(S, j_w, w, i) **then**
5:             $S' = $ Insertion (S, j_w, w, i);
6:             end process;
7:          end if
8:       end if
9:       **if** $i \mathrel{!}= o$ **then**
10:          **if** Cnd_1(S, j_o, o, i) and Cnd_2(S, j_o, o, i) **then**
11:             $S' = $ Insertion (S, j_o, o, i);
12:             end process;
13:          end if
14:       end if
15:    end for
16: **end for**

Cnd_1(S, j_{sm}, sm, i) (line 4 and line 10) allows verifying that the mutated solution (S') will have equal or better quality than the initial solution (S). In this way, Cnd_1 checks out that the sum of the processing time resulted from the insertion in the intervened machines i and sm (w or o) will be less than or equal to the sum of their processing times without performing the insertion. Hence, for each job j_w, Cnd_1(S, j_w, w, i) returns TRUE if $C_w - p_{wj_w} + C_i + p_{ij_w} \leq C_w + C_i$, where C_w and C_i represent the time that machines w and i require to process their assigned jobs, respectively, while p_{wj_w} and p_{ij_w} depict the processing time that machines w and i require to process job j_w, respectively. Otherwise, it returns

FALSE. In the same way, for each job j_o, Cnd_1(S, j_o, o, i) returns TRUE if $C_o - p_{oj_o} + C_i + p_{ij_o} \leq C_o + C_i$, where C_o and C_i represent the time that machines o and i require to process their assigned jobs, respectively; while p_{oj_o} and p_{ij_o} depict the processing time that machines o and i require to process job j_o, respectively. Otherwise, it returns FALSE.

On the other hand, Cnd_2(S, j_{sm}, sm, i) (line 4 and line 10) checks out that the mutated solution (S') will have equal or better quality than the initial solution (S). Cnd_2 verifies that the processing time C_i of the machine i with the new job, either j_w or j_o, will be less than or equal to the current makespan C_{max}. Therefore, for each job j_w, Cnd_2(S, j_w, w, i) returns TRUE if $C_i + p_{ij_w} \leq C_{max}$. Otherwise, it returns FALSE. Similarly, for each job j_o, Cnd_2(S, j_o, o, i) returns TRUE if $C_i + p_{ij_o} \leq C_{max}$. Otherwise, it returns FALSE.

In this way, the function Insertion(S, j_{sm}, sm, i) (lines 5 and 11) is applied to S if and only if a job j (j_w or j_o) satisfies the two conditions (Cnd_1 and Cnd_2). The rearrangement process ends once an insertion is performed (lines 6 and 12), but if none of the jobs satisfied the three conditions, the mutated solution would remain with its genetic material without any modification.

On the other hand, the rearrangement heuristic Assemble uses two functions. The first one is the Insertion(S, j_{sm}, sm, i) that works similarly to the above rearrangement heuristic. Additionally, it incorporates a second function called Interchange that seeks to exchange each job of the selected machines with each job of the other machines in an attempt to reduce the processing time of the selected machines. Algorithm 10 contains the procedure of the rearrangement heuristic Assemble. We denote S' = Interchange(S, j_{sm}, sm, j_i, i) the solution derived from S by exchanging job j_{sm} (j_w and j_o) from the selected machine sm (w or o) with each job j_i in machine i. Like the Insertion rearrangement heuristic, Assemble loops through the jobs j_w and j_o of the machines w and o selected with the machine selection strategy Worst Random (line 1). Thus, for each pair of jobs (j_w and j_o), this algorithm goes through the m machines (line 2). In this fashion, first, it tries to insert the jobs j_w of the worst machine w and j_o of the other machine o into every machine i different from machines w and o (line 3 and line 9) according to the two conditions described in Algorithm 9: Cnd_1 and Cnd_2 (line 4 and line 10). Next, it attempts to interchange the same jobs j_w and j_o with each job j_i in every machine i (line 15) different from machine w and o (line 16 and line 22), validating two conditions: Cnd_3 and Cnd_4 (line 17 and line 23).

Cnd_3(S, j_{sm}, sm, j_i, i) (line 17 and line 23) allows verifying that the mutated solution (S') will have equal or better quality than the initial solution (S). In this way, Cnd_3 checks out that the processing time resulted from the exchange in the intervened machines i and sm (w or o) will be less than or equal to the sum of their processing times without swapping their jobs. Hence, for each job j_w, Cnd_3(S, j_w, w, j_i, i) returns TRUE if $(C_w - p_{wj_w} + p_{wj_i}) + (C_i - p_{ij_i} + p_{ij_w}) \leq C_w + C_i$, where C_w and C_i represent the time that machines w and i require to process their assigned jobs, respectively; p_{wj_w} and p_{ij_i} depict the processing time that machines w and i require to process jobs j_w and j_i, respectively; p_{wj_i} p_{ij_w} indicate the processing time that machines w and i require to process job j_i and j_w, respectively. Otherwise, it returns FALSE. In the same way, for each job j_o, Cnd_3(S, j_o, o, j_i, i) returns TRUE if $(C_o - p_{oj_o} + p_{oj_i}) + (C_i - p_{ij_i} + p_{ij_o}) \leq C_o + C_i$, where C_o and C_i represent the time that machines o and i require to process their assigned jobs, respectively; p_{oj_o} and p_{ij_i} depict the processing time that machines o and i require to process jobs j_o and j_i, respectively; and p_{oj_i} and p_{ij_o} indicate the processing time that machines o and i require to process job j_i and j_o, respectively. Otherwise, it returns FALSE.

On the other hand, the condition Cnd_4(S, j_{sm}, sm, j_i, i) (line 17 and line 23) validates that the processing time resulting from the interchange in the intervened machines i and sm (w or o) will be less than or equal to the current makespan (C_{max}) of the initial solution S. Hence, for each job j_w, Cnd_4(S, j_w, w, j_i, i) returns TRUE if $(C_w - p_{wj_w} + p_{wj_i} \leq C_{max})$ and $(C_i - p_{ij_i} + p_{ij_w} \leq C_{max})$. Otherwise, it returns FALSE. Similarly, for each job j_o, Cnd_4(S, j_o, o, j_i, i) returns TRUE if $(C_o - p_{oj_o} + p_{oj_i} \leq C_{max})$ and $(C_i - p_{ij_i} + p_{ij_o} \leq C_{max})$. Otherwise, it returns FALSE.

Algorithm 10 Rearrangement heuristic Assemble

Input: A solution S and two machines w and o.
Output: A mutated solution S'.
1: **for all** job $j_w \in w$ & $j_o \in o$ **do**
2:     **for** machine i in S **do**
3:         **if** $i\ !=w$ **then**
4:             **if** Cnd_1(S, j_w, w, i) and Cnd_2(S, j_w, w, i) **then**
5:                 S' = Insertion (S, j_w, w, i);
6:                 end process;
7:             **end if**
8:         **end if**
9:         **if** $i\ !=o$ **then**
10:             **if** Cnd_1(S, j_o, o, i) and Cnd_2(S, j_o, o, i) **then**
11:                 S' = Insertion (S, j_o, o, i);
12:                 end process;
13:             **end if**
14:         **end if**
15:         **for** job j_i in i **do**
16:             **if** $i\ !=w$ **then**
17:                 **if** Cnd_3(S, j_w, w, j_i, i) and Cnd_4(S, j_w, w, j_i, i) **then**
18:                     S' = Interchange (S, j_w, w, j_i, i);
19:                     end process;
20:                 **end if**
21:             **end if**
22:             **if** $i\ !=o$ **then**
23:                 **if** Cnd_3(S, j_o, o, j_i, i) and Cnd_4(S, j_o, o, j_i, i) **then**
24:                     S' = Interchange (S, j_o, o, j_i, i);
25:                     end process;
26:                 **end if**
27:             **end if**
28:         **end for**
29:     **end for**
30: **end for**

The Assemble process ends once an operation, either the insertion or the interchange, is accomplished (lines 6, 12, 19, and 25). If none of the jobs met the two conditions, the mutated solution remains with its genetic material without any modification.

In this way, two variants of the operator with the best characteristics identified in the two previous stages (i.e., removing one job from two machines selected with the strategy Worst Random and re-inserting such jobs with the Min() heuristic) were created, one for each rearrangement heuristics presented in this section: Insertion and Assemble. The performance of the two variants, called Insertion and Assemble, was evaluated using the methodology mentioned above, i.e., starting from an initial population of 100 individuals that are subsequently mutated during 500 generations and using the same seed. Table 4 holds the experimental results obtained by the two mutation operators generated in this phase. Moreover, Table 4 includes the performance of the Download mutation operator, the original GGA operator described in Section 2.5, to compare the degree of improvement provided by the variants of the operator proposed in this section. For a comprehensive analysis, the performance of the operators was analyzed clustering the instances with the criteria used in the previous stages: number of jobs n, number of machines m, distribution of processing times p_{ij}, and the 1400 instances together. Thus, each column shows the performance of each assessed operator for the different criteria used to group the instances, highlighting in bold the results obtained by the best mutation operator.

As can be observed in Table 4, the best variant is that with the rearrangement heuristic Assemble, which for each pair of jobs first tries the insertion and then the interchange. The variants with the rearrangement heuristics Insertion and Assemble reached an average RPD of 0.0552 and 0.0395, respectively. However, it is important to note that the two versions of the mutation operators presented in this section outperformed the original Download mutation operator of the GGA studied that reached an average RPD of 0.1139, as well as the four state-of-the-art operators, which had an average RPD above 0.1.

Table 4. Comparison of mutation operators with the rearrangement heuristics Insertion and Assemble and the Download operator using RPD.

	Instance Set	Insertion	Assemble	Download
n	100	0.0306	**0.0185**	0.0730
	200	0.0480	**0.0280**	0.1125
	500	0.0631	**0.0441**	0.1328
	1000	0.0793	**0.0671**	0.1383
m	10	0.0612	**0.0416**	0.1261
	20	0.0617	**0.0429**	0.1258
	30	0.0497	**0.0366**	0.1076
	40	0.0507	**0.0376**	0.1054
	50	0.0528	**0.0382**	0.1048
P_{ij}	$U(1,100)$	0.0523	**0.0407**	0.2307
	$U(10,100)$	0.0538	**0.0331**	0.1862
	$U(100,120)$	0.0286	**0.0176**	0.0358
	$U(100,200)$	0.0750	**0.0362**	0.1072
	$U(1000,1100)$	0.0150	**0.0100**	0.0182
	JobsCorr	0.0664	**0.0654**	0.0892
	MacsCorr	0.0952	**0.0728**	0.1304
	1400 instances	0.0552	**0.0394**	0.1139

5. Comparing GGA with the Old and the New Mutation Operators

Given the knowledge gained from the experimental study, we propose a mutation operator called 2-Items Reinsertion. This operator randomly chooses two jobs from two different machines selected with the strategy Worst Random to release them and later reinsert them with the allocation heuristic Min(). Furthermore, it employs the rearrangement heuristic Assemble, based on insertion and interchange operations. The rearrangement process is only applied if, after releasing and reinserting the jobs, the genetic material of the mutated solution has not been modified.

To assess the 2-Items Reinsertion mutation operator performance, we run two variants of the state-of-the-art GGA for $R||C_{max}$ [1]. One with the old mutation operator (the Download mutation operator), i.e., the state-of-the-art GGA and the Enhanced GGA (EGGA) that uses the 2-Items Reinsertion mutation instead of the Download operator to evaluate their performance over the 1400 benchmark instances. For an equivalent comparison, the effectiveness and efficiency of both GGA variants were compared by using the same parameter configuration, i.e., the one proposed by Ramos-Figueroa et al. [1]. Table 5 contains the parameter values utilized for the population size $|P|$, number of individuals selected for the crossover n_c, number of individuals selected for the mutation n_m, elite population size $|B|$, and maximal number of generations max_gen. In this way, we analyze the strengths and weaknesses of the 2-Items Reinsertion mutation operator, distinguishing the quality of the solutions found by each GGA variant, their search time, as well as their ability to escape from local optima.

Table 5. Parameter configuration.

Parameter	Value
$|P|$	100
n_c	20
n_m	83
$|B|$	20
max_gen	500

For a fair comparison, both algorithms were programmed in the Rust language and were compiled using Visual Studio in the 64-bits mode. The experiments were performed on a computer with an Intel Core i5 (3.10 GHz), and 16 GB in RAM. Similar to Ramos-Figueroa et al. [1], for each instance, a single execution of the algorithms was run, with the same initial seed for the random number generation.

5.1. Comparing the effectiveness of GGA with the old and the new mutation operators

To measure the effectiveness of the designed 2-Items Reinsertion mutation operator, we applied the two GGA variants to the 1400 test instances and measured the improvement degree in the quality of the solutions found by each algorithm based on the RPD. Table 6 contains the experimental results. The first and second columns indicate the criteria used to group the test instance based on the number of jobs n, the number of machines m, the processing time distribution p_{ij}, and the 1400 instances together. On the other hand, the remaining columns contain the average RPD obtained by each metaheuristic algorithm for the four grouping criteria, respectively. Finally, this table highlights in bold the results obtained by the best GGA for each group of instances.

Table 6. Comparison of the state-of-the-art GGA and the EGGA presented in this work using RPD.

	Instance Set	GGA	EGGA
n	100	0.0391	**0.0176**
	200	0.0565	**0.0224**
	500	0.0665	**0.0291**
	1000	0.0724	**0.0441**
m	10	0.0512	**0.0220**
	20	0.0606	**0.0306**
	30	0.0559	**0.0275**
	40	0.0596	**0.0308**
	50	0.0657	**0.0306**
p_{ij}	$U(1, 100)$	0.0719	**0.0465**
	$U(10, 100)$	0.0853	**0.0361**
	$U(100, 120)$	0.0278	**0.0092**
	$U(100, 200)$	0.0820	**0.0229**
	$U(1000, 1100)$	0.0131	**0.0036**
	JobsCorr	0.0522	**0.0380**
	MacsCorr	0.0780	**0.0419**
	1400 instances	0.0586	**0.0283**

Table 6 illustrates that the EGGA showed a better performance than the state-of-the-art GGA using any criteria to group the test instances. Furthermore, it is worth noting that the EGGA reaches an average RPD considerably lower than the state-of-the-art GGA by solving the 1,400 test instances, with 0.028 and 0.059, respectively. Additionally, we applied the Wilcoxon rank-sum test to assess whether the differences in the RPD achieved by both GGAs for the 1,400 test instances are statistically significant. The Wilcoxon rank-sum is a non-parametric test that compares two algorithms without assuming a normal distribution, even for small sample sizes [44]. Table 7 presents the results obtained by the Wilcoxon rank-sum for the RPD values reached by both algorithms in the benchmark considered with a 95%-confidence level. For a comprehensive comparison, we generated a hypothesis test for the RPD achieved by both GGAs in groups of instances sorted according to the number of jobs n, the number of machines m, the distribution of the processing times p_{ij} of the instances, and the complete benchmark (1400 instances). In this way, the first column indicates the criterion used to compare the algorithms, the second one contains the classes covered for each grouping criterion, and the last column indicates the p-values obtained by the Wilcoxon test.

Table 7. p-values for the Wilcoxon test for GGA and EGGA.

	Instance	p-Value
n	100	7.10×10^{-26}
	200	6.70×10^{-43}
	500	2.30×10^{-46}
	1000	8.16×10^{-29}
m	10	4.57×10^{-39}
	20	1.63×10^{-29}
	30	2.98×10^{-21}
	40	3.51×10^{-20}
	50	3.37×10^{-25}
P_{ij}	$U(1, 100)$	1.13×10^{-12}
	$U(10, 100)$	1.59×10^{-49}
	$U(100, 120)$	2.03×10^{-33}
	$U(100, 200)$	1.01×10^{-51}
	$U(1000, 1100)$	2.25×10^{-37}
	JobsCorr	2.19×10^{-15}
	MacsCorr	4.44×10^{-27}
	1400 instances	5.44×10^{-120}

Table 7 indicates that the EGGA is indeed statistically better than the state-of-the-art GGA considering the *RPD* that they reached for the test benchmark for all the groups of instances considered since all p-values are less than the level of significance $\alpha = 0.05$.

Finally, in order to graphically show the suitability of the designed mutation operator, the experimental study presented in Section 2.5 was repeated but this time for the impact analysis of crossover and mutation rates on the EGGA. In this way, the EGGA that incorporates the 2-Items Reinsertion mutation operator was run with the same 9 configurations, i.e., $Conf_1$: $n_c = 20$, $n_m = 20$, $Conf_2$: $n_c = 20$, $n_m = 40$, ... $Conf_9$: $n_c = 60$, $n_m = 60$. Figure 8 presents a bar graph with the results obtained from this study, where each bar depicts one of the 9 configurations grouped according to the number of mutated solutions (n_m), and each pattern indicates the number of selected individuals for the crossover process (n_c): squares = 20, waves = 40, and circles = 60. As Figure 8 indicates, the EGGA performance is mainly related to the number of individuals considered for the mutation processes n_m in such a way that the performance of the EGGA improves (lower *RPD*) as the number of mutated solutions increases. Similarly, as the number of selected individuals for the crossover process n_c increases, the GGA performance improves but to a lesser degree.

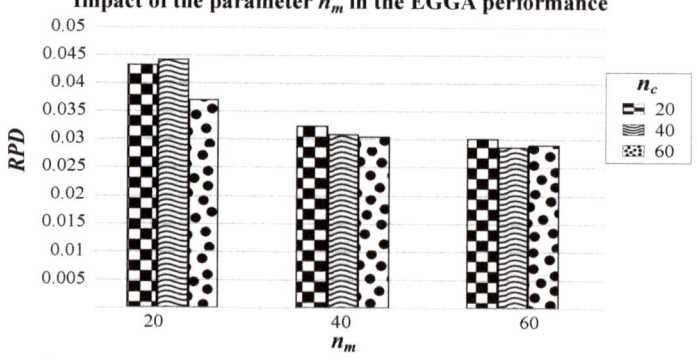

Figure 8. Impact analysis of the parameters: number of individuals selected for crossover n_c and number of mutated solutions n_m in the EGGA final performance.

The behavior mentioned above shows the suitability of the 2-Items Reinsertion mutation, which is the operator with the biggest impact on EGGA final performance and improves it considerably. Thus, the EGGA behavior is quite similar to the one presented by the GGA-CGT [28], where the mutation operator has the greatest positive impact on the final performance of this algorithm.

5.2. Comparing the Efficiency of GGA with the Old and the New Mutation Operators

After analyzing the effectiveness of the EGGA, we evaluate the implications associated with the computational time of using the 2-Items Reinsertion mutation operator. Table 8 includes the experimental results. Like Table 6, the first and second columns describe the characteristics used to cluster the instances: the number of jobs n and machines m, the processing time distribution p_{ij}, and the 1400 instances together. Thus, the following columns contain the average time in seconds obtained by the state-of-the-art GGA and the EGGA for each instance set, respectively.

Table 8. Comparison of the state-of-the-art GAA and the EGGA based on the time (time in seconds).

	Instance	GGA	EGGA
n	100	1.2	5.71
	200	1.2	5.68
	500	1.24	5.49
	1000	1.36	9.44
m	10	1.26	8.71
	20	1.24	7.66
	30	1.21	6.94
	40	1.19	6.33
	50	1.17	5.79
p_{ij}	$U(1,100)$	1.25	34.09
	$U(10,100)$	1.25	14.04
	$U(100,120)$	1.25	2.52
	$U(100,200)$	1.25	2.88
	$U(1000,1100)$	1.25	2.71
	JobsCorr	1.25	1.50
	MacsCorr	1.25	1.69
	1400 instances	1.25	8.49

Table 8 shows that the 2-Items Reinsertion mutation operator causes the EGGA to be much slower. Said computational cost is closely related to the rearrangement strategy Assemble, incorporated to avoid, as far as possible, becoming stuck in a local optima. Although the computational cost of this strategy is high, it is also too useful, since the properties and characteristics of the addressed problem make the mutation operator by itself incapable of avoiding local optima., mainly in the instances with processing times generated in the ranges $U(1,100)$ and $U(10,100)$, where the average times increased from 1.25 to 34.09 and 14.04 seconds, respectively. To review such algorithmic behavior, we analyzed the average generation in which the state-of-the-art GGA and the EGGA find the best solution for each test instance.

Table 9 shows that the GGA becomes quickly trapped in local optima in generation 16 on average, while the EGGA shows a better ability to deal with the landscape characteristics of the $R||C_{max}$ search space, finding its best solutions in generation 362 on average. In this way, Table 9 shows the importance of incorporating the 2-Items Reinsertion mutation operator to the GGA since, although the computational cost is high, it provides to the EGGA a better exploration capability during the search process.

Table 9. Comparison of the state-of-the-art GAA and the EGGA based on the generation in which the best solution in population is improved.

	Instance	GGA	EGGA
n	100	9.27	358.34
	200	8.00	369.31
	500	8.00	380.83
	1000	17.09	362.54
m	10	16.35	358.46
	20	13.69	359.06
	30	11.79	359.78
	40	11.05	360.96
	50	10.01	362.20
P_{ij}	$U(1,100)$	64.80	218.56
	$U(10,100)$	8.00	305.34
	$U(100,120)$	8.00	360.44
	$U(100,200)$	8.00	391.96
	$U(1000,1100)$	8.00	390.13
	JobsCorr	8.00	474.82
	MacsCorr	8.00	392.95
	1400 instances	16.11	362.03

From this study, we can conclude that it is still necessary to improve the performance of the EGGA and study its other operators, evaluation function, and stop criteria in order to better explore the search space, since it also becomes stuck in local optima, although not as soon as the original GGA. Additionally, we will focus on analyzing the properties and characteristics of the instances in the sets $U(1,100)$ and $U(10,100)$, where the EGGA stagnates sooner and requires a longer processing time since the rearrangement heuristic is used more times during the solution process of instances with those characteristics.

6. Conclusions and Paths of Work

The GGA has become one of the most outstanding metaheuristics for the solution of combinatorial optimization problems related to the partition of a set of items into different subsets. The development of a GGA involves the definition of variation operators adapted to work at the group level. The main goal of this paper was to promote the design of intelligent operators for GGAs as a more suitable way to obtain high-performance GGAs that incorporate knowledge of the problem-domain.

We present a systematic experimental examination to gain insights into the importance of each phase involved in the mutation operator of a GGA designed to solve the Parallel-Machine scheduling problem with unrelated machines and makespan minimization ($R||C_{max}$), analyzing whether different strategies actually contribute to the performance of the operator. The overall procedure of a grouping mutation operator for $R||C_{max}$ comprises: (1) selecting one or more machines; (2) selecting one or more jobs from each of the selected machines; and (3) reinserting the selected jobs in some of the machines. In order to learn something about each of these three algorithmic components, this work covered the analysis of each component in isolation by evaluating distinct strategies to deal with it. In this way, the study covered the evaluation of four state-of-the-art grouping mutation operators, thirty-five operators with different numbers of machines and jobs handled, four machine selection strategies, and two rearrangement heuristics for the reinsertion of the selected jobs. The experimental results suggested that the mutation operator with the best performance: (1) selects two machines, one of the machines with the worst C_i value and one random machine; (2) selects one random job from each of the selected machines; and (3) reinserts the selected jobs in two stages. First, for each job, each machine is checked in an attempt to insert the job in the machine with the lowest C_i value. Second, if the first stage yields the original solution, a rearrangement heuristic is applied to attempt to reduce the processing time of the selected machines by trying to insert one of their jobs into the other machines or to exchange one of their jobs with one job of the other machines.

The knowledge gained from the systematic study was used to design a new grouping mutation operator, called 2-Items Reinsertion. The new operator was incorporated into the state-of-the-art GGA (replacing the original mutation operator) to solve 1400 benchmark instances, showing significant differences with an improvement rate of 52%. These results underline the importance of evaluating the performance of the different components of the GGA operators.

We are aware that the current performance of the Enhanced GGA (EGGA) is still far from reaching the performance of state-of-the-art algorithms for $R||C_{max}$. However, the improvements achieved with the approach proposed in this work are quite promising. Therefore, we believe that with the design and implementation of experimental approaches such as the one presented in this paper we can further improve the performance of EGGA by studying the behavior of other genetic components, such as the population initialization strategy, the selection mechanism, the crossover operator, the replacement mechanism, and the objective function. In this order of ideas, the study of the final performance obtained by the EGGA for the $R||C_{max}$ problem revealed that there still are benchmark instances that show a high degree of difficulty; for these instances, the included strategies in the EGGA do not appear to lead to better solutions. Future work will consist of studying the different components of each operator and technique included in the EGGA, designing a better crossover operator, implementing an efficient reproduction technique, and analyzing the EGGA behavior to understand the impact of each strategy when solving different instances of the $R||C_{max}$ problem. We are also developing a new fitness function that will allow us to discriminate between solutions with the same C_{max} value but with a different exploitation of the machine's processing time. The knowledge gained from the analysis of each component of the grouping mutation operator for the $R||C_{max}$ problem can help us gain a better understanding of the performance of other heuristics for this problem and opens up an interesting range of possibilities for future research on other Parallel-Machine Scheduling variants. It is expected that the study presented in this paper represents a guideline to carry out similar systematic experimental examinations to analyze the components of other GGAs. This knowledge can be used to develop new intelligent operators for solving NP-hard grouping problems.

Author Contributions: Conceptualization, O.R.-F., M.Q.-C., E.M.-M. and N.C.-R.; methodology, O.R.-F. and M.Q.-C.; software, O.R.-F.; validation, O.R.-F. and M.Q.-C.; formal analysis, M.Q.-C.; investigation, O.R.-F. and M.Q.-C.; resources, O.R.-F.; writing—original draft preparation, O.R.-F.; writing—review and editing, O.R.-F., M.Q.-C., E.M.-M. and N.C.-R.; visualization, O.R.-F. and M.Q.-C.; supervision, E.M.-M. and M.Q.-C.; project administration, M.Q.-C. All authors have read and agreed to the published version of the manuscript.

Funding: This research received no external funding.

Conflicts of Interest: The authors declare no conflict of interest. The funders had no role in the design of the study; in the collection, analyses, or interpretation of data; in the writing of the manuscript, or in the decision to publish the results.

References

1. Ramos-Figueroa, O.; Quiroz-Castellanos, M.; Mezura-Montes, E.; Schütze, O. Metaheuristics to solve grouping problems: A review and a case study. *Swarm Evol. Comput.* **2020**, *53*, 100643. [CrossRef]
2. Garey, M.R. A Guide to the Theory of NP-Completeness. In *Computers and Intractability*; W. H. Freeman and Company: New York, NY, USA, 1979.
3. Sels, V.; Coelho, J.; Dias, A.M.; Vanhoucke, M. Hybrid tabu search and a truncated branch-and-bound for the unrelated parallel machine scheduling problem. *Comput. Oper. Res.* **2015**, *53*, 107–117. [CrossRef]
4. Fanjul-Peyro, L. Models and an exact method for the unrelated parallel machine scheduling problem with setups and resources. *Expert Syst. Appl. X* **2020**, *5*, 100022. [CrossRef]
5. Bitar, A.; Dauzère-Pérès, S.; Yugma, C. Unrelated parallel machine scheduling with new criteria: Complexity and models. *Comput. Oper. Res.* **2021**, *132*, 105291. [CrossRef]
6. Moser, M.; Musliu, N.; Schaerf, A.; Winter, F. Exact and metaheuristic approaches for unrelated parallel machine scheduling. *J. Sched.* **2022**, *25*, 507–534. [CrossRef]

7. Shim, S.O.; Kim, Y.D. Minimizing total tardiness in an unrelated parallel-machine scheduling problem. *J. Oper. Res. Soc.* **2007**, *58*, 346–354. [CrossRef]
8. Terzi, M.; Arbaoui, T.; Yalaoui, F.; Benatchba, K. Solving the Unrelated Parallel Machine Scheduling Problem with Setups Using Late Acceptance Hill Climbing. In Proceedings of the Asian Conference on Intelligent Information and Database Systems, Phuket, Thailand, 23–26 March 2020; pp. 249–258.
9. Arroyo, J.E.C.; Leung, J.Y.T.; Tavares, R.G. An iterated greedy algorithm for total flow time minimization in unrelated parallel batch machines with unequal job release times. *Eng. Appl. Artif. Intell.* **2019**, *77*, 239–254. [CrossRef]
10. Diana, R.O.M.; de Souza, S.R. Analysis of variable neighborhood descent as a local search operator for total weighted tardiness problem on unrelated parallel machines. *Comput. Oper. Res.* **2020**, *117*, 104886. [CrossRef]
11. Yepes-Borrero, J.C.; Villa, F.; Perea, F.; Caballero-Villalobos, J.P. GRASP algorithm for the unrelated parallel machine scheduling problem with setup times and additional resources. *Expert Syst. Appl.* **2020**, *141*, 112959. [CrossRef]
12. Arnaout, J.P. A worm optimization algorithm to minimize the makespan on unrelated parallel machines with sequence-dependent setup times. *Ann. Oper. Res.* **2020**, *285*, 273–293. [CrossRef]
13. Ezugwu, A.E.; Akutsah, F. An improved firefly algorithm for the unrelated parallel machines scheduling problem with sequence-dependent setup times. *IEEE Access* **2018**, *6*, 54459–54478. [CrossRef]
14. Lei, D.; Liu, M. An artificial bee colony with division for distributed unrelated parallel machine scheduling with preventive maintenance. *Comput. Ind. Eng.* **2020**, *141*, 106320. [CrossRef]
15. Zheng, X.l.; Wang, L. A two-stage adaptive fruit fly optimization algorithm for unrelated parallel machine scheduling problem with additional resource constraints. *Expert Syst. Appl.* **2016**, *65*, 28–39. [CrossRef]
16. Afzalirad, M.; Shafipour, M. Design of an efficient genetic algorithm for resource-constrained unrelated parallel machine scheduling problem with machine eligibility restrictions. *J. Intell. Manuf.* **2018**, *29*, 423–437. [CrossRef]
17. Jaklinović, K.; Đurasević, M.; Jakobović, D. Designing dispatching rules with genetic programming for the unrelated machines environment with constraints. *Expert Syst. Appl.* **2021**, *172*, 114548. [CrossRef]
18. Lei, D.; Yuan, Y.; Cai, J.; Bai, D. An imperialist competitive algorithm with memory for distributed unrelated parallel machines scheduling. *Int. J. Prod. Res.* **2020**, *58*, 597–614. [CrossRef]
19. Bitar, A.; Dauzère-Pérès, S.; Yugma, C.; Roussel, R. A memetic algorithm to solve an unrelated parallel machine scheduling problem with auxiliary resources in semiconductor manufacturing. *J. Sched.* **2016**, *19*, 367–376. [CrossRef]
20. Wu, X.; Che, A. A memetic differential evolution algorithm for energy-efficient parallel machine scheduling. *Omega* **2019**, *82*, 155–165. [CrossRef]
21. De, P.; Morton, T.E. Scheduling to minimize makespan on unequal parallel processors. *Decis. Sci.* **1980**, *11*, 586–602. [CrossRef]
22. Davis, E.; Jaffe, J.M. Algorithms for scheduling tasks on unrelated processors. *J. ACM* **1981**, *28*, 721–736. [CrossRef]
23. Kumar, V.; Marathe, M.V.; Parthasarathy, S.; Srinivasan, A. A unified approach to scheduling on unrelated parallel machines. *J. ACM JACM* **2009**, *56*, 28. [CrossRef]
24. Lin, Y.; Pfund, M.; Fowler, J. Minimizing makespans for unrelated parallel machine scheduling problems. In Proceedings of the 2009 IEEE/INFORMS International Conference on Service Operations, Logistics and Informatics, Chicago, IL, USA, 22–24 July 2009; pp. 107–110.
25. Ghirardi, M.; Potts, C.N. Makespan minimization for scheduling unrelated parallel machines: A recovering beam search approach. *Eur. J. Oper. Res.* **2005**, *165*, 457–467. [CrossRef]
26. Fanjul-Peyro, L.; Ruiz, R. Iterated greedy local search methods for unrelated parallel machine scheduling. *Eur. J. Oper. Res.* **2010**, *207*, 55–69. [CrossRef]
27. Glass, C.; Potts, C.; Shade, P. Unrelated parallel machine scheduling using local search. *Math. Comput. Model.* **1994**, *20*, 41–52. [CrossRef]
28. Quiroz-Castellanos, M.; Cruz-Reyes, L.; Torres-Jimenez, J.; Gómez, C.; Huacuja, H.J.F.; Alvim, A.C. A grouping genetic algorithm with controlled gene transmission for the bin packing problem. *Comput. Oper. Res.* **2015**, *55*, 52–64. [CrossRef]
29. Carmona-Arroyo, G.; Quiroz-Castellanos, M.; Mezura-Montes, E. Variable Decomposition for Large-Scale Constrained Optimization Problems Using a Grouping Genetic Algorithm. *Math. Comput. Appl.* **2022**, *27*, 23. [CrossRef]
30. Alharbe, N.; Aljohani, A.; Rakrouki, M.A. A Fuzzy Grouping Genetic Algorithm for Solving a Real-World Virtual Machine Placement Problem in a Healthcare-Cloud. *Algorithms* **2022**, *15*, 128. [CrossRef]
31. Falkenauer, E. The grouping genetic algorithms-widening the scope of the GAs. *Belg. J. Oper. Res. Stat. Comput. Sci.* **1992**, *33*, 2.
32. Ramos-Figueroa, O.; Quiroz-Castellanos, M.; Mezura-Montes, E.; Kharel, R. Variation Operators for Grouping Genetic Algorithms: A Review. *Swarm Evol. Comput.* **2020**. [CrossRef]
33. Ibarra, O.H.; Kim, C.E. Heuristic algorithms for scheduling independent tasks on nonidentical processors. *J. ACM JACM* **1977**, *24*, 280–289. [CrossRef]
34. Cuadra, L.; Aybar-Ruíz, A.; Del Arco, M.; Navío-Marco, J.; Portilla-Figueras, J.A.; Salcedo-Sanz, S. A Lamarckian Hybrid Grouping Genetic Algorithm with repair heuristics for resource assignment in WCDMA networks. *Appl. Soft Comput.* **2016**, *43*, 619–632. [CrossRef]
35. Singh, K.; Sundar, S. A new hybrid genetic algorithm for the maximally diverse grouping problem. *Int. J. Mach. Learn. Cybern.* **2019**, *10*, 2921–2940. [CrossRef]

36. Ülker, Ö.; Özcan, E.; Korkmaz, E.E. Linear linkage encoding in grouping problems: Applications on graph coloring and timetabling. In Proceedings of the International Conference on the Practice and Theory of Automated Timetabling, Brno, Czech Republic, 30 August–1 September 2006; pp. 347–363.
37. Chen, C.H.; Lu, C.Y.; Lin, C.B. An intelligence approach for group stock portfolio optimization with a trading mechanism. *Knowl. Inf. Syst.* **2020**, *62*, 287–316. [CrossRef]
38. Mutingi, M.; Mbohwa, C. Home Healthcare Worker Scheduling: A Group Genetic Algorithm Approach. In Proceedings of the World Congress on Engineering, London, UK, 3–5 July 2013; Volume 1.
39. Vin, E.; De Lit, P.; Delchambre, A. A multiple-objective grouping genetic algorithm for the cell formation problem with alternative routings. *J. Intell. Manuf.* **2005**, *16*, 189–205. [CrossRef]
40. Fukunaga, A.S. A new grouping genetic algorithm for the multiple knapsack problem. In Proceedings of the 2008 IEEE Congress on Evolutionary Computation (IEEE World Congress on Computational Intelligence), Hong Kong, China, 1–6 June 2008; pp. 2225–2232.
41. Erben, W. A grouping genetic algorithm for graph colouring and exam timetabling. In Proceedings of the International Conference on the Practice and Theory of Automated Timetabling, Konstanz, Germany, 16–18 August 2000; pp. 132–156.
42. Yasuda, K.; Hu, L.; Yin, Y. A grouping genetic algorithm for the multi-objective cell formation problem. *Int. J. Prod. Res.* **2005**, *43*, 829–853. [CrossRef]
43. Balasch-Masoliver, J.; Muntés-Mulero, V.; Nin, J. Using genetic algorithms for attribute grouping in multivariate microaggregation. *Intell. Data Anal.* **2014**, *18*, 819–836. [CrossRef]
44. Wilcoxon, F. Individual comparisons by ranking methods. In *Breakthroughs in Statistics*; Springer: Berlin/Heidelberg, Germany, 1992; pp. 196–202.

Disclaimer/Publisher's Note: The statements, opinions and data contained in all publications are solely those of the individual author(s) and contributor(s) and not of MDPI and/or the editor(s). MDPI and/or the editor(s) disclaim responsibility for any injury to people or property resulting from any ideas, methods, instructions or products referred to in the content.

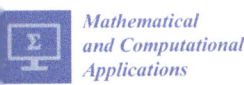

Article

The Hypervolume Newton Method for Constrained Multi-Objective Optimization Problems

Hao Wang [1,*], Michael Emmerich [1], André Deutz [1], Víctor Adrián Sosa Hernández [2] and Oliver Schütze [3]

[1] Leiden Institute of Advanced Computer Science, Leiden University, 2333 CA Leiden, The Netherlands
[2] School of Engineering and Sciences, Tecnológico de Monterrey, Av. Lago de Guadalupe Km 3.5, Atizapán de Zaragoza, Mexico City 52926, Mexico
[3] Computer Science Department, Cinvestav-IPN, Mexico City 07360, Mexico
* Correspondence: h.wang@liacs.leidenuniv.nl

Abstract: Recently, the Hypervolume Newton Method (HVN) has been proposed as a fast and precise indicator-based method for solving unconstrained bi-objective optimization problems with objective functions. The HVN is defined on the space of (vectorized) fixed cardinality sets of decision space vectors for a given multi-objective optimization problem (MOP) and seeks to maximize the hypervolume indicator adopting the Newton–Raphson method for deterministic numerical optimization. To extend its scope to non-convex optimization problems, the HVN method was hybridized with a multi-objective evolutionary algorithm (MOEA), which resulted in a competitive solver for continuous unconstrained bi-objective optimization problems. In this paper, we extend the HVN to constrained MOPs with in principle any number of objectives. Similar to the original variant, the first- and second-order derivatives of the involved functions have to be given either analytically or numerically. We demonstrate the applicability of the extended HVN on a set of challenging benchmark problems and show that the new method can be readily applied to solve equality constraints with high precision and to some extent also inequalities. We finally use HVN as a local search engine within an MOEA and show the benefit of this hybrid method on several benchmark problems.

Keywords: multi-objective optimization; hypervolume indicator; newton method; evolutionary algorithms; constraint handling; hypervolume scalarization

1. Introduction

Multi-objective optimization problems (MOPs)—i.e., problems where several objectives have to be optimized concurrently –naturally arise in many applications (e.g., [1–4]). As an example, in many portfolio problems, one is interested in maximizing the expected return and social responsibility or sustainability while minimizing the risk to a financial portfolio ([5,6]). In multi-objective optimization, we distinguish between the decision space, which contains the vectors of decision variables, and the objective space, which is the k dimensional real vectors and comprises the images of the vector-valued objective function. A typical approach to the solution of MOPs is to compute or approximate the non-dominated (or efficient) set with respect to the Pareto dominance order (the image of which in the objective space is called the Pareto front). One important characteristic of (continuous) MOPs is that in regular cases, the Pareto front is a manifold of $k-1$ dimensions, where k denotes the number of objective functions. In general, it is possible that parts of the Pareto front are of lower dimension, but the Pareto front is never more than $k-1$ dimensions. Since, in the continuous case, the non-dominated set and the Pareto front can contain infinitely many points, it is usually approximated by a finite set of points. In particular, in the area of evolutionary multi-objective optimization (EMO), many performance indicators have been proposed that propagate optimal approximations of the Pareto front (e.g., [7–10]). While their definitions slightly differ, most have in mind to obtain (more or less) evenly spread solutions along the Pareto front.

Interestingly, with the *hypervolume indicator* [10], there exists an indicator that does not require the knowledge of the location of the true Pareto front. Still, its maximization leads to well-distributed approximation sets consisting of only non-dominated solutions. In this work, by "well-distributed", we mean the objective points have good coverage of the Pareto front and are gap-free when the population size is large. At the maximum of the hypervolume indicator, the density of objective points is inversely proportional to the local curvature of the Pareto front [11]. Here is where the idea of set-scalarization comes into play. In set-scalarization methods, rather than focusing on the improvement of single points of the approximation set, the focus is on the optimization of a fixed cardinality set as an entity concerning a set-based indicator, e.g., the hypervolume indicator. The objective function of the set-scalarization method, in our case, the hypervolume indicator, provides a mapping from the set of fixed cardinality sets in the decision space to a scalar that has to be maximized. Due to the properties mentioned above of the hypervolume indicator, the resulting set will provide a well-distributed set of points on the Pareto front.

Multi-objective evolutionary algorithms (MOEAs) have long since adopted the idea of set-scalarization. The so-called indicator-based MOEAs (e.g., [12–14]) use performance indicators to guide the search, e.g., by indicator-based selection. In numerical methods, the set scalarization approach was first addressed in gradient-based hypervolume maximization [15–19] and in the maximization of the Averaged Hausdorff Metric [14]). More recently, the approach was generalized to second-order methods with the Hypervolume Newton Method (HVN), a set scalarization-based Newton–Raphson method for the maximization of the hypervolume indicator value of a given MOP (e.g., [20,21]). However, this method has only been discussed for unconstrained and bi-objective optimization problems, which limits its application.

In this paper, we extend the HVN for constrained MOPs with a general number of objectives. To this end, we present the HVN for equality-constrained problems and further discuss a straightforward active set method to handle inequalities. Since the HVN is highly local, we also discuss the hybridization of this method with an MOEA. Finally, we present numerical results indicating the strength of the novel approaches.

The remainder of this paper is organized as follows: in Section 2, we present the necessary background required for understanding the sequel, and we review the related work. In Section 3, we present the HVN for constrained multi-objective optimization problems. Section 4 presents the numerical results of the constrained HVN as a standalone algorithm and a local search strategy within a hybrid evolutionary algorithm. Finally, we conclude and give possible paths for future research in Section 5.

2. Background and Related Work

2.1. Notations

We will always denote a finite Pareto approximate set by $\mathbf{X} = \{\mathbf{x}^{(1)}, \mathbf{x}^{(2)}, \ldots, \mathbf{x}^{(\mu)}\} \subseteq \mathbb{R}^n$. When differentiating a set function, e.g., the hypervolume, over the input set, we often concatenate the points in $\mathbf{X}$ into a much longer vector, i.e., $\mathbf{X} = [\mathbf{x}^{(1)\top}, \mathbf{x}^{(2)\top}, \ldots, \mathbf{x}^{(\mu)\top}]^\top \in \mathbb{R}^{\mu n}$. To make our discussion less cumbersome, we abuse the notation $\mathbf{X}$ slightly such that it can be interpreted as a finite set in $\mathbb{R}^n$ or an $\mathbb{R}^{\mu n}$-vector, depending on the context. (See [16] for a detailed formal discussion of the mapping between fixed cardinality sets and vectors.) We will explain the meaning of $\mathbf{X}$ on the spot whenever it is unclear from the text. We will always denote by ∇ and ∇^2 the gradient/Jacobian and Hessian operators on real-valued functions, respectively, when the domain of such a function is clear from the text. Otherwise, we take the derivative operator $\partial/\partial \mathbf{X}$. When expressing the Hessian matrix, we will use the numerator layout for matrix calculus notations [22].

2.2. Multi-Objective Optimization

A real-valued multi-objective optimization problem (MOP) involves minimizing multiple objective functions simultaneously, i.e., $F = (f_1, \ldots, f_k), f_i : \mathcal{X} \to \mathbb{R}, \mathcal{X} \subseteq \mathbb{R}^n, i \in \{1, \ldots, k\}$. For every $\mathbf{y}^{(1)}$ and $\mathbf{y}^{(2)} \in \mathbb{R}^k$, we say $\mathbf{y}^{(1)}$ weakly dominates $\mathbf{y}^{(2)}$ (written as

$\mathbf{y}^{(1)} \preceq \mathbf{y}^{(2)}$) iff $y_i^{(1)} \leq y_i^{(2)}$, $i \in [1 \ldots k]$. The Pareto order $\prec$ on $\mathbb{R}^k$ is defined: $\mathbf{y}^{(1)} \prec \mathbf{y}^{(2)}$ iff. $\mathbf{y}^{(1)} \preceq \mathbf{y}^{(2)}$ and $\mathbf{y}^{(1)} \neq \mathbf{y}^{(2)}$. A point $\mathbf{x} \in \mathcal{X}$ is called efficient or (Pareto) optimal iff. $\nexists \mathbf{x}' \in \mathcal{X}(F(\mathbf{x}') \prec F(\mathbf{x}))$. The set P_Q of all Pareto optimal solutions of a MOP is called the Pareto set, and its image $F(P_Q)$ is called the Pareto front. Typically, i.e., under certain (mild) assumptions on the model, one can assume that the Pareto set and front of a given continuous MOP form at least locally an object of dimension $k-1$ ([23]).

The Pareto order can also be extended to the family of sets [10], i.e., we say $A \prec B$ iff. $\forall \mathbf{y} \in B \exists \mathbf{y}' \in A(\mathbf{y}' \prec \mathbf{y})$. The set of all efficient points of $\mathcal{X}$ is called the *efficient set*. The image of the efficient set under F is called the *Pareto front*. Multi-objective optimization algorithms (MOAs) often employ a finite multiset $\mathbf{X} = \{\mathbf{x}^{(1)}, \ldots, \mathbf{x}^{(\mu)}\}$ to approximate the efficient set, whose image under F is denoted by $\mathbf{Y}$. Multi-objective optimization is an active research field that has produced many algorithms for the approximation of the entire Pareto set/front of a given MOP. There exist, for instance, scalarization methods, and mathematical programming techniques that transform the given MOP into an auxiliary scalar optimization problem (SOP) (e.g., [24]). Via solving a clever sequence of such SOPs, one can obtain in many cases suitable Pareto front approximations (e.g., [25–28]). In [29], a Newton method is proposed for multi-objective optimization. Next to these point-wise iterative local search strategies there exist global set-based algorithms such as cell-to-cell mapping techniques and subdivision techniques ([30–32]) as well as specialized evolutionary algorithms ([33–36]). There exist in particular indicator-based evolutionary algorithms (IBEAs) that aim for Pareto front approximations of a given performance indicator (e.g., [12–14]). Widely used performance indicators are the Generational Distance (GD [7]), the Inverted Generational Distance and variants ([8,37,38]), the averaged Hausdorff distance Δ_p ([9,39,40]), and the Hypervolume indicator, which we will use in this work and briefly review in the next section.

Finally, there exist multi-objective continuation methods that make use of the fact that the solution set forms at least locally a manifold (e.g., [23,41–46]).

2.3. Hypervolume Indicator and Its First-Order Derivatives

The hypervolume indicator (HV) [10,47] is defined as the Lebesgue measure of the compact set dominated by a Pareto approximation set $\mathbf{Y} \subset \mathbb{R}^k$ and cut from above by a reference point $\mathbf{r}$:

$$\text{HV}(\mathbf{Y}; \mathbf{r}) = \lambda_k(\{\mathbf{p} \colon \exists \mathbf{y} \in \mathbf{Y}(\mathbf{y} \prec \mathbf{p}) \wedge \mathbf{p} \prec \mathbf{r}\}),$$

where λ_k denotes the Lebesgue measure in $\mathbb{R}^k$. HV is Pareto compliant, i.e., for all $\mathbf{Y} \prec \mathbf{Y}'$, $\text{HV}(\mathbf{Y}; \mathbf{r}) > \text{HV}(\mathbf{Y}'; \mathbf{r})$, and is extensively used to assess the quality of approximation sets to the Pareto front, e.g., in SMS-MOEA [12] and multi-objective Bayesian optimization [48]. Being a set function, it is cumbersome to define the derivative of HV. (The derivative of a set function is not defined for an arbitrary family of sets. For some special cases, it can be defined directly, e.g., on Jordan-measurable sets [49].) Therefore, we follow the generic set-based approach for MOPs [16], which considers a finite approximation sets of size μ vectors as a point in $\mathbb{R}^{\mu n}$, i.e., $\mathbf{X} = [\mathbf{x}^{(1)^\top}, \mathbf{x}^{(2)^\top}, \ldots, \mathbf{x}^{(\mu)^\top}]^\top \in \mathbb{R}^{\mu n}$. Similarly, the image of $\mathbf{X}$ under F can also be represented by a $\mathbb{R}^{\mu k}$-vector: $\mathbf{Y} = [F(\mathbf{x}^{(1)})^\top, F(\mathbf{x}^{(2)})^\top, \ldots, F(\mathbf{x}^{(\mu)})^\top]^\top$. In this sense, the objective function F is also extended as follows:

$$\mathbf{F} \colon \mathcal{X}^\mu \to \mathbb{R}^{\mu k}, \mathbf{X} \mapsto [F(X_1, \ldots, X_n), F(X_{n+1}, \ldots, X_{2n}), \ldots, F(X_{(\mu-1)n+1}, \ldots, X_{\mu n})]^\top.$$

Taking $\mathbf{F}$, we can express the hypervolume indicator as a function on $\mathbb{R}^{\mu n}$:

$$\mathcal{H}_\mathbf{F} \colon \mathbb{R}^{\mu n} \to \mathbb{R}_{\geq 0}, \quad \mathbf{X} \mapsto \text{HV}(\mathbf{F}(\mathbf{X}); \mathbf{r}).$$

We will henceforth omit the reference point **r** in $\mathcal{H}_\mathbf{F}$ for simplicity. It is straightforward to express the gradient of $\mathcal{H}_\mathbf{F}$ with respect to $\mathbf{X}$ using the chain rule as reported in our previous works [16,19]: $\nabla \mathcal{H}_\mathbf{F}(\mathbf{X}) = (\partial \mathcal{H}_\mathbf{F}/\partial \mathbf{F})(\partial \mathbf{F}/\partial \mathbf{X})$, in which we also discussed the time complexity of computing the hypervolume gradient. It is noted here that an alternative to the computation of the gradient of the entire set, it was also suggested to compute only the gradient of a single point with respect to the hypervolume indicator; this approach is referred to as hypervolume scalarization [50].

2.4. Hypervolume Hessian and Hypervolume Newton Method

Here, we assume F is at least twice continuously differentiable. In general, the Hessian matrix of the hypervolume indicator can be expressed as follows:

$$\nabla^2 \mathcal{H}_\mathbf{F} = \frac{\partial}{\partial \mathbf{X}}\left(\frac{\partial \mathcal{H}_\mathbf{F}}{\partial \mathbf{F}}\frac{\partial \mathbf{F}}{\partial \mathbf{X}}\right) = \left[\frac{\partial}{\partial \mathbf{X}}\left(\frac{\partial \mathcal{H}_\mathbf{F}}{\partial \mathbf{F}}\right)\right]^\top \frac{\partial \mathbf{F}}{\partial \mathbf{X}} + \frac{\partial \mathcal{H}_\mathbf{F}}{\partial \mathbf{F}}\frac{\partial^2 \mathbf{F}}{\partial \mathbf{X} \partial \mathbf{X}^\top}$$

$$= \nabla \mathbf{F}^\top \frac{\partial^2 \mathcal{H}_\mathbf{F}}{\partial \mathbf{F} \partial \mathbf{F}^\top} \nabla \mathbf{F} + \frac{\partial \mathcal{H}_\mathbf{F}}{\partial \mathbf{F}}\frac{\partial^2 \mathbf{F}}{\partial \mathbf{X} \partial \mathbf{X}^\top}. \qquad (1)$$

Note that in the above expression, $\partial^2 \mathcal{H}_\mathbf{F}/\partial \mathbf{F} \partial \mathbf{F}^\top$ and $\partial^2 \mathbf{F}/\partial \mathbf{X} \partial \mathbf{X}^\top$ denote the Hessian matrix of the hypervolume indicator with respect to objective points and of the objective function **F**, respectively. In our previous work [21], we derived the analytical expression of $\nabla^2 \mathcal{H}_\mathbf{F}$ for bi-objective cases and analyzed the structure and properties of the hypervolume Hessian matrix. In addition, we implemented a standalone hypervolume Newton (HVN) algorithm for unconstrained MOPs. Moreover, we have shown that the Hessian $\nabla^2 \mathcal{H}_\mathbf{F}$ is a tridiagonal block matrix in bi-objective cases and provided the non-singularity condition thereof, which states the Hessian is only singular on a null subset of $\mathbb{R}^{\mu n}$ [21], thereby ascertaining the safety of applying the HVN method.

The analytical expression of the Hessian matrix for higher dimensions contains the derivatives $\partial \mathcal{H}_\mathbf{F}/\partial x_i^{(\ell)} \partial x_j^{(m)}$, $m = 1, \ldots, \mu, \ell = 1, \ldots, \mu, i = 1, \ldots, n, j = 1, \ldots, n$. To compute these derivatives analytically, the chain rule can be applied (see [21]). In [21]. However, the Hessian matrix of the second mapping—from the points in the objective space $(\mathbf{y}^{(1)}, \ldots, \mathbf{y}^{(k)})$ to the hypervolume indicator—was only given analytically for two dimensions. The Hessian matrix of this second mapping can be generalized to k dimensional objective spaces, and it is continuous in regular cases. Here, we will only sketch the construction of this matrix and leave the detailed analysis for future research. It is known that in the N-dimensional case, the first derivatives $\partial \operatorname{HV}/\partial y_i$ are given by the $(k-1)$-dimensional Lebesgue measure of the $k-1$ dimensional faces of the attainment surface that separates the dominated space from the non-dominated space (see Figure 1, $\partial \operatorname{HV}/\partial y_3^{(1)}$). These faces themselves have a derivative that is given by the $(k-2)$-dimensional Lebesgue measure of the $k-2$-dimensional segments (or patches) at the boundary of these faces, which are also changing continuously with y_i (see Figure 1, examples $\partial \operatorname{HV}/\partial y_1^{(1)} \partial y_3^{(1)}$ and $\partial \operatorname{HV}/\partial y_2^{(2)} \partial y_3^{(1)}$). Note that points in the objective space need to be in a general position to guarantee differentiability; otherwise, one-sided differentiability applies and one of the two derivatives, i.e., when the derivative with perturbed coordinate falls to the dominated subspace, it is always zero [16].

In this work, however, rather than investigating in detail the analytical and computational properties of the Hessian for more than two objective functions, we compute the second-order derivative $\partial^2 \mathcal{H}_\mathbf{F}/\partial \mathbf{F} \partial \mathbf{F}^\top$ with the automatic differentiation (AD) method [51] and focus on solving equality-constrained MOPs using the Hessian matrix of the hypervolume indicator.

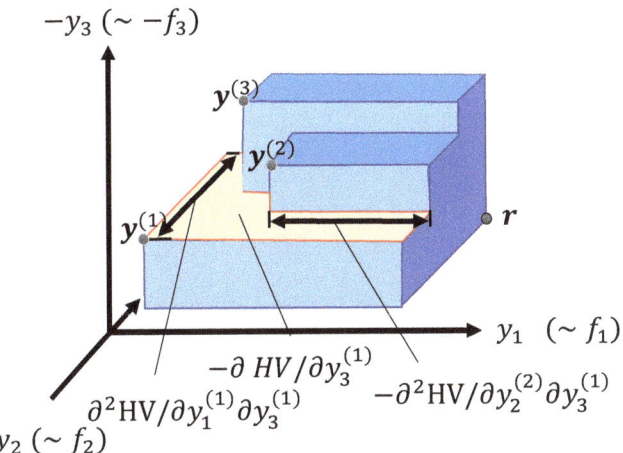

Figure 1. Example of a hypervolume indicator Hessian computation in three-dimensional objective space with a collection of points $\{\mathbf{y}^{(1)}, \mathbf{y}^{(2)}, \mathbf{y}^{(3)}\}$ and reference point **r**.

3. Hypervolume Newton Method for Constrained MOPs

In this section, we first describe the base method of HVN for the treatment of equality constrained MOPs and will then discuss how to deal with inequalities and with dominated points that may be computed during the run of the Newton method.

3.1. Handling Equalities

Consider a continuous equality-constrained MOP of the form

$$\begin{aligned} \min_{\mathbf{x} \in \mathcal{X}} \quad & F(\mathbf{x}), \\ \text{s.t.} \quad & h(\mathbf{x}) = 0, \end{aligned} \qquad (2)$$

where $h(\mathbf{x}) = (h_1(\mathbf{x}), \dots, h_p(\mathbf{x}))^\top$, and $h_i : \mathbb{R}^n \to \mathbb{R}$, $i = 1, \dots, p$, being the i-th equality constraint. The objective map is defined by $F : \mathcal{X} \subset \mathbb{R}^n \to \mathbb{R}^k$, where $f_i : \mathcal{X} \subset \mathbb{R}^n \to \mathbb{R}$ is the i-the individual objective to be considered in the MOP. The feasible set is given by:

$$Q = \{\mathbf{x} \in \mathcal{X} \ : \ h(\mathbf{x}) = 0\}. \qquad (3)$$

The set (population) based hypervolume optimization problem we are considering in this work is the following one:

$$\max_{\substack{X \subset Q \\ |X| = \mu}} \text{HV}(F(X)), \qquad (4)$$

where $\text{HV}(F(X))$ denotes the value of the hypervolume for a given set $X = \{\mathbf{x}^{(1)}, \dots, \mathbf{x}^{(\mu)}\}$ of magnitude $\mu \in \mathbb{N}$, where each $\mathbf{x}^{(i)} \in \mathbb{R}^n$. Note that the set $X \subset Q$ can be interpreted as a point in $R^{\mu n}$ (via considering $\mathbf{X} = (x_1^{(1)}, \dots, x_n^{(1)}, x_1^{(2)}, \dots, x_n^{(2)}, \dots, x_1^{(\mu)}, \dots, x_n^{(\mu)}))$, and hence, problem (4) can be identified by a scalar objective optimization problem of dimension μn.

The feasibility of X (i.e., $X \subset Q$) is identical to

$$h_i(\mathbf{x}^{(j)}) = 0, \quad i = 1, \dots, p, \, j = 1, \dots, \mu. \qquad (5)$$

For the related set-based equality constraints, we define for $i \in \{1, \dots, p\}$ and $j \in \{1, \dots, \mu\}$

$$h_{i,j} : \mathbb{R}^{\mu n} \to \mathbb{R}, \qquad h_{i,j}(\mathbf{X}) = h_i(\mathbf{x}^{(j)}). \qquad (6)$$

For checking the feasibility of all decision points, we define $\bar{h}: \mathbb{R}^{\mu n} \to \mathbb{R}^{pn}$ via

$$\bar{h}(\mathbf{X}) = \begin{pmatrix} h_{1,1}(\mathbf{X}) \\ h_{2,1}(\mathbf{X}) \\ \vdots \\ h_{p,1}(\mathbf{X}) \\ h_{1,2}(\mathbf{X}) \\ h_{2,2}(\mathbf{X}) \\ \vdots \\ h_{p,2}(\mathbf{X}) \\ \vdots \\ h_{p,n}(\mathbf{X}) \end{pmatrix} =: \begin{pmatrix} \bar{h}_1(\mathbf{X}) \\ \bar{h}_2(\mathbf{X}) \\ \vdots \\ \bar{h}_p(\mathbf{X}) \\ \bar{h}_{p+1}(\mathbf{X}) \\ \bar{h}_{p+2}(\mathbf{X}) \\ \vdots \\ \bar{h}_{2p}(\mathbf{X}) \\ \vdots \\ \bar{h}_{pn}(\mathbf{X}) \end{pmatrix}, \tag{7}$$

then its Jacobian is given by

$$\bar{H} := \nabla \bar{h}(\mathbf{X}) = \mathrm{diag}\left(H(\mathbf{x}^{(1)}), \ldots, H(\mathbf{x}^{(\mu)})\right) \in \mathbb{R}^{\mu p \times \mu n}, \tag{8}$$

where

$$H(\mathbf{x}^{(i)}) = \begin{pmatrix} \nabla h_1(\mathbf{x}^{(i)})^\top \\ \vdots \\ \nabla h_p(\mathbf{x}^{(i)})^\top \end{pmatrix} \in \mathbb{R}^{p \times n}. \tag{9}$$

The Karush-Kuhn-Tucker (KKT) equations of the problem (4) hence read as

$$\begin{aligned} \nabla \mathcal{H}_\mathbf{F}(\mathbf{X}) + \bar{H}^\top \lambda &= 0 \\ \bar{h}(\mathbf{X}) &= 0, \end{aligned} \tag{10}$$

for a Lagrange multiplier (or the dual variable) $\lambda \in \mathbb{R}^{\mu p}$ which directly leads to the root finding problem

$$G: \mathbb{R}^{n(\mu+p)} \to \mathbb{R}^{n(\mu+p)}$$

$$G(\mathbf{X}, \lambda) = \begin{pmatrix} \nabla \mathcal{H}_\mathbf{F}(\mathbf{X}) + \bar{H}^\top \lambda \\ \bar{h}(\mathbf{X}) \end{pmatrix} = 0, \tag{11}$$

where $\lambda \in \mathbb{R}^{\mu n}$. The Jacobian of G at $(X, \lambda)^T$ is given by

$$DG(\mathbf{X}, \lambda) = \begin{pmatrix} \nabla^2 \mathcal{H}_\mathbf{F}(\mathbf{X}) + \mathbf{M} & \bar{H}^\top \\ \bar{H} & 0 \end{pmatrix} \in \mathbb{R}^{\mu(n+p) \times \mu(n+p)}, \tag{12}$$

where

$$\mathbf{M} = \sum_{j=1}^{\mu p} \lambda_i \nabla^2 \bar{h}_j(\mathbf{X}) \in \mathbb{R}^{\mu n \times \mu n}. \tag{13}$$

Denoting by $\mathbf{X}_t \in \mathbb{R}^{\mu n}$ and $\lambda_t \in \mathbb{R}^{\mu p}$, the variables in iteration t, a Newton step for problem (11) is given by

$$\begin{pmatrix} \mathbf{X}_{t+1} \\ \lambda_{t+1} \end{pmatrix} = \begin{pmatrix} \mathbf{X}_t \\ \lambda_t \end{pmatrix} - DG(\mathbf{X}_t, \lambda_t)^{-1} G(\mathbf{X}_t, \lambda_t). \tag{14}$$

In our computations, we have omitted M in DG. A Newton step is hence obtained by solving

$$\begin{pmatrix} \nabla^2 \mathcal{H}_\mathbf{F}(\mathbf{X}_t) & \bar{H}^\top \\ \bar{H} & 0 \end{pmatrix} \begin{pmatrix} \mathbf{X}_{t+1} - \mathbf{X}_t \\ \lambda_{t+1} - \lambda_t \end{pmatrix} = -\begin{pmatrix} \nabla \mathcal{H}_\mathbf{F}(\mathbf{X}_t) + \bar{H}^\top \lambda_t \\ \bar{h}(\mathbf{X}_t) \end{pmatrix}. \tag{15}$$

3.2. Handling Inequalities

In order to handle inequalities, we have chosen an active set approach which we will discuss in the following. This approach is straightforward; however, it has led to satisfying results in our computations, in particular when the initial candidate set was computed by the evolutionary algorithm.

Assume problem (2) contains inequalities of the form

$$g(x) \leq 0, \tag{16}$$

where $g(x) = (g_1(x), \ldots, g_m(x))^\top$ and $g_i : \mathbb{R}^n \to \mathbb{R}$, $i = 1, \ldots, m$, is the i-th inequality constraint. Analogous to the equality-constrained case, we define the feasibility of $\mathbf{X} = (x_1^{(1)}, \ldots, x_n^{(1)}, x_1^{(2)}, \ldots, x_n^{(2)}, \ldots, x_1^{(\mu)}, \ldots, x_n^{(\mu)})$ by

$$g_i(\mathbf{x}^{(j)}) \leq 0, \quad i = 1, \ldots, m, \ j = 1, \ldots, \mu. \tag{17}$$

Define for $i \in \{1, \ldots, m\}$ and $j \in \{1, \ldots, \mu\}$

$$g_{i,j} : \mathbb{R}^{\mu n} \to \mathbb{R}, \quad g_{i,j}(\mathbf{X}) = g_i(\mathbf{x}^{(j)}) \tag{18}$$

and $\bar{g} : \mathbb{R}^{\mu n} \to \mathbb{R}^{mn}$ by

$$\bar{g}(\mathbf{X}) = \begin{pmatrix} g_{1,1}(\mathbf{X}) \\ h_{2,1}(\mathbf{X}) \\ \vdots \\ h_{m,1}(\mathbf{X}) \\ h_{1,2}(\mathbf{X}) \\ h_{2,2}(\mathbf{X}) \\ \vdots \\ h_{m,2}(\mathbf{X}) \\ \vdots \\ h_{m,n}(\mathbf{X}) \end{pmatrix} =: \begin{pmatrix} \bar{g}_1(\mathbf{X}) \\ \bar{g}_2(\mathbf{X}) \\ \vdots \\ \bar{g}_m(\mathbf{X}) \\ \bar{g}_{m+1}(\mathbf{X}) \\ \bar{g}_{m+2}(\mathbf{X}) \\ \vdots \\ \bar{g}_{2m}(\mathbf{X}) \\ \vdots \\ \bar{g}_{mn}(\mathbf{X}) \end{pmatrix}. \tag{19}$$

The active set we have used is as follows: if for an inequality constraint it holds

$$\bar{g}_l(\mathbf{X}) > -\text{tol} \tag{20}$$

for a given tolerance tol > 0 at $\mathbf{X}$, then we impose the equality

$$\bar{g}_l(\mathbf{X}) = 0, \tag{21}$$

(i.e., it will be added to the set of equalities) while all other inequalities are disregarded at $\mathbf{X}$.

3.3. Handling Dominated Points

Since Newton's method tends to realize relatively longer steps, it often occurs that some decision points are dominated after a Newton step/iteration. Therefore, it is necessary to discuss how the equality-constrained HVN method behaves in this case. For the reason that will become clear during our discussion, we will investigate two scenarios: (1) *infeasible and dominated points* and (2) *feasible but dominated points*.

For the first scenario, we consider the simplest case, where $p = 1$ and there is only one dominated point. Without loss of generality, we can assume that for an approximation set $\mathbf{X} = \{\mathbf{x}^{(1)}, \mathbf{x}^{(2)}, \ldots, \mathbf{x}^{(\mu)}\} \subseteq \mathcal{X}$, $\mathbf{x}^{(1)}$ is dominated by at least one of the remaining $\mu - 1$

points (as the indices are assigned to **X** arbitrarily). Denoting by $\mathbf{X}^{(-1)}$ the approximation set after removing $\mathbf{x}^{(1)}$, we can express the constraint function on $\mathbf{X}^{(-1)}$ as:

$$\bar{h}^*(\mathbf{X}^{(-1)}): \mathbb{R}^{(\mu-1)n} \to \mathbb{R}^{\mu-1}, \quad \mathbf{X}^{(-1)} \mapsto \left(\bar{h}_2^*(\mathbf{X}^{(-1)}), \bar{h}_3^*(\mathbf{X}^{(-1)}), \ldots, \bar{h}_\mu^*(\mathbf{X}^{(-1)})\right)^\top,$$

$$\bar{h}_j^*(\mathbf{X}^{(-1)}): \mathbb{R}^{(\mu-1)n} \to \mathbb{R}, \quad \mathbf{X}^{(-1)} \mapsto h(\mathbf{x}^{(j)}), \quad j \in [2\ldots\mu].$$

Note that we are only considering the special case of one constraint, i.e., $p = 1$. The root finding problem G can re-expressed in the following form, equivalent to Equation (11):

$$G(\mathbf{X},\lambda) = \begin{pmatrix} \lambda_1 \nabla h(\mathbf{x}^{(1)}) \\ \nabla \mathcal{H}_F\left(\mathbf{X}^{(-1)}\right) + \sum_{j=2}^\mu \lambda_j \nabla \bar{h}_j^*(\mathbf{X}^{(-1)}) \\ h(\mathbf{x}^{(1)}) \\ \bar{h}^*(\mathbf{X}^{(-1)}) \end{pmatrix}.$$

Let $\mu' = \mu - 1$ and $\mathbf{H}\left(\mathbf{X}^{(-1)}\right) = [\nabla \bar{h}_2^*(\mathbf{X}^{(-1)}), \ldots, \nabla \bar{h}_\mu^*(\mathbf{X}^{(-1)})] \in \mathbb{R}^{\mu' n \times \mu'}$, we express the derivative of G as a block matrix:

$$DG(\mathbf{X},\lambda) = \begin{bmatrix} \lambda_1 \nabla^2 h(\mathbf{x}^{(1)}) & \mathbf{0}_{n \times \mu' n} & \nabla h(\mathbf{x}^{(1)}) & \mathbf{0}_{n \times \mu'} \\ \mathbf{0}_{\mu' n \times n} & \nabla^2 \mathcal{H}_F\left(\mathbf{X}^{(-1)}\right) + \sum_{j=2}^\mu \nabla^2 \bar{h}_j^*\left(\mathbf{X}^{(-1)}\right) & \mathbf{0}_{\mu' n \times 1} & \mathbf{H}\left(\mathbf{X}^{(-1)}\right) \\ \nabla h(\mathbf{x}^{(1)})^\top & \mathbf{0}_{1 \times \mu' n} & 0 & \mathbf{0}_{1 \times \mu'} \\ \mathbf{0}_{\mu' \times n} & \mathbf{H}\left(\mathbf{X}^{(-1)}\right)^\top & \mathbf{0}_{\mu' \times 1} & \mathbf{0}_{\mu' \times \mu'} \end{bmatrix}.$$

Note that the upper left 2×2 block equals $\nabla^2 \mathcal{H}_F(\mathbf{X}) + \sum_{i=1}^\mu \nabla^2 h_i^-(\mathbf{X})$. The inverse of DG can be obtained by applying the Schur complement recursively (first consider the block partition indicated above and then apply it again to each partition), provided that both $\nabla^2 h(\mathbf{x}^{(1)})$ and $\nabla^2 \mathcal{H}_F\left(\mathbf{X}^{(-1)}\right)$ are non-singular.

After simplification, the inverse of DG admits the following form:

$$[DG(\mathbf{X},\lambda)]^{-1} = \begin{bmatrix} \left(\mathbf{I}_{n \times n} - (\mathbf{g}^\top \mathbf{A}\mathbf{g})^{-1} \mathbf{A}\mathbf{g}\mathbf{g}^\top\right)\mathbf{A} & \mathbf{0}_{n \times \mu' n} & (\mathbf{g}^\top \mathbf{A}\mathbf{g})^{-1} \mathbf{A}\mathbf{g} & \mathbf{0}_{n \times \mu'} \\ \mathbf{0}_{\mu' n \times n} & \mathbf{B}\left(\mathbf{I} - \mathbf{H}(\mathbf{H}^\top \mathbf{B}\mathbf{H})^{-1} \mathbf{H}^\top \mathbf{B}\right) & \mathbf{0}_{\mu' n \times 1} & \mathbf{0}_{\mu' n \times \mu'} \\ (\mathbf{g}^\top \mathbf{A}\mathbf{g})^{-1} (\mathbf{A}\mathbf{g})^\top & \mathbf{0}_{1 \times \mu' n} & -(\mathbf{g}^\top \mathbf{A}\mathbf{g})^{-1} & \mathbf{0}_{1 \times \mu'} \\ \mathbf{0}_{\mu' n \times n} & \mathbf{0}_{\mu' \times \mu' n} & \mathbf{0}_{\mu' \times 1} & -(\mathbf{H}^\top \mathbf{B}\mathbf{H})^{-1} \end{bmatrix},$$

where $\mathbf{g} = \nabla h(\mathbf{x}^{(1)}), \mathbf{A} = [\lambda_1 \nabla^2 h(\mathbf{x}^{(1)})]^{-1}, \mathbf{H} = \mathbf{H}(\mathbf{X}^{(-1)})$, and

$$\mathbf{B} = \left[\nabla^2 \mathcal{H}_F\left(\mathbf{X}^{(-1)}\right) + \sum_{j=2}^\mu \nabla^2 \bar{h}_j^*\left(\mathbf{X}^{(-1)}\right)\right]^{-1}.$$

The first row of blocks is of particular interest to us since it determines the search step of $\mathbf{x}^{(1)}$. It is obvious that

$$\begin{aligned} \Delta \mathbf{x}^{(1)} &= -\left([DG(\mathbf{X},\lambda)]^{-1}\right)_{[1:n,1:\mu(n+1)]} G(\mathbf{X},\lambda) \\ &= -\left(\lambda_1 \left(\mathbf{I}_{n \times n} - (\mathbf{g}^\top \mathbf{A}\mathbf{g})^{-1} \mathbf{A}\mathbf{g}\mathbf{g}^\top\right) \mathbf{A}\mathbf{g} + h(\mathbf{x}^{(1)}) (\mathbf{g}^\top \mathbf{A}\mathbf{g})^{-1} \mathbf{A}\mathbf{g}\right) \qquad (22) \\ &= -\frac{h(\mathbf{x}^{(1)})}{\nabla h(\mathbf{x}^{(1)})^\top [\nabla^2 h(\mathbf{x}^{(1)})]^{-1} \nabla h(\mathbf{x}^{(1)})} [\nabla^2 h(\mathbf{x}^{(1)})]^{-1} \nabla h(\mathbf{x}^{(1)}), \end{aligned}$$

where notation $(\mathbf{M})_{[1:n,1:\mu(n+1)]}$ takes rows from 1 to n and columns from 1 to $\mu(n+1)$ in matrix $\mathbf{M}$. Similarly, the search step of the dual variable is:

$$\begin{aligned}
\Delta \lambda_1 &= -\left([DG(\mathbf{X},\boldsymbol{\lambda})]^{-1}\right)_{[\mu n+1,1:\mu(n+1)]} G(\mathbf{X},\boldsymbol{\lambda}) \\
&= -\lambda_1 \left(\mathbf{g}^\top \mathbf{A}\mathbf{g}\right)^{-1} (\mathbf{A}\mathbf{g})^\top \mathbf{g} + \left(\mathbf{g}^\top \mathbf{A}\mathbf{g}\right)^{-1} h(\mathbf{x}^{(1)}) \\
&= \lambda_1 \left(\frac{h(\mathbf{x}^{(1)})}{\nabla h(\mathbf{x}^{(1)})^\top [\nabla^2 h(\mathbf{x}^{(1)})]^{-1} \nabla h(\mathbf{x}^{(1)})} - 1\right).
\end{aligned} \qquad (23)$$

Now, consider the function $\hat{h}(\mathbf{x}) = h^2(\mathbf{x})/2$, whose first- and second-order derivatives are:

$$\nabla \hat{h}(\mathbf{x}) = h(\mathbf{x}) \nabla h(\mathbf{x}), \quad \nabla^2 \hat{h}(\mathbf{x}) = h(\mathbf{x}) \nabla^2 h(\mathbf{x}) + \nabla h(\mathbf{x}) \nabla h(\mathbf{x})^\top.$$

The global minimum/maximum of $\hat{h}$ corresponds to the feasible set, i.e., $h(\mathbf{x}) = 0$. Hence, Newton iterations that optimize $\hat{h}$ will equivalently find the feasible set. Computing the Newton direction of $\hat{h}$, we have:

$$\begin{aligned}
&-\left[\nabla^2 \hat{h}(\mathbf{x})\right]^{-1} \hat{h}(\mathbf{x}) \\
&= -[h(\mathbf{x}) \nabla^2 h(\mathbf{x})]^{-1} \left(\mathbf{I}_{n\times n} - \frac{\nabla h(\mathbf{x}) \nabla h(\mathbf{x})^\top [h(\mathbf{x}) \nabla^2 h(\mathbf{x})]^{-1}}{1 + \nabla h(\mathbf{x})^\top [h(\mathbf{x}) \nabla^2 h(\mathbf{x})]^{-1} \nabla h(\mathbf{x})}\right) h(\mathbf{x}) \nabla h(\mathbf{x}) \\
&= -\frac{h(\mathbf{x})}{h(\mathbf{x}) + \nabla h(\mathbf{x})^\top [\nabla^2 h(\mathbf{x})]^{-1} \nabla h(\mathbf{x})} [\nabla^2 h(\mathbf{x})]^{-1} \nabla h(\mathbf{x}).
\end{aligned} \qquad (24)$$

Setting $\mathbf{x} = \mathbf{x}^{(1)}$ in the above equation and comparing it to Equation (22), we notice that the Newton direction of $\hat{h}$ and the hypervolume Newton step $\Delta \mathbf{x}^{(1)}$ only differ by a scalar, which can be neglected in practice since we implement a step-size control to re-scale the search step (see the following sub-section). Therefore, we conclude that for infeasible and dominated points, our HVN method (Equation (15)) only considers the constraint function and moves such decision points to the feasible set rapidly (ideally at quadratic speed when the point is close to the feasible set). This satisfactory property allows for handling infeasible and dominated points without modifying our HVN method.

In addition, due to this nice property, an infeasible point will eventually lie on the feasible set, where it can still be dominated if other feasible points exist. This is precisely the second scenario of our discussion, in which the hypervolume of feasible but dominated points will be zero. To move such points, we propose to employ the famous *non-dominated sorting* [36] procedure, where we partition all feasible points into "layers" of mutually non-dominated ones (formally, anti-chains of Pareto order) and compute the Newton direction for each layer (using Equation (15)) regardless of other dominating layers. In this manner, the HVN method can move all feasible points along the feasible set for achieving a good distribution.

3.4. The HVN Method for Constrained MOPs

Taking the above considerations regarding the HVN method, in this section, we aim to devise and implement a standalone HVN algorithm, which is outlined in Algorithm 1. First, we check if any decision point is feasible (i.e., $\mathbf{h}(\mathbf{x}) = \mathbf{0}$ for some $\mathbf{x}$), where the feasibility can be tested numerically with a pre-defined small threshold (e.g., 10^{-4} used in this work) for the equality constraints. Then, we employ the non-dominated sorting point procedure [36] to partition the feasible points $\mathbf{X}_f$ into "layers" of mutually non-dominated ones, where the Newton direction (Equation (15)) is calculated separately on each layer. Taking L for the indices of points in a layer and $\mathbf{X}_f[L]$ for the subset indexed by L, we express this partitioning as $\mathbf{X}_f[L_1] \prec \mathbf{X}_f[L_2] \prec \cdots \prec \mathbf{X}_f[L_q], \forall i \neq j (L_i \cap L_j = \emptyset), \cup_i L_i \subseteq [1\ldots\mu]$. Note that the dominance relation for the remaining infeasible and dominated points is not well-defined, considering the equality constraints since they are incomparable to the feasible ones (also among themselves). In this case, we simply merge them into the first layer L_1 and compute the Newton direction thereof, which can be justified by the observation in Equations (22) and (24). The resulting search direction of the infeasible and dominated points is a Newton direction of the function $h^2/2$. In this treatment, a special case arises when there are no feasible points, usually in the first several iterations of the algorithm.

Algorithm 1: Standalone hypervolume Newton algorithm for equality-constrained MOPs

1 **Input:** F: multi-objective function, h: equality constraints, $\mathbf{X}_0$: initial approximation set, B: maximal iterations;
2 **if** $\mathbf{X}_0$ *is not given* **then**
3   sample $\mathbf{X} = \left\{\mathbf{x}^{(1)}, \mathbf{x}^{(2)}, \ldots, \mathbf{x}^{(\mu)}\right\} \subseteq \mathcal{X}$ uniformly at random
4 **else**
5     $\mathbf{X} \leftarrow \mathbf{X}_0$
6 $\mathbf{Y} \leftarrow \left\{F(\mathbf{x}^{(1)}), F(\mathbf{x}^{(2)}), \ldots, F(\mathbf{x}^{(\mu)})\right\}$;
7 $\mathbf{H} \leftarrow \left\{h(\mathbf{x}^{(1)}), h(\mathbf{x}^{(2)}), \ldots, h(\mathbf{x}^{(\mu)})\right\}$;
8 $\lambda \leftarrow \{\mathbf{1}_{1\times p}/\mu, \ldots, \mathbf{1}_{1\times p}/\mu\}$ and $|\lambda| = \mu$;   ▷ initialize dual variables
9 $\varepsilon \leftarrow 10^{-4}$;
10 **for** $c = 1, 2, \ldots, B$ **do**
11     $S \leftarrow \emptyset$;   ▷ indices for the feasible subset
12   **for** $i \in [1 \ldots \mu]$ **do**   ▷ check the feasibility
13   **if** $\max\left\{|h_1(\mathbf{x}^{(i)})|, \ldots, |h_p(\mathbf{x}^{(i)})|\right\} \leq \varepsilon$ **then** $S \leftarrow S \cup \{i\}$;
14     $L_1, L_2, \ldots, L_q \leftarrow \text{NON-DOMINATED-SORTING}(\mathbf{X}[S])$;   ▷ $\mathbf{X}_f = \mathbf{X}[S]$
15     $L_1 \leftarrow L_1 \cup ([1..\mu] \setminus S)$;
16   **for** $L \in \{L_1, L_2, \ldots, L_q\}$ **do**
17        $\nabla^2 \mathcal{H}_\mathbf{F}(\mathbf{X}[L]) \leftarrow \text{HYPERVOLUME-HESSIAN}(\mathbf{X}[L], \mathbf{Y}[L])$;   ▷ Equation (1)
       // Equation (15)
18        $\Delta_L \leftarrow \text{NEWTON-STEP}(\nabla^2 \mathcal{H}_\mathbf{F}(\mathbf{X}[L]), \nabla^2 h(\mathbf{X}[L]), \nabla h(\mathbf{X}[L]), \mathbf{H}[L], \lambda[L])$;
       // See Section 3.4
19   Determine the step-size σ_L with Armijo's backtracking line search;
       // Apply Newton step to the primal-dual pair
20        $(\mathbf{X}[L], \lambda[L]) \leftarrow (\mathbf{X}[L], \lambda[L]) + \sigma_L \Delta_L$;
21     $\mathbf{Y} \leftarrow \left\{F(\mathbf{x}^{(1)}), F(\mathbf{x}^{(2)}), \ldots, F(\mathbf{x}^{(\mu)})\right\}$;
22     $\mathbf{H} \leftarrow \left\{h(\mathbf{x}^{(1)}), h(\mathbf{x}^{(2)}), \ldots, h(\mathbf{x}^{(\mu)})\right\}$;
23 **return** $\mathbf{X}$;

Finally, another important aspect is the step-size control for each Newton step. We propose maintaining individual step-sizes for each partition, which is determined using the well-known Armijo's backtracking line search [52]. In detail, this method starts with an initial step-size σ_0 and tests whether the Euclidean norm of $G(\mathbf{X}, \lambda)$ has sufficiently decreased after applying the Newton step to the primal-dual pair $(\mathbf{X}, \lambda)$. Since Newton's direction for equality-constrained problems (Equation (15)) is not necessarily an ascent direction for the hypervolume, we take the Euclidean norm $||G(\mathbf{X}, \lambda)||$ as the convergence measure since (1) the optimality condition is $G(\mathbf{X}, \lambda) = 0$ (Equation (11)) and (2) the Newton step is always a descent direction of $||G(\mathbf{X}, \lambda)||$. Let $\mathbf{Z} = (\mathbf{X}^\top, \lambda^\top)^\top$ be the primal-dual variable and $\Delta \mathbf{Z} = -[DG(\mathbf{Z})]^{-1} G(\mathbf{Z})$, then we have $(\frac{d}{d\sigma} ||G(\mathbf{Z} + \sigma \Delta \mathbf{Z})||)|_{\sigma=0} = -||G(\mathbf{Z})|| \leq 0$. If the test fails, then we halve the step-size and repeat the test. Notably, for infeasible and dominated points, the test checks if the value of the squared constraint value is sufficiently decreased as the HVN method computes the Newton direction of $h^2/2$ for those points. In our implementation, we use maximally six iterations of such tests, resulting in a minimal step-size of $\sigma_0/64$. As for the initial step-size σ_0, the commonly used value $\sigma_0 = 1$ often leads to Newton steps that jump out of the decision space when the Newton direction is large or the point is in the vicinity of the decision boundary. Therefore, we set it to the minimum of one and the maximal step-size that the primal vector **X** can take without leaving the decision space, i.e., $\sigma_0 = \min\{1, \sigma_{\max}\}$. The value of $\sigma_{\max}$ can be calculated in a straightforward way when the decision space is a convex and compact subset of $\mathbb{R}^n$, e.g., a hyperbox.

3.5. Computational Cost

The above method requires the knowledge of the Jacobian and the Hessian of both objective and constraint functions. In this work, we have used automatic differentiation (AD) techniques [53]. Note that finite differences can also be utilized when the AD-computation is not applicable. The AD-computation takes maximally four times the used multiply–add operations taken in evaluating the function value [54]. Hence, to make a fair comparison between HVN and MOEA methods, we will take 4 function evaluations (FEs) and $4 + 6n$ FEs to quantify the computational cost of each AD-computed Jacobian and Hessian, respectively. In total, the number of FEs consumed in each iteration comprises:

$$\#\text{FEs}: \underbrace{\mu}_{F} + \underbrace{\mu}_{h} + \underbrace{4\mu}_{\nabla F} + \underbrace{4\mu}_{\nabla h} + \underbrace{(4+6n)\mu}_{\nabla^2 F} + \underbrace{(4+6n)\mu}_{\nabla^2 h} + \underbrace{6(4\mu + 4\mu)}_{\text{step-size control}} = (69 + 12n)\mu,$$

which amounts to computations of function evaluation, constraint evaluation, Jacobian of the objective function and the constraint, Hessian of the objective function and the constraint, and the backtracking line search of the step-size. Computing the hypervolume Hessian takes $\Theta((\mu n)^3)$ time in addition to the AD-computation of derivatives in Equation (1). For solving Equation (15), we use Cholesky decomposition, which has a computational complexity of $O((\mu(n+p))^3)$. It is certainly desired either to have an analytic expression of the HV Hessian or to exploit the block diagonal structure this matrix will certainly have for AD, which we, however, have to leave for future research.

We have implemented the standalone algorithm in Python, which is accessible at https://github.com/wangronin/HypervolumeDerivatives (accessed on 1 November 2022).

4. Numerical Results

In this section, we present some numerical results of the HVN both as standalone algorithms as well as a local search engine within the NSGA-III algorithm.

4.1. HVN as Standalone Algorithm

We showcase the behavior of the proposed Newton method as a standalone method on three example problems:

(P1): $F(\mathbf{x}) = \left[(x-1)^2, (x+1)^2\right]^\top$,

$h(\mathbf{x}) = x^2 - 1$, $\mathcal{X} = [-2, 2]^2$, $\mathbf{r} = [20, 20]^\top$.

(P2): $F(\mathbf{x}) = \left[(\mathbf{x} - (1,1,0)^\top)^2, (\mathbf{x} - (1,-1,0)^\top)^2, (\mathbf{x} - (-1,1,0)^\top)^2\right]^\top$,

$h(\mathbf{x}) = \left(\mathbf{x} - \left(\frac{2\sqrt{3}}{3} - 1, 0, -1.5\right)^\top\right)^2 - 1$, $\mathcal{X} = [-2, 2]^3$, $\mathbf{r} = [38, 38, 38]^\top$.

(P3): $F(\mathbf{x}) = \left[(\mathbf{x} + (1,1,1)^\top)^2, (\mathbf{x} + (1,0,0)^\top)^2, (\mathbf{x} + (2,2,-4)^\top)^2\right]^\top$,

$g(\mathbf{x}) = -x_0$, $\mathcal{X} = [-4, 4]^3$, $\mathbf{r} = [90, 90, 90]^\top$.

Importantly, we will use different initializations of the decision points that are specific to each problem in order to investigate the behavior of the standalone HVN with respect to the characteristic of each problem; We do not aim to provide a unified and systematic initialization method for the standalone HVN in this section. Note that problem P3 defines an inequality constraint on the first component x_0 of the decision point, where the feasible set is $\{\mathbf{x} \in \mathcal{X}: x_0 \geq 0\}$, and the optimum lies on the active set of g, i.e., $x_0 = 0$. This problem is meant to test if the proposed HVN algorithm can manage to solve inequality-constrained problems where the optimum is on the active set of the constraint. To measure the empirical performance of the HVN algorithm, we take the Euclidean norm $||G(\mathbf{X}, \lambda)||$ since the Newton direction is not necessarily an ascent direction for the hypervolume.

Moreover, since it is well-known that the Newton-like method can be affected by choice of initial solutions, we investigate the performance of the HVN algorithm on problem P1 with three different initializations. Specifically, in the two-dimensional decision space, we create $\mu = 50$ initial decision points on the line segment $x_2 = x_1 - 2, x_1 \in [0, 2]$, where we determine the value of x_1 by (i) taking evenly spaced points (linear), (ii) logistic-transformed evenly spaced points (which makes the points denser around the tails of the line segment), or (iii) logit-transformed evenly spaced points (higher density of points in the middle). The results are illustrated in Figure 2 and Table 1, which shows a set of well-distributed points on the feasible set in the objective space (the red dashed sphere) for all three initializations. In addition, the empirical convergence rate is quadratic regardless of the choice of initialization methods, as reported in Table 1.

Table 1. The evolution of $||G(\mathbf{X}, \lambda)||$ on problems P1 with three different initialization strategies.

	Linear	Logistic	Logit
1	4.23×10^1	4.55×10^1	4.20×10^1
2	2.33×10^1	2.54×10^1	2.27×10^1
3	8.81×10^0	1.01×10^1	8.52×10^0
4	8.19×10^0	7.82×10^0	8.30×10^0
5	2.29×10^0	2.17×10^0	2.29×10^0
6	1.06×10^{-1}	8.77×10^{-2}	1.11×10^{-1}
7	1.91×10^{-4}	3.48×10^{-4}	1.93×10^{-3}
8	7.38×10^{-10}	7.05×10^{-7}	1.03×10^{-5}
9	1.76×10^{-14}	1.06×10^{-12}	1.55×10^{-10}
10	1.62×10^{-14}	1.79×10^{-14}	2.33×10^{-14}

The results on problem P2 are depicted in Figure 3 and Table 2 for three different sizes $\mu \in \{20, 40, 60\}$ of the approximation set. The initial decision points are sampled uniformly at random in the convex hull of three points $(1, 1, 0)^\top, (1, -1, 0)^\top$, and $(-1, 0, 0)^\top$. Whereas the final approximation set is well-distributed in the objective space, we observe that empirical convergence of $||G(\mathbf{X}, \lambda)||$ is considerably rugged in the first 20–25 iterations, after which quadratic convergence appears. This is indeed attributed to the fact that decision points often become dominated in the first couple of iterations on this problem, resulting in zero hypervolume gradient thereof and hence quite a large norm of $||G(\mathbf{X}, \lambda)||$. Nevertheless, the proposed treatment of those dominated points (Algorithm 1), which is based on the non-dominated sorting procedure, is capable of bringing the dominated points to the active set with a quadratic speed. Similarly, the same ruggedness is seen in the convergence chart of problem P3 (shown in Figure 4). On this problem, we again take the setting $\mu \in \{20, 40, 60\}$, and the initial decision points are sampled uniformly at random in the feasible space of $[0, 4] \times [-4, 4]^2$. We extend the HVN algorithm slightly for this inequality-constrained problem in the following way: whenever the decision points are feasible, i.e., $g(\mathbf{x}) \leq 0$, and quite distant from the active set ($g(\mathbf{x}) = 0$, shown as the red plane in Figure 4), we ignore the constraint function when computing the Newton step. When the feasible decision points are sufficiently close to the active set (the distance is less than 10^{-4} in our implementation), we consider $g(\mathbf{x})$ an equality constraint and utilize Equation (15) to compute the Newton step.

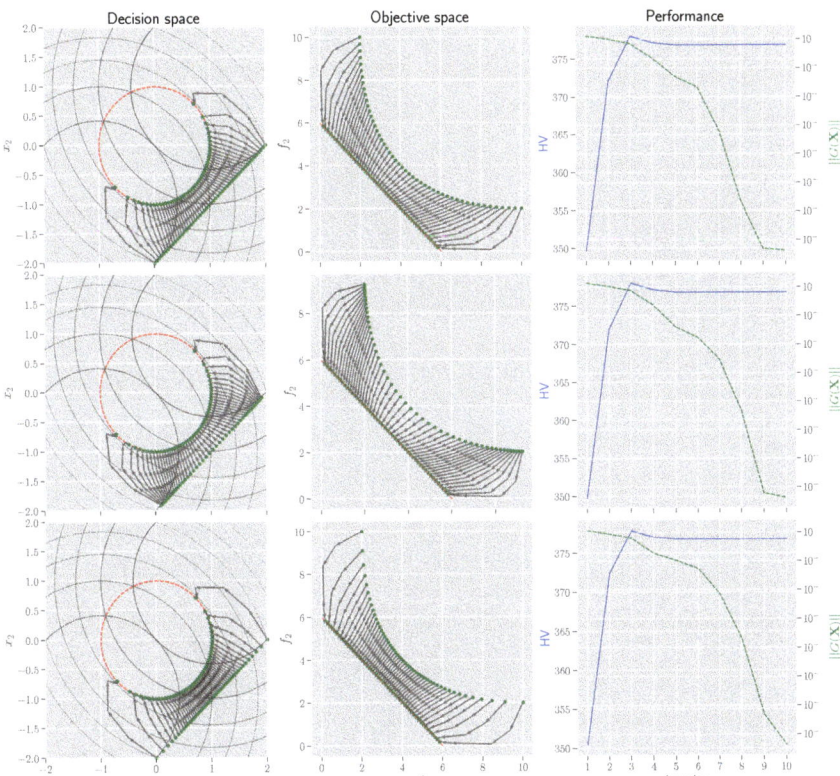

Figure 2. On problem P1, the convergence of the HVN method is shown for three different initializations of the starting approximation set ($\mu = 50$)—linear (**top row**), logistic (**middle**), and logit spacing (**bottom**). We depict the final approximation set (**left column**; green stars), the corresponding objective points (**middle column**; green stars), and the evolution of the HV value and $\|G(\mathbf{X}, \lambda)\|$ (**right column**).

Moreover, we test the standalone HVN method on large-scale, complicated MOPs. We choose the well-known DTLZ problems with one spherical constraint [55,56] with $\mu = 200$ decision points, resulting in a relatively large Hessian matrix (for an 11-dimensional decision space and one constraint, the $DG(\mathbf{X}, \lambda)$ object is of size 2400×2400). In this case, we use sparse matrix operations for computation efficiency, exploiting the sparsity of the Hessian. Since the DTLZ problems are highly multi-modal, the initial approximation set is generated in a local vicinity of the Pareto set, i.e., $\mathbf{X}^* + 0.02\mathcal{U}(0, 1)$, where $\mathbf{X}^*$ is sampled uniformly at random on the Pareto set. We execute the standalone HVN method for 15 iterations and illustrate the result in Figure 5. In the plot, we observe well-distributed final points (green dots) in contrast to non-uniform initial ones (black crosses), showing the standalone HVN works properly as a local method for large-scale problems.

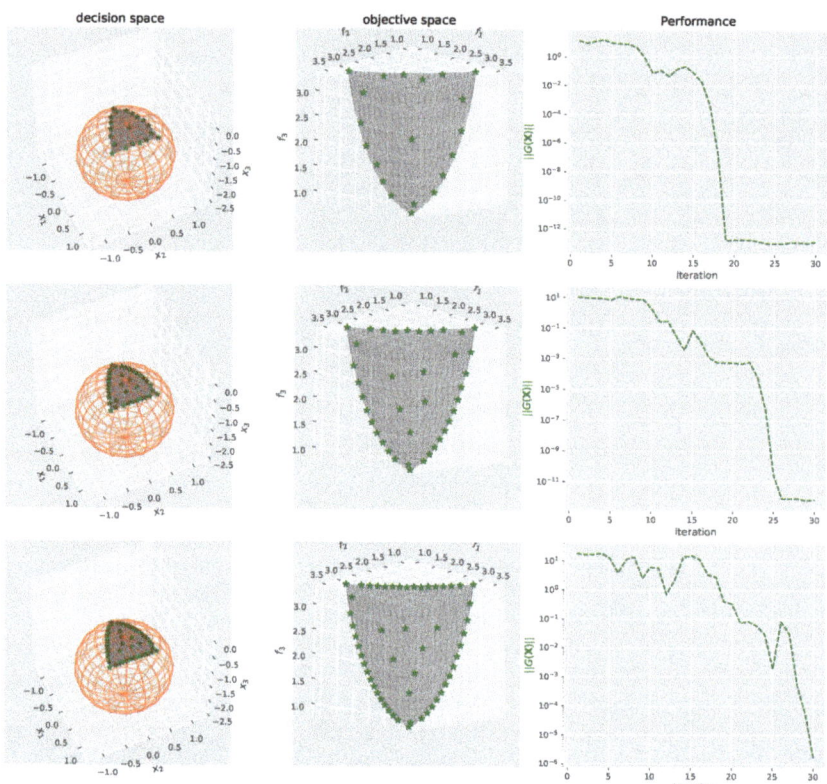

Figure 3. On problem P2 with a spherical constraint, we depict for three sizes of the approximation set ($\mu \in \{20, 40, 60\}$; from **top** to **bottom**), the final approximation set (**left column**; green stars), the corresponding objective points (**middle column**; green stars), and the evolution of the HV value and $\|G(\mathbf{X}, \lambda)\|$ (**right column**). The initial points are sampled uniformly at random in the convex hull of three points $(1, 1, 0)^\top$, $(1, -1, 0)^\top$, and $(-1, 0, 0)^\top$.

Table 2. The evolution of $\|G(\mathbf{X}, \lambda)\|$ on problems P2 and P3.

	Problem P2			Problem P3		
	$\mu = 20$	$\mu = 40$	$\mu = 60$	$\mu = 20$	$\mu = 40$	$\mu = 60$
1	1.365×10^1	1.055×10^1	18.036836	1.433×10^3	569.121097	438.983791
2	9.454×10^0	9.259×10^0	16.083916	9.368×10^2	541.523806	434.703270
3	1.247×10^1	8.977×10^0	16.403643	1.197×10^3	444.774066	365.952443
4	1.589×10^1	8.628×10^0	18.052126	9.522×10^2	261.636562	362.014326
5	9.791×10^0	6.888×10^0	12.364802	6.194×10^2	212.841570	341.897644
6	8.618×10^0	1.123×10^1	3.899254	5.232×10^2	145.076665	254.253017
7	8.024×10^0	8.779×10^0	11.323440	3.557×10^2	103.986300	240.719767
8	4.737×10^0	7.632×10^0	13.320606	2.419×10^2	57.592159	165.603954
9	9.037×10^{-1}	7.090×10^0	2.543622	1.511×10^2	12.628821	109.411195
10	7.393×10^{-2}	1.816×10^0	5.984437	8.527×10^1	0.104307	70.516402
11	1.182×10^{-1}	2.660×10^{-1}	5.749496	3.732×10^1	0.097777	41.699152
12	4.399×10^{-2}	2.877×10^{-1}	0.702964	3.248×10^0	0.097013	19.525977
13	1.535×10^{-1}	3.232×10^{-2}	2.240449	2.008×10^0	0.096634	0.447690
14	2.299×10^{-1}	3.694×10^{-3}	13.274468	1.829×10^0	0.096256	0.257345

Table 2. Cont.

	Problem P2			Problem P3		
	$\mu = 20$	$\mu = 40$	$\mu = 60$	$\mu = 20$	$\mu = 40$	$\mu = 60$
15	7.425×10^{-2}	7.159×10^{-2}	15.201915	5.425×10^{-2}	0.005277	2.066379
16	1.572×10^{-2}	1.378×10^{-2}	11.273571	1.735×10^{-1}	0.002934	2.016149
17	4.216×10^{-4}	1.231×10^{-3}	3.318978	6.372×10^{-6}	0.001602	1.019636
18	1.630×10^{-7}	5.630×10^{-4}	2.818340	9.702×10^{-3}	0.001552	0.944297
19	1.674×10^{-13}	5.454×10^{-4}	0.400360	9.373×10^{-5}	0.001528	4.904926
20	1.733×10^{-13}	5.411×10^{-4}	0.335107	2.546×10^{-8}	0.001522	2.937413
21	1.803×10^{-13}	4.697×10^{-4}	0.074058	7.243×10^{-12}	0.001516	3.118031
22	1.761×10^{-13}	5.901×10^{-4}	0.081798	8.897×10^{-12}	0.001139	0.336917
23	1.384×10^{-13}	6.140×10^{-5}	0.057776	6.654×10^{-12}	0.001072	0.004270
24	1.020×10^{-13}	4.508×10^{-7}	0.029809	7.210×10^{-12}	0.001010	0.000866
25	9.765×10^{-14}	2.759×10^{-11}	0.001956	5.851×10^{-12}	0.000994	0.000489
26	9.788×10^{-14}	7.794×10^{-13}	0.081949	5.851×10^{-12}	0.000990	0.000477
27	1.177×10^{-13}	7.767×10^{-13}	0.031275	5.851×10^{-12}	0.000954	0.000459
28	1.176×10^{-13}	7.688×10^{-13}	0.000492	5.851×10^{-12}	0.128140	0.000460
29	1.052×10^{-13}	5.918×10^{-13}	0.000053	5.851×10^{-12}	0.252721	0.000460
30	1.314×10^{-13}	6.821×10^{-13}	0.000002	5.851×10^{-12}	0.022233	0.000460

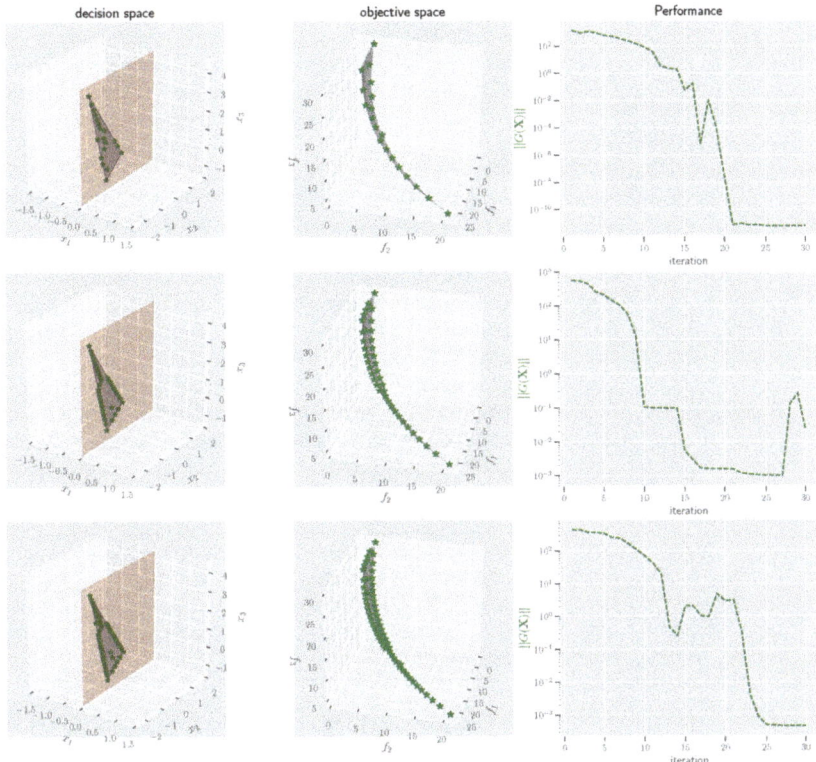

Figure 4. On problem P3 with a spherical constraint, we depict for three sizes of the initial approximation set ($\mu \in \{20, 40, 60\}$; from **top** to **bottom**), the final approximation set (**left column**; green stars), the corresponding objective points (**middle column**; green stars), and the evolution of the HV value and $\|G(\mathbf{X})\|$ (**right column**). The initial decision points are sampled uniformly at random in the feasible space of $[0,4] \times [-4,4]^2$.

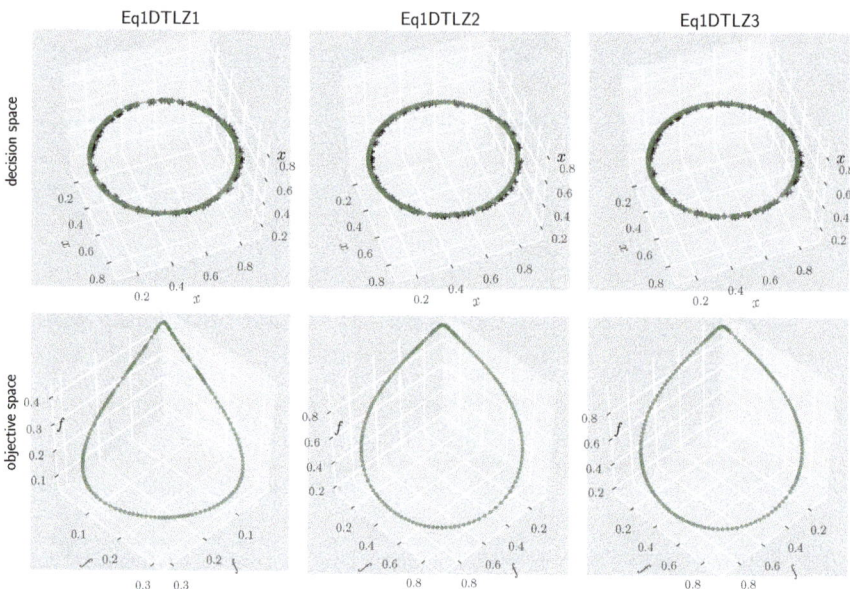

Figure 5. On Eq-DTLZ1-3 problems, the HVN method starts from a small local perturbation (black crosses) of the Pareto set (sphere in the decision space), i.e., $\mathbf{X}^* + 0.02\mathcal{U}(0,1)$, where $\mathbf{X}^*$ (of size 200) is sampled uniformly at random on the Pareto set. The final approximation set of the HVN method is depicted as green points. Only the first three search dimensions are shown for the decision space.

4.2. HVN within NSGA-III

In this section, we investigate the empirical performance of the HVN algorithm on more complicated, equality-constrained DTLZ (Eq-DTLZ) problems [55,56] and their inverted counterparts (Eq-IDTLZ). As Newton-like algorithms are local methods, running the standalone algorithm (Algorithm 1) will stagnate at local Pareto sets. Therefore, we hybridize the HVN algorithm with an MOEA, in which we first execute the MOEA for a pre-defined budget to overcome the local optimum and get close to the global Pareto set, and then initialize the HVN algorithm from the final approximation set of the MOEA to make local refinements. We summarize this hybrid approach in Algorithm 2. Notably, in line 3, we transfer the whole approximation set (rather than only the non-dominated points) to HVN upon the termination of MOEA since the standalone HVN method is able to move dominated points towards the feasible set at quadratic speed, as proven in Section 3.3.

Algorithm 2: Hybridization of HVN and MOEA

1 **Input:** F: multi-objective function, $\mathbf{h}$: equality constraints, B_1: #iteration for MOEA, B_2: #iteration for HVN;
2 $\mathbf{X} \leftarrow \text{MOEA}(F, \mu, \mathbf{h}, B_1)$;   ▷ `X is the entire approximation set`
3 $\mathbf{X}' \leftarrow \text{HVN}(F, \mathbf{h}, \mathbf{X}, B_2)$;   ▷ `Algorithm 1`
4 **return** $\mathbf{X}'$;

The following empirical study aims to check whether the hybridization approach can achieve a better final approximation set/front than an MOEA alone under the same computation budget. As for the test problem, a single spherical constraint $h(\mathbf{x}) = (x_1 - 0.5)^2 + (x_2 - 0.5)^2 - 0.16$ is imposed on problems DTLZ1 − 4. The decision space is $[0,1]^{11}$, the reference point is $\mathbf{r} = (1,1,1)^\top$ for HVN, and the approximation set is of size 200. Here, we choose the well-known NSGA-III algorithm [34,35], where the equality constraints are handled using the adaptive ε-constraint handling technique. We utilize the implementation in the Pymoo library: https://pymoo.org/constraints/eps.html (accessed on 1 November 2022). The method considers a solution feasible subject to a small ε threshold, which decreases linearly to zero. The initial value of ε is set to the average constraint value of the initial population. In our experiment, we control the ε decrease to zero after 50% of the iterations of NSGA-III. In addition, we use Das and Dennis's approach [28] to generate well-spaced reference directions (18 partitions which lead to 190 directions) for NSGA-III. As for its hyperparameters, we use the default setting: $\eta = 30$ and $p = 1$ for simulated binary crossover and $\eta = 20$ for polynomial mutation. Furthermore, the hybrid algorithm first executes NSGA-III with $\mu = 200$ for 1000 iterations and then runs the HVN method for 10 iterations. In HVN, the total function evaluations and AD operations take ca. 270 s CPU time on an Intel(R) Core(TM) i5-8257U CPU. Considering the CPU time of a single function evaluation, which is on average ca. 5.6×10^{-5} s measured on the same hardware, the total function evaluations plus the AD operations are equivalent to roughly $270/5.6 \times 10^{-5} \approx 4.8 \times 10^5$ FEs. Therefore, the total budget of the hybrid algorithm is roughly $4.8 \times 10^5/200 + 1000 \approx 3400$ iterations. We will execute the standalone NSGA-III algorithm for the same iterations to keep the fairness of comparisons.

We first depict one example of the final approximation set (only the non-dominated subset is shown) in Figure 6 for both methods, where we clearly observe that the hybridization achieves much more non-dominated points than NSGA-III. Second, we show, in Table 3, the hypervolume indicator value and the number of final non-dominated points for both algorithms obtained from 15 independent runs. In addition, we compute the above metrics for the hybrid algorithm right before the HVN phase starts (NSGA-III (1000) in the table), showing the progress that HVN manages to make. From the results, we conclude that the hybrid algorithm significantly improves upon the hypervolume metric and outputs substantially more non-dominated points than NSGA-III alone. We conjecture that the observed advantage of the hybrid algorithm is very likely attributed to HVN's ability to move dominated points to the feasible set with quadratic convergence (see Section 3), which disregards the objective function and thereby its multi-modal landscape.

Table 3. On Eq-DTLZ1-4 and Eq-IDTLZ1-4 problems, the sample mean and standard error of the hypervolume (HV) value and the number of final non-dominated (ND) points over 15 independent runs for each algorithm. The hypervolume values are computed with reference point $(1,1,1)^\top$ for all problems except Eq-DTLZ4, Eq-IDTLZ3, and Eq-IDTLZ4, which we use $(1.2, 5 \times 10^{-3}, 5 \times 10^{-4})^\top$, $(800, 800, 700)^\top$, and $(-0.4, 0.6, 0.6)^\top$, respectively. The initial population is $\mu = 200$ for all algorithms. Hybridization = NSGA-III (iter = 1000) + HVN (iter = 10), which consumes roughly the same CPU time on function evaluations with NSGA-III for 3400 iterations (see caption of Figure 6 for the detail).

	Eq-DTLZ1		Eq-DTLZ2		Eq-DTLZ3		Eq-DTLZ4	
Algorithm	HV	#ND	HV	#ND	HV	#ND	HV	#ND
NSGA-III (1000)	$0.867 \pm 1.4 \times 10^{-3}$	28.4 ± 0.7	$0.297 \pm 1.9 \times 10^{-3}$	32.7 ± 0.9	$0.292 \pm 1.9 \times 10^{-3}$	26.0 ± 1.0	$8.4 \times 10^{-4} \pm 7.0 \times 10^{-5}$	12.3 ± 0.8
Hybridization	$0.876 \pm 2.4 \times 10^{-4}$	80.9 ± 2.0	$0.324 \pm 3.6 \times 10^{-4}$	95.3 ± 1.9	$0.321 \pm 6.6 \times 10^{-4}$	75.2 ± 2.4	$1.1 \times 10^{-3} \pm 5.1 \times 10^{-5}$	200.0 ± 0.0
NSGA-III (3400)	$0.873 \pm 4.5 \times 10^{-4}$	38.5 ± 1.3	$0.304 \pm 9.2 \times 10^{-4}$	32.6 ± 0.9	$0.301 \pm 1.1 \times 10^{-3}$	30.1 ± 0.7	$9.2 \times 10^{-4} \pm 5.2 \times 10^{-5}$	14.5 ± 0.6

	Eq-IDTLZ1		Eq-IDTLZ2		Eq-IDTLZ3		Eq-IDTLZ4	
Algorithm	HV	#ND	HV	#ND	HV	#ND	HV	#ND
NSGA-III (1000)	$0.517 \pm 1.8 \times 10^{-2}$	23.2 ± 0.5	$3.224 \pm 2.0 \times 10^{-2}$	74.1 ± 1.2	$1.5 \times 10^9 \pm 8.0 \times 10^6$	81.7 ± 1.6	$8.4 \times 10^{-4} \pm 7.0 \times 10^{-5}$	12.3 ± 0.8
Hybridization	$0.534 \pm 1.5 \times 10^{-3}$	112.1 ± 2.1	$3.388 \pm 1.7 \times 10^{-2}$	198.2 ± 0.4	$1.6 \times 10^9 \pm 5.4 \times 10^6$	197.1 ± 0.4	$1.1 \times 10^{-3} \pm 5.1 \times 10^{-5}$	200.0 ± 0.0
NSGA-III (3400)	$0.529 \pm 2.9 \times 10^{-4}$	33.4 ± 0.4	$3.359 \pm 4.7 \times 10^{-3}$	88.3 ± 0.4	$1.5 \times 10^9 \pm 2.5 \times 10^6$	92.1 ± 0.8	$9.2 \times 10^{-4} \pm 5.2 \times 10^{-5}$	14.5 ± 0.6

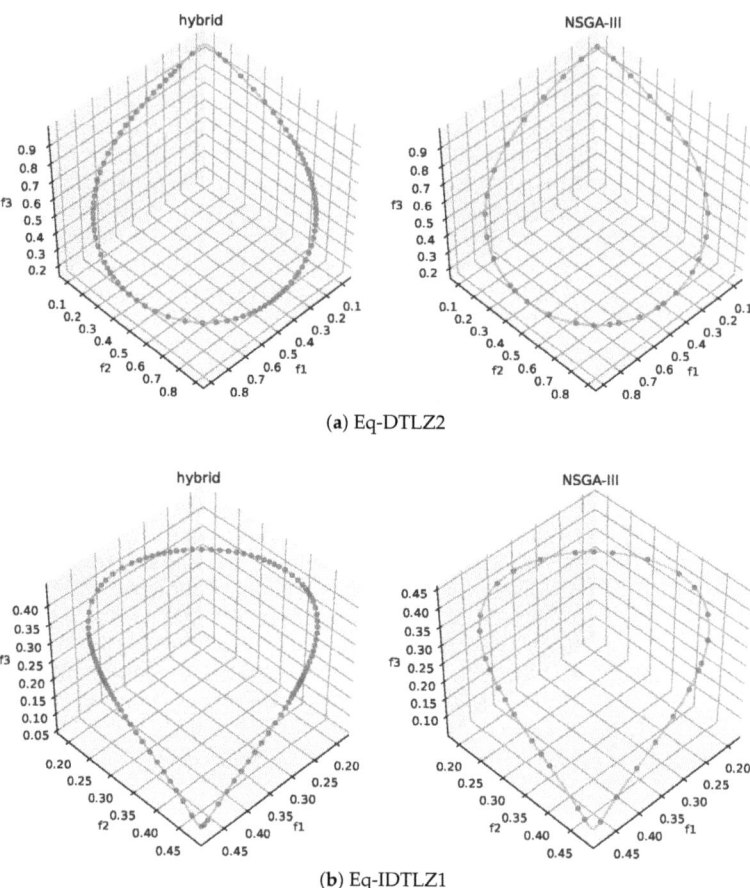

Figure 6. On the Eq-DTLZ2 (**a**) and the Eq-IDTLZ1 (**b**) problem, we compare the hybridization of HVN and NSGA-III to NSGA-III with roughly the same budget: for the former, the hybrid algorithm first executes NSGA-III with $\mu = 200$ for 1000 iterations and then runs the HVN method for 10 iterations. In HVN, the total function evaluations and AD takes ca. 270 s CPU time on an Intel(R) Core(TM) i5-8257U CPU, which corresponds to ca. 4.8×10^5 FEs. Hence, for the latter, we set 3400 (=$4.8 \times 10^5 / 200 + 1000$) iterations in total for $\mu = 200$. We use the same hyperparameter setting for the standalone NSGA-III and the one used in the hybridization. The decision space is $[0, 1]^{11}$, and the reference point is $(1, 1, 1)^\top$ for HVN.

5. Conclusions

In this paper, we propose a hypervolume Newton method for equality-constrained multi-objective optimization problems (MOPs) under the assumption that both the objective and the constraint functions are twice continuously differentiable. Based on previous works on set-oriented hypervolume Hessian matrix and hypervolume Newton (HVN) method for unconstrained MOPs, we propose, in this paper, the generalization of the HVN for equality-constrained problems and also elaborate a treatment for inequality-constrained based on an active set approach, which regards an inequality function as equality if the constraint values are within some small tolerance. In addition, we devised and tested two resulting algorithms: the standalone HVN method as an efficient local optimizer and a hybridization of the HVN and an MOEA for solving complicated and multi-modal MOPs. Moreover, in detail, we discuss the search direction for dominated points obtained from the set-oriented

Newton step in which we prove that for dominated and infeasible points, the computed search step is the Newton step of the squared equality constraint function. Therefore, our HVN method can efficiently steer the non-dominated and dominated decision points.

We first illustrate the empirical behavior of the standalone algorithm on three simple MOPs, where we observe quadratic convergence of the two-norm of the root finding problem G. Then, on highly multi-modal DTLZ problems with one spherical constraint (Eq-DTLZ), we tested the local convergence of the standalone HVN algorithm with a relatively large approximation set ($\mu = 200$) by initializing the approximation set in the neighborhood around the Pareto set, which shows a fast convergence to well-distributed points on the feasible set. Finally, we benchmark the hybrid algorithm against NSGA-III on Eq-DTLZ1-4 and Eq-IDTLZ1-4 problems, in which we observe that with roughly the same computational budget, the hybrid algorithm achieves substantially more non-dominated points in the final population, which leads to significantly higher hypervolume values. We conjecture that such an advantage is attributed to (1) the fast local convergence of the HVN method and (2) HVN's ability to move infeasible and dominated points.

For future works, we contemplate (1) testing the hybridization of the HVN method with other EMOAs for more than three objectives, e.g., SMS-EMOA, to investigate the benefit of the HVN method in a broader setup; (2) comparing the hybrid HVN method to other state-of-the-art algorithms, e.g., MOEA/D (decomposition-based), EHVI-EGO (Bayesian optimization), or the average Hausdorff distance-based Newton method (mathematical optimization) on complex, or even real-world MOPs with multiple non-linear constraint functions; (3) investigating the analytical expression (as sketched in Figure 1) and computation of the hypervolume Hessian matrix, which can reduce the computation cost of the HVN method; (4) devising generic methodologies to handle inequality constraints for the HVN method, which will make it more applicable in practice; (5) extending the HVN to methods that provide non-zero sub-gradients for dominated points as in [17,18]; and (6) incorporating a surrogate-assisted method for tackling high-dimensional and complex problems, e.g., as in [57].

Author Contributions: Conceptualization, O.S., H.W., A.D., M.E. and V.A.S.H.; methodology, O.S. and H.W.; software, M.E. geometrical analysis, and visualization, H.W. and V.A.S.H.; validation, H.W., M.E. and O.S.; formal analysis, H.W., O.S. and M.E.; investigation, H.W. and O.S.; resources, O.S.; data curation, H.W.; writing—original draft preparation, all; writing—review and editing, all; visualization, H.W.; supervision, O.S. and M.E.; project administration, O.S. All authors have read and agreed to the published version of the manuscript.

Funding: This research received no external funding.

Data Availability Statement: We have hosted all the data sets of this work on Zenodo: https://doi.org/10.5281/zenodo.7509148.

Acknowledgments: We dedicate this work to Kalyanmoy Deb for his pioneering, inspiring, and fundamental contributions to the evolutionary multi-objective optimization (EMO) community, and particularly for his famous non-dominated sorting procedure, which plays a crucial role in this work in order to efficiently handle dominated points that can be generated throughout the Newton iteration.

Conflicts of Interest: The authors declare no conflict of interest.

References

1. Stewart, T.; Bandte, O.; Braun, H.; Chakraborti, N.; Ehrgott, M.; Göbelt, M.; Jin, Y.; Nakayama, H. Real-World Applications of Multiobjective Optimization. In *Proceedings of the Multiobjective Optimization, Lecture Notes in Computer Science*; Slowinski, R., Ed.; Springer: Berlin/Heidelberg, Germany, 2008; Volume 5252; pp. 285–327.
2. Deb, K. Evolutionary multi-objective optimization: Past, present and future. In Proceedings of the GECCO '20: Proceedings of the 22th annual Conference on Genetic and Evolutionary Computation, Cancún, Mexico, 8–12 July 2020; pp. 343–372.
3. Aguilera-Rueda, V.J.; Cruz-Ramírez, N.; Mezura-Montes, E. Data-Driven Bayesian Network Learning: A Bi-Objective Approach to Address the Bias-Variance Decomposition. *Math. Comput. Appl.* **2020**, *25*, 37. [CrossRef]

4. Frausto-Solis, J.; Hernández-Ramírez, L.; Castilla-Valdez, G.; González-Barbosa, J.J.; Sánchez-Hernández, J.P. Chaotic Multi-Objective Simulated Annealing and Threshold Accepting for Job Shop Scheduling Problem. *Math. Comput. Appl.* **2021**, *26*, 8. [CrossRef]
5. Utz, S.; Wimmer, M.; Hirschberger, M.; Steuer, R.E. Tri-criterion inverse portfolio optimization with application to socially responsible mutual funds. *Eur. J. Oper. Res.* **2014**, *234*, 491–498. [CrossRef]
6. Estrada-Padilla, A.; Lopez-Garcia, D.; Gómez-Santillán, C.; Fraire-Huacuja, H.J.; Cruz-Reyes, L.; Rangel-Valdez, N.; Morales-Rodríguez, M.L. Modeling and Optimizing the Multi-Objective Portfolio Optimization Problem with Trapezoidal Fuzzy Parameters. *Math. Comput. Appl.* **2021**, *26*, 36. [CrossRef]
7. Van Veldhuizen, D.A. *Multiobjective Evolutionary Algorithms: Classifications, Analyses, and New Innovations*; Technical report; Air Force Institute of Technology: Kaduna, Nigeria, 1999.
8. Coello, C.A.C.; Cortés, N.C. Solving Multiobjective Optimization Problems Using an Artificial Immune System. *Genet. Program. Evolvable Mach.* **2005**, *6*, 163–190. [CrossRef]
9. Schütze, O.; Esquivel, X.; Lara, A.; Coello, C.A.C. Using the averaged Hausdorff distance as a performance measure in evolutionary multiobjective optimization. *IEEE Trans. Evol. Comput.* **2012**, *16*, 504–522. [CrossRef]
10. Zitzler, E.; Thiele, L.; Laumanns, M.; Fonseca, C.M.; da Fonseca, V.G. Performance assessment of multiobjective optimizers: An analysis and review. *IEEE Trans. Evol. Comput.* **2003**, *7*, 117–132. [CrossRef]
11. Auger, A.; Bader, J.; Brockhoff, D.; Zitzler, E. Theory of the hypervolume indicator: Optimal μ-distributions and the choice of the reference point. In Proceedings of the Foundations of Genetic Algorithms, 10th ACM SIGEVO International Workshop, FOGA 2009, Orlando, FL, USA, 9–11 January 2009; Garibay, I.I., Jansen, T., Wiegand, R.P., Wu, A.S., Eds.; ACM: New York, NY, USA, 2009; pp. 87–102. [CrossRef]
12. Beume, N.; Naujoks, B.; Emmerich, M.T.M. SMS-EMOA: Multiobjective selection based on dominated hypervolume. *Eur. J. Oper. Res.* **2007**, *181*, 1653–1669. [CrossRef]
13. Bader, J.; Zitzler, E. HypE: An Algorithm for Fast Hypervolume-Based Many-Objective Optimization. *Evol. Comput.* **2011**, *19*, 45–76. [CrossRef]
14. Schütze, O.; Domínguez-Medina, C.; Cruz-Cortés, N.; de la Fraga, L.G.; Sun, J.Q.; Toscano, G.; Landa, R. A scalar optimization approach for averaged Hausdorff approximations of the Pareto front. *Eng. Optim.* **2016**, *48*, 1593–1617. [CrossRef]
15. Emmerich, M.; Deutz, A.; Beume, N. Gradient-Based/Evolutionary Relay Hybrid for Computing Pareto Front Approximations Maximizing the S-Metric. In *Proceedings of the Hybrid Metaheuristics*; Bartz-Beielstein, T., Blesa Aguilera, M.J., Blum, C., Naujoks, B., Roli, A., Rudolph, G., Sampels, M., Eds.; Springer: Berlin/Heidelberg, Germany, 2007; pp. 140–156.
16. Emmerich, M.; Deutz, A.H. Time Complexity and Zeros of the Hypervolume Indicator Gradient Field. In Proceedings of the EVOLVE—A Bridge between Probability, Set Oriented Numerics, and Evolutionary Computation III EVOLVE 2012, Mexico City, Mexico, 7–9 August 2012; Studies in Computational Intelligence; Schuetze, O., Coello, C.A.C., Tantar, A., Tantar, E., Bouvry, P., Moral, P.D., Legrand, P., Eds.; Springer: Berlin/Heidelberg, Germany, 2012; Volume 500, pp. 169–193. [CrossRef]
17. Wang, H.; Ren, Y.; Deutz, A.; Emmerich, M. On steering dominated points in hypervolume indicator gradient ascent for bi-objective optimization. In *NEO 2015*; Springer: Berlin/Heidelberg, Germany, 2017; pp. 175–203.
18. Deist, T.M.; Maree, S.C.; Alderliesten, T.; Bosman, P.A. Multi-objective optimization by uncrowded hypervolume gradient ascent. In *Proceedings of the International Conference on Parallel Problem Solving from Nature*; Springer: Berlin/Heidelberg, Germany, 2020; pp. 186–200.
19. Wang, H.; Deutz, A.H.; Bäck, T.; Emmerich, M. Hypervolume Indicator Gradient Ascent Multi-objective Optimization. In Proceedings of the Evolutionary Multi-Criterion Optimization—9th International Conference, EMO 2017, Münster, Germany, 19–22 March 2017; Trautmann, H., Rudolph, G., Klamroth, K., Schütze, O., Wiecek, M.M., Jin, Y., Grimme, C., Eds.; Springer: Berlin/Heidelberg, Germany, 2017; Volume 10173, pp. 654–669. [CrossRef]
20. Sosa Hernández, V.A.; Schütze, O.; Emmerich, M. Hypervolume maximization via set based Newton's method. In *EVOLVE-A Bridge between Probability, Set Oriented Numerics, and Evolutionary Computation V*; Springer: Berlin/Heidelberg, Germany, 2014; pp. 15–28.
21. Sosa-Hernández, V.A.; Schütze, O.; Wang, H.; Deutz, A.H.; Emmerich, M. The Set-Based Hypervolume Newton Method for Bi-Objective Optimization. *IEEE Trans. Cybern.* **2020**, *50*, 2186–2196. [CrossRef] [PubMed]
22. Petersen, K.B.; Pedersen, M.S. The matrix cookbook. *Tech. Univ. Den.* **2008**, *7*, 510.
23. Hillermeier, C. *Nonlinear Multiobjective Optimization: A Generalized Homotopy Approach*; Springer Science & Business Media: Berlin/Heidelberg, Germany, 2001; Volume 135.
24. Miettinen, K. *Nonlinear Multiobjective Optimization*; Springer Science & Business Media: Berlin/Heidelberg, Germany, 2012; Volume 12.
25. Klamroth, K.; Tind, J.; Wiecek, M. Unbiased Approximation in Multicriteria Optimization. *Math. Methods Oper. Res.* **2002**, *56*, 413–437. [CrossRef]
26. Fliege, J. Gap-free computation of Pareto-points by quadratic scalarizations. *Math. Methods Oper. Res.* **2004**, *59*, 69–89. [CrossRef]
27. Eichfelder, G. *Adaptive Scalarization Methods in Multiobjective Optimization*; Springer: Berlin/Heidelberg, Germany, 2008.
28. Das, I.; Dennis, J.E. Normal-Boundary Intersection: A New Method for Generating the Pareto Surface in Nonlinear Multicriteria Optimization Problems. *SIAM J. Optim.* **1998**, *8*, 631–657. [CrossRef]

29. Fliege, J.; Drummond, L.G.; Svaiter, B.F. Newton's method for multiobjective optimization. *SIAM J. Optim.* **2009**, *20*, 602–626. [CrossRef]
30. Dellnitz, M.; Schütze, O.; Hestermeyer, T. Covering Pareto Sets by Multilevel Subdivision Techniques. *J. Optim. Theory Appl.* **2005**, *124*, 113–155. [CrossRef]
31. Hernández, C.; Naranjani, Y.; Sardahi, Y.; Liang, W.; Schütze, O.; Sun, J.Q. Simple Cell Mapping Method for Multi-objective Optimal Feedback Control Design. *Int. J. Dyn. Control.* **2013**, *1*, 231–238. [CrossRef]
32. Sun, J.Q.; Xiong, F.R.; Schütze, O.; Hernández, C. *Cell Mapping Methods—Algorithmic Approaches and Applications*; Springer: Berlin/Heidelberg, Germany, 2019.
33. Zhang, Q.; Li, H. MOEA/D: A Multi-objective Evolutionary Algorithm Based on Decomposition. *IEEE Trans. Evol. Comput.* **2007**, *11*, 712–731. [CrossRef]
34. Deb, K.; Jain, H. An Evolutionary Many-Objective Optimization Algorithm Using Reference-Point-Based Nondominated Sorting Approach, Part I: Solving Problems With Box Constraints. *IEEE Trans. Evol. Comput.* **2014**, *18*, 577–601. [CrossRef]
35. Jain, H.; Deb, K. An Evolutionary Many-Objective Optimization Algorithm Using Reference-Point Based Nondominated Sorting Approach, Part II: Handling Constraints and Extending to an Adaptive Approach. *IEEE Trans. Evol. Comput.* **2014**, *18*, 602–622. [CrossRef]
36. Deb, K.; Agrawal, S.; Pratap, A.; Meyarivan, T. A fast and elitist multiobjective genetic algorithm: NSGA-II. *IEEE Trans. Evol. Comput.* **2002**, *6*, 182–197. [CrossRef]
37. Ishibuchi, H.; Masuda, H.; Nojima, Y. *A Study on Performance Evaluation Ability of a Modified Inverted Generational Distance Indicator*; Association for Computing Machinery: New York, NY, USA, 2015. [CrossRef]
38. Dilettoso, E.; Rizzo, S.A.; Salerno, N. A Weakly Pareto Compliant Quality Indicator. *Math. Comput. Appl.* **2017**, *22*, 25. [CrossRef]
39. Rudolph, G.; Schütze, O.; Grimme, C.; Domínguez-Medina, C.; Trautmann, H. Optimal averaged Hausdorff archives for bi-objective problems: theoretical and numerical results. *Comput. Optim. Appl.* **2016**, *64*, 589–618. [CrossRef]
40. Bogoya, J.M.; Vargas, A.; Schütze, O. The Averaged Hausdorff Distances in Multi-Objective Optimization: A Review. *Mathematics* **2019**, *7*, 894. [CrossRef]
41. Schütze, O.; Dell'Aere, A.; Dellnitz, M. On Continuation Methods for the Numerical Treatment of Multi-Objective Optimization Problems. In *Proceedings of the Practical Approaches to Multi-Objective Optimization*; Number 04461 in Dagstuhl Seminar Proceedings; Branke, J., Deb, K., Miettinen, K., Steuer, R.E., Eds.; Internationales Begegnungs- und Forschungszentrum (IBFI): Schloss Dagstuhl, Germany, 2005. Available online: http://drops.dagstuhl.de/opus/volltexte/2005/349 (accessed on 1 November 2022).
42. Martin, B.; Goldsztejn, A.; Granvilliers, L.; Jermann, C. On continuation methods for non-linear bi-objective optimization: towards a certified interval-based approach. *J. Glob. Optim.* **2014**, *64*, 3–16. [CrossRef]
43. Martín, A.; Schütze, O. Pareto Tracer: A predictor-corrector method for multi-objective optimization problems. *Eng. Optim.* **2018**, *50*, 516–536. [CrossRef]
44. Schütze, O.; Cuate, O.; Martín, A.; Peitz, S.; Dellnitz, M. Pareto Explorer: A global/local exploration tool for many-objective optimization problems. *Eng. Optim.* **2020**, *52*, 832–855. [CrossRef]
45. Beltrán, F.; Cuate, O.; Schütze, O. The Pareto Tracer for General Inequality Constrained Multi-Objective Optimization Problems. *Math. Comput. Appl.* **2020**, *25*, 80. [CrossRef]
46. Bolten, M.; Doganay, O.T.; Gottschalk, H.; Klamroth, K. Tracing Locally Pareto-Optimal Points by Numerical Integration. *SIAM J. Control. Optim.* **2021**, *59*, 3302–3328. [CrossRef]
47. Zitzler, E.; Thiele, L. Multiobjective Optimization Using Evolutionary Algorithms—A Comparative Case Study. In Proceedings of the Parallel Problem Solving from Nature—PPSN V, 5th International Conference, Amsterdam, The Netherlands, 27–30 September 1998; Lecture Notes in Computer Science; Eiben, A.E., Bäck, T., Schoenauer, M., Schwefel, H., Eds.; Springer: Berlin/Heidelberg, Germany, 1998; Volume 1498, pp. 292–304. [CrossRef]
48. Emmerich, M.; Yang, K.; Deutz, A.H.; Wang, H.; Fonseca, C.M. A Multicriteria Generalization of Bayesian Global Optimization. In *Advances in Stochastic and Deterministic Global Optimization*; Pardalos, P.M., Zhigljavsky, A., Zilinskas, J., Eds.; Springer: Berlin/Heidelberg, Germany, 2016; Volume 107, pp. 229–242. [CrossRef]
49. DiBenedetto, E.; Debenedetto, E. *Real Analysis*; Springer: Berlin/Heidelberg, Germany, 2002.
50. Paquete, L.; Schulze, B.; Stiglmayr, M.; Lourenço, A.C. Computing representations using hypervolume scalarizations. *Comput. Oper. Res.* **2022**, *137*, 105349. [CrossRef]
51. Margossian, C.C. A Review of Automatic Differentiation and its Efficient Implementation. *WIREs Data Mining Knowl. Discov.* **2019**, *9*, e1305. [CrossRef]
52. Nocedal, J.; Wright, S.J. *Numerical Optimization*; Springer: Berlin/Heidelberg, Germany, 1999. [CrossRef]
53. Baydin, A.G.; Pearlmutter, B.A.; Radul, A.A.; Siskind, J.M. Automatic Differentiation in Machine Learning: A Survey. *J. Mach. Learn. Res.* **2017**, *18*, 153:1–153:43.
54. Griewank, A.; Walther, A. *Evaluating Derivatives—Principles and Techniques of Algorithmic Differentiation*, 2nd ed.; SIAM: Philadelphia, PA, USA, 2008. [CrossRef]
55. Cuate, O.; Uribe, L.; Lara, A.; Schütze, O. A benchmark for equality constrained multi-objective optimization. *Swarm Evol. Comput.* **2020**, *52*, 100619. [CrossRef]

56. Cuate, O.; Uribe, L.; Lara, A.; Schütze, O. Dataset on a Benchmark for Equality Constrained Multi-objective Optimization. *Data Brief* **2020**, *29*, 105130. [CrossRef]
57. Fu, C.; Wang, P.; Zhao, L.; Wang, X. A distance correlation-based Kriging modeling method for high-dimensional problems. *Knowl. Based Syst.* **2020**, *206*, 106356. [CrossRef]

Disclaimer/Publisher's Note: The statements, opinions and data contained in all publications are solely those of the individual author(s) and contributor(s) and not of MDPI and/or the editor(s). MDPI and/or the editor(s) disclaim responsibility for any injury to people or property resulting from any ideas, methods, instructions or products referred to in the content.

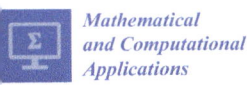

Article

COVID-19 Data Analysis with a Multi-Objective Evolutionary Algorithm for Causal Association Rule Mining

Santiago Sinisterra-Sierra [1], Salvador Godoy-Calderón [1] and Miriam Pescador-Rojas [1,2,*]

[1] Centro de Investigación en Computación, Instituto Politécnico Nacional, Ciudad de México 07738, Mexico
[2] Escuela Superior de Cómputo, Instituto Politécnico Nacional, Ciudad de México 07320, Mexico
* Correspondence: mpescadorr@ipn.mx

Abstract: Association rule mining plays a crucial role in the medical area in discovering interesting relationships among the attributes of a data set. Traditional association rule mining algorithms such as *Apriori*, FP growth, or Eclat require considerable computational resources and generate large volumes of rules. Moreover, these techniques depend on user-defined thresholds which can inadvertently cause the algorithm to omit some interesting rules. In order to solve such challenges, we propose an evolutionary multi-objective algorithm based on NSGA-II to guide the mining process in a data set composed of 15.5 million records with official data describing the COVID-19 pandemic in Mexico. We tested different scenarios optimizing classical and causal estimation measures in four waves, defined as the periods of time where the number of people with COVID-19 increased. The proposed contributions generate, recombine, and evaluate patterns, focusing on recovering promising high-quality rules with actionable cause–effect relationships among the attributes to identify which groups are more susceptible to disease or what combinations of conditions are necessary to receive certain types of medical care.

Keywords: association rule mining; causality measures; multi-objective evolutionary algorithm; COVID-19 data

1. Introduction

The coronavirus (COVID-19) pandemic has affected societies around the world for more than two years now since 11 March 2020, when the World Health Organization recognized the pandemic [1]. However, unlike similar phenomena experienced several times in human history, this pandemic has been meticulously documented, with millions of records about almost any conceivable aspect of the phenomenon's mechanics, including hospital occupation, infection and death rates, medical care protocols, and medication availability. Even government reactions, safety measures taken, social responsibility, and economic consequences have also been recorded [2]. The availability of this enormous amount of data poses an opportunity to test traditional data mining and knowledge discovery techniques and algorithms, as well as design and test new ones. Association rule mining is the most widely used technique when the goal is to reveal behavioral patterns in phenomena.

As is always the case, both private institutions and government agencies focus their attention only on mined information that is considered useful, namely behavioral patterns that can suggest some course of action to take. In that sense, traditional association rule mining is not enough, and causal rules are needed. Instead of discovering associations that have only strong statistical presence in the data set, causal rule mining aims to discover causality relations that hold in the studied phenomenon, particularly relations that can bring some degree of certainty about the future effects to indicate the rule evaluation measures and regulations established to cope with a situation.

From the computational viewpoint, data sets consisting of thousands of millions of records are not the ideal scenario for performing data mining. Exhaustive search techniques are evidently not an option. More efficient ways to traverse the data and analyze huge search spaces must be selected, but huge search spaces are the specialty of bio-inspired meta-heuristics, which in part explains why some recent papers have used diverse meta-heuristics as the guiding tool to perform data mining [3]. In this paper, we present a new evolutionary algorithm specifically designed to serve both traditional and causal association rule mining. This model allows a more focused data search and offers the user a set of parameters for increased flexibility over the intended mining process. We tested our model with the official COVID-19 pandemic database from the Mexican government [4].

The authors of this article state that the application of artificial evolution processes in this work only partially falls under the field of medicine since no diagnosis, prescription, or treatment decisions are involved. Our mining process only analyzes data from previously treated patients, and an evolutionary algorithm is used as a dynamic model of the studied phenomenon. Moreover, neither the identification nor the interpretation of any rule mined from the database can modify the results of the real phenomenon.

The remainder of this paper is organized as follows. First, we state the conceptual and theoretical basis of the research in Section 2 (Background and Basic Concepts). These include basic concepts about association rule mining, causality relations described by mined rules, and some of the evaluation functions traditionally used to assess the nature and strength of identified causality relations. Then, in Section 3 (Related Previous Works), we briefly review some of the most relevant publications relating to association rule mining and evolutionary algorithms, both as a prediction tool and as a guide for the mining process. Section 4 (Proposal) describes the architecture, mathematical foundations, and implementation details of the proposed causal mining algorithm. This section dives into the artificial evolution process, recombination, and mutation operators, as well as the nuances of the mining process. Section 5 (Experiments and Results) shows the designs of different experimentation scenarios, the conditions of each experiment, the obtained results, and their interpretation. Finally, we draw some relevant conclusions in Section 6.

2. Background and Basic Concepts

2.1. Association Rule Mining

Association rule mining is a set of data analysis techniques aiming to discover the interesting but implicit relational patterns present in a data set. Usually, the data set is expressed in an attribute-value language, and the relations found are expressed as association rules. An *association rule* is a logical expression with the following structure:

$$A_1 \land A_2 \land \ldots \land A_m \rightarrow C_1 \land C_2 \land \ldots \land C_n,$$

where both the antecedent (A_i) and the consequent (C_j) are conjunctive clauses with terms called selectors (item sets). Association rules can be read as "when A_1 and ... and A_m occur in the data set, C_1 and ... and C_n also occur".

In traditional association rule mining, a rule is considered interesting if it reveals an association between its antecedent and its consequent with a strong statistical presence (in the source or mine). Since interesting associations can occur in several different ways, evaluation functions are defined for each rule so that the evaluation obtained precisely measures the strength of the association described by the rule. Consequently, there are several measures for assessing the rules discovered during a mining process, such as the classical functions of $support(supp)$, $confidence(conf)$, and *lift* defined by Equations (1)–(3), respectively [5]. Traditional association rule mining algorithms seek to find all rules that exceed certain user-defined thresholds for one or more of these functions:

$$supp(A \rightarrow C) = \frac{|A \cap C|}{|U|} \qquad (1)$$

$$conf(A \rightarrow C) = \frac{supp(A \rightarrow C)}{supp(C)} = \frac{P(A \cap C)}{P(C)} \qquad (2)$$

$$lift(A \rightarrow C) = \frac{supp(A \rightarrow C)}{supp(A) \cdot supp(C)} = \frac{conf(A \rightarrow C)}{supp(C)} \quad (3)$$

Here, the support (*supp*) function defined in the above equations computes the quotient of the number of records containing both the A and C item sets and the total number of records (*U*).

A different scenario is found in causal association rule mining. Causal association rules can be read as "The simultaneous occurrence of A_1 and A_2 and ... and A_m, causes (is the cause for) the occurrence of C_1 and C_2 and ... and C_n". In causal association rule mining, a rule is considered interesting when it reveals a cause–effect relation between its antecedent and its consequent. Additionally, a causal rule must offer a degree of actionability; that is, it should be possible to modify the situation modeled by the antecedent in order to obtain some specific and predictable effect on the situation modeled by the consequent. Therefore, a causal rule is interesting when it describes a strong causality relation and it has high actionability. However, evaluating those properties is not a trivial task, and that is why the causality relationship has always been elusive to modeling.

Causality has historically been studied from several different perspectives. Within the computational view, actionability is the most important property of a causal model [6]. From the artificial intelligence perspective, Judea Pearl [7] pointed out that an autonomous intelligent system trying to build a model of its environment cannot rely exclusively on preprogrammed causal knowledge. It must have the ability to transform perceptual observations into cause–effect relations. By describing causal relations among the variables considered, a causal model allows estimating new environment states as a result of specific modifications on the causal conditions. In this work, we apply the following causal models to help in the identification and magnitude estimation of the causal effects as well as preview possible actions that could modify the consequent by changing the antecedent.

2.1.1. Absolute Risk (*AR*)

In a control case study to verify the hypothesis that "*A* causes *C*", it must first be clear that both the presence and the absence of *A* have measurable effects on *C*. A balanced sample with two data groups is created: the first one, the experimental group with the causal conditions being studied (antecedent *A*), models the rule $A \rightarrow C$, and the second one, the control group without the antecedent, models the rule $\neg A \rightarrow C$. The sample must be balanced. For each observation within the experimental group, there must be another observation within the control group (i.e., both groups must have the same support). Once the control case sample is constructed, the occurrence of the consequent *C* is computed within both groups, and the *confidence* of $A \rightarrow C$ is used as the *Experimental Event Rate* ($EER = conf(A \rightarrow C)$), while the *confidence* of $\neg A \rightarrow C$ is used as the *Control Event Rate* ($CER = conf(\neg A \rightarrow C)$). Both *event rates* must then be compared. When the comparison is measured as $EER - CER$, the result is labeled the *Absolute Risk* [8] (see Equation (4)). Its range is $[-1, 1]$. A value greater than zero indicates that the antecedent has a causal effect on the consequent:

$$AR(A \rightarrow C) = conf(A \rightarrow C) - conf(\neg A \rightarrow C) = \frac{supp(A \rightarrow C) - supp(\neg A \rightarrow C)}{supp(C)} \quad (4)$$

2.1.2. Probability of Sufficiency (*PS*)

The probability of sufficiency (*PS*) measures the capacity of *A* to produce *C* when *A* is absent [7]. Equations (5) and (6) represent this measure:

$$PS = \frac{AR}{1 - CER} \quad (5)$$

$$PS = \frac{conf(A \rightarrow C) - conf(\neg A \rightarrow C)}{1 - conf(\neg A \rightarrow C)} = \frac{supp(A \rightarrow C) - supp(\neg A \rightarrow C)}{supp(C) - supp(\neg A \rightarrow C)} \quad (6)$$

2.1.3. Population Attributable Fraction (PAF)

The population attributable fraction (*PAF*) or population impact is an evaluation measure used to study the impact of exposure to a specific variable in the population [9]. In data mining, the population refers to the total number of records that show the consequent *C*, the effect being studied. The formula to calculate the impact on the population, proposed by Miettinen [10], is given in Equation (7). The measure involves the support of *C* and the relative risk. The population impact measure has a causal interpretation which indicates the estimated fraction of all observations of the consequent that did not occur when the antecedent also did not occur:

$$AF_p = supp(C) \cdot (1 - \frac{1}{RR}) \tag{7}$$

$$AF_p = supp(C) \cdot \left(1 - \frac{conf(\neg A \to C)}{conf(A \to C)}\right) = supp(C) \cdot \left(1 - \frac{supp(\neg A \to C)}{supp(A \to C)}\right) \tag{8}$$

2.2. Discrete Multi-Objective Optimization Problems

Consider a discrete multi-objective optimization problem (DMOP) with m objective functions (f_i, $i = 1, \ldots, m$) and n decision variables (x_j, $j = 1, \ldots, n$). The goal of multi-objective optimization is to minimize all objectives simultaneously. Mathematically, it can be described as follows:

$$\text{minimize } \vec{f}(\vec{x}) = [f_1(\vec{x}), f_2(\vec{x}), \ldots, f_m(\vec{x})]^T \tag{9}$$
$$\text{subject to } x \in \mathcal{S}$$

where $\mathcal{S} = \{\vec{x} \in \mathbb{N}\}$ is the feasible search space and $\vec{x} = [x_1, x_2, \ldots, x_n]^T \in \mathcal{S}$ is the vector of the decision variables. Each $f_i : \mathbb{N}^n \to \mathbb{R}$, $i \in \{1, \ldots, m\}$ is an objective function. Let us assume that we have two vectors $\vec{u}, \vec{v} \in \mathbb{R}^m$. Then, we say that $\vec{u}$ *dominates* $\vec{v}$ (denoted by $\vec{u} \prec \vec{v}$) if $u_i \leq v_i$ for every $i \in \{1, \ldots, m\}$, and $u_j \neq v_j$ for at least one index $j \in \{1, \ldots, m\}$. We say that a decision variable vector $\vec{x}^* \in \mathcal{S}$ is *Pareto optimal* if no other $\vec{x} \in \mathcal{S}$ such that $\vec{f}(\vec{x}) \prec \vec{f}(\vec{x}^*)$ exists.

The *Pareto Optimal Set* (POS) is defined by $POS = \{\vec{x} \in \mathcal{S} | \vec{x}^* \text{ is Pareto optimal}\}$. The $\vec{x}^*$ vector corresponds to the *non-dominated solutions*. The *Pareto Optimal Front* (POF) is defined by $POF = \{\vec{f}(\vec{x}) \in \mathbb{R}^n | \vec{x} \in POS\}$. We thus wish to determine the POS from the $\mathcal{S}$ set of all the decision variable vectors that satisfy Equation (9). The *dominance* phenomenon occurs in the decision variable (POS) and the objective function (POF) spaces. From here on, each time we mention *Pareto dominance*, we are referring to the same concept in both spaces.

3. Related Previous Works

This Section shows a review of some related previous works focused on association rule mining in COVID-19 data sets. Two groups were defined: (1) works related to traditional assessment measures (support, confidence, and lift) optimized by classical algorithms such as *Apriori*, FP growth, and Eclat and (2) works that simultaneously optimize more than one association measure function with evolutionary algorithms.

Recently, the work of Cortes et al. in [11] provided an extensive review of the state-of-the-art machine learning techniques and data mining algorithms for predicting the COVID-19 pandemic. Their paper analyzed the role of diverse data mining techniques in classification, regression, text analysis, clustering, and association. Another comprehensive study is the work of Flora et al. [12] with a review of machine learning modeling. There, association rule mining was used as a knowledge discovery tool in the analysis of vaccines and the identification of potential risk factors.

The work of Zicheng Shan and Wei Miao [13] proposed a data mining algorithm based on association rules for the diagnosis and treatment of COVID-19 patients. During the study, some disadvantages of the proposed algorithm were found because of the delicate data preprocessing required in order to improve the efficiency of the *Apriori* algorithm.

Moreover, the authors reported notably low values in some association-measure functions such as *support* and *confidence*.

Wasiq et al. [14] proposed a framework for identifying patterns and class associations between demographic attributes and COVID-19 death rates across different regions of the world. Their approach suggested a workflow (pipeline) that includes data preprocessing, class association learning, clustering, and data analysis to discover significant association patterns.

In [15], Tandan et al. showed a comparative study of association rule mining works using the *Apriori*, FP growth, and Eclat algorithms to discover symptom patterns by age, gender, chronic condition, and mortality status among COVID-19 patients. Their study optimized the *support*, *confidence*, and *lift* measures one by one, in order to determine a ranking of symptoms and chronic conditions of COVID-19 patients.

In [16–18], a multi-objective genetic association rule mining algorithm based on NSGA-II was proposed. These pioneering works introduced new concepts such as *comprehensibility*, *surprise*, *interestingness*, and *confidence* as useful measures for extracting interesting rules. However, these studies were only tested on small data sets with categorical or numerical attributes and never with mixed attribute values.

The work of Luna et al. [19] introduced the first grammar-guided genetic programming approach for mining association rules from relational databases. The performance of this algorithm was checked using both synthetic relational data and a real-world database, but this work focused only on *support* and *confidence* measures.

In this paper, we propose a causal association rule mining process guided by an evolutionary algorithm with non-standard recombination and mutation operators. The proposed algorithm was designed precisely to be used on a COVID-19 official database in order to learn the behavior of the contagion and hospitalization phenomena during the pandemic. The causality nature of the mined rules ensures a certain degree of *actionability* that decision makers can leverage while combating the COVID-19 pandemic.

4. Proposal

In this section, we describe the mining methodology proposed to extract association rules in a COVID-19 data set. Figure 1 shows the principal steps for our proposal, while the following subsections describe the details for each one.

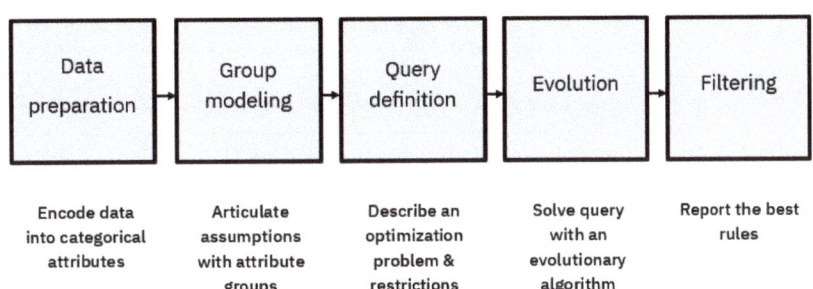

Figure 1. The rule mining process.

4.1. Data Preparation

Experimentation was performed with an official pandemic database generated by the Mexican government [4]. At the moment of performing these experiments, the database was composed of records from 1 January 2020 to 1 April 2022. The total number of records within this period was 15,578,792 with 37 attributes.

Numerical data were discretized using the quintile-based technique [20] in order to provide the following properties in the information:

- Uniform support: Each selector had approximately the same support, which was 20%.

- Reduced impact of outliers: Quantile-based discretization accumulates outliers in two ranges, assigning very low values to the first quintile and very high values to the last quintile.
- Pareto principle, or the 80-20 rule: This empirical principle states that 80% of the incidence of a factor is attributable to 20% of the observations [21].

4.2. Group Modeling

The set of all attributes initially used to describe the data is manually clustered in order to define smaller groups of attributes with related semantics. The user can select any two attribute groups to be related as the antecedent and consequent, starting a causal mining process. This selection helps to narrow the mining process to causal rules with a specific kind of *actionability*. Table 1 shows the sets of attributes manually selected that define a semantic group. Here, the term comorbidities refers to the previous illnesses that a person has suffered, such as diabetes or hypertension.

Table 1. Sets of attributes for each semantic group.

ID	Attributes
Comorbidities	Asthma, cardiovascular disease, COVID-19, diabetes, chronic obstructive pulmonary disease (COPD), hypertension, immunosuppression, pneumonia, obesity, chronic kidney disease
Age and gender	Age, Gender
Location	Location of hospital, sector
Medical care and outcome	Intubation, in intensive care unit (ICU), deceased, hospitalized

Table 2 summarizes the number of attributes in each group, the number of possible selectors, and the total number of possible combinations or rules to estimate the search space size for each scenario. In Table 3, we consider three *scenarios*, with each one defined by a pair of related attribute groups and a target optimization function (used as fitness criteria). The search space contains all possible association rules according to the number of attributes and selectors. Moreover, we considered four periods of time called waves, with each one representing the increase in the number of people with COVID-19. Finally, we applied the process of association rule mining in the following intervals (see Table 4).

Table 2. Description of the number of attributes and selectors in COVID-19 data set.

Attribute Group	No. of Attributes	No. of Selectors	Possible Combinations
Comorbidities	13	43	134,217,727
Clinical care	3	66	3266
Medical care	4	12	224
Age and gender	2	7	17

Table 3. Experimentation scenarios with search space size.

Scenario	Antecedent Group	Consequent Group	Search Space Size
A	Age and gender	Comorbidities	2,281,701,359
B	Comorbidities	Medical care	30,064,770,848
C	Location	Comorbidities	438,355,096,382

Table 4. Periods of time in which the number of people with COVID-19 increased.

Wave	Initial Date	End Date	Records
1	2020-02-16	2020-09-26	1,955,291
2	2020-09-27	2021-04-17	4,604,490
3	2021-06-06	2021-10-23	4,220,735
4	2021-12-19	2022-03-05	3,027,248

4.3. Query Definition by Optimization Problem

We defined three discrete multi-objective optimization problems (DMOPs). In all three cases, the association-measure functions showed a conflict when optimizing them simultaneously. Additionally, we included three constraints to obtain correct and complete association rules:

- Support greater than zero: The association rule must be true for at least one record. In the formal definition of optimization problems, this is stated as $supp(A \to C) > 0$.
- Absolute positive effect: An association rule with an absolute positive effect and with a value greater than zero indicates that observing the antecedent increases the probability of observing the consequent, thus rejecting rules in which the antecedent inhibits the consequent. Formally, in optimization problems, this is stated as $AR(A \to C) > 0$.
- Statistical significance: The odds ratio must be statistically significant; that is, the lower bound of its 95% confidence interval must be greater than or equal to one. Formally, in problems of optimization, this is stated as $CI_{OR}^{inf}(A \to C) \geq 1$.

DMOP-1. Classic association rule mining aims to obtain rules with the highest possible support, confidence, and lift. However, simultaneously optimizing these measures is impossible because a sustained increase or decrease in one does not guarantee behavior in the same direction in the other two. The formal definition of the optimization problem for this query is described by Equation (10):

$$\begin{aligned} &\text{maximize } supp(A \to C) \\ &\text{maximize } conf(A \to C) \\ &\text{maximize } lift(A \to C) \\ &\text{subject to } supp(A \to C) > 0, \\ &AR(A \to C) > 0, \\ &CI_{OR}^{inf}(A \to C) \geq 1. \end{aligned} \qquad (10)$$

DMOP-2. From a logical perspective, a biconditional expression $(A \leftrightarrow C)$ can be interpreted as "A if and only C" or "A is a necessary and sufficient condition for C". Its truth value is equivalent to the expression $(A \to C) \wedge (C \to A)$. The sufficiency condition falls to the association rule $A \to C$, interpreted as "A is a sufficient condition for C". The sufficiency condition is considered to be satisfied if the causal effect of $A \to C$ is large enough. On the other hand, to satisfy the necessary condition of the biconditional expression, the causal effect of $C \to A$ must be considered as well (see Equation (11)):

$$\begin{aligned} &\text{maximize } AR(A \to C) \\ &\text{maximize } AR(C \to A) \\ &\text{subject to } supp(A \to C) > 0, \\ &AR(A \to C) > 0, \\ &CI_{OR}^{inf}(A \to C) \geq 1. \end{aligned} \qquad (11)$$

DMOP-3. In this problem, we seek to find the rules that maximize susceptibility, a measure that quantifies the capacity of the antecedent to produce the consequent, and the population attributable fraction, a measure that indicates the proportion of observations of the consequences that were caused by the antecedent (see Equation (12)):

$$\begin{aligned}
&\text{maximize } PS(A \rightarrow C) \\
&\text{maximize } AF_p(A \rightarrow C) \\
&\text{subject to } supp(A \rightarrow C) > 0, \\
&\quad AR(A \rightarrow C) > 0, \\
&\quad CI_{OR}^{inf}(A \rightarrow C) \geq 1.
\end{aligned} \quad (12)$$

4.4. Evolution Proposal and Heuristically Guided Mining

Since direct exhaustive search strategies are not an option for mining a large data set, a heuristically guided mining mode is used. When in this mode, previous knowledge about the structure of the data is fed to a meta-heuristic optimization which evolves a set of specific patterns with the adequate structure to be *Pareto front* elements in the process of optimizing a selected objective function (i.e., *absolute risk*, *relative risk*, or any other).

The evolutionary algorithm proposed herein performs artificial evolution based on NSGA-II [22]. Some arguments for using NSGA-II include its mechanisms for solving combinatorial optimization problems with two and three objective functions [23], particularly the following:

- The non-dominated sorting of solutions based on the Pareto dominance concept assigns a ranking to the non-dominated members of the population.
- A crowding distance strategy for assessing the density of individuals surrounding a particular solution allows for preserving a better population diversity.

Our proposal controls the selector structure of each pattern, allowing the system to answer specific user questions to discover association rules with particular semantics. In addition, the regulation of the search space *exploration/exploitation* process allows the generation of a wide range of causal rule complexities, from very simple rules with only one selector in the antecedent and consequent to more elaborate rules with the antecedent and consequent formed by several selectors. Once these patterns are known to have optimal structures and values, the mining system can directly search for these patterns in the actual data set. This has the effect of speeding up the mining process.

In order to guarantee the statistical significance of causal rules, two criteria are proposed. First, a *diversity preservation* criterion will be used as an essential evolution guide in the algorithm. Second, a statistical significance test on the set of causal rules mined is used.

Rule Evolution

The proposed algorithm evolves a population of selector lists as any other artificial evolution process would. Each list represents a possible association rule in the data set. The structure of those lists is straightforward, as is the structure of association rules. Each list has two main sections representing the *antecedent* and *consequent* of the rule, and then each section may have one or more subsections in correspondence with the selectors that conform it. The label and domain of all attributes are considered background knowledge, so the proper validation restrictions can be applied every time a new selector enters the expression.

During successive generations, the algorithm selects individuals from its population based on their fitness and applies recombination and mutation operators to generate new individuals, which are also evaluated by their aptitude. As the population size is fixed to N individuals, each new generation is selected from the best fit rules among previously known and newly generated rules:

- The stop criterion for the evolution process is triggered after 100 generations without improvement in the fitness value of the fittest rule.

- Recombination: This generates new individuals (new rules) from a pair of previously known rules $A_1 \to C_1$ and $A_2 \to C_2$, referred to as the *ancestor* rules. Four new individuals are created using the following recombination modalities:
    1. Interchange: The antecedent and consequent from the ancestor rules are interchanged. Two new individuals are created: $A_1 \to C_2$ and $A_2 \to C_1$.
    2. Set operations: The *union* ($\cup$), *intersection* ($\cap$), and *symmetric difference* ($\triangle$) operators are applied to the sets of selectors in the antecedent and consequent of the ancestor rules. For each one of those set operators, the antecedent of new rules results from applying the operator on sets A_1 and A_2, and the consequent results from applying the same operator on sets C_1 and C_2. Selectors with repeated attributes are pruned, as well as all cases that result in an empty antecedent or consequent. At most, three new individuals are created with this recombination process.
- Mutation: Each new rule generated by any recombination method is subjected to either an *extension* or a *contraction* transformation to introduce variability into the population. The *extension* randomly adds a new selector not previously present in the rule, while the *contraction* randomly prunes a selector from the rule.
- Elitism: The non-dominated sorting and crowding distance methods used by NSGA-II [22] are adopted to select the fittest rule and preserve the diversity of the population.

5. Experiments and Results

We designed two main experiments. The first one explored the association rules in the complete data set (15,578,792 records). Here, our data mining methodology described in the previous section was applied while considering the three scenarios (A, B, and C) illustrated in Table 3. In this experiment, we intended to solve a single-objective optimization problem to find the best (maximum) values for each association measure function (equations described in Section 2.1) and validate the convergence of our proposed algorithm. Table 5 shows each case's fitness mean (and standard deviation). The best values are shown in boldface. We considered 10 executions with different seeds for random generation. We established this number of executions for two reasons: the data mining process is computationally expensive, and we corroborated that after 10 executions, there was no variation in the results for the majority of the scenarios (standard deviation equals zero). In the classical measures, the best association rules reached a support function value that was low in each case's fitness means (rather than 0.6), and the lift function was variable in these three scenarios. In the causal association measures, the functions of the probability of sufficiency and attributable fraction reported low values in scenarios A and C, respectively. In general, scenario B reported the maximum values for the association measures.

The second experiment had two purposes: (1) solve the DMOP described in Section 4.3 in order to compare the classic and causal association rule models as adequate and feasible tools for analyzing the COVID-19 pandemic phenomenon and (2) find association rules along four different and well-defined time periods (labeled as waves) to clearly characterize the behavior and tendencies of each contagion wave. Then, we applied our genetic algorithm in the three scenarios and the four waves for each DMOP. Then, we filtered the experimental results using criteria that selected non-dominated rules.

Table 5. The maximum mean values found by an evolutionary algorithm for each objective function.

Classical Measures	Scenarios		
	A	B	C
Support	0.322 (0)	0.588 (0)	0.365 (0.021)
Confidence	0.655 (0)	0.993 (0)	0.880 (0.119)
Lift	7.696 (0)	33.967 (0)	41.11 (31.003)

Causal Measures	Scenarios		
	A	B	C
Probability of Sufficiency	0.272 (0)	0.869 (0)	0.823 (0.094)
Attributable Fraction	0.739 (0)	0.891 (0)	0.245 (0.019)
Absolute Risk	0.293 (0)	0.941 (0)	0.951 (0.019)
Reciprocal Absolute Risk	0.913 (0)	0.935 (0)	0.377 (0.031)

Table 6 reports the mean and standard deviation (in parenthesis) of the number of non-dominated rules found after 10 executions for each case. We can note that scenarios A and B, related to the comorbidities, age, gender, medical care, and outcome, were very consistent in the non-dominated rules. In contrast, scenario C (location and comorbidities) showed more variation in the association rules found.

Table 6. The mean of the non-dominated rules found for each DMOP in all scenarios.

Scenario	DMOP	W1	W2	W3	W4	A
A	1	28 (0)	28 (0)	29 (0)	26 (0)	27 (0)
	2	9 (0)	28 (0)	14 (0)	15 (0)	9 (0)
	3	13 (0)	15 (0)	13 (0)	14 (0)	11 (0)
B	1	38 (0)	40 (0)	39 (0)	40 (0)	39 (0)
	2	16 (0)	21 (0)	24 (0)	28 (0)	20 (0)
	3	23 (0)	22 (0)	23 (0)	28 (2.34)	21 (0)
C	1	16.4 (1.14)	16.8 (1.789)	18.2 (1.09)	10.2 (0.83)	16 (0.70)
	2	9.6 (1.51)	13.4 (1.14)	10.8 (1.64)	3 (0.70)	8.8 (1.64)
	3	10.6 (1.14)	12.6 (2.40)	11.4 (0.54)	8.2 (1.30)	11.2 (1.09)

Figures 2–4 show the obtained Pareto front with the levels of the maximum values reached by interesting rules according to causal measures. For Scenario B, DMOP-1, and DMOP-2, the mined rules were very similar. We appreciated some differences in scenarios B and C, where the absolute risk function, reciprocal absolute risk, population attributable fraction, and probability of sufficiency reported low values in the last period, called wave 4. Here, we can understand these results as a positive effect of the vaccine on the population.

Table 7 reports the same non-dominated association rules discovered for the classic and causal measures in scenarios A and B. Both logical models for the data mining process found the same patterns demonstrating that causal measures can find interesting rules as a classical model. According to the results, the diseases with the greatest influence on the association rules found for the time periods called waves were diabetes, hypertension, pneumonia, and COPD. The ages of the patients were directly related to the diseases. Therefore, the majority of the population older than 53 had the highest comorbidity statistics as the most vulnerable sector. From the viewpoint of the association measures, we observed that the numerical values for the causal measures were more evident. Unlike these, the support and confidence numerical values were very small.

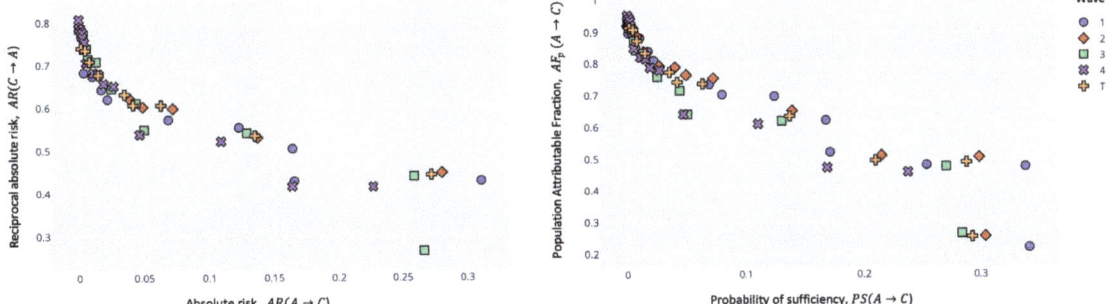

Figure 2. Obtained Pareto fronts of DMOP-2 (absolute risk and reciprocal absolute risk) and DMOP-3 (probability of sufficiency and population attributable fraction) for all waves in Scenario A. The antecedent group is age and gender, and the consequent group is comorbidities.

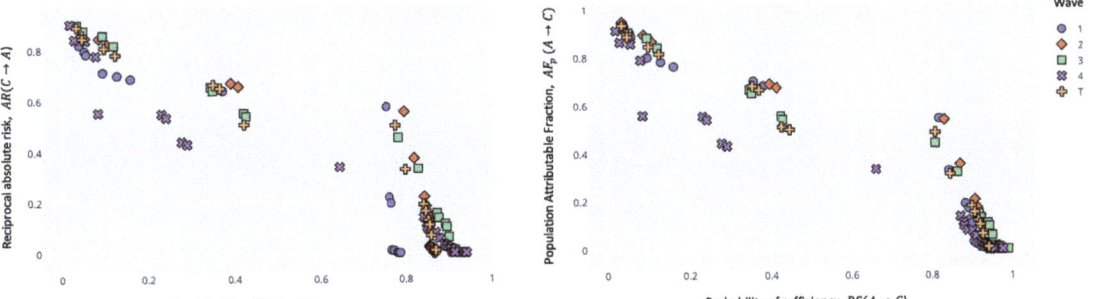

Figure 3. Obtained Pareto fronts of DMOP-2 (absolute risk and reciprocal absolute risk) and DMOP-3 (probability of sufficiency and population attributable fraction) for all waves in Scenario B. The antecedent group is comorbidities, and the consequent group is medical care.

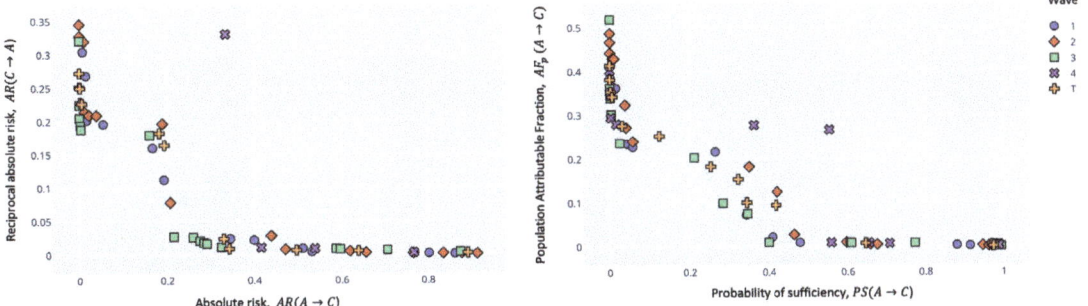

Figure 4. Obtained Pareto fronts of DMOP-2 (absolute risk and reciprocal absolute risk) and DMOP-3 (probability of sufficiency and population attributable fraction) for all waves in Scenario C. The antecedent group is location, and the consequent group is comorbidities.

All supplementary material for this research can be found in https://github.com/sinisterra/mscgp (accessed on 1 November 2022). There, we provide the Python code used to generate all experiments.

Table 7. The best association rules were obtained in scenarios A (age and gender → comorbidities) and B (comorbidities and medical care). The evolutionary algorithm found these rules in the last population generated.

AGE ^53.0 ->DIABETES ^HYPERTENSION ^PNEUMONIA					
Measure	W1	W2	W3	W4	T
Support	0.0178	0.0095	0.0041	0.0027	0.0071
Confidence	0.075	0.042	0.026	0.016	0.037
Lift	3.3361	3.7296	5.1588	4.9639	4.2691
Absolute Risk	0.0686	0.04	0.0252	0.0155	0.0354
Reciprocal Absolute Risk	0.5711	0.6184	0.6439	0.6776	0.6304
Prob. Sufficiency	0.069	0.0401	0.0252	0.0155	0.0355
Attributable Fraction	0.7337	0.7878	0.7574	0.8139	0.7725
AGE >53.0 ->DIABETES ^HYPERTENSION					
Measure	W1	W2	W3	W4	T
Support	0.045	0.0345	0.0218	0.0206	0.0288
Confidence	0.188	0.154	0.141	0.121	0.15
Lift	2.9746	3.2525	4.3939	3.9651	3.6786
Absolute Risk	0.1642	0.1373	0.1291	0.1092	0.1354
Reciprocal Absolute Risk	0.5038	0.5296	0.5402	0.5212	0.5338
Prob. Sufficiency	0.1683	0.1396	0.1307	0.1106	0.1375
Attributable Fraction	0.6201	0.6501	0.618	0.609	0.633
AGE >53 ->HYPERTENSION ^PNEUMONIA					
Measure	W1	W2	W3	W4	T
Support	0.0324	0.0173	0.0072	0.0048	0.0129
Confidence	0.136	0.077	0.047	0.028	0.067
Lift	3.2169	3.6087	4.9252	4.7907	4.1133
Absolute Risk	0.1229	0.0721	0.044	0.027	0.0631
Reciprocal Absolute Risk	0.5532	0.5971	0.6104	0.6497	0.605
Prob. Sufficiency	0.1245	0.0724	0.0441	0.027	0.0633
Attributable Fraction	0.6962	0.7529	0.7147	0.7786	0.7357
AGE >53.0 ->HYPERTENSION					
Measure	W1	W2	W3	W4	T
Support	0.094	0.0766	0.0467	0.0465	0.0624
Confidence	0.393	0.342	0.303	0.273	0.327
Lift	2.5102	2.7453	3.6076	3.225	3.0653
Absolute Risk	0.3108	0.2804	0.2589	0.2271	0.2722
Reciprocal Absolute Risk	0.4279	0.4466	0.4385	0.4142	0.4419
Prob. Sufficiency	0.3387	0.2988	0.2708	0.238	0.2879
Attributable Fraction	0.4743	0.5037	0.4748	0.457	0.488
HYPERTENSION ^PNEUMONIA ->HOSPITALIZATION					
Measure	W1	W2	W3	W4	T
Support	0.0378	0.0196	0.0087	0.0052	0.0148
Confidence	0.897	0.912	0.92	0.873	0.904
Lift	5.3062	10.4193	16.4679	23.7918	11.7312
Absolute Risk	0.7602	0.8426	0.8721	0.8414	0.8411
Reciprocal Absolute Risk	0.2186	0.2213	0.1553	0.1396	0.1905
Prob. Sufficiency	0.8809	0.9055	0.9156	0.869	0.8979
Attributable Fraction	0.1896	0.2063	0.1481	0.1353	0.1788

Table 7. *Cont.*

	DIABETES ^PNEUMONIA ->HOSPITALIZATION				
Measure	W1	W2	W3	W4	T
Support	0.0337	0.0163	0.0077	0.0042	0.0127
Confidence	0.905	0.919	0.925	0.881	0.911
Lift	5.3528	10.4933	16.5565	23.9939	11.8201
Absolute Risk	0.7645	0.846	0.876	0.8479	0.846
Reciprocal Absolute Risk	0.1952	0.1848	0.1371	0.1148	0.1639
Prob. Sufficiency	0.8896	0.9122	0.9207	0.8765	0.905
Attributable Fraction	0.1685	0.1717	0.1306	0.1111	0.1534
	PNEUMONIA ->HOSPITALIZATION				
Measure	W1	W2	W3	W4	T
Support	0.1016	0.0497	0.0257	0.0127	0.0395
Confidence	0.83	0.836	0.813	0.668	0.815
Lift	4.9114	9.5507	14.5584	18.1962	10.5679
Absolute Risk	0.7536	0.7958	0.7819	0.6433	0.7751
Reciprocal Absolute Risk	0.576	0.5571	0.4547	0.3386	0.5021
Prob. Sufficiency	0.8163	0.8292	0.807	0.6594	0.8071
Attributable Fraction	0.5453	0.5405	0.4433	0.3324	0.487

6. Conclusions

In this research, we used NSGA-II mechanisms for guiding an association rule mining process to learn the behavior of the COVID-19 contagion phenomenon at a country-wide scale from an official government database in Mexico. Our mining algorithm includes non-classical crossover and mutation operators that have shown certain reliability for optimizing both classical and causal rule evaluation measures. Using artificial evolution as a guide to the mining process, we designed three experimentation scenarios as multi-objective optimization problems and considered the four officially identified waves of contagion.

Each experiment correctly found the rules with the maximum values for *support*, *confidence*, *lift*, *absolute risk*, and *probability of sufficiency* in a DMOP context. Since all those values were obtained under the constraint of having a *confidence interval* greater than or equal to one, they all had a strong correspondence with the concept of *interesting* rules expressed at the end of the Introduction section. Therefore, all mined rules identified the strongest associations between the antecedent and consequent in the database. The rules mined in DMOP-1 experiment were *interesting* in the classic mining sense, while the rules mined in the DMOP-2 and DMOP-3 experiments were *interesting* in the causal mining sense. The set of all rules mined during each experiment constituted the *learned behavioral model* of the studied phenomenon and brought forth interesting information about the phenomenon's behavior.

The main contributions made by this work are the following:

- Design and testing of a new evolutionary algorithm for association rule mining with enough flexibility to integrate domain knowledge in order to solve single-objective and multi-objective association rule mining problems;
- The inclusion of a causal model to restate the semantics of the search process by providing a measure of the actionability of mined rules;
- The inclusion of a set of proposed crossover and mutation operators into the mining process.

Some of the next steps considered in this research include the following:

- Extending the evolution process with logical expressions;
- Incorporating a target group discovery algorithm;
- Considering the opposite optimization criteria to generate interesting rules;
- Including the proposed algorithm in other case studies.

Supplementary Materials: The supporting information is shared and available online by visiting https://github.com/sinisterra/mscgp.

Author Contributions: S.S.-S., S.G.-C. and M.P.-R. have contributed equally in conceptualization, methodology, and formal analysis; software and validation S.S.-S. All authors have read and agreed to the published version of the manuscript.

Funding: This research was funded by Secretaría de Investigación y Posgrado (SIP-IPN) through projects/grants SIP-20230252 and SIP-20230105.

Acknowledgments: The authors wish to acknowledge and gratefully thank Consejo Nacional de Ciencia y Tecnología (CONACyT) and Instituto Politécnico Nacional (IPN).

Conflicts of Interest: The authors declare no conflict of interest.

References

1. Sohrabi, C.; Alsafi, Z.; O'Neill, N.; Khan, M.; Kerwan, A.; Al-Jabir, A.; Iosifidis, C.; Agha, R. World Health Organization declares global emergency: A review of the 2019 novel coronavirus (COVID-19). *Int. J. Surg.* **2020**, *76*, 71–76. [CrossRef] [PubMed]
2. López, L.; Rodó, X. The end of social confinement and COVID-19 re-emergence risk. *Nat. Hum. Behav.* **2020**, *4*, 746–755. [CrossRef] [PubMed]
3. Telikani, A.; Gandomi, A.H.; Shahbahrami, A. A survey of evolutionary computation for association rule mining. *Inf. Sci.* **2020**, *524*, 318–352. [CrossRef]
4. De Salud, S. COVID-19 Pandemic Data Set from Mexico. 2022. Available online: https://datos.gob.mx/busca/dataset/informacion-referente-a-casos-covid-19-en-mexico (accessed on 7 December 2022).
5. Fürnkranz, J.; Gamberger, D.; Lavrač, N. *Foundations of Rule Learning*; Cognitive Technologies; Springer: Berlin/Heidelberg, Germany, 2012. [CrossRef]
6. Pearl, J.; Mackenzie, D. *The Book of Why: The New Science of Cause and Effect*; Basic Books: New York, NY, USA, 2018.
7. Pearl, J. *Causality: Models, Reasoning, and Inference*; Cambridge University Press: Cambridge, UK; New York, NY, USA, 2000.
8. Hernán, M.A.; Robins, J.M. *Causal Inference: What If*; CRC Press: Boca Raton, FL, USA, 2020; p. 311.
9. Mansournia, M.A.; Altman, D.G. Population attributable fraction. *BMJ* **2018**, *360*, k757. [CrossRef] [PubMed]
10. Miettinen, O.S. Proportion of disease caused or prevented by a given exposure, trait or intervention. *Am. J. Epidemiol.* **1974**, *99*, 325–332. [CrossRef] [PubMed]
11. Cortés-Martínez, K.V.; Estrada-Esquivel, H.; Martínez-Rebollar, A.; Hernández-Pérez, Y.; Ortiz-Hernández, J. The State of the Art of Data Mining Algorithms for Predicting the COVID-19 Pandemic. *Axioms* **2022**, *11*, 242. [CrossRef]
12. Flora, J.; Khan, W.; Jin, J.; Jin, D.; Hussain, A.; Dajani, K.; Khan, B. Usefulness of Vaccine Adverse Event Reporting System for Machine-Learning Based Vaccine Research: A Case Study for COVID-19 Vaccines. *Int. J. Mol. Sci.* **2022**, *23*, 8235. [CrossRef] [PubMed]
13. Shan, Z.; Miao, W. COVID-19 patient diagnosis and treatment data mining algorithm based on association rules. *Expert Syst.* **2021**, e12814. [CrossRef] [PubMed]
14. Wasiq, K.; Abir, H.; Ahmed, K.S.; Mohammed, A.J.; Raheel, N.; Panos, L. Analysing the impact of global demographic characteristics over the COVID-19 spread using class rule mining and pattern matching. *R. Soc.* **2021**, *8*, 201823.
15. Tandan, M.; Acharya, Y.; Pokharel, S.; Timilsina, M. Discovering symptom patterns of COVID-19 patients using association rule mining. *Comput. Biol. Med.* **2021**, *131*, 104249. [CrossRef] [PubMed]
16. Wakabi-Waiswa, P.P.; Baryamureeba, V. Extraction of interesting association rules using genetic algorithms. *Adv. Syst. Model. ICT Appl.* **2007**. Available online: https://www.researchgate.net/publication/255610299_Extraction_of_interesting_association_rules_using_genetic_algorithms (accessed on 1 November 2022).
17. Anand, R.; Vaid, A.; Singh, P.K. Association rule mining using multi-objective evolutionary algorithms: Strengths and challenges. In Proceedings of the 2009 World Congress on Nature and Biologically Inspired Computing (NaBIC), Coimbatore, India, 9–11 December 2009; pp. 385–390. [CrossRef]
18. Martín, D.; Rosete, A.; Alcalá-Fdez, J.; Herrera, F. A multi-objective evolutionary algorithm for mining quantitative association rules. In Proceedings of the 2011 11th International Conference on Intelligent Systems Design and Applications, Cordoba, Spain, 22–24 November 2011; pp. 1397–1402.
19. Luna, J.M.; Cano, A.; Ventura, S. Genetic Programming for Mining Association Rules in Relational Database Environments. In *Handbook of Genetic Programming Applications*; Springer International Publishing: Cham, Switzerland, 2015; pp. 431–450. [CrossRef]
20. Elhilbawi, H.; Eldawlatly, S.; Mahdi, H. The Importance of Discretization Methods in Machine Learning Applications: A Case Study of Predicting ICU Mortality. In *Advanced Machine Learning Technologies and Applications*; Chang, K.C., Hassanien, A.E., Mincong, T., Eds.; Springer International Publishing: Cham, Switzerland, 2021; Volume 1339, pp. 214–224. [CrossRef]
21. Tanabe, K. Pareto's 80/20 rule and the Gaussian distribution. *Phys. A Stat. Mech. Its Appl.* **2018**, *510*, 635–640. [CrossRef]

22. Deb, K.; Pratap, A.; Agarwal, S.; Meyarivan, T. A fast and elitist multiobjective genetic algorithm: NSGA-II. *IEEE Trans. Evol. Comput.* **2002**, *6*, 182–197. [CrossRef]
23. Shanu, V.; Millie, P.; Vaclav, S. A Comprehensive Review on NSGA-II for Multi-Objective Combinatorial Optimization Problems. *IEEE Access* **2021**, *9*, 57757–57791. [CrossRef]

Disclaimer/Publisher's Note: The statements, opinions and data contained in all publications are solely those of the individual author(s) and contributor(s) and not of MDPI and/or the editor(s). MDPI and/or the editor(s) disclaim responsibility for any injury to people or property resulting from any ideas, methods, instructions or products referred to in the content.

Knowledge Transfer Based on Particle Filters for Multi-Objective Optimization

Xilu Wang and Yaochu Jin *

Faculty of Technology, Bielefeld University, 33619 Bielefeld, Germany
* Correspondence: yaochu.jin@uni-bielefeld.de

Abstract: Particle filters, also known as sequential Monte Carlo (SMC) methods, constitute a class of importance sampling and resampling techniques designed to use simulations to perform on-line filtering. Recently, particle filters have been extended for optimization by utilizing the ability to track a sequence of distributions. In this work, we incorporate transfer learning capabilities into the optimizer by using particle filters. To achieve this, we propose a novel particle-filter-based multi-objective optimization algorithm (PF-MOA) by transferring knowledge acquired from the search experience. The key insight adopted here is that, if we can construct a sequence of target distributions that can balance the multiple objectives and make the degree of the balance controllable, we can approximate the Pareto optimal solutions by simulating each target distribution via particle filters. As the importance weight updating step takes the previous target distribution as the proposal distribution and takes the current target distribution as the target distribution, the knowledge acquired from the previous run can be utilized in the current run by carefully designing the set of target distributions. The experimental results on the DTLZ and WFG test suites show that the proposed PF-MOA achieves competitive performance compared with state-of-the-art multi-objective evolutionary algorithms on most test instances.

Keywords: particle filter; multi-objective optimization; transfer learning

1. Introduction

Many real-world applications in economics, mechanics and engineering can be formulated as multi-objective optimization problems (MOPs) that simultaneously optimize two or more objective functions [1]. The basic statement of an MOP for a minimization task can be formulated as

$$\min \quad \mathbf{F}(\mathbf{x}) = \{f_1(\mathbf{x}), f_2(\mathbf{x}), \cdots, f_m(\mathbf{x})\} \\ \mathbf{x} \subseteq \Omega \tag{1}$$

where $\Omega \subseteq \mathbb{R}^D$ is the decision space of decision variables, $\mathbf{x} = (x_1, x_2, \cdots x_D)$ is a decision vector with D denoting the number of decision variables, $\mathbf{F}(\mathbf{x})$ consists of m objective functions, and m is the number of objectives.

Usually, different objectives are conflicting with each other, which means that a decision vector that decreases the values of f_m may increases that of f_n. As a result, it is impossible to find only one solution that can optimize all the objectives simultaneously; however, a set of optimal solutions that trade off between different objectives are known as Pareto optimal solutions. The whole set of Pareto optimal solutions in the decision space is called the Pareto set (PS), and the projection of PS in the objective space is called the Pareto front. Various types of algorithms have been proposed for solving MOPs.

For example, the scalarization technique is one of the most popular methods and is used to convert an MOP into a single optimization problem. Scalarization can be achieved by the global criterion method [2], the weighted min-max method [3,4], the ϵ-constraint method [5] and reference point methods [6].

Another popular approach is based on evolutionary algorithms (EAs), which have been applied successfully to many real-world complex optimization problems [7,8]. Over the past decades, a large number of multi-objective evolutionary algorithms (MOEAs) have been proposed, such as nondominated sorting genetic algorithm II (NSGA-II) [9], multi-objective evolutionary algorithm based on decomposition (MOEA/D) [10], reference vector guided evolutionary algorithm (RVEA) [11] and strength Pareto evolutionary algorithm 2 (SPEA2) [12]. More recently, many variants have been proposed to further enhance the optimization performance of MOEAs and extend them to many-objective optimization problems, such as NSGA-III [13], θ-DEA [14] and MOEA/DD [15].

Particle filter (PF), also known as sequential Monte Carlo (SMC), is a class of importance sampling and resampling techniques designed to simulate from a sequence of probability distributions, and this has gained popularity over the last decade to solve sequential Bayesian inference problems. With the notable exception of linear-Gaussian signal-observation models, the PF theory has become the dominated approach to solving the state filtering problem in dynamic systems. Applications of particle filter theory have expanded to diverse fields, such as object tracking [16], navigation and guidance [17] and fault diagnosis [18].

Recently, particle filters have been extended for optimization [19,20] by utilizing the ability to track a sequence of distributions. In order to deal with a global optimization problem, generally, a sequence of artificial dynamic distribution is designed to employ the particle filter algorithm [21,22]. The crucial element in particle filter optimization (PFO) is how to design the system dynamic function by formulating the optimization problem as a filtering problem, which forces the set of particles to move toward the promising area containing optima.

Although PFO has shown promising performance in certain applications, current PFO methods only work for single-objective optimization problems [23]. As many real-world problems involve multiple objectives to be optimized simultaneously, it is interesting to extend PFO to MOPs. To fill this gap, we make an effort to extend the scope of the application of PFO to multi-objective cases. To achieve this, we propose a novel particle-filter-based multi-objective optimization algorithm (PF-MOA) by transferring knowledge acquired from the search experience.

The key insight adopted here is that, if we can construct a sequence of target distributions that can balance the multiple objectives and make the degree of the balance controllable, we can approximate the Pareto optimal solutions by simulating each target distribution via particle filters. Inspired by the ability of SMC samplers to sample sequentially from a sequence of probability distributions [24], we design a particle filter to perform the optimization. The method of importance updating in particle filters makes it possible to leverage the knowledge readily available for the previous subproblem to optimize the current subproblem, guiding the new particles to concentrate on the more promising area found thus far. As a result, PF-MOA offers an efficient solution to optimize MOPs by tracking the Pareto optimal solutions on the Pareto front via a particle filter.

The rest of this paper is organized as follows. Section 2 presents a brief introduction to particle filters and the application to single-objective optimization. In Section 3, a particle-filter-based multi-objective optimization method is proposed. Numerical simulations are conducted in Section 4, where the results are presented and discussed. Finally, our conclusions are drawn in Section 5.

2. Background

2.1. Particle Filter

Consider the discrete-time nonlinear state-space models relating a hidden state x_k to the observations y_k:

$$x_k = g(x_{k-1}, u_k), k = 1, 2, \ldots,$$
$$y_k = h(x_k, v_k), k = 0, 1, \ldots,$$
(2)

where k is the sample number; $x_k \in R^{n_x}$ is the state; $y_k \in R^{n_y}$ are the observations; $u_k \in R^{n_x}$ and $v_k \in R^{n_y}$ are the system and observation noise, respectively; and n_x and n_y are the dimensions of x_k and y_k, respectively. We assume u_k and v_k are independent and identically distributed (i.i.d.) sequences, independent of each other and also independent of the initial state x_0, which has the probability density function (p.d.f.) p_0. Let $p(x_k \mid x_{k-1})$ denote the transition density, and $p(y_k \mid x_{k-1})$ denote the likelihood function.

The goal of filtering is to estimate the conditional density,

$$b_k(x_k) \triangleq p(x_k \mid y_{0:k}), \quad k = 0, 1, \ldots \tag{3}$$

where $y_{0:k} = \{y_0, \ldots, y_k\}$, for all the observations from time 0 to k. The conditional density $b_k(x_k)$ can be derived recursively via the Chapman–Kolmogorov equation and Bayes rule as follows:

$$\begin{aligned} b_k(x_k) &= \frac{p(y_k \mid x_k) p(x_k \mid y_{0:k-1})}{p(y_k \mid y_{0:k-1})} \\ &= \frac{p(y_k \mid x_k) \int p(x_k \mid x_{k-1}) b_{k-1}(x_{k-1}) dx_{k-1}}{\int p(y_k \mid x_k) p(x_k \mid y_{0:k-1}) dx_k} \end{aligned} \tag{4}$$

Since $b_k(x_k)$ is unknown, we generate the particles by sampling from another known density $q(x_k \mid y_{0:k})$ and adjust the weights of the samples to obtain an estimate of $b_k(x_k)$. This approach is known as importance sampling, and the density $q(x_k \mid y_{0:k})$ is referred to as the importance density. Hence, it is easy to see that, in order to approximate $p(x_k \mid y_{0:k})$, for samples $\{x_k^i, i = 1, \ldots, N\}$ drawn i.i.d. from $q(x_k \mid y_{0:k})$, their weights should be

$$w_k^i \propto \frac{p(x_k^i \mid y_{0:k})}{q(x_k^i \mid y_{0:k})} \tag{5}$$

where $\propto$ means proportional to, and the weights should be normalized.

To perform the estimation recursively, we used the Bayes rule to derive the following recursive equation for the conditional density:

$$\begin{aligned} b_k(x_k) &\triangleq p(x_k \mid y_{0:k}) \\ &= \frac{p(x_k, y_k \mid y_{0:k-1})}{p(y_k \mid y_{0:k-1})} \\ &\propto p(y_k \mid x_k) \int p(x_k \mid x_{k-1}) p(x_{k-1} \mid y_{0:k-1}) dx_{k-1} \\ &\propto \int p(y_k \mid x_k) p(x_k \mid x_{k-1}) b_{k-1}(x_{k-1}) dx_{k-1} \end{aligned} \tag{6}$$

where $p(y_k \mid y_{0:k-1}, x_k) = p(y_k \mid x_k)$ and $p(x_k \mid y_{0:k-1}, x_{k-1}) = p(x_k \mid x_{k-1})$ both follow from the Markovian property of model Equation (12), the denominator $p(y_k \mid y_{0:k-1})$ does not explicitly depend on x_k and k, and $\propto$ means that $p(x_k \mid y_{0:k})$ is the normalized version of the right-hand side. The state transition density $p(x_k \mid x_{k-1})$ is induced from the state equation in Equation (12) and the distribution of the system noise u_{k-1}, and the likelihood $p(y_k \mid x_k)$ is induced from the observation equation in Equation (12) and the distribution of the observation noise v_k. Substituting Equation (6) into Equation (5), we find

$$w_k^i \propto \frac{p(y_k \mid x_k^i) p(x_k^i \mid x_{k-1}^i)}{q(x_k^i \mid y_{0:k})} p(x_{k-1}^i \mid y_{0:k-1}), \tag{7}$$

If the importance density $q(x_k \mid y_{0:k})$ is chosen to be factored as

$$q(x_k \mid y_{0:k}) = q(x_k \mid x_{k-1}, y_k) q(x_{k-1} \mid y_{0:k-1}) \tag{8}$$

Moreover, to avoid sample degeneracy, new samples are resampled i.i.d. from the approximate conditional density $\hat{p}(x_k \mid y_{0:k})$ at each step; hence, the weights are reset to $w_{k-1}^i = 1/N$, and

$$w_k^i \propto \frac{p(y_k \mid x_k^i) p(x_k^i \mid x_{k-1}^i)}{q(x_k^i \mid x_{k-1}^i, y_k)}, i = 1, \ldots, N \tag{9}$$

In the plain particle filter, the importance density $q(x_k \mid x_{k-1}^i, y_k)$ is chosen to be the state transition density $p(x_k \mid x_{k-1}^i)$, which is independent of the current observation y_k, yielding

$$w_k^i \propto p(y_k \mid x_k^i), i = 1, \ldots, N \tag{10}$$

The plain particle filter recursively propagates the support points and updates the associated weights. The algorithm is as follows in Algorithm 1:

Algorithm 1 General particle filter.

1: Initialization: Sample $\{x_0^i\}_{i=1}^N$ i.i.d. from an initial p.d.f. p_0. Set $k = 1$.
2: Importance Sampling/Propagation: Sample x_k^i from $p(x_k \mid x_{k-1}^i), i = 1, \ldots, N$.
3: Bayes Updating: Receive new observation y_k. The conditional density is approximated by $\hat{p}(x_k \mid y_{0:k}) = \sum_{i=1}^N w_k^i \delta(x - x_k^i)$, where w_k^i is computed according to Equation (10).
4: Resampling: Sample $\{x_k^i\}_{i=1}^N$ i.i.d. from $\hat{p}(x_k \mid y_{0:k})$.
5: $k \leftarrow k + 1$ and go to step 2.

2.2. Particle Filter Optimization for Global Optimization

We consider the global optimization problem:

$$x^* \in \arg\max_{x \in \mathcal{X}} H(x) \tag{11}$$

where x is a vector of n decision variables, $\mathcal{X}$ is the search space, and the objective function H is a bounded deterministic function. We denote the optimal function value as H^*, i.e., there exists an x^* such that $H(x) \leq H^* \triangleq H(x^*), \forall x \in \mathcal{X}$.

Many of the simulation-based global optimization methods, such as the estimation of distribution algorithms (EDAs) [25,26], covariance matrix adaptation evolution strategy [27], cross-entropy (CE) method [28], model reference adaptive search (MRAS) method [29] and particle filter optimization (PFO), fall into the category of model-based methods. They share the similarities of iteratively repeating the following two steps: let g_k be a probability distribution on x at the k-th iteration of an algorithm:

- Randomly generate a set/population of candidate solutions $X^{(k)}$ from an intermediate distribution g_k over the solution space.
- Update the intermediate distribution g_k using the candidate solutions to obtain a new distribution g_{k+1}; increase k by 1 and reiterate from step 1.

The underlying idea is to construct a sequence of iterates (probability distributions) g_k with the hope that $g_k \to g^*$ as $k \to \infty$, where g^* is a limiting distribution that assigns most of its probability mass to the set of optimal solutions. Thus, it is the probability distribution (as opposed to candidate solutions as in instance-based algorithms) that is propagated from one iteration to the next [30].

The main idea of PFO is to formulate the optimization problem as a filtering problem, then particle filter construction appears as a natural candidate for the reformulation of the global optimization problem as a filtering problem. More specifically, the optimization problem Equation (11) can be formulated as a filtering problem by constructing an appropriate state-space model. Let the state-space model be

$$\begin{aligned} x_k &= x_{k-1}, \quad k = 1, 2, \ldots, \\ y_k &= H(x_k) - v_k, \quad k = 0, 1, \ldots, \end{aligned} \quad (12)$$

where the optimal solution is a static state to be estimated, x_k is the unobserved state, y_k is the observation, v_k is the observation noise that is an i.i.d. sequence, and the conditional density of the state approaches a delta function concentrated on the optimal solution as the system evolves.

We assume that v_k has a p.d.f. $\varphi(\cdot)$, and then the transition density is

$$p(x_k \mid x_{k-1}) = \delta(x_k - x_{k-1}) \quad (13)$$

where δ denotes the Dirac delta function. The likelihood function is

$$\begin{aligned} p(y_k \mid x_k) &= \varphi(H(x_k) - y_k) \\ &= \varphi(H(x_{k-1}) - y_k) \end{aligned} \quad (14)$$

Substituting Equations (13) and (14) into the recursive equation of conditional density Equation (6), we obtain

$$b_k(x_k) = \frac{\varphi(H(x_k) - y_k) b_{k-1}(x_k)}{\int \varphi(H(x_k) - y_k) b_{k-1}(x_k) dx_k} \quad (15)$$

The intuition of model Equation (12) is that the optimal solution x^* is an unobserved static state, while we can only observe the optimal function values $y^* = H(x^*)$ with some noise. Equation (15) implies that, at each iteration, the conditional density (i.e., b_{k-1}) is tuned by the performance of solutions to yield a new conditional density (i.e., b_k) for drawing candidate solutions at the next iteration.

It should be expected that, if y_k increases with k, the conditional density b_k will come closer to the density of x_k, i.e., a Dirac delta function concentrated on x^*. From the viewpoint of filtering, b_k is the posterior density of x_k that approaches the density of x_k. From the optimization viewpoint, b_k is a density defined on the solution space that becomes increasingly concentrated on the optimal solution as k increases. The framework of general particle filter optimization is given in Algorithm 2.

Algorithm 2 General particle filter optimization framework.

1: Initialization: Sample $\{x_0^i\}_{i=1}^N$ i.i.d. from an initial p.d.f. p_0. Set $k = 1$.
2: Importance Sampling/Propagation: Sample x_k^i from $p(x_k \mid x_{k-1}^i), i = 1, \ldots, N$.
3: Bayes Updating: Take y_k to be the sample function value of $H(x_k^i)$ according to a certain rule. Compute the weight w_k^i for sample x_k^i according to $w_k^i \propto \varphi(H(x_k^i) - y_k), i = 1, 2, \ldots, N_k$ and normalize the weights such that they sum up to 1.
4: Resampling: Sample $\{x_k^i\}_{i=1}^N$ i.i.d. from $\hat{p}(x_k \mid y_{0:k})$.
5: $k \leftarrow k + 1$ and go to step 2.

Generally, the PFO algorithms can be differentiated from each other by the definitions of the target p.d.f. and of the proposal p.d.f. A specific definition of the target and proposal p.d.f. determines how the objective function is implanted in the sampling process and how the random samples (i.e., candidate solutions) are generated, respectively. For example, while a uniform distribution is adopted as the likelihood function $p(y_k \mid x_{k-1})$ in [22,31], the Boltzmann distribution is another choice in defining the target distribution for PFO methods [21].

3. Proposed Algorithm

3.1. Algorithm Framework

As mentioned above, particle filter optimization methods have been applied to single-objective optimization problems by reformulating an optimization problem into a filtering problem. In this work, we make an effort to extend the scope of application of PFO to multi-objective cases. It is well-known that a Pareto optimal solution to a MOP, under mild conditions, could be an optimal solution of a scalar optimization problem in which the objective is an aggregation of all the objectives [10]. That is to say, MOPs can be formulated as a task of searching a set of Pareto optimal solutions, each of which corresponds to a scalar optimization subproblem with a certain degree of tradeoff among the objectives in an MOP.

With the insight into the decomposition strategy in the context of MOPs, it makes sense to construct a series of target distributions corresponding to a number of scalar objective optimization subproblems, and then the particle filter is adopted to simulate these distributions so that the Pareto optimal solutions can be obtained based on the samples yielded from simulations. There are two main issues: (1) how to design a series of proxy target pdfs for MOPs and (2) how to effectively simulate these p.d.fs via SMC. In the following, we seek answers to these problems and propose a particle filter optimization method for solving multiobjective optimization problems, which will be elaborated in the following. The framework of the proposed PF-MOA is outlined in Algorithm 3.

Algorithm 3 Particle filter multiobjective optimization.

Input: N: the number of particles; K: the number of subproblems; set the maximum number of fitness evaluation $FE^{max} = N * K$;
Output: particles in the archive D;
1: Initialization: Generate a uniform spread of K weight vectors λ for the Tchebycheff approach; optimize the first subproblem and obtain N particles $\{x_0^i\}_{i=1}^N$ to be evaluated on objective functions; save the particles in D; set $z^* = (z_1^*, ..., z_K^*)$ with $z_i^* = \min f_i(x)$; set $k = 1$ and $FE = N$;
2: **while** $FE \leqslant FE^{max}$ **do**
3:    **for** $k = 1, \ldots, K$ **do**
4:       //Computing the k-th subproblem//
5:       Calculate the subproblem with the k-th weight vector according to Equation (16): $g^{tch}(x \mid \lambda^k, z^*) = \max_{1 \leq i \leq m}\{\lambda_i^k(f_i(x) - z_i^*)\}$.
6:       Update the reference point z^*.
7:       //Computing the target pdf associated with the k-th subproblem//
8:       Calculate the corresponding k-th target pdf according to Equation (17): $\tilde{\pi}_k(x) \triangleq \frac{\pi_k(x)}{C_k}$ and $\pi_k(x) = \exp\{-g^{tch}\}$.
9:       **for** $i = 1, \ldots, N$ **do**
10:          //Importance Updating//
11:          Compute the weight $\hat{\omega}_k^i$ for each sample x_k^i according to Equation (18), $\hat{\omega}_k^i = \begin{cases} \tilde{\pi}_k(x_k^i), & \text{if } k = 1 \\ \tilde{\pi}_k(x_k^i)/\tilde{\pi}_{k-1}(x_k^i), & \text{otherwise.} \end{cases}$
12:       **end for**
13:       Normalize the weights such that they sum up to 1;
14:       Resampling: Generate N i.i.d. samples by setting $\tilde{x}^i = x_k^j$ with probability $\hat{\omega}_k^j, j = 1, \ldots, N$. Then, set $x_k^i = \tilde{x}^i, \hat{\omega}_k^i = 1/N$, for $\forall i$.
15:       Calculate the mean of particles $\bar{x}_k$ and the best particle x_k^* obtained thus far.
16:       Particle move: Generate new particles x' using genetic operators on $\bar{x}_k$ and x_k^*, shown in Algorithm 4.
17:       Update the reference point z^*.
18:       Save the particles $\{x_k^i\}_{i=1}^N$ to D.
19:    **end for**
20:    Update $k = k + 1, FE = FE + N$;
21: **end while**
22: Return the particles in D;

3.2. The Design of Target Distribution

Based on the theoretical foundation of sequential Monte Carlo samplers [24], SMC allows us to perform global optimization and sequential Bayesian estimation by sequentially sampling from a sequence of probability distributions that are defined on a common space. Specifically, similar to simulated annealing [32], we can move from a tractable distribution to a distribution of interest through a sequence of artificial intermediate distributions. Consequently, the convergence results are available for SMC samplers [33]. As two or more conflicting objectives are involved in an MOP in Equation (1), the design of the target p.d.f. is different from that in single-objective optimization problems.

To approach to the Pareto optimal set, a set of proxy target pdfs are needed, each of which corresponding to a specific amount of balance among the objectives. To this end, we adopted a decomposition strategy to decompose an MOP into a number of scalar optimization subproblems, followed by designing a target p.d.f. for each single-objective subproblem. More specifically, let $\lambda^1, ..., \lambda^K$ be a set of even spread weight vectors, and let $\mathbf{z}^*$ be the reference point. An MOP with m objectives, i.e., Equation (1), can be decomposed into K scalar/single-objective optimization subproblems using the Tchebycheff (TCH) decomposition [10], and the objective function of the jth subproblem is

$$\min_{\mathbf{x} \in \Omega} g^{\text{tch}}\left(\mathbf{x} \mid \lambda^j, \mathbf{z}^*\right) = \max_{1 \leq i \leq m} \left\{ \lambda_i^j (f_i(\mathbf{x}) - z_i^*) \right\} \tag{16}$$

where m is the number of objectives, $\mathbf{z}^* = (z_1^*, ..., z_m^*)$ with $z_i^* = \min f_i(\mathbf{x} \mid \mathbf{x} \in \Omega)$ is the reference point, $\lambda^j = \left(\lambda_1^j, ..., \lambda_m^j\right)$ with $\sum_{i=1}^m \lambda_i = 1$ and $\lambda_i \geq 0$ is the weight vector, and f_i and $\mathbf{x}$ are the objective function and decision vector, respectively.

In this way, for each Pareto optimal solution $\mathbf{x}^*$ of an MOP, there exists a weight vector λ such that $\mathbf{x}^*$ is the optimal solution of a subproblem (Equation (16)), and each optimal solution of the subproblem is Pareto optimal to the MOP. As a result, to obtain a set of different Pareto optimal solutions of an MOP, one can solve a set of single-objective optimization problems with different weight vectors defined by Equation (16) or any other decomposition approaches. Note that g^{tch} is continuous of λ, the optimal solution of $g^{\text{tch}}(\mathbf{x} \mid \lambda^i, \mathbf{z}^*)$ should be close to that of $g^{\text{tch}}(\mathbf{x} \mid \lambda^j, \mathbf{z}^*)$ if λ^i and λ^j are close to each other. Therefore, any information about these g^{tch} with weight vectors close to λ^i should be helpful for optimizing $g^{\text{tch}}(\mathbf{x} \mid \lambda^i, \mathbf{z}^*)$.

Obtaining a set of single-objective subproblems, a set of target p.d.fs $\tilde{\pi}_1(\mathbf{x}), \tilde{\pi}_2(\mathbf{x}), ..., \tilde{\pi}_K(\mathbf{x})$ corresponding to the subproblems are constructed as follows,

$$\begin{aligned}\tilde{\pi}_k(\mathbf{x}) &\triangleq \frac{\pi_k(\mathbf{x})}{C_k}, k = 1, 2, ..., K \\ \pi_k(\mathbf{x}) &= \exp\left\{-g^{\text{tch}}\right\}\end{aligned} \tag{17}$$

where K is the number of target p.d.fs (in our case, K equals to the number of the weight vector), C_k is a normalizing constant which ensures $\tilde{\pi}_k(\mathbf{x})$ to be a qualified pdf whose integral equals 1. According to Equations (16) and (17), each p.d.f. corresponds to a specific degree of balance between each objective using the weight vectors.

3.3. The Sampling Procedure

Given the target p.d.fs, the particle filter appears as a natural candidate for the simulation of these target distributions. The first subproblem is optimized, and then the particle filter is used to track the sequence of target distributions that correspond to a set of scalar subproblems. This has three main steps: importance updating, resampling and particle move. The importance updating step takes the current distribution $\tilde{\pi}_k$ (corresponding to a subproblem) as the target distribution and takes the previous distribution $\tilde{\pi}_{k-1}$ (corresponding to the previous subproblem) as the proposal distribution.

Thus, given that the previous samples are updated in proportion to $\tilde{\pi}_k(\cdot)/\tilde{\pi}_{k-1}(\cdot)$, the new empirical distribution formed by samples is already distributed approximately according to $\tilde{\pi}_{k-1}$, and the weights of these weighted samples will closely follow $\tilde{\pi}_k$. The resampling step redistributes the samples such that they all have equal weights. The particle move step is performed on each particle to update their locations towards the promising region so that we can follow the target distribution of each subproblem as closely as possible.

Note that, instead of updating particles according to a transition equation as in Equation (12), a Metropolis sampling method associated with genetic operators is adopted to sample new particles as the transition equation in the MOPs is unknown.

From the perspective of multi-objective optimization, the advantage of the proposed PF-MOA can be explained by tracking the Pareto optimal solutions on the Pareto front and making the search more efficient. The reason is that the importance weight of particles in the proposed PF-MOA is updated according to the difference between the current and the previous distributions (which correspond to two related subproblems). As we mentioned in Section 3.2, any information about these g^{tch} with weight vectors close to λ^i should be helpful for optimizing $g^{tch}(x \mid \lambda^i, z^*)$. The method of importance updating makes it possible to leverage the knowledge readily available for the previous subproblem to optimize the next subproblem, guiding the new particles to concentrate on the more promising area found thus far.

More specifically, while the normalization of the weights and the resampling of the particles are the typical operations in Algorithm 2, the calculation of the importance weight for the i-th particle according to the set of target distributions is as follows,

$$\tilde{\omega}_k^i = \begin{cases} \tilde{\pi}_k(x^i), & \text{if } k = 1 \\ \tilde{\pi}_k(x^i) / \tilde{\pi}_{k-1}(x^i), & \text{otherwise.} \end{cases} \quad (18)$$

Through the resampling step, we eliminate/duplicate samples with low/high importance weights, respectively, avoiding the issue of particle degeneracy.

3.4. Particle Move

After the resampling step, a Metropolis sampling method based on genetic operators is proposed to promote the divergence of particles as summarized in Algorithm 4. As we demonstrate in Section 2.2, the state transition as function is assumed $x_k = x_{k-1}$ in the state space model when solving global optimization problems. If a particle filter is applied to this model directly, with no particle move, the resulting algorithm would be equivalent to importance sampling from the initial sampling distribution directly to the posterior in a single step. This would be problematic if the initial sampling distribution was located in a different region of parameter space entirely, particularly in the context of MOPs. Hence, a Metropolis sampling method for generating new particles is proposed to assist the particle filter to simulate these target pdfs by exploiting the promising region.

The resampling step together with the Metropolis sampling step prevents sample degeneracy or, in other words, maintains the sample diversity and, thus, the exploration of the solution space. To make use of the search information obtained by the particle filter, the mean of particles $\bar{x}_k$ and the best particle x_k^* obtained thus far are identified and assumed to be close to the optimum. The new/displacement particles x' will hence be generated around the promising region using genetic operators, i.e., the typical mutation and crossover operators. Subsequently, the displacement will be either accepted or rejected according to a dynamically calculated probability, called the acceptance probability. In the proposed PF-MOA, the acceptance probability for the displacement of the i-th particle (x^i) is calculated by

$$\rho = \min\{\tilde{\pi}_k(x') / \tilde{\pi}_k(x^i), 1\}. \quad (19)$$

Algorithm 4 A Metropolis sampling method based on genetic operators.

Input: The current particles $\{x_k^i\}_{i=1}^N$ and the current target pdf $\tilde{\pi}_k$, the mean of particles $\bar{x}_k$ and the best particle x_k^* obtained thus far.
Output: the new particles;
1: **for** $i = 1 : N$ **do**
2:    Perform the genetic operator on $\bar{x}_k$ and x_k^* and generate a new particle x'.
3:    Calculate acceptance probability via Equation (19) and replace x_k^i by x' with

$$x_k^i = \begin{cases} x', & \text{with probability } \rho \\ x_k^i, & \text{with probability } 1 - \rho \end{cases} \quad (20)$$

4:    Update $x_k^* = x'$, if $\tilde{\pi}_k(x') > \tilde{\pi}_k(x_k^*)$.
5: **end for**
6: Return updated particles;

4. Comparative Studies

In this section, numerical experiments are conducted on nine three-objective benchmark problems taken from the DTLZ test suite. To examine the efficiency of the proposed strategies, the proposed PF-MOA is compared with state-of-the-art multi-objective evolutionary algorithms, NSGA-II [9], RVEA [11], MOEA/D [10], NSGA-III [13], MOEA/DD [15] and θ-DEA [14]. Our code is available at https://github.com/xw00616/PF-MOA (accessed on 1 November 2022).

In the following section, we begin with briefly introducing the test problems and performance metrics adopted in our paper. Afterwards, the details of the experimental settings concerning the four compared algorithms are described. Lastly, the experimental results together with the Wilcoxon rank sum test are presented and discussed.

4.1. Test Problems

In our experiments, the proposed algorithm is compared with three state-of-the-art multi-objective optimization algorithms on DTLZ [34] and WFG [35] test suites with three objectives. The number of decision variables for the DTLZ test instances is set to $D = M + K - 1$, where $K = 5$ is adopted for DTLZ1, $K = 10$ is used for DTLZ2 to DTLZ6, and $K = 20$ is employed in DTLZ7. The number of decision variables for the WFG test instances is set to 12. M represents the number of objectives; here, we set $M = 3$.

4.2. Performance Metrics

The inverted generational distance (IGD) [36] metric and hypervolume (HV) [37] metric are adopted to assess the performance of the algorithms. IGD and HV provide a combined information of the convergence and diversity of the obtained set of solutions. The PlatEMO toolbox [38] is used to calculate values of the performance metric in our experiments. Let P^* be a set of uniformly distributed solutions sampled from objective space along the theoretical Pareto front. Let P be an obtained approximation to the Pareto front. Let P^* be a set of uniformly distributed solutions sampled from objective space along the theoretical Pareto front. IGD measures the inverted generational distance from P^* to P, defined as

$$IGD(P^*, P) = \frac{\sum_{v \in P^*} d(v, P)}{|P^*|} \quad (21)$$

where $d(v, P)$ is the minimum Euclidean distance between v and all points in P. The smaller IGD value, the better the achieved solution set is.

HV calculates the volume of the objective space dominated by an approximation set P and dominates P^* sampled from the PF.

$$HV = \text{volume}\left(\cup_{i=1}^j \vartheta_i\right) \quad (22)$$

where ϑ_i represents the hypervolume contribution of the i-th solutions relative to the reference points. All HV values presented in this paper are normalized to $[0,1]$. Algorithms achieving a larger HV value are better.

4.3. Experimental Settings

We ran each algorithm on each benchmark problem 20 independent times, and the Wilcoxon rank sum test was calculated to compare the mean of 20 running results obtained by PF-MOA and by the compared algorithms at a significance level of 0.05. Symbols "(−)", "(+)" and "(≈))" indicate that the proposed algorithm shows significantly better, worse and similar performance than the compared algorithm, respectively.

The PF-MOA was implemented in MATLAB R2019a on an Intel Core i7 with 2.21 GHz CPU, and the compared algorithms were implemented in PlatEMO toolbox [38]. The general parameter settings in the experiments are given as follows: (1) The maximum number of function evaluations $FE_{max} = 10,000$. (2) For PF-MOA: the population size was set to 100 and the maximum number of generations was set to 100. (3) For the three multiobjective evolutionary algorithms: the population size was set to 100 and the maximum number of generations was set to 100. The specific parameter settings for each compared algorithm were the same as recommended in their original papers.

4.4. Experimental Results

The statistical results in terms of IGD and HV values obtained by the four algorithms are summarized in Table 1 and Table 2, respectively. For the DTLZ test problems, it is apparent that the proposed PF-MOA achieved the best approximate Pareto front on all test problems except for DTLZ6 and DTLZ7 (NSGA-II obtained the best IGD values). The reason behind this may be that DTLZ6 has a plenty of disconnected Pareto optimal regions in the decision space, and DTLZ7 has a discontinuous Pareto front. Hence, it is challenging to design proper target distributions in PF-MOA, which further degrades PF-MOA's performance.

According to the Wilcoxon rank sum test, the proposed algorithm significantly outperformed the compared algorithms on most of the test problems. For the WFG test instances, PF-MOA showed significantly better performance than the algorithms under comparison on six out of nine test instances, confirming the promising performance of the proposed PF-MOA. More specifically, taking WFG5 as an example, the objective multimodality was combined with landscape deception, and the proposed PF-MOA showed the worst performance compared with the other algorithms.

A possible explanation for this is that the deceptive objectives may impact the design of the target distributions, and the information form the previous subproblem does not provide sufficient information to help the algorithm generate good tradeoff solutions for the current subproblem. Moreover, similar observations can be made from Table 2.

To further illustrate the performance of the proposed algorithm, the obtained Pareto front for each algorithm is illustrated in Figure 1. We observed that the proposed method can find a set of well-converged and diverse Pareto optimal solutions, thereby, confirming the effectiveness of the particle filter in the PF-MOA.

Table 1. Statistical results of the IGD values obtained by NSGA-II, RVEA, MOEA/D, MOEA/DD, NSGA-III, θ-DEA and PF-MOA with the same number of real function evaluations.

Problem	D	MOEA/D	NSGA-II	RVEA	NSGA-III	MOEA/DD	θ-DEA	PF-MOA
DTLZ1	7	2.41e-1 (3.56e-1) −	4.00e-1 (4.17e-1) −	4.67e-1 (2.83e-1) −	1.86e-1 (1.73e-1) ≈	3.51e-1 (2.36e-1) −	2.22e-1 (3.58e-1) −	1.27e-1 (7.06e-2)
DTLZ2	12	5.48e-2 (2.21e-4) −	6.96e-2 (2.44e-3) −	5.59e-2 (6.45e-4) −	5.51e-2 (2.45e-4) −	5.54e-2 (1.95e-4) −	5.48e-2 (4.76e-5) −	4.11e-2 (1.01e-2)
DTLZ3	12	1.18e+1 (6.40e+0) −	1.02e+1 (6.66e+0) −	1.63e+1 (5.65e+0) −	1.04e+1 (2.75e+0) −	2.22e+1 (1.07e+1) −	1.06e+1 (1.10e+0) −	1.79e+0 (3.79e+0)
DTLZ4	12	4.89e-1 (3.50e-1) +	1.15e-1 (1.44e-1) +	5.59e-2 (5.89e-4) +	5.51e-2 (1.20e-4) +	5.55e-2 (7.39e-4) +	5.49e-2 (7.99e-5) +	6.48e-1 (2.32e-1)
DTLZ5	12	3.23e-2 (7.34e-4) −	6.10e-3 (3.36e-4) −	8.45e-2 (1.70e-2) −	1.27e-2 (2.16e-3) −	3.13e-2 (1.03e-3) −	3.01e-2 (2.18e-3) −	3.87e-3 (1.21e-3)
DTLZ6	12	2.09e-1 (3.93e-1) −	3.58e-2 (1.61e-1) −	1.46e-1 (1.42e-1) +	1.89e-2 (2.42e-3) +	1.00e-1 (1.39e-1) +	3.81e-2 (1.71e-3) +	7.63e-1 (3.62e-1)
DTLZ7	22	2.19e-1 (1.99e-1) +	1.13e-1 (6.90e-2) +	2.02e-1 (5.32e-2) +	1.61e-1 (1.39e-1) +	4.29e-1 (2.44e-1) +	9.62e-2 (5.39e-3) +	7.45e+0 (6.91e-1)
WFG1	12	6.84e-1 (1.00e-1) +	5.72e-1 (8.19e-2) +	7.62e-1 (8.89e-2)	1.03e+0 (3.60e-2) ≈	1.51e+0 (6.12e-3) −	1.01e+0 (4.76e-2) ≈	1.82e+0 (1.41e-1)
WFG2	12	3.33e-1 (7.77e-2) −	2.24e-1 (9.68e-3) −	2.16e-1 (1.22e-2) −	1.75e-1 (7.12e-3) −	1.91e-1 (9.10e-3) −	1.60e-1 (2.81e-3) −	2.03e-1 (2.65e-2)
WFG3	12	3.55e-1 (1.24e-1) −	1.29e-1 (2.21e-2) −	2.65e-1 (2.41e-2) −	1.65e-1 (1.40e-2) −	3.79e-1 (1.12e-1) −	1.43e-1 (1.99e-2) +	2.18e-1 (1.51e-2)
WFG4	12	2.91e-1 (1.25e-2) −	2.82e-1 (1.04e-2) −	2.69e-1 (7.74e-3) −	2.32e-1 (1.67e-3) −	2.48e-1 (3.02e-3) −	2.29e-1 (1.10e-3) −	1.60e-1 (2.68e-2)
WFG5	12	2.73e-1 (9.26e-3) +	2.85e-1 (1.22e-2) +	2.61e-1 (7.34e-3) +	2.37e-1 (2.13e-3) +	2.52e-1 (1.05e-3) +	2.36e-1 (1.38e-3) +	6.87e-1 (2.43e-2)
WFG6	12	3.44e-1 (2.25e-2) −	3.29e-1 (1.92e-2) −	3.37e-1 (2.06e-2) −	2.78e-1 (2.12e-2) −	3.04e-1 (2.23e-2) −	2.67e-1 (1.35e-2) −	1.71e-1 (3.38e-2)
WFG7	12	4.17e-1 (5.34e-2) −	2.83e-1 (1.04e-2) ≈	2.89e-1 (1.33e-2) −	2.32e-1 (1.13e-3) −	2.66e-1 (1.56e-2) −	2.29e-1 (8.96e-4) ≈	2.63e-1 (5.54e-2)
WFG8	12	3.78e-1 (2.51e-2) −	3.75e-1 (1.02e-2) +	3.74e-1 (1.39e-2) +	3.20e-1 (5.91e-3) +	3.37e-1 (7.67e-3) +	3.16e-1 (6.32e-3) +	5.48e-1 (3.59e-2)
WFG9	12	3.70e-1 (6.98e-2) −	2.84e-1 (2.24e-2) −	2.78e-1 (3.30e-2) −	2.38e-1 (3.51e-2) −	2.61e-1 (1.63e-2) −	2.35e-1 (4.19e-3) −	1.21e-1 (2.11e-2)
+/−/≈		6/10/0	7/8/1	6/10/0	5/7/4	5/10/1	6/8/2	

Table 2. Statistical results of the HV values obtained by NSGA-II, RVEA, MOEA/D, MOEA/DD, NSGA-III, θ-DEA and PF-MOA with the same number of real function evaluations.

Problem	D	MOEA/D	NSGA-II	RVEA	NSGA-III	MOEA/DD	θ-DEA	PF-MOA
DTLZ1	7	6.21e-1 (3.49e-1) −	3.60e-1 (4.02e-1) −	2.12e-1 (2.86e-1) −	4.57e-1 (3.40e-1) −	2.27e-1 (3.15e-1) −	5.78e-1 (3.33e-1) −	9.28e-1 (7.50e-2)
DTLZ2	12	5.55e-1 (6.99e-4) −	5.29e-1 (7.43e-3) −	5.51e-1 (2.97e-3) −	5.55e-1 (6.66e-4) −	5.54e-1 (8.13e-4) −	5.56e-1 (5.04e-4) −	6.91e-1 (1.01e-4)
DTLZ3	12	0.00e+0 (0.00e+0) −	0.00e+0 (0.00e+0) −	0.00e+0 (0.00e+0) −	0.00e+0 (0.00e+0) −	0.00e+0 (0.00e+0) −	0.00e+0 (0.00e+0) −	2.00e-1 (1.27e-2)
DTLZ4	12	2.91e-1 (1.12e-1) ≈	4.96e-1 (8.42e-2) +	5.53e-1 (1.39e-3) +	5.56e-1 (8.24e-4) +	5.55e-1 (1.45e-3) +	5.55e-1 (4.87e-4) +	2.48e-1 (1.32e-1)
DTLZ5	12	1.82e-1 (4.00e-4) −	1.98e-1 (3.78e-4) −	1.48e-1 (4.11e-3) −	1.93e-1 (1.91e-3) −	1.82e-1 (2.29e-4) −	1.83e-1 (6.22e-4) −	4.87e-1 (2.51e-4)
DTLZ6	12	1.77e-1 (3.83e-3) +	1.99e-1 (1.59e-4) +	1.35e-1 (2.14e-2) +	1.90e-1 (1.28e-3) +	1.54e-1 (4.42e-2) +	1.81e-1 (1.71e-3) +	0.00e+0 (0.00e+0)
DTLZ7	22	2.32e-1 (9.16e-3) +	2.47e-1 (3.41e-3) +	2.06e-1 (2.69e-2) +	2.39e-1 (1.33e-2) +	2.11e-1 (1.70e-2) +	2.53e-1 (1.69e-3) +	0.00e+0 (0.00e+0)
WFG1	12	3.72e-1 (2.30e-2) −	4.91e-1 (4.72e-2) −	4.58e-1 (2.91e-2) −	4.60e-1 (1.22e-2) ≈	2.82e-1 (5.79e-3) −	4.61e-1 (1.74e-2) ≈	4.78e-1 (1.41e-2)
WFG2	12	8.20e-1 (3.14e-2) −	9.07e-1 (6.22e-3) −	8.93e-1 (1.12e-2) −	9.09e-1 (2.33e-3) −	8.93e-1 (1.04e-2) −	9.16e-1 (4.92e-3) −	9.59e-1 (1.32e-2)
WFG3	12	2.71e-1 (2.63e-2) −	3.77e-1 (5.82e-3) −	2.97e-1 (1.68e-2) −	3.53e-1 (9.30e-3) −	2.57e-1 (4.44e-2) −	3.61e-1 (1.62e-2) −	4.78e-1 (2.11e-2)
WFG4	12	4.91e-1 (1.41e-2) −	5.01e-1 (6.63e-3) −	5.17e-1 (2.21e-3) −	5.26e-1 (2.51e-3) −	5.19e-1 (3.28e-3) −	5.32e-1 (1.82e-3) −	9.51e-1 (5.11e-3)
WFG5	12	4.77e-1 (8.04e-3) ≈	4.81e-1 (2.91e-3) +	4.98e-1 (3.27e-3) +	5.06e-1 (4.35e-3) +	4.94e-1 (5.37e-3) +	5.05e-1 (3.61e-3) +	4.43e-1 (2.63e-2)
WFG6	12	4.45e-1 (1.90e-2) −	4.41e-1 (1.06e-2) −	4.65e-1 (7.82e-3) −	4.72e-1 (1.58e-2) −	4.55e-1 (2.01e-2) −	4.80e-1 (1.21e-2) −	6.01e-1 (1.63e-2)
WFG7	12	4.41e-1 (2.54e-2) −	5.10e-1 (4.93e-3) −	5.18e-1 (7.89e-3) −	5.31e-1 (2.05e-3) −	5.11e-1 (1.06e-2) −	5.35e-1 (1.96e-3) −	7.63e-1 (1.54e-2)
WFG8	12	4.11e-1 (1.73e-2) −	4.23e-1 (3.71e-3) −	4.31e-1 (1.01e-2) −	4.40e-1 (2.75e-3) −	4.30e-1 (7.56e-3) −	4.44e-1 (6.64e-3) −	7.33e-1 (2.24e-2)
WFG9	12	3.87e-1 (5.17e-2) −	4.84e-1 (7.56e-3) −	4.95e-1 (1.15e-2) −	5.02e-1 (4.90e-3) −	4.92e-1 (7.97e-3) −	5.07e-1 (7.91e-3) −	9.38e-1 (6.11e-3)
+/−/≈		6/10/0	7/8/1	2/12/2	4/11/1	4/12/0	4/11/1	

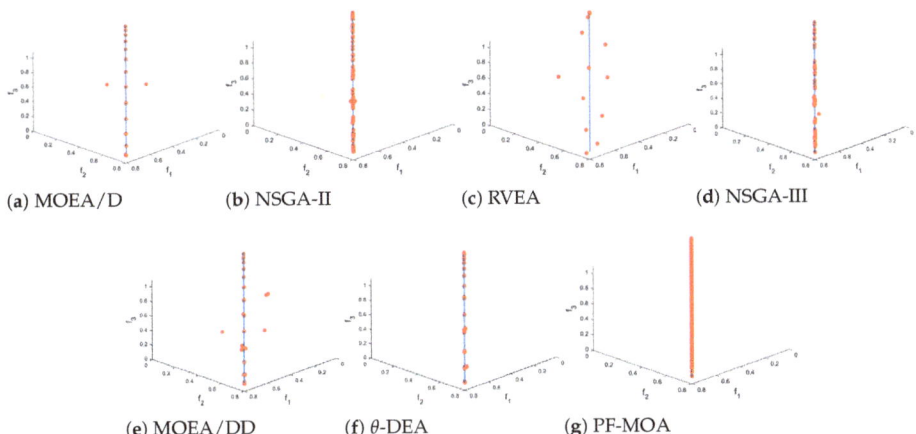

(a) MOEA/D (b) NSGA-II (c) RVEA (d) NSGA-III

(e) MOEA/DD (f) θ-DEA (g) PF-MOA

Figure 1. The Pareto front obtained by the compared algorithms on DTLZ5.

5. Conclusions

In this paper, we extended the particle filter optimization method from single-objective optimization to multiobjective optimization. The Tchebycheff decomposition was used to decompose a multi-objective optimization into a set of single-objective problems so that a sequence of target distribution was defined. Subsequently, the particle filter was adopted to simulate these target distributions by using its tracking ability, and genetic operators were employed to perform the particle move. The experimental results on the DTLZ test suite showed the promising performance of PF-MOA compared with three state-of-the-art multi-objective evolutionary algorithms.

However, PF-MOA cannot effectively solve certain problems with discontinuous optimization problems, such as DTLZ6 and DTLZ7. The reason may be that PF-MOA always searches around the best particle, thereby, reducing the diversity of all the particles; however, the lack of diversity cannot be addressed by the resampling step, which should be considered in future work. Moreover, for real-world multiobjective optimization problems, uncertainty is an unavoidable issue, and it directly affects the optimization performance. As the filtering methods have been successfully applied to noisy MOPs, the particle filter may benefit MOEAs for solving MOPs with uncertainty.

Author Contributions: Conceptualization, X.W. and Y.J.; methodology, X.W.; software, X.W.; validation, X.W.; formal analysis, X.W.; investigation, X.W.; resources, X.W.; data curation, X.W.; writing—original draft preparation, X.W.; writing—review and editing, X.W. and Y.J.; visualization, X.W.; supervision, Y.J.; project administration, Y.J.; funding acquisition, Y.J. All authors have read and agreed to the published version of the manuscript.

Funding: This research received no external funding.

Conflicts of Interest: The authors declare no conflict of interest.

References

1. He, C.; Huang, S.; Cheng, R.; Tan, K.C.; Jin, Y. Evolutionary Multiobjective Optimization Driven by Generative Adversarial Networks (GANs). *IEEE Trans. Cybern.* **2021**, *51*, 3129–3142. [CrossRef]
2. Marler, R.T.; Arora, J.S. Survey of multi-objective optimization methods for engineering. *Struct. Multidiscip. Optim.* **2004**, *26*, 369–395. [CrossRef]
3. Kaliszewski, I. A modified weighted Tchebycheff metric for multiple objective programming. *Comput. Oper. Res.* **1987**, *14*, 315–323. [CrossRef]
4. Tseng, C.; Lu, T. Minimax multiobjective optimization in structural design. *Int. J. Numer. Methods Eng.* **1990**, *30*, 1213–1228. [CrossRef]
5. Miettinen, K. *Nonlinear Multiobjective Optimization*; Springer Science & Business Media: Berlin/Heidelberg, Germany, 2012; Volume 12.
6. Ogryczak, W. A goal programming model of the reference point method. *Ann. Oper. Res.* **1994**, *51*, 33–44. [CrossRef]
7. Jin, Y.; Wang, H.; Chugh, T.; Guo, D.; Miettinen, K. Data-driven evolutionary optimization: An overview and case studies. *IEEE Trans. Evol. Comput.* **2018**, *23*, 442–458. [CrossRef]
8. Dasgupta, D.; Michalewicz, Z. *Evolutionary Algorithms in Engineering Applications*; Springer Science & Business Media: Berlin/Heidelberg, Germany, 2013.
9. Deb, K.; Pratap, A.; Agarwal, S.; Meyarivan, T. A fast and elitist multiobjective genetic algorithm: NSGA-II. *IEEE Trans. Evol. Comput.* **2002**, *6*, 182–197. [CrossRef]
10. Zhang, Q.; Li, H. MOEA/D: A multiobjective evolutionary algorithm based on decomposition. *IEEE Trans. Evol. Comput.* **2007**, *11*, 712–731. [CrossRef]
11. Cheng, R.; Jin, Y.; Olhofer, M.; Sendhoff, B. A reference vector guided evolutionary algorithm for many-objective optimization. *IEEE Trans. Evol. Comput.* **2016**, *20*, 773–791. [CrossRef]
12. Zitzler, E.; Laumanns, M.; Thiele, L. SPEA2: Improving the strength Pareto evolutionary algorithm. *TIK-Report* **2001**, *103*. [CrossRef]
13. Deb, K.; Jain, H. An evolutionary many-objective optimization algorithm using reference-point-based nondominated sorting approach, part I: Solving problems with box constraints. *IEEE Trans. Evol. Comput.* **2013**, *18*, 577–601. [CrossRef]
14. Yuan, Y.; Xu, H.; Wang, B.; Yao, X. A new dominance relation-based evolutionary algorithm for many-objective optimization. *IEEE Trans. Evol. Comput.* **2015**, *20*, 16–37. [CrossRef]
15. Li, K.; Deb, K.; Zhang, Q.; Kwong, S. An evolutionary many-objective optimization algorithm based on dominance and decomposition. *IEEE Trans. Evol. Comput.* **2014**, *19*, 694–716. [CrossRef]

16. Zhang, T.; Xu, C.; Yang, M.H. Multi-task correlation particle filter for robust object tracking. In Proceedings of the IEEE Conference on Computer Vision and Pattern Recognition, Honolulu, HI, USA, 21-26 July 2017; pp. 4335–4343.
17. Cappello, F.; Sabatini, R.; Ramasamy, S.; Marino, M. Particle filter based multi-sensor data fusion techniques for RPAS navigation and guidance. In Proceedings of the 2015 IEEE Metrology for Aerospace (MetroAeroSpace), Benevento, Italy, 4–5 June 2015; pp. 395–400.
18. Orchard, M.E.; Vachtsevanos, G.J. A particle-filtering approach for on-line fault diagnosis and failure prognosis. *Trans. Inst. Meas. Control* **2009**, *31*, 221–246. [CrossRef]
19. Schutte, J.F.; Reinbolt, J.A.; Fregly, B.J.; Haftka, R.T.; George, A.D. Parallel global optimization with the particle swarm algorithm. *Int. J. Numer. Methods Eng.* **2004**, *61*, 2296–2315. [CrossRef]
20. Hou, Y.; Hao, G.; Zhang, Y.; Gu, F.; Xu, W. A multi-objective discrete particle swarm optimization method for particle routing in distributed particle filters. *Knowl.-Based Syst.* **2022**, *240*, 108068. [CrossRef]
21. Ji, C.; Zhang, Y.; Tong, M.; Yang, S. Particle filter with swarm move for optimization. In Proceedings of the International Conference on Parallel Problem Solving from Nature, Dortmund, Germany, 13–17 September 2008; Springer: Berlin/Heidelberg, Germany, 2008; pp. 909–918.
22. Zhou, E.; Fu, M.C.; Marcus, S.I. A particle filtering framework for randomized optimization algorithms. In Proceedings of the 2008 Winter Simulation Conference, Miami, FL, USA, 7–10 December 2008; pp. 647–654.
23. Martí, L.; Garcia, J.; Berlanga, A.; Coello, C.; Molina, J.M. *On Current Model-Building Methods for Multi-Objective Estimation of Distribution Algorithms: Shortcommings and Directions for Improvement*; Department of Informatics, Universidad Carlos III de Madrid: Madrid, Spain, 2010; Tech. Rep. GIAA2010E001.
24. Del Moral, P.; Doucet, A.; Jasra, A. Sequential monte carlo samplers. *J. R. Stat. Soc. Ser. B (Stat. Methodol.)* **2006**, *68*, 411–436. [CrossRef]
25. Larrañaga, P.; Lozano, J.A. *Estimation of Distribution Algorithms: A New Tool for Evolutionary Computation*; Springer Science & Business Media: Berlin/Heidelberg, Germany, 2001; Volume 2.
26. Doerr, B.; Krejca, M.S. Significance-based estimation-of-distribution algorithms. *IEEE Trans. Evol. Comput.* **2020**, *24*, 1025–1034. [CrossRef]
27. Hansen, N.; Müller, S.D.; Koumoutsakos, P. Reducing the time complexity of the derandomized evolution strategy with covariance matrix adaptation (CMA-ES). *Evol. Comput.* **2003**, *11*, 1–18. [CrossRef]
28. Rubinstein, R.Y.; Kroese, D.P. *The Cross-Entropy Method: A Unified Approach to Combinatorial Optimization, Monte-Carlo Simulation and Machine Learning*; Springer Science & Business Media: Berlin/Heidelberg, Germany, 2013.
29. Hu, J.; Fu, M.C.; Marcus, S.I. A model reference adaptive search method for global optimization. *Oper. Res.* **2007**, *55*, 549–568. [CrossRef]
30. Hu, J.; Wang, Y.; Zhou, E.; Fu, M.C.; Marcus, S.I. A survey of some model-based methods for global optimization. In *Optimization, Control, and Applications of Stochastic Systems*; Springer: Berlin/Heidelberg, Germany, 2012; pp. 157–179.
31. Zhou, E.; Fu, M.C.; Marcus, S.I. Particle filtering framework for a class of randomized optimization algorithms. *IEEE Trans. Autom. Control* **2013**, *59*, 1025–1030. [CrossRef]
32. Guilmeau, T.; Chouzenoux, E.; Elvira, V. Simulated annealing: A review and a new scheme. In Proceedings of the 2021 IEEE Statistical Signal Processing Workshop (SSP), Rio de Janeiro, Brazil, 11–14 July 2021; pp. 101–105.
33. Dai, C.; Heng, J.; Jacob, P.E.; Whiteley, N. An invitation to sequential Monte Carlo samplers. *J. Am. Stat. Assoc.* **2022**, 1–38. [CrossRef]
34. Deb, K.; Thiele, L.; Laumanns, M.; Zitzler, E. Scalable multi-objective optimization test problems. In Proceedings of the 2002 Congress on Evolutionary Computation, CEC'02 (Cat. No. 02TH8600), Honolulu, HI, USA, 12–17 May 2002; Volume 1, pp. 825–830.
35. Huband, S.; Hingston, P.; Barone, L.; While, L. A review of multiobjective test problems and a scalable test problem toolkit. *IEEE Trans. Evol. Comput.* **2006**, *10*, 477–506. [CrossRef]
36. Bosman, P.A.; Thierens, D. The balance between proximity and diversity in multiobjective evolutionary algorithms. *IEEE Trans. Evol. Comput.* **2003**, *7*, 174–188. [CrossRef]
37. Zitzler, E.; Brockhoff, D.; Thiele, L. The hypervolume indicator revisited: On the design of Pareto-compliant indicators via weighted integration. In Proceedings of the International Conference on Evolutionary Multi-Criterion Optimization, Matsushima, Japan, 5–8 March 2007; pp. 862–876.
38. Tian, Y.; Cheng, R.; Zhang, X.; Jin, Y. PlatEMO: A MATLAB platform for evolutionary multi-objective optimization [educational forum]. *IEEE Comput. Intell. Mag.* **2017**, *12*, 73–87. [CrossRef]

Disclaimer/Publisher's Note: The statements, opinions and data contained in all publications are solely those of the individual author(s) and contributor(s) and not of MDPI and/or the editor(s). MDPI and/or the editor(s) disclaim responsibility for any injury to people or property resulting from any ideas, methods, instructions or products referred to in the content.

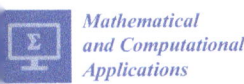

Article

Many-Objectives Optimization: A Machine Learning Approach for Reducing the Number of Objectives

António Gaspar-Cunha [1,*], Paulo Costa [1], Francisco Monaco [2] and Alexandre Delbem [2]

1 Institute of Polymers and Composites, University of Minho, 4800-058 Guimarães, Portugal
2 Institute of Mathematics and Computer Science, University of São Paulo, São Paulo 05508-060, Brazil
* Correspondence: agc@dep.uminho.pt

Abstract: Solving real-world multi-objective optimization problems using Multi-Objective Optimization Algorithms becomes difficult when the number of objectives is high since the types of algorithms generally used to solve these problems are based on the concept of non-dominance, which ceases to work as the number of objectives grows. This problem is known as the curse of dimensionality. Simultaneously, the existence of many objectives, a characteristic of practical optimization problems, makes choosing a solution to the problem very difficult. Different approaches are being used in the literature to reduce the number of objectives required for optimization. This work aims to propose a machine learning methodology, designated by FS-OPA, to tackle this problem. The proposed methodology was assessed using DTLZ benchmarks problems suggested in the literature and compared with similar algorithms, showing a good performance. In the end, the methodology was applied to a difficult real problem in polymer processing, showing its effectiveness. The algorithm proposed has some advantages when compared with a similar algorithm in the literature based on machine learning (NL-MVU-PCA), namely, the possibility for establishing variable–variable and objective–variable relations (not only objective–objective), and the elimination of the need to define/chose a kernel neither to optimize algorithm parameters. The collaboration with the DM(s) allows for the obtainment of explainable solutions.

Keywords: objectives reduction; data mining; multi-objective optimization; many objectives

1. Introduction

Real-world optimization problems are usually multiobjective, in which multiple conflicting objectives must be taken into account simultaneously. Manly, there are two ways to tackle these types of problems, scalarization functions and population-based algorithms. The use of scalarization functions presented some drawbacks, which led to the development of population-based metaheuristics that use the concept of Pareto-dominance and niching to evolve a population of solutions in the direction of the Pareto-optimal front [1,2].

There are at least three basic types of population-based algorithms commonly employed to solve Multiobjective Optimization Problems MOPs, namely, evolutionary algorithms, swarm-based methods, and colony-based algorithms, which can use the dominance concept, the metric indicators, or the decomposition strategy [3]. In most of these algorithms, a random initial population of solutions is generated and the new populations are consecutively obtained by selection and variation strategies until a stop criterion is met. It is expected from this procedure that the successive populations evolve towards, or to a good approximation of, the Pareto-optimal frontier. In each one of these populations, complex relations exist between the Decision Variables (DVs) and the objectives, as well as between DVs and DVs and objectives and objectives.

These algorithms work well when the number of objectives is low; however, as the number of objectives grows, the percentage of non-dominated solutions decreases, making it difficult for an algorithm based on Pareto-dominance to work effectively, a problem that is known as the curse of dimensionality. There is no consensus on the number of objectives for which this problem occurs; some authors indicate this number as ten [4] and others as four [5], but in reality, these difficulties arise when the number of objectives is four or more.

Two different methods are used to deal with this problem, either using relaxed forms of Pareto optimality or reducing the number of objectives [5]. The reduction of the number of objectives is useful either for the search process or for the decision-making process during and/or at the end of the optimization.

In previous years, some work related to objective reduction for many objectives optimization was proposed in the literature, which can be sub-divided into four different categories: (i) methods in which the aim is to maintain the dominance relation for the non-dominated solutions [6,7]; (ii) methods based on unsupervised feature selection [8]; (iii) methods based into a comparative analysis between the results obtained when the number of objectives is reduced [9]; (iv) methods based on data mining [5,10–12]; and methods based on the use of multi-objective formulations [13]. These approaches will be presented in more detail here.

Brockoff and Zitzler [6,7] suggested the use of two different approaches for objectives reduction, which are based on the definition of two types of problems. The first problem aims to obtain the minimum objective subset that produces a certain error (δ), designated by δ-MOSS problem (δ- Minimum Objective Subset problem), and the second problem aims to obtain an objective subset of a predefined size (k) with the minimum possible error, designated by k-EMOSS problem. For each one of these cases, two algorithms were presented, an exact and a greedy algorithm, characterized for maintaining the dominance relation. They were tested using different knapsack problems and the DTLZ2, DTLZ5, and DTLZ7 benchmark problems for different numbers of objectives.

In López et al. [8], a methodology based on unsupervised feature selection was proposed to address the δ-MOSS and k-EMOSS problems. A correlation matrix obtained from the non-dominated set is used to divide the objective set into homogeneous neighbourhoods. Then, based on the idea that if the distance between the objectives is higher, this signifies that those objectives are more conflicting. Thus, only the objectives in the centre of those neighbourhoods are chosen and the others are discarded. The algorithms were validated by comparing the results obtained with those of the reference [7].

Singh et al. [9] proposed an algorithm, designated by the Pareto Corner Search Evolutionary Algorithm (PCSEA) that, instead of searching for the complete Pareto front, searches for the corners of the Pareto front based on a ranking scheme. Those solutions are used to identify the relevant objectives and the others are discarded. Some benchmark problems and two engineering problems were used to show the performance of the methodology proposed.

Deb and Saxena [10] suggested an approach based on Principal Component Analysis (PCA) for the same purpose of objectives reduction, considering the hypothesis that if two objectives are negatively correlated, they are conflicting. In this way, they maintain the objectives that can explain most of the variance in the objective space, which are the most positive and the most negative of the eigenvectors of the correlation matrix. The authors designated this method as PCA-NSGAII. Afterwards, due to the problem of misinterpreting the data when it lies in sub-manifolds, a new proposal is made based on nonlinear dimensionality reduction [11]. For that purpose, the authors developed two new algorithms to replace the linear PCA, one based on correntropy [14] and the other on Maximum Variance Unfolding (MVU). However, the method lacks information on the means by which objective reduction alters the dominance structure, cannot guarantee the preservation of the dominance relation and provides no measure to specify how much the dominance relation changes when objectives are disregarded. The different procedures proposed were applied to solve DTLZ2 and DTLZ5 benchmark problems for different numbers of objectives.

Later, the same group, Saxena et al. [5], proposed a framework for using linear and nonlinear objective reduction algorithms, namely, L-PCA and NL-MVU-PCA, which are based on machine learning techniques, PCA and MVU, to remove the secondary higher-order dependencies in the non-dominated solutions. The idea was very similar to that of given in previous work by the same authors [10,11], but this time, they proposed a reduction of the number of algorithm parameters and an error measure. The algorithms were tested on a broad range of problems and the results were compared with others in the literature. Based on the same methodology, Sinha et al. [15] proposed an iterative procedure to reduce the objectives in which a Decision Maker (DM) chose the best solutions. The methodology was applied to solve some real-world problems, namely storm drainage and car-side impact. Finally, Duro et al. [12] proposed to extend the methodology presented in reference [5] to rank all objectives by a preference order, as well as to solve the δ-MOSS and k-EMOSS problems, i.e., to obtain the smallest set of objectives that can originate the same POF, and the smallest objective set corresponding to a minimum pre-defined error and the objective sets of a certain size that originates a minimum error.

The main drawback of all these methodologies based on PCA is that they need to use a kernel and, as a consequence, to optimize the kernel parameters. The characteristics of this methodology, NL-MVU-PCA, were compared with the one proposed in the present paper at the end of the next section.

Yuan et al. [13] proposed a methodology based on the use of multi-objective evolutionary algorithms to solve a MOOP formulation. The authors applied this approach to some benchmark problems and two real optimization problems. In both cases, the calculation of the objective functions is based on simple analytical equations where the computational cost is not relevant when compared with the problems that we intend to solve here, which are based on numerical calculation. Therefore, besides performance, this type of methodology will not be explored in the present work.

The present paper aims to propose a method for objectives reduction based on data mining that:

1. can be applied independently on the type and the size of the data and the shape of the Pareto-optimal front,
2. is independent from the choice/definition of the algorithm parameters,
3. considers the relations DVs-DVs and objectives-objectives (and not only the relations between the DVs and objectives), and
4. can provide explainable results for a DM that is a non-expert in optimization or machine learning.

The central aim of the works cited above was to find a reduced set of objectives that could exactly reproduce the results from the original set. Thus, only the redundant objectives could be discarded after a reduction process. That is not the aim of the present work, since our purpose is to apply the proposed methodology to real-world and complex problems where the relations between DVs and the objectives are complex, and the objectives are, in general, partially redundant. Thus, redundancy is not a helpful criterion to eliminate an objective.

For that purpose, a methodology was developed to capture those complex relations and define the relative importance of the objectives based on the determination of the objectives–objectives relations. Doing this makes it possible to determine objectives that can be discarded but with a certain error. In other words, the approximation of the Pareto optimal found (with the reduced number of objectives) has some error when compared with the approximation to the optimal Pareto front (when using all the objectives). Simultaneously, the redundant objectives are also eliminated. Such an approach has at least two significant advantages. First, it aids an optimization algorithm in finding a POF estimate; second, it makes it easier to explain the results found to the DM.

The contents of the paper are as follows: in Section 2, the concepts of machine learning and the methodology proposed are presented; in Section 3, the methodology is tested using some benchmarks; in Section 4, the methodology is applied in a real polymer extrusion problem and the results obtained are discussed and, finally, the conclusions are stated in Section 5.

2. Machine Learning Approach

2.1. Concepts

Bandaru et al. [4] reviewed several proposals from Statistics, Data Mining, and Machine Learning to improve optimization techniques for MaOPs. The approaches usually apply data-driven methods to the solutions in a non-dominated set. The authors arranged the proposals based on the knowledge representation and summarized them into three main classes: (i) Descriptive Statistics, (ii) Visual Data Mining and (iii) Machine Learning itself. Those methods have an origin outside the MOO literature. Thus, they usually are not applied to find properties between variables, objectives, and the non-dominated set. In general, the relatively complex nature of those relations makes their performance inadequate for MaOPs. Other drawbacks relate to some classes of real-world MaOPs that require interactions with a practitioner due to the complexity of the system modelled or for a stakeholder making decisions. Usually, such classes of problems also involve raw or observed data or small datasets (due to the expensiveness of generating, collecting, or simulating samples) involving different data types, varying from continuous to nominal variables. This way, methods that produce explainable models and work with distinct data types are essential for those real-world problems. The strategies proposed by Duro et al. [12] and Bandaru et al. [16] have overcome some of those challenges, including an interactive approach for dealing with two and three objectives and pattern recognition from nominal variables. Another proposal facing those challenges is FS-OPA, initially designed for multidimensional analysis focused on MaOPs. FS-OPA generates explainable (explicit) models, has a relatively low computational cost (aiming at working with high dimensional decisions and objective spaces), and can deal with different data types and their mixtures.

First, this paper compares the principal features of an extension of FS-OPA to the NL-MVU-PCA approach (Duro et al. [12]) for determining the essential objective set. NL-MVU-PCA learns a Kernel matrix by unfolding a high-dimensional data manifold subject to local constraints that preserve the local isometry. Then, eigenvalues are used to identify the principal dimensions that should correspond to a set of conflicting objectives. On the other hand, FS-OPA uses no manifold learning; it maps the problem's fundamental structures into one or more phylograms (not a Cartesian graphical representation). FS-OPA employs data clustering, but not in the usual way, since it instantiates DAMICORE [17], a pipeline with Normalized-compressions distance (NCD), Neighbor-Joining (NJ), and Fast Newman algorithm, that produces intermediate representations enabling the detection of the strongest associations of dimensions. The embedding produced by FS-OPA does not focus on reducing the decision (or objective) space; otherwise, it augments the space by adding new variables, the internal nodes of the phylogram (while the terminal nodes correspond to the original variables). The phylogram construction also searches for preserving the isometry for different neighborhood sizes. Finally, FS-OPA can obtain similar results as manifold learning (i.e., the determination of the essential dimensions) by finding the closest common ancestors in a phylogram (a clade) and the frequency of common ancestors between clades (obtained from several phylograms by data resampling). Such ancestors highlight the principal relationships between variables and/or objectives.

Second, this paper applies the extension FS-OPA to the MOO of extruders, which requires dealing with the relatively poor data from initial populations of an MOEA. In other words, there is an assumption that the solutions belonging to a specific Pareto-optimal front have some characteristics that identify the optimal behavior of the process considered. The critical question is to know if it is possible, from a set of random solutions, as the initial population of an MOEA, to extract information about the complex relationship between the DVs and the objectives and between objectives and objectives. Therefore, the idea is to capture this type of information using data mining methods from multivariate data, independently of its location on the objectives or decision variables spaces, i.e., if the data represents or is not optimal (or near optimal) solutions. Moreover, no distinction between DVs and objectives will be made.

2.2. FS-OPA

The foundations of FS-OPA are based on two methodologies that deal with large-scale and multidimensional data of any type, named DAMICORE [17] and FS-OPA [18]. The latter is a pipeline involving methods from Information Theory, Complex Networks, and Phylogenetic Inference, aiming at revealing hidden relationships of objects from an unstructured (raw) dataset. It runs in three main Steps: (S1) given a metric of similarity, build a distance matrix comparing every two objects; (S2) convert the matrix into a phylogenetic tree by connecting close objects according to hierarchical levels of similarity; (S3) apply a community detection process to group near subtrees into clusters. Figure 1 shows a set of generic objects x_i. The elements d_{ij} of the distance matrix correspond to a measure of dissimilarities between objects xi and x_j, according to some given metric. The matrix is broken down into a tree, where the distance between any two objects (leaves) corresponds to the sum of the lengths of the branches connecting them. Finally, the third step merges objects strongly connected (according to the tree topology) into a community, generating a set of different similarity clusters.

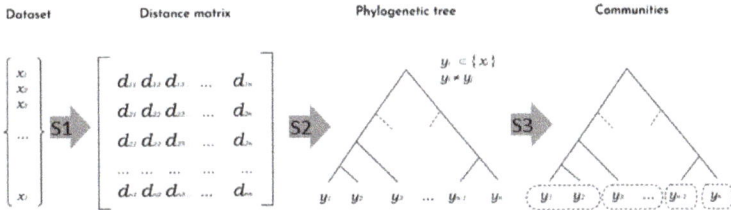

Figure 1. The tree-steps of the pipeline DAMICORE (reproduced from [18]).

The first implementation of DAMICORE used three specific algorithms for S1, S2, and S3 (Figure 1), respectively, Normalized Compression Distance (NCD) [19], as it works with for any data type and mixed types; Neighbor-Joining (NJ) [20], widely employed in bioinformatics; and Fast Newman (FN) [21], that constructs a graph partition using a greedy algorithm based on a bottom-up strategy for maximizing the graph modularity function [22]. The pipeline with NCD, NJ, and FN possesses some distinctive properties. NCD makes DAMICORE a data-type agnostic method; in the sense that it works with any object (continuous, discrete, categorical-ordinal, and nominal variables, texts, images, audio, etc.) and a mixture of data types.

DAMICORE has some properties that make it proper for dealing with problems with a low level of previous knowledge, carried out by non-experts, or that would require a large multidisciplinary team of experts. First, it can run without any data pre-processing (such as filtering, outlier detection, feature extraction, parameter setup, and knowledge of the problem domain). Second, it requires no parameters setup to run and is therefore not biased toward arbitrary tuning constants. Naturally, pre-processing steps and some execution options may improve the DAMICORE performance. Its success in such a challenge has been checked for problems in a variety of fields, such as software-hardware co-design [23–25], compiler optimization [26], student profiling in e-learning environments [27,28], identification of phytopathology from sensor data [29], systematic literature review, identification of cross-cut concerns [30], and electrical distribution systems [31].

A Feature Sensitivity (FS) analysis aims to make salient the principal features of a problem (that may differ from selecting the main components), facing common challenges in some classes of real-world problems. For example, the quality of observed data, the database consistency and representativeness, and the discovery of interactions between features and their contributions to each target or objective are hard to check from a raw dataset with low previous domain knowledge. Thus, such a scope differs from those where the standard feature selection algorithms have usually succeeded. Moreover, an FS strategy is expected to aid in learning the fundamental structures of a complex problem from scratch. The learned structures can induce a probabilistic model used by optimization algorithms, such as in the Estimation of Distribution Algorithms [32]. In this research, we use phylogram-based models since they can work with small datasets, they are computationally efficient, and there is an optimization approach designed to use such models: Optimization based on Phylogram Analysis (OPA).

Figure 2 shows a diagram summarizing OPA and its use of the FS analysis. Such a combination is called FS-OPA. The two main FS steps are (A) "Salienting Samples (SS) according to a criterion" and (B) applying DAMICORE to construct a phylogram-based model. SS ranks the samples according to each of the M criteria (or non-dominated fronts), producing the sets of selected samples (Figure 3), denoted BC1 (the samples in the best quantile according to Criterion 1), BC2, ..., BCM. DAMICORE constructs a phylogram (a rough model) from BCi, i = 1, ..., M, generating M models (BC1-based model, ..., BCM-based model). Then, a consensus strategy produces a unified phylogram-based model. An OPA cycle completes when the unified model generates new samples.

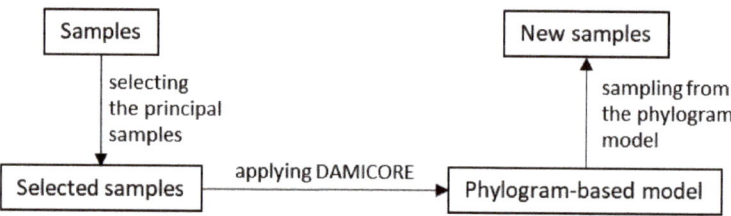

Figure 2. Diagram of the Optimization based on Phylogram Analysis—OPA.

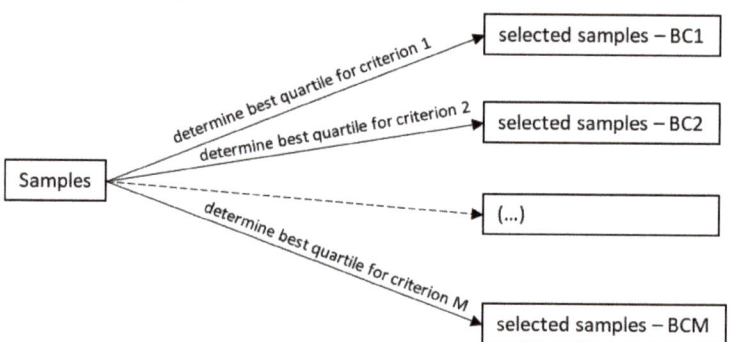

Figure 3. SS procedure that obtains the selected samples is shown in Figure 2.

OPA performance has been verified for relatively complex combinatorial mono- and multi-objective optimization problems [32]. Basic proofs concerning (stochastic) convergence to optima and time–space complexity have been provided [32,33].

2.3. Comparison of FS-OPA with NL-MVU-PCA for MaOPs Data-Driven Structural Learning

NL-MVU-PCA is the primary method used by Duro et al. [12] for finding the essential objective set in MaOPs. Such a scheme also runs PCA based on the objective–function correlation matrix, aiming to improve objectives' preference ranking. On the other hand, NL-MVU-PCA maximizes the variance in objective space while preserving the local isometry (common property in dimensionality reduction through embedding's). NL-MVU-PCA is computationally more complex than PCA since the former solves an optimization problem. The non-linear (NL) approach performs the optimization of the Kernel (Gram) matrix values by minimizing the Maximum Variance Unfolding (MVU) to find the best mapping that preserves the geometric properties of each neighbourhood.

Table 1 synthesizes some relevant properties of NL-MVU-PCA and FS-OPA for MaOPs. The latter analyses three types of associations: variable-variable (producing results similar to the Gibbs measure for Ising Models or Markov Random fields [34]), objective–objective (the dissimilarities, when found, can favour the construction of (non-dominated) front distributions [35]), and the variable–objective (that may benefit inference as Markov Blankets [36]). The former works on the objective space for space reduction to determine the essential objective set [12]. FS-OPA also has other properties that are relevant for some classes of real-world problems: (i) it preserves the original variable space, which favours non-experts interpretability; (ii) it works with any data type (continuous, discrete, categorical—not only ordinal, but also nominal data, addressed by Bandaru et al. [4]) and mixed types (proper for multiple heterogeneous databases with observed data); (iii) it has a relatively low time complexity; (iv) and, finally, it has generated applicable models when applied to learn from small datasets [17,23–31].

Table 1. NL-MVU-PCA and FS-OPA for multidimensional data-driven structural learning applied to real-world MaOPs.

Category	Types		NL-MVU-PCA	FS-OPA
Analyses	Objective-objective		X	X
	Variable-variable			X
	Variable-objective			X
	Objective space reduction		X	
	Sensitivity			X
Priors	Kernel function usage		X	Not necessary
	Parameter optimization		X [#]	Not necessary
Variable and objective representation	Continuous		X	X
	Discrete (integers, real intervals)		X	X
	Ordinal		X	X
	Nominal		X	X
	Mixed			X
Explainability	Implicit		X	
	Explicit (The Why)			X
User-friendliness	Stakeholders can easily run FS-OPA and understand results even for a large number of variables and/or objectives			X
Scalability	Time-complexity	Usual cases	$O(M^3 q^3)$ *	$O(l^3)$ **
		The worst case	$O(M^6)$	$O(nl^2 + l^3)$
	Sample-size support		Empirical	Theoretical and empirical

* M is the number of objectives, and q is the number of clusters; ** l is the number of variables and objectives, and n is the number of data resamples; [#] Reference [5] shows that one can avoid parameter optimization for a new problem by choosing $q = M - 1$ for NL-MVU-PCA.

Reference [5] shows the use of NL-MVU-PCA for a mixed-variable problem, the gearbox problem (with continuous and discrete variables and continuous objectives). NL-MVU-PCA works on the (continuous) objective vectors for the gearbox problem. It differs from the meaning of mixed in Table 1, which relates to both the variable and objective representation (important for the "explicit explainability"), i.e., the mixture may include data vectors simultaneously from both spaces with different types. Moreover, FS-OPA can naturally work with any number of combinations of data types due to its foundation on NCD.

Concerning Explainability, "Explicit" means to provide a knowledge representation (with clues for "The Why" as the potential influence of variables on objectives) that benefits decision-maker interaction, while "Implicit" refers to the capacity to reveal the objectives' relative importance for an optimization problem, e.g., by ranking them.

The Feature Sensitivity (FS) analysis of FS-OPA aims at finding the variable and/or objective data-driven interactions to construct structural (graph-based) and probabilistic modelling. Probabilistic results are fundamental when dealing with the odds of bias in observed data or small-data sampling. Explainability is also essential for some classes of real-world problems, mainly those concerning decisions by stakeholders. Moreover, a user-friendly tool (instantiating the FS-OPA methodology) is relevant for real-world applications involving practitioners or stakeholders who are not optimization or artificial intelligence experts. Variable–variable and variable–objective interactions can also benefit practitioners' comprehension (The Why), increasing their confidence. Finally, the phylogram-based representation of those interactions has scaled up the understanding of results for some problems with dozens of variables or objectives (note that the interactive data mining approach proposed by Bandaru et al. [4] works with two or three objectives).

Table 1 also shows the time complexity for usual cases and the worst case to estimate the overhead of both procedures. The number of clusters in NL-MVU-PCA relates to the number of constraints to maintain the local isometry (M q; but in the worst case $q = M - 1$, resulting in M2) [12]. FS-OPA with usual resampling is $O(l^3)$ since $n \leq 1$ (as in leave-one-out resampling) [34]. Moreover, $l = M$ in a space analysis only uses objectives. Thus, the time complexities of FS-OPA and NL-MVU-PCA have a ratio $(n + M)/M^4$ (l/q^3) of running time for $l = M$ in the worst case (in the usual case).

Another relevant factor is the minimal samples required to ensure reliable findings. Usually, the sample size for the PCA-based approach is empirically determined. FS-OPA has a theoretical model to decide the minimal amount of samples that guarantees high confidence in the results, which has been empirically corroborated for relatively complex problems in the decision space of binary variables [32].

2.4. FS-OPA Framework

Figure 4 shows a flowchart of the global procedure of FS-OPA to reduce the number of objectives. Two options exist (i) automatic procedure, and (ii) procedure with the intervention of the DM(s). In the first case, the selection of the number of objectives to be used in the optimization is defined by the program automatically, using the table of the distance between objectives and applying the following rules:

1. choose the objective(s) of the less distant clusters;
2. choose one objective of the more distant (single) cluster;
3. choose one objective from each of the remaining clusters.

In the second case, the selection is made by the DM(s), using both the phylogram and the table with the distance of objectives–objectives, as follows:

1. choose the objective(s) of the less distant clusters;
2. choose one objective of the more distant (single) cluster;
3. choose objective(s) from each of the remaining clusters taking into account, also, the phylogram and the knowledge of the DM(s) about the process.

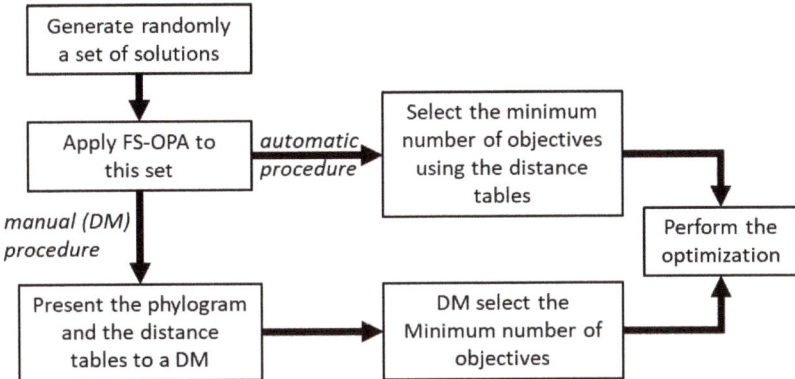

Figure 4. The general procedure of FS-OPA for the reduction of the number of objectives.

The reasons for rules 1 and 2 are different: the less distant cluster is the one that transports more information concerning the entire process, since it is near most of the decision variables, while the more distant cluster, besides everything, also has some information about the process that cannot be lost. The idea is that the intermediate clusters, selected by rule 3, have some information regarding the process that is already present in the objectives selected by rules 1 and 2, and thus, the objectives that can be discarded are those that belong to these clusters.

Both cases will be illustrated in the next section using a practical example. However, there are advantages and disadvantages to using one or the other. The first procedure provides the final solution directly, but the DM(s) does not take part in the process, which can imply some discomfort and distrust with the solution found. This does not happen when, after the analysis of the initial population of solutions, the DM(s) is confronted with relevant information about the process and, given these intermediate results, is asked about a possible way to advance. We are facing a situation in which the results may be explainable to the DM(s).

3. Examples of Application: DTLZ Benchmark Problems

A strategy to deal with many-objective real-world complex optimization problems (e.g., those with no explicit objective functions) is prioritizing objectives. In the case of unknown priorities, their relative importance can be estimated from samples of the decision space, as proposed in this paper. Such prioritization has a certain resemblance to the problem of determining the essential objective set, since a redundant objective has low priority.

The DTLZ problems (with and without redundant objectives) have been used to test the method's capacity to find such a set and to evaluate algorithms for many-objective optimization. Some algorithms have succeeded in finding the set from samples in POF, near POF, or, for example, from the last generation of an NSGAII run, although more recently, some of them failed for new challenging problems with other types of redundancies, as shown in [37]. This way, evaluating how much FS-OPA can estimate objectives' relevance for DTLZs from a random population (or from the first fronts of it) may be useful, since they are well-known problems.

Figure 5A illustrates an FS-OPA output for unconstrained DTLZ5, also used by Duro et al. [12] for explaining the capacity of their method to find redundant objectives (objectives $f_1, f_2, f_3, f_4, f_5, f_6, f_7, f_8$, and f_9 are linearly correlated in DTLZ5). A random population of size 31 with samples normalized and Euclidian distance was used to obtain a distance matrix. SS procedure in Figure 3 was not applied. The output of Figure 5A shows variables and objectives arranged into a phylogram with leaf nodes (the objects under analysis) composing clusters (similarly to the end of the pipeline in Figure 1)—they are identified by the same color.

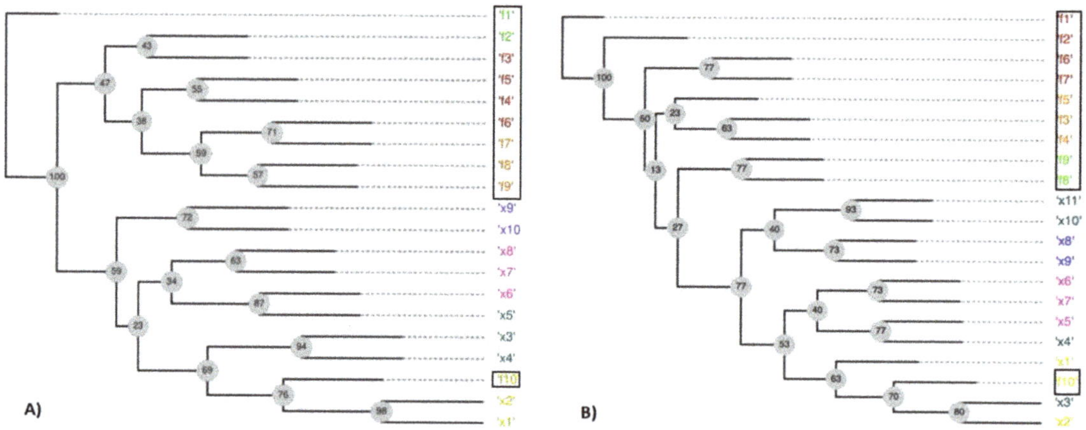

Figure 5. Phylogram and the clusters found: (**A**) for unconstrained DTLZ5 with 10 objectives and (**B**) for constrained DTLZ5 (2,10).

Objective functions $f_1, \ldots, f_9$ are partitioned into three neighbor clusters ($\{f_1, f_2\}$, $\{f_3, f_4, f_5, f_6\}$, and $\{f_7, f_8, f_9\}$) in the phylogram structure; while f_{10} is together with the leaf nodes, corresponding to variables. The phylogram structure aggregates $f_1, \ldots,$ and f_9 into the same subtree, while f_{10} is isolated from the other objectives in the complementary subtree. The unique node with the label "100" (another type of result from a tree consensus) splits the phylogram into those two subtrees. Such a label ("100") means that the leaf nodes f_{10} and $x_1, \ldots, x_{10}$, and f_{10} were in the same subtree (with the remaining leaf nodes in the complementary subtree) in 100% of all the constructed phylograms, independently of each subtree topology in a phylogram. Such an interpretation suggests a hypothesis: f_{10} is weakly correlated to the other objectives, which are significantly associated with themselves. Thus, f_{10} and one of the other objectives could compose an essential objective set; this result is consistent with the DTLZ5 problem structure.

Figure 5B shows the proposed phylogram for DTLZ5(2,10) with constraints (Saxena et al. [5]). It requires an additional variable, x_{11}, to generate samples outside POF, as samples used to construct a phylogram from Figure 5A. The phylogram from Figure 5B shows that f_{10} is isolated in a subtree, while $f_1, \ldots, f_9$ are in the complementary subtrees. Such a result suggests that f_{10} and f_1 (for example) would enable proper POF estimates; this result agrees with the DTLZ5(2,10) problem structure.

Figure 6 shows the phylograms obtained by FS-OPA for DTLZs 1–4 obtained from random populations of size 31 as a way to check if the FS-OPA clues about the objective relationships are plausible.

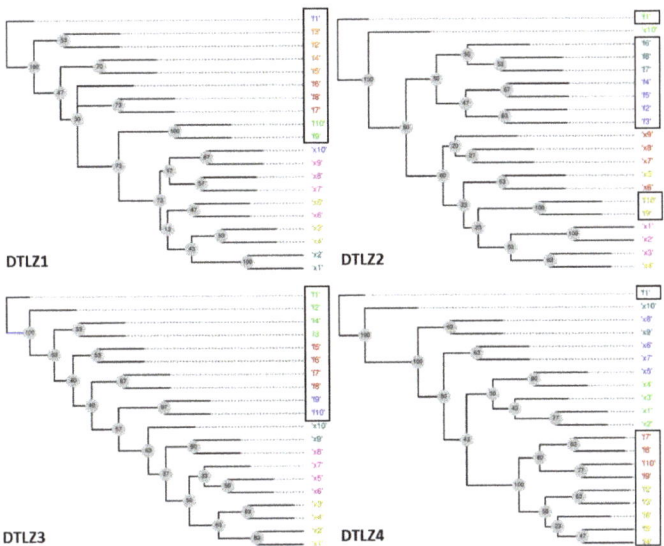

Figure 6. Phylogram and the clusters found for DTLZ1 to DTLZ4 with 10 objectives.

Given that these problems do not have redundant objectives, the unique possibility is to present some clue about the prioritization of objectives, considering that a reduction in the number of objectives only can be made with a certain error, as explained before. For example, the behaviours of functions DTLZ1, DTLZ2, and DTLZ3 are very similar. The simultaneous analysis of the clusters found and of the distances between objectives and the decision variables show that objectives can be portioned in the following sets:

- DTLZ1: $\{f_1\}$, $\{f_2, f_3, f_4, f_5\}$, $\{f_6, f_7, f_8\}$, $\{f_9\}$ and $\{f_{10}\}$;
- DTLZ2: $\{f_1\}$, $\{f_2, f_3, f_4, f_5\}$, $\{f_6, f_7, f_8\}$, $\{f_9\}$ and $\{f_{10}\}$;
- DTLZ3: $\{f_1\}$, $\{f_2, f_3, f_4\}$, $\{f_5, f_6, f_7, f_8\}$, $\{f_9\}$ and $\{f_{10}\}$;
- DTLZ4: $\{f_1\}$, $\{f_2, f_3, f_4\}$, $\{f_5, f_6\}$ and $\{f_7, f_8, f_9, f_{10}\}$;

This signifies that a possible hierarchization of the objectives for these problems can be made by selecting, in the first step, a single objective of the groups identified above and then, by selecting all the others to a second level.

In addition, all the objectives in the phylograms found for DTLZ2 and DTLZ4 are not in a subtree without a variable. That may mean that the disagreement of objectives of those two problems is more salient from an initial random sampling.

However, the objective of this paper is not only to define the minimum number of objectives that can be used without error but also to identify the situations where the reduction can be done with a certain error. Anyway, a deep analysis will be necessary here, which is outside of the scope of the present paper.

The FS-OPA also produces other outputs (useful for human comprehension of some classes of real-world problems), which are explored in Sections related to the extrusion problem.

4. Polymer Extrusion Problem

4.1. The Problem to Solve

To demonstrate the complexity of this system regarding the modelling program and the interrelations between the decision variables and the objectives, some details are given here. However, the system is much more complex, as can be seen in the following references [38–41].

Figure 7A shows an axial cut of the extruder and die fitted with a barrier screw. The sequence of the physical phenomena developing typically along the screw is also represented, and comprises [38–40]: (i) gravity conveying of the solid material in the hopper; (ii) drag solids conveying in the first screw turns; (iii) development of a thin film of melted material separating the solids from the surrounding metallic walls; (iv) melting of the solid plug, with physical separation of the solid plug from the melt pool; (v) melt conveying following a relatively complex regular helical flow pattern; vi) pressure flow through the die. Figure 7B shows the complex flow pattern quantified by the velocity fields and the temperature profile in the Conventional Screw (CS) and Maillefer Barrier Screw (MBS), while Figure 7C shows the complete system geometry used in the calculations.

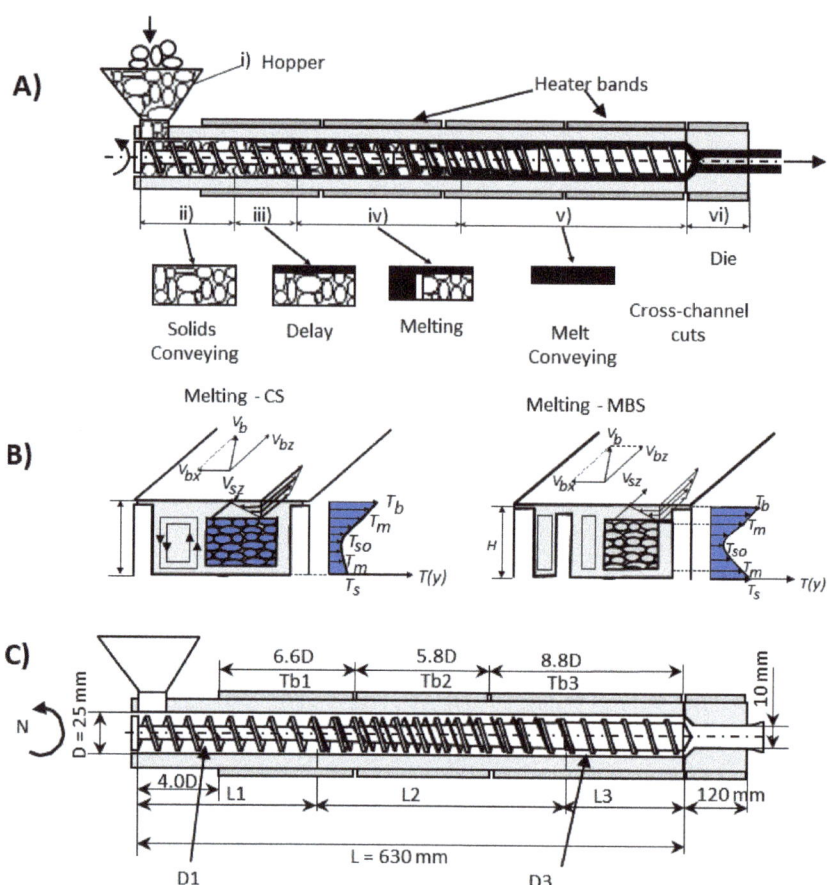

Figure 7. Single screw extrusion: (**A**) plasticating phases; (**B**) melting mechanism in CS (left) and MBS (right); (**C**) specific system geometry used in the calculations.

The aim is to determine if the best solution is to use a CS or an MBS for fixed and/or for changing operating conditions and, simultaneously, to optimize the corresponding geometry.

The following equations represent the momentum and energy equations for the melted region of the channel (melting and melt conveying in Figure 7), which resulted from some specific simplifications of the general tri-dimensional (3D) set of equations. These equations were solved numerically, considering a 2D space representing the cross-screw channel (X and Y directions) for small increments along the channel (Z direction). However, it is necessary to note that all the regions identified above and in Figure 7 have different thermomechanical models that must be put together using the appropriate boundary conditions. This is a very complex system in which the polymer properties, the operating conditions of the machine, and the screw geometry contribute in a complex way to measure the process performance quantified by the objectives (see Table 2).

Table 2. Optimization objectives, aim of optimization and range of variation.

Objectives	Aim	x_{min}	x_{max}
Output—Q (kg/hr)	Maximize	1	20
Length for melting—L (m)	Minimize	0.1	0.9
Melt temperature—T (°C)	Minimize	150	210
Power consumption—$Power$ (W)	Minimize	0	9200
WATS	Maximize	0	1300
Viscous dissipation—$Viscous$	Minimize	0.9	1.2

For example, to only illustrate the complexity of this process and the corresponding numerical modelling, Equation (3) shows the melt rate per unit of channel length (Φ) that represents the quantification of solids material that changes the physical state to melt in each of the increments along the screw channel. However, we must take into account that it is an analytical model that resulted from further simplifications of Equations (1) and (2). For more details of the model used, the reader is referred to references [41–43].

$$\frac{\partial P}{\partial z} = \frac{\partial}{\partial y}\left(\eta \frac{\partial V_z}{\partial x}\right) + \frac{\partial}{\partial y}\left(\eta \frac{\partial V_z}{\partial y}\right) \tag{1}$$

$$\rho_m\, C_s\, V_z(y) \frac{\partial T}{\partial z} = k_m \left(\frac{\partial^2 T}{\partial x^2} + \frac{\partial^2 T}{\partial y^2}\right) + \eta\, \dot{\gamma}^2 \tag{2}$$

$$\Phi = \left(\left\{\frac{V_{bx}\rho_m\left[k_m(T_b - T_m) + \frac{\eta}{2}V_j^2\right]}{2\left[C_s(T_m - T_{s0}) + C_m(T_{avg} - T_m) + h\right]}\right\}\right)^{1/2} \tag{3}$$

The variables in these equations represent the polymer properties, operating conditions and flow variables: ρ_m is the melt density, k_m is the melt thermal conductivity, h is the melting entropy, C_m and C_s are specific heat of melt and solids, respectively, T_m is the melting temperature, η is the melt viscosity, T_{so} and T_c are the solids and the barrel temperatures, $\dot{\gamma}$ is the shear rate, T is the melt temperature in each node of the mesh, T_{avg} is the average temperature of the melt, V_z is the melt velocity in the Z direction, V_s is the solid velocity in the y direction, and V_{bx} is the barrel velocity in the X direction.

Therefore, the performance of the process depends on the polymer properties, machine operating conditions and geometry. In the present example, a Low-Density Polyethylene (LDPE) is used, and for the operating conditions, two situations are considered, as shown in Table 3, i.e., in some cases, they are fixed, and in one of the cases, they are also considered as a DVs. The DVs are the operating conditions and the geometrical parameters as identified in Tables 3 and 4, respectively.

Table 3. Cases studied for LDPE—only in case 7 the operating are used as decision variables.

Case	Operating Conditions	Decision Variables				
		N (rpm)	Tb1 (°C)	Tb2 (°C)	Tb3 (°C)	Geometry
1	Constant	40	140	150	160	Table 4
2	Constant	60	140	150	160	Table 4
3	Constant	80	140	150	160	Table 4
4	Variable	[40, 80]	[140, 160]	[150, 170]	[160, 200]	Table 4

Math. Comput. Appl. 2023, 28, 17

Table 4. Geometrical parameters of both CS and MBS screws.

Screw Type		Decision Variables							
CS	case	L1	L2	H1	H3	P	e	Hf	wf
MBS		L1_	L2_	H1_	H3_	P_	e_		
Interval	[0, 1]	[100, 400]	[170, 400]	[18, 22]	[22, 26]	[25, 35]	[3, 4]	[0.1, 0.6]	[3, 4]

The performance of the machine was quantified using six objectives, two to maximize (output and degree of mixing) and four to minimize (length of screw required to melt the polymer, melt temperature at the exit, mechanical power consumption required to rotate the screw, and viscous dissipation quantified as the ratio between the melt temperature and the fixed barrel temperature), as shown in Table 2.

The geometrical parameters involved in the description of both types of screws are shown in Table 4. Since only one screw can be used each time in the machine, an additional decision variable was added, identified as "case," to trigger the decision variables corresponding to one of the types of screws, i.e., when case ranges in the interval [0.0, 0.5] the decision variables of the conventional screw are used, while when case ranges in the interval [0.5, 1.0], the other screw is considered. Consequently, the total number of decision variables is 15.

For each case studied (Table 3), 11 optimization runs are made for statistical comparison using the hypervolume (HV) and the Inverted Generational Distance (IGD).

4.2. Results and Discussion

The FS-OPA analysis for Cases 1 and 4 are presented in Figure 8 and Tables 5 and 6. The results were very similar, generating the same three groups of objectives, (Q, L), (Power, WATS), and (T, TTb). The application of the methodology defined in Section 2.4 allows for identifying the objectives Q, Power, WATS, and T to be used in the optimization after reduction (see Tables 5 and 6): (i) the objectives with lower distance. Power and WATS; (ii) one objective of the cluster with higher distance, T; and (iii) one objective of the remaining cluster, Q. It is clear, also, that instead of T, it is possible to select TTb, and instead of Q, it is possible to select L.

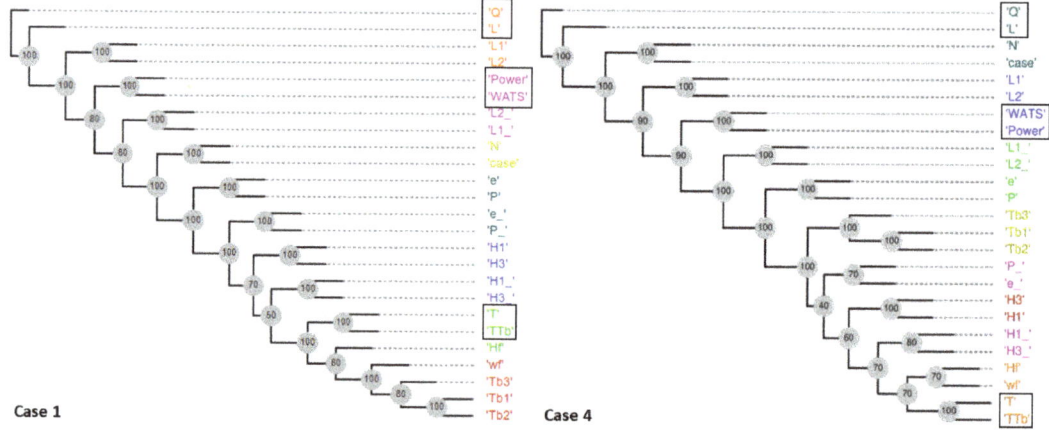

Figure 8. Phylograms for Cases 1 and 4 (Table 3).

Table 5. Distances between the objectives for Case 1.

	'Q'	'L'	'T'	'Power'	'WATS'	'TTb'	Average
'Q'	0.00	0.07	0.73	0.27	0.27	0.73	**0.345**
'L'	0.07	0.00	0.73	0.27	0.27	0.73	**0.345**
'T'	0.73	0.73	0.00	0.67	0.67	0.07	**0.478**
'Power'	0.27	0.27	0.67	0.00	0.07	0.67	**0.325**
'WATS'	0.27	0.27	0.67	0.07	0.00	0.67	**0.325**
'TTb'	0.73	0.73	0.07	0.67	0.67	0.00	**0.478**

Table 6. Distances between the objectives for Case 4.

	'Q'	'L'	'T'	'Power'	'WATS'	'TTb'	Average
'Q'	0.00	0.08	1.00	0.42	0.42	1.00	0.480
'L'	0.08	0.00	1.00	0.42	0.42	1.00	0.480
'T'	1.00	1.00	0.00	0.83	0.83	0.08	0.620
'Power'	0.42	0.42	0.83	0.00	0.08	0.83	0.430
'WATS'	0.42	0.42	0.83	0.08	0.00	0.83	0.430
'TTb'	1.00	1.00	0.08	0.83	0.83	0.00	0.620

To assess the capacity of using only the four objectives selected, the optimization results obtained using SMS-EMOA provided with the problem with these four objectives will be compared with the case with the initial six objectives using the Pareto-optimal fronts obtained after 100 generations for a population of 100 individuals in each generation and 11 runs with different seeds values are made for statistical comparison. Additionally, this comparison will be made with a situation with three objectives one of each of the clusters found, specifically Q, WATS, and T.

Figures 9 and 10 show the Pareto-optimal fronts found in each one of the cases (Case 1 and Case 2) using the three sets of objectives: (i) all objectives; (ii) objectives Q, Power, WATS, and T; (iii) objectives Q, WATS, and T. The results are, apparently, very similar when comparing the cases with six and four objectives. In the other situation, with three objectives, the multi-objective optimization algorithm is clearly lost, since the final solution found alternates in the different runs between one type of screw and the other (i.e., between the CS and the MBS). The results for Cases 2 and 3 are very similar to those presented here and, thus, no specific discussion is made here.

By using the 11 runs performed for each case studied, the Hypervolume (HV) and the Inverted Generational Distance (IGD) were applied and the results are presented in Table 7, where it is possible to see the average and the percentage of losses when the number of objectives is reduced [42–44]. To calculate IGD, all Pareto-optimal solutions found in each run were put together in a pool and the non-dominated solutions of this pool were used for comparison.

As shown in Table 7, it is possible to conclude that the use of four objectives (Q, Power, WATS, and T) does not significantly deteriorate the final solutions found, the maximum difference found is 11.6%, which, for a process like the extrusion process, and taking into account a final population of 100 solutions, is not expressive. Additionally, the differences in the IGD value are too small, indicating that at least the solutions found for the case of four objectives are near the best solution found in the 11 runs. The results found for the situation with three objectives corroborate the results shown in Figures 9 and 10.

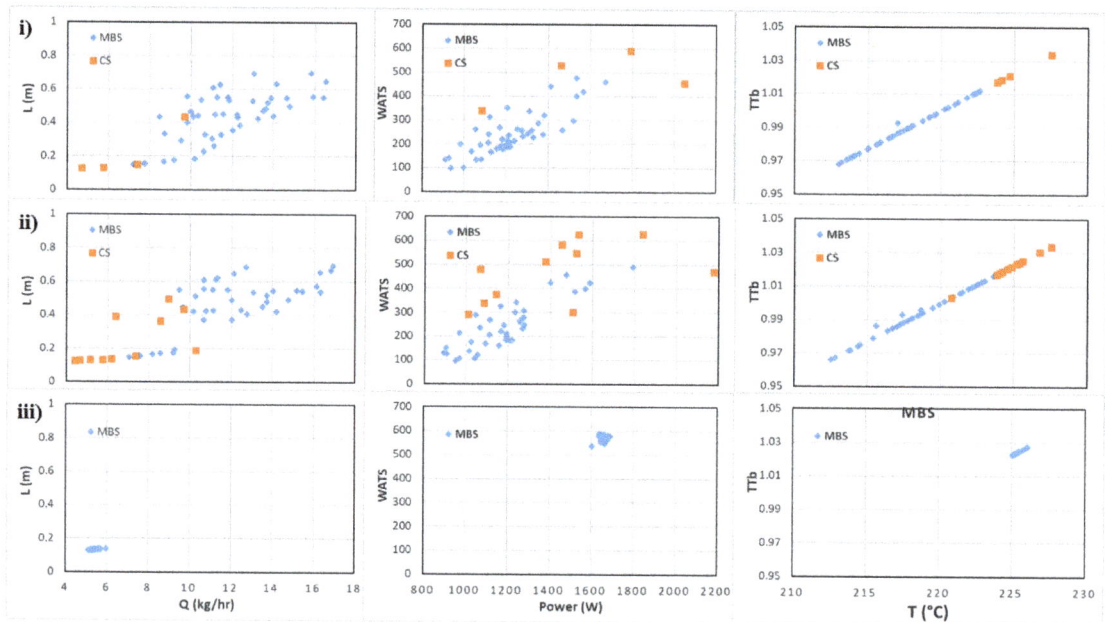

Figure 9. Pareto-optimal fronts after 100 generations for the pair of objectives identified in Figure 8 for Case 1.

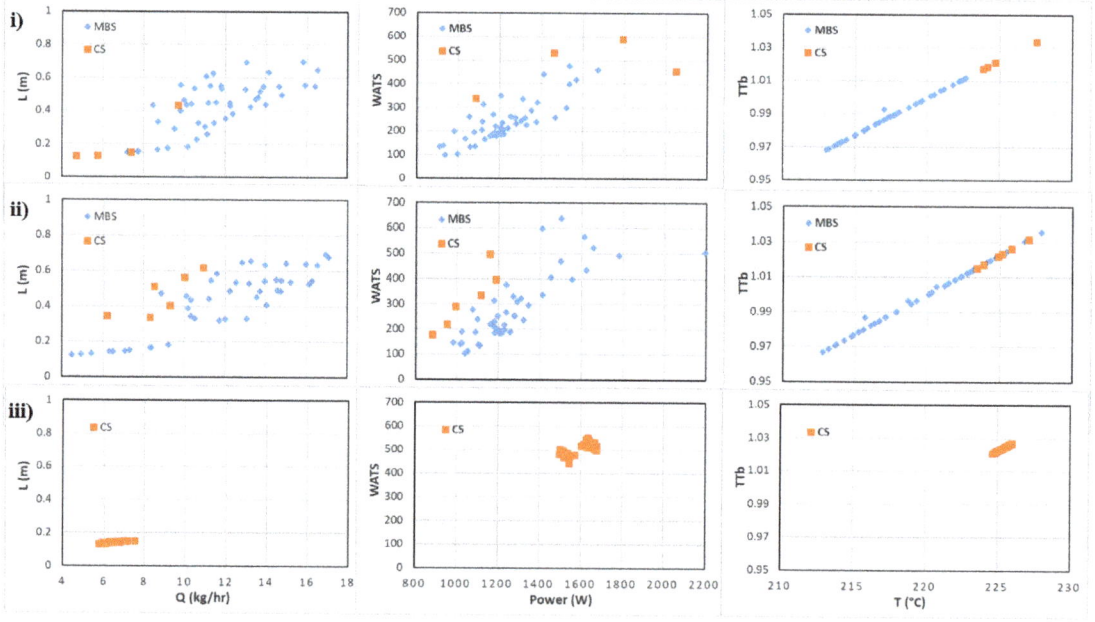

Figure 10. Pareto-optimal fronts after 100 generations for the pair of objectives identified in Figure 8 for Case 7.

Table 7. Performance comparison using Hypervolume and IGD for the total number of objectives and the automatic reduction to four and three objectives (between brackets the standard deviation, and loss percentage relative to six objectives) for the four cases studied.

Case Study	Metric	6 Objectives	4 Objectives (Q, Power, WATS, T)	3 Objectives (Q, WATS, T)
1	HV	0.21518 (0.008145)	0.19148 (0.012324) −11.0%	0.02555 (0.024707) −88.1%
	IGD	0.10966 (0.004972)	0.11159 (0.003607) −1.76%	0.66727 (0.143866) −508%
2	HV	0.23233 (0.013760)	0.20867 (0.010411) −10.2%	0.04689 (0.028991) −79.8%
	IGD	0.10966 (0.004972)	0.11205 (0.003526) −2.17%	0.69042 (0.105262) −529%
3	HV	0.24809 (0.006384)	0.21932 (0.014301) −11.6%	0.04598 (0.0285391) −81.5%
	IGD	0.11076 (0.005756)	0.11326 (0.006315) −2.25%	0.69042 (0.105262) −523%
4	HV	0.24809 (0.006384)	0.22911 (0.009955) −7.7%	0.01967 (0.011256) −92.1%
	IGD	0.11076 (0.005756)	0.11431 (0.007949) −3.21%	0.72078 (0.046369) −550%

Finally, it is important to point out that during this process, the DM(s) play an important role in the procedure. Indeed, they have some intervention when selecting the objectives. For example, it is necessary to opt for Q or L, two objectives from the same cluster having apparently the same importance in the process. In this case, an informed DM will make the option for Q because this objective is the output of the machine and is directly linked with the economic issue of the problem, while L is the length for melting that is related to the quality of the product obtained; however, this quality is also quantified by WATS, which was already selected by the algorithm. This example shows the importance of the DM(s) that simultaneously help the optimization process and are informed about the process of obtaining the results.

5. Conclusions

A methodology for reducing the number of objectives for many-objective optimization problems using population-based algorithms is proposed. This approach, based on machine learning, is an improvement over similar state-of-the-art methodologies; namely, it allows analysis of the relations variable–variable and variable–objective relations (and not only objective–objective), does not need kernel function choice and parameters optimization, allows for obtaining explainable solutions to assist the decision maker with interpreting the results, its time complexity is also low, and it supports theoretical and empirical sample sizes.

The approach showed its potential to reduce the number of objectives by capturing the complex relations between the different objectives with an additional possibility, which is to capture the objective-variable relations. This is done by applying the methodology to a set of benchmark and real-world problems. The comparison of the Pareto-optimal fronts obtained with another machine learning approach in the literature allows for the conclusion that its performance is very competitive, but with the great advantage of being much easier to use. Additionally, there is the possibility of strong interaction with the DM(s).

The application of the proposed approach to a difficult real-world problem has proven that it is automatically possible to reduce the number of objectives by losing only around ten percent of the Pareto-optimal frontier obtained, for the case of 100 individuals in the population. The use of a second possibility, which is to require the intervention of the decision maker during the process, e.g., when selecting the objectives to be considered in the optimization, can be very useful because the person interested can see how the process works and interpret the results obtained. Finally, an important characteristic of the method proposed is the capacity to explain the solutions found.

Author Contributions: Conceptualization, A.G.-C., F.M. and A.D.; methodology, A.G.-C., F.M. and A.D.; software, P.C.; investigation, A.G.-C. and A.D.; resources, A.G.-C.; data curation, A.G.-C.; writing—original draft preparation, A.G.-C. and A.D.; writing—review and editing, A.G.-C.; visualization; supervision, A.G.-C. and A.D.; project administration, A.G.-C. and A.D.; funding acquisition, A.G.-C., F.M. and A.D. All authors have read and agreed to the published version of the manuscript.

Funding: This research was funded by POR Norte under the PhD Grant PRT/BD/152192/2021. The authors also acknowledge the funding by FEDER funds through the COMPETE 2020 Programme and National Funds through FCT (Portuguese Foundation for Science and Technology) under the projects UID-B/05256/2020, and UID-P/05256/2020, the Center for Mathematical Sciences Applied to Industry (CeMEAI) and the support from the São Paulo Research Foundation (FAPESP grant No 2013/07375-0, the Center for Artificial Intelligence (C4AI-USP), the support from the São Paulo Research Foundation (FAPESP grant No 2019/07665-4) and the IBM Corporation.

Data Availability Statement: Not applicable.

Conflicts of Interest: The authors declare no conflict of interest.

References

1. Deb, K. *Multi-Objective Optimization using Evolutionary Algorithms*; Wiley: Chichester, UK, 2001.
2. Carlos, A.; Coello, C.; Gary, B.L.; David, A.V.V. *Evolutionary Algorithms for Solving Multi-Objective Problems*, 2nd ed.; Springer: New York, NY, USA, 2007.
3. Boussaïd, I.; Lepagnot, J.; Siarry, P. A survey on optimization metaheuristics. *Inf. Sci.* **2013**, *237*, 82–117. [CrossRef]
4. Bandaru, S.; Ng, A.H.C.; Deb, K. Data mining methods for knowledge discovery in multi-objective optimization: Part A—Survey. *Expert Syst. Appl.* **2017**, *70*, 139–159. [CrossRef]
5. Saxena, D.K.; Duro, J.A.; Tiwari, A.; Deb, K.; Zhang, Q. Objective Reduction in Many-Objective Optimization: Linear and Nonlinear Algorithms. *IEEE Trans. Evol. Comput.* **2013**, *17*, 77–99. [CrossRef]
6. Brockhoff, D.; Zitzler, E. Are All Objectives Necessary? On Dimensionality Reduction in Evolutionary Multiobjective Optimization. In *Lecture Notes in Computer Science*; Springer: Berlin/Heidelberg, Germany, 2006; pp. 533–542. [CrossRef]
7. Brockhoff, D.; Zitzler, E. Objective Reduction in Evolutionary Multiobjective Optimization: Theory and Applications. *Evol. Comput.* **2009**, *17*, 135–166. [CrossRef]
8. López, J.A.; Coello, C.C.A.; Chakraborty, D. Objective reduction using a feature selection technique. In Proceedings of the 10th Annual Conference on Genetic and Evolutionary Computation—GECCO '08, Atlanta, GA, USA, 12–16 July 2008. [CrossRef]
9. Singh, H.K.; Isaacs, A.; Ray, T. A Pareto Corner Search Evolutionary Algorithm and Dimensionality Reduction in Many-Objective Optimization Problems. *IEEE Trans. Evol. Comput.* **2011**, *15*, 539–556. [CrossRef]
10. Deb, K.; Saxena, D.K. Searching for Pareto-optimal solutions through dimensionality reduction for certain large-dimensional multi-objective optimization problems. In Proceedings of the 2006 IEEE Congress on Evolutionary Computation (CEC'2006), Vancouver, BC, Canada, 16–21 July 2006; IEEE: Vancouver, BC, Canada, 2006; pp. 3353–3360.
11. Saxena, D.K.; Deb, K. Non-linear Dimensionality Reduction Procedures for Certain Large-Dimensional Multi-Objective Optimization Problems: Employing Correntropy and a Novel Maximum Variance Unfolding. In *Evolutionary Multi-Criterion Optimization*; Obayashi, S., Deb, K., Poloni, C., Hiroyasu, T., Murata, T., Eds.; Springer: Berlin/Heidelberg, Germany, 2007; Volume 4403. [CrossRef]
12. Duro, J.A.; Saxena, K.D.; Deb, K.; Zhang, Q. Machine learning based decision support for many-objective optimization problems. *Neurocomputing* **2014**, *146*, 30–47. [CrossRef]
13. Yuan, Y.; Ong, Y.-S.; Gupta, A.; Xu, H. Objective Reduction in Many-Objective Optimization: Evolutionary Multiobjective Approaches and Comprehensive Analysis. *IEEE Trans. Evol. Comput.* **2018**, *22*, 189–210. [CrossRef]
14. Gunduz, A.; Principe, J.C. Correntropy as a novel measure for nonlinearity tests. *Signal Process.* **2009**, *89*, 14–23. [CrossRef]
15. Sinha, A.; Saxena, D.K.; Deb, K.; Tiwari, A. Using objective reduction and interactive procedure to handle many-objective optimization problems. *Appl. Soft Comput.* **2013**, *13*, 415–427. [CrossRef]
16. Bandaru, S.; Ng, A.H.C.; Deb, K. Data mining methods for knowledge discovery in multi-objective optimization: Part B—New developments and applications. *Expert Syst. Appl.* **2017**, *70*, 119–138. [CrossRef]
17. Sanches, A.; Cardoso, J.M.; Delbem, A.C. Identifying merge-beneficial software kernels for hardware implementation. In Proceedings of the International Conference on Reconfigurable Computing and FPGAs (ReConFig), Cancun, Mexico, 30 November–2 December 2011; pp. 74–79.
18. Gholi Zadeh Kharrat, F.; Shydeo Brandão Miyoshi, N.; Cobre, J.; Mazzoncini De Azevedo-Marques, J.; Mazzoncini de Azevedo-Marques, P.; Cláudio Botazzo Delbem, A. Feature sensitivity criterion-based sampling strategy from the Optimization based on Phylogram Analysis (Fs-OPA) and Cox regression applied to mental disorder datasets. *PLoS ONE* **2020**, *15*, e0235147. [CrossRef]
19. Lui, L.T.; Terrazas, G.; Zenil, H.; Alexander, C.; Krasnogor, N. Complexity Measurement Based on Information Theory and Kolmogorov Complexity. *Artif. Life* **2015**, *21*, 205–224. [CrossRef] [PubMed]

20. Saitou, N.; Nei, M. The neighbor-joining method: A new method for reconstructing phylogenetic trees. *Mol. Biol. Evol.* **1987**, *4*, 406–425. [PubMed]
21. Newman, M.E. Fast algorithm for detecting community structure in networks. *Phys. Rev. E* **2004**, *69*, 066133. [CrossRef] [PubMed]
22. Newman, M.E. Modularity and community structure in networks. *Proc. Natl. Acad. Sci. USA* **2006**, *103*, 8577–8582. [CrossRef]
23. Silva, B.D.A.; Cuminato, L.A.; Delbem, A.C.B.; Diniz, P.C.; Bonato, V. Application-oriented cache memorybconfiguration for energy efficiency in multi-cores. *IET Comput. Digit. Tech.* **2015**, *9*, 73–81. [CrossRef]
24. Silva, B.A.; Delbem, A.C.B.; Deniz, P.C.; Bonato, V. Runtime mapping and scheduling for energy efficiency in heterogeneous multi-core systems. In Proceedings of the International Conference on Reconfigurable Computing and FPGAs, Mayan Riviera, Mexico, 7–9 December 2015; pp. 1–6.
25. Martins, L.G.A.; Nobre, R.; Delbem, A.C.B.; Marques, E.; Cardoso, J.M.P. A clustering-based approach for exploring sequences of compiler optimizations. In Proceedings of the 2014 IEEE Congress on Evolutionary Computation (CEC), Beijing, China, 6–11 July 2014; pp. 2436–2443. [CrossRef]
26. Martins, L.G.; Nobre, R.; Delbem, A.C.; Marques, E.; Cardoso, J.M. Exploration of compiler optimization sequences using clustering-based selection. In Proceedings of the 2014 SIGPLAN/SIGBED Conference on Languages, Compilers and Tools for Embedded Systems, Edinburgh, UK, 11 December 2014; p. 63.
27. Moro, L.F.S.; Lopes, A.M.Z.; Delbem, A.C.B.; Isotani, S. Os desafios para minerar dados educacionais de forma rápida e intuitiva: O caso da damicore e a caracterização de alunos em ambientes de elearning. In Proceedings of the XXXIII Congresso da Sociedade Brasileira de Computação, Workshop de Desafios da Computação Aplicada à Educação, Maceio, Brazil, 23–26 July 2013; pp. 1–10.
28. Moro, L.F.; Rodriguez, C.L.; Andrade, F.R.H.; Delbem, A.C.B.; Isotani, S. Caracterização de Alunos em Ambientes de Ensino Online: Estendendo o Uso da DAMICORE para Minerar Dados Educacionais. *An. Workshops CBIE* **2014**, 1–10. [CrossRef]
29. Ferreira, E.J.; Melo, V.V.; Delbem, A.C.B. Algoritmos de estimação de distribuição em mineração de dados: Diagnóstico do greening in citrus. In Proceedings of the II Escola Luso-Brasileira de Computação Evolutiva, Guimarães, Portugal, 11–14 July 2010.
30. Martins, L.G.A.; Nobre, R.; Cardoso, J.A.M.P.; Delbem, A.C.B.; Marques, E. Clustering-based selection for the exploration of compiler optimization sequences. *ACM Trans. Archit. Code Optim* **2016**, *13*, 8:1–8:28. [CrossRef]
31. Mansour, M.R.; Alberto, L.F.C.; Ramos, R.A.; Delbem, A.C. Identifying groups of preventive controls for a set of critical contingencies in the context of voltage stability. In Proceedings of the IEEE International Symposium on Circuits and Systems (ISCAS), Beijing, China, 19–23 May 2013; pp. 453–456.
32. Soares, A.; Râbelo, R.; Delbem, A. Optimization based on phylogram analysis. *Expert Syst. Appl.* **2017**, *78*, 32–50. [CrossRef]
33. Martins, J.P.; Delbem, A.C.B. Reproductive bias, linkage learning and diversity preservation in bi-objective evolutionary optimization. *Swarm Evol. Comput.* **2019**, *48*, 145–155. [CrossRef]
34. Goutsias, J.K. Mutually compatible Gibbs random fields. *IEEE Trans. Inf. Theory* **1989**, *35*, 1233–1249. [CrossRef]
35. Fonseca, C.M.; Guerreiro, A.P.; López-Ibáñez, M.; Paquete, L. On the Computation of the Empirical Attainment Function. In Proceedings of the 6th International Conference on Evolutionary Multi-Criterion Optimization (EMO 2011), Ouro Preto, Brazil, 5–8 April 2011; Takahashi, R.H.C., Deb, K., Wanner, E.F., Greco, S., Eds.; Springer: Berlin/Heidelberg, Germany, 2011; Volume 6576. [CrossRef]
36. Pearl, J.; Geiger, D.; Verma, T. Conditional independence and its representations. *Kybernetika* **1989**, *25*, 33–44.
37. Zhen, L.; Li, M.; Cheng, R.; Peng, D.; Yao, X. Multiobjective test problems with degenerate Pareto fronts. *arXiv* **2018**, arXiv:1806.02706.
38. Gaspar-Cunha, A. *Modelling and Optimisation of Single Screw Extrusion Using Multi-Objective Evolutionary Algorithms*, 1st ed.; Lambert Academic Publishing: London, UK, 2009.
39. Gaspar-Cunha, A.; Covas, J.A. The Plasticating Sequence in Barrier Extrusion Screws Part I: Modeling. *Polym. Eng. Sci.* **2014**, *54*, 1791–1803. [CrossRef]
40. Gaspar-Cunha, A.; Covas, J.A. The Plasticating Sequence in Barrier Extrusion Screws Part II: Experimental Assessment. *Polym. Plast. Technol. Eng.* **2014**, *53*, 1456–1466. [CrossRef]
41. Gaspar-Cunha, A.; Monaco, F.; Sikora, J.; Delbem, A. Artificial intelligence in single screw polymer extrusion: Learning from computational data. *Eng. Appl. Artif. Intell.* **2022**, *116*, 105397. [CrossRef]
42. Hisao, I.; Hiroyuki, M.; Yuki, T.; Yusuke, N. Modified distance. In *Evolutionary Multi-Criterion Optimization*; Gaspar-Cunha, A., Antunes, C.H., Coello Coello, C., Eds.; Springer International Publishing: Cham, Switzerland, 2015; pp. 110–125.
43. Fonseca, C.M.; Paquete, L.; López-Ibáñez, M. An improved dimension sweep algorithm for the hypervolume indicator. In Proceedings of the 2006 Congress on Evolutionary Computation (CEC 2006), Vancouver, BC, Canada, 16–21 July 2006; pp. 1157–1163. [CrossRef]
44. Pymoo: Multi-objective Optimization in Python. Available online: https://pymoo.org/misc/indicators.html#nb-hv (accessed on 5 November 2022).

Disclaimer/Publisher's Note: The statements, opinions and data contained in all publications are solely those of the individual author(s) and contributor(s) and not of MDPI and/or the editor(s). MDPI and/or the editor(s) disclaim responsibility for any injury to people or property resulting from any ideas, methods, instructions or products referred to in the content.

Article

Single-Loop Multi-Objective Reliability-Based Design Optimization Using Chaos Control Theory and Shifting Vector with Differential Evolution

Raktim Biswas [†] and Deepak Sharma [*,†]

Department of Mechanical Engineering, Indian Institute of Technology Guwahati, Guwahati 781039, Assam, India
* Correspondence: dsharma@iitg.ac.in; Tel.: +91-361-2582661
† These authors contributed equally to this work.

Abstract: Multi-objective reliability-based design optimization (MORBDO) is an efficient tool for generating reliable Pareto-optimal (PO) solutions. However, generating such PO solutions requires many function evaluations for reliability analysis, thereby increasing the computational cost. In this paper, a single-loop multi-objective reliability-based design optimization formulation is proposed that approximates reliability analysis using Karush-Kuhn Tucker (KKT) optimality conditions. Further, chaos control theory is used for updating the point that is estimated through KKT conditions for avoiding any convergence issues. In order to generate the reliable point in the feasible region, the proposed formulation also incorporates the shifting vector approach. The proposed MORBDO formulation is solved using differential evolution (DE) that uses a heuristic convergence parameter based on hypervolume indicator for performing different mutation operators. DE incorporating the proposed formulation is tested on two mathematical and one engineering examples. The results demonstrate the generation of a better set of reliable PO solutions using the proposed method over the double-loop variant of multi-objective DE. Moreover, the proposed method requires 6×–377× less functional evaluations than the double-loop-based DE.

Keywords: multi-objective reliability-based design optimization; shifting vector approach; reliability analysis; chaos control theory; differential evolution

1. Introduction

The design optimization mostly keeps design variables and parameters deterministic. It ignores the fact that uncertainties can arise owing to manufacturing variations, dimensional inaccuracy, boundary conditions, material properties, and improper loading conditions, which can lead to the infeasibility of the solution obtained through deterministic optimization. Therefore, it is necessary to consider these uncertainties in designing the process to maintain safety and the quality of the solution. Reliability-based design optimization (RBDO) [1,2] is a mathematical tool that is used for obtaining such reliable optimal solutions for problems involving uncertainties. It also enables engineers to identify solutions effectively for complex applications in the fields of the automotive, civil, mechanical, and aerospace industries [3,4]. In RBDO, the uncertainties are manifested by converting the deterministic constraints to probabilistic constraints. This is accomplished by applying a probability operator to performance functions or to limit-state functions in the literature. A generalized single-objective RBDO formulation is given in Equation (1).

$$\begin{aligned} \text{Minimize} \quad & f(\mu_X), \\ \text{subject to} \quad & P[G_i(\mathbf{X}) \geq 0] \leq P_{f_i}^T = \Phi(-\beta_i^T), \quad i = 1, \ldots, I, \\ & \mu_X^{(L)} \leq \mu_X \leq \mu_X^{(U)}, \end{aligned} \quad (1)$$

where $f(\mu_X)$ is the objective function, $G_i(X)$ is the i-th performance/constraint function, and μ_X is the mean value vector of random variable vector $X \in \mathbb{R}^n$, where n is the number of random design variables. L and U in the superscript of μ_X represent the lower and upper limits of the vector. $\Phi(\cdot)$ represents the standard normal cumulative distribution function, β_i^T is the target reliability index of the i-th performance function, and $P[\cdot]$ is the probability operator that represents the failure probability of performance function ($G_i(X) \geq 0$) that should be less than the target failure probability ($P_{f_i}^T$).

Equation (1) demonstrates that solving a single-objective RBDO requires a nested-loop procedure [2], where the outer optimization loop involves the inner-loop for reliability analysis. The reliability analysis can be performed using simulation-based methods [5] and analytical methods [6] on probabilistic performance function to obtain its failure probability. The simulation-based methods show better accuracy with an expense of computational cost [7], such as Monte Carlo simulation (MCS) [5], subset simulation [8], importance sampling [9], and Latin-hypercube sampling [9]. On the other hand, analytical methods are known for their computational efficiency, such as most-probable point (MPP)-based methods, in which the sub-optimization problem is solved for each performance function to obtain their respective MPP. The MPP-based methods can be broadly divided into the performance measurement approach (PMA) [10] and the reliability index approach (RIA) [6]. The optimum solution obtained using PMA and RIA is known as the most probable target point (MPTP) and the most probable failure point (MPFP), respectively. Many advanced methods have been developed to estimate the MPTP and MPFP of performance functions, and they are categorized as double-loop methods, decoupled-loop methods, and single-loop methods.

The classical double-loop methods [11,12] involve a nested optimization loop, where the inner-loop performs reliability analysis and the outer-loop is used for obtaining design solutions. All the random variables are transformed to standard normal variables [13] for performing reliability analysis. Since the nested optimization loop is computationally expensive, the reliability analysis loop (inner-loop) is decoupled and performed separately in decoupled-loop methods [14–17]. Some advanced and efficient reliability-based frameworks were also proposed based on isogeometric analysis [18,19]. The reliability analysis itself is considered as an computationally expensive procedure. Therefore, single-loop methods [20] have been proposed, in which approximate reliability analysis is performed. Different concepts such as Karush-Kuhn Tucker (KKT) conditions and quantile approximation are used to approximate MPTP that can eliminate the reliability analysis loop. The adaptive conjugate single-loop approach (AC-SLA) [21], the enhanced single-loop method (ESM) [22], the chaotic single-loop approach (CSLA) [23], the single-loop shifting vector method (SLShV-CG) [24], the sequential single-loop reliability optimization and confidence analysis method (SROCA) [25], and the approximate single-loop chaos control method (ASLCC) [26] are a few recently developed single-loop methods. Recently, some efficient evolutionary RBDO methods are also proposed to obtain the global reliable solution [27,28].

It has been found that many real-world engineering problems consist of more than one objective, which are conflicting in nature [29], and can also have uncertainties. Evolutionary algorithms are found to be promising for solving deterministic multi-objective optimization problems (MOOPs) because they can generate Pareto-optimal (PO) solutions in one run. However, these evolutionary algorithms need to be modified for generating reliable PO solutions for multi-implemented as a design optimization algorithm, and inverse reliability was performed. objective reliability-based design optimization (MORBDO) problems. To address uncertainty in MORBDO, Deb et al. [3] used a non-dominated sorting genetic algorithm (NSGA-II) [30] for design optimization, and Fast RIA for reliability analysis. A multi-objective differential evolution (MODE) [31] was also Simulation-based techniques are also used for reliability analysis and are coupled with double-loop methods. For example, a radial basis function was used for approximating the responses of the performance function and was coupled with MCS to implement reliability analysis. NSGA-II was used to obtain PO solutions for solving the multi-objective and multi-case [32] RBDO problem. In another study, MCS and NSGA-II were coupled with entropy weighted grey relational analysis for design optimization [33] to solve the control arm problem. The multi-objective optimization design of the control arm was carried out using the Kriging surrogate model. Sun et al. [34] proposed a radial basis function-based surrogate modeling that was implemented with Latin-hypercube sampling for sensitivity analysis. MCS and multi-objective particle swarm optimization (PSO) were coupled for obtaining the reliable PO solutions. In another study, a multiple response surface method-based artificial neural network was implemented for reliability analysis [35], and a dynamic multi-objective particle swarm optimization algorithm was proposed for obtaining PO solutions. A worst-case scenario was used with fuzzy sets for reliability analysis, and a real-coded population-based incremental learning [36] was implemented with DE for obtaining the PO solutions. A multi-objective robust optimization [37] was proposed, in which the design problems consisted of parametric uncertainties involving both random and interval variables. NSGA-II was implemented to generate robust PO solutions, and MCS was performed to evaluate the impact responses of the mixed uncertainties. Constrained NSGA-II was also implemented to solve the MORBDO problem [38]. It was coupled with the hybrid method using the Kriging surrogate metamodel for reliability analysis.

A time-dependent reliability-based robust design optimization (TRBRDO) problem [39] was solved using NSGA-III [40] and the dimension reduction method. It was developed by constructing an extreme value model using the sparse grid-based stochastic collocation method for time-dependent reliability analysis. A Bayesian multi-objective RBDO [41] was proposed to solve problems involving aleatory and epistemic uncertainties. Multi-objective PSO was implemented for obtaining PO solutions, and Bayesian interference was used for reliability analysis. Another method using nested loop was proposed to solve RBDO problems [42], in which the outer-loop was performed using multi-objective PSO, and the inner-loop was solved using surrogate modeling with MCS sampling. A two-layer nested optimization problem was proposed based on a decoupling strategy. The inter-generation projection genetic algorithm was employed in the inner-loop, and the multi-objective genetic algorithm [43] was implemented at the outer-loop for solving the MORBDO problem. Another multi-objective RBDO [44] was solved by converting it into a single-objective RBDO problem. This was achieved by assigning weights to the objectives based on quantitative analysis and evidence theory. The reliability analysis was estimated using the PMA method.

From the literature, it can be seen that most of the MORBDO methods focus on PMA, RIA, MCS, or surrogate modeling for reliability analysis, and they are based on double-loop or decoupled-loop methods, which make them computationally expensive. Since evolutionary algorithms are population-based methods and require many functional evaluations, a single-loop method for solving MORBDO can improve the computational efficiency. Moreover, single-loop methods that are solved using steepest descent search to estimate MPTP are often stuck with periodic oscillation [26,45] for highly nonlinear functions. This leads to the motivation of this paper, in which a new MORBDO formulation is proposed, based on adaptive multi-objective DE. An adaptive mutation scheme is used for selecting different variants of mutations for exploration in the search space. Both trial and target vectors take part in the MORBDO formulation to estimate the reliable PO solutions. The following are the contributions of the paper.

- A single-loop MORBDO formulation is developed by using a shifting vector approach for achieving feasibility quickly, and by using chaos control theory for estimating MPTP effectively for better convergence.
- An adaptive multi-objective differential evolution is developed by performing two variants of mutation by estimating a heuristic parameter through hypervolume computation.

- The formulation is further developed by incorporating target and trial vectors of differential evolution for better exploration of the search space.

The proposed method is tested on three benchmark examples from the literature. The results are compared with a double-loop variant of multi-objective differential evolution using PMA for reliability analysis.

The organization of the paper is as follows. In Section 2, a brief discussion on multi-objective RBDO, PMA, chaos control method, single-loop method, and shifting vector approach are presented. The proposed single-loop multi-objective reliability-based design optimization method is discussed in Section 3, along with its implementation. The adaptive mutation scheme and the detailed steps of multi-objective differential evolution are also discussed in this section. Numerical examples are solved and discussed in Section 4. Finally, the paper is concluded in Section 5 with a note on future work.

2. Preliminaries

2.1. Multi-Objective Reliability-Based Design Optimization

A generalized MORBDO formulation can be written as

$$\begin{aligned}
\text{Minimize} \quad & f_m(\mu_\mathbf{X}), & m = 1,\ldots,M, \\
\text{subject to} \quad & P[G_i(\mathbf{X}) \geq 0] \leq P_{f_i}^T = \Phi(-\beta_i^T), & i = 1,\ldots,I, \\
& \mu_\mathbf{X}^{(L)} \leq \mu_\mathbf{X} \leq \mu_\mathbf{X}^{(U)},\ \mathbf{X}^{(L)} \leq \mathbf{X} \leq \mathbf{X}^{(U)},
\end{aligned} \quad (2)$$

where $f_m(\cdot)$ is the m-th conflicting objective function that is written using the mean value ($\mu_\mathbf{X}$) of the random variable ($\mathbf{X}$). $\mathbf{X}^{(L)}$ and $\mathbf{X}^{(U)}$ are the upper and lower limits on $\mathbf{X}$. Solving Equation (2) generates a set of reliable PO solutions in the design space. The reliability analysis is performed on the probabilistic performance function to estimate the failure probability by solving a multidimensional integral, as given in Equation (3).

$$P_{f_i} = P[G_i(\mathbf{X}) \geq 0] = \int \cdots \int_{G_i(\mathbf{X}) \geq 0} f_\mathbf{X}(\mathbf{X}) d\mathbf{X}, \quad (3)$$

where $f_\mathbf{X}(\mathbf{X})$ is the joint probability density function of $\mathbf{X}$. Solving this multidimensional integral is difficult, and therefore, it is approximated with reliability analysis [7]. The first-order reliability method (FORM) [6] and second-order reliability method (SORM) [46] are analytical methods for reliability analysis. Both FORM and SORM estimate the reliability index β that represents the minimum distance from the origin to the performance function in the standard normal space. The reliability index β can be obtained by solving a sub-optimization problem, and the reliability (R) can be estimated using $\Phi(\beta)$ (R = $1 - P_f = 1 - \Phi(-\beta) = \Phi(\beta)$). Due to its computational efficiency and stability in generating a reliable solution, PMA is widely used to solve the sub-optimization problem [47].

2.2. Performance Measure Approach (PMA)

PMA estimates the failure probability of performance function $G(\mathbf{X})$ by finding MPTP in the standard normal space (U-space). After transforming $G(\mathbf{X})$ to the U-space using the Rosenblatt transformation [13], the MPTP can be estimated using the steepest descent direction. When all the random variables are independent, the joint cumulative distribution function (CDF) is calculated via the product of the marginal CDFs. The Rosenblatt transformation is given as

$$\Phi(u_i) = F_{X_i}(x_i) \implies u_i = \Phi^{-1}(F_{X_i}(x_i)), \quad (4)$$

where $F_{X_i}(x_i)$ is the marginal CDF of X_i and $\Phi(\cdot)$ is the CDF of the standard normal random variable. After transforming variables to the standard normal space by using Equation (4), MPTP is calculated by performing the following sub-optimization problem.

$$\begin{aligned} \text{Minimize} \quad & G(\mathbf{U}), \\ \text{subject to} \quad & \|\mathbf{U}\| = \beta^T, \end{aligned} \tag{5}$$

where $\mathbf{U}$ is the random variable in the standard normal space, and β^T is the target reliability index for the performance function $G(\mathbf{U})$. To efficiently obtain the optimum solution of Equation (5), the advanced mean value algorithm is used and the expression is presented in Equation (6).

$$\mathbf{U}^{(k+1)} = \beta^T \frac{\nabla G(\mathbf{U})}{\|\nabla G(\mathbf{U})\|}. \tag{6}$$

If the performance function value at MPTP is less than or equal to zero, it is satisfied for the given target reliability, as presented in Equation (2).

2.3. The Chaos Control Method

It has been observed that PMA performs well for simple nonlinear performance functions, but it fails to converge for highly nonlinear performance functions. To overcome this issue, chaos control theory [45] was proposed based on a stability transformation method [48]. The modification is achieved while updating the iterative point $\mathbf{U}^{(k+1)}$ of Equation (5). The formulation for estimating the iterative point via the chaos control (CC) method is as follows.

$$\begin{aligned} \mathbf{U}_{CC}^{(k+1)} &= \mathbf{U}_{CC}^{(k)} + \lambda \mathbf{C}[\mathbf{F}(\mathbf{u}^{(k)}) - \mathbf{U}_{CC}^{(k)}], \\ \mathbf{F}(\mathbf{u}^{(k)}) &= \mathbf{U}^{(k+1)} = \beta^T \frac{\nabla G(\mathbf{U})}{\|\nabla G(\mathbf{U})\|}, \end{aligned} \tag{7}$$

where $\mathbf{U}_{CC}^{(k)}$ is the MPTP calculated using CC method in the k-th iteration; $\mathbf{C}$ is the involutory matrix with only one element in each row and is assumed as identity matrix $\mathbf{I}$ for simplicity. The matrix $\mathbf{C}$ is usually selected to stabilize the unstable fixed point of the chaotic dynamical system in Equation (7). The chaos control factor λ is determined according to the eigenvalues of the original system's Jacobian matrix, and the value is considered within interval $[0,1]$. When λ is considered as one, the formulation of the CC method is similar to Equation (5) and can have the same issue as discussed earlier. Therefore, a small value of λ is considered for stable convergence. $\mathbf{F}$ is the vector of the response function that is estimated via nonlinear mapping with respect to the iterative values of $\mathbf{U}^{(k+1)}$, as shown in Equation (7). Although the CC method eliminates the issue of oscillation in the convergence of MPTP, it is considered to be an inefficient process. Therefore, a modified chaos control (MCC) [12] was proposed. The modification is achieved by extending the iterative search to the β-hypersphere that is at the constraint boundary in the standard normal space. Thus, MPTP is located on the constraint boundary, and convergence is improved by controlling the tangential step size instead of the radial step size, which was the case for the CC method. The formulation of MCC is given as

$$\begin{aligned} \tilde{\mathbf{n}}^{(k+1)} &= \mathbf{U}_{CC}^{(k)} + \lambda \mathbf{C}[\mathbf{F}(\mathbf{u}^{(k)}) - \mathbf{U}_{CC}^{(k)}], \\ \mathbf{U}_{MCC}^{(k+1)} &= \beta^T \frac{\tilde{\mathbf{n}}^{(k+1)}}{\|\tilde{\mathbf{n}}^{(k+1)}\|}, \end{aligned} \tag{8}$$

where $\tilde{\mathbf{n}}^k$ is the modified search direction updated using $\mathbf{U}_{CC}^{(k+1)}$ of Equation (7). $\mathbf{U}_{MCC}^{(k+1)}$ is the MPTP evaluated using the MCC method.

2.4. Single-Loop Method

The single-loop method (SLM) [20] has been proposed to approximate the reliability analysis of the double-loop method, and establish an equivalent deterministic performance function that is computationally efficient. The approximate MPTP is estimated by using the KKT optimality conditions of Equation (5), and is given in Equation (9).

$$\nabla G(\mathbf{U}) - \hat{\lambda} \nabla H(\mathbf{U}) = 0, \tag{9}$$

where $\hat{\lambda}$ is the Lagrange multiplier, and $H(\mathbf{U}) = \|\mathbf{U}\|^2 - \beta_i^{T^2}$ after squaring both sides of the equality constraint of Equation (5). Using Equation (9) and $\nabla H(\mathbf{U}) = 2\mathbf{U}$ yields $\nabla G(\mathbf{U}) - 2\mathbf{U}\hat{\lambda} = 0$. After simplification, $\mathbf{U}$ can be written as $\frac{\nabla G(\mathbf{U})}{2\hat{\lambda}}$, and multiplying it with $\|\nabla G(\mathbf{U})\|$ in the numerator and denominator, and further simplifying, we obtain

$$\mathbf{U} = \frac{\|\nabla G(\mathbf{U})\|}{2\hat{\lambda}} \frac{\nabla G(\mathbf{U})}{\|\nabla G(\mathbf{U})\|} = \beta^T \alpha, \tag{10}$$

where $\alpha = \frac{\nabla G(\mathbf{U})}{\|\nabla G(\mathbf{U})\|}$ is the unit gradient direction, and $\beta^T = \frac{\|\nabla G(\mathbf{U})\|}{2\hat{\lambda}}$ is a constant at the optimal solution $\mathbf{U}^*$. The gradient is calculated in U-space and the random design variables lie in the X-space. Therefore, the transformation from X-space to U-space is used for the evaluation of approximate MPTP, using the following relationship.

$$\mathbf{X} = \mu_{\mathbf{X}} + \sigma_{\mathbf{X}}\mathbf{U}, \tag{11}$$

where $\sigma_{\mathbf{X}}$ is the standard deviation of $\mathbf{X}$. Substituting $\mathbf{U}$ from Equation (10) in Equation (11) and using the chain rule, we obtain MPTP in the X-space as

$$\mathbf{X}_{MPTP} = \mu_{\mathbf{X}} + \sigma_{\mathbf{X}}\beta\alpha = \mu_{\mathbf{X}} + \sigma_{\mathbf{X}}\beta^T \frac{\sigma_{\mathbf{X}}\nabla_{\mathbf{X}} G(\mathbf{X})}{\|\sigma_{\mathbf{X}}\nabla_{\mathbf{X}} G(\mathbf{X})\|}, \tag{12}$$

where $\mathbf{X}_{MPTP}$ is the MPTP of the performance function $G(\mathbf{X})$.

2.5. Shifting Vector Approach

The concept of the shifting vector ($\mathbf{S}_i^{(k)}$) has been proposed [14] to decouple the double-loop structure of the RBDO problem. It separates the optimization and reliability analysis loop and performs it sequentially in the sequential optimization and reliability assessment (SORA) [14] method. Using this process, the computational efficiency of SORA has been improved as compared to the double-loop method. The concept of the shifting vector is used to shift the violated performance function towards the feasible direction. It is given as

$$\mathbf{S}_i^{(k)} = \mu_{\mathbf{X}}^{(k-1)} - \mathbf{X}_{i,MPTP}^{(k-1)} \tag{13}$$

where $(\mathbf{S}_i^{(k)})$ is the shifting vector at the k-th iteration, $\mathbf{X}_{i,MPTP}^{(k-1)}$ is the MPTP for the i-th constraint, and $\mu_{\mathbf{X}}^{(k-1)}$ is the mean of the random variable $\mathbf{X}$ in the $(k-1)$-th iteration. Figure 1 shows the schematic diagram of the shifted constraint based on the MPTP. It can be seen that $(\mathbf{S}_i^{(1)})$ is estimated based on $\mathbf{X}_{i,MPTP}^{(1)}$ and $\mu_{\mathbf{X}}^{(1)}$, and the shifted constraint is evaluated at $\mu_{\mathbf{X}}^{(1)} - (\mathbf{S}_i^{(1)})$ until the reliability of the constraint is achieved. Here, the shifting vector $(\mathbf{S}_i^{(k)})$ is generated via an iterative process that helps to estimate the feasibility of the performance function until its reliability is satisfied.

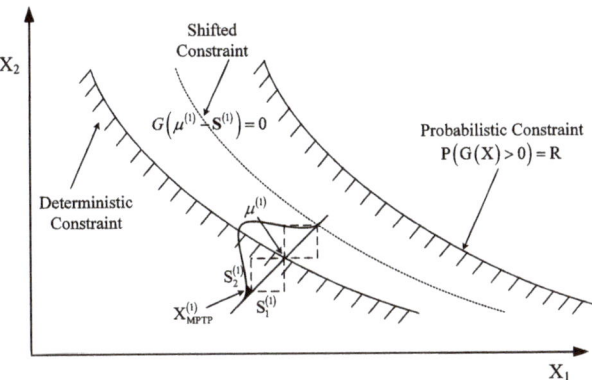

Figure 1. Shifting vector approach.

3. The Proposed Method and Its Implementation

3.1. Single-Loop MORBDO Formulation Using Chaos Control and the Shifting Vector Approach

The single-loop MORBDO formulation can be written using the approximate MPTP given in Equation (12) as

$$
\begin{aligned}
&\text{Min. } f_m(\mu_X), && m = 1, \ldots, M, \\
&\text{s.t.: } G_i(X_{i,MPTP}^{(k)}) \leq 0, && i = 1, \ldots, I, \\
&\text{where } X_{i,MPTP}^{(k)} = \mu_X^{(k)} + \beta_i^T \sigma_X \alpha_{i,X}^{(k)}, \\
&\alpha_{i,X}^{(k)} = \frac{\sigma_X \nabla G_{i,X}(X_{i,MPTP}^{(k-1)})}{\|\sigma_X \nabla G_{i,X}(X_{i,MPTP}^{(k-1)})\|}, \\
&\mu_X^{(L)} \leq \mu_X \leq \mu_X^{(U)},
\end{aligned}
\tag{14}
$$

where $X_{i,MPTP}^{(k)}$ is the approximate MPTP of the 'i' performance function at the k-th iteration, and $\alpha_{i,X}^{(k)}$ is the unit gradient vector of the performance function 'i' with respect to random variable (X). In Equation (14), the probabilistic performance functions of Equation (2) are converted into deterministic performance functions, which eliminate the MPTP search of the inner-loop at every iteration. Thus, the computational efficiency can be improved significantly. It is to be noted that the steepest descent search is used to evaluate the approximate MPTP, which has a tendency to oscillate during convergence [45].

In the proposed formulation, chaos control theory replaces the steepest descent search for approximating MPTP. The concept of the shifting vector approach is incorporated to formulate a novel single-loop MORBDO formulation, as shown in Equation (15).

$$
\begin{aligned}
&\text{Min. } f_m(\mu_X), && i = 1, \ldots, M, \\
&\text{s.t.: } G_i(\Psi^{(k)}) \leq 0, && i = 1, \ldots, I, \\
&\text{where } \Psi^{(k)} = \begin{cases} X_{i,MPTP}^{(k)}, & \forall \text{ target vectors,} \\ \mu_U^{(k+1)} - S_i^{(k+1)}, & \forall \text{ trial vectors,} \end{cases} \\
&S_i^{(k+1)} = \mu_X^{(k)} - X_{i,MPTP}^{(k)}, \\
&X_{i,MPTP}^{(k)} = T^{-1}(U) = \mu_X^{(k)} + \sigma_X U_{i,SLCC}^{(k)}, \\
&\mu_X^{(L)} \leq \mu_X \leq \mu_X^{(U)},
\end{aligned}
\tag{15}
$$

where $\mathbf{U}_{i,SLCC}^{(k)}$ is the approximate MPTP in the U-space that is estimated using the MCC method. $\boldsymbol{\mu}_{\mathbf{U}}^{(k+1)}$ is the trial vector of differential evolution in the U-space in the $(k+1)$-th iteration. In the proposed formulation, the performance function $G_i(\boldsymbol{\Psi}^{(k)})$ includes both $\mathbf{X}_{i,MPTP}^{(k)}$ and $(\boldsymbol{\mu}_{\mathbf{U}}^{(k+1)} - \mathbf{S}_i^{(k+1)})$, which are used for evaluating the performance function for each target vector and trial vector, respectively. The vector $(\boldsymbol{\mu}_{\mathbf{U}}^{(k+1)} - \mathbf{S}_i^{(k+1)})$ shifts the violated performance function towards a feasible direction for the population of trial vectors. $\mathbf{U}_{i,SLCC}^{(k)}$ in the standard normal space is given in Equation (16).

$$\mathbf{U}_{i,SLCC}^{(k)} = \beta_i^T \frac{\mathbf{U}_i^{(k-1)} + \lambda_i^{(k)} \mathbf{C}[\mathbf{U}_i^{(k)} - \mathbf{U}_i^{(k-1)}]}{\|\mathbf{U}_i^{(k-1)} + \lambda_i^{(k)} \mathbf{C}[\mathbf{U}_i^{(k)} - \mathbf{U}_i^{(k-1)}]\|}, \qquad (16)$$

where $\mathbf{U}_i^{(k)}$ and $\mathbf{U}_i^{(k-1)}$ are the MPTPs estimated for the i-th constraint in the k-th and $(k-1)$-th generations, respectively. The value of $\mathbf{U}_{i,SLCC}^{(k)}$ is calculated after the transformation, as given in Equation (17).

$$\mathbf{U}_i^{(k)} = T(\mathbf{X}_i^{(k)}) = (\mathbf{X}_i^{(k)} - \boldsymbol{\mu}_\mathbf{X})/\sigma_\mathbf{X}. \qquad (17)$$

The proposed single-loop MORBDO formulation given in Equation (15) is developed based on a single-loop methodology that eliminates the integrated reliability analysis involved in double-loop formulation, as given in Equation (2). The approximated formulation for reliability analysis is established through KKT optimality conditions, where the search direction is calculated by using modified chaos control theory. Furthermore, the shifting vector is integrated with the single-loop MORBDO formulation that uniquely involves the target and trial vectors of differential evolution.

3.2. Multi-Objective Differential Evolution with Adaptive Mutation Scheme

Differential evolution (DE) [49] is a population-based meta-heuristic algorithm that works with a set of vectors and optimizes an optimization problem by iteratively improving each vector based on an evolutionary process. It explores the design space by maintaining a population of vectors and creating new vectors by combining existing ones. It starts with a random generation of vectors, which are referred to as target vectors, $\boldsymbol{\mu}_\mathbf{X}^{(k)}(t)$, in which t represents the t-th target vector, and k represents the k-th generation counter. Since DE is used for solving the MORBDO problem, the notation for vector is kept the same as the mean value of the random variable. Each target vector ($\boldsymbol{\mu}_\mathbf{X}^{(k)}(t)$) is transformed to the mutant vector ($\boldsymbol{\mu}_\mathbf{V}^{(k+1)}(t)$) using the randomly chosen vectors ($\boldsymbol{\mu}_{\mathbf{r}_1}^{(k)}(t)$), ($\boldsymbol{\mu}_{\mathbf{r}_2}^{(k)}(t)$) and ($\boldsymbol{\mu}_{\mathbf{r}_3}^{(k)}(t)$). In this paper, an adaptive mutation scheme is used, in which the mutation vector ($\boldsymbol{\mu}_\mathbf{V}^{(k+1)}(t)$) is generated, either by using a random vector or the best vector. The scheme for generating ($\boldsymbol{\mu}_\mathbf{V}^{(k+1)}(t)$) is given in Equation (18).

$$\boldsymbol{\mu}_\mathbf{V}^{(k+1)}(t) = \begin{cases} \boldsymbol{\mu}_{\mathbf{r}_1}^{(k)}(t) + \hat{F} \times (\boldsymbol{\mu}_{\mathbf{r}_2}^{(k)}(t) - \boldsymbol{\mu}_{\mathbf{r}_3}^{(k)}(t)), & \zeta > \epsilon, \\ \boldsymbol{\mu}_{\text{best}}^{(k)}(t) + \hat{F} \times (\boldsymbol{\mu}_{\mathbf{r}_2}^{(k)}(t) - \boldsymbol{\mu}_{\mathbf{r}_3}^{(k)}(t)), & \text{otherwise,} \end{cases} \qquad (18)$$

where $\mathbf{r}_1 \neq \mathbf{r}_2 \neq \mathbf{r}_3$ are the three randomly chosen vectors from the current population, and $\hat{F}$ is the scaling factor. The variant "DE/rand/bin/1" is found to be effective in exploring the search space during the initial generations because the mutant vector is generated a using random vector. When DE starts converging towards the Pareto-optimal front, the "DE/best/bin/1" variant replacing $\boldsymbol{\mu}_{\mathbf{r}_1}^{(k)}(t)$ to $\boldsymbol{\mu}_{\text{best}}^{(k)}(t)$ can improve the convergence. The $\boldsymbol{\mu}_{\text{best}}^{(k)}(t)$ vector for each target vector is found by calculating the Euclidean distance of the t-th target vector with respect to all non-dominated target vectors in the objective space. The closest non-dominated target vector is selected as $\boldsymbol{\mu}_{\text{best}}^{(k)}(t)$ for the t-th target vector. Since both the variants have their own merits, a heuristic convergence parameter (ζ) is proposed that can help DE to use either of these variants, depending on the user-defined parameter ϵ. The parameter ζ is calculated using the hypervolume (HV) performance indicator [50] that is given as

$$\zeta = I_H^{(k)} - I_H^{(k-1)}, \tag{19}$$

where $I_H^{(k)}$ and $I_H^{(k-1)}$ are the hypervolume calculated with respect to the non-dominated target vectors in the (k) and $(k-1)$ generations. It is noted that the non-dominated target vectors in the $(k-1)$ and (k) generations are normalized together for estimating the hypervolume with respect to the dominated point. Thereafter, the trial vector ($\boldsymbol{\mu}_U^{(k+1)}(t)$) is created for each target vector ($\boldsymbol{\mu}_X^{(k)}(t)$), which is given as

$$\boldsymbol{\mu}_U^{(k+1)}(t_j) = \begin{cases} \boldsymbol{\mu}_V^{(k+1)}(t_j) & \text{if } r \leq p_c \text{ or } j = rnbr(i), \\ \boldsymbol{\mu}_X^{(k)}(t_j) & \text{if } r > p_c \text{ and } j \neq rnbr(i), \end{cases} \tag{20}$$

where subscript j with t in $\boldsymbol{\mu}_X^{(k)}(t_j)$, $\boldsymbol{\mu}_V^{(k+1)}(t_j)$, and $\boldsymbol{\mu}_U^{(k+1)}(t_j)$ represent the j-th component of the target, mutant, and trial vectors, respectively. r is a random number between 0 and 1, p_c is the crossover rate, and $rnbr(i)$ is a randomly chosen index $\in \{1, 2, \ldots, n\}$, which ensures that $\boldsymbol{\mu}_U^{(k+1)}(t_j)$ obtains at least one component from $\boldsymbol{\mu}_V^{(k+1)}(t_j)$. Thereafter, all target vectors and trial vectors are combined ($\boldsymbol{\mu}_X^{(k)} \cup \boldsymbol{\mu}_U^{(k+1)}$) to find the rank of the combined population using the non-dominated sorting [30] of NSGA-II. The crowding distance is also calculated for maintaining the diversity for the selection of the next generation of target vectors. The best N target vectors for the next generation are selected by using the environmental selection scheme of NSGA-II [30]. Multi-objective DE is terminated if the generation counter (k) is more than the total number of generations (K). Otherwise, the generation loop continues till the termination condition becomes satisfied.

3.3. Steps for Implementation

In this section, the steps for implementing DE with an adaptive mutation scheme for the proposed MORBDO formulation are presented, which are as follows.

1. **Input**: population size (N), number of variables (n), total number of generations (K), scaling factor ($\hat{F}$), probability of crossover (p_c), standard deviation (σ) for random variables, and target reliability index for constraints (β^T), generation counter ($k = 1$).
2. Initialize random population ($P(k)$) that comprises target vectors ($\boldsymbol{\mu}_X^{(k)}$).
3. For each target vector ($\boldsymbol{\mu}_X^{(k)}(t)$) of ($P(k)$):
    3.1 Calculate the objective function values, $f_m(\boldsymbol{\mu}_X^{(k)}(t))$.
    3.2 Calculate MPTP for each performance function (i) using Equations (15) and (16), and estimate shifting vector $\mathbf{S}_{i,\mu_X}^{(k+1)} = \boldsymbol{\mu}_X^{(k)} - \mathbf{X}_{i,MPTP}^{(k)}$.
    3.3 Calculate the constraint violation of each performance function using the MPTP that is estimated through the chaos control theory given in Equation (15).
4. If ($k > K$), terminate. Otherwise, continue to Step 5.
5. Generate mutant vectors ($\boldsymbol{\mu}_V^{(k+1)}$) using the scheme given in Equation (18).
6. Generate trial vectors ($\boldsymbol{\mu}_U^{(k+1)}$), as given in Equation (20).
7. For each trial vector:
    7.1 Calculate the objective function, $f_m(\boldsymbol{\mu}_U^{(k+1)}(t))$.

7.2 Calculate MPTP ($\hat{\mathbf{X}}_{i,MPTP}^{(k+1)}$) and shifting vector for each performance function (i) using Equations (15) and (16), and $\mathbf{S}_{i,\mu_U}^{(k+2)} = \boldsymbol{\mu}_U^{(k+1)} - \hat{\mathbf{X}}_{i,MPTP}^{(k+1)}$, and estimate the constraint violation of $G_i(\boldsymbol{\mu}_U^{(k+1)} - \mathbf{S}_{i,\mu_X}^{(k+1)})$.

7.3 Calculate the constraint violation of each performance function using the MPTP that is estimated through chaos control theory as given in Equation (15).

8 Combine target and trial vectors, and perform non-dominated sorting and estimate the crowding distance.

9 Update target vectors ($\boldsymbol{\mu}_X^{(k+1)}$) for the next generation using the environmental selection of NSGA-II. It should be noted that the corresponding MPTPs and shifting vector are stored in Step 7 for utilizing them in the next generation. Set $k = k + 1$ and go to Step 4.

4. Numerical Examples

In this section, three mathematical examples and one engineering example are solved to demonstrate the performance of the proposed method. All the examples consist of two objective functions, along with the nonlinear performance functions. The proposed method is abbreviated as SLMDE since it is developed via a single-loop method using multi-objective DE. The results of SLMDE are compared with double-loop multi-objective differential evolution (DLMDE). It is noted that PMA is used with DLMDE for reliability analysis. The reliable PO solutions are generated via both methods for different values of the target reliability index (β^T). HV performance indicator values and number of function evaluations are used to compare the outcome. Both the methods are run 30 times with different initial populations. The standard deviation (SD) is also evaluated to see the dispersion of HV values. The Wilcoxon signed-rank test at a 5% significance level is also used to determine the difference for the statistical significance between SLMDE and DLMDE. The parameters of SLMDE and DLMDE are as follows: the scaling factor ($\hat{F}$) is taken as 0.3, the crossover probability (p_c) is 0.9, the population size (N) is 200, and the total number of generations (K) is 100 for the first example, 250 for the second example, and 200 for the car side impact example. The chaos control factor (λ) is considered as 0.2 [26]. The user-defined parameter (ϵ) in Equation (18) is considered as 10^{-3}. The MATLAB R2016b platform is used for developing both methods.

4.1. Example 1

The first MORBDO example [3] consists of two objectives that are developed using two independent random normal variables with a standard deviation of 0.03. The example is subjected to two linear performance functions that are shown in Equation (21).

$$\begin{aligned}
&\min: f_1(\boldsymbol{\mu}_X) = \mu_{x_1}, \\
&\min: f_2(\boldsymbol{\mu}_X) = \frac{1 + \mu_{x_2}}{\mu_{x_1}}, \\
&\text{s.t.: } P[G_i(\mathbf{X}) > 0] \leq \phi(-\beta_i^T), \quad i = 1, 2, \\
&G_1(\mathbf{X}) = x_2 + 9x_1 - 6, \\
&G_2(\mathbf{X}) = -x_2 + 9x_1 - 1, \\
&0.1 \leq \mu_{x_1} \leq 1, \ 0 \leq \mu_{x_1} \leq 5.
\end{aligned} \quad (21)$$

Table 1 presents the best, median, and worst values of HV obtained via SLMDE and DLMDE. SLMDE has converged to better values of HV for different β^T values. This indicates that SLMDE generates a better set of PO solutions for the given example. It is to be noted that for a larger value of β^T, the HV value becomes reduced, as compared to the lower β^T value. This is because a larger value of β^T signifies a high degree of reliability that makes the obtained PO solutions more conservative and pushes them away from the deterministic PO front inside the feasible region.

Table 1. Best, median, and worst HV values obtained by both methods are presented for Example 1 for different values of β^T. The best performances are highlighted in bold font.

β^T	SLMDE	DLMDE	β^T	SLMDE	DLMDE	β^T	SLMDE	DLMDE
1.0	**0.8100** 0.8075$^+$ 0.8065	0.8067 0.8048 0.7772	2.0	**0.7998** 0.7982$^+$ 0.7971	0.7754 0.7739 0.7550	3.0	**0.7908** 0.7879$^+$ 0.7869	0.7422 0.7411 0.7247
SD	9×10^{-4}	0.0063	SD	6×10^{-4}	0.0042	SD	7×10^{-4}	0.0054

Figure 2 demonstrates the PO solutions obtained by both methods for different values of β^T. The reliable PO solutions shown in Figure 2a,b correspond to the median HV values from Table 1. It can be seen that for larger values of β^T, the PO solutions become conservative and move inside the feasible region. The same figure also demonstrates that some solutions coincide with the deterministic PO front that is located at the bottom right. This is because for those solutions, the target reliability is satisfied for the performance function $G_1(\mathbf{x})$.

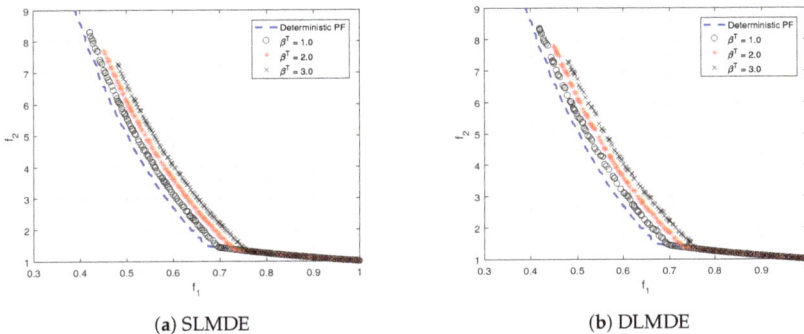

(a) SLMDE (b) DLMDE

Figure 2. The obtained PO solutions by both methods for example 1 for different β^T values.

The computational efficiencies of both methods are measured with the help of a number of function evaluations that are presented in Table 2. It can be seen that the proposed method requires 202,000 function evaluations, which is only 14.85% of DLMDE. This is because SLMDE is based on a single-loop method, where the reliability of the performance function is estimated using KKT optimality conditions. On the other hand, DLMDE performs PMA for reliability estimation, which requires many function evaluations. Since the number of iterations for PMA is kept fixed, the number of function evaluations is the same for DLMDE with different values of β^T.

Table 2. Number of function evaluations required by both methods for example 1.

β^T	SLMDE	DLMDE
1.0	202,000	1,360,000
2.0	202,000	1,360,000
3.0	202,000	1,360,000

The Wilcoxon test results are shown in the same table with symbols ($+, =, -$). The symbol '$+$' suggests a significantly better performance of SLMDE over DLMDE. Other symbols '$-$' and '$=$' suggest a significantly bad performance and an equivalent performance of SLMDE over DLMDE, respectively. It can be seen from the table that SLMDE shows a significantly better performance over DLMDE.

The progress of HV and heuristic convergence parameter ζ with respect to iterations are shown in Figure 3. It can be seen that there are some initial fluctuations in both HV and ζ, which subsidise after 10 generations and stabilize after 50 generations.

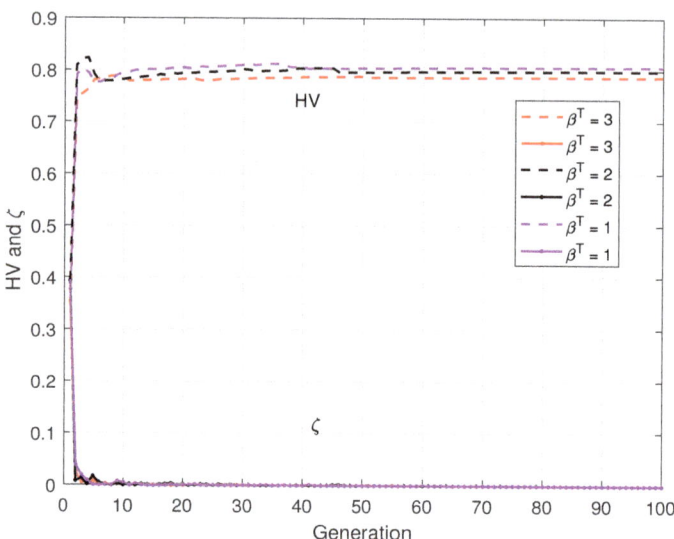

Figure 3. Progress of hypervolume and ζ of SLMDE with respect to number of generations for example 1.

4.2. Example 2

The second example [51] consists of two objective functions which are highly nonlinear. It has four linear and two nonlinear performance functions that are developed using two independent random normal variables, each with a standard deviation of 0.3. The RBDO formulation of this example is given in Equation (22).

$$\begin{aligned}
\text{min: } & f_1(\boldsymbol{\mu_X}) = -[25(\mu_{x_1} - 2)^2 + (\mu_{x_2} - 2)^2 + (\mu_{x_3} - 1)^2 + (\mu_{x_4} - 4)^2 + (\mu_{x_5} - 1)^2], \\
\text{min: } & f_2(\boldsymbol{\mu_X}) = [\mu_{x_1}^2 + \mu_{x_2}^2 + \mu_{x_3}^2 + \mu_{x_4}^2 + \mu_{x_5}^2 + \mu_{x_6}^2], \\
\text{s.t.: } & P[G_i(\mathbf{X}) > 0] \leq \phi(-\beta_i^T), \quad i = 1, \ldots, 6 \\
& G_1(\mathbf{X}) = x_1 + x_2 - 2, \\
& G_2(\mathbf{X}) = 6 - x_1 - x_2, \\
& G_3(\mathbf{X}) = 2 - x_2 + x_1, \\
& G_4(\mathbf{X}) = 2 - x_1 + 3x_2, \\
& G_5(\mathbf{X}) = 4 - (x_3 - 3)^2 - x_4, \\
& G_6(\mathbf{X}) = (x_5 - 3)^2 + x_6 - 4, \\
& 0 \leq \mu_{x_1}, \mu_{x_2}, \mu_{x_6} \leq 10, \ 1 \leq \mu_{x_3}, \mu_{x_5} \leq 5, \ 0 \leq \mu_{x_4} \leq 6.
\end{aligned} \quad (22)$$

Table 3 presents the statistical values of HV obtained via both methods. In can be seen that SLMDE has converged to better values of HV for different β^T values. This indicates that SLMDE generates a better set of PO solutions for this given example. In this case, a similar observation can also be made where for larger values of β^T, the HV values becomes reduced. This is due to the fact that larger values of β^T signify a larger degree of reliability, which leads to the generation of conservative PO solutions. The Wilcoxon test results are shown in the same table with symbols $(+, =, -)$. It can be seen from the table that SLMDE shows a significantly better performance over DLMDE.

Figure 4 shows the reliable PO solutions generated in the run, corresponding to a median HV value from Table 3. It can be seen that for larger β^T, PO solutions move inside the feasible region and away from the deterministic PO front. The spread of solutions is less in the case of SLMDE for $\beta^T = 1.0$. The solutions are nicely distributed in the case of DLMDE. The shift of the solutions is more for larger values of β^T, which leads to smaller values of HV that can be seen from Table 3.

Table 3. Best, median, and worst HV values obtained by both methods are presented for Example 2 for different values of β^T. The best performances are highlighted in bold font.

β^T	SLMDE	DLMDE	β^T	SLMDE	DLMDE	β^T	SLMDE	DLMDE
	0.9118	0.9017		0.6234	0.6119		0.4027	0.3929
1.0	0.9028$^+$	0.8906	2.0	0.6181$^+$	0.6025	3.0	0.3945$^+$	0.3777
	0.8853	0.8293		0.5999	0.5953		0.3776	0.3680
SD	**0.0065**	0.0153	SD	0.0065	**0.0056**	SD	0.0074	**0.0080**

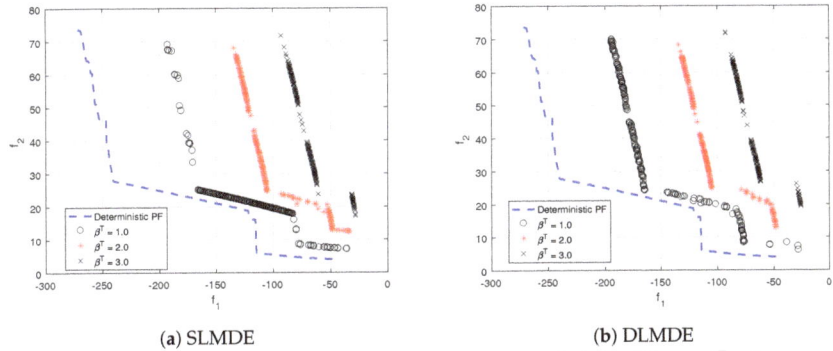

(a) SLMDE (b) DLMDE

Figure 4. The PO solutions obtained via both methods for example 2, for different β^T values.

Table 4 presents the computational efficiency of both methods. The proposed method only requires 3,915,600 function evaluations, which is only 3.5–2.7% of DLMDE. It suggests that DLMDE needs many function evaluations because PMA is performed for reliability estimation.

Table 4. Number of function evaluations required by both methods for Example 2.

β^T	SLMDE	DLMDE
1.0	3,915,600	111,424,992
2.0	3,915,600	132,344,016
3.0	3,915,600	145,249,728

Figure 5 shows the progress of HV and ζ with respect to the number of generations. It can be seen that there are fluctuations for all values of β^T until the termination criterion is achieved. The initial fluctuations can also be observed for ζ, which subsidize after 150 generations.

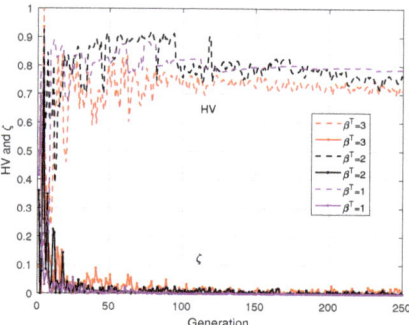

Figure 5. Progress of hypervolume and ζ of SLMDE with respect to the number of generations for example 2.

4.3. Car Side Impact Example

The car side impact [3] example is considered as an engineering RBDO example, which is formulated by using 2 objectives and 10 performance functions. It consists of 11 random design variables that are normally distributed and that are grouped into random variables $(x_1, \ldots, x_7)$ and random parameters $(x_8, \ldots, x_{11})$. The details of the variables with their standard deviation values are given in Table 5. The RBDO formulation is presented in Equation (23). The mathematical expressions for each function are given in Table 6.

$$
\begin{aligned}
&\min: f_1(\mu_X) \equiv \text{Structural weight,} \\
&\min: f_2(\mu_X) \equiv \text{Average rib deflection,} \\
&\text{s.t.:} \ P[G_i(X) > 0] \leq \phi(-\beta_i^T), \quad i = 1, \ldots, 10 \\
&G_1(X) = \text{Abdomen load} \leq 1\text{KN,} \\
&G_2(X) = V * Cupper \leq 0.32\text{m/s,} \\
&G_3(X) = V * Cmiddle \leq 0.32\text{m/s,} \\
&G_4(X) = V * Clower \leq 0.32\text{m/s,} \\
&G_5(X) = \text{Upper rib deflection} \leq 32\text{mm,} \\
&G_6(X) = \text{Middle rib deflection} \leq 32\text{mm,} \\
&G_7(X) = \text{Lower rib deflection} \leq 32\text{mm,} \\
&G_8(X) = \text{Pubic force} \leq 4\text{KN,} \\
&G_9(X) = \text{Velocity of V-Pillar} \leq 9.9\text{mm/ms,} \\
&G_{10}(X) = \text{Front door velocity of V-Pillar} \leq 15.7\text{mm/ms,} \\
&0.5 \leq \mu_{x_1}, \mu_{x_3}, \mu_{x_4} \leq 1.5,\ 0.45 \leq \mu_{x_2} \leq 1.35,\ 0.875 \leq \mu_{x_5} \leq 2.625, \\
&0.4 \leq \mu_{x_6} \leq 1.2,\ 0.4 \leq \mu_{x_7} \leq 1.2,\ 0.192 \leq \mu_{x_8}, \mu_{x_9} \leq 0.75.
\end{aligned} \quad (23)
$$

The statistical values of the HV values obtained from both methods with respect to different β^T are presented in Table 7. The proposed method has converged to larger values of HV for all β^T values. This signifies a better distribution of PO solutions of SLMDE as compared to DLMDE. The observation of reducing HV values with larger β^T values remains the same. The Wilcoxon test results are shown in the same table with symbols $(+, =, -)$. It can be seen from the table that SLMDE shows significantly better, bad, and equivalent performances over DLMDE for $\beta^T = 1, 2$ and 3, respectively.

The obtained reliable PO solutions for both methods are shown in Figure 6. As observed with previous examples, for larger values of β^T, the PO solutions start moving away from the deterministic PO front inside the feasible region.

Table 8 presents the computational efficiency of both methods. In this example, SLMDE requires only 4,623,000, the number of function evaluations, which is only 0.3–0.26% that of

DLMDE. Since SLMDE performs an approximate reliability estimation by using the KKT optimality conditions, it saves many function evaluations compared to DLMDE. Figure 7 shows a similar progress for HV and ζ with respect to the number of generations. There are initial fluctuations for all values of β^T, which subside after 80 generations.

Table 5. Details of design variables and their standard deviation values.

Design Variable	Standard Deviation
x_1: Thickness of B-pillar inner	0.03
x_2: Thickness of B-pillar reinforcement	0.03
x_3: Thickness of floor side inner	0.03
x_4: Thickness of cross members	0.03
x_5: Thickness of door beam	0.03
x_6: Thickness of door beltline reinforcement	0.03
x_7: Thickness of roof rail	0.03
x_8: Material of B-pillar inner	0.006
x_9: Material of floor side inner	0.006
x_{10}: Barrier height	10
x_{11}: Barrier hitting position	10

Table 6. The objectives and performance functions of Example 3.

$f_1(\mu_X)$:	$1.98 + 4.9x_1 + 6.67x_2 + 6.98x_3 + 4.01x_4 + 1.78x_5 + 0.00001x_6 + 2.73x_7$,
$f_2(\mu_X)$:	$(G_5(X) + G_6(X) + G_7(X))/3$,
$G_1(X)$:	$1.16 - 0.3717x_2x_4 - 0.00931x_2x_{10} - 0.484x_3x_9 + 0.01343x_6x_{10}$,
$G_2(X)$:	$0.261 - 0.01598x_1x_2 - 0.188x_1x_8 - 0.0198x_2x_7 + 0.0144x_3x_5 + 0.0008757x_5x_{10}$
	$+ 0.08045x_6x_9 + 0.00139x_8x_{11} + 0.00001575x10x11$
$G_3(X)$:	$0.214 + 0.00817x_5 - 0.1318x_1x_8 - 0.0704x_1x_9 + 0.030998x_2x_6 - 0.018x_2x_7 + 0.0208x_3x_8$
	$+ 0.121x_3x_9 - 0.00364x_5x_6 + 0.0007715x_5x_{10} - 0.0005354x_6x10 + 0.00121x_8x_{11}$
	$+ 0.00184x_9x_{10} - 0.018x_2^2$
$G_4(X)$:	$0.74 - 0.61x_2 - 0.163x_3x_8 + 0.001232x_3x_{10} - 0.166x_7x_9 + 0.227x_2^2$
$G_5(X)$:	$28.98 + 3.818x_3 - 4.2x_1x_2 + 0.0207x_5x_{10} + 6.63x_6x_9 - 7.77x_7x_8 + 0.32x_9x_{10}$
$G_6(X)$:	$33.86 + 2.95x_3 + 0.1792x_{10} - 5.057x_1x_2 - 11.0x_2x_8 - 0.0215x_5x_{10} - 9.98x_7x_8 + 22x_8x_9$
$G_7(X)$:	$46.36 - 9.9x_2 - 12.98x_1x_8 + 0.1107x_3x_{10}$
$G_8(X)$:	$4.72 - 0.5x_4 - 0.19x_2x_3 - 0.01228x_4x_{10} + 0.009325x_6x10 + 0.000191x_{11}^2$
$G_9(X)$:	$10.58 - 0.674x_1x_2 - 1.958x_2x_8 + 0.02054x_3x_{10} - 0.0198x_4x_{10} + 0.028x_6x_{10}$
$G_{10}(X)$:	$16.45 - 0.489x_3x_7 - 0.843x_5x_6 + 0.0432x_9x_{10} - 0.0556x_9x_{11} - 0.000786x_{11}^2$

Table 7. Best, median, and worst HV values obtained via both methods, presented for car side impact example for different values of β^T. The best performances are highlighted in bold font.

β^T	SLMDE	DLMDE	β^T	SLMDE	DLMDE	β^T	SLMDE	DLMDE
	0.8256	0.8216		**0.7175**	0.7104		**0.5208**	0.5200
1.0	**0.8245**$^+$	0.8211	2.0	**0.7137**$^-$	0.7095	3.0	**0.5145**$^=$	0.5142
	0.8235	0.8196		**0.7078**	0.7070		**0.4996**	0.4912
SD	5×10^{-4}	4×10^{-4}	SD	0.0021	0.0040	SD	0.0050	0.0082

Table 8. Number of function evaluations required by both methods for car side impact example.

β^T	SLMDE	DLMDE
1.0	4,623,000	1.467×10^9
2.0	4,623,000	1.6970×10^9
3.0	4,623,000	1.7342×10^9

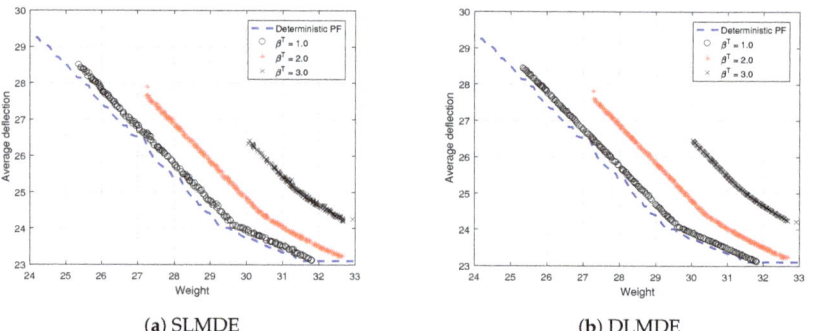

(a) SLMDE (b) DLMDE

Figure 6. The obtained PO solutions by both methods for car side impact example for different β^T values.

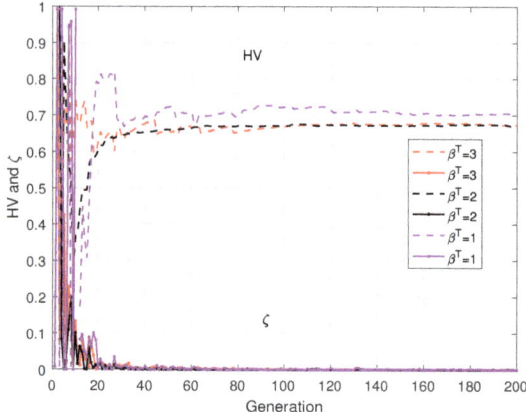

Figure 7. Progress of hypervolume and ζ of SLMDE with respect to number of generations for car side impact problem.

4.4. Example 4

The fourth example [44] consists of two objective functions and both of them are quadratic functions. The example has a linear performance function developed with three independent random normal variables. The RBDO formulation is given in Equation (24).

$$\begin{aligned}
&\min: f_1(\boldsymbol{\mu_X}) = (\mu_{x_1} - 1)^2 + (\mu_{x_2} - 2)^2 + (\mu_{x_3} - 3)^2, \\
&\min: f_2(\boldsymbol{\mu_X}) = \mu_{x_1}^2 + 2\mu_{x_2}^2 + 3\mu_{x_3}^2, \\
&\text{s.t.:} \ P[G_i(\mathbf{X}) > 0] \leq \phi(-\beta_i^T), \ i = 1, \\
&G_1(\mathbf{X}) = x_1 + x_2 + x_3 - 1, \\
&0.1 \leq \mu_{x_i} \leq 6, \ i = 1, 2, 3.
\end{aligned} \quad (24)$$

where $x_1 \sim N(1, 0.05)$, $x_2 \sim N(2, 0.1)$, and $x_3 \sim N(3, 0.15)$.

Table 9 presents the statistical values of HV obtained via SLMDE and DLMDE. It can be observed that in most of the cases, SLMDE converged to better values of HV for different β^T. The HV values become reduced with larger values of β^T. The Wilcoxon test results are shown in the same table with symbols (+, =, −). It can be seen from the table that SLMDE shows an equivalent performance with DLMDE for $\beta^T = 2$ and 3, and a bad performance for $\beta^T = 1$.

Table 9. Best, median, and worst HV values obtained by both methods are presented for example 4 for different values of β^T. The best performances are highlighted in bold font.

β^T	SLMDE	DLMDE	β^T	SLMDE	DLMDE	β^T	SLMDE	DLMDE
	0.7733	**0.7751**		**0.7416**	0.7413		**0.6834**	0.6833
1.0	0.7723⁻	**0.7721**	2.0	0.7407⁼	**0.7405**	3.0	0.6826⁼	**0.6828**
	0.7380	**0.7585**		**0.7297**	0.7091		0.6439	**0.6799**
SD	0.0100	**0.0028**	SD	**0.0035**	0.0059	SD	0.0103	**0.0080**

Figure 8 shows the reliable PO solutions generated in the run corresponding to the median HV value obtained via both methods for different values of β^T. As observed in the previous examples, for larger β^T, PO solutions move inside the feasible region, away from the deterministic PO front.

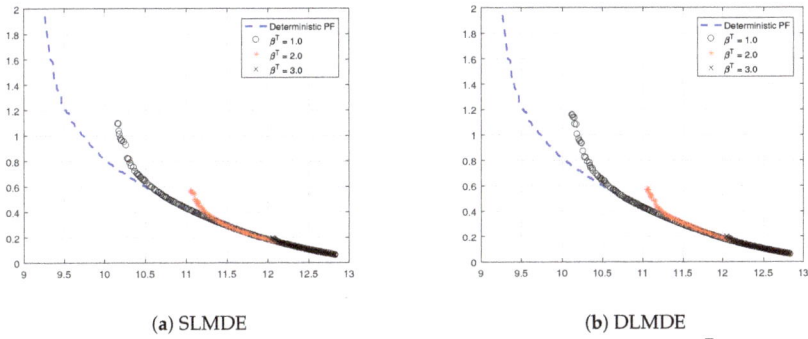

(a) SLMDE (b) DLMDE

Figure 8. The PO solutions obtained via both methods for example 4 for different β^T values.

Table 10 presents the computational efficiencies of both methods. The proposed method requires only 50% of function evaluations as that of DLMDE. Figure 9 also shows similar observations for HV and ζ during the progress of the generations. There is an initial fluctuation which reduces after 20 generations.

Table 10. Number of function evaluations required by both methods for Example 4.

β^T	SLMDE	DLMDE
1.0	280,000	520,000
2.0	280,000	520,000
3.0	280,000	520,000

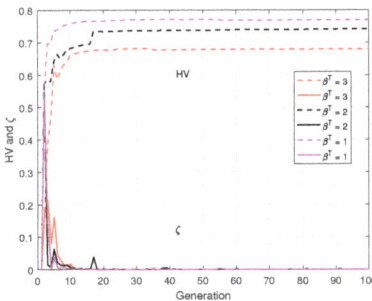

Figure 9. Progress of hypervolume and ζ of SLMDE with respect to number of generations for Example 4.

5. Conclusions

A single-loop multi-objective reliability-based design optimization has been proposed for generating reliable PO solutions quickly. It was developed by applying KKT optimality conditions to PMA for generating an approximate expression of MPTP. The search direction of approximate MPTP was modified via chaos control theory. The concept of the shifting vector approach was implemented with the novel formulation to include both target and trial vectors. DE was made adaptive, using the heuristic parameter that helped DE to perform different mutation operators. The proposed SLMDE was tested on three mathematical and one engineering bi-objective RBDO examples. It was found that SLMDE generated more reliable PO solutions for all examples compared to DLMDE. The results demonstrate that the convergence of SLMDE takes less function evaluations than DLMDE. For all four examples, the SLMDE was able to generate better HV values. For example 2, a lot of fluctuations during the progress of hypervolume can be observed, which stabilize gradually. The user-defined parameter ζ shows stable progress for all the examples. In the future, the proposed method can be modified for quick convergence by incorporating quantile approximation for reliability analysis. The proposed method can also be tested on other real-world examples having many nonlinear functions.

Author Contributions: Conceptualization: R.B. and D.S.; methodology: R.B.; validation: R.B.; formal analysis: R.B. and D.S.; investigation: R.B.; writing—original draft preparation: R.B.; writing—review and editing: R.B. and D.S.; visualization: R.B.; supervision: D.S. All authors have read and agreed to the published version of the manuscript.

Funding: This research received no external funding.

Conflicts of Interest: The authors declare no conflicts of interest.

Abbreviations

The following abbreviations are used in this manuscript:

MORBDO	Multi-objective reliability-based design optimization
MPTP	Most probable target point
SLCC	Single-loop chaos control
DE	Differential evolution
KKT	Karush-Kuhn Tucker optimality conditions
HV	Hypervolume performance indicator
SLMDE	Single-loop multi-objective differential evolution
DLMDE	Double-loop multi-objective differential evolution
PMA	Performance measure approach

References

1. Aoues, Y.; Chateauneuf, A. Benchmark study of numerical methods for reliability-based design optimization. *Struct. Multidiscip. Optim.* **2010**, *41*, 277–294. [CrossRef]
2. Tu, J.; Choi, K.K.; Park, Y.H. A New Study on Reliability-Based Design Optimization. *J. Mech. Des.* **1999**, *121*, 557–564. [CrossRef]
3. Deb, K.; Gupta, S.; Daum, D.; Branke, J.; Mall, A.K.; Padmanabhan, D. Reliability-Based Optimization Using Evolutionary Algorithms. *IEEE Trans. Evol. Comput.* **2009**, *13*, 1054–1074. [CrossRef]
4. Yu, X.; Du, X. Reliability-based multidisciplinary optimization for aircraft wing design. *Struct. Infrastruct. Eng.* **2006**, *2*, 277–289. [CrossRef]
5. Pradlwarter, H.; Schuëller, G. Local Domain Monte Carlo Simulation. *Struct. Saf.* **2010**, *32*, 275–280. [CrossRef]
6. Hasofer, A.M.; Lind, N.C. Exact and Invariant Second-Moment Code Format. *J. Eng. Mech. Div.* **1974**, *100*, 111–121. [CrossRef]
7. Madsen, H.; Krenk, S.; Lind, N. *Methods of Structural Safety*; Dover Publication, Inc.: Mineola, NY, USA, 1986.
8. Song, S.; Lu, Z.; Qiao, H. Subset simulation for structural reliability sensitivity analysis. *Reliab. Eng. Syst. Saf.* **2009**, *94*, 658–665. [CrossRef]
9. Choi, S.K.; Grandhi, R.; Canfield, R.A. *Reliability-Based Structural Design*; Springer: London, UK, 2007. [CrossRef]
10. Youn, B.D.; Choi, K.K.; Du, L. Enriched Performance Measure Approach for Reliability-Based Design Optimization. *AIAA J.* **2005**, *43*, 874–884. [CrossRef]
11. Youn, B.D.; Choi, K.; Park, Y. Hybrid Analysis Method for Reliability-Based Design Optimization. *J. Mech. Des.* **2003**, *125*, 221–232. [CrossRef]

12. Meng, Z.; Li, G.; Wang, B.P.; Hao, P. A hybrid chaos control approach of the performance measure functions for reliability-based design optimization. *Comput. Struct.* **2015**, *146*, 32–43. [CrossRef]
13. Rosenblatt, M. Remarks on a Multivariate Transformation. *Ann. Math. Stat.* **1952**, *23*, 470–472. [CrossRef]
14. Du, X.; Chen, W. Sequential optimization and reliability assessment method for efficient probabilistic design. *J. Mech. Des.-Trans. ASME* **2004**, *126*, 225–233. [CrossRef]
15. Cheng, G.; Xu, L.; Jiang, L. A sequential approximate programming strategy for reliability-based structural optimization. *Comput. Struct.* **2006**, *84*, 1353–1367. [CrossRef]
16. Zou, T.; Mahadevan, S. A direct decoupling approach for efficient reliability-based design optimization. *Struct. Multidiscip. Optim.* **2006**, *31*, 190. [CrossRef]
17. Hao, P.; Wang, Y.; Liu, C.; Wang, B.; Wu, H. A novel non-probabilistic reliability-based design optimization algorithm using enhanced chaos control method. *Comput. Methods Appl. Mech. Eng.* **2017**, *318*, 572–593. [CrossRef]
18. Hao, P.; Yang, H.; Wang, Y.; Liu, X.; Wang, B.; Li, G. Efficient reliability-based design optimization of composite structures via isogeometric analysis. *Reliab. Eng. Syst. Saf.* **2021**, *209*, 107465. [CrossRef]
19. Hao, P.; Wang, Y.; Ma, R.; Liu, H.; Wang, B.; Li, G. A new reliability-based design optimization framework using isogeometric analysis. *Comput. Methods Appl. Mech. Eng.* **2019**, *345*, 476–501. [CrossRef]
20. Liang, J.; Mourelatos, Z.; Tu, J. A Single-Loop Method for Reliability-Based Design Optimization. *Int. J. Prod. Dev.* **2008**, *5*, 76–92. [CrossRef]
21. Meng, Z.; Keshtegar, B. Adaptive conjugate single-loop method for efficient reliability-based design and topology optimization. *Comput. Methods Appl. Mech. Eng.* **2018**, *344*, 95–119. [CrossRef]
22. Keshtegar, B.; Hao, P. Enhanced single-loop method for efficient reliability-based design optimization with complex constraints. *Struct. Multidiscip. Optim.* **2018**, *57*, 1731–1747. [CrossRef]
23. Meng, Z.; Yang, D.; Zhou, H.; Wang, B. Convergence control of single loop approach for reliability-based design optimization. *Struct. Multidiscip. Optim.* **2018**, *57*, 1079–1091. [CrossRef]
24. Biswas, R.; Sharma, D. A single-loop shifting vector method with conjugate gradient search for reliability-based design optimization. *Eng. Optim.* **2021**, *53*, 1044–1063. [CrossRef]
25. Hao, P.; Yang, H.; Yang, H.; Zhang, Y.; Wang, B. A sequential single-loop reliability optimization and confidence analysis method. *Comput. Methods Appl. Mech. Eng.* **2022**, *399*, 115400. [CrossRef]
26. Biswas, R.; Sharma, D. An approximate single-loop chaos control method for reliability based design optimization using conjugate gradient search directions. *Eng. Optim.* **2021**, *55*, 382–398. [CrossRef]
27. Meng, Z.; Rıza Yıldız, A.; Mirjalili, S. Efficient decoupling-assisted evolutionary/metaheuristic framework for expensive reliability-based design optimization problems. *Expert Syst. Appl.* **2022**, *205*, 117640. [CrossRef]
28. Biswas, R.; Sharma, D. A single-loop reliability-based design optimization using adaptive differential evolution. *Appl. Soft Comput.* **2023**, *132*, 109907. [CrossRef]
29. Deb, K. *Multi-Objective Optimization Using Evolutionary Algorithms*, 1st ed.; Wiley: Chichester, UK, 2001.
30. Deb, K.; Pratap, A.; Agarwal, S.; Meyarivan, T. A fast and elitist multiobjective genetic algorithm: NSGA-II. *IEEE Trans. Evol. Comput.* **2002**, *6*, 182–197. [CrossRef]
31. Lobato, F.S.; Gonçalves, M.S.; Jahn, B.; Cavalini, A.A.; Steffen, V. Reliability-Based Optimization Using Differential Evolution and Inverse Reliability Analysis for Engineering System Design. *J. Optim. Theory Appl.* **2017**, *174*, 894–926. [CrossRef]
32. Sun, G.; Zhang, H.; Fang, J.; Li, G.; Li, Q. Multi-Objective and Multi-Case Reliability-Based Design Optimization for Tailor Rolled Blank (TRB) Structures. *Struct. Multidiscip. Optim.* **2017**, *55*, 1899–1916. [CrossRef]
33. Jiang, R.; Sun, T.; Liu, D.; Pan, Z.; Wang, D. Multi-Objective Reliability-Based Optimization of Control Arm Using MCS and NSGA-II Coupled with Entropy Weighted GRA. *Appl. Sci.* **2021**, *11*, 5825. [CrossRef]
34. Sun, G.; Zhang, H.; Wang, R.; Lv, X.; Li, Q. Multiobjective reliability-based optimization for crashworthy structures coupled with metal forming process. *Struct. Multidiscip. Optim.* **2017**, *56*, 1571–1587. [CrossRef]
35. Song, L.K.; Fei, C.W.; Wen, J.; Bai, G.C. Multi-objective reliability-based design optimization approach of complex structure with multi-failure modes. *Aerosp. Sci. Technol.* **2017**, *64*, 52–62. [CrossRef]
36. Sleesongsom, S.; Bureerat, S. Multi-Objective, Reliability-Based Design Optimization of a Steering Linkage. *Appl. Sci.* **2020**, *10*, 5748. [CrossRef]
37. Li, F.; Sun, G.; Huang, X.; Rong, J.; Li, Q. Multiobjective robust optimization for crashworthiness design of foam filled thin-walled structures with random and interval uncertainties. *Eng. Struct.* **2015**, *88*, 111–124. [CrossRef]
38. Dammak, K.; Hami, A.E. Multi-objective reliability based design optimization using Kriging surrogate model for cementless hip prosthesis. *Comput. Methods Biomech. Biomed. Eng.* **2020**, *23*, 854–867. [CrossRef]
39. Yu, S.; Wang, Z.; Wang, Z. Time-Dependent Reliability-Based Robust Design Optimization Using Evolutionary Algorithm. *ASCE-ASME J. Risk Uncertain. Eng. Syst. Part B Mech. Eng.* **2019**, *5*, 020911. [CrossRef]
40. Deb, K.; Jain, H. An Evolutionary Many-Objective Optimization Algorithm Using Reference-Point-Based Nondominated Sorting Approach, Part I: Solving Problems With Box Constraints. *IEEE Trans. Evol. Comput.* **2014**, *18*, 577–601. [CrossRef]
41. Celorrio, L.; Patelli, E. Reliability-Based Design Optimization under Mixed Aleatory/Epistemic Uncertainties: Theory and Applications. *ASCE-ASME J. Risk Uncertain. Eng. Syst. Part A Civ. Eng.* **2021**, *7*, 04021026. [CrossRef]

42. Zafar, T.; Zhang, Y.; Wang, Z. An efficient Kriging based method for time-dependent reliability based robust design optimization via evolutionary algorithm. *Comput. Methods Appl. Mech. Eng.* **2020**, *372*, 113386. [CrossRef]
43. Liu, X.; Fu, Q.; Ye, N.; Yin, L. The multi-objective reliability-based design optimization for structure based on probability and ellipsoidal convex hybrid model. *Struct. Saf.* **2019**, *77*, 48–56. [CrossRef]
44. Qiu, J.; Luo, H. Multiobjective reliability-based design optimization approach using the gray system and evidence theory. *J. Mech. Sci. Technol.* **2022**, *36*, 1789–1797. [CrossRef]
45. Yang, D.; Yi, P. Chaos control of performance measure approach for evaluation of probabilistic constraints. *Struct. Multidiscip. Optim.* **2009**, *38*, 83–92. [CrossRef]
46. Breitung, K. Asymptotic Approximations for Multinormal Integrals. *J. Eng. Mech.* **1984**, *110*, 357–366. [CrossRef]
47. Ramu, P.; Qu, X.; Youn, B.D.; Haftka, R.; Choi, K. Inverse reliability measures and reliability-based design optimisation. *Int. J. Reliab. Saf.* **2006**, *1*, 187–205. [CrossRef]
48. Pingel, D.; Schmelcher, P.; Diakonos, F. Stability transformation: A tool to solve nonlinear problems. *Phys. Rep.-Rev. Sect. Phys. Lett.* **2004**, *400*, 67–148. [CrossRef]
49. Storn, R.; Price, K. Differential Evolution—A Simple and Efficient Heuristic for global Optimization over Continuous Spaces. *J. Glob. Optim.* **1997**, *11*, 341–359. [CrossRef]
50. Brockhoff, D.; Friedrich, T.; Neumann, F. Analyzing Hypervolume Indicator Based Algorithms. In Proceedings of the 10th International Conference, Dortmund, Germany, 13–17 September 2008; Rudolph, G., Jansen, T., Beume, N., Lucas, S., Poloni, C., Eds.; Springer: Berlin/Heidelberg, Germany, 2008; pp. 651–660.
51. Osyczka, A.; Kundu, S. A new method to solve generalized multicriteria optimization problems using the simple genetic algorithm. *Struct. Optim.* **1995**, *10*, 94–99. [CrossRef]

Disclaimer/Publisher's Note: The statements, opinions and data contained in all publications are solely those of the individual author(s) and contributor(s) and not of MDPI and/or the editor(s). MDPI and/or the editor(s) disclaim responsibility for any injury to people or property resulting from any ideas, methods, instructions or products referred to in the content.

MDPI
St. Alban-Anlage 66
4052 Basel
Switzerland
Tel. +41 61 683 77 34
Fax +41 61 302 89 18
www.mdpi.com

Mathematical and Computational Applications Editorial Office
E-mail: mca@mdpi.com
www.mdpi.com/journal/mca

www.ingramcontent.com/pod-product-compliance
Lightning Source LLC
LaVergne TN
LVHW070147100526
838202LV00015B/1906